MEMOIRS O

THE LIFE AND TIMES

OF

SIR CHRISTOPHER HATTON, K.G.,

VICE-CHAMBERLAIN AND LORD CHANCELLOR TO
QUEEN ELIZABETH.

INCLUDING HIS CORRESPONDENCE WITH THE QUEEN AND OTHER
DISTINGUISHED PERSONS.

BY SIR HARRIS NICOLAS, G. C. M. G.

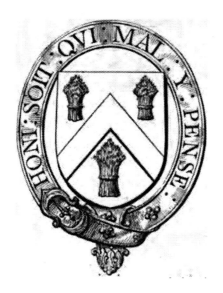

LONDON:

RICHARD BENTLEY, NEW BURLINGTON STREET,

Publisher in Ordinary to Her Majesty.

M.DCCC.XLVII.

PREFACE.

———

Of Sir Christopher Hatton, Gentleman Pensioner,
Captain of the Guard, Vice-Chamberlain, and Lord Chancellor to Queen Elizabeth, and her distinguished personal
Favourite, less was known than of almost any other
Statesman of that period. This neglect of a very remarkable person probably arose from the notion that he was a
mere Courtier, whose life presented no incidents to instruct, and few to amuse mankind. Though noticed by
Naunton, Fuller, Lloyd, and Lodge, as well as in all
general Biographical Collections, no attempt was made
to give a detailed account of Hatton's career, until
Lord Campbell wrote a Memoir of him in "The Lives
of the Lord Chancellors and Keepers of the Great
Seal of England." Since the appearance of that work,
the transcript of a manuscript, entitled "Booke of Letters receaved by Sir Christopher Hatton, Vice-Cham-
berlayne to the Quene's Majestie, from sundry parsons, and
procured by him to be written in this same Booke," was
placed in the Editor's hands, for the purpose of being
printed with the usual illustrative Notes.

It of course became desirable to ascertain whether any other Letters from or relating to HATTON could be found, besides those in that manuscript; and whether LORD CAMPBELL's Memoir had rendered any other account of his life unnecessary. Numerous Letters, and some of the highest interest, were discovered in the State Paper Office, consisting principally of his secret Letters to the Queen; and there are a few others in the British Museum. The examination of the Memoir in the " Lives of the Lord Chancellors" shewed it to be remarkable for omissions and for errors, while it seems that an unfair, if not prejudiced, view is there taken of HATTON's character. Under these circumstances, it was determined to write an entirely new LIFE OF HATTON, and to illustrate it by the Correspondence in the " Letter Book," as well as by Letters from other sources.

The present Memoir contains every fact relating to SIR CHRISTOPHER HATTON that could be found, together with every Letter from him of which the existence is known. It will be seen that LORD CAMPBELL's statements have been treated with the freedom, and it is hoped with the candour, that should characterize all literary investigations ; and his Lordship is of all men the last to wish that Historical truth should be in any degree sacrificed to feelings of courtesy. His Lordship's mistakes as to facts are placed beyond dispute ; and it only remains for the public to decide upon the justice or injustice of his estimate of HATTON's talents and character.

So far from being a vain, idle " scapegrace," with few acquirements and less talents, and the mere ornament of a Court, HATTON took a prominent part in all State affairs; and his opinion on public transactions received great consideration from LORD BURGHLEY, LEICESTER, WALSINGHAM, and all the other Ministers. He was for many years what is now termed the Leader of the House of Commons; and if he did not adorn the Woolsack, to which he was unexpectedly raised, by great legal learning, he had the modesty and good sense to consult eminent lawyers in cases of magnitude, and obtained the respect of the public by the equity and impartiality of his decisions. Unlike that of many great legal luminaries of his age, his own conduct was pure with respect to bribes; and, long before he was made Chancellor, he dismissed his old Secretary because he had taken some small fees from persons who had solicited his Master's favour.

SIR CHRISTOPHER HATTON was the constant resource of the unfortunate, knowing on such occasions no distinction of Religion; "in whose cause," he nobly said, "neither searing nor cutting was to be used." He was the frequent intercessor in cases of persecution; the patron and, better still, the friend of literary men, who repaid his kindness by the only means in their power, thanks,— "the Exchequer of the Poor,"—in the dedications of their works. All that is known of HATTON proves that his heart and disposition were amiable, his temper mild, and his judgment less biassed by the prejudices of his age than that of most of his contemporaries.

The Correspondence in the "Letter Book" consists mostly of Letters to HATTON on a great variety of subjects, both public and private, from QUEEN ELIZABETH, SIR CHRIS-

TOPHER HATTON himself, LORD BURGHLEY, the DUKE of NOR-
FOLK, LORD CHANCELLOR BROMLEY, the LORD KEEPER BACON,
and the EARLS of LEICESTER, ARUNDELL, and SUSSEX; the
COUNTESSES of SUSSEX, BEDFORD, and DERBY; ARCHBISHOPS
GRINDALL, SANDYS, WHITGIFT, and LOFTUS; AYLMER, BISHOP
of LONDON; LORDS BUCKHURST, and GREY of WILTON; DR.
MATHEW, afterwards Archbishop of York; LORD HENRY
HOWARD, afterwards Earl of Northampton; SIR PHILIP SID-
NEY, SIR FRANCIS WALSINGHAM, SIR AMIAS PAULET; SIR
THOMAS HENEAGE, Treasurer of the Chamber; Secretary
DAVISON, SIR JOHN STANHOPE, the Poet CHURCHYARD,
CHARLES ARUNDELL; STUBBES, the author of "The Gaping
Gulf," for which he lost his hand; CARTWRIGHT and NOR-
TON, the well-known polemical writers; THEODORE BEZA,
&c. Many of these Letters, as might be expected, throw
much new light upon the history of the times, as well as
on the characters and conduct of the writers themselves.

But the Letters to which the greatest interest attaches
are from HATTON to the QUEEN, which have hitherto entirely escaped observation, and which certainly breathe
the devotion and tenderness of a Lover rather than the
humility and duty of a Subject. These documents, and
some others in this Collection, will probably raise a strong
doubt upon her Majesty's right to her favourite and well-
known designation.

The "Letter Book" formerly belonged to Mr. UPCOTT,
but its previous history is unknown. It was purchased
at the sale of his manuscripts, by the Trustees of the
British Museum, and now forms the "Additional MS.
15891." Its genuineness is beyond suspicion, and the

collection was apparently made before SIR CHRISTOPHER
HATTON became Lord Chancellor, there being no Letters
relating to him after 1587, and that dignity is not attributed to him in the title. The letters seem to have been
copied by his Secretary, Mr. SAMUEL COX, who shews the
flattering opinion he entertained of his own epistolary
talents by the insertion of so many of his own learned,
but prolix and pedantic epistles, that it was necessary
to consign many of them to an Appendix. It may perhaps be wished that a few other Letters had been placed
with them.

The Editor begs leave to offer his best thanks to his
friends Sir CHARLES GEORGE YOUNG, Garter, and to ALBERT
WILLIAM WOODS, Esq., Lancaster Herald, for much useful
information ; and his thanks are likewise due to ROBERT
LEMON, Esq., and H. C. HAMILTON, Esq., for their zealous
and obliging aid in selecting from the comparatively
speaking unexplored Historical stores in the State Paper
Office, all that related to SIR CHRISTOPHER HATTON.

TORRINGTON SQUARE,
  30th November, 1846.

CONTENTS.

b

1578 *continued.*

1578 *continued.*

b 2

CONTENTS.

CONTENTS.

1581 *continued.*

1581 *continued.*

1582 *continued.*

1582 *continued.*

1583 *continued.*

1584 *continued.*

1585.

1589 *continued.*

APPENDIX.

c

THE

LIFE AND TIMES

OF

SIR CHRISTOPHER HATTON.

ERRATA.

P. 26, line 36, note, for " 5th," *read* " 7th " of June.

P. 63, line 23, *dele* " and Hatton is said to have consulted the latter in all important cases," Dr. *Dale* having been there mistaken for Dr. *Swale.* A similar error occurs in p. 250, line 4.

P. 128, line 33, note, for " 1759," *read* " 1579."

said to have had a sixth son, Wolfaith, Lord of Hatton in that county, from whom descended, through a long series of Knights and Esquires of some local but of little general fame, Piers or Peter Hatton, of Quisty Birches in Cheshire, whose third son, Henry Hatton, founded a new line by marrying, in the reign of Henry the Seventh, Elizabeth, the sister and eventually sole heiress of William Holden, of Holdenby in Northamptonshire, Esq. Their eldest son, John Hatton, settled at Holdenby, and had three sons, William, the eldest;

VOL. I.   B

John Hatton, of Gravesend in Kent, ancestor of the Viscounts Hatton, now represented by the Earl of Winchelsea and Nottingham; and Christopher. William Hatton, the eldest son, had, by Alice Saunders, an only daughter, Dorothy, who married John Newport, of Horningham in Warwickshire, Esquire, and three sons, viz. Francis and Thomas, who both died young[a] and unmarried; and CHRISTOPHER, who, as heir to his brothers, succeeded to the estates at Holdenby,[b] and made the name of Hatton historical, if not imperishable.

CHRISTOPHER HATTON was born at Holdenby in 1540,[c] and was left an orphan at the age of six years, by the death of his father in August 1546.[d] It does not appear how long he enjoyed a mother's care; nor can it be ascertained precisely when, by the deaths of his two elder brothers, he succeeded to the family inheritance, but probably before he became of age. There is some reason to believe that his maternal uncle, William Saunders, superintended his education; but nothing of his early life is known until he entered as a Gentleman Commoner at St. Mary's Hall, Oxford,[e] when he was probably about fifteen or sixteen years old. He quitted the University without a degree, and became a member of the Inner Temple on the 26th of May 1560, on which occasion he was described "of

[a] Francis, the eldest son, was fourteen years old in 1548; but he and his next brother, Thomas, are stated to have died in their youth, in the Herald's Visitations of Northamptonshire, in the College of Arms, and British Museum.
[b] Pedigree of Hatton in Baker's History of Northamptonshire.
[c] On his monument he is said to have been fifty-one at his death in November 1591.

[d] Esch. 1 Edw. VI. Part II. No. 22; by which it was found that William Hatton, Gentleman, was seized in fee of the manor of Holdenby, &c.; that his wife Alice survived him; that he died on the 28th of August, 38 Hen. VIII., 1546; and that Francis Hatton was his son and heir, and was then fourteen years old and upwards.
[e] Wood's Athen. Oxon. ed. Bliss. i. 582.

Holdenby in Northamptonshire;"* which tends to show
that he was then in possession of those estates.   Some
of his biographers have said that he did not enter the
Temple with a view of studying the law as a profession; but, as has been justly observed, that report
was probably invented to increase the wonder,[b] if not
the obloquy, which his appointment as Lord Chancellor
created.   It is supposed that Hatton was never called
to the bar; but, though no proof of the fact exists,
it may nevertheless have occurred.   He became eligible
to be called within five, if not three years after his
admission as a student; and, as no book is ·pre-
served in which "calls" are registered before 1567,
Hatton may have been made a barrister between
1565 and 1567; but he was never either a Reader
or a Bencher of his Inn.[c]

The next occasion on which any notice of Hatton has

* Inner Temple Register of Ad-
missions.

[b] Lodge's Memoir of Sir Christopher Hatton.

[c] From the information, very oblig-
ingly supplied, of Edw. H. Martin,
Esq., Under-Treasurer of the Inner
Temple.   Lord Campbell, in his
"Lives of the Lord Chancellors,"
vol. ii. pp. 136, 139, says positively
that Hatton was never called to the
bar.   His Lordship gives a very minute account of Hatton's early career; but as the Editor has not had
the good fortune to find the slightest
authority for any one of those statements, and as none is cited (except
Justice Shallow's description of his
own life in Clement's Inn), he can
only observe, that, according to Lord
Campbell, Hatton was "idle and
volatile" as a child, and "imbibed
with difficulty from a domestic tutor
the first rudiments of knowledge;"
that he had already shown "the
vanity which always distinguished
him; and, being much spoiled as
the child of his father's old age, he
succeeded in prevailing upon the indulgent squire to enter him a Gentleman Commoner at St. Mary's Hall,
although the additional expense thus
incurred could ill be afforded."   Upon
this it must be observed, that the expense could not have much affected
the "indulgent squire," nor could
"the news of the manner in which"
his son "dedicated himself to dancing" at the Temple "have caused
heavy hearts under the paternal roof
in Northamptonshire," inasmuch as
Hatton's father died when he was
only six years old.   "While at college," his Lordship proceeds to say,
"he was exceedingly popular with
his companions, but he spent much
more time in fencing and archery than
in perusing Aristotle and Aquinas;
and, from the fear of being plucked,
he left Oxford without trying for a

been discovered is remarkable, as it was to a similar festivity that he owed his fortunes. In 1561 the Inner Temple celebrated Christmas by a splendid masque, in which the part of " Master of the Game" was played by " Christopher Hatton." The scene was honoured with the presence of Lord Robert Dudley, afterwards the celebrated Earl of Leicester, who under the title of " Palaphilos," held the mimic rank of Constable and Marshal.[a]

Hatton was then in the twenty-first year of his age, handsome, tall, and graceful in his person, of elegant manners, and an accomplished dancer—qualities that never failed to please the eye and gratify the taste of Queen Elizabeth. Neither the exact time nor the occasion upon which he first appeared before his Sovereign is known, but it is said to have been in one of those masques which the Templars often presented to the Queen. " He came to Court," says Sir Robert Naunton, on the authority of Sir John Perrot, " by the galliard, for he came thither as a private gentleman

degree." At the Temple he was "in truth a noted roisterer and swashbuckler; hearing the chimes at midnight, knowing where the *bona robas* were, and sometimes lying all night in the Windmill in St. George's Fields ; but while he spent much of his time in dicing and gallantry, there were two amusements to which he particularly devoted himself, and which laid the foundation of his future fortune. The first was dancing, which he studied under the best masters, and in which he excelled beyond any man of his time : the other was the stage : he constantly frequented the theatres ... and he himself used to assist in writing masques, and took a part in performing them." First Edition, ii. 136 : Second Edition, ii. 138.

Lord Campbell's horror of Hatton's being a good dancer, from its apparent inconsistency with the gravity of forensic, not to say judicial, duties, might not have been quite so great had he remembered that dancing was then not merely tolerated, but exacted from lawyers. On the 6th of February, 7 Jac. 1610, " the under-barristers of Lincoln's Inn were, by decimation, put out of commons for example's sake, because the whole bar offended by not dancing on Candlemas-day preceding, according to the ancient order of this Society, when the judges were present ; with this, that, if the like fault were committed afterwards, they should be fined or disbarred." Dugdale's Origines Juridiciales, Ed. 1680, p. 346.

[a] Dugdale's Origines Juridiciales, Ed. 1680, pp. 150.

of the Inns of Court in a masque, and for his acti-
vity and person, which was tall and proportionable,
taken into the Queen's favour." This statement, which
has been generally adopted, though probable in itself,
may have originated in envy; or Naunton may have
been misinformed, as his account of Hatton is very
erroneous.[a] It is, however, to some extent supported
by Camden, whose candour was no less great than
his learning; who says, that, " being young and of a
comely tallness of body and countenance, he got into
such favour with the Queen that she took him into
her band of fifty Gentlemen-pensioners."[b]

The precise date of Hatton's appointment as a Gentleman-pensioner has not been discovered; nor has
that of his promotion to the situation of Gentleman
of the Privy Chamber been ascertained, and which,
like his subsequent higher offices in the Queen's service,
Camden says he owed to the " modest sweetness of his
manners." It is, however, nearly certain that he attracted the Queen's notice, and was made one of the Gen-

[a] Fragmenta Regalia, p. 30, printed in 1641. Naunton says, Hatton
was *first* made Vice-Chamberlain,
whereas he had previously held three
other offices.

[b] Annals of Queen Elizabeth, ed.
1630, book iv. p. 34. Lord Campbell's account of Hatton's removal
from the Temple to the Court wants
only the *authority* for his Lordship's
statement to be interesting ;—" The
tender heart of Elizabeth was at once
touched by his athletic frame, manly
beauty, and graceful air; and she
openly expressed her high admiration of his dancing. An offer was
instantly made by her to admit him
of the band of Gentlemen-pensioners. He expressed great unwillingness to renounce all his prospects in
the profession of the law, but informed her that he had incurred
debts which were beginning to be
troublesome to him. She advanced
him money to pay them off,—at the
same time (*more suo*) taking a bond
and statute-merchant to repay her
when he should be of ability. He
little thought he should ever hear
of these securities, which afterwards
were supposed to be the cause of his
death." 2nd ed., vol. ii. page 140.
However well founded this narrative
may be in other parts, it will be seen
hereafter that the sum for which
Hatton was pressed by the Queen,
and which is said to have hastened
his death, had nothing whatever to
do with his early debts, nor with
those imaginary "bonds" or "statute-
merchant."

tlemen-pensioners between March and June 1564; for
though his name does not occur in the Roll of the Band,
made at Lady-day in that year, yet on the 30th of June
1564 [a] a warrant was issued to the Master of the Armoury,
commanding him " to cause to be made one armour complete, fit for the body of our well-beloved servant Christopher Hatton, one of our Gentlemen-pensioners, he pay-
ing according to the just value thereof," [b] and which was
probably the usual order for the equipment of persons
appointed to that situation. In 1568 Hatton was one
of the "gentlemen of the Inner Temple" who wrote a
tragedy called " Tancred and Gismund," which was
acted before the Queen, apparently by the authors of
the piece. [c] His contribution was the fourth act; to
which, when the play was printed in 1592, his name
was thus affixed—" Composuit Chr. Hatton."

[a] Seven Rolls of the names of Gentlemen-pensioners in the reign of Elizabeth, before 1580, have been found; viz. those of 3rd, 5th, 6th, 15th, 19th, 20th, and 21st Eliz., all of which (except that of the 5th, which is in the State Paper Office) are in the Rolls House. The name of "Christopher Hatton" occurs only in the Rolls of the 12th, 15th, and 19th Eliz.

[b] Original in the State Paper Office.

[c] Lord Campbell (ii. 138) says, but without giving his authority, that Hatton "did not act in this piece himself." The point is not very material; but the dedication by its editor Wilmot, in 1592, as well as the other introductory matter, show that it was performed by the authors. To the fair dedicatees, Lady Mary Petre and Lady Ann Grey, the editor says: "So, amongst others, these gentlemen, which with what sweetness of voice, liveliness of action they then expressed it, they which were of her Majesty's Right Honourable maidens can testify." Wilmot's friend Webb, who requested him to print it, says, " The tragedy was by them" (the Inner Temple gentlemen) "most pithily framed, and no less curiously acted, in view of her Majesty, by whom it was then as princely accepted." . . . . . "The brave youths that then, to their high praises, so feelingly performed the same in action, did shortly after lay up the book unregarded, or perhaps let it run abroad, (as many parents do their children once past dandling,) not respecting so much what hard fortune might befal it, being out of their fingers, as how their heroical wits might again be quickly conceived with new inventions of like worthiness, whereof they have been ever since wonderful fertile." The names of the actors are not prefixed to the play; but to the first act is added the signature "G. Al.," and to the second, "Per Hen. No."

In April 1568, Hatton exchanged his hereditary manors of Holdenby with the Queen for the site of the abbey and demesne lands of Sulby; but on the same day she granted him a lease of the manors of Holdenby for forty years.[a] From this time the Royal bounty flowed upon him in so copious a stream as to excite wonder, if not suspicion; for he had performed no service to the State, and to meritorious public servants Elizabeth was parsimonious, if not mean, in the distribution of rewards. It is said that the favours lavished upon Hatton excited the displeasure, if not the jealousy, of Leicester; and that, in ridicule of the accomplishment which first attracted the Queen's notice, he proposed to introduce a dancing-master, who excelled the young pensioner. But Elizabeth drew a proper distinction between the merit of an artist and the skill of an amateur: " Pish!" she said contemptuously, " I will not see your man;—it is his *trade!*"[b] On the 27th of July in that year he was appointed Keeper of Eltham Park, and of the Park of Horne. In 1569 the farm of the chapel of Monkton in Pembrokeshire was granted to him; and he was one of the Justices of the Peace in Northamptonshire.[c] In February 1570 he obtained the reversion of the office of Queen's Remembrancer in the Exchequer;[d] and, in 1571, an inn near Temple Bar called " the Ship," lands in Yorkshire and Dorsetshire, and the wardship of a minor were granted to him.[e]

[a] Rot. Patent. 10 Eliz.; Baker's Northamptonshire, i. 195.

[b] Miss Strickland's Life of Queen Elizabeth, vol. vi. p. 336; but the fair authoress does not give her authority.

[c] List of Justices of the Peace in October 1569, in the State Paper Office. In a list of " Gentlemen under the Marquis of Northampton " in 1569, the name of " Hatton " was underlined by Cecil.—Ibid.

[d] This grant was repeated in May 1572.

[e] Rot. Patent. 11, 12, 13, Eliz., passim.

Hatton was returned to parliament for Higham Fer-
rers[a] in April 1571, but there is nothing to show that
he took any part in its proceedings. In May 1571, he
distinguished himself as one of the challengers in " a
solemn tournay and barriers," before the Queen at Westminster; his colleagues being the Earl of Oxford, Mr.
Charles Howard, and Sir Henry Lee, "who did very
valiantly, but the chief honour was given to the Earl
of Oxford."[b] In 1572 he presented his Royal mistress,
apparently for the first time, with a New-year's gift,
consisting of a jewel of pizands of gold adorned with
rubies and diamonds, and flowers set with rubies,
with one pearl pendant, and another at the top.[c] From
this time Hatton, like the rest of the Court, never
failed to make a similar offering to the Queen on New-
year's day, obtaining in return silver-gilt plate; and
it is deserving of remark, that while the largest quantity
of plate ever given, even to the highest personage,
never exceeded two hundred, and was seldom more
than fifty ounces,[d] Hatton always received four hundred
ounces on those occasions. Between February and July
1572, grants were made to him of woods in Here-
fordshire, of the manor of Frampton in Dorsetshire, of
the reversion of the house of the monastery de Pratis
in Leicestershire, of the stewardship of the manor of

[a] Willis' Notitia Parliamentaria.
[b] Nichols' Progresses of Queen
Elizabeth, i. 276.
[c] Ibid. 295.
[d] See the lists in Nichols' Progresses of Queen Elizabeth, vols. ii.
and iii. passim. The earliest is in
1578. The Keeper of the Great
Seal received 34 ounces; Leicester,
then Master of the Horse, 100; the
Lord Admiral, 22; the Chancellor
of the Duchy, 30; Sir Francis Walsingham, 60; the Treasurer of the
Household, 25; the Comptroller, 24;
the Archbishop of York, 35; Lord
Howard, 104; Countesses, 18 to 50;
Lord Howard, 104; and the Earl of
Ormonde, 165 ounces, which is the
largest quantity given except "to
Sir Christopher Hatton, Vice-Chamberlain and Captain of the Guard,"
who received 400 ounces.

Wendlingborough in Northamptonshire, and of the wardship of two more minors.[*]

Though Hatton had then been at least eight years attached to the Court, his name has not been found in any correspondence of the period; and his career seems to have been marked only by the extraordinary favour and liberal bounty of the Queen. That his position rendered him an object of envy, cannot be doubted; but he seems to have made more friends and fewer enemies than any other Royal favourite.

Literary men found in him a kind and generous patron; and his influence with the Queen had enabled him to lay some of the highest personages in the State under obligations. An affecting proof of his friendship for the Duke of Norfolk, who was condemned for high treason on the 16th of January 1572, but whose greatest crime was a design to marry the Queen of Scots, is afforded by a passage in the letter which that unfortunate nobleman wrote to his son, Philip Earl of Surrey, on the 20th of that month: "Mr. Hatton is a marvellous constant friend, one that I have been much beholden unto. Write unto him and seek his goodwill, and I believe you shall find him assured." To this circumstance may be attributed the insertion of the following letter, from the Duke to his son, in Hatton's "Letter book." It was intended that Norfolk should have been executed on the 2nd of February, and early in the morning of that day he wrote this pathetic letter in his Bible; but he was then respited, and not put to death until the 2nd of June. The young Earl of Surrey naturally revered the book so bequeathed to him, and wrote in it, "Phi-

[*] Rot. Pat. 14 Eliz.

lip Surreye and this booke ought no waye be separated, but be together alwayes; and I Philip Surreye testify the same, beinge written with myne owen hande."[a]

THOMAS DUKE OF NORFOLK TO HIS SON, PHILIP EARL OF SURREY.

Now, my dear son Philip, the hour is come that your earthly father must bid you farewell: and so I do with a right goodwill, as well yourself as also your loving wife, my well-beloved daughter; your two brethren, my dear children; and mine own sweet daughter, with your pretty sisters-in-law.[b] For I have, by my most earnest prayers to Almighty God, for His dear Son's sake Jesus Christ, committed you wholly over to His divine Majesty; whose grace if you call for earnestly, with a constant faith in Christ only, no doubt you shall receive more mercy and goodness at His hands than my natural affection unto you can either think for or wish you. Besides, I have by most humble petition to my most gracious sovereign Lady, Queen, and Mistress,[c] offered you

[a] Harleian MSS. 6991, where another copy, differing slightly from the one in the text, occurs. Copies of the Duke's letter to his children on the 20th of February, bidding them farewell in the most tender terms, and advising them as to their conduct in life, as well as of the letter of that date to his son, are in the Harleian MSS. 787, 4808, &c., and they may all have been printed.

[b] By his first wife, Mary, only child of Henry Fitz-Alan, Earl of Arundel, he had his son and heir, Philip Howard, then styled Earl of Surrey, who inherited the earldom of Arundel from his mother. Though then very young, he was married to Anne, eldest daughter of Thomas, and sister and co-heir of George Lord Dacre of Gillesland, and he died a prisoner in the Tower, under sentence of death for treason, in November 1595. By his second wife, Margaret, daughter and heiress of Thomas Lord Audley of Walden, the Duke of Norfolk left two sons, viz. Thomas, ancestor of the Earls of Suffolk and Berkshire, and William, ancestor of the Earls of Carlisle, and of Mr. Howard of Corby. Both Thomas and William Howard married daughters of Lord Dacre and sisters of their half-brother the Earl of Arundel's wife, and a daughter Margaret, who became the wife of Robert Earl of Dorset. The Duke married a third wife, who died in 1569, and by whom he had no issue, but who left two daughters by her first husband.

[c] This petition is in Hayne's State Papers, p. 166. In the Duke's letter to the Queen, of the 23rd of January, called his "confession," he gratefully acknowledges her "intended goodness to his unfortunate brats." Ibid. p. 168.

(as poor orphans cast away) unto the comfort of her Highness' most merciful goodness; to whom with your hearts, if
you have not minds fully bent, as your abilities will serve you,
to make some satisfaction for me your father's disobedience.
Instead of well-wishing you, I pray God send you short lives;
but I hope, as it may be an example unto you to take heed
of undutifulness, so you will remember this my last charge.
And because by mine own experience I know how forgetful
youth is, and for fear lest your young years (which I have
most unhappily overthrown) should utterly sink for want of
bridling, I have by my earnest petition chosen for you my
children one* that I hope will be to you another myself: not
that I can claim any so great kindness at his hands by desert,
(who have been ever beholden to him, and I never able to
pleasure him,) but for the former experience that I have had
of his friendship; and now, lastly, when friendship was most
tried, that it pleased him, at my fervent request, to be your
adoptive father. It is, methinks, no little comfort unto me,
at this time of my death, that I have so well bestowed you,
first, to the protection of the most merciful God; secondly,
to the most gracious and pitiful heart of my most redoubted
Queen and Mistress; thirdly, to the care of so friendly and
vigilant a nobleman, now your earthly father. I write briefly
now, because my mind is wholly bent upon that which I
have more care of than of yourselves: have regard to my
meaning, and not to my uncouthed sentences, or perhaps
unapt words. I have written to you at length heretofore,
which perhaps is come to your hands ere this. Remember
my former lessons, as well as if I should repeat them anew.
They be but short; but, if you follow them, you shall find
them sweet, and best for your souls' health, and for your
worldly profit and quietness. Be obedient to your new good
father, and to those other my friends that in my letters I
have recommended unto you; and be advised by such of my
servants as have been trustiest unto me, for they are able
to give you that counsel which shall be fittest for you to

* Lord Burghley.

follow.   I write thus much unto you in this place of the
Book, because by godly Job you may learn to be patient in
this adversity that my desert hath now laid upon you, and say
with that good man the one-and-twentieth verse in his first
chapter; and on the other side, of the Psalms of good King
David, you may select and see many sentences again for the
comfort of your afflicted minds.   But the true cause why I
send you this Book is, to the end you may study it well, and
live accordingly, for so shall you be thought to fear to do evil.
O God, forgive me, I beseech Him, all my misdeeds! If I had
done as I now counsel you, this misfortune had not chanced;
and yet behold the mercifulness of God, for although I was
called but at the eleventh hour, yet I hope I have taken
that instruction of this Book of Life as hath made me fit to
battle against the devil, death, and all worldly temptations.
God grant, for His mercy's sake in my Saviour Jesus Christ,
that I may so strongly in spiritual grace continue till my
last breath!   O Philip, is not this then a worthy Book, that,
if you ply it worthily, will keep thee ever from deadly sin?
and yet if thou fall, by the frailty of Adam's flesh, in this
Book thou mayest find comfort to be again and again renewed
and reconciled to Jesus Christ.   Read this Book, study it,
and meditate upon it, and the Lord will bless you, not only
in this world, but also in the world to come, where *nova
facta sunt omnia*, and where I most humbly beseech Him
to grant us a joyful meeting.   That is the only kingdom.
Pray most effectually for the long preservation of our most
gracious Queen, for our Lord save her! If aught should chance
otherwise than well to her noble person, your misery shall be
doubled, and your back friends perchance strengthened.   Beware of factions (whereof there be too many), if you love
your own life, or will save that little that by hap is left
you.   Farewell, my dear son! as you may think, when you
see how much time I have bestowed upon you at this instant,
when time is more precious unto me than all the good in the
world.   And the Lord bless you all, my dear children!   I
wish this to the rest as well as to you, and send you all His
grace, which is no ways to be obtained but by faith in Jesus

Christ; in which faith the Lord of His merciful goodness strengthen you now and evermore, Amen! The 2nd of February, which, within four hours after, might have been written with my heart's blood. Remember my lessons, and forget me. Written between four and five of the clock by me your earthly woeful father, but joyful. I most humbly thank the Lord, that I hope my time draweth so near that my soul shall enjoy bliss, and leave this crooked lump of sinful flesh.

Sometime NORFOLK, now THOMAS HOWARD.[a]

In May 1572, Hatton was elected a Knight of the Shire for Northampton, and he continued to represent that county[b] until he became Lord Chancellor. On the 13th of July Lord Burghley was made Lord High Treasurer; Lord William Howard, Lord Privy Seal; the Earl of Sussex, Lord Chamberlain; and Sir Thomas Smith, Secretary of State. On the same occasion the office of Captain of the Guard becoming vacant by Sir Francis Knollys being made Treasurer of the Household, he was succeeded by Hatton,[c] who still retained the situation of Gentleman of the Privy Chamber and of Gentleman-pensioner.

Though large beneficial grants had been made to Hatton, no important office, nor any honour, for he was not even Knighted until five years after this period, had been conferred upon him; yet the Queen's regard for him was so notorious, that he was considered to rival the Earl of Leicester in her favour, and scandal was equally rife with respect to them both. The earliest allusion that has been found to these injurious reports shows how prevalent they must have been. In August 1570,

[a] Additional MSS. 15891 fo. 149.   [c] Stow, p. 672. Nichols' Progresses, i. 307.
[b] Willis' Notitia Parliamentaria.

several persons were tried, and some executed at Norwich, for treasonable speeches and designs. "They had set out four proclamations: one was touching the wantonness of the Court;" and one of the conspirators called Marsham, having said that "my Lord of Leicester had two children by the Queen," was sentenced to lose both his ears, or pay a fine of one hundred pounds.[a] Among the traitorous speeches of a person called Mather, in 1571, according to Berney's written confession to Lord Leicester, was, that the Queen "desireth nothing but to feed her own lewd fantasy, and to cut off such of her nobility as were not perfumed and court-like to please her delicate eye, and place such as were for her turn, meaning dancers, and meaning you my Lord of Leicester, and one Mr. Hatton, whom he said had more recourse unto her Majesty in her privy chamber than reason would suffer if she were so virtuous and well-inclined as some noiseth her; with other such vile words as I am ashamed to speak, much more to write."[b] In a letter from Archbishop Parker to Lord Burghley, in September 1572, he says he was credibly informed that some man had, in his examination by the Mayor of Dover and Mr. Sommers, uttered "most shameful words against her" (the Queen), namely, that the Earl of Leicester and Mr. Hatton should be such towards her as the matter is so horrible that they would not write down the words, but would have uttered them in speech to your lordship if ye could have been at leisure."[c]

But there were far more distinguished and more

[a] Lodge's "Illustrations of British History," 8vo. vol. i. pp. 514, 515.
[b] Murdin's State Papers, p. 204.
[c] Lansdowne MSS. 15, art 43.

Orig., printed in Strype's Life of Archbishop Parker, ed. Oxon. vol. ii. p. 127; and in Wright's "Queen Elizabeth and her Times," i. 440.

virulent calumniators of the Queen than these obscure people.

Mary Queen of Scots' charges must be here repeated, however disgusting or untrue. In her celebrated letter to Elizabeth, she says, that the Countess of Shrewsbury had expressed regret " que vous ne vous contentiez de maistre Haton et un autre de ce royaulme;" but had forgotten her honour with Simyer, as well as with the Duke d'Anjou, his master. " Quant au dict Haton, que vous le couriez a force, faisant si publiquement paroitre l'amour que luy portiez, qui luy mesmes estoit contreint de s'en retirer, et que vous donnastes un soufflet a Kiligreu pour ne vous avoir ramene le dict Haton, que vous avviez envoiay rappeler par luy, s'etant desparti en chollere d'auveques vous pour quelques injures que luy auviez dittes pour certiens boutons d'or qu'il auvoit sur son habit. Qu'elle auvoit travaille de fayre espouser au dit Haton la feu Comtesse de Lenox sa fille, mays que de creinte de vous, il ne osoit ententre." Mary then says that the Earl of Oxford dared not cohabit with his wife " de peur de perdre la faveur qu'il esperoit recepvoir par vous fayre l'amour;" that she was lavish towards all such people, " et ceulx qui se mesloient de telles mesnees, comme a un de vostre chambre, Gorge,"[a] to whom she had given three hundred pounds of rent, " pour vous avoir apporte les nouvelles du retour de Haton."[b]

[a] Query if the William Gorge or Gorges, who was for many years one of the Gentlemen-pensioners.

[b] Murdin's State Papers, 558. The admirers of Mary affect to doubt the authenticity of this letter, which is said to have been printed from the original; but the opportunity of exasperating Elizabeth, whom she hated, and at the same time injuring Lady Shrewsbury, whom she detested, — a double revenge, too tempting to a vindictive and injured woman to be lost, and perfectly consistent with Mary's temper, — explains away most of the objections taken to it. It receives some support from Lady Shrewsbury's stepson, Gilbert Talbot, having informed

Cardinal Allen, in his " Admonition to the Nobility and People of England and Ireland," in 1588, charges her, in the coarsest terms, with having intrigued with Leicester and " with divers others," and speaks of her " unlawful, long concealed, or fained issue."[a]

To these facts may be added, that the notoriety of Elizabeth's incontinence was alleged by the Duke of Anjou as his reason for refusing to marry her;[b] and that one of Lord Burghley's objections to her marrying Leicester was, that " it would be thought that the slanderous speeches of the Earl with the Queen have been true."[c]

Extraordinary evidence on this delicate subject is afforded by the following letter to Hatton, from his friend Edward Dyer,[d] written a few weeks after the before-mentioned examination at Dover, and by the still more remarkable letters from Hatton to the Queen, which will be afterwards given. The letter from Dyer proves that whatever may have been the nature of Elizabeth's regard for Hatton, it was perfectly well known to his friends; and that, a rival having appeared, Hatton was thrown into the shade. He therefore con-

---

his father of the Queen's flirtation with the Earl of Oxford in 1573.

[a] Cardinal Allen's charges are abridged and translated in a note to Lingard's History of England, 8vo. vol. viii. p. 535.

[b] In a Letter from the Queen Mother, Catherine de Medicis, to De la Motte Fenelon, the French ambassador, (Ed. Cooper, vol. vii. p. 179,) she said, " Et pour venir au poinct, c'est que mon fils m'a faict dire par le Roy qu'il ne la veut jamais espouser, quand bien elle le voudroit, d'aultant qu'il a tousjours si mal oui parler de son honneur, et en a veu des lettres escriptes de tous les am-

bassadeurs, qui y ont esté, qu'il penseroit estre déshonnoré et perdre toute la réputation qu'il pense avoir acquise."

[c] Hayne's State Papers, p. 444.

[d] Edward Dyer was one of the many dependants of the Earl of Leicester. He was occasionally employed in the Queen's service, and was rewarded in 1596 by the appointment of Chancellor of the Order of the Garter, when he was Knighted; and died about 1607. An account of Dyer, by the Editor of this work, will be found in " Davison's Poetical Rhapsody," ed. 1826, where this letter was first printed.

sulted Dyer as to the means of maintaining or recovering his position in the Queen's favour. Finding that Hatton contemplated the dangerous plan of reproaching Elizabeth for the change in her sentiments, he earnestly advised him not to adopt so perilous a course; and, if the expressions used by Dyer are to receive their usual interpretation, it is difficult to disbelieve the reports which were then so prevalent.   Hatton's rival was apparently the young and eccentric Earl of Oxford, who had lately married the daughter of Lord Burghley, and whom he cruelly treated in revenge for her father's having refused his request to intercede with the Queen for the Duke of Norfolk.   As Oxford, besides his illustrious descent, was distinguished for the same personal qualities as those which obtained the Queen's favour for Hatton,* his jealousy is not surprising;—

MR. DYER TO MR. HATTON.

Sir, After my departure from you, thinking upon your case as my dear friend, I thought good to lay before you mine opinion in writing somewhat more at large than at my last conference I did speak.   And I do it of goodwill, for you need no counsel of mine I know right well.   But one that standeth by shall see more in the game than one that is much more skilful, whose mind is too earnestly occupied. I will not recite the argument, or put the case as it were, for it needeth not; but go to the reasons, such as they be. First of all, you must consider with whom you have to deal, and what we be towards her; who though she do descend very much in her sex as a woman, yet we may not forget her place, and the nature of it as our Sovereign.   Now if a man, of secret cause known to himself, might in common reason challenge it, yet if the Queen mislike thereof, the world

* *Vide* page 23, *post.*

followeth the sway of her inclination; and never fall they
in consideration of reason, as between private persons they
do.   And if it be after that rate for the most part in causes
that may be justified, then much more will it be so in causes
not to be avouched.   A thing to be had in regard; for
it is not good for any man straitly to weigh a general disal-
lowance of her doings.

That the Queen will mislike of such a course, this is my
reason: she will imagine that you go about to imprison
her fancy, and to warp her grace within your disposition;
and that will breed despite and hatred in her towards you:
and so you may be cast forth to the malice of every envious
person, flatterer, and enemy of yours; out of which you
shall never recover yourself clearly, neither your friends, so
long as they show themselves your friends.

But if you will make a proof (*par ver vramo,* [a] as Spanish
phrase is) to see how the Queen and he will yield to it, and
it prosper, go through withal; if not, to change your course
suddenly into another more agreeable to her Majesty, I can
like indifferently of that.   But then you must observe this,
that it be upon a by-occasion, for else it were not convenient
for divers reasons that you cannot but think upon.

But the best and soundest way in mine opinion is, to put
on another mind; to use your suits towards her Majesty in
words, behaviour, and deeds; to acknowledge your duty,
declaring the reverence which in heart you bear, and never
seem deeply to condemn her frailties, but rather joyfully to
commend such things as should be in her, as though they
were in her indeed; hating my Lord of Ctm[b] in the Queen's
understanding for affection's sake, and blaming him openly
for seeking the Queen's favour.   For though in the beginning
when her Majesty sought you (after her good manner), she
did bear with rugged dealing of yours, until she had what
she fancied, yet now, after satiety and fulness, it will rather
hurt than help you; whereas, behaving yourself as I said

---

[a] *Sic.*   Query *Por verrano?* a Portuguese proverb,—to see daylight
through obscurity.   [b] Query Oxford ?

before, your place shall keep you in worship, your presence in favour, your followers will stand to you, at the least you shall have no bold enemies, and you shall dwell in the ways to take all advantages wisely, and honestly to serve your turn at times.   Marry, thus much I would advise you to remember, that you use no words of disgrace or reproach towards him to any; that he, being the less provoked, may sleep, thinking all safe, while you do awake and attend your advantages.

Otherwise you shall, as it were, warden him and keep him in order; and he will make the Queen think that he beareth all for her sake, which will be as a merit in her sight; and the pursuing of his revenge shall be just in all men's opinions, by what means soever he and his friends shall ever be able.

You may perchance be advised and encouraged to the other way by some kind of friends that will be glad to see whether the Queen will make an apple or a crab of you, which, as they find, will deal accordingly with you; following if fortune be good; if not, leave, and go to your enemy: for such kind of friends have no commodity by hanging in suspense, but set you a fire to do off or on,—all is one to them; rather liking to have you in any extremity than in any good mean.

But beware not too late of such friends, and of such as make themselves glewe between them and you, whether it be of ignorance or practice.   Well, not to trouble you any longer, it is very necessary for you to impart the effect of this with your best and most accounted friends, and most worthy to be so; for then you shall have their assistance every way; who, being made privy of your council, will and ought in honour to be partners of your fortune, which God grant to be of the best.   The 9th of October 1572.   Your assured poor friend to command,   EDW. DYER.[a]

Though the original letter does not exist, there is no reason to doubt the accuracy of the transcript.   It occurs among the copies of many other letters and docu-

---

[a] In the Harleian MSS. 787, fol. 88.

ments of the period, which were found in the possession
of Mr. Dell, who had been Secretary to Archbishop
Laud. The internal evidence of its genuineness is
strong; and becomes still stronger when compared with
Dyer's other letters, especially with his letter to Lord
Leicester some years later,* giving him advice respecting
his proceedings in the Low Countries. The danger which
it might be supposed would attend any person who ventured to commit such sentences to writing, if they really
had the meaning which they seem to bear, is some
reason for suspecting the letter, or for giving a very
different construction to the passages; but the Queen's
attachment to Hatton was so notorious that it accounts
for Dyer's recommending Hatton to consult his "best
and most accounted friends" on the subject.

Though there is no date to the following letter from
Hatton to the Queen, and though he fell under her displeasure on subsequent occasions, there can be little
doubt that it was written at this period; and it shews
the ostensible cause of his loss of favour. It is super-
scribed with this cypher, instead of the proper address;—

MADAM, In striving to withstand your violent course of
evil opinion towards me, I might perhaps the more offend

* Memoir of Sir Edward Dyer, in "Davison's Poetical Rhapsody," ed.
1826, vol. i. p. lxxix.

you, because the truth of my cause disagreeth with the rigour of your judgment. But the bitterness of my heart in humble complaints I trust you will hear, for your goodness and justice sake. May it therefore please you, my faults are said to be these;—unthankfulness, covetousness, and ambition.

To the first, I speak the truth before God, that I have most entirely loved your person and service; to the which, without exception, I have everlastingly vowed my whole life, liberty, and fortune. Even so am I yours, as, whatever God and you should have made me, the same had been your own; than which I could, nor any can, make larger recompense. This I supposed to have been the true remuneration of greatest good turns, because I know it balanceth in weight the greatest good wills. Neither hath the ceremony of thanksgiving any way wanted, as the world will right fully witness with me; and therefore in righteousness I most humbly pray you condemn me not. Spare your poor prostrate servant from this pronounced vengeance.

To the second, I ever found your largess before my lack, in such plenty as I could wish no more, so that by craving I never argued myself covetous; if any other way it appeared, let it be of folly and not of evil mind that so I have erred: yet God knoweth I never sought nor wished more wealth than to live worthily in your most sacred service, without mixture of any other opinion, purpose, or matter. I trust therefore in your holy heart this truth shall have his settled place. God for His mercy grant it may so be.

To the third, God knoweth I never sought place but to serve you; though indeed, to shield my poor self, both nature and reason would have taught me to ask refuge at your strong and mighty hand. These late great causes that most displeased your nobles, as of the Duke of N. and Q. of S.,* the Acts of Parliament for religion, and other strange courses in those things taken, were all laid on my weak shoulders; under which when I shall fall, behold then the wretched man how he shall pass all pointed at. But to my purpose, if ever

* Duke of Norfolk and Queen of Scots: *vide* p. 9, *ante.*

I inordinately sought either honour, or riches, place, calling, or dignity, I pray to God that hell might swallow me. Believe not, I humbly beseech you for your wisdom and worthiness, the tale so evil told of your most faithful: be not led by lewdness of others to lose your own, that truly loveth you. These most unkind conceits wonderfully wring me: reserve me more graciously to be bestowed on some honourable enterprise for you; and so shall I die a most joyful man and eternally bound to you.

But would God I might win you to think well according with my true meaning; then should I acquiet my mind, and serve you with joy and further hope of goodness. I ask right of Her will do no wrong; and yet this hard hap doth follow me, that I must make prayer for the blessing that every man hath without demand or asking. I fear your too great trouble in reading this blotted letter. I will therefore with my most dutiful submission pray for your long and happy life. I pray God bless you for ever.

Your despairing most wretched bondman,

CH. HATTON.[a]

Early in May 1573, Hatton was seriously ill; and, however much the Queen's regard for him may have been lessened, his indisposition certainly revived her affection. On the 11th of that month Mr. Gilbert Talbot wrote a letter to his father, the Earl of Shrewsbury, filled with news; and it affords so much curious information on the state of the Court, that a few sentences will be extracted, besides the one immediately relating to Hatton:—
" My Lord Treasurer, even after the old manner, dealeth with matters of the State only, and beareth himself very uprightly. My Lord Leicester is very much with her Majesty, and she sheweth the same great good affection to him that she was wont: of late, he hath endeavoured

---

[a] Autograph in the State Paper Office.

to please her more than heretofore.   There are two
sisters now in the Court that are very far in love with
him, as they have been long, my Lady Sheffield and
Frances Howard:[a] they of like striving who shall love
him better are at great wars together, and the Queen
thinketh not well of them, and not the better of him;
by this means there is spies over him.   My Lord of Sussex goeth with the tide, and helpeth to back others; but
his own credit is sober, considering his estate: he is very
diligent in his office, and takes great pains.   My Lord
of Oxford is lately grown into great credit; for the
Queen's Majesty delighteth more in his personage, and
his dancing and valiantness, than any other.   I think
Sussex doth back him all that he can; if it were not for his
fickle head, he would sure pass any of them shortly.   My
Lady Burghley[b] unwisely has declared herself (as it were)
jealous, which is come to the Queen's ear; whereat she
hath been not a little offended with her, but now she is
reconciled again.   At all these love matters my Lord
Treasurer winketh, and will not meddle any way.   Hatton is sick still; it is thought he will very hardly recover his disease, for it is doubted it is in his kidneys:
the Queen goeth almost every day to see how he doth.
Now is there devices, chiefly by Leicester (as I suppose),
and not without Burghley's knowledge, how to make
Mr. Edward Dyer as great as ever was Hatton; for now,
in this time of Hatton's sickness, the time is convenient.
It is brought thus to pass: Dyer lately was sick of a
consumption, in great danger; and, as your Lordship
knoweth, he hath been in displeasure these two years: it

---

[a] Daughters of William Lord Howard of Effingham.   The Earl of Leicester married the former, and the
Earl of Hertford the latter.

[b] The Earl of Oxford's mother-in
law.

was made the Queen believe that his sickness came because of the continuance of her displeasure towards him,
that, unless she would forgive him, he was like not to
recover; and hereupon her Majesty hath forgiven him,
and sent unto him a very comfortable message: now he is
recovered again, and this is the beginning of this device.
These things I learn of such young fellows as myself."[a]

On the 23rd of May, Lord Talbot informed his father
that the Queen was desirous of making a progress to Bristol, but that it was wished to dissuade her from going so
far on account of the unseasonableness of the weather; and
he added, "Mr. Hatton, by reason of his great sickness, is
minded to go to the Spa for the better recovery of his
health."[b]   On the 29th of May an order was signed by
the Privy Council for allowing Hatton " to pass over
the seas for recovery of his health,"[c] and the deep
solicitude which the Queen felt about him was shewn
by her causing him to be accompanied by Dr. Julio,
the eminent Court physician.   Hatton took leave of
Elizabeth on the 3rd of June; and few letters have

[a] Shrewsbury Papers in the College of Arms, F. fo. 79, printed in
Lodge's " Illustrations of British
History," 8vo., vol. ii. pp. 17, 18.
[b] Hunter's History of Hallamshire, p. 84.   Mr. Hunter has erroneously assigned this letter to 1574,
because in that year the Queen visited
Bristol. Strype (ed. Oxford, ii. 449)
and Mr. Nichols (Progresses, i.
388) have fallen into a similar mistake by supposing that Hatton went
to Spa in 1574.   Referring to a letter from Francis Talbot, dated 28th
June 1574, in which he says the
Queen " had been melancholy disposed a good while, which should
seem that she is troubled with
weighty causes," Strype says, "but,
notwithstanding, that month she began her progress. . . . . . Mr. Hatton (not well in health) took this
opportunity to get leave to go to the
Spaw, and Dr. Julio (a great Court
physician) with him ; whereat the
Queen shewed herself very pensive,
and very unwilling to grant him
leave, for he was a favourite.   These
are some of the contents of a private
letter of the Lord Talbot to the Earl
his father." It is certain that Hatton
returned to England in the autumn
of 1573, and that he did not go to
Spa in 1574 ; and, consequently,
both Strype and Mr. Hunter have
mistaken the date.   Strype has also
misrepresented the contents of Lord
Talbot's letter of the 23rd of May
[1574] quoted in the text.
[c] Privy Council Books.

ever been published more curious than those written by him to her Majesty during his absence, which now for the first time see the light.   It appears that she had given him the singular appellation of " Lids " or " Lyddes;"* that he sometimes subscribed his letters with a cypher; and that those which he wrote to her had no other address than another cypher.   The style of his correspondence is that of an ardent and successful lover, separated by distance and illness from a mistress, rather than that of a Subject to his Sovereign.

On the 5th of June, Hatton wrote the following reply to some letters which he had received from the Queen, though only two days had elapsed since he quitted her presence:

If I could express my feelings of your gracious letters, I should utter unto you matter of strange effect.   In reading of them, with my tears I blot them.   In thinking of them I feel so great comfort, that I find cause, as God knoweth, to thank you on my knees.   Death had been much more my advantage than to win health and life by so loathsome a pilgrimage.

The time of two days hath drawn me further from you than ten, when I return, can lead me towards you.   Madam, I find the greatest lack that ever poor wretch sustained.   No death, no, not hell, no fear of death shall ever win of me my consent so far to wrong myself again as to be absent from you one day.   God grant my return.   I will perform this vow.   I lack that I live by.   The more I find this lack, the

* Some expressions in his letters tend to shew that the name was "lids," i. e. "eyelids;" and, if so, Hatton's were perhaps peculiar.

further I go from you.   Shame whippeth me forward.
Shame take them that counselled me to it.   The life (as you
well remember), is too long that loathsomely lasteth.   A true
saying, Madam.   Believe him that hath proved it.   The great
wisdom I find in your letters, with your Country counsels are
very notable, but the last word is worth the bible.   Truth,
truth, truth.   Ever may it dwell in you.   I will ever deserve
it.   My spirit and soul (I feel) agreeth with my body and life,
that to serve you is a heaven, but to lack you is more than
hell's torment unto them.   My heart is full of woe.   Pardon
(for God's sake) my tedious writing.   It doth much diminish
(for the time) my great griefs.   I will wash away the faults of
these letters with the drops from your poor Lydds and so
inclose them.   Would God I were with you but for one hour.
My wits are overwrought with thoughts.   I find myself
amazed.   Bear with me, my most dear sweet Lady.   Passion
overcometh me.   I can write no more.   Love me ; for I love
you.   God, I beseech thee witness the same on the behalf of
thy poor servant.   Live for ever.   Shall I utter this familiar
term (farewell)?   yea, ten thousand thousand farewells.   He
speaketh it that most dearly loveth you.   I hold you too
long.   Once again I crave pardon, and so bid your own poor
Lidds farewell.   1573 June.

Your bondman everlastingly tied,   CH. HATTON.[*]

Soon after Hatton arrived at Antwerp he again
wrote to the Queen:

THE time is (as it were) hallowed with me, wherein I may
in this sort exercise my devotion towards you and ease the
travails of my mind, which I continually find too much over-
burdened with the fears and cares that affection layeth upon
it.   Let it not, therefore, with you, Madam, be labour and
trouble to read these rude lines, that proceed from me with so

[*] Autograph in the State Paper
Office.   This letter must have been
written on the 5th of June, because
Hatton says it was the second day
since he quitted the Court ; and in
his letter of the 17th of that month
he says that it was the *twelfth* day
since he had seen the Queen.

pure and holy a thought. I fear you will be offended
with my boldness, but I know you will excuse me in
your goodness. I fear you will mislike that I find no other
matter to discourse unto you: in good faith, if I could
find a more worthy action, I would deliver it unto you; but
accept this, Madam, for in the world (above this) there is
nothing. This is the twelfth day since I saw the brightness
of that Sun that giveth light unto my sense and soul. I wax
an amazed creature.   Give me leave, Madam, to remove
myself out of this irksome shadow, so far as my imagination
with these good means may lead me towards you, and let me
thus salute you: Live for ever, most excellent creature; and
love some man, to shew yourself thankful for God's high
labour in you.   I am too far off to hear your answer to this
salutation; I know it would be full of virtue and great wisdom, but I fear for some part thereof I would have but small
thanks.   Pardon me; I will leave these matters, because I
think you mislike them.

Madam, I have received great honour in these Countries
for the love they bear you, or rather their fear of your greatness.   I perceive they are careful to exercise all good parts,
how unworthy so ever the person be unto whom they use
them; but of these things, and others, I have advertised Mr.
Heneage, whose report of the same I humbly beseech you to
hear.   I would I saw your world at home, how some seek
that I have done, which they shall find never.   Some hope
well and haste them on, but waste shall be their hire; and
some despair, whom I allow the wisest, but not the most
happy of these men.   But, Madam, forget not your Lidds that
are so often bathed with tears for your sake.   A more wise man
may seek you, but a more faithful and worthy can never have
you.   Pardon me, my most dear sweet Lady, I will no more
write of these matters. I wish you like welfare your presence
might give me; it is, I assure you, the best farewell that ever
was given you.   Antwerp, the 17th of June 1573.

Yours all and ever yours,

CH. HATTON.[a]

* Autograph in the State Paper Office.   No address or superscription.

The following letter to the Queen is without a date, but it was probably sent from Spa, in July or in the early part of August. It may however have been written at an earlier period, and before Hatton left England. Though it is not possible to explain all the extraordinary passages, there can be no doubt that he represents himself as the Queen's sheep, that the "branch" was a jewel she had sent to him, and that the "boar" with which he contrasts her "sheep" was the Earl of Oxford, whose crest was a boar :—

THE lack I feel doth make me know your greatest worth. I speak in the presence of God. I find my body and mind so far divided, as, yourself shall judge, that melancholy (conceived by this unwonted absence) hath made myself forget myself. Your Mutton is black; scarcely will you know your own, so much hath this disease dashed me. I pray God, you may believe my faith. It is the testament of your greatest excellencies. It might glad you (I speak without presumption), that you live so dearly loved with all sincerity of heart and singleness of choice. I love yourself. I cannot lack you. I am taught to prove it by the wish and desire I find to be with you. Believe it, most gracious Lady, there is no *illud mitius*, you are the true felicity that in this world I know or find. God bless you for ever. The branch of the sweetest bush I will wear and bear to my life's end. God doth witness I feign not. It is a gracious favour, most dear and welcome unto me. Reserve it to the Sheep, he hath no tooth to bite; where[as] the Boar's tusk may both rase and tear. The branch of brass with your most notable word and sentence, I desire exceedingly to have. But your judgment most pleaseth me, that you cannot esteem the untrue esteemer. Pardon me, most humbly on my knees I beseech you.   The abundance of my heart carrieth me I know not to what purpose ; but guess you (as the common proverb is), and I will grant.   I guess by my servant you should not be well, which troubleth me greatly.   I humbly pray you that I may know it, for then will I presently come, whatever befal me. Humbly on the knees of my soul, I pray God bless you for ever.   Your slave and *EveR*[a] your own,

 [b]

On the 10th of August Hatton wrote to the Queen under the signature of " Lyddes," in reply to a letter which he had received from her inclosed in one to Mr. Heneage :

MADAM, as your most rare works confirm in me an irremoveable faith, so is my love and band enlarged to an infinite serviceable thankfulness.   The lining of Mr. Heneage letter warmeth the heart's blood with joys above joys.   Full sweet will such a life be, that by so noble a sweet creature is with so glad and kind devotion asked at the Almighty's hands.   God grant it you.   Not for myself I ask it; but that your everlasting bondman, with pure love and careful diligent faith, may everlastingly serve you.   God grant him grace to give you as small trouble as you give him most inestimable

---

[a] The *E* and *R* are capitals, and are so written by him in a subsequent letter, evidently in allusion to the Queen's initials, — Elizabetha Regina.

[b] Autograph in the State Paper Office.

great cause of the contrary. I trust with discretion to correct all frail humour. Give your pardon of things bypast, and I will even it by amendments to follow. The contentment of mind you give me doth most of all re-cure me. By your great bounty and most liberal charge I purchase life and health withal. By your oft messengers, carriers of your endless cares for my recovery's sake, I enjoy so great a comfort in life as never God hath blessed man withal before. For all these I can yield you nothing but the beggar's phrase, though indeed the best thanks, God save your life for ever, and bless you with His glorious thanks for your divine merits towards me your so poor and discomforted despairing servant. My dear Lady, I amend: some proof thereof hath Julio[a] sent unto you. I find cause to think that much greater effects will follow. God be blessed in all His works, and you in your most Royal gifts. Upon the knees of my heart I most humbly commend my most faithful love and service unto you. Adieu, most dear sweet Lady. This 10th of August 1573. All and *EveR* yours, your most happy bondman, LYDDES.[b]

[a] Doctor Julio the physician.

[b] Autograph in the State Paper Office. Though the inquiry after letters from Queen Elizabeth to Hatton has not been successful, it has brought to light parts of two very remarkable documents, which may possibly have been the " gracious letters" to which he alludes (p. 26), because in one of them she speaks of the health of the person to whom it was addressed ; both were written at the same time; and the conclusion of the second of them may have been the " last word," which he says was " worth the Bible." If these extracts were really made from letters to Hatton, they tend to negative the injurious impressions created by other circumstances, and they ought, therefore, to be here inserted. In the Editor's opinion, however, they did not form parts of the Queen's letters to him; but they shew, at all events, that she sometimes repressed improper wishes, and they are extremely curious in themselves:—

" Even such good health my friend as never can appair is wished may fall unto your share by one even wholly yours, if he can be such a one, that scant is found to be his own. Your curious care to know what grief incumbred my breast together with the remedy that may cure the sore, is harder for me to utter than write. If my guest were not worse than his lodging, the rest were not worse than the travail. And lest my paraphrase agree not with my text, I will make mine own exposition. The constitution of my mind's vessel is not so evil framed, as whereupon grievous diseases or perilous maladies have taken hold. I find not the mixture so evil made as that any one element of all four, overruleth so his fellows, as that the rest may envy his hap. Since but one other part the divine power hath

The exact time of Hatton's return to England is not known, but it must have been before October in this year; for, on the 11th of that month, a religious enthusiast, named Peter Burchet, a student of the Middle Temple, deemed it a matter of conscience to assassinate Hatton,[a] because he had made himself obnoxious to the Puritans, by whom he was considered "a wilful Papist, and hindereth the glory of God so much as in him lieth;"[b] but, mistaking Captain Hawkins[c] of the Queen's

given us for the best, it followeth then that there must be the plaint, or gone is all the moan. If your request, that seldom I deny, had not enforced a custom newly made, it would have pleased me well that you should not forget how hardly green wounds suffer their toucher's hand ; but since a nay your firm friend can scarce be brought to make you, the upper scale you shall touch to sound the depth shall serve the feeler's part. When I a gathering make of common paths and trades and think upon the sundry sorts of travellers in them both, I find a muse no greater, when multitudes be gathered and faces many one, amongst the which not two of all be found alike ; then wonder breeds in me, how all this worldly mass so long is made to hold, where never a mould is framed alike, nor never a mind agrees. And were it not that heavenly power overcometh human philosophy, it would content me well to remember that an evil is much better the less while it endureth."

* * * * *

"A question once was asked me thus. Must aught be denied a friend's request? Answer me yea or nay. It was said—Nothing. And first it is best to scan what a friend is, which I think nothing else but friendship's harbour. Now it followeth what friendship is, which I deem to be one uniform consent of two minds, such as virtue links and

naught but death can break. Therefore I conclude that the house that shrinketh from his foundation shall down for me ; for friend leaves he to be, that doth demand more than the giver's grant with reason's leave may yield. And if so, then my friend no more; my foe. God send thee mend. And if needly thou must will, yet at the least no power be thine to atchieve thy desire. For where minds differ and opinions swerve, there is scant a friend in that company. But if my hap have fallen in so happy a soil, as one such be found that wills but that beseems, and I be pleased with that he so allows, I bid myself farewell,—and then I am but his."—Contemporary copies in the State Paper Office, indorsed "A couple of letters of the Qū, endited and written at one time."

[a] Sir Thomas Smith, writing to Lord Burghley on the 15th of October 1573, says, "It is said here that divers times within this fortnight, both by words and writings, Mr. Hatton hath been admonished to take heed to himself, for his life was laid in wait for." Wright's Queen Elizabeth and her Times, i. 492.

[b] Burchet's (or, as he wrote his name, Byrchet) autograph confession in the Lansdowne MSS., 17. art. 88.

[c] The celebrated navigator Sir John Hawkins ; but neither Campbell nor Prince notice the circumstance in their accounts of his life.

navy for his intended victim, Burchet struck that officer with his dagger, as he was riding with Sir William Winter near Temple Bar towards Westminster. The wound, though severe, was not mortal; and, Burchet being sent to the Tower, he there murdered his keeper. As the false humanity of considering every fanatical assassin necessarily insane was not then in fashion, or, as a learned authority expresses it, "as they did not then stand on such niceties," [a] the criminal was justly condemned, and as properly executed.[b] Whether from indignation at the act, or terror at the danger from which her favourite had so narrowly escaped, Elizabeth ordered a commission to be issued for executing Burchet by martial law; and she was with some difficulty persuaded from so illegal a measure.[c]

Only one letter of the year 1573 occurs in Hatton's Letter-book. The Lord Deputy of Ireland, Sir William Fitzwilliam, had, with the consent of the majority of the Council, improperly granted a full pardon to a man accused of slaying a gentleman; and they had, moreover, complained of Sir Edward Fitton, one of the Council and Treasurer of Ireland, for having objected to the pardon. The Queen severely reprimanded the Deputy, and told the Council that they ought not servilely to adopt his views, but to advise him when they thought he was mistaken; and she highly applauded Fitton for his firmness. The comparison which she draws between the severity of Henry the Eighth on a similar occasion, and her own " moderate reign and government," is amusing;—

[a] Lord Campbell.
[b] Stow's Annals, 677. Strype's Annals, ed. Oxford, 427, 428. Camden's Annals, b. ii. p. 62.
[c] Camden's Annals, and Ellis's Original Letters, second series, vol. iii. p. 27.

THE QUEEN TO THE DEPUTY AND COUNCIL OF IRELAND.

RIGHT trusty and well-beloved, and trusty and well-beloved, we greet you well. We have received your letter of the 12th of June, in the which, for the matter of pardon granted, and also touching Sir Edward Fitton, having read and considered the whole that you have written, and likewise that he hath written, of that matter unto us, we cannot but mislike that you the Deputy should be so hasty to give such and so general a pardon upon the slaying of a gentleman: for, where the corrupt jury of the coroner's quest did find it but *se defendendo*, it may easily appear that was no true verdict, and that it was a murther; or else you would not in that case have made out a general pardon, but a particular pardon upon the indictment, and, of course, as in like cases are wont. But this pardon is so general, that all treasons, murders, and other enormities, and transgressions of laws be pardoned, and from the friend of the man murdered all prosecution of law taken away, such a one as we ourself (for we have seen the copy of it) would be afraid to grant, nor have not granted (to our knowledge) at any time since the first day of our reign: for it is not unknown to our Council here, and to all that have any doings with us, how seldom, and with what difficulty and conscience we be brought to pardon any man where suspicion of murther and malice pretensed is; and how curious we be to be informed of the matter when any of our subjects be slain, before we will condescend to discharge any man of it. That discretion we looked for in you our Deputy, and therefore we put you in that place, lest the blood of the man slain should cry vengeance upon us and our realm not doing justice for it, and that the punishment of the murder should be a terror to others to adventure upon the like. But if you our Deputy should overslip yourself in this, either by hastiness or temerity, yet, as it appeareth, you the rest of our Council there have done as little your duties to God and us, in that you would put your hands unto it; as, whatsoever the Deputy therein for the time

D

should do and allow, you would straight run into the same
rashness, and affirm it with subscription of your hands as
applauders of our Deputy. You be put there to be grave
and sage advisers, to temper such sudden affections either
the one way or the other, of love or of hatred, as may chance
to our Deputy, being but a man made of flesh and blood,
who cannot lightly be without them; and to have regard to
God first, and then to our honour and the surety and good
government of our realm. Sir Edward Fitton seemeth to
us a true and a good Counsellor, who, seeing so unreasonable
a pardon so unadvisedly granted, made stay of it to bring it
unto you our Deputy to be better advised of it, not resisting, but discreetly requiring more mature consultation; and
for this you will agree to put him to that shame as to commit
him for a contemner of your doings, imputing rashness unto
him in that behalf, where, in truth, he honoured us, in requiring more deliberation and regard than was had, to be had
in justice, the which is clean taken away by that rash and
unjust pardon. He refused to sit with you, and he had
cause so to do; for it appeareth you are all rather followers
of the Deputy's affections, than careful ministers of justice or
of our honour. If you had done well, you should have done
as he did, requiring the Deputy to stay to take better advisement: so should you have showed more care of justice, of
our honour, and of the good government of that our realm,
than of following the hasty affection of our Deputy. You
are adjoined to him from us as Counsellors, and in one
commission, not to follow one head, or whatsoever the Deputy
willeth; but to consider what is just and reason to be done,
and so agree with him and set to your hands, and no otherwise; and therefore be you more than one, that, if need be,
one may temper the other. Nicholas White, as appeareth
by your letter, not daring to dissent against so running a consent, yet showed his conscience not to consent to affection,
and would prescribe no punishment to that fact, which in his
conscience he thought to be the duty of a good Counsellor
to do. If this had been in our father's time, who removed a

Deputy thence for calling of one of the Council dissenting
from his opinion 'churl,' you may soon conceive how it
would have been taken. Our moderate reign and government can be contented to bear this, so you will take this for
a warning, and hereafter have before your eyes, not the will
or pleasure of our Deputy or any other Counsellor, but first
God's honour, and then justice and our service, which is
always joined to the good government of the realm, not
following in any respect any private quarrels or affections.
And as to you our Deputy, we shall hereafter write our mind
more at large: so will we not forget to give thanks to our
good cousin, the Earl of Kildare, for his good service. And
we could be content that the Earl of Ormond were at home.
We have written to Sir Edward Fitton, willing him to join
with you in Council and take his place again; and do wish
that, all sinister affections laid apart, you do join all in one
to do that which may be to the honour of God and of our
service, to the execution of justice, and to the good government of that realm. Given under our signet at our manor
of Greenwich, the 29th of June 1573, the 15th year of our
reign.*

The Queen visited Bristol in August 1574, attended by
Leicester, Hatton, and the other officers of her household.
Churchyard, the prolific versifier, from whom several
letters occur, published an account of her reception in
the second edition of his book, called " Churchyard's
Chips," which he dedicated to " the Right Worshipful,
his tried and worthy friend, Master Christopher Hatton,
Esquire, Captain of the Queen's Majesty's Guard, and
Gentleman of her Highness's Privy Chamber." His
motive for thus inscribing his work he thus explains:
" The long liking and goodwill, with the fast friendship I find in you, good Master Hatton, procures my
pen presently to perform that I promised no small

Additional MSS. 15891, f. 22.

time since, touching a book of all my English verses in metre. The offer whereof came from myself, not for the goodness of the matter, but for the perfectness of the person to whom I meant to dedicate my work." It was in this year that Hatton, with the approbation of the Queen, first applied to Dr. Cox, Bishop of Ely, for the lease of the episcopal house in Ely Place, Holborn. The bishop made, however, so vigorous though fruitless a defence of the property of his See,[a] as to call forth this well-known reprimand from the Queen:

" Proud Prelate ! I understand you are backward in complying with your agreement, but I would have you know, that I who made you what you are can unmake you; and if you do not forthwith fulfil your engagement, by God I will immediately unfrock you.

" ELIZABETH."[b]

Hatton was then so much in debt, that in December of this year Mr. Walsingham communicated the Queen's commands to Lord Burghley, that, of the note of the hundred pounds land that was given to him by Hatton, he should apply fifty pounds of it, as he might think most fit for her to part with, to him, " for that she is content to bestow so much on him presently towards the payment of his debts."[c]

In the year 1575 few notices have been found of Hatton. He presented his usual New-year's gift to the Queen, and her favour to him was manifested by large

---

[a] Strype's Annals, ed. Oxford, i. 501, 502, 533, 541; ii. 259, 564, 584.

[b] There are so many versions of this pithy letter that its authenticity becomes doubtful. No better authority has been found for it than the Gentleman's Magazine, vol. lxxix.

pt. i. p. 136, where the above copy of it is printed from " the Register of Ely."

[c] Original letter from Walsingham to the Lord Treasurer, 12th December 1574. Lansdowne MSS. 18, art. 96.

grants. In January he obtained lands in several counties : in August the manor of Chapel Brompton in Northamptonshire was given to him; and, on the 5th of December, Elizabeth settled four hundred pounds a year upon him for life, which donations were followed in the next year by the gift of Corfe Castle in Dorsetshire, and other lands in various parts of England.[a]

One of the few occasions on which Hatton appears in Parliamentary proceedings occurred in the Parliament which met in February 1575-6. Mr. Peter Wentworth, one of the members for Tregony, made a speech which astonished the pliant Commons. To advert to the acts of the Crown or to the state of the Country, except in terms of praise, was to speak "unreverend and undutiful words of the Queen." Wentworth was sequestered; and placed in the custody of the Sergeant-at-arms. A committee, of which Hatton was one, was appointed to investigate the affair. It made a report on the 9th; and the offender was sent,[b] almost as a matter of course, to the Tower.[c] On the 12th of March, Hatton was the bearer of a gracious message from the Queen, announcing that her Majesty was pleased to remit her "justly occasioned displeasure," and to refer the enlargement of the party to the House.[d] During that Parliament Hatton obtained a private Act for the assurance of his lands.[e]

---

[a] Rot. Patent. 17 & 18 Eliz. It appears from the Sydney Papers, vol. i. p. 159, that Hatton had also enjoyed a monopoly in Ireland, which expired about January 1576-7, the granting of which was "thought to be of no benefit to that country."

[b] Lord Campbell (ii. 140) says, Hatton moved Wentworth's committal to the Tower. His committal was moved by the Treasurer of the Household, not by Hatton. Commons' Journals, i. 104.

[c] Commons' Journals, i. 104.

[d] Ibid. p. 114 ; and Parliamentary History, i. 802.

[e] Statutes of the Realm, vol. iv. pt. i. p. 607.

On the 26th of August 1576, Hatton wrote to Lord
Burghley, from Northamptonshire, in reply to a letter
in which the Lord Treasurer had thanked him for his
reception at his house, and advised him to return to the
Court. It is obvious that Hatton was then in bad health
and depressed spirits.

TO LORD BURGHLEY.

MY MOST HONOURABLE GOOD LORD, Your letters declare
the great goodness of your noble nature. I have neither
deserved your thanks, nor can be grateful as I am most
bound unto you. I will love and honour you as your virtue
bindeth me, and every honest man that is subject to our most
gracious Sovereign. I have scarcely had health, Sir, since
my coming to this country; so that, enjoying not myself, I
could little joy in those small things I have. Sir Thomas
Cecil,[a] I thank him, is pleased to be with me; whereof, I assure your Lordship, I take great comfort. He is faithful,
good, and honest. I pray God you may live long to joy in
him and his. I most humbly thank your Lordship for your
loving and grave counsel. I will return to my most bounden
and dutiful service ever so soon as possibly I can; your
honourable wish for the stay of my poor house is that I
pray to God for, but yet it doth not so please Him that it may
come to pass. Thus, leaving to cumber your good Lordship
with my simple occasions, I most humbly take my leave.
Dene,[b] this 26th of August 1576. Your good Lordship's most
bound.   CHR. HATTON.[c]

The year 1577 was an important era in Hatton's
life. On the 11th of November he was appointed Vice-
Chamberlain of the Queen's Household, and sworn of
the Privy Council;[d] and in the same month he re-

---

[a] Lord Burghley's eldest son.

[b] Hatton's writing is very illegible.
This word may be either "Dean"
in Northamptonshire, or "Done."

[c] Lansdowne MSS. 22, art. 82.
Autograph.

[d] "At Windsor, 11th November
1577. This day Christopher Hat-

ceived the honour of Knighthood from the hands of his Royal mistress at Windsor Castle. That dignity was on the same occasion conferred upon Walsingham, one of the Secretaries of State, and upon Thomas Heneage, Treasurer of the Chamber.[a] He also received in the same year an additional grant of lands in many counties.[b] The only letter that is known to exist from Hatton in 1577 is of little other value than from its showing that he was then in possession of Ely House, of which he obtained a formal grant from the Crown in June in the ensuing year.[c]

TO LORD BURGHLEY.

RIGHT HONOURABLE AND MY VERY GOOD LORD, I understand that my friend Arden Waferer (whom I have required to be busy all this day about certain necessary affairs of mine at my house in Ely Place and elsewhere) is warned this morning to appear before your Honour in the Exchequer Chamber, for what cause I know not; but I know the man so well, and have known him for these fourteen or fifteen years, even since my first coming to the Inner Temple, (where we were some time both together,) that I verily think he will be well able to answer all matters that any his adversaries shall object against him. Notwithstanding, for so much as my business require present and speedy dispatch, (which, without him, being of long acquainted therewithal, cannot well be done,) if therefore your good Lordship will show me the favour presently to give him liberty to attend my causes, I shall think myself much beholding to your Honour; and I will undertake that he shall always be ready, moreover, to wait upon your Honour whensoever your good Lordship

ton, Esquire, Captain of her Majesty's Guard, was sworn Vice-Chamberlain and one of the Privy Council, and Mr. Doctor Wilson one of her Highness's Principal secretaries."— Privy Council Books.

[a] Cotton MSS. Claudius, C. III.
[b] Rot. Patent. 19 Eliz.
[c] Ibid. 20 Eliz.

shall appoint me to send him unto you. And so, beseeching
your Honour to stand his good Lord, and to grant my said
suit, and not to take displeasure with him, although perchance my occasions cause him to wait somewhat the later
upon your Honour, (as the bearer hereof shall more largely
declare to your Honour,) with my humble commendations I
take my leave of your good Lordship. Court, this 13th of
June 1577. Your good Lordship's most bound during life,

CH. HATTON.[a]

The Hatton Letter-book contains only one letter
written in 1577, and which was from the Lord Keeper
Bacon to the Queen on the state of public affairs. That
venerable statesman, who offered his opinions in a similar manner on at least two other occasions,[b] died in
February 1579.

THE LORD KEEPER TO THE QUEEN.

MY MOST GRACIOUS SOVEREIGN, I with all humbleness
pray pardon of your Majesty that I presume by letter to do
that, which bounden duty and service requireth to be done in
person. O good Madam, not want of a willing heart and
mind, but an unable and an unwieldy body, is the only cause
of this. And yet the body, such as it is, every day and
hour is, and ever shall be, at your Majesty's commandment ;
and so should they be, if I had a thousand as good as any man
hath, mine allegiance and a number of benefits hath so sundry
ways bounden me. The causes that make me now write
to your Majesty be the dangerous and perilous times, that
have continued long, and do now, in my judgment, daily
greatly increase. For as the two mighty and potent princes,
your neighbours, and surely your inward enemies, were the
less to be doubted as long as they had their hands full at
home ; so doubtless, as they prevail against those that kept
them occupied, (which, as I understand, they do greatly,) do
the perils and dangers to your Majesty's state hasten and grow

[a] Lansdowne MSS. 25, art. 22.   [b] In November 1577, and May
Original.   1578. Harleian MSS. 168, f. 91, 93.

on as greatly.   Their wills be ready, only these letts defer
their opportunity; which being now taken away, it is easy
to judge that with conjunct force and fury they will execute
their wills, full of enmity and revenge: for seeing your Majesty hath had evident proof of their ill dispositions towards
you by their practices, and that in weighty matters in the
midst of their troubles, when they were not able to do you
any hurt; what then is to be looked for when opportunity
and ability shall concur?   Again, it is to be doubted, that,
when they shall begin to stir coals, there be many both at
home and abroad that will put oil to this fire; and the rather,
because of the glorious and plausible pretext that they pretend to have to serve their purpose.   Most gracious Sovereign, I have been so inquieted with these things when I
entered into the consideration of them, (whether of over-much
fearfulness by nature, or over-great jealousy of your Highness's estate, I know not,) that I could not choose but now at
the last to utter to your Majesty that which I have oft
intended, and yet never done, partly for fear, and partly
in hope that things would prove better, which I see daily
prove worse and worse.   And, if remedy be not foreseen
in time, I doubt it will prove very hard to be holpen by any
counsel to my understanding.   And the best remedies that I
can think of be these, nevertheless submitting them with all
humbleness to your Majesty's most grave and wise consideration: The first remedy is, to make Scotland as sure to your
Majesty as may be; for so, beside the aid you may have by
them, that great peril of annoyance by France will be removed: and the better to understand what is best to be foreseen and provided, both for theirs and your surety, methinks
it best that some wise men were sent to confer with the
Regent and his adherents by your Majesty, and that such
counsel as shall be agreed upon in that conference be sent to
your Highness to be considered of, and by you allowed or
amended.   Then resteth nothing but to have it carefully
executed; and, ... handling of this, great care would be
taken that the . . . . who groweth now to years, be

not transported, but . . . . nance of such as shall
be most assured to your Majesty.* And for the better bringing of this to pass, I most humbly beseech your Highness,
that such and so many pensions may be granted as may best
bring it to good effect. Surely I think that every thousand
pounds that shall be thus bestowed will save you a hundred
thousand ; and it may be doubted, whether (if this be undone) any money will be able to bear off the danger. As
to the second remedy, because the annoyance from Spain
is like to grow by the Low Countries, I see no way so sure
for your Majesty as to keep the Prince of Orange in heart
and life; for methinks his estate towards Spain, and the
Regent's towards France, stand both in one predicament, and
therefore require both one course. The States of the Low
Countries are so divided, that how trust may be reposed in
them where one trusteth not another, I see not. Marry, if it
might be brought to pass by counsel from hence that the
Duke of Arschot and the States might govern the countries
according to their liberties, and the Prince to have the rule
of their martial matters, this of all others were the surest
way : otherwise, whilst the States be in deliberation, it may
be doubted that their overthrow may happen. The third
remedy is, to have your musters kept and continued, and
their certificates carefully perused and wants supplied, so
as your captains, men, munition, and armour may be in
readiness against all suddens. Thus I have troubled your
Majesty, I confess, longer than perchance it needeth, considering chiefly your own understanding and wisdom, and
therewith the grave, wise, and careful counsellors daily attendant about you. But, good Madam, how can these things
discharge me of my duty, judging of these times as I do ?
And although I have before this time signified to some of my
Lords what I have thought in your matters of state, yet
seeing now the danger increasing, I could not satisfy my own

---

* The lacunæ in the text are occasioned by part of the MS. being torn.
The passage in the Harleian MS.
168, reads thus : "Great care is to
be had that the young King, growing
now in years, be not transported into
France, and that he may for a time
be in the governance of such as be
the most assured to your Majesty."

heart without an advertisement to your self, most humbly praying pardon of the length of my letter, my shaking hand being so ill, and the rather because I mean not to trouble your Majesty often without your license and good favour. Thus, wishing to your Highness all felicity both of mind and body, I forbear any further to trouble your Majesty at this time. From Gorhambury, the 15th of September 1577.

Your Majesty's most humble subject and servant,

BACON.[a]

From the year 1577 Sir Christopher Hatton took a prominent part in State affairs.   The Privy Council was then also, what has since been termed, the "Cabinet Council;" and the interest which he felt in public business was probably the cause of his having had transcribed, not only his private correspondence, but also many letters addressed to other persons on subjects of importance.   The letters in his "Letter Book" consequently begin about this period; and they afford as much information on the policy of the Country, and the persons employed in her service, as on his own character and conduct.

The first letter of the year 1578 was to Sir Christopher Hatton from Mr. Davison, who was employed in various negotiations, and became Secretary of State in 1586, but who is now best known as the victim of Queen Elizabeth's dissimulation respecting the execution of Mary Queen of Scots.   In February 1576, Davison was sent on a mission to the Low Countries; and, in July 1577, was appointed the Queen's agent at Antwerp.[b]

[a] Additional MSS. 15891, f. 1. Another copy of this letter, but with some variations, is in the Harleian MS. 168, f. 52. Lodge, in his memoir of Sir Nicholas Bacon, says that an autograph draught of it is in the Harleian collection, but it has not been found.

[b] His instructions and great part of his correspondence while in Holland are in the Harleian MSS. 285, 287 ; Cottonian MSS. Galba, C. vi ;

MR. DAVISON TO SIR CHRISTOPHER HATTON.

SIR, The Duke of Alençon having (as I credibly learn) received advice from some of his favourers here that her Majesty should either be utterly altered, or at the least so coldly affected to embrace the cause of this country as that there was great appearance she should break off with the States under pretext of their refusing to deliver her the Isle of Walcheren for assurance, hath hereupon taken occasion to dispatch hither in post one Lafugiere, a gentleman of his, to renew his old practice and offer of assistance unto the States, in hope it will be now accepted, partly in respect of their necessity, and partly to show that he proceedeth with the greater sincerity and good will towards them.   He seemeth content to offer them *la carte blanche,* and to accept what conditions they themselves will prescribe.   The gentleman had his audience with the Prince on Thursday and Friday last, with whom he hath been very earnest and full of persuasion to induce an acceptation of his master's offered goodwill; but he hath yet no other comfort than general compliments.   Neither do I think that the Prince, or the rest that be of judgment, considering how much they ought to suspect the offers of such a Prince, their neighbour, (a born enemy, a Prince ambitious, the next heir to the crown of France, one that pretendeth a right and interest to the greatest part of this country, and that hath long sought to invest himself in the government thereof,) will in any sort incline to this proposition, unless it be to use him as an instrument to divert the succours which the enemy hath and may have from that side, till they be so provided as they need not doubt them.   And yet thus much I may assure your Honour, that the long suspense and uncertainty of her Majesty's

Titus, B. ii. and B. vii; Lansdowne MSS. 2442, in the British Museum: but the above, and the other letters to Hatton, do not appear to be in those collections. A Life of Davison, who died in great poverty in December 1608, was published by the Editor of this work in 1823.

resolution (considering the necessity whereunto the affairs
are here reduced, the promise which her Majesty had made
them, the hope and comfort wherein she had so long entertained them, making them reject the former offers of the
Duke, and neglect other means which they might have used
for their relief,) hath begun such a jealousy and alteration
in divers of the greatest that were before enemies to the
part of France, as, fearing that her Majesty's long delay
will in fine bring an absolute denial, are now the first that
would persuade that course.   And, to say truly, some of the
wisest here attend such a desperate resolution, if her Highness should indeed abandon them.   For, seeing the King of
Spain hath resolutely determined to prosecute the war
against them with all extremity, that he hath an army
strong at their gates, composed of the expertest captains
and soldiers of Christendom, that he hath, for the better
attaining and effecting his purpose, concluded a truce with
the Turk, and solicited the succour and assistance of the
Pope, the French King, the Swisses, the Dukes of Savoy
and Lorrain, with divers other princes and potentates of
Italy and Germany, conjured enemies to the cause of the
Low Countries, (against whose forces it shall be hard for
them to resist without the help and succour of some of
their neighbours,) they must of necessity strengthen themselves with the alliance of some one or other that may be
able and apt to protect them.   Now, amongst all their
neighbours, it is indubitable that there is no one whose
assistance may be so much profitable and little dangerous
unto them as the help of the Queen our sovereign, France
being justly suspected, and the calling in of such a protector perilous, the Emperor both unable and unassured,
and the rest of the Princes of Germany hirelings and
coldly affected.   And therefore have they first addressed
themselves unto her Majesty, of whose favour the interest
she hath in the success of their troubles, and the experience they have of her bounty and clemency, hath not a
little increased their hope and presumption; in satisfy-

ing whereof if her Majesty fail them, such is their hatred
against the Spaniard, as, rather than they will be forced to
fall under the yoke of their insupportable tyranny, they will
run any fortune, be it never so desperate; and especially
that of France, which though all men esteem full of peril,
yet will they make it a counsel without counsel, when they
cannot otherwise choose.   Now, seeing that her Majesty can
neither abandon them without the certain peril as well of
herself as of them, and seeing that to suspend their hope
and her deliberations any longer shall be as inconvenient
for both, (for as there is nothing more dangerous in matters
of state than to be uncertain and doubtful in deliberation,
so is there nothing more unfitting to the time and present
condition of their affairs,) it should in my poor judgment,
under the correction of your Honour, be much the more
profitable and honourable for her Majesty the sooner that
she giveth them her determination ; for, if she mind to assist
them, it shall be the more acceptable and available unto
them the more timely her succour cometh to do them good,
and it shall make their obligation so much the greater
towards her Majesty, and her merit consequently the greater
in that respect, if the medicine be timely applied, ere that
the grief be grown to any hard or rather impossible cure.
For as the house is easily maintained and repaired that
is yet strong and in good plight, but being ruined and
fallen is of far greater charge and travail to be redressed
and restored to its former estate; and as the sickness is
the less to be feared, the less that the body is feeble
and weak : so shall it be an easier matter to support and
entertain the state of these countries whilst they be strong
and united, than, being once weakened and dismembered, to
restore them to their former condition.   On the other side,
if her Majesty have no will to embrace the cause, it were
better they knew it betimes than too late; because it shall
make them the more diligent and resolute to take some
other course for the supply of their necessity, where now
their suspended hope doth make them both negligent, un-

certain, and irresolute, a thing amongst others most perilous for them.   Now, though I may seem to go too far in judging whether of these two resolutions her Majesty were best to take, yet shall it not be much amiss that I tell your Honour what I observe upon the inclination of things hard.   To cast them off cannot, in my poor judgment, but bring forth a general astonishment in the people, an alteration in the nobility, a confusion of the present union and agreement of the Provinces, an advancement of the affairs and hopes of the enemy, a hazard, or rather a certainty, of losing the hearts of this people; which will be so much the more perilous to her Majesty in that she shall continue, notwithstanding, in the hatred of Spain, and so gain unto herself the enmity of both, and friendship of neither; and that which is more, so far unlikely it is that her Majesty in not assisting them shall eschew war, as she shall rather defer it than otherwise, to her greater disadvantage.   For the scope of the Holy League of these Catholic Princes, long since projected, often renewed, and now like to be put in execution, doth manifestly appear to reach, not only to the subverting of these countries in particular, but also to the ruin of all such as make profession of the Reformed Religion in general; amongst whom as her Majesty occupieth the chiefest place, so is she the mark they principally shoot at; holding it for a maxim, that if she, being the chiefest protectrix of our Religion, were once supplanted, they should the more easily prevail over the rest.   Now if this be true, as it is too apparent to be called into doubt, I leave to the discourse of others, whether her Majesty's own surety do will her to look to the cause of this country betimes, or not.   There resteth now to be considered in what sort her Majesty may best assist them.   Some men perhaps are of opinion that it were better done underhand with the loan of some money than with men; or, if with men at all, that it were better some few should be passed over by stealth than openly; alleging further reason, that if her Majesty do send over any great forces

under the charge of a personage of quality, it shall draw
her into an open war against both the Kings of Spain and
France, with the one, in respect of the injury which he shall
presume to have therein received, with the other, in regard
of the jealousy and doubt which he may conceive of our
neighbourhood, having once set footing in such a country
as this is; and therefore they conclude, that to eschew a war
so chargeable, so uncertain and dangerous, it were better
her Majesty should assist them underhand than openly.
But against these reasons may be produced others of far
more moment and consideration in my rude advice.   One is,
that to give them any manner of succour underhand shall
not be so profitable for her Majesty as if she proceeded
roundly and openly; partly because her Majesty, entering
into the action openly, shall the sooner obtain that she desireth, which is a peace.   For of how much the greater difficulty the King of Spain shall find his enterprise, so much
the more easily will he be brought to a peace: partly because
both her Majesty's merit towards these countries, and their
obligation and duty, shall be the greater; and partly, (that
which is not of least consideration,) because her Majesty may
have, without her charge, a convenient army of her own
subjects, trained and experienced in the wars of this country, of whom she may be the better served in all occasions
that may occur hereafter; whereas they be now, of all other
nations, the most inexpert and ignorant in that behalf.
Another reason is, that it shall not be so honourable for
her Majesty, because she hath already passed her promise;
in performing whereof she shall show a zeal to the cause
of her poor neighbours, a resolution in counsel, a stedfast-
ness in promise, a magnanimity in execution.   The contrary
whereof may be perhaps noted and condemned in her Majesty if she should do otherwise. Besides that, it is apparent
she should no less offend, nor show a less evil affection to the
King of Spain, if she should in any sort assist them underhand.   Lastly, seeing it is a resolution here to serve themselves with strangers, I think there is no man would counsel

her Majesty to lend them money, to entertain the French, the
Scots, or other foreign nations, and to keep her own subjects unemployed; the reasons being so manifest as they need
no disputation.   So as by these few circumstances it may appear how much fitter it were for her Majesty to succour
them openly, and with her men, conducted by some personage of quality that may keep them in discipline and good
order, than either to send over any small troops by stealth,
which is ill; or to assist them with money without men,
which is much worse.   As for the fear which some men
apprehend of an invasion pretended in England or Ireland,
upon occasion whereof they would infer a necessity for her
Majesty to keep her men at home, it is not to be doubted
but that the King of Spain, so long as he hath his hands full
in the Low Countries, shall be an enemy more terrible in
opinion than in effect unto us.   And as for France, how easily
her Majesty might keep them occupied at home, every man
that hath any acquaintance with the state of that country
can tell.   In sum, it is in her Majesty's hands to prevent
and divert, if she list, any peril that possibly may threaten
her estate by the one Prince or the other.   Lastly, to speak
of the condition of this war in general, such is the nature
and strength of the country, so many and so inexpugnable
be the towns and holds in the same, and so resolute and
desperate is the condition of the people, as there is no man
of judgment but thinketh the enterprise of infinite difficulty,
being assisted of her Majesty, and abiding united among
themselves; a thing never more hoped and less doubted than
since the defeat of their camp.   Since which misadventure
they have buried and compounded all their private differences,
and have showed an universal resolution to withstand the
common enemy.   So as the King of Spain being deceived
of his chief hope, which was to have sowed such a division
and zizany* amongst them as that he might have set them one

---

* The word is not very legible,
but it was probably "zizany," from
zizanium, cockle or darnel.   "Cum
autem dormirent homines, venit ini-
micus ejus, et superseminavit *zizania*
in medio tritici, et abiit."   Matt.
xiii. 25.

against the other, and so have had the better market of both, without which hope it is indubitable he would never have taken this war in hand; and finding, besides, the infinite charge, peril, and difficulty to entertain as well a great navy by sea, as an army by land, without which his enterprise is desperate, and with it in manner hopeless, having no one port in the whole country at his devotion, no mean to re-dress a second navy when the first is miscarried, besides a number of other difficulties; it is not to be doubted but that once within the year he will be glad of a peace, though it cost him very dearly. And therefore I conclude, that if her Majesty's surety, honour, profit, and necessity may move her, she will no doubt go forward with her promise and good disposition to assist these countries, whose union or disjunction, prosperity or peril, dependeth upon her resolu-tion. And thus, submitting my opinion to the judgment and correction of your Honour, I most humbly take my leave. Antwerp, the 8th of March 1577 [1577-8.]

W. Davison.*

A letter from Lord Burghley, in April, shows the Prime Minister in correspondence with one of his col-leagues respecting the Queen's tooth-ache; and, as the courtly physicians were afraid to inform her of the necessity of extracting the tooth, Burghley suggests that Hatton should undertake the delicate task, who pro-bably, as the writer expected, did so by placing the letter itself in the Queen's hands;—

TO SIR CHRISTOPHER HATTON.

Mr. Vice-Chamberlain, I heard of her Majesty's indispo-sition by some pain in her head; and then how can any of her poor members, having life by her as our head, be without pain? If my coming thither might either diminish her pain, or be thought convenient, I would not be absent; although

* Additional MS. 15891, f. 23.

in grief I am present, and do most heartily beseech God to deliver her from all grief, praying you to let me know of her Majesty's amendment: not doubting but you are careful by the physicians to provide the remedy, which is said to be only the withdrawing of some one tooth that is touched with some humorous cause, and, except that be removed, her Majesty's pain shall not be quit. And though her Highness doth not or will not so think, yet I assure you it is said that the physicians do of knowledge affirm it, howsoever they forbear to impart it unto her. Besides my prayer, I cannot tell what to yield for her Majesty's ease more than this information; praying you to examine the truth, and further truth to her Majesty's service, and to her ease in this point. 21st April 1578.   Yours assuredly,

W. BURGHLEY.[a]

Doctor John Aylmer, Bishop of London, the learned tutor of Lady Jane Grey, a celebrated divine and bitter enemy of the Puritans, was a frequent correspondent of the Vice-Chamberlain; and perhaps prelatical hypocrisy was never more painfully shown than in some of his letters. His efforts to place Doctor Chatterton in the See of Chester were successful, but not until late in the following year. "One Goodman," to whom the Bishop so discourteously alludes, was no doubt Dr. Christopher Goodman, a violent non-conformist, who printed a pamphlet at Geneva in 1558, entitled "How superior powers ought to be obeyed of their subjects," which Warton describes as being "an absurd and factious pamphlet against Queen Mary";—

TO SIR CHRISTOPHER HATTON.

SIR, I have been an importunate suitor to my Lord of Leicester and you in the behalf of Mr. Doctor Chader-

---

[a] Additional MSS. 15891, f. 42ᵇ.

ton for his preferment to the Bishoprick of Chester; not so much for my affection to the man, as for the good I know he might do in the Church of God, both for his singular learning, as also in respect of his zeal to bridle disordered persons.   It may please you, therefore, at my request to help to dispatch the poor man, and send a governor to that place; which I fear, as an unruly family without a steward, will, by this long delay* that hath happened, be hardly drawn to good order.   There is in that country one Goodman, who wrote against the government of women, a man not unknown to her Majesty; who, in this vacation, I doubt, will build one way more than the Bishop shall a good while be able to pull down in that kind of curiosity.   I pray God bless you and make you happy in His grace, and in all other prosperity.   From Fulham, the 29th of April 1578.   Your Honour's most assured to command in Christ,

JOHN LONDON.[b]

Doctor Edmund Grindall, who was made Archbishop of Canterbury in 1576, having fallen under the Queen's displeasure for refusing to sanction the marriage of Dr. Julio,[c] the favourite physician and dependant of Leicester, with another man's wife, he was sequestered from his See and confined to his house.   Hatton had, it appears, used his influence, though in vain, to restore him to the Queen's favour, and was thus thanked for his exertions :—

TO SIR CHRISTOPHER HATTON.

SIR, Although your long and instant travail to her Majesty for my benefit is not yet come to such fulness of effect as you desire and I have long wished for, yet do I think myself especially bounden to give you most hearty thanks, and that in as ample manner as if I presently enjoyed the

---

* The See of Chester fell vacant by the death of Bishop Downman in December 1577.

[b] Additional MSS. 15891, f. 54[b].
[c] Vide pp. 24, 30, *ante.*

fruition of the end of my suit; for that I do right well understand of your continual, honourable, and most friendly cares and travails for me, by the which, as also by your sundry comfortable messages at divers times sent unto me, I am brought into an assured hope by your good means to recover her Majesty's grace and favour in time convenient, (the limitation whereof I wholly refer to her Majesty's good will and pleasure,) much to the quieting and comforting of my mind, so long afflicted for the want of the same.　Your honourable and friendly dealing herein I shall not fail carefully to lay up in the treasury of a thankful memory. And so, taking my leave, I heartily commend you to the grace of God.　From Lambeth, the 2nd of May 1578.

Yours in Christ,　　EDM. CANTUAR.*

Mr. Davison wrote to the Privy Council about the affairs of the Low Countries on the 8th of May;—

I WROTE lately unto your Lordships from Gant, and what hath succeeded since you may somewhat particularly understand by this bearer.　The traffic with the Duke of Alençon doth very much confound their opinions here. Four or five thousand arquebusiers of his troops, coming through France in twelve days from about Rochelle, are already entered the country, and ere this (as it is doubted) possessed of Quesny, by the mean of the Count Labaine, who hath in plain terms let the States understand that he thinketh it fit to receive them in for divers respects which he allegeth, wherein he doth rather express his sentence, than desire their advice or direction.　The Baron of Aribigny is in the town, whose partiality that way doth make the matter never a whit the better　The Duke's Commissioners are sent for to come to Brusselles for the more commodious proceeding in their negociation with the States; but their answer is not yet returned.　Whatsoever opinion is had at home of this action, it is here held a thing indubitable that this practice

* Additional MSS. 15891, f. 30.

will go forward. Your Lordships do much better perceive than I, both the offence and defence of these States, and the danger of either. The offence, in my rude observation, must be either for the enemy or for himself, both which do threaten some unhappy consequent. Their defence on the other side must be either in respect of their common cause, or of his own particular profit. The first is generally suspected, the second is certainly believed. Now whether we do in this behalf mean well or ill, the success cannot but greatly touch both them and us : them, because from one tyranny they shall run to another, or return to the same ; and us, in that the weakening of our friends and allies must of necessity weaken our estate. Once, however, the French proceed, whether in favour of the Spaniard or of themselves, it is like to be the seed of a languishing war, and the beginning of great alteration ; for they must here, in fine, either resolve to return and reconcile themselves with the King of Spain, or to commit themselves unto the hands of some other master, or else translate their State into a government popular or aristocratical. The first they seem now resolved never to do ; of the other, the question is not yet decided. Some, and a great part, (I will put your Lordships out of doubt,) are resolute to change their master, and to take the French ; others to change their government, abandoning both them and the other. But for debate and disputation, it will not be long ere this matter grow to execution. We may hereof, in the mean time, rather conjecture than in any sort assure the success. I shall not need to tell your Lordships, who can sufficiently shun the danger, how much this matter importeth the looking to; but thus much I think I may safely say, that the sooner it be met withal, the better. Your Lordships can now perceive whether her Majesty's forbearing of her open declaration have diverted the French; or whether it hath not rather advanced their purpose, with the hazard of her friends, and perhaps prejudice to herself. But, as it becomes me not, so will I wade no further in this discourse. Only this I

wish, that she may not be constrained, in fine, to fall into
this action with her greater incommodity and disadvantage
than if she had entered into it sooner, though if it might be
with her Majesty's surety and honour, I could rather pray
she might not have to do with it at all, either early or late.
I do live here utterly ignorant of the success of things in a
Court; and though I have of late in this special matter given
your Lordships sundry advice, yet have I received no manner
of direction how to govern myself. If your Lordships do
think herein I may do any service at all, I would beseech
the same to let my ignorance be repaired; knowing what a
maim it is in service abroad to understand nothing, and
seldom from home.   Of the late accident of Maesterich, of
the apprehension of three councillors at Gant whilst I was
there, of the proclaiming of an inhibition against the exercise
of religion either publicly or secretly, with other particular
occurrents, I think Mr. Rogers can at length inform your
Lordships. Concluding, therefore, with my hearty prayer for
your Lordships' long and prosperous lives, I most humbly
take my leave. From Antwerp, the 8th May 1578.

W. DAVISON.*

The Bishop of London's character is exhibited in
the following letter. It would seem, and which is confirmed by a subsequent letter, that one of Hatton's relations, or friends, had felt the effects of Aylmer's perse-
cuting spirit. It appears also that Hatton was the me-
dium of communicating the Queen's wishes on the prelate's proceedings towards her recusant subjects;—

TO SIR CHRISTOPHER HATTON.

SIR, I had written unto you before this for divers
causes, and especially to give you most hearty thanks for
that mild and calm manner of expostulation which you used
with me in our last conference, but that the next day after

* Additional MSS. 15891, f. 18.

I fell very sick, and so continued for five or six days together; out of which feebleness as soon as I any whit recovered, I thought good to salute you with a line or two,
partly to signify unto you that I will not forget to commend,
both to God in my prayers and to all men in speech, that
rare conquest that by great wisdom you have had over your
affections, which by the motions of flesh and blood must
needs have been set on fire marvellously against me, had not
a natural instinct of heavenly and Christian philosophy and
wisdom quenched the flame thereof; and partly to ask your
honourable advice in one branch of that speech that passed
between you and me; which was, whether it were not the
safest and profitablest way to cut off (even as her Majesty
termed it) and to correct offenders on both sides which
swerve from the right path of obedience, which I set up as
the mark to aim at, purposing to discipline both the Papist
and the Puritan in anything wherein (disobeying her Majesty's laws) they may be indifferently touched. By which
course of proceeding I do not doubt but I shall do that service to her Majesty, in suppressing these dangerous people,
which shall well content her, and bring great unity of government to the Church, which her Majesty in her godly
wisdom so much thirsteth after. It was her Majesty's pleasure that I should understand her mind by you in these
things. Let me therefore intreat your Honour to afford me
some direction, in a word or two, how you think good I
should deal in these matters, and then you shall see that I
shall so guide the helm as the ship shall keep the best and
safest course. Thus hoping you will remember me in this
point, that *principis indignatio mors est,* I leave at this time to
trouble you any further; remaining most faithfully at your
commandment. From Fulham, the 28th of May 1578. Your
Honour's most bound *in Christo,* JOHN LONDON.*

The annexed letter from Walsingham refers to the
attempts of an adventurer, called Stukeley, who, with

* Additional MSS. 15891, f. 38.

the assistance of the Pope, from whom he had received the title of Marquis of Leinster, and the command of eight hundred Italians, attempted to excite a rebellion in Ireland.   He arrived with these troops at Lisbon ; " but," says Camden, " the more potent power of the Divine counsel frustrated those designs against England and Ireland."[a] ;—

TO SIR CHRISTOPHER HATTON.

Sir, I like well of her Majesty's course, being very considerate and such as answereth to the place she holdeth ; and therefore do mind at the next dispatch to acquaint either the Deputy or the Governor for the time being with this her Majesty's resolution.   It needeth no present dispatch, for that her letters to the Nobility of that Realm are not yet signed : in the delivery whereof there may be that order taken, as the Nobility of that Realm may be contained in their good devotion, and encouraged (in case any thing shall be attempted) to do that which in duty they ought ; without public notification, by proclamation or otherwise, of any fear conceived here that so weak an instrument as Stukeley is shall be able to prevail against a Prince of her Majesty's power, armed with the goodwill of her subjects in that Realm, as she doubted not but that she is.   Thus much I thought good to scribble unto you, referring the rest to this bearer, and yourself to God's good keeping.   From the Court, the 3rd of June 1578.   Yours most assuredly,

FRA. WALSINGHAM.[b]

Upon the following disgraceful letter no comment could be too severe.   Bishop Aylmer's proceedings seem to have disgusted both the Queen and Hatton ; and the spiritual tyrant appears in the too common character of a Court sycophant.   His " travails for the government of women," to which he alludes, was a tract, printed in 1559,

---

[a] Annals, ed. 1630, p. 93.   [b] Additional MSS. 15891, f. 35.[b]

called " An Harborowe for faithful and trewe subjects against the late blowne blaste concerning the government of women," and which is said to have been an able answer to John Knox's " First blast of the trumpet against the monstrous regiment of women." It may be inferred, from one passage in this letter, that Aylmer, who was only Archdeacon of Lincoln when he was elected to the See of London, in March 1577, owed his mitre to Hatton;—

TO SIR CHRISTOPHER HATTON.

Sir, I have much desired, and yet do, to receive some line or two from you in writing, only to persuade me that your displeasure is appeased, as I found it was at our last meeting, much to my comfort and more to your honour; but chiefly that I might have some little inkling that her Majesty standeth my gracious Lady, without the obtaining whereof, what joy can I have in myself? what courage to execute this painful service, which is more than the burthen of Atlas? or what lively comfort can I, being as a dead trunk, conceive before I take such nourishment as the root sendeth up to the tree, and as the head, which the natural philosophers term *principium motus et sensus*, conveyeth to the sinews, and so strengtheneth and confirmeth the body. I beseech you, Sir, vouchsafe so to deal with me as I may not live but with her Majesty's good liking; otherwise I shall go on like a horse that is spurred and not cherished, and so in the end shall fall under the burthen. If my fighting against the beasts at Ephesus, my travails that I took when I was twenty years younger than I am now for the Government of Women, my continual setting forth of her Majesty's infinite gift from God and unspeakable deserts towards us, have merited nothing; yet it is the honour of a Prince to breathe life into dead bodies, and, after the cold and dead winter, to cheer the dry earth with the fresh and lively spring time. I study with my eyes on my book, and my mind is in the Court; I preach without spirit; I trust not of God, but of my Sovereign, which is God's lieutenant, and so another God unto me—for of such it is said *Vos estis dii;* I eat without stomach, I sleep without rest, I company without comfort, and live as one dead. You labour daily to your great commendation to cherish other Bishops set up by others, and will you throw down him whom you have set up yourself? You think the fault that is past can never be recompensed. If that be your conceit, assure yourself it will redound the more to your honour and reputation if you can freely forgive it. Cæsar was sorry that Cato had killed himself, because he could not make him bound to him by forgiving and delivering him. Let Cæsar's noble mind be in you, though Cato's mind be not in me; and think that it shall be the more honourable for you, and make my band the greater, if you forget and forgive me, whom I commit to God's good providence. From Fulham, the 8th of June 1578.

Your Honour's to command *in Christo,*

JOHN LONDON.[a]

In June, Walsingham was sent with Lord Cobham on a mission to the Netherlands, with the hope, in conjunction with the Imperial and French ministers, of terminating hostilities there; but the negotiation failed, and they returned to England a few months after. Walsingham being on his way to meet Lord Cobham at Cobham Hall near Rochester, wrote the following letter to Hatton. The opportunity of making a firm alliance with Scotland, so strongly pressed in this letter, was the recent removal of the Regent Morton, and the transfer of the government to the young King, who had sent the Abbot of Dumfermline to acknowledge, " with most grateful remembrance, Queen Elizabeth's benefits towards him." [b]

[a] Additional MSS. 15891, f. 38.[b]   [b] Camden's Annals, book ii. p. 91.

TO SIR CHRISTOPHER HATTON.

SIR, Finding you absent from Court at the time of my leave-taking, I desired our good friend Mr. Heneage to acquaint you with certain public causes worthy of your knowledge and furtherance, which I would have been glad to have imparted by mouth. I nothing doubt but that you will have care of them, especially to further a straiter knot of amity between this crown and Scotland. I find her Majesty in that point, to rest upon some nice terms; which I hope, by your good persuasion, will be removed. Surely, Sir, if her Majesty let slip this opportunity, I fear we shall estrange Scotland from us unrecoverably; and how perilous that will be, I leave to your good consideration. For my particular, in my absence, I promise that friendship unto myself at Mr. Vice-Chamberlain's hands that he would look to receive from me, being in like case. And so, wishing unto you as to my own self, I commit you to God. At Gravesend, in haste, the 16th of June 1578.

Yours most assuredly,   FRA. WALSINGHAM.[a]

Bishop Aylmer's next letter to Hatton relates to some acts of intolerance similar to those before mentioned. By the Bishop's authority Mr. Roper's house had been searched, and " vestments, albes, and such trumpery," found in it.[b] If, as there seems little doubt, the Mr. John Harrington was the author of the papers published under the title of " Nugæ Antiquæ," Aylmer was little indebted to his friendship, for the anecdotes there related of the prelate are more curious than creditable.

[a] Additional MSS. 15891, f. 44[b].   [b] Minutes of the Privy Council of the 13th of January 1577-8.

BISHOP AYLMER TO SIR CHRISTOPHER HATTON.

SIR, You have borne so much with me, that I were to blame if I should not for your sake bear with your friends, among whom Mr. John Roper hath, chiefly in respect of you, and partly by seeing and confessing his own oversight, won at my hands both forgiving and forgetting of all the injuries which he offered me; which were in number not many, but in likelihood to hurt me of such force, as, if your good-nature by bearing, and your wisdom in judging, had not holpen, the weakest must have gone to the wall. It may please you then to remember, not for his hurt but for my discharge, and for the confirmation of your good opinion, that I am none of those that will deal doubly with any man, and much less with such a friend as you are. These be the points : first, his complaining on me to the Council, wherein he did me great wrong; for God himself knoweth, and your Honour can testify, that I wrote to you that we two, if it pleased you, should hear and order it, meaning and dealing simply. Besides, I was so free from the rifling of his house, that, upon the receipt of your letters, I despatched a pursuivant at midnight to call them back. The matter grieved me so much the more, for that I was blamed in the hottest time of the paroxysm between you and me ; and where he reported that he was, or should be, called by my means, I inquired of it, but I found no such matter ; and to be sure it should not be done, I forewarned the Archdeacon and my Chancellor, that, if any such thing should happen, I might be made privy to it. He wrote unto you that he was called before the Commissioners. Upon search, I found no such meaning. I left it not so, but inquired again of the Archdeacon; he knew nothing. I sought to learn who were his officers; in the end, it was Doctor Forde and Babam. I asked of them; they were ignorant. In the end, I found by their clerks that Doctor Forde had excommunicated them. Thus I was fain to play the spaniel, not

for his sake, for I was angry with him, but because I would
justify myself to you, my honourable friend; and so will I
stand to my justification in all things towards you, (one excepted,) wherein no wager of law is to be admitted. And
therefore, I pray you, Sir, henceforth let me answer before
you suspect, and I warrant you no crack shall be found in
my friendship. I joy that your Honour beginneth to put
Mr. John Harrington in the calendar of your friends; I assure
it appertaineth,) but for the security and preservation of
you, you shall find him honest, wise, faithful, constant, and
no universal friend to depend upon many, but fast where
he maketh his choice. I pray your Honour bear with my
long letters, for I cannot be short in so long a tragedy. God
bless and prosper you, for, God willing, I mind to stand and
fall with you. I speak it unfeignedly. From Fulham, the
17th of June 1578.

   Your Honour's most assured in Christ, as most bounden,
                              JOHN LONDON.*

   As soon as Walsingham arrived at Cobham Hall, he
sent a trustful person to Hatton with the following
letter ;—

SIR FRANCIS WALSINGHAM TO SIR CHRISTOPHER HATTON.

   GOOD MR. VICE-CHAMBERLAIN, For that your leisure oftentimes will not serve you to acquaint me with such things as
were fit for me to know in furtherance of her Majesty's
service, I have made choice of this gentleman, being wise,
honest, and discreet, and one that desireth good and sound
friendship between us, as well for the advancement of her
Majesty's service as our own particular, to repair unto you,
and to receive from you such matter as you shall think
fit to be communicated unto me in respect of my present
charge ; which, standing as it doth upon hard terms, had
need of all furtherance. If the matter itself and my skill

   * Additional MSS. 15891, f. 37.

did answer unto my care, then would I promise all good success; but the matter (by letting slip the opportunity of time, which overthroweth all good causes,) is so far out of frame, as I can hardly conceive any hope of good issue; which is no small grief unto me, considering the zeal and desire I have to do her Majesty some acceptable service, especially in a cause that concerneth her Majesty's safety so much as this doth.   I can but commit the success to God, who, blessing my travail, may make me an instrument to do that which is contrary to man's expectation; which I wish not for my own glory, (for to him will I render it to whom her, which I prefer before all worldly respects.   And so, wishing unto you as to my own self, I commit you to God's good keeping.   At Cobham Hall, the 17th of June 1578.

Yours assuredly,   FRA. WALSINGHAM.

I pray you, Sir, let this gentleman enjoy your good countenance, who doth love and honour you.[*]

The matter to which the next two letters relate has not been ascertained.   Mr. Cox was Hatton's secretary; and many remarkably well written letters occur from him to his patron.   Dr. Aubrey and Dr. Dale were eminent civilians; and Hatton is said, when Chancellor, to have consulted the latter in all important cases.

MR. COX TO SIR CHRISTOPHER HATTON.

MAY IT PLEASE YOUR HONOUR, Having heard the opinion of Mr. Doctor Aubrey, and likewise of Mr. Dale, I find the law to be this for the matter of false depositions: *Secunda assertio, extra judicium, non enervat effectum primi dicti in judicio, etiamsi testis hoc dicat in articulo mortis.* The reason that the law giveth is, *propter venerantiam juramenti et judicis.* There is therefore thus much to be said for the sick man's protestation on his death-bed, *quod valde*

[*] Additional MSS. 15891, f. 43.

minuitur fides primi dicti, sed non omnino tollitur: so that
if there were no more but this man alive deposed, *nec adhuc
lata sit sententia,* then no doubt his last protestation in his
sickness is of more credit than his first deposition; but, if
there were two more sworn as well as he, their depositions
are still of force, *ratione qua supra.* If there were but
one besides this sick man deposed *in eodem judicio, non
valebit primum juramentum,* because *fides alterius diminuitur,*
and there must be two lawful witnesses at the least. The
words of the law at large are these: *Quando primum dictum testis est dictum in judicio, et secundum extra judicium,
si sententia fuit lata per primum dictum, non revocatur sententia. Si sententia non est adhuc lata, detrahitur primo dicto
per secundum, et in hoc ultimo casu diminuitur fides testis
per secundum dictum, sed non tollitur.* It was four of the
clock before Mr. Doctor Aubrey came from the Court of
the Admiralty, so that I could not make that speed in the
return of my answer which haply your Honour expected. I
read the law myself, and desired Mr. Aubrey to turn over
more books than one, because I would be sure of the soundest
resolution. I beseech God to bless your Honour with the
increase of His manifold graces now and ever.   From the
Arches, the 20th of June 1578.

   Your Honour's most humble and obedient poor servant,
                                          SA. COX.[a]

   Dr. Aubrey himself wrote soon after to Hatton on the
subject;—

DR. WILLIAM AUBREY TO SIR CHRISTOPHER HATTON.

SIR, For answer to the question propounded unto me by
Mr. Cox, I make bold with your honourable favour to return this resolution: That respect ought to be had rather of
the first judicial and sworn deposition of a witness than of his
extra-judicial and unsworn revocation thereof in his death-

----
[a] Additional MSS. 15891, f. 54.

bed ; for the law doth judge, in regard of the reverence that ought to be had of an oath, and of the magistrate, that the witness did depose the truth at the first, and doth not give credit to the revocation, as a thing presumed to be procured by the contrary party, whom the first deposition did prejudice. Yet such revocation made in the article of death doth greatly weaken the first deposition, and there may concur with that revocation such vehement presumptions and probabilities as may induce a Judge to give no credit to the first deposition. But, setting circumstances aside, the first judicial deposition by virtue of oath is to be followed. And thus, in haste for satisfying my duty to your Honour, I humbly take my leave.

 Your Honour's most bounden at commandment,

W. AUBREY.*

Queen Elizabeth's wavering policy towards the Low Countries, and her unwillingness to advance money to aid the States in their struggle for independence, caused Walsingham so much anxiety, that he wrote privately to Hatton, as well as officially to the Council ;—

SIR FRANCIS WALSINGHAM TO SIR CHRISTOPHER HATTON.

SIR, Your honourable and friendly dealing towards me, confirmed by divers of my friends, especially by Mr. Tremayne, doth give me just cause to be thankful for the same. But herein I had rather yield satisfaction in deeds than in words. I am greatly grieved, considering the perilous state this Country standeth in, to find her Majesty so strangely affected as she is. I hope, when her Highness shall have duly considered (upon perusing our letters sent as well to herself as to my Lords) what dangerous inconveniences are likely to follow, and to what confusion these Countries will come unto, if she withdraw her gracious assistance, she will then prefer her safety and honour before her treasure ; protesting unto you before God, that, if her Majesty do not

* Additional MSS. 15891, f. 57^b.

look unto it in time, yea, and that out of hand, I see no
remedy but the French will be masters of the Country.
Seeing the peril so great, and knowing how careful you
are of her Majesty's honour and safety, I do assure myself
that you will take the matter in such sort to heart as the
cause importeth.   Sorry I am to see by your letters her
Majesty's indisposition to deal effectually in the Scottish
causes.[a] If the parties presently repaired thither be sent
away with evil satisfaction, farewell the quietness and good
days of England.   If I stood (as I hear I do not) in her
Majesty's good grace, which is no small grief unto me, considering with what mind I serve, I would then discharge my
duty plainly unto her, touching the sending away of Dumfermline well satisfied.   But my state standing as it doth,
having no hope to do good, I think it wisdom to forbear to
offend.   And so, for other matters referring you unto our
general letter sent to my Lords, I commit you to God.   At
Antwerp, the 23rd of June 1578.

Your assured friend to his poor power,

FRAN. WALSINGHAM.[b]

As Hatton did not quite understand the communication that was made to him by Mr. Heneage respecting
the affairs of Scotland[c], Walsingham again wrote to him
on the subject from Canterbury;—

SIR FRANCIS WALSINGHAM TO SIR CHRISTOPHER HATTON.

SIR, I perceive the message I sent you by Mr. Heneage
touching the nobleman that is to be sent out of Scotland,
seemed somewhat dark unto you, being not made acquainted
with the last letters sent from Mr. Bowes, remaining in Mr.
Secretary Wilson's hands.   You shall therefore do well to
send for them, and upon the view of the same to take that
course that to your good judgment shall seem most apt to
knit the two Crowns in perfect amity.   I am the more importunate in this cause, for that at my departure I found a

---

[a] Vide p. 60, 68.   [b] Additional MSS. 15891, f. 45[b].

[c] Vide page 60, ante.

strange disposition in her Majesty (things at home and abroad
duly considered) touching the entering into any straiter degree of amity with Scotland, as a matter dishonourable to
join in any treaty with that Crown during the Queen's life. If
her Majesty would call to mind her former proceeding in the
causes of that Country since the deposition of the Queen,
as the maintenance of such as were the deposers of her, the
prosecuting of her friends, the disposing of her of the castle
of Edinburgh, and the retaining of her prisoner; all these
actions being grounded on reason and justice, considering
the title she pretendeth to this Crown, and the actual rebellion she procured here within the Realm, there is no cause
why her Majesty should now make a conscience to strengthen
herself with the amity of Scotland. Such scruples of conscience are rather superstitious than religious. Scotland is
the postern-gate to any mischief or peril that may befal to
this Realm. It will therefore behove her Majesty to look
well to it. The Scot is a proud nation: if you refuse his
friendship when he offereth it, you shall miss it when you
would have it: and therefore it greatly importeth her Majesty to look substantially to the matter; for to my judgment it toucheth her as nearly as the conservation of her
Crown amounteth unto. I am afraid I am too troublesome
to you in this matter of Scotland; and, though the Country
be cold, I can neither think nor speak of it but in heat.
By a letter received this last night from Mr. Secretary, I
perceive that Monsieur's man is dispatched with good satisfaction; her Majesty doth deal therein very providently; it
behoveth her (the time duly considered) to lose no advantage that by God's goodness is offered unto her. He will
serve for a good counterpoise of his brother's malice, which
I always noted to be great, not only towards her Majesty,
but to the whole Nation. I may not forget to acquaint
you with the honourable entertainment the Lord Cobham
and I have received at Mr. Justice Manwood's house in his
absence; the same being performed not only very bountifully, but also most orderly. The man is greatly loved and

esteemed here, for his uprightness and integrity, of the best sort of the gentlemen of this shire; which is a most apparent argument of his good and just dealings amongst them: and therefore it were great pity that the malice of some few for their particulars should blemish the credit of a man of his sufficiency for her Majesty's service, and so well able for living to bear the countenance of a place of credit. And so, with most hearty thanks for the assurance of your good friendship, I commit you to God's good keeping. At Canterbury, the 27th of June 1578.

Your most assuredly,　　　　Fra. Walsingham.[a]

The date of the following letter from Lord Leicester to Hatton is fixed by Mr. Gilbert Talbot having written to his father, on the 3rd of May 1578, " My Lord of Leicester threateneth to come to Buxton this summer." . . . . . On Monday or Tuesday next her Majesty goeth to Lord Compton's house at Tottenham; and so to my Lord Treasurer's at Theobald's, and there tarrieth three or four days; and from thence to Wanstead, and there four or five days."[b]　At Wanstead, a seat of Leicester's, she was received by Philip Sidney, and entertained by a dramatic interlude, written by him for the occasion, called " A Contention between a Forester and a Shepherd for the May-Lady," and printed at the end of the Arcadia.[c]

THE EARL OF LEICESTER TO SIR CHRISTOPHER HATTON.

I humbly thank God to hear of the increase of her Majesty's good health, and am most glad that she took that happy medicine that wrought so well with her, as I perceive by your letter it did. I trust it will help to prolong and perfect that which we all daily pray for. I hope now, ere long,

---

[a] Additional MSS. 15891. Though the date in the Letter-Book is 1579, it was certainly a mistake for 1578.

[b] Lodge's Illustrations of British History, 8vo. vol. ii. p. 98.

[c] Nichols's Progresses, ii. 94 where the piece is reprinted.

to be with you, to enjoy that blessed sight which I have been so long kept from. A few of these days seem many years, and I think I shall feel a worse grief ere I seek so far a remedy again.   I thank God, I have found hitherto great ease by this bath, and hope it will make me a long while the better able to do my duty for attendance.   One thing hath troubled me not a little, to hear that her Majesty should come to Wanstead, and her .=.[a] not there to receive her.   I fear that little liking to it she had before will through too, too many more faults, breed her less love hereafter.   If my wishing could have served, yea, or a little sooner knowing of it had come, I think St. Anne should have had a short farewell. But God grant I may hear that her Majesty doth both well rest, and find all things else there to her good contentment; and that the good man Robert,[b] she last heard of there, were found at his beads, with all his *aves*, in his solitary walk. Well, good Captain, I hope you have supplied that which is almost impossible, without her great especial goodness, to be done.   I am now at a point with St. Anne here, and will hie me home as fast as I can, not disobeying the great charge you have laid upon me: at which Mr. Doctor Baily doth not take a little advantage, specially because the late hot weather is now here returned again, having had three or four days of great heat now together.   It will, I suppose, make me a little the more obedient also.   I have sent you a letter which I received yesterday from Casimir; it is of no new date.   You may see what he writes, and how earnestly.   Since my hap is not to be in so honourable a voyage, nor   ,[c] I would be most glad that my nephew[d] might go to Casimir; and if he may not as from her Majesty, yet after the other sort you say her Majesty could like of.   I beseech you further it, and I shall be most glad it may be obtained.   I long to hear of Mr. Walsingham's news; by this you have all, I am sure.   I

---

[a] The copyist originally wrote,— " and I not there;" but the " I " is deleted, and the above symbol, which occurs elsewhere, and which is thus proved to indicate Leicester, is written over it in another hand.

[b] Himself.

[c] An unintelligible abbreviation occurs here.

[d] Philip Sydney.

will trouble you no further, but to wish you as myself, and
hope shortly to see you. From Buxton's, this 9th of July.

Yours assured ever,   R. LEICESTER.[*]

Davison made another report of the affairs of the
Low Countries, in his usual prolix style, on the 23rd
of July;—

MR. DAVISON TO SIR CHRISTOPHER HATTON.

SIR, I have so long forborne to write unto your Honour,
as I wot not well with what reason to excuse myself that
shall not rather accuse me, considering mine obligation towards you in many respects. But I doubt not mine error
shall obtain your pardon, the rather in that it hath not grown
from any want of duty. Of the present condition of things
with us, I can write nothing that your Honour may not
amply understand from my Lords here. The Duke of
Alençon being at Mons, is the matter which doth at this
time most perplex and confound our opinions. Such as consider the power of France, the unquiet humour of that
nation, their ready disposition to fish in the troubled streams
of their neighbours, the occasion that this war doth offer unto
them both to make their profit abroad and to throw the fire
out of their State at home, together with the inclination of
some part of this Country to embrace them, do hold the enterprise of singular moment and danger: others measuring the
same by the age and quality of the Duke, by the supposed
difference between him and his brother, by the firm amity
between the two Kings, by the lightness and negligence proper to that nation, by the nature and strength of these Countries, and in some by the difficulties which great attempts do
commonly meet withal, do think it a matter not much to be
feared, unless it tend to the deceiving of these States, in
advancing the affairs of the Spaniard. But what is like to
be the success is the harder to judge, in that it dependeth on
accidents uncertain, and on the will and affection of a nation

* Additional MSS. 15891, f. 53.

most inconstant. He hath, since his arrival at Mons, written to divers towns and persons particularly, and to the States generally, disguising the cause of his coming down to be wholly for their succour; but as they might very well spare help, so are the most parts loath to embrace the same, unless it be with better caution than is looked for. Howbeit, the matter is now grown to that point, that either they must accept him as a friend, or reject him as an enemy, a question sure very hard to determine: for if they receive him in this sort he desires, which is to have the commandment of their forces jointly with his own, they must either depose the Archduke, or at the least abridge his authority, either of which will be hard to do but with an outward offence and inward confusion; besides that, they must put their fortune into the hands of a stranger, and, that which is more, of a born enemy, of whom they have infinitely to suspect, and nothing to trust unto other than a French promise. So as, be it that he run a course for the Spaniard, which some suspect, or that he pretend to serve his own turn, which is rather believed, (for other object than one of these two undoubtedly he hath not,) the danger is apparent. On the other side, if they should reject him, the doubt is that either he will take part openly with the Spaniard, or else, for the first induction, impatronize himself of Hainault, which he holdeth as already at his devotion, and so have the gap opened to invade and dismember the rest of the Country; either of which inconveniences were hard for them to fall into, though in common reason they cannot eschew the one or the other, unless the remedies be all the sooner applied. The Duke, to blear the eyes of this people, hath already put himself in action, and sent Bussy d'Amboise with three thousand men to the siege of Maubeuge, not far from Mons, wherein is a garrison of the enemies; his drift being chiefly, under that colour, to draw his prepared forces (which by his ministers are bruited to be about four thousand horse and fifteen thousand footmen) the rather into Hainault; and yet, in the mean time, gives out that he doth nothing but with the liking and

knowledge of her Majesty, whose name and credit he useth
as a cloak to colour his ambitious and deceitful pretext, as
will better appear with time, and is partly to be judged already by the ·manner of dealing of his ministers with my
Lords here.   He hath, since his arrival at Mons, sent one
Monsieur de Beauier towards Casimir to make fair weather
with him, but, of all his demonstrations, the scope and drift
resteth suspicious; and thus much for that matter.   The
Baron of Preinder, last ambassador for the Emperor, is departed towards his master: the other seems in mind to repair
towards Don John, to see if there be yet any hope of peace,
whereby to prevent the danger which the Country is like
to fall into by the proceeding of this war; the remedy whereof
resteth, as it seems, in the retire of Don John, and yielding
up the places he occupieth into the hands of the States, who
are otherwise jealous and indisposed to enter into any treaty
of peace, presuming it shall tend on his part to the gaining
of time, and wearying of them with entertaining an army so
chargeable as they have presently in the field, rather than
to any good and sound composition.   Their army, composed
of eight thousand horse and nine thousand footmen, (besides
the regiment of our nation and those which yet rest in garrison, through a lack of money to draw them to the camp,) are
lodged still within a mile of Liege, between the two rivers
called the Little and Great Nethe, from whence it is thought
they shall remove within a day or two.   The enemy hath
retired the most part of his forces into garrison, pretending,
as some think, to make a war defensive, leaving the field
another while to the States: his forces are esteemed to be
five thousand horse and twenty-five thousand footmen, accounting the companies as complete, which indeed they are
not.   He hath abandoned Soigny in Hainault, wherein the
Count Lalam hath put garrison: the like it is thought he
pretends to do with Dyest and Arschot, from whence he
hath withdrawn his munition and artillery, even to the small
iron pieces.   Compiegne certainly affirmed to be rendered to
the States of Guelders, who are in hope of like composition

with Dewenter. Casimir should as yesterday begin his musters besides Zutphen. The Gauntois, on Sunday morning last, surprised by a stratagem the town of Ipre in Flanders, which (with them of the three members) is now at their devotion. The towns of Hainault, Artois, Lisle, Douay, and Orchies, (being practised by the letters of Monsieur,) have written hither to the States to know how they should govern themselves; whom the States have in their answer required to refer themselves to the general resolution of the Provinces. Thus, being as weary with writing as I think your Honour will be of reading my tedious letter, I end with the offer of my humble service, commending your Honour to the protection of the Almighty. Antwerp, the 22nd of July 1578.

Your Honour's humbly at commandment,
W. DAVISON.[*]

On the 23rd of July Walsingham wrote again to Hatton respecting his mission;—

SIR FRANCIS WALSINGHAM TO SIR CHRISTOPHER HATTON.

SIR, How we have proceeded here in our charge, what little good is like to follow thereof, and how things do stand here, this bearer, Mr. Sommers, is able sufficiently to inform you. I have amongst other things prayed him to acquaint you with my opinion touching the town of Sluse, which I wish were in her Majesty's hands in pawn for the money already lent, and that which hereafter her Majesty is to furnish them withal, as well to withdraw them from the French as to keep them from being overrun by the Spaniards. If I do not mistake it, they have put their towns in that strength as the King of Spain is too old to see the end of these wars; so that they may have, during their troubles, some convenient support from hence, which they shall not lack elsewhere, if we do not make sure with them betimes. And yet the matter may be so ordered as neither her Majesty shall enter into an

---

[*] Additional MSS. 15891, f. 107.

actual war, nor yet remain unsatisfied of such treasure as she shall furnish them withal. To make this probable unto you requireth the setting down of many circumstances which I would be loath to commit to paper, but do reserve them to acquaint you withal at my return; which by your good and friendly furtherance I hope will be with speed, seeing no necessary cause of stay here at this present, as yourself shall perceive by this bearer's report. By her Majesty's especial commandment I wrote unto her in a private letter what I could discover touching the Prince of Orange's intention concerning these Countries; which in effect was, as far as I can gather, he meaneth never to be subject to the King of Spain; that he purposeth to annex them to the Empire; that he is not otherwise inclined to the French than to serve his own turn; and lastly, that, though he gave out the contrary, he had rather enjoy the Country himself, than either French, Spaniard, English, or Almayne. I know her Majesty will and hath acquainted you with all, and therefore I pray you advise her to keep the matter secret, especially that it be not known to come from me. And so, beseeching you to commit this letter to the fire, I commend you to God's good keeping. At Antwerp, the 23rd of July 1578.

Yours most assuredly, FRA. WALSINGHAM.[a]

Sir Amias Paulet, the writer of the following letter, was then ambassador at Paris; and, as will appear from subsequent letters, soon after used Sir Christopher Hatton's influence to obtain his recall, in which he succeeded in January 1579; but Paulet did not return to England until the spring of that year.

SIR AMIAS PAULETT TO SIR CHRISTOPHER HATTON.

It may please your Honour to hold me excused that I write not more often unto you, which proceedeth only of want of matter worthy of you; the root and spring of our

[a] Additional MSS. 15891, f. 36.

actions here being derived into the Low Countries, from whence the news of France must be expected hereafter. Our only open doings consist in the assembly of men of war, which march daily, and want nothing but money; and he may perchance be assisted with Captains of good credit very shortly. Our secret drifts and devices are composed of two divers factions, and tend to two divers ends: the one, and the mightier, seeking to disturb this voyage by all means possible; the other, and the greater in number, sparing nothing that may advance the same. Ambassadors are gone to Monsieur from the Pope, the State of Venice, and the Duke of Savoy, to dissuade this journey. Monsieur is the only man that must decide this question, and some think that he will not be dissuaded. If you in England can bridle the French ambition, all will be well; many here being of opinion that your own means will make you able, and that the necessity of the time will constrain others to yield to your counsel. The Marshal de Biron will not be quiet in Guienne; and what may ensue of his doings there, it is yet uncertain. I leave to trouble your Honour any further, committing you to the merciful protection of the Almighty. From Paris, the 26th of July 1578.

Your Honour's to command,   A. POWLETT.*

Walsingham's proceedings in Holland gave great displeasure to Elizabeth; and the ensuing vindication of his conduct, to Hatton is remarkable for the boldness and honesty of the expressions;—

SIR FRANCIS WALSINGHAM TO SIR CHRISTOPHER HATTON.

SIR, I most heartily thank you for letting me understand by Mr. Tremayne the causes whereon hath grown her Majesty's offence. And though I hope I shall be able sufficiently to satisfy her at my return, yet in the mean time it is an intolerable grief unto me to receive so hard measure at her Majesty's hands, as if I were some notorious offender.

* Additional MSS. 15891, f. 39.

Surely, Sir, it standeth not with her Majesty's safety to deal
so unkindly with those that serve her faithfully.   There
is a difference between serving with a cheerful and languishing mind.   If there hath lacked in us either care, faithfulness, or diligence, then were we worthy of blame.   It is
very hard to judge there, (without understanding all necessary circumstances,) what is fit to be done here.   When our
doings shall come to examination, I hope the greatest fault
we may be charged withal is, that we have had more regard
to her Majesty's honour and safety than to her treasure;
wherein we have dealt no worse with her than with ourselves,
having for her service sake engaged ourselves £5000 thick;
which doing of ours being offensively taken, doth make the
burthen the heavier.   Thus, Sir, you see, as my good friend,
I am bound to open unto you my grief.   For our proceedings here, I refer you to the letters directed to my Lords.
And so, with most hearty thanks for your faithful, friendly
dealing towards me, I commit you to God's good keeping.
Written with a weary hand and a wounded mind.   At
Antwerp, the 29th of July 1578.

Your most assured friend,

FRA. WALSINGHAM.[*]

It appears from Dr. Toby Mathew's reply to a letter
from Sir Christopher Hatton that he wished to examine
the records of Christ-Church College, Oxford.   Dr.
Mathew, who was afterwards Archbishop of York, was
then President of St. John's, and Canon of Christ-
Church.

DR. MATHEW TO SIR CHRISTOPHER HATTON.

My bounden duty humbly remembered to your Honour.
Immediately upon my repair hither I dealt with my company
for the search of such evidences as your letter mentioneth.
We are all not only contented a perfect view be had of all

[*] Additional MSS. 15891, f. 43b.

the muniments we have, but would be right glad, every one of us, that aught might be found therein to profit or pleasure your Honour. And if I might understand by this bearer, Mr. Mainwaring, (a man most willing and well able to do you much honour,) when it would like you to send hither to see the search made, (the sooner the better in my opinion,) I would provide our officer for that purpose should not fail to be present. For mine own particular, I assure you, Sir, I think myself greatly benefited that it pleaseth you in any thing to use my poor service; which is, and shall be, and is so bound to be, at your commandment. And even thus I humbly commend the continuance and increase of your honour to the gracious blessing of Almighty God. From Christ-Church in Oxon, 22nd August 1578.

Your Honour's humble and bounden,

TOBIE MATHEWE.*

Mr. Stanhope, of Harrington in Northamptonshire, the writer of the next letter, and ancestor of the Earls of Chesterfield, was then a Gentleman of the Privy Chamber. He succeeded Hatton as Vice-Chamberlain, was raised to the peerage by King James the First, and left issue two daughters, besides his son and heir, Charles, second Lord Stanhope; but no marriage took place between any of his children and those of Lord Scrope of Bolton. Hatton's "fair house" was Holdenby, which he rebuilt in imitation of Lord Burghley's seat of Theobald's;—

MR. STANHOPE TO SIR CHRISTOPHER HATTON.

SIR, The continuance of your former courtesies emboldeneth me to salute you with these few lines, which humbly recommend unto you his goodwill whom your virtue and friendship have won to be yours in all he may; praying you

* Additional MSS. 15891, f. 35.

to accept the offer of an honest mind in good part, till either
occasion give more proof, or time more power, to perform that
which the whilst must rest in promise. In my journey
from London I had a little sight afar off of your fair house,
which I had then gone to view better, had I not been tied
to such a charge as I could not well part from till I came to
my cousin Thomas Markham's house, where I assure you,
Sir, there was as great plenty of every good thing that might
welcome his friends as could be devised; and as well can his
wife skill to entertain them, as I have seen. From thence,
after two or three days' rest, I took my daughter with me to
my brother's house; where leaving her, I came to Carlisle to
finish in some sort or other with my Lord Scrope our former
agreement touching the match of our children, whom I find,
as ever, so still desirous to proceed according to our first
intent; and therefore have agreed to meet his Lordship again
a month hence, in a progress which he intendeth into Lan-
cashire, where the young couples may see one another, and,
after a little acquaintance, may resolve accordingly. Wherefore, Sir, I humbly pray you to present my humblest service
to her Majesty's gracious acceptance, imparting to her Highness our proceeding therein, and the cause of my stay here
upon this occasion; who either am otherwise to be counter-
manded by her Majesty, or else to finish this matter as conveniently as I may, and then to return and make an end of
the remainder of my few years in her Highness's service,
whereunto I have ever from the first both vowed myself
and it; most humbly praying the Almighty to prosper and
defend her ever, to the only comfort of all her true loving
servants and subjects, as it hath from the first pleased Him to
bless her above all others with the excellency of most rare
and singular virtues. Your letter was very welcome to my
Lord Scrope, and, I can assure you, you may dispose of him
as of your honourable constant friend; who is so much the
more worthy accounting of, as he is her Majesty's very true
and faithful servant, and the carefullest to discharge the place
committed to him with all diligence that may be, as may well

appear; for that, of so rude and untamed people as these have
been, I think her Majesty hath in few places better ordered
or more obedient subjects.   And yet surely, Sir, I must say
that I am very glad I know no truer nor lovinger people to
her Majesty anywhere than are generally over all these north
parts as I have travelled; so as, if their landlords and governors
be honest men, there is no doubt but the rest will show themselves very dutiful: the which I pray God we may all have
ever the grace to do.   And so, humbly praying you again to
pardon my long troubling you, I recommend my service to
your devotion, and your health to the favour of the Almighty.
From Carlisle, the 5th of August, 1578.

   Yours most humbly to his power,   JOHN STANHOPE.[*]

Walsingham's next letter to Hatton exhibits the Vice-
Chamberlain in a very amiable light;—

TO SIR CHRISTOPHER HATTON.

SIR, Your most friendly standing in my defence where it
might do me most good, and your comfortable letter written
to my poor comfortless wife, do minister unto me just cause
to acknowledge myself greatly beholden unto you, praying
you to make account of me as of a most constant and assured
friend in all fortunes.   The desire that now her Majesty hath
to understand of my doings at Mons, the speedy answer
she requireth unto her last letters, and the sufficiency of
this bearer, Mr. Somers, who hath been acquainted with all
our proceedings here, which I have prayed him to impart
unto you, doth force me to be much shorter than otherwise
I would have been if leisure had served.   As you dispatch
this bearer with comfortable or uncomfortable answer, so
are these people here either to depend or utterly to fall away
from you, wherein also there is to be used great expedition.
God therefore direct her Majesty's heart to do that which

* Additional MSS. 15891, f. 39[b].

may be for her honour and safety, to whose protection I commit you.   At Antwerp, the 16th of August 1578.

Your most assured friend,   Fra. Walsingham.[a]

In July the Queen set out upon one of her usual Progresses, and the Vice-Chancellor of Cambridge, hearing that her Majesty intended to honour that University with a visit, wrote to Lord Burghley, its Chancellor, apprising him of the manner in which they intended to show their respect, and asking his opinion on other points relating to her reception.   Burghley, in his answer, advised them to provide gloves, with a few verses on a paper affixed, for the Earls of Leicester and Oxford and the Lord Chamberlain; adding, " that for himself he could spare them, so that if Mr. Vice-Chamberlain might have a pair with some verses, it should do well to conciliate his goodwill, being a lover of learned men." [b]   On the 26th of that month the Vice-Chancellor and heads of houses waited upon the Queen at Audley End, when the gloves were presented.   Gabriel Harvey, a scholar, orator, and poet, wrote a volume of Latin verses on the occasion; the fourth book of which he divided into three parts, and dedicated the first to Lord Oxford, the second to Sir Christopher Hatton, and the third to Philip Sidney.[c]

On the accession of Elizabeth's suitor, Henry Duke of Anjou, to the Crown of France, in May 1574, the title of Anjou was conferred upon his brother, Francis Duke of Alençon, who was then about twenty years old, and had for some time succeeded Henry as a candidate for the Queen's hand, though she was more than double his own age.   This ridiculous alliance occupied the

[a] Additional MSS. 15891, f. 35b.   [b] Nichols's Progresses, ii. 110.
[c] Ibid. ii. 111.

public attention for some years; and in 1578, Camden says, " the Duke of Anjou, though his mind were bent upon the Netherland war, yet to show that he could attend both martial and love matters both at once, prosecuteth his marriage with Queen Elizabeth, which he had begun to sue for whilst he was Duke of Alençon; and first Bacheville being sent for, this cause came to the Queen in her progress at Melford, Cordall's house in Suffolk." [a]   Elizabeth visited Sir Thomas Cordall, the Master of the Rolls, at Melford, early in August[b], attended by the Earl of Oxford, Lord Hunsdon, Sir Christopher Hatton, and others of her Court; and, a few days after, the Earl of Sussex expressed his opinions to the Queen respecting her marriage in the following long letter :[c]—

THE EARL OF SUSSEX'S LETTER TO HER MAJESTY.

IT MAY PLEASE YOUR MOST EXCELLENT MAJESTY, Upon Tuesday last, in the morning, about seven o'clock, Monsieur de Bussy came hither to me, and told me, that, hearing (as he was to pass through London) I was come hither from the Court, he would acquaint me with his negociation, for that he doubted that the messenger sent from Mr. Walsingham, since his coming from Monsieur, was not come to your Majesty before my coming from the Court. The substance of his speech consisted upon two points. The one, that Monsieur dealt with such sincerity in the matter of the marriage as it rested in your Majesty to dispose of him therein as should please your self. The other, that he would be directed by your Majesty in his action of the Low Countries; hoping that in both these your Majesty would have such respect

---

[a] Annals, b. ii. p. 90.
[b] Nichols's Progresses, ii. 113—116.
[c] Some passages, which are obliterated in the transcript in Hatton's " Letter Book," have been supplied from the copy in Lodge's Shrewsbury Papers, vol. ii. p. 107, et seq.

to his honour and state as the great affection which he bare
to your person did deserve. He made a long discourse of the
hard dealing that had been divers times used towards Monsieur in France, and of the jealousies that from time to time
were put into the heads of his mother and brother by personages of great quality, that sought their own greatness by
his hinderance. He also declared that Monsieur, by these
occasions, was necessarily detained from showing himself to
be himself; but being now in free place, and at his full
liberty, he would make his value and resolute mind known
to all the world. And so concluded how necessary it was for
him to seek greatness abroad, to continue thereby his greatness and surety at home ; and therefore was come into the
Low Countries to be directed wholly by your Majesty, where
he might receive and follow your directions without the stay
or lett of any other person; which he would do with as great
sincerity as could be required. He did not directly say that
Monsieur looked to be made great either by his marriage
with you or by his actions in the Low Countries; but surely
his whole discourse was oftentimes intermingled with such
speeches as I might certainly gather that Monsieur's meaning was to be great by the one of these means or by both,
and that it were a dishonour to him and a peril to lack both,
and so return home worse than he came forth. This was the
substance of his speech unto me, which I thought my duty
to declare unto your Majesty as briefly as I could. And now,
remembering your Majesty's pleasure to be that upon all
occasions I should be bold to write to you my opinion, I
thought it my duty upon this occasion to write somewhat,
humbly beseeching your Majesty to accept my plain and true
meaning therein. To enter into this matter, I must first lay
this foundation (which I think to be as sure as man can lay),
that Monsieur hath determined to seek to make himself
great either by the marriage of your Majesty or by the possession of the Low Countries, or by both; and that the
French King and the Queen Mother to deliver him out of
France will by all the possible means that may, help to

further and advance his greatness in this sort for their own benefit, quiet, and surety, and the avoiding of all fires, troubles, and perils at home.   And if Monsieur by your Majesty be put from his hope in both these, and no sure peace concluded before, betwixt the King of Spain and the States, then will he turn over all his forces to aid Don John, and seek his greatness and surety by martial actions that way, and by the friendship of the King of Spain, rather than with dishonour and peril to return home in worse case than he came forth.   Wherein also, or in any other action abroad, there is no doubt but his mother and brother will further him what they may, to keep him occupied abroad, and thereby to avoid the peril at home.   This foundation being thus laid, it is fit to consider of the commodities and incommodities of every of them; that is to say, of the marriage, of the alienating of the Low Countries, and of the French assisting of Don John.

Touching the marriage, (if your Majesty in your own heart can like of it, which I will leave to God and you,) I find these commodities to follow.   Your alliance with the house of France, whereby, besides all likelihood that the French King will not attempt anything to the prejudice of you and his brother, you shall be assured by yourself and by your husband to have such a party in France as the French King shall not be able, nor shall not dare to attempt, directly or indirectly, anything against you.   You shall take away and suppress all practices for competition, for Popery, or any other seditious cause, at home or abroad; and so shall you at home and abroad assure your person and your state from all perils that by man's judgment might grow anyways to you by France.   You shall also, by the help of your husband, be able to compel the King of Spain to take reasonable conditions of his subjects in the Low Countries, and the States to take reasonable conditions of their King, so as he may have that which before God and man doth justly belong to him, and they may enjoy their liberties, freedoms, and all other things that is fit for their quiet and surety in their

bodies, goods, consciences, and lives; whereby you shall avoid
great effusion of Christian blood, and shall have the honour
and reward due in this world, and by God, to so gracious,
godly, and Christian actions. And herewith, for the more
surety of all persons and matters, yourself may have in your
own hands some maritime part to be by you kept at the
charge of the King of Spain, and your husband may have
some frontier towns in like sort, and both to be continued
for such a number of years as may bring a settling of surety
in all respects; by which means you shall also be delivered
from perils at home and abroad that may grow from the King
of Spain. And if you like not of this course in dealing for
the Low Countries, you may join with your husband, and so
between you attempt to possess the whole Low Countries,
and draw the same to the Crown of England, if you have
any child by him; or, if you have none, to divide them
between the realms of England and France, as shall be
metest for either. But, to be plain with your Majesty, I
do not think this course to be so just, so godly, so honourable,
nor, when it is looked into the bottom, so sure for you and
your state, as the other, although at the first sight it do
perhaps carry in show some plausibility. It is also most
likely, and a matter certainly to be expected, that, if God
will incline your heart to marriage, He will also bless you
with children; whereby both you for your time shall be
settled in the chair of surety, and all matters that might be
kindled by mischievous fires shall go away in the smoke,
et erunt cogitationes malorum sicut somnia. And, by the leaving behind you of a successor of your own body, you shall
leave surety and quiet to your realm; you shall avoid Christian bloodshed, like to grow by civil wars; you shall dis-
burden your conscience; you shall receive at God's hand your
just desert for so godly a care, and your fame shall exceed
upon the earth. So as, to be short, by your marriage you
shall give law to France, Spain and Low Countries, England,
Scotland, and, in effect, to all Christendom; you shall settle
your state surely at home; you shall be strongly friended

abroad; you shall be in estimation over all the world; you shall have a husband as a servant and defender of all your causes present; you shall be like a serpent in the sight of the .evil, and like a dove in the sight of the good; you shall be the peacemaker to all Christendom; your fame shall exceed all other Princes that were ever in Europe; and God will bless you as His own chosen vessel both in this world and in the world to come: which be the commodities that be like to grow by your marriage at this present.

The incommodities which may grow for lack of your marriage be fittest to be left to be by your Majesty considered of by their contraries, whereby, and by the knowledge of your own heart, you may best judge of them; and be such as my heart trembleth to think of them, and I pray God I never live to see them. The incommodities, dangers, and difficulties that have been remembered might grow by your marriage be these: 1. Your own mislike to marriage, which might breed a discontented life hereafter. 2. The difficulty of the choice of a person that might in all respects content your mind. 3. The danger that a foreign Prince might with time and by degrees bring this realm to his own possession, being your husband. 4. The danger that if your husband should come to be a King of a foreign country, necessity would constrain him to his own from yours, and keep you in your own from him, and so by absence the comfort expected by marriage should lack. 5. The danger that, if you should have but one son by him, he should be heir of both kingdoms; and then would be himself in the greatest, and rule the other by a viceroy, which England cannot bear. 6, 7. The difficulty of religion. The charge that should grow to the realm by the maintenance of your husband. 8, 9. The general mislike which Englishmen have to be governed by a stranger. The danger of your person if your husband should but fraudulently seek you first, to possess by treason another after. To all which such answers have also been remembered as follow: The first and second receive not the counsel of others, but must be directed by yourself, whereby

you be to follow only the counsel of your own heart, whereunto all men must leave you ; for it is the judgment of your
own heart that may make it ill to you, which no other man
can say to be but good of itself, if your heart can like of
it. The third is a peril that must have a long time of drift
ere it come to pass, and indeed can never take effect if God
take not all senses away both from you and all the states
of your realm ; and therefore a peril in talk and no peril in
matter, as appeareth by the King of Spain married to Queen
Mary. The fourth is not yet in this man, neither doth any
man know that it ever shall be, and therefore no peril, but
accidental; but if it did fall out indeed that he should be
a King of himself, and thereby his own country require his
presence, and your country require your presence, yet is it
not therefore necessary that you should be always absent the
one from the other ; for, as by the amity of both Kingdoms
both shall remain in the greater surety, so by that occasion
and the vicinity of them you may have the better cause to be
often together without danger to either of you, as appeared
by King Philip, who came divers times to Queen Mary, and
remained with her certain months, even in his greatest times
of wars with the French King. The fifth rather seemeth to
bring honour than peril, and yet is but a supposition, and no
matter certain ; for it is a hard case to make an assignment
that you shall have a child, and but one only child. And yet,
if it so fall out, an Englishman, born in England and King
thereof, born in his own realm, should also be King of
France, as heretofore with great honour hath been ; and it
should not be that a Frenchman, born in France, King thereof, should also be King of England, which never was before.
And so, reducing this matter to the example that hath been,
it will be honour, and not peril, that shall grow thereby. The
sixth hath always been answered that the exercise of his religion should (so long as he should continue it) be private to
himself and a few of his own nation, without admitting any
Englishmen to it ; and he should also accompany you to the
exercise of your religion in convenient times, which can bring

no peril to your person or state, nor hath been thought to be
so intolerable as it should break your marriage, but only by
such as picked quarrel rather to your marriage than to religion, whereof the world hath had good proof. . The seventh
shall rather bring gain than charge, for he hath a great pa-
trimony of his own to spend here. The example appeareth
by King Philip. The eighth doth not carry a truth, for
the realm is to be governed as it was before, and so was it in
the time of King Philip; and then the people shall have no
cause to mislike, but rather a great cause of liking, when
both your person, your realm, and all your people shall by
this means be assured from all dangers. The ninth inferreth
a treasonable dealing not to be thought of by a Christian
Prince, much less to be executed, and that carrieth no reasonable sense with it, that a Christian Prince, possessed
of your godly, virtuous, wise, beautiful, and peerless person,
and of all your kingdoms therewith, should have in his heart
to be by treason delivered of you, and that he hath by you,
to seek to get the same again by another person so far inferior to you. And, therefore, of a Christian Prince I dare
not have any such thought; and he that thinketh of this can
think of anything that he thinketh can hinder your marriage.
And so I leave to your Majesty to consider at your pleasure
of the commodities and incommodities of your marriage, and
of the incommodities that are like to come if you marry not.
Touching the alienating of the Low Countries to the French,
the incommodities be these: The uniting of the whole into
one Prince's hands, which being divided, either party hath
been able to match the other, and so by their division the
realm of England hath never lacked a friend of the one;
which hath been a principal stay and surety to England,
and by uniting of both will be a manifest and present danger
and peril. The great forces both by land and sea that the
French shall have when they shall possess both, where the
French may attempt what they will, and shall have power to
execute their will. The great danger that may grow to all
Europe by the greatness of the French. The perils that may

grow in particular to your Majesty by the French maintenance of competition, Popery, faction, and other civil divisions within the realm, and by withdrawing of England from
your devotion.   The disturbing of all your traffic, and impos-
ing thereupon of all taxes at the pleasure of the French.   The
stop of vent of all inward commodities, and the mutinying of
the people that shall lack work.   The bringing of the realm
into a perpetual servitude of tributes or other worse matter,
which discommodities, how they may be encountered with
any of our commodities, I do not see.   By the joining of
Monsieur with Don John, and no sure peace concluded between the King of Spain and the States, I see no commodities to grow, but these incommodities manifestly to ensue.
Either the whole suppression of the Low Countries by the
Spanish tyranny, and thereby your Majesty to be subject to
many of the perils before rehearsed in the cause of France,
both for your person, realm, and traffic; or else your Majesty
to make yourself the head of the war, and so to enter into
that which my simple head seeth no possibility for you to
maintain, nor knoweth no way how to bring you out of it:
which two generalities have so many particular perils depending on them, as neither I can think of all, neither is it
fit, for tediousness, to trouble you with those I think of;
seeing your Majesty doth better know them, and deeplier
judge of them than I can think.   What may be done to
procure a sure peace between the King and the States, I
know not; seeing I see such diffidence on both sides, and
no likelihood that the States will either yield to reasonable
conditions, or have any disposition to any reasonable peace.
But if there might be such a peace made as in honour, truth,
justice, and conscience were fit, both for the King and the
subjects before God and man, and sufficient to France of
the continuance thereof, then do I surely think that many
of the perils before rehearsed might be avoided for the time.
But, if no such peace be made, then it were fit the States
(being not able to defend themselves) must cast themselves
into either your defence or into the defence of France, where-

upon depend the perils before written. Thus have been bold to touch at this time such matter as true and faithful duty doth find, and to put your Majesty in remembrance of; most humbly beseeching your Highness, that, seeing it is now time that all men should shake off particular respects, and yield themselves wholly to that which is best for your service, the surety of your person, and the benefit of your realm, you will pardon me at this present for the delivering to you by writing that which in substance I have often before spoken, and, having by absence the commodity of speech taken from me, am forced, for the faithful discharge of my duty, to deliver it rather by pen than by mouth, with my most humble prayer to God that He may long preserve your Majesty to your own heart's contentation, and to put into your heart to do that which shall be most for His glory, and for your Majesty's honour and surety.   The 28th of August 1578.

Your Majesty's most humble and faithful subject and servant,   T. SUSSEX.

The decision of the Council on the affairs of the Low Countries, and its treatment of the Scottish ambassadors towards the beginning of September in this year, were equally unsatisfactory to Walsingham, who declared his sentiments to Hatton on both points with his usual candour;—

TO SIR CHRISTOPHER HATTON.

SIR, If it be good to have these Countries possessed by the French, and alienated in goodwill from the Crown of England, then have you returned Mr. Sommers with a very good dispatch; but if nothing can be more prejudicial to the state of the Realm than such a resolution as may minister just cause of alienation, then have you committed a most dangerous, I will not say an irreparable error: for surely those people mean no longer to depend upon your uncertainties, who are the more grieved for that they shall be forced thereby to have recourse to a most perilous remedy, such as may be termed *medicina morbo deterior*. We do what we can to help the matter, and to stay them from taking any desperate course. We put them in some hope, that upon our return, when her Majesty by us shall be thoroughly informed of the state of their affairs, she will take some other resolution that shall be to their comfort; which, though it breedeth some contentment in them for a time, yet when they weigh the uncertainty of your former proceedings, and how subject they are to changes, and how dangerous it is for certain diseases to be relieved by uncertain remedies, they then despair to receive any good from them. Her Majesty shall never have the like occasion offered to do them good, as she might, by yielding the relief they demanded ; the estate of their affairs standing then upon making, or marring: but things past cannot be called back again. Seeing your proceedings with them of Scotland, by sending away their ministers discontented, maketh me the less to wonder at your dealings with those of these Countries. The consideration of both doth give me just cause to think that there hangeth over that Realm, which hitherto hath been blest under her Majesty's government with a rare quietness, some most fearful storm; and the rather, I am led so to conceive, for that I am informed by Mr. Sommers, that no Prince could be more faithfully and earnestly dealt withal by Counsellors than her Majesty hath been by hers, wherein he telleth me no man could treat more effectually than yourself. When the advice of grave and faithful Counsellors cannot prevail with a Prince of her Majesty's rare judgment, it is a sign that God hath closed up her heart from seeing and executing that which may be for her safety; which we that love her, and depend of her fortune, cannot but with grief think of: particularly my Lord Cobham and I have cause to think ourselves most unfortunate, to be employed in a legation that is like to have so hard an issue; but I hope the world can witness that there lacked no goodwill in us to do that which duty and our calling required. Thus, wanting presently any other matter to impart unto you, I commit you to God's protection.   From Antwerp, the 9th of September 1578.

Your very loving assured friend,

FRAN. WALSINGHAM.[a]

None of Hatton's friends enjoyed more of his confidence than Sir Thomas Heneage, the Treasurer of the Queen's Chamber; and some remarkable letters from him occur.   The annexed, however, is unimportant:—

TO SIR CHRISTOPHER HATTON.

SIR, To say nothing to you, now I go further from you, agrees not with my mind, nor, methinks, were good manner: yet hearing nothing from you, I have the less to trouble you with; and if at any time for myself I trouble you at all, it is not the nature of my will, but the pricking of my need that is the cause thereof.   Going now about my journey, which will occupy me above a fortnight, I send this bearer principally to bring me word truly from you, that are like to know best, how her Majesty's perfect health (which of late hath been more accumbered than she careth for) now presently standeth: for loving her more than my life, I care for her health more than my own, and am in little quiet when I hear that any thing impeacheth it.   Next her Majesty, that yourself do well, is that I most desire to hear from you, and most heartily wish.   And so commend me humbly to you, and us both to God's best keeping.   From Copthall, very hastily, this 15th of September 1578.

Your own at commandment,

THOS. HENEAGE.[b]

The particulars of the "controversy" mentioned in the following letter from the Earl of Sussex have not been ascertained, but it seems to have been of a public rather than personal nature:—

[a] Additional MSS. 15891, f. 41[b].   [b] Additional MSS. 15891, f. 56.

THE EARL OF SUSSEX TO SIR CHRISTOPHER HATTON.

GOOD MR. VICECHAMBERLAIN, I am sorry to perceive that there was some matter fallen out of controversy between you and Mr. Paginton, fearing it might have bred some other disquiet; but, understanding by your letters how discreetly you have dealt therein, and how well her Majesty resteth satisfied therewith, I am greatly eased of that fear; and for my own part do like well that he tasteth some smart for his arrogant using of a Counsellor, which in right is due to him and to all others in the same predicament, although not always expected in like sort. Seeing the treaty by the three Princes, ambassadors take theffect, I would be glad to hear of a better sequel of the Emperor's sole treaty. I hope the report of the King of Portugal's overthrow is not true. I do hear of late that the Queen's Majesty hath been somewhat ill-disposed: if it be so, God shortly give her perfect health; for with her good estate we all breathe and live, and without that we all stifle and perish. This soil bringeth forth no matter worth writing, and therefore for this time I end, and wish to you, good Mr. Vicechamberlain, as to myself. From Bath, the 20th of September 1578.

Your assured friend,   T. SUSSEX.[a]

When the following letter was written, Hatton was in attendance on the Queen at Loughton Hall in Essex, the seat of Mr. Francis Stonard, whence she proceeded to the Earl of Leicester's house at Wanstead, where the progress ended :[b]—

TO LORD BURGHLEY.

MY VERY GOOD LORD, In consideration that her Majesty is not willing to hearken to any other suit made unto her by Sir John Smythe for his better enabling and recompense of

[a] Additional MSS. 15891, f. 31.   [b] Nichols's Progresses, ii. 222.

his service, her Highness is well pleased to release unto him the mortgage of his lands upon the debt which he oweth her, with this order, that your Lordship shall take good bonds of him for the payment of 2000*l.* at Michaelmas come twelve-months; to the end, that his said lands being set free from mortgage, he may, either by making sale of them, or some other convenient means, endeavour to discharge and satisfy the debt the sooner. And whereas Mr. Secretary told your Lordship, that all his lands should stand bound for the said debt, there was no other meaning in it, than that by the bonds abovesaid his whole livelihood should be liable to her Majesty's execution; as the morrow, waiting upon your Lordship at dinner, I will give you to understand more at large. In the mean while, with my very hearty commendations, I commit your good Lordship to the Almighty. From the Court, at Mr. Stoner's, the 21st September 1578.

Your good Lordship's most bound poor friend,

CHR. HATTON.[a]

Walsingham's next letter was written soon after his return from the Low Countries. He was probably only restrained by respect or fear from adding another epithet to " hatred," when speaking of the Queen's " wooing matters," for it must have been a subject of ridicule throughout Europe :—

SIR FRANCIS WALSINGHAM TO SIR CHRISTOPHER HATTON.

SIR, I know by the inclosed from Mr. Davison, you shall be thoroughly informed what alterations are happened in the Low Countries since our departure from thence. God dealeth most lovingly with her Majesty in taking away her enemies; it requireth at her hands thankfulness, which is the only sacrifice He attendeth[b] from her. By the reason of her indisposition, being continually troubled with the pain in her

---

[a] Autograph in the State Paper Office.   [b] *i. e.* expects.

face, there hath as yet been no consultation for the Low
Country causes. I find her Highness greatly altered from
that I left her touching those causes, so that I am out of
hope of any good resolution; for the which I am very sorry,
knowing that upon this resolution dependeth either the conservation or alienation of the Low Country people's hearts
from her Majesty. The French ambassador, having received
letters from the King and the Duke of Anjou, requireth
audience. I would to God her Majesty would forbear the
entertaining any longer the marriage matter. No one thing
hath procured her so much hatred abroad as these wooing
matters, for that it is conceived she dallieth therein. I have
discharged my duty in that behalf, but in very temperate
sort, for that she hath been heretofore jealous of my liking
of her marriage; and therefore cannot speak so frankly as
others may. Finding her Majesty daily subject to the pain
in her face, she was content, through my persuasion, that her
physicians should confer with some of the best experimented
physicians in London, which was performed accordingly; but
yet are they not resolved either touching the disease, nor the
remedy. Thus, Sir, (as my leisure will give me leave,) have
I scribbled unto you such things as I think meet for your
knowledge; and so commit you to God. At Richmond, the
9th of October 1578.

Your most assured friend,

FRA. WALSINGHAM.

I should yesterday have moved you, at the request of my
brother Dodington, to appoint some day of access unto you
for the Bishop of London; as also to recommend unto you
Mr. Manwood, to be by your good means furthered to the
Chief Baronry[b]; both which I forgot, and am therefore charged
with my unmindfulness of my friends. I pray you let me

* Sic, sed quære " misliking ;" or it
may mean that the Queen suspected
he did not like her intended marriage.

[b] Sir Roger Manwood succeeded
to the office, but was not appointed
until the 24th of January 1579.

hear from you, or else perhaps we may be both blamed. And so God keep you.

Your assured friend,   Fʀᴀ. Wᴀʟsɪɴɢʜᴀᴍ.[a]

Mr. Edmund Tremayne, the writer of the annexed letter, appears to have been the person of those names who is deservedly memorable for his fidelity; and if so, he was the second son of Thomas Tremayne, an Esquire of a very ancient family in Devonshire, and entered the service of Edward Earl of Devon, afterwards created Marquis of Exeter. When that nobleman and the Princess Elizabeth were sent to the Tower, on suspicion of being privy to Wyat's rebellion, Tremayne was placed on the rack to extort from him a confession of their guilt; but he bore the torture without compromising either of them: and after Elizabeth came to the throne, she rewarded him with many marks of favour, and appointed him a Clerk of the Privy Council.[b]   He married Eulelia, daughter of Sir John St. Leger, by Katherine, daughter of George Lord Abergavenny, who appears to have been his mother-in-law, the " little lady" with a " noble mind" of whom he speaks so kindly :—

TO SIR CHRISTOPHER HATTON.

Mᴀʏ ɪᴛ ᴘʟᴇᴀsᴇ ʏᴏᴜʀ Hᴏɴᴏᴜʀ, Though no man be more unwilling to trouble his friend with suits than myself, yet in such a case as this is, of my poor mother-in-law, which differeth not much from the state of a widow or an orphan, not to be remedied but by the help of a worthy gentleman that will do it of his benevolence, I am bold to press upon your Honour, to whom if it were known as it is to me what a noble mind there is within that little body, I am assured you would not but use all means to keep her from calamity.

[a] Additional MSS. 15891, f. 44ᵇ.   [b] Prince's Worthies of Devon, Ed. 1810, p. 740.

If her husband were in state, as he hath been within these twenty years, that little lady were easily induced to bestow upon her Majesty at an instant a present as great as this that she now desireth, rising to her Majesty to be paid by years. Besides the marriage of her daughter, I have been ever singularly bound unto her; and in my greatest adversity I found in her a rare disposition to travail for my comfort. And therefore, besides the relief of the hard estate of her husband and herself, the good that she shall receive by my means shall greatly pleasure me and increase my band towards you. I have no doubt your Honour will do what you can. If her Majesty cannot like to pardon the debt, I hope yet her Highness will be pleased at the least to respite it, without danger to incur further forfeiture. If nothing else will be had, yet, I beseech you, vouchsafe the poor gentlewoman a dispatch with her Majesty's good favour; which of late days hath been the especial comfort of her life, and the least doubt thereof, I assure you, will shorten her days and hasten her death. I am very loath to trouble you with many words, and yet much desire her good success in that she sueth for. In hope whereof, craving pardon of my boldness, I humbly take my leave. From Aukerwick, the 17th of October 1578.

Your Honour's most assured at commandment,

E. TREMAYNE.[a]

The following letter from the Earl of Leicester has no date; and as he incurred the Queen's displeasure,—the only fact mentioned in it,—on more than one occasion, there is nothing to prove when it was written. It probably, however, referred to Elizabeth's anger on being informed of his second marriage, in September 1578, to Lettice, widow of Walter Earl of Essex, and daughter of Sir Francis Knollys. The letter occurs among those of 1578 and 1579; but as the letters are copied without

[a] Additional MSS. 15891, f. 34b.

much regard to their dates, little reliance can be placed
on its position;—

MR. VICECHAMBERLAIN, Even as I had dined, Wrothe,
my Lord Chamberlain's man, came to me that immediately
I should come to the Court.   My Lord of Hunsdon was with
me, to whom he did the like message and other of her Majesty's Council I perceived were sent for also, whereby I conceived the message was general for some Council causes.   I
did make show I would come presently; but I partly desired my Lord of Hunsdon, as I do now most earnestly to
you, to excuse me that I forbear to come, being, as I wrote
to you this morning, troubled and grieved both in heart and
mind.   I am not unwilling, God knows, to serve her Majesty wherein I may, to the uttermost of my life, but most
unfit at this time to make repair to that place, where so many
eyes are witnesses of my open and great disgraces delivered
from her Majesty's mouth.   Wherefore, if by silence it may
be passed over, (my calling for being but in a general sort,) I
pray you let it be so; otherwise, to be commanded for her
Majesty's service, I will be most ready to it, if in time I
may know it.   Fare you well.   In haste, this afternoon, one
of the clock.

Your very assured,   R. LEICESTER.[a]

No information that can be relied upon has been found
respecting Gerard de Marini, the writer of the following letter, and nothing is known of the "fault" for
which he asks Hatton's pardon:—

SIR, I could wish that these my dutiful lines should attend
some time of your Honour's leisure before they should presume to trouble you; but knowing how hardly they may

[a] Additional MSS. 15891, f. 54^b.

then find such opportunity, as I crave they might, to present
my humble service to your noble favour, I fear me they shall
be constrained to press more boldly into your presence than
becometh them, unless they should, through pusillanimity,
leave that unperformed for which they come ; in which case,
I trust your wonted courtesy will hold them favourably excused.   After they have kissed your virtuous hands (as with
due reverence I also do in heart), they are first most humbly
to desire in my behalf your honourable pardon for my long
silence; and then to represent unto the same the good and
due remembrance which I have of all the favours which your
goodness hath bestowed on me at my divers needs, for which
as I acknowledge myself most bounden unto your Honour,
so am I, and will be always, ready to employ the uttermost of
my small power in your service, and repute it a great grace
when you would vouchsafe to command it.   Hastily, and to
conclude; they shall advertise you that I shall ever have in
mind to beseech Almighty God for the preservation of your
happy estate, with increase of honour, fruition of your contentation, and all perfect felicity.   Thus having confessed
my fault, desired pardon, and insinuated my duty unto your
Honour, with most lowly request of continuance of your
accustomed favour towards me, I now think it meet to forbear to interrupt your honourable affairs any longer.   From
Paris, the 23rd of October 1578.

        Your Honour's most affectionate poor servant,
                        GHERARDE DE MARINI.[a]

In November, the Archbishop of Canterbury renewed
his application that Hatton would again intercede for
him with the Queen :—

TO SIR CHRISTOPHER HATTON.

SIR, As the remembrance of your honourable friendship
and travails for me in this my long distress do restrain me

        [a] Additional MSS. 15891.

from importunity, so the respect of my duty towards her Majesty, and the great desire I have to recover her gracious favour, will not suffer me long to be silent; but still, at convenient opportunity, to renew my old suit unto you for the continuance of your honourable intercession for me to her Majesty, for the attaining of her princely benign goodness. I do assure myself that your Honour pretermitteth no convenient time, and so I understand also by relation from some of my very good friends; but yet have I been bold, for these respects which I tell you, to pray you to do that which of your own honourable inclination you are always most willing to do. So, ceasing further to trouble you at this present, I heartily commend you to the grace of God. From Lambeth, this 15th of November 1578.

Yours in Christ, EDM. CANTUAR.[a]

The "cousin Cheke," who brought Mr. Davison's next letter to Hatton, was Sir Henry Cheke, some time Secretary to the Council in the North, first cousin to Davison's wife, and nephew of Mary, daughter of Peter Cheke, of the Isle of Wight, Lord Burghley's first wife:—

TO SIR CHRISTOPHER HATTON.

SIR, This bearer, my cousin Cheke, can so particularly inform your Honour of our success at Ghent, together with such other particularities as have occurred since my last, as I forbear by him to trouble you with a long letter; and the rather, because the subject presently offered is such as I am sure would little delight you. I beseech your Honour, therefore, to excuse this my shortness; and at all times to dispose of my poor service as of him that resteth faithfully at your Honour's devotion, whom I most humbly commend to the grace and providence of God. From Bruges, the 18th of November 1578.

Your Honour's humbly bounden,

W. DAVISON.[b]

[a] Additional MSS. 15891, f. 30[b].   [b] Ibid. 15891, f. 106[b].

Sir Amias Paulet wrote to Hatton from Paris, in December, informing him of the approaching arrival of Simyer to negotiate the Queen's marriage with the Duke of Anjou, and who arrived in January following.[*] Paulet's letter shows also the distracted state of France :—

TO SIR CHRISTOPHER HATTON.

It may please your Honour to pardon my long silence, which I could excuse in reasonable manner, if I did not believe that your good opinion of me would not easily admit any sinister impression; and therefore presume upon your favourable interpretation, I will say no more but that in my last packet my leisure would not permit me to write unto any other than to the Secretaries, saving two or three words to my Lord of Leicester; and, in my other dispatch, I may say truly, that I know no matter worthy of you; and now it must suffice you to be advertised that Simyer hath taken his leave of the King, and cometh unto you accompanied with ten or twelve gentlemen, and his whole train, esteemed to amount to forty horse, or near thereabouts. The Protestants continue in their accustomed jealousies, and especially of [? the] Queen-Mother, whose painful journey into Languedoc hath been with small profit hitherunto, the Protestants refusing to come to any conference with her. The other subjects of the Realm seem to be no better satisfied, requiring with threatenings to be restored to their ancient form of government. They will pay as in the time of Louis the Twelfth, and no more. It may be doubted lest this discontentment have such furtherers and favourers as will bring the same to some dangerous issue; and I would believe it, if I did not think that by the cunning and policy of some great personages the full rage of this storm will fall upon the Protestants. It seemeth that the King is not greatly troubled with these alterations, and it perchance fareth with him as with those who, being sick in extremity, feel not their own

* Lodge, Illustrations of British History, ii. 143.

sickness. His troubles and dangers are so thick and so many as he cannot easily judge which requireth the speediest remedy. The game is already begun in Gascony, where La Reulle hath been lately surprised by the Catholics, not without some slaughter. It may please your Honour to be mindful of my revocation; wherein you shall show your good-will towards me, and shall bind me to be at your commandment, as knoweth the Almighty, who always preserve your Honour. From Paris, the 6th of December 1578.

.Your Honour's to command,   A. PAULETT.[a]

It appears from the following letter that Lord Burghley had disapproved of some suit of Hatton's arising out of a grant which the Queen had made to him:—

FROM SIR CHRISTOPHER HATTON TO LORD BURGHLEY.

MY VERY GOOD LORD, I humbly thank you for your most honourable letters. I am fully persuaded that duty to her Majesty, and not any other private respect to me or against me, hath led you into the course you hold. I heartily commend you for it, and reverence you in that, as in the rest of your faithful and most diligent dealings in this estate, you rightly deserve, and I in truth am bound to witness.

My poor case hath no defence ; *demisso vultu dicendum, rogo.* I ask, because I want: my reward is made less, but I confess my unworthiness. I do my service with diligence and travail, according to God's gift in me ; and therefore in charitable goodness I should not in any reasonable cause be so contemptuously rejected. Evil men are made examples; but I, that made no offence, should not be punished for Grey's fault. I seek a debt which grew to me through her Majesty's reward; but your Lordship's direction will lead me to further charge, without any comfort of her Majesty's care and goodness in the gift she made to relieve me. But, Sir, if this be for her general service, I, in my little particular, most humbly submit myself not only without offence towards

[a] Additional MSS. 15891, f. 108.

your Lordship, but with sincere and hearty good liking of your Lordship's proceedings; and, touching my present state, I will justify it to be reasonable and every way agreeable with my duty and estate. How it is hindered, I hear by her Majesty; but by whom I know not: but I know and feel it is an easy thing to do harm, and therefore will pray to God to give us grace to do good each to other, while we may. I hope your Lordship will not hinder me, because my doings are direct in this suit; I offered her Majesty what I am able, to the advancement of her ordinary revenue. I did acknowledge my gain, through her goodness, for my comfortable relief. I made your Lordship privy, and you misliked not. But now this little is thought too much, and so do content myself with what shall please her I am most bound to. I humbly beseech your Lordship not to conceive so hardly of me, that I will so rashly forget my duty toward you.

I love you according to your worthiness, and I will serve you for your goodness towards me heretofore, so long as I live. No cause shall lead me to mislike you, for I believe in my heart you will do nothing but that is good and honourable. And so, with the commendation of my faithful goodwill, I humbly take my leave. This 14th day of December 1578.

Your good Lordship's most bound poor friend,

CHRISTOPHER HATTON.*

Doctor Thomas Bynge, the writer of the next letter, was Master of Clare Hall, Cambridge, and was the Chancellor of that University in 1572 and 1578:—

TO SIR CHRISTOPHER HATTON.

THOUGH I doubted not, Right Honourable, but this bearer would not only advertise your Honour sufficiently of his late success in our election of Fellows, but also report of my duty therein accordingly; yet I was right glad to take the occasion by him to be the presenter thereof myself; the

* Murdin's State Papers, p. 318.

rather, for that I am therewithal to render to your Honour my most humble thanks for the great courtesy which your Honour vouchsafed me this last summer at the Court at Audley End;[a] whereby I have ever sithence accounted myself so much indebted unto your Honour, that I heartily wish my poor service in any respect could be such as might seem worthy your Honour's acceptation. Howbeit, what it is, or how simple soever it is, I am to crave that it would please you to reckon it to be at your commandment. And so, most humbly taking my leave, I commit your Honour to the blessed tuition of the Almighty. From Cambridge, this 24th of December 1578.

Your Honour's humbly at commandment,

THO. BYNGE.[b]

Sir Amias Paulet's first letter to Hatton, in 1579, is only remarkable for the notice it contains of the Order of Saint Esprit, which was instituted by Henry the Third, on the 30th of December 1578 :—

TO SIR CHRISTOPHER HATTON.

IT may please your Honour to bear with these few lines until my hand shall be strengthened with the news of my successor; and I trust to trouble you with longer letters, if any good occasion be ministered. This Christmas yieldeth no new thing worthy of the writing, and this winter season serveth for a bridle to our French humours; and yet the same break out in some places into dangerous accidents. In Provence, no quietness; open wars in Languedoc, in Guyenne, towns surprised of both sides; and yet Queen Mother persisteth to urge a conference, whereof no good effect is expected. Burgoigne, Normandy, and other provinces are nothing appeased, and will accept no moderation of their demands; and some think that the King shall be forced to yield to the malice of the time. The new Order of Knighthood hath been celebrated with great solemnity; and although

---

[a] Vide *ante*.   [b] Additional MSS. 15891, f. 46.

this Order be especially affected by Knights of the Romish
religion, yet the Bishop of Rome hath not yet allowed thereof,
and his ambassador hath refused to assist at the ceremonies.
The Duke of Guise will see the next spring before he come
to the court.   I am advertised divers ways of your friendly
furtherance to my revocation; most humbly praying you to
take hold upon every good occasion occurring. And thus I
commit your Honour to the merciful tuition of the Almighty.
From Paris, the 12th of January 1578 [1578-9].

Your Honour's to command,   A. POULETT.[*]

The departure of the Duke of Anjou from the Low
Countries, in February, was announced to Hatton, with
other intelligence, by Mr. Davison, on the 8th of that
month :—

TO SIR CHRISTOPHER HATTON.

SIR, If I seem slow in remembering your Honour with my
letters, I beseech you excuse it with the want of leisure,
which doth many times restrain my will.   Now, in part to
make the amends, the best news I can send unto your Honour
is the flight of the Duke of Anjou from hence to Alençon, I
wot not whether with his greater discontentment, or this
Country's good liking.   He was appointed to stay a time at
La Fere, upon the frontier of Picardy; but that deliberation
was suddenly altered upon the return of his secretary out
of England.   His ambassador remaining here doth, notwithstanding, make great instance to have the Deputies of all
the Provinces assembled, to deliberate upon the renouncing
of their subjection to the King of Spain, and accepting of his
master for their Prince, in case they do intend to change
masters, as they have often borne him in hand.   But this
motion is not without impediments.   The new solicited peace
hangeth in suspense.   The Emperor's ambassador is returned
once again to the enemy to break with him in that behalf,
upon whose success dependeth the burying or reviving of the

* Additional MSS. 15891, f. 34.

Duke of Anjou's motion. The Marquis of Haurech is employed in Artois to hinder the intended reconcilement of those frontier provinces with the enemy, where it is doubted he shall effect little. In Flanders the boors have taken arms against the soldiers in respect of the spoils committed amongst them, and have this last week disarmed two companies of French, and defeated three companies of Scots with one Campbell their colonel, in the villages of Isegem and Mespelare, between Alst and Dendremond. The rest of the soldiers do upon this accident fortify themselves as they best may for their surety and defence, and I doubt the mischief will not rest where it is. A cornet of the D. Casimer's reystres hath been this last week defeated about Guyeck upon the Maes, by the enemy; the Walloons lie yet in Meinen and Cassels, attending their first two months' pay promised them by the accord. The enemy is passed to the hither side of the Maes, having abandoned the enterprise of Guelder, which he made a countenance to besiege. Some think his drift is, to cut off as many as he can of the States' reystres, and other forces, which lie straggling over the country. The Colonels of that Nation do solicit hard for pay, but hitherto to little purpose. If they be dismissed ill-contented as they are yet, it is doubted they will take a sluttish farewell. Here is news out of Spain of the death of another of the King's sons, the certainty thereof may be known of his ambassador Mendoza. Here, commending your Honour to the providence of the Almighty, I most humbly take my leave. At Antwerp, the 8th of February 1578-9.

Your Honour's humbly at commandment,

W. DAVISON.[a]

Queen Elizabeth's instructions to Sir Amias Paulet, which are not dated, but were probably sent about February in this year, respecting her marriage with the Duke of Anjou, are extremely interesting, and bear evident marks of having been dictated by Elizabeth herself.

[a] Additional MSS. 15891, f. 37[b].

After stating her objections to the conditions proposed by Simyer, she expresses her suspicion that the youthful suitor sought her " fortune" and not her " person," in terms which a wealthy heiress would now use towards a lover who had shewn rather too much attention to the marriage-settlement.   The hint that the Duke ought to have come to England, and the satirical allusion to the discreditable termination of his proceedings in the Low Countries, are very neatly conveyed, while the complacency with which she adverts to her own attractions, personal and mental, is perfectly characteristic.   Her praise of Simyer, whom Camden calls " a most choice courtier, exquisitely skilled in love toys, pleasant conceits, and court dalliances," will not pass unnoticed by those who remember the Queen of Scots' remark respecting her conduct towards him[a]:—

THE QUEEN TO SIR AMIAS PAULET.

TRUSTY &c., Finding De Simyer, at a certain late conference between him and some of our Council about the treaty of marriage between the Duke his master and us, to insist very peremptorily upon certain articles that have always heretofore been denied to such Princes as in former time have sought us in way of marriage, as also to the King, the said Duke's brother, (a thing falling out far contrary to our expectation,) considering that before his repair hither we caused one of our Secretaries to advertise him (upon view of certain letters of his directed to the King's ambassador here, by which he signified unto him that he was to repair hither about the interview and the concluding of the articles,) that our meaning was not to enter into any treaty of articles, being resolved not to yield to any other than were before agreed on between us and other Princes that have sought . . . . . .[b] like

[a] Vide *ante.*   [b] The MS. is torn away in these and other places.

case, and therefore advised him to forbear to . . . . if
he were sent to any such end; only thus . . . . that
in case any of the said articles were doubtful or obscure, to
explain and make them more clear.   We have therefore
thought meet, for that we know not what to judge of such a
strainable kind of proceeding, even at that time when to
our seeming we were growing to a conclusion touching the
interview, to acquaint you therewith, to the end that you
may let both the King and Monsieur know what we conceive
thereof.   And for that you may the more substantially and
fully deal therein, you shall understand that the articles,
upon which he did at the said conference with certain of
our Council insist, were three.   The first, that the said Duke
might jointly have authority with us to dispose of all things
donative within this our Realm and other our dominions.
The second, that he might be, after marriage, crowned King;
offering certain cautions, that nothing should be done thereby
to the prejudice of our Realm.   And lastly, that he might
have threescore thousand pounds' pension during his life.
Touching the first, the inconveniencies were laid before him
by our said Council, who declared unto him that it was a
matter that greatly toucheth our Regality, insomuch as Monsieur might have thereby *vocem negativam ;* and also, that,
in the marriage between the King of Spain and our late
sister, the contents of that demand was by an especial article
prohibited in the treaty between them, which afterwards was
ratified by Parliament: yet was he not without great difficulty drawn to desist from urging us to yield our consent
therein, notwithstanding he was plainly given to understand
that our consenting thereto could not but breed a dangerous
alienation of our Subjects' goodwill from us.   And, for the
other two articles, it was showed unto him, that, the consideration of the said articles being committed to our whole
Council, it was by them after long deliberation had thereon
resolved, that they were not presently to be granted or considered of, but by the Counsel of the whole Realm in Parliament, without whose consent they could no wise be accorded

unto, and therefore thought meet to be held in suspense until
the Duke's coming over; with which answers he not resting
satisfied, did still peremptorily insist in pressing the granting
of the same, plainly protesting as well to ourself as to our
Council, that though he had very ample and large authority
to treat and deal in the cause, yet durst he not take upon him
(considering what curious eyes there were bent to behold his
actions.and doings in this cause) to qualify the said articles.
And th . . . would no otherwise be satisfied unless he might
have our private allowance and assurance that the said . . . .
articles should be both pro . . . . ed by consent of Parliament; wherein, though it was very . . . .
unto him, ... dishonourable it would be for us to give any
such private assurance in a matter that rested in the allowance
and consent of others, and how much the same would mislike
our subjects that any such thing should be yielded unto before such time as it were seen what contentment of our persons might grow by the interview, yet did he not forbear still
to press us therein. Whereupon, we finding that by no persuasion that could be used, either by us or by our Council,
he could be induced to allow of our answers, both we and
certain of our Council did plainly let him know that such a
kind of insisting upon such articles as had been denied to
other Princes, (specially having before his repair hither let
him understand that our meaning was not to alter former
articles, but only to clear such as were obscure and doubtful,)
did minister unto us just cause of suspicion, either to think
that they had no mind of further proceeding (by standing
upon such hard points as in reason we could not yield unto),
or else that they sought this match to some other end than
hitherto hath been by them pretended, having always heretofore, as well by letters as by most earnest speeches and
protestations, given out, that not our fortune but our person was the only thing that was sought: which, upon the conclusion seeming to fall out otherwise, as manifestly appeareth
by their insisting upon points chiefly incidental, and depending
upon our fortune, giveth us just cause to suspect that the

mark that is shot at, is our fortune and not our person; for
if the affection were so great as is pretended, neither would
the Duke have directed him, his Minister, to have stood upon
so hard conditions, nor himself made so great difficulty to
have come over and seen us without standing upon so many
ceremonies, being persuaded that a Duke of Anjou could
receive no dishonour by taking a journey to see a Queen of
England, whatsoever success the end of his coming took;
when as, at the least, there could not but grow thereby increase of friendship.   For we are well assured that his repair
unto us could not be accompanied with harder success (we
will not say with so great dishonour) than his late voyage
into the Low Countries; and therefore we saw no cause why
the one might not be performed with as little difficulty as the
other, if they were both sought with like goodwill and devotion.   It was also declared unto him, that if they had to deal
with a Princess that had either some def . . . . of body, or
some other notable defect of nature, or l . . . . ts of
the mind fit for one of our place and quality, such a kind of
strainable proceeding (carrying a greater show of profit than
of goodwill) might in some sort have been tolerated.   But,
considering how otherwise, our fortune laid aside, it hath
pleased God to bestow His gifts upon us in good measure,
which we do ascribe to the Giver, and not glory in them as
proceeding from ourselves, (being no fit trumpet to set out
our own praises,) we may in true course of modesty think
ourself worthy of as great a Prince as Monsieur is, without
yielding to such hard conditions as by persons of greater
quality than himself (being denied upon just cause) hath not
been stood upon.   And so we concluded with him, that
seeing we saw apparently by their course of proceeding that
we were not sought either with that affection or to that end
we looked for, that we had just cause to think ourselves in
this action not so well dealt with as appertained to one of
our place and quality; having not without great difficulty
won in ourself a disposition to yield to the match, in case
upon the interview there should grow a liking of our persons.

Wherein we showed him, that if. the Duke his master knew what advertisements were received from Foreign parts, what effectual persuasions were used towards us at home, to dissuade us from the same, and how carefully we travailed to win our subjects to allow thereof (who are not the best affected to a Foreign match), he should then see what wrong he had done us (we will not say unto himself) to stand so much upon terms of profit and reputation. Assuring him therefore, that seeing we saw we had just cause to doubt that there was not that account made of our plain and friendly dealing in this action towards him that we looked for, and as we conceived that we have deserved, that the Duke his master should perhaps hereafter hardly draw us to yield so far forth as we have already done, unless we should find him, and that by effects, to be otherwise affected towards us than as yet we can perceive he is; wishing him therefore, and rather advising him, to proceed in the other matches that by some of his nearest friends are (as we be not ignorant of) embraced, whereof it should seem, by the manner of dealing, both he and they have better liking. And as for the gentleman himself, De Simyer, whom we found greatly grieved for that he saw we could not allow of his insisting upon the said articles as a matter very offensive unto us, we did assure him that we had no cause to mislike of him, who . . . . in no other sort than either he was directed; . . . . otherwise, (though his authority were large,) he could not, without peril to himself, in respect of such as are not the best affected towards him, follow his own discretion and affection to the cause ; having found in him otherwise so great fidelity towards his master, so rare a sufficiency and discretion in one of his years in the handling of the cause, and so great devotion towards the match itself, as we had both great reason to like of him, as also to wish that we had a subject so well able to serve us. And therefore we would have you let both the King and the Duke his master understand how well we conceive of the gentleman, and how happy his master may think himself to have so rare a servant.

Having thus at large laid before you the whole course of our late proceeding with De Simyer, and the effect of such speech as both by ourself and our Council have been delivered unto ·him, we nothing doubt but that you will report the same both to the King and to the Duke in that good sort as both they may be induced to see their error, and we discharged of such calumniations as perhaps by such as are maliciously affected towards us in that Court may be given out against us.

YOUR SOVEREIGN.[*]

In February, and again in March, Hatton was made acquainted by Sir Amias Paulet with what had taken place in France; but those letters are not of much interest:—

TO SIR CHRISTOPHER HATTON.

IT may please your Honour to be advertised that I have received your courteous and friendly letters of the 20th of the last, and may perceive by her Majesty's letters of the same date, signifying her gracious pleasure touching my revocation, that your travail in my behalf hath been no less friendly than effectual.   This is not the first time that I have tasted of your favour; and can remember, and will not forget, that at some other time it hath pleased you to use me with like roundness.   I presume to find you in this good disposition towards me at my coming into England, where I trust to be shortly by your good furtherance; and here, and there, will be always at your commandment.   No change here of late. The governor chased out of Provence.   La Reulle rendered to the Protestants.   Queen Mother urgeth the conference, and yet no hope of any good success to ensue.   The Deputies of the Provinces are here, attending the King's resolution, and continue peremptory in their demands.   The castle of Beaucaire is in danger to be rendered to Domville.   The return of Monsieur into those parts will discover the humours

[*] Additional MSS. 15891, f. 6ᵇ.

of this unquiet people, and now perchance the King will be more careful to conserve the goodwills of his subjects. As knoweth the Almighty, who always preserve your Honour. From Paris, the 9th of February 1578 [1578-9].

Your Honour's to command,   A. POWLETT.[a]

TO SIR CHRISTOPHER HATTON.

It may please your Honour to give me leave to trouble you sometimes with the occurrents of these parts during the time of my abode here; which I trust will be the shorter by your good means, wherein I have tasted of your favour already, and do not doubt of the continuance thereof. The troubles of Guienne and Languedoc are said to be appeased, and many things granted in the favour of the Protestants; so as Queen Mother returneth to the Court, and now it is likely that those of the religion here shall pass this year in quietness. Queen Mother is resolved to see Monsieur before she come hither, and perchance will do her good-will to bring him with her. We say here that Monsieur will be in England very shortly, and that the King alloweth of his journey. The Provinces continue their complaints; and now the other Provinces, which had yet said nothing, make haste with double diligence to overtake the foremost. The murmuring is great, and cannot end without danger or loss. The Duke of Guise is reconciled, and will be at the Court within seven or eight days. The Low Countries must look for a fresh assault, to which purpose the Spaniard is said to make great preparations by sea and land. I would think myself happy if I might be the messenger of my next advertisements from hence. And thus, resting at your commandment, I commit your Honour to the mercy of the Highest. From Paris, the 10th of March 1578 [1578-9].

Your Honour's to command,   A. POWLETT.[b]

Neither the date nor the circumstances mentioned in this letter have been precisely ascertained. It is evi-

---

[a] Additional MSS. 15891, f. 47[b].   [b] Additional MSS. 15891, f. 55.

dent that Hatton had taken an active part in suppressing some riots near London; and, from the remark that
the affair was not "a trifling Pale matter," it is probable
that the riots were those which are thus mentioned by
Stow,* and that this letter was written early in April,
1579—:" A° 1579.   The 4th of May were arraigned at
Barnet in Hartfordshire certain men of Northall Mims,
and the parts near adjoining, for *pulling down a pale* at
Northall, late set up (on the common ground) by the
Earl of Warwick.   Eight of them were condemned: two
were brent in the hand, two were hanged betwixt Barnet
and Whetstone, and other four condemned remained
prisoners in Hartford Gaol long after," &c.   This conjecture is the more likely to be correct from Hatton being
then with Sir Ralph Sadler, whose seat was in Hertfordshire, not far from the scene of the disturbance,
which evidently arose from an attempt to inclose a common.   The subject is again noticed in another letter.

TO SIR CHRISTOPHER HATTON.

I must begin with her Majesty's commandment, as duty
bindeth me; which is to signify unto you, Mr. Vicechamberlain, in how gracious part she taketh this your careful and
diligent service done for the dispersing and quieting of these
rebellious and tumultuous persons lately gathered together
in those parts.   Her Highness hath been informed of the
great pains you have taken, of the wise and discreet orders
which you have prescribed, as well for the establishing of
good and assured ways to prevent any further inconvenience
by these lewd people for their proceeding, as to search
out what hath been the cause, as also their further intent
in following this enterprise.   These your doings, I assure
you, she takes in most gracious sort.   And, leaving to tell
you what particularities she understandeth of your doings

* Annals, p. 685.

by sundry means, I must let you know what her express
pleasure is for herself to do.   Albeit she was most desirous
to hear of your speedy return, having brought all things
to so good pass as you have done, yet being advertised of
your travail and watch you have sustained in this business,
she would have you in anywise rest you at least all day
to-morrow, notwithstanding some of us did let her know
that her former desire to have you to return was written
by us unto you before; and hath charged me thus specially to signify her pleasure that she would have you
take some rest ere you put yourself to travel again; and
for that purpose hath she sent this bearer with her own
commandment to you beside, who can also declare unto
you how acceptable your service is unto her: and thus
much by her Majesty's direction.   Now, Sir, to the matter; for my part I think you in a most happy hour to
prevent so great and dangerous a mischief as this lewd
enterprise was like to have grown unto, both to her Majesty's person and to her estate.   I perceive you find it
was more than a trifling Pale matter; and I fear, if this
be not made a full example, you shall hear of far more
greater of this sort: but her Majesty is bent to make her
subjects know that she can and will mix justice with mercy.
It is time, you see, for us to look further into the dispositions of the common people further off, when so near
hand they will so audaciously take the Prince's authority
into their hands.   I trust you have been the instrument
to save both treasure and blood, and that is a happy piece
of service.   For my brother's private respect and mine,
wherein you have showed yourself a most faithful friend,
I will say no more, but, what may lie in so small powers
to requite, either you must be sure of it, or God send
shame upon us.   I will here end, and pray God to send
you all good hap, even as I can wish for myself; and refer
the rest to this bearer, who must excuse my brother, for
that it was late, and I willed him not to stay for any letter
from him, for he was a-bed and asleep, and now past 11

o'clock, and besides troubled with his gout. God be with you, and commend me to Sir Ralph Sadler. Your most assured,   Ro. Leicester.[a]

Walsingham also wrote to Hatton about the riots in Hertfordshire ; and his letter proves not only that he was familiarly called by the Queen her " Mutton," but that the term was well known to the Court ;—

TO SIR CHRISTOPHER HATTON.

Sir, I acquainted her Majesty this afternoon with the particular letters you sent me, who did very greatly commend your discreet manner of proceeding ; and willed me to let you understand, that, upon report made unto her of an outrage committed upon certain of Sir John Brockett's sheep, she feareth greatly her Mutton, lest he should take some harm amongst those disordered people. I am glad, Sir, that matters are so well appeased that her Majesty may be merry withal, and no further cause of your absence from hence; at whose return, upon conference with you, her Majesty and my Lords mean to take order for the extending of such punishment upon the offenders as the quality of their offences requireth, and may serve for a terror to others. And so, praying you, good Mr. Vice-Chamberlain, to commend me to Sir Ralph Sadler, your colleague, I commend you to God's good protection. At the Court, the 23rd of April 1579.

FRAN. WALSINGHAM.

Postscript. We are at this present so troubled with St. George's ceremonies,[b] as we cannot thoroughly consult upon matters of substance.[c]

Several curious letters occur from Henry Howard, who was apparently the second son of Henry Earl of Surrey,

---

[a] Additional MSS. 15891, f. 46[b].
[b] The observance of the Feast of St. George by the Knights of the Garter.
[c] Additional MSS. 15891, f. 36[b].

and was created Earl of Northampton by James the First. His eminent talents did not procure him any share of the Queen's favour until the latter part of her reign, though he used all the usual arts to propitiate her. It is not certain that this curious letter, which was accompanied by a present for the Queen, was addressed to Hatton, whose relationship to Howard has not been traced;—

FROM HENRY HOWARD.

As I have ever been too well acquainted with my own defects to challenge any place among the chosen, so, lest by negligence I might be cast among the reprobate, I thought good (my own dear Cousin) to require your favour in presenting my humble service to her Majesty, with assured warrant that a number, which have made more curtesies, have not said so many prayers for her Majesty as I have done since her departure from this place; for men's minds are never more inclined to contemplate than while the senses are suspended from their chief felicity. There is no bush nor flower in this garden which yieldeth not a comfort or a corrysine. Violets are gathered to make conserve. Rosemary begins to bloom, but it is too common. Primroses seem more pleasant for their season, than sweet by their favour. Eglantine hath ten delights for every other's one, if it had no prickles; and heartsease is so raised upon the tops of the walls as I cannot reach it. The grace which cometh from the windows is most welcome, for by this mean I can say what was, though wiser men than I can hardly tell what shall be. Every favour brings a thirst, but the streams retire; and every fancy putteth us in hope of fruit, but Tantalus is famished. This sharp sauce to my sweet conceits enforceth me to write and seek that comfort, by assurance of her Majesty's good health, which cannot be conceived by my deepest meditations in her absence. And though among so many heaps of dainty presents as other men's abundance may bring forth according to the merit of her Majesty's great bounty, this simple pledge

and token of my duty may be driven to shrink aside, and
hide itself for fear of some disgrace; yet, if it please her to
conceive that some things are as welcome for their figure as
other for their weight, and that the sender of this token
deemeth not the richest crown in Europe worthy of that
head which closeth in itself the treasures of true wisdom, and
letteth out the springs of happy government, I doubt not
but her Majesty will accept the same *ex congruo*, though
neither I nor anything of mine can claim her favour *ex con-
digno*. The fancy, many years agone, hath been derived from
the Franciscans; but I am much deceived if, by the turning
of one loop or two, her Majesty may not convert it to a
truelove's knot. The mean I know, but not the manner,
further than that I am assured that no woman of less virtue,
grace, and beauty than the best can make this change, because it passeth more by skill than sleight, by wisdom than
by hazard: only this I promise, that whatsoever knot her
Majesty doth bind shall be my fast in faith; and whatsoever
band her fancy shall not like, shall be my loose at liberty.
And thus, my dear Cousin, requiring you in my behalf to kiss
that sacred hand, whose print is here, though the pattern be
not extant; and withal to recommend my faith, my life, and
service to herself, who bindeth me more ways than she shall
ever know, I take my leave, kissing the soil where her foot
hath left impression of so rare a personage. From Whitehall, this 1st of May 1579.   H. HOWARD.*

It does not appear who the person was to whom
Dr. Bynge gave the following letter of introduction to
Sir Christopher Hatton:—

TO SIR CHRISTOPHER HATTON.

SIR, Your honourable message that it pleased you to send
me by Mr. Hamond, a Fellow of our House, doth draw me
eftsoons to renew that duty which I justly acknowledge I owe
unto you. And therewithal I have taken further boldness

* Additional MSS. 15891, f. 96ᵇ.

even to be a solicitor to your Honour in the behalf of another; wherein, nevertheless, if I seem perhaps to presume too far as I am humbly to crave pardon for the same, so upon monition I shall be easily reformed: and yet at this present I could hardly avoid to yield to the petition of this bearer, who, being an humble suitor unto your Honour, desired only my testimony in furtherance of his cause; the report whereof as I leave to himself, so for his person I can truly say, that I know him to be both discreet and learned, and, in the faculty, fit for the room he desireth. He is this year to proceed Doctor, and hath to that end already done acts in the public schools. Now, if his good hap may be such as to find favour with your Honour, I shall be doubly glad: first, for my friend's sake, whose preferment I wish; next, for myself, in that my dutiful meaning hath been well accepted at your Honour's hands. Even thus humbly taking my leave, I commend your Honour to God's most blessed tuition. From Cambridge, the 6th of May 1579. Your Honour's humbly to be commanded,   THO. BYNGE.[a]

The unfortunate Archbishop of Canterbury again besought Hatton's intercession with the Queen in May of this year. The great man to whom he alludes was the Duke of Anjou: —

TO SIR CHRISTOPHER HATTON.

SIR, The consultation about the coming of yonder great man (being a cause of greatest importance) hath long occupied her Majesty and your Honours of her Council; in which time I thought it my duty to abstain from troubling you with suit in my private cause. That Foreign matter being (as I hear) clearly laid aside, so good opportunity of time being offered, I am bold to renew my suit, praying your Honour to renew your intercession to her Majesty for my

[a] Additional MSS. 15891, f. 55.

restitution to her favour and execution of mine office. I trust that the remembrance of my two years' restraint of liberty in this my old and sickly age will move her Majesty to some commiseration over me, according to her accustomed most gracious inclination to all benignity, goodness, and clemency, and the rather by your honourable and good mediation. So, ceasing further to trouble your Honour at this time, I heartily commend the same to the grace of God. From Lambeth, the 22nd of May 1579. Yours in Christ,

EDM. CANTUAR.[a]

On the 17th of July a circumstance occurred which placed the lives of the Queen, the Earl of Lincoln, the French ambassador Simyer, and Sir Christopher Hatton in some danger. Being in her private barge on the Thames, between Deptford and Greenwich, accompanied by those persons, a shot was fired out of a boat, which struck one of the rowers within six feet of her Majesty, and passed through both his arms. The wound was so severe as to cause him to scream piteously; but the Queen did not lose her presence of mind in the slightest degree, and giving her scarf to the wounded man, bid him be of good cheer, saying, he should want for nothing. When it was insinuated to Elizabeth that it was an attempt to murder her or Simyer, she magnanimously observed, "she could believe nothing of her people which parents would not believe of their children;" and though the author of the accident was condemned and brought out for execution, he was pardoned.[b] A few days after this affair, the Duke of Anjou arrived privately in England, and came unexpectedly to Greenwich, where he had some secret conferences with the

[a] Additional MSS. 15891, f. 31b.
[b] Stow's Annals, p. 685. There is little doubt it was entirely accidental. Speed, 1159.

Queen, and returned soon after to France, " being seen but of few.[a]

Although Hatton did not become High Steward of Cambridge until after the Earl of Leicester's death in 1588, he seems to have taken much interest in the affairs of the University long before that event:—

DR. BYNGE TO SIR CHRISTOPHER HATTON.

UPON receipt of your Honour's letters directed to me, and to other Assistants and Visitors of Gonville and Caius College, in the behalf of Mr. Booth, one of the Fellows of that House, who found himself grieved with some hard proceeding (as he took it) of the Master and certain other of the Fellows there in a cause of defamation against him, for further examination whereof we were required by your Honour to call before us the parties different, the better to understand the truth of that matter. May it please your Honour to be advertised that, upon Saturday last, being met together about that business, and intending, according to the purport of your Honour's letters, to send for the Master of the College and other parties, Mr. Booth there, in presence of us all, made earnest request that we would not enter to deal further that way, alleging that otherwise he might incur the danger of perjury, by reason of a statute of their House whereby it is ordained, as he said, that no Fellow ought to decline the order of the Master and the Company unless they do it by appellation, and that to be made unto none other Judge but to their Visitors only. Upon this his information I stayed to proceed, and wished him to use advice of some that might sufficiently direct him in his doings. What course he is resolved to take I know not; but this much I thought best to advertise your Honour, remaining ready to yield unto the same what duty I can: and so most humbly I take my leave. From Cambridge, the 3rd of August 1579. Your Honour's humbly at commandment,   THO. BYNGE.[b]

---

[a] Camden's Annals, b. ii. p. 96.   [b] Additional MSS. 15891, f. 33[b].

Lord Burghley having gone into Northamptonshire in August, he transmitted his opinion on the affairs of Ireland and the Low Countries to one of his Colleagues, and apparently to Secretary Walsingham, in the following letter. James Fitzmaurice, who had raised a rebellion in Munster, went to France and thence to Spain for assistance, and landed from three ships with two priests, to one of whom, called Nicholas Saunders, the Pope had given a consecrated banner, and some soldiers at St. Mary Wick, in Kerry, where he erected a fort. He placed his vessels close under it, where they were gallantly boarded and taken by one of the Queen's vessels, commanded by Captain Courtenay[a].

LORD BURGHLEY TO MR. SECRETARY WALSINGHAM.

Sir, I most heartily thank you for acquainting of me with your advertisements both from Ireland and the Low Countries, which came hither to me this foul rainy morning, being Sunday, at Althorpe. I do return all your letters, having made Mr. Chancellor[b] acquainted therewith. And for the matters of Ireland, I am of opinion that it is still necessary that the ships should go on, and that they should be double-manned, for to be able to set two or three shot on land, as occasion should serve, and as the Justice might think meet: for if the enemy tarry still at the Dingle, it must be the force of the ships that must remove them; for, as I remember, there is no good access by land through Kerry to approach the Dingle; whereof my Lord of Ormond can best inform you. If the enemy should not now be removed, from his settling in Ireland, though presently his forces be small, yet his holding, and taking of footing and of a haven, would be dangerous to receive from Foreign parts further forces to offend her Majesty; whereof I am very jealous, if discon-

---

[a] Camden's Annals.   [b] Sir Walter Mildmay, Chancellor of the Exchequer.

tentation grow betwixt France and us upon a breach of this
interview, or if the King of Spain shall be free from his
troubles in the Low Countries, and have his will there for
religion. This small entry of Fitzmorris will be a gate for
any of those two Princes to offend her Majesty in Ireland in
recompence of former offences offered unto them. And,
besides that, the sufferance of Fitzmorris with his Papistical
forces, and offers for restoring of religion, will undoubtedly
be a continual comfort to all lewd and discontented people
of Ireland; whereof I think three parts of four, or rather
nine parts of ten, are for matter of religion evil satisfied with
the English Government: and thus you see I cannot forbear
to write my conceit, submitting it nevertheless to the better
judgment of others. For the Low Countries, I think surely
you shall find that the articles of peace sent from Cologne will
draw all the people to accept the conditions, saving only the
people that are well devoted in religion; so as surely the war
that shall continue will be for religion: and I pray God they
that are Protestants be not also divided among themselves by
provocation of the Lutheran Princes of Germany. When
I consider the articles of Cologne, and the accord of Gant
established, (whereby Holland and Zealand are to continue
their religion, and the strangers to depart,) I could rather
yield to the acceptation of these articles than to have the war
continue; wherein if the Prince should quail, then surely the
pacification of Gant will also fall. I pray you, Sir, with my
hearty commendations, tell Mr. Vice-Chamberlain that Mr.
Chancellor and I, in our way to Northampton, mean to survey his house at Holdenby, and, when we have done, to fill
our bellies with his meat, and sleep also, as the proverb is,
our bellies-full all Monday at night; and on Tuesday in the
morning we will be at Northampton where after noon we
mean to hear the babbling matters of the town for the causes
of religion, wishing that we may accord them all both in
mind and actions; at the least we will draw them all to follow
one line by the rule of the Queen Majesty's laws, or else to
procure the contrariant to feel the sharpness of the same laws.

And so, praying you to commend us humbly to all our good Lords and others of the Council, we also do pray for her Majesty's prosperity in all her actions.   From Althorpe, the 9th of July [August*] 1579.

Your assured loving friend,   W. BURGHLEY.[b]

Despatches having reached Burghley relating to Ireland after he had written the preceding letter, he answered them in the afternoon of the same day :—

TO SECRETARY WALSINGHAM.

SIR, This morning afore dinner I wrote to you in answer of your letters, by which you made mention of your direction to Bland and to Mr. Tremayne to stay some part of the victualling, upon some opinion that you conceived of the smallness of James Fitzmorris' forces.   And now this afternoon I have received your later letters, with copies of writings from the Lord Justice and Waterhouse, by which I see that the peril is presently greater than before appeared, but surely no greater than in time coming would prove if the matter be not at the first rooted up, as by my forenoon's writing to you I did pronounce.   But now no cost is to be spared nor time lost, for, if haste be made with the ships, I hope they shall come thither before the Pope's nuncio and Saunders shall return with their supplies from Spain ; which surely they will, with their large reports of their likelihood of success for the matter of religion, procure out of Spain under colour of the clergy and holy-house of Spain with connivance of the King Catholic.   Therefore, the more haste be used with the ships, the more sure to withstand the new supply ; and the forces of footmen from England are as necessary to withstand the inward revolts in Munster, where-

---

* The date of " July" in the " Letter Book" is certainly a mistake.   Burghley says the day he wrote was "Sunday."   The 9th of July did *not*, and the 9th of August *did* fall on *Sunday*.   Moreover Burghley says he should sleep at Holdenby on Monday ; and on Monday the 10th of August he wrote to Hatton from that place.   See also Hatton's letter of the 9th of *August*, welcoming him to Holdenby.

[b] Additional MSS. 15891, f. 110[b].

in I fear more the authority and rooted malice of Sir John of Desmond than the untruth of his brother. The departing thither of the Earl of Ormond is worth the sending of five hundred men: the loss of Davill[a] is very great. Mr. Chancellor is privy to this my writing, in testimony whereof I have required his subscription.

W. BURGHLEY.[b]

Pursuant to the intention announced in one of the preceding letters, Lord Burghley went to Sir Christopher Hatton's new mansion at Holdenby, and its owner not being able to receive his distinguished guest in person, he welcomed him there by the following letter. As Holdenby was built in imitation of Burghley's seat at Theobalds, he requested his Lordship to mention to the surveyor any improvements that might occur to him:—

TO LORD BURGHLEY.

MY SINGULAR GOOD LORD, I yield you as friendly and thankful a welcome as may be given you by any man or in any place in this world. I fear me that as your Lordship shall find my house unbuilt and very far from good order, so through the newness you shall find it dampish and full of evil air; whereof I pray God your health be not impeached. Before God, Sir, I take great comfort of your most honourable courtesy to visit your poor friend in so kind manner. I pray God I may deserve it by my true service towards you. I humbly beseech you, my honourable Lord, for your opinion to the surveyor of such lacks and faults as shall appear to you in this rude building, for as the same is done hitherto in direct observation of your house and plot at Tyball's, so I earnestly pray your Lordship that by your good corrections at this time, it may prove as like to the same as it

[a] Henry Davill, " an English gentleman and stout soldier," and Arthur Carter, Lieutenant of the Marshal of Munster, were murdered in their bed at Traly by John Desmond, who afterwards killed all Davill's servants: and boasting of the deed to Father Saunders, the priest commended it " as a sweet sacrifice in the sight of God."—Camden.

[b] Additional MSS. 15891, f. 111.

hath ever been meant to be. I beseech you, Sir, use patience
in your too too rude entertainment, and think how much he
doth honour and love you that would have wished it to have
been much better and fit for so honourable a personage.
Your Lordship will pardon my lack of presence to attend on
you, because you know my leave cannot be gotten. God
bless you for ever my good Lord, and a thousand and ten
thousand times I humbly bid you farewell. Mr. Secretary
telleth me he hath written the news unto you, and, therefore,
I will no further trouble your good Lordship. Her most excellent Majesty hath good health, God be praised for it; and
hath commanded me to write her most gracious and loving
commendations unto you. Order is in part given to prepare against Monsieur's coming. And thus my honourable
good Lord I humbly bid you my dutiful farewell. Greenwich, this 9th of August 1579. Your Lordship's most bound,

CHR. HATTON.[a]

Before Lord Burghley left Holdenby, he wrote to
thank its owner for his hospitality; and his description
of the house shows its magnificence. In a postscript he
acknowledged Hatton's letter of the 9th:—

LORD BURGHLEY TO SIR CHRISTOPHER HATTON.

SIR, I may not pass out of this good house without thanks
on your behalf to God, and on mine to you, nor without
memory of her Majesty, to whom it appeareth this goodly,
perfect, though not perfected work is consecrated; and all
this I do in mind largely conceive, and in writing do mean
but to touch, because I am hastened to Northampton, and
I will reserve matter to enlarge at my return, to yourself. I
came yesterday in the afternoon to your house with Sir
Walter Mildmay, who came with very good will to visit this
house. I was first met on the way with Mr. Colshill, and
your good uncle Mr. Saunders,[b] your cousin Mr. Tate, and

---

[a] Autograph in the Lansdowne
MS. 28, art. 63, addressed to "The
Right Honourable my singular good
Lord the Lord High Treasurer of
England, at Holdenby."

[b] William Saunders of Harrington, his mother's brother.

others, and then with a great multitude of your gentlemen and servants, all showing themselves, as by your direction, glad of my coming. But approaching to the house, being led by a large, long, straight fair way, I found a great magnificence in the front or front pieces of the house, and so every part answerable to other, to allure liking. I found no one thing of greater grace than your stately ascent from your hall to your great chamber; and your chambers answerable with largeness and lightsomeness, that truly a Momus could find no fault. I visited all your rooms high and low, and only the contentation of mine eyes made me forget the infirmity of my legs. And where you were wont to say it was a young Theobalds, truly Theobalds I like as my own; but I confess it is not so good as a model to a work, less than a pattern, and no otherwise worthy in any comparison than a foil. God send us both long to enjoy Her, for whom we both meant to exceed our purses in these. And so I end with my prayer for her health, and thanks humbly for her Majesty's remembrance of me her weak Spirit.[a] From a monument of her Majesty's bountifulness to a thankful servant, that is, from Holdenby Queen Elizabeth's memory, by Sir Christopher Hatton her faithful servant and counsellor. 10th August 1579.

Yours most assuredly, W. BURGHLEY.

Postscript.—The abundant memorials of your house had almost made me forget to thank you for your kind letter, which came to me in the midst of a sumptuous supper.[b]

The disturbances in Ireland, to which Sir Thomas Heneage alludes in the following letter, have been already mentioned. That Queen Elizabeth translated parts

---

[a] Queen Elizabeth had a peculiar name for most of her ministers and favourites; Burghley was her "Spirit," Walsingham was her "Moon," and Lady Norris was her "Crow." There is some reason for supposing that Leicester was called her "Turk,"

and Hatton was certainly "Lyddes" and her "Mutton."

[b] Additional MSS. 15891, f. 32. The date in the Letter Book is "19th of August, 1578," but it was obviously a mistake of the copyist.

of Seneca is well known ; and a copy of her translation
of the 107th Epistle, which she gave to her god-son,
Sir John Harington, in 1567, is printed in the " Nugæ
Antique :"—

TO SIR CHRISTOPHER HATTON.

SIR, Being here yet much worse than I looked for, and, I
think, than you would have me, it would make me the better
to know that you did well, and her Majesty did best; for
which cause I have sent my man unto you. How the fire
made by the rebels and runagates in Ireland now grows to
flame, (yet I trust but like a wisp of straw,) the Country
takes knowledge of, and I doubt not but the Court takes
care of. Her Majesty, of those that love her, shall have
leave to think of these things according to her wisdom, but
not to take thought for them according to their wrong. So
may these things rather touch her than trouble her. And
surely, Sir, by the great goodness of God, which hath led her,
and whereon she leaneth, and by her Highness' fore-ordained
felicity and virtue, whereof we have tasted, I am persuaded
that there is no mischief nor harm meant her but shall turn
to her honour ; so as that shall be verified of her that Seneca
wrote wisely, and her Majesty translated more sweetly,—of
adversity and virtue, *illustrat dum vexat*, it graces whom it
grates. More lines my bad health will not afford you, but
more goodwill shall no man alive bear you ; which I beseech
you to accept until I can send you a better token. And the
Lord of Life send you long life with great honour, accompanied with most continuance and contentation. From Copthall, the 12th of August 1579. Your own so bound,

T. HENEAGE.[*]

The first letter from Philip Sidney to Hatton related
to his memorable quarrel with the Earl of Oxford, the
particulars of which, though fully described by Lord

---

[*] Additional MSS. 15891, f. 36ᵇ.

Brooke,* are imperfectly told by later biographers. While Sidney was playing in the Tennis Court belonging to the Palace, Oxford came in, and after some conversation, peremptorily ordered him to quit the place.   Sidney having refused to comply with so rude a request, the Earl twice called him a "puppy."   Sidney then gave him the lie, which Lord Brooke gravely says he had a right to do, inasmuch as puppies are the produce of dogs, and not of men, and then left the ground.   Not hearing from Oxford in the manner he expected after so public an insult, Sidney sent on the following day " to awake him out of his trance," and thus incited, the Earl challenged him.   The matter was immediately taken up by the Privy Council, who tried in vain to induce Sidney to make submission; and the Queen herself remonstrated with him on the impropriety of quarrelling with so high a personage.   But he properly felt that he was the guardian of his own honour, and having positively declined to make any concessions, withdrew from the Court, to his sister, the Countess of Pembroke's seat at Wilton, and there composed the ,' Arcadia."

TO SIR CHRISTOPHER HATTON.

SIR, The great advantage which I have by the singular goodness and friendship it pleaseth you to show me (which in truth I do, and have a good while reputed amongst the chief ornaments of my life and fortune,) makes me find myself at as much disadvantage when my heart, longing to show myself grateful, can present nothing which may be serviceable unto you.   But as I know, and have well found, that you do esteem a true goodwill of some value, in that kind

---

* Lord Brooke does not say when this affair occurred. Dr. Zouch assigns it to the year 1580; but if the date of this letter be correct, it took place in August 1759.

only can I show myself, and assure you that the little that I am, is and shall be at all times and fortunes so to be disposed by you as one that hath promised love, and is bound by desert to perform it. This is all therefore I can say; though you lose me, you have me. As for the matter depending between the Earl of Oxford and me, certainly, Sir, howsoever I might have forgiven him, I should never have forgiven myself if I had lain under so proud an injury as he would have laid upon me; neither can anything under the sun make me repent it, nor any misery make me go one half-word back from it. Let him therefore, as he will, digest it. For my part, I think tying up makes some things seem fiercer than they would be. Sir, let me crave still the continuance of my happiness in your favour and friendship; and I will ever pray unto God, that, among those I most honour, I may ever see you have prosperous causes of contentment. 28th August 1579. Your Honour's to be commanded, even by duty,

PHILIP SIDNEY.[a]

Nicholas Saunders, the writer of the following letter to one of the sons of the Earl of Clanrickard, and probably to his second son John Burgh, afterwards created Lord Leitrim, was the celebrated priest before mentioned,[b] who aided Fitzmaurice in his rebellious proceedings in Ireland, and to whom the Pope entrusted the consecrated banner. In the " Letter Book" this letter is thus described :—

THE SEDITIOUS LETTER OF THE MOST TRAITOROUS REBEL, SAUNDERS, TO THE SON OF THE EARL OF CLANRICKARD.

THE more I am unacquainted, the more I am to be borne withal; forsomuch as I write, not for any private commodity of my own, but rather for yours and the Commonwealth's. God, permitting your father (for whose preservation I heartily pray) to be taken prisoner, meant to warn you, his son, to

---

[a] Additional MSS. 15891, fo. 31[b].   [b] Vide p. 121, ante.

provide as well for his liberty as your own. Look then which
is the safest way for both, and that are you bound to take.
Protections of men are neither liberally always granted, nor
faithfully always kept, nor available when the granter dieth ;
and least of all to be trusted when they are granted for fear.
The protection of God is that which can never fail ; and there
is no way under heaven sooner to obtain God's protection than
. . . . . . the defence of God's honour. For if you will . . .
. . . . protection of him that hazardeth his goods and life
. . . . . . what will God do, or rather what will He not do,
for him who fighteth and warfareth for His glory? Now-a-
days the heretics, as you know, do so violently oppress God's
honour in this world, that they overthrow His temples and
places, cast down His altars, take away His sacrifice, deny
His priesthood, burn His image, abandon His vicar, contemn
His sacraments, and, by false pretence of God's word, cut off
and wipe away whole books of the Holy Scriptures. They
also refuse to come to General Councils, to keep unity of
faith with other Christian Princes and Countries, to follow
the ancient Doctors of the Church, and, to say all at once,
they would have none other judge, rule, or law to be tried
by than their own fantasy and sensuality. And what a dishonour to God and to our Saviour Jhesu Christ is it, that He,
instituting a kingdom in this world which is commonly
called His Church, should be thought to leave it so disordered that there should be in it neither altar for God's service, nor any chief pastor or governor to whom the rest of the
Christians should be bound to obey. Would any good or
wise man order such a commonweal in any part of the world?
If, then, they make our Saviour Christ so ungodly as not to
leave an altar whereupon we might offer sacrifice to His
Father, and so indiscreet as not to leave an order and a Judge
to end all our controversies—if this opinion be to the great
dishonour both of God and of Christ His Son, our Saviour,
seeing we fight against them that do and teach these blasphemies, and seeing we fight against them, not of our own
heads, but by the most lawful authority of him to whom, as

to the true successor of St. Peter the Prince of the Apostles, Christ committed the keys of the kingdom of heaven, that is to say, the supreme government of His Church, which is a kingdom not of earth but of heaven ; if it please you to join with us in this holy quarrel, (as I pray God to give you His grace so to do, and without His grace it cannot be done as it ought,) you shall doubtless be under the protection of Almighty God, and of that Prince whom God shall set up in place of this Usurper that now unjustly reigneth, and of God's Vicar, who will see every man rewarded for the service that he doth to the Church.   You also shall deserve well of your Country, which, having fed and nourished you, requireth you again that you help to deliver her from the tyranny of heretics.   The time yet is such that you may deserve thanks and reward; but when our aid is come, which we look for daily, when the Scottish and English nobility are in . . . . as we doubt not they will be shortly, and when . . . . . . begin to invade England itself, as divers of the self English nobility labour and procure,—afterward I say it shall be small thank before God and man to be of our company, seeing that the very heretics will then hold with us, at the least for fear of us.   Certainly God meaneth better to your Worship if you know the time of His merciful calling and gracious visitation.   Touching the controversy of inheritance which is said to be betwixt your brother and you, where may you hope to know that better decided than in his Holiness's camp, where so wise and discreet governors be as you know the Earl's brethren are?   There lack not also other grave and learned men whose advice may be profitable in that behalf.   Once, whatsoever service I may do you, either in counselling or testifying your readiness in this cause, or otherwise, it shall never fail, God willing ; whom I beseech to direct and prosper you in all your doing.   The 23rd of September 1579.   Yours to command always,

NICHOLAS SAUNDERS.*

* Additional MSS. 15891, f. 8.

Though there is ample evidence of the aversion of the people of this Country to the Queen's marriage with the Duke of Anjou, it is nowhere more strikingly shown than in the annexed letter from the Bishop of London :—

TO SIR CHRISTOPHER HATTON.

RIGHT HONOURABLE, I thank God your travail and mine with the preacher hath taken good effect; and the instructions which you ministered unto him were very zealously and, I doubt not, profitably remembered, and with such earnestness advisedly uttered, that it hath much stayed the heady, confirmed the good and the wise in the great good opinion conceived generally of her Majesty, and somewhat quenched the sparks of murmuring, misliking, and misconstruing of matters of State, wherewith the seditious libeller had kindled many of the busier sort. The preacher accused stoutly, and sharply reproved the author of this seditious pamphlet of arrogancy and lack of charity; that he, being a private man, durst so far presume to look into the secret bosom of Princes' councils and high Magistrates, and to meddle with matters both above his reach, and that did not belong unto him;
. . . . . that so uncharitably he would or could . . . .
not only conceive himself, but set abroach . . . . evil
and ingrate a conceit . . . .
thing that should tend* . . . .
of the Gospel, which she hath both carefully and happily maintained ever since her entry into her most gracious reign ; and that he or any man should think or mistrust her that she will not continue ever herself, and the same wherein she hath been bred, and adventured so far with the misliking of the greatest Potentates in Europe, with many arguments tending to that end : accusing also some of the people of curiosity and unkindness, that they could not read as much in the book of her Majesty's dealing in government, written by the experience of twenty sweet peaceable years, to confirm them

---

* These lacunæ are caused by the MS. being torn.

in a good and assured opinion of her great love and care over
them, to comfort and to warrant them in the good continuance thereof, as they could learn out of such a seditious
treaty, devised and hatched by some green head to make
them to doubt of her who giveth unto us all most apparent
shows and demonstrations, that, as she hath been bred and
brought up in Christ, entered and reigned by Christ, so she
will live and die in Christ, &c.   Whereat the people seemed,
even as it were with a shout to give God thanks; and, as far
as I could perceive, took it very well, that she was commended for that her zeal and constancy.   I have understood
since the sermon, that as the people well liked of the commendation attributed to her Majesty with the great hope of
her continuance, so, to say plainly, they utterly bent their
brows at the sharp and bitter speeches which he gave against
the author of the book; of whom they conceive and report
that he is one that feareth God, dearly loveth her Majesty,
entered into this course being carried with suspicion and jealousy of her person and safety.   Whereby I perceive that
any that bend their pen, wit, knowledge, or speech against
the foreign Prince, is of them counted a good patriot and
pius subditus; and, so long as their eye is fixed upon her,
they find themselves as it were ravished: but looking aside
at the stranger, (though without cause peradventure,) they
are like them that by long looking on the sun, their eyes
are become so dazzled that they judge everything else to
be monstrous.   Of the people of London I hope well, that
by the good instructions of the preachers they will stay themselves from all outrages.   But I am informed that abroad in
the country (and the further off the worse) the preachers are
. . . . in speech against Monsieur, and the people to . . . .
edit to hear any blemish in that nation.   But I have sent
for some of them, and would send for more, but that I am
afraid to have too many irons in the fire at once; for, if
by sending for them in the country the Londoners should understand of the grudging and groaning abroad, it would make
them the worse, and I am greatly careful of my own flock.

Of one synod and conventing of the ministers yesterday this
fell out, that upon my discourse to them in recital of the
Queen's Majesty's zeal and good nature, blessed gifts of
wisdom, learning, and happy government, many of them
wept, and drew down my tears for company, which was not
the best part of an orator; but, in the end, some of them
told me that they could not but move their people to prayer
and fasting for her Majesty's good estate, which they feared
was now like to be in great peril, praying God upon the
knees of their hearts that they might be deceived. Whereby,
to tell you truth, there is singular love towards her, and great
heartburning towards him. To mitigate that their evil opinion, I showed a piece of the Tocsin, bitterly written against
the massacre of the French Protestants, wherein the very
Protestants do appeal to Monsieur, and also to her Majesty,
for their patrociny and defence against the tyranny of the
enemies; which wrought somewhat with them, but not so
much as I wished. Thus, praying you to bear with Mr. Cox's
so long tarrying, (for I could not but with some leisure gather
any likelihood of the people's and preachers' humours,) I bid
your Honour most heartily farewell. From Fulham, this
28th of September 1579. Your Honour's most assured at
commandment, JOHN LONDON.[a]

A large part of the correspondence in the " Letter
Book" is without any date; and the difficulty of ascer-
taining in what years letters were written which contain no particular fact, and allude to obscure transactions, is extremely great. In many cases it is indeed
impossible to fix the precise date of such letters; and
there is scarcely any better reason for assigning the following ones to this period, than that they occur among
others of the years 1578 and 1579; but which, as has
been before observed, cannot be relied upon as proof that
they actually belong to those years.

[a] Additional MSS. 15891, f. 5.

Dr. Humfrey, Dean of Gloucester, the Queen's Professor of Divinity, and President of Magdalen College, Oxford, the writer of the two following letters to Hatton, was appointed to that Deanery in March 1570; and, some time after, he wrote to complain of an infraction of the liberty of his Church by the Mayor's having executed civil processes within its precincts:—

TO SIR CHRISTOPHER HATTON.

MY DUTY HUMBLY REMEMBERED. Some occasions have lately fallen out, of great importance and of no small weight, especially to the church of Gloucester, and presently a grief to me, a poor Dean of a very poor company during her Majesty's pleasure; which state I could be glad to maintain and further for the best, and no way diminish. The substance and circumstances I will not particularly declare, because it is an incumbrance to your Honour, and Mr. Oldsworth our solicitor, a good gentleman and a wise lawyer, can certify you thereof; and we have already signified the matter to the body of the Right Honourable Privy Council. It is in effect a new attempt of the Mayor of Gloucester and others lately against our old liberties, in arresting a gentleman of my Lord of Leicester's within our own precinct, in beating and imprisoning our servants and officers defending the privilege, and other many outrages in articles specified, which touch generally all Cathedral churches. And because I know your Honour of yourself well inclined to the preservation of right, and hath of your goodness accepted the patronage of our Church, I beseech you let the matter be examined, either by your Honour or by the ecclesiastical commission, at your pleasure: and I will shortly attend you of purpose. In your other matter in Southwark order is taken, as at my coming I will declare. The Lord Jesus preserve us. Oxon, Nov. 13. Your Honour's to command, L. HUMFREY.*

<hr>

* Additional MSS. 15891, fo. 118.

Sir Christopher Hatton's nephew, mentioned by Dr. Humfrey, was William Newport, the son of his only sister, who was born about 1565, and who seems, when this letter was written, to have belonged to Magdalen College. On his uncle's death, he succeeded to his estates, and assumed the name and arms of Hatton. Dr. Humfrey was made Dean of Winchester in October 1580, which promotion was probably the fulfilment of the Vice-Chamberlain's promise alluded to in this letter:—

TO SIR CHRISTOPHER HATTON.

It may be your Honour desireth to hear from your nephew, being far from us; and therefore I could not but certify you of his welfare and well-doing at this time by this messenger. The continuance of them both I wish in the Lord, the Giver of all grace, and will further as I may. I perceive, for the French, Mr. Gyles taketh good pains; and the gentleman will learn well both that and other things, if he may have time, and good and godly instructions. I may not forget thanks in humble manner to your Honour, for that I am by friends certified of your good meaning and late promise for my preferment: which as it is before desert of my part, and of small acquaintance with me or my qualities, so must I account the more of your goodness; hoping, for the one, you shall find me not unmindful, and touching the other, upon further knowledge and experience you shall have no cause to repent for any good word or deed bestowed on me. This benefit, above all things, I humbly request of you; that, whatsoever bruit or complaint cometh to you against me, (as the malice of this world is great, yea, against the greatest, and spareth not us poor men,) it would please you to hear my answer before credit be given. It was the worthy virtue of great Alexander, and it is one of the best and wisest parts in a nobleman; whereof nothing doubting of yourself, I cease,

desiring the Lord long to preserve your Honour in all prosperity.   Your Honour's to command,

LAUR. HUMFREY.[a]

It is impossible to say whether the annexed letter
from Henry Howard preceded or followed the one before
inserted :—[b]

TO SIR CHRISTOPHER HATTON.

SIR, It may please you to understand, that as it grieved
me not a little to perceive by your most courteous and
honourable lines that any man could deal so hardly and unjustly with me as to report unto a person of your quality
how forward I had been in preferring discourtesy so near
unto a place, the very sight whereof alone were able to stir
up a reverend and dutiful respect in any well-disposed mind,
so can I not esteem this as the least of many your most
friendly favours towards me, that you, whom I desire to
satisfy in any doubt, vouchsafe to call me to mine answer
before you yield to their unjust reports, which seek to cover
with the greatness of their countenance, in comparison of
me, what cannot be defended in the presence of a better than
us both.   Wherefore at this time I will only complain unto
yourself as mine assured friend, that all respects of duty
which I used in that place, perhaps against my nature, (which
sometime is no less ready to reject a wrong than other men
to proffer it,) cannot so far shield me from reproof but that
my greatest merit is perverted to my most disgrace : and to
suffer wrong is not supposed to be punishment enough for
me, unless I be accused of a double guilt in suffering.   This
six years' space I have remained in this Court without so
much as proffer of disgrace to any man.   I look for nothing
but the grace and favour of the Queen (which till the last
drop of my blood I will deserve by duty).   To my friend I
seek to be reputed constant, and as open to my enemy.   No
day passeth over without some wrong conceits, which need

---

[a] Additional MSS. 15891, f. 56.   [b] Vide p. 116, *ante*.

no other answer but their own uncertainty. Mine able friends
are few, my mighty foes are many; the plight wherein I came
first to the Court I keep in every man's belief that disdaineth
not so poor a friend. And notwithstanding false reports and
wrong surmises of divers sects, the time is yet to come that
either I was touched with default in duty to my Prince, or in
desert to my approved friend. Wherefore, good Mr. Vice-
Chamberlain, let these examples move you to believe, that,
after so long harbour in a calm, I find but small delight in
storms of quarrel, further than I am enforced by discourtesy;
which I love as ill to bear as to proffer : assuring you, that if
their lives, which sought to lead you from well-wishing towards me by this report, were so precisely looked into, their
causes canvassed, their steps observed, and their dealings deciphered, as mine have been these many years, either they
would not be thought so clear, or I should not be accounted
and reputed faulty. But because I mean so quickly to attend
on you myself, and my defence requireth some discourse, I
crave no more but that you will suspend your judgment
either way till you hear what may be answered. God I take
to witness, and as many as were present, that in this matter I
gave no more cause of just offence to any man than he that
was as far from Greenwich at that instant as myself was
from London. And touching my well-meaning to yourself,
I beseech you humbly to persist in this conceit, that as I
never faulted towards you in any thought, so can you not
employ me further than my service shall be ready to discharge
your pleasure. There were no cause for me to wade in this
apology, were it not that proof hath taught me in what bitter
sort some persons have dealt with me, whom you hold in
great account too, far meaner than yourself in calling, and
weaker in authority. Notwithstanding, as an honest, plain,
and constant course fears no encounter; so doubt I not, by
good desert, to let you understand the difference between my
friendly meaning and the malice of mine enemies. Thus
humbly craving pardon for my posting lines, and reposing
that assured trust in your upright and honourable friendship

that you will not otherwise advise me than may stand with honour, which I am resolute to keep unstained till the last spark of my life, I recommend both myself and all I have to your devotion. In haste, from my lodging at Ivy Bridge.[a]
Your Honour's faithful and assured friend at commandment,

HENRY HOWARD.[b]

There is nothing to show when the following letter was written:—

SIR THOMAS HENEAGE TO SIR CHRISTOPHER HATTON.

SIR, Because I am to no man more bound, I am of no man more bold, than of yourself, whereby in good right no man hath more interest in me; and though my state and fortune make my letters less worth unto you than I would, yet your great goodness to me is your praise and my band; and my true good-will shall never fail to love and honour you to the uttermost of my power. Wishing you all you would, now and ever,

Your own, most bound at commandment,

T. HENEAGE.[c]

The next letter of the series refers to a proceeding which stands disgracefully conspicuous in the annals of Queen Elizabeth's reign. From religious as well as patriotic feelings the French marriage was, as so many of these letters show, extremely unpopular in England; and in the autumn of this year a pamphlet was published by a gentleman of Lincoln's Inn, called John Stubbes, " with " what Camden calls " a stinking style," entitled " The Discovery of a Gaping Gulph wherein England is like to be swallowed by another French marriage, if the Lord forbid not the bans by letting her Majesty see the sin and the punishment thereof;" [d] in which the alliance was

[a] Near Plymouth.
[b] Additional MSS. 15891, f. 40[b].
[c] Additional MSS. 15891, f. 46[b].
[d] Small octavo, August 1579.

denounced as dangerous to the Protestant religion, and
the French Prince and nation were grossly abused.   A
proclamation immediately appeared, defending Monsieur,
and declaring that the book "was nothing else but a
fiction of traitors, to raise envy abroad and sedition
at home," and commanding it to be publicly burnt.
The Queen's vengeance fell upon its author, the publisher, and the printer, who, under an Act passed in
the reign of Philip and Mary " against seditious words
and rumours,"* were condemned to lose their right
hands.   The printer was pardoned; but Stubbes, and
Paget the publisher, both underwent this barbarous
punishment in the market-place at Westminster on the
3rd of November.   Camden says he was present, and
that " their right hands were cut off with a cleaver
driven through the wrist with the force of a beetle;"
and that, as soon as the execution was over, Stubbes took
off his hat with his remaining hand, and exclaimed with
a loud voice " God save the Queen!"   Well indeed may
Camden be believed that " the multitude standing about
was altogether silent: either out of horror of this new
and unwonted punishment; or else out of pity towards
the man, being of most honest and unblameable report;
or else out of hatred of the marriage, which most men
presaged would be the overthrow of religion."   It is remarkable that both Camden and Stow should assign this
transaction to the year 1581.ᵇ   Though Hatton had
taken an active part in Stubbes' prosecution, he nevertheless applied to him to intercede with the Queen
for his release from further persecution.

* Stat. 1 & 2 Phil. & Mar. cap. 3.
ᵇ In Park's edition of the " Nugæ
Antiquæ," some curious papers relating to Stubbes' work and punishment occur.

TO SIR CHRISTOPHER HATTON.

SIR, The round dealing which your Honour used at my first
examination, and your severe sifting out of that fault which
bred me all my woe, doth not, for all that, affray me from
coming to your Honour with some hope of pitying me, now
fallen into the extremity of affliction. For as your service to
her Majesty's commandment, and place in high counsel, required at that time all diligence and wisdom to discover the
author of so great offence to her Highness; whereupon hath
also followed a time for Justice to do that which was her part
in giving and executing judgement according to law; so
now I humbly pray that it may not seem out of time for the
poor offender, after his pains endured, to sue for pity, and to
crave that Mercy might save so much as Justice hath left;
which thing, next under God, lieth in her Majesty's gracious
hands to do. For truly, Sir, though my imprisonment hath
been long; mine expense great, even to the disordering and
almost undoing of my poor estate; the cutting off my hand
and healing most painful and dangerous, the perpetual want
thereof a loss most piteous and inestimable; yet is the continuance of her Highness's indignation more to my heart's
grief, and pincheth me more nearly than all the rest.   And,
indeed, as under this burden I can but fall; so, if it might
please her Majesty of her accustomed and great grace to
release me thereof, the greatness of that new joy would
swallow up all mine old sorrows.   I humbly beseech your
Honour to say for me that you found me no perverse examinate.   For albeit upon the first examination the terror of a
Prince's wrath made me tremble to accuse myself, yet did I,
without any accuser, after a while lay myself open.   The
judgement-seat, which gave sentence against my fault, will
yet testify my humble and dutiful reverence throughout all
my defence and answering for myself.   The scaffold of execution can witness my loyal care to give all good example of
meet obedience; insomuch as, notwithstanding the bitter pain
and doleful loss of my hand immediately before chopped off,

I was able, by God's mercy, to say with heart and tongue, before I left the block, these words, "God save the Queen!" I dare report myself to my very keepers, under whom I was severally a prisoner, what was my obedience ever unto them in regard of her Majesty, in whose name I was committed; as also for all my other usage, how far it was from any working or practice for intelligence with any by message or writing, whereof I thank God I had no need. But all these duties are such, and so due, as their desert endeth in the doing of them, and reacheth no further than the very performing. It will affect her tender royal heart to understand that my poor wife and little child, who had no community with me in the fault, have yet their society and satiety in these lamentable troubles; in whose favour I humbly crave the rather your mediation. But this the only thing that I can put in your Honour's hands wherewith to move her Majesty's mercy, even my poor heart sorrowing to have offended and troubled her Majesty's person, laws, and state, humbling itself at her feet in all submission, and vowing henceforth such religious and careful obedience as may show how much I love that most honourable, profitable, and necessary ordinance of God, wherein we are commanded to obey our sovereign magistrates, especially the government of the Queen of England, by whom the Lord hath dispensed such benefits to our country, both bodily and spiritually, as five hundred years past cannot speak of. If in tender mercy of these things, or rather by natural motion of her Majesty's natural clemency, it may please her to show some grace, she shall enlarge the number of her benefits towards him, whose duty of humble thankfulness is already owing unto her Majesty in such measure as it cannot be increased. And if by your mean I may obtain so great a good as is the relief of her heavy offence and of my grievous imprisonment, your Honour may so be a mean also to save my life, which, in these terms of extremity, hasteth fast to an end. The Lord bless her Majesty with health and peace, with long life and honour; and grant you the grace of God, and continuance of her

Highness's favour, by serving the Lord and her in all single--ness of heart, which is the truest honour!   From the house of my strait imprisonment, the 1st of December 1579.

Your Honour's humble suitor and suppliant,

JHO. STUBBES.[a]

Very few particulars of Sir Christopher Hatton in the year 1580, except what may be derived from his correspondence, have been preserved.   Though generally supposed to have been unfavourable to the Queen's marriage, his letters do not convey that impression; and the Archbishop of York, writing to the Earl of Shrewsbury from London, in March of this year, says, " the Earl of Leicester, Mr. Hatton, and Mr. Walsingham have earnestly moved her Majesty to go forward with the marriage as her most safety." [b]   In June, a private conference took place with the French Ambassador at Nonsuch, at which only Leicester and Hatton were present, but in the evening they were joined by Lord Burghley. [c]   In July a slanderous book was secretly printed at Paris, similar to one called a " Treatise of Treasons," being a requital of the attacks made on Monsieur, to which the lives, being no doubt scurrilous accounts, of Leicester and Hatton were added.[d]   The only grant which is recorded to have been made to Hatton in this year was that of Keeper of the Manor of Pleasaunce, in Kent, for life. [e]

The first letter to Sir Christopher Hatton in 1580 is from Mr. Davison, respecting some monopoly that had been granted to the Vice-Chamberlain, which proved injurious to the merchants of the Low Countries:—

[a] Additional MSS. 15891, f. 25ᵇ.
[b] Lodge's Illustrations, ii. 162.
[c] Strype's Annals, ii. 319.
[d] Letter from William Parry to Lord Burghley, in the State Paper Office.
[e] Rot. Patent. 22 Eliz.

MR. DAVISON TO SIR CHRISTOPHER HATTON.

SIR, I should do a wrong to the sufficiency of this bearer, your Honour's servant, to write you any news by him, that may particularly inform you of the course of our doings here. Only hereof I have thought it my duty to acquaint your Honour in a word or two, that on Thursday night last his Highness sent unto me a couple of counsellors, known to this bearer, to communicate with me a complaint against the patent of one Typper, containing an exclamation of wrongs under that pretext offensive to the merchants of this Country trading to England. Though I knew not then that the matter did any way touch your Honour, yet made I them such answer as you may see by my letters to Mr. Secretary; which not satisfying them, it seems they are in mind to send over some one or other to seek redress of her Majesty. If your Honour should relent in the cause, I doubt not but you and the rest of my Lords there will, in regard thereof, take order that her Majesty's subjects trading hither may be uncumbered of such wrongs as are from time to time offered them here; for, otherwise, I see not but that they will rather increase than diminish. Of this, and all other particularities, this bearer may more at large inform your Honour: of whom, with remembrance of my duty, I most humbly take my leave. At Antwerp, the 21st of February 1579 [1580]. Your Honour's humble to command,   W. DAVISON.[*]

A letter from Sir Nicholas Wooderooffe, the Lord Mayor of London, to Hatton, shows that courtiers had so frequently applied for the Freedom of the City for their dependants, that it was at last necessary to refuse the request:—

[*] Additional MSS. 15891, f. 42^b.

TO SIR CHRISTOPHER HATTON.

IT may please your Honour, I have imparted to my brethren your letters of request for the Freedom of London
to be granted to Richard Bateman, wherein we thank you
that you so honourably refer the same to our customs,
orders, and considerations. Surely, Sir, our granting of
Freedom is by the excess thereof grown grievous to the
Commons of this City, being already so overpressed with
multitudes, that the meaner sort are not able to live one
by another. Wherefore, the rather for that we lately
granted one in like sort at your request, and, upon our letters signifying the hardness of those grants to our Citizens,
you were contented so to esteem the matter, and to promise
forbearing to press us with the like; it may please you to
take in good part that in our consideration we have not
thought convenient for the City to increase the number of
Freemen with admitting Bateman into that Society.   And
so I commit your Honour to the tuition of the Almighty.
At London, the 11th of February 1579 [1580].   Your
Honour's assured,   NICHOLAS WOODROFFE, Mayor.[a]

Four very interesting letters occur in the "Letter
Book," from Margaret Countess of Derby, one to the
Queen, and three to Sir Christopher Hatton, which bring
to light another instance of Queen Elizabeth's rigour
to those who had the misfortune of sharing the Blood
Royal. This "poor wretched abandoned lady," as she
touchingly calls herself, was the only surviving child of
Henry Clifford second Earl of Cumberland, by his first
wife Eleanor, daughter and co-heiress of Charles Duke
of Suffolk, by Mary Queen of France, daughter of King
Henry the Seventh ; and she was consequently first
cousin, once removed, to Queen Elizabeth. She married, in February 1555, Henry Stanley fourth Earl of
Derby, by whom she had four sons, of whom Ferdi-

[a] Additional MSS. 15891, f. 56b.

nando and William were successively Earls of Derby;
became a widow in 1594, and died in 1596. These
letters contain the only notice that has been found of
the Countess of Derby's having incurred the Queen's
displeasure, and which probably arose from some suspicion of her conduct in relation to the succession. It
appears that she was long a prisoner, though she was
never publicly accused of any crime. None of those
letters have any date; but the following letter from the
Countess to Sir Francis Walsingham, in another collection, shows that they must have been written about
May 1580 ; and, as they cannot be assigned to their
precise dates, it has been thought advisable to place
them together. Hatton was, she says, the only person
in the Court that had shown any compassion for her;
and he exerted himself successfully in obtaining some
alleviation of her sufferings.

THE COUNTESS OF DERBY TO SIR FRANCIS WALSINGHAM.

RIGHT HONOURABLE, If but one and not many afflictions
and troubles were laid upon me at once, I would then endeavour myself to bear therewith, and forbear for remedy
thereof to trouble any of my good friends. Sickness and
weakness in my body and limbs I have of long time been
accustomed to suffer; and, finding small remedy after proof of
many, lastly upon information of some about me that one
Randall* had a special remedy for the cure of my disease by
applying of outward things, I had him in my house from
May until August next following, in which time I found
some ease by his medicines: but since I have understood by
report that man to have lived in great wickedness, wherewith
it hath pleased God to suffer him among other not a little to
plague me with his slanderous tongue whilst he lived. What
repentance he took thereof before his death God knoweth.

* Stow mentions the execution of a William Randall for conjuring towards the end of 1580 ; but the impostor alluded to above was dead when this letter was written.

Good Sir, the heavy and long-continued displeasure which her Majesty thereby, and by the accusation of some others, hath laid upon me, doth more vex my heart and spirit than ever any infirmity have done my body. And yet I ever have, do, and will confess that her Majesty hath dealt both graciously and mercifully with me in committing of me unto such a place where is wholesome and good air, without the which I had perished; and unto such a person, whom I find, as he is, my good kinsman. The last affliction tormented my soul with the continual clamour and outcry of many of my poor creditors, for whom I find no remedy unless it may please her Highness to license my Lord and me to sell so much land of my inheritance as may discharge the same; whereof though her Highness be in reversion, yet be there about twenty persons inheritable thereunto as heirs of the body of my grandfather Charles Duke of Suffolk. I humbly pray you to be a means unto her Highness herein, and for her Majesty's clemency and mercy to be extended towards me, whom I take the High God to witness, that I ever have feared and loved, and so will continue whilst my life endureth. Thus committing myself to your good consideration, and us both to God, I cease to trouble you. May 1580.

Her Majesty's prisoner and your assured friend,

M. DERBY.[a]

COUNTESS OF DERBY TO SIR CHRISTOPHER HATTON.

SIR, Your honourable dealing hath bound me so much unto you as it is unpossible you should make a gentlewoman more beholding unto you than I am; for the liberty which I have attained unto at her Majesty's hands (whose feet I lie under) I do freely acknowledge to have only proceeded from her goodness by your honourable mediation. You are the sole person in Court that hath taken compassion on me, and hath given comfort unto my careful heart, and, under God, kept life itself within my breast. All these noble kindnesses are derived from your virtue and good favour

---

[a] Copy, in the Harleian MSS. 787, f. 16.

towards me, a poor wretched abandoned lady, no way able
to yield you thankfulness worthy thereof.   You are the
rock I build on.   That made me yesterday so bold to send
Bessy Lambert unto you to deliver you at large the state
of my body and the poverty of my purse, whom you heard
with that willingness as I am double and treble beholding
unto you, and humbly thank you for it.   I well hoped by
your good means unto her Majesty to have placed myself in
that air that I best agree withal.   These sudden faintings
and overcomings which I am seldom out of, have so weakened and afflicted my feeble body since my coming hither,
that I am many times as a woman brought to death's door
and revived again beyond all expectation.   My cousin Sackford* hath built him a house at Clerkenwell, which is not
yet thoroughly finished.   I would be very gladly his tenant;
for the air, as I take it, cannot be much unlike to that of his
house at St. John's : but I hear now they die of the sickness
round about it, so that though I could and would, yet I
dare not adventure to take it ; but I hope it will stay ere it
be long, and in the mean while I purpose to provide me of
some house about Highgate to remain in until Michaelmas.
If I can find out any, I will embolden myself upon your
pleasure to trouble you with my letters, beseeching you to
move her Majesty for mercy and favour towards me when
time shall serve you ; for in effect, as I am now, I live dying,
and death were much better welcome unto me than life, if
I must be still in her Highness' misliking.   Pardon me, I
pray you, for my tedious lines ; and God send you as much
happiness as ever had noble gentleman.   Your most bounden
friend,   .   MARGARET DERBY.[b]

COUNTESS OF DERBY TO SIR CHRISTOPHER HATTON.

SIR, I am altogether most beholden unto you for your
honourable care of my man's miserable cause, whose adversary God amend ; neither is his better void of enemies.

Mr. Sackford, Master of Re-   in the Sidney Papers, also calls him
quests. Sir Henry Sidney, in a letter   his cousin.
          .   [b] Additional MSS. 15891, f. 84[b].

But God alone can revenge the injury, and regard his innocency. Myself at this instant sickly, in heart perplexed, and in mind as it were exiled, somewhat amazed, but not altogether amated. In good sooth, the hope of her Highness' favour is only my relief; the regard of her gracious goodness towards me in my suit shall most comfort me and depress the rage of my enemy. Well, to God and our good Queen I commit both cause and creature; and yourself, my friend, bind me ever yours. Thus, scribbling rudely, I leave hastily, but heartily, with my loving salutations. Yours as faithfully as you to me,   MARGARET DERBY.[a]

COUNTESS OF DERBY TO SIR CHRISTOPHER HATTON.

I HAVE sent you by this bearer my loyal and most humble lines unto her most excellent Majesty, which I beseech you of all nobleness of mind, for that you may see the wretched estate of a poor woman therein described, and my unableness to perform so great a part of duty by pen as is due, and should have been done before this time. That now you will vouchsafe I may commend me to your honourable aid and favour for the amendment of anything which you shall find amiss in my letter to her Majesty: which I beg for God's sake that you will do, even as you tender justice and the dignity of the place that you are called unto. When you have seen it I expect the return of it, with your pleasure and good advice; which when I have written as well as I can, I will speedily send it you again to be exhibited to her Majesty, whom God long preserve, and send you great happiness in honour. Your bounden friend,

·   MAR. DERBY.[b]

COUNTESS OF DERBY TO QUEEN ELIZABETH.

MY DREAD AND GRACIOUS SOVEREIGN, most renowned in all clemency and justice, I do prostrate myself, and most humbly crave that it will please your Highness favourably to read, and mercifully to conceive of these few lines and

---

[a] Additional MSS. 15891, f. 32.   [b] Additional MSS. 15891, f. 69[b].

wretched estate of a very poor distressed woman, whose heart, God knoweth, hath long been overwhelmed with heaviness through the great loss of your Majesty's favour and gracious countenance, which heretofore right joyfully I did possess; the only want whereof hath made me eat my tears instead of bread, and to endure all griefs beside that your gracious high wisdom may imagine. But, most dear Sovereign, I confess and acknowledge that I have found great mercy and goodness at your hands, in that, of your merciful consideration, you sent me to the house of your Majesty's grave officer the Master of Requests, my very good friend and kinsman; and now from thence it hath pleased your Highness, according to your accustomed benignity and rare goodness, to give order unto your honourable Counsellors, the Lord Chancellor and Mr. Vice-Chamberlain, for my delivery to Isleworth House: for all which sweet branches from the tree of your Majesty's mercy I am, and so take myself to be, most dutifully bounden and thankful unto your Highness, as I trust they will testify whom I besought with unfeigned tears upon my knees to be earnest mediators to your Majesty for more plenty of your most noble favour, pity, and mercy towards me; without the good hope whereof I do account myself, and heart and mind, to be as in the black dungeon of sorrow and despair. And therefore, with more of loyalness of heart than my pen can express, I lie most humbly at your gracious feet, and pray to God that shortly my heavy and dry sorrows may be quenched with the sweet dew and moisture of your Majesty's abundant grace and virtue.   Your Majesty's most woful and miserable thrall,   .   MAR. DERBY.*

Sir Walter Mildmay, the writer of the annexed letter, was Chancellor of the Exchequer. Of the disorder mentioned in this and some other letters, a correspondent of the Earl of Shrewsbury gave an account on the 1st of July:—" We have here in London, and at

* Additional MSS. 15891, f. 72.

the Court, a new strange sickness. It does grieve men in the head, and with a stitch over the stomach. Few do die thereof, and yet many are infected. I do hear it credibly reported that forty students of Lincoln's Inn were taken with the said malady within the space of twenty-four hours. At the Court, the Lady Lincoln, the Lady Howard, the Lady Stafford, the Lady Leighton, are at this instant troubled therewithal. The Lord Lumley is sick there, and many of the inferior sort"[a]:—

TO SIR CHRISTOPHER HATTON.

Sir, According to her Majesty's pleasure, I mean to attend upon my Lord Treasurer and you to-morrow at eight of the clock in the morning; albeit I thought it my duty to let you know what hath happened. In the very next house to mine, here in this town, one is dead of the plague, and another sick; so as, whether it were convenient that I should meet with you or no, in respect of your continual access to her Majesty's presence, I am doubtful, and refer the same to your consideration. That occasion doth hasten me out of town sooner than I thought, and therefore it may please you to send me your opinion. The matter of your meeting will be well enough performed without me; but I say not this to be excused from any service of her Majesty, to whom I owe all that I have, and my life too. Thus, praying to receive some few lines from you for answer, I commend you and all your actions to God's merciful government. From London, the 30th of June 1580. Your most assured and faithful friend to my power,   Wa. Mildmay.[b]

The following letter without a date from the Earl of Sussex, the Lord Chamberlain, was perhaps written about this time:—

[a] Lodge's Illustrations, ii. 174.   [b] Additional MSS. 15891, f. 34.

TO SIR CHRISTOPHER HATTON.

Good Mr. Vice-Chamberlain, I do most heartily thank
you for your letter, and am very sorry that her Majesty is
forced to remove by an infectious accident; but better in my
opinion to make any remove to a clear place, than in any
respect to remain in the danger of the infection, which by
degrees may grow nobody knoweth how near to herself,
whom God always defend from that, and from all other evils.
I am sorry that my unhappy accident, and the state of my
own body, do at this time keep me from doing of her Majesty
any service in that place: nevertheless I rest ready to do any
thing that an absent man may do; and will pray to God to
preserve her in all good contentation.

Your assured friend,

T. Sussex.*

A letter from Hatton to Lord Burghley, in July of
this year, contains two facts relating to his history of
some value, namely, that his estate had been entirely
ruined, and that he ascribed its restoration to Burghley's favour; meaning, no doubt, that the Lord Treasurer
had rather encouraged than opposed the Queen's repeated grants to him of lands and monopolies:—

TO LORD BURGHLEY.

My singular good Lord, My term in the impost of wines
draweth (after this year) to expiration. I have therefore
humbly moved her Majesty for the renewing of my lease;
in the which I earnestly beseech you of your good favour
towards me. The course I hold is, to pass my bill according
with my present demise verbatim, upon the same covenants
and rents expressed in this book already passed, if so, with
your Lordship's good advice, it may like her Majesty to grant

* Additional MSS. 15891, f. 88.

it to me. I humbly pray your Lordship that you will advertise me your good pleasure herein, and give me leave to go
on with the suit as it may please your Lordship to direct me.

I do acknowledge with all thankfulness the recovery of my
poor estate, in effect all entirely ruined, to have grown out
of your great goodness and favour towards me; for the
which I will honour and serve you and yours so long as God
giveth life in this world. And thus, with the remembrance
of my bounden duty, I pray God bless your Lordship for
ever. Oatlands, this 22nd of July 1580. Your good Lordship's most bound,   CHR. HATTON.[a]

Two more of the Vice-Chamberlain's extraordinary
letters to the Queen were written during his absence
from the Court in this year; but the annexed is not
quite so romantic as some of his former ones:—

TO THE QUEEN'S MOST ROYAL MAJESTY.

△   △

I MOST humbly with all dutiful reverence beseech your
sacred Majesty to pardon my presumption in writing to your
Highness. Your kingly benefits, together with your most
rare regard of your simple and poor slave, hath put this passion into me to imagine that for so exceeding and infinite
parts of unspeakable goodness I can use no other means of
thankfulness than by bowing the knees of my own heart with
all humility to look upon your singular graces with love and
faith perdurable.

I should sin, most gracious Sovereign, against a holy ghost
most damnably, if towards your Highness I should be found
unthankful. Afford me the favour, therefore, most dear
Lady, that your clear and most fair eyes may read and register
these my duties, which I beseech our God to requite you
for.

[a] Autograph in the State Paper Office.

The poor wretch my sick servant receiveth again his life, being as in the physician's opinion more than half-dead, through your most princely love of his poor Master, and holy charitable care, without respect of your own danger, of the poor wretch. We have right Christian devotion to pray for your Highness, which God for His mercy's sake kindle in us for ever to the end of our lives.

I should not dissemble, my dear Sovereign, if I wrote how unpleasant and froward a countenance is grown in me through my absence from your most amiable and royal presence, but I dare not presume to trouble your Highness with my not estimable griefs, but in my country I dare avow this fashion will full evil become me. I hope your Highness will pardon my unsatisfied humour, that knoweth not how to end such complaints as are in my thoughts ever new to begin; but duty shall do me leave off to cumber your heavenlike eyes with my vain babblings. And, as most nobly your Highness preserveth and royally conserveth your own poor creature and vassal, so shall he live and die in pure and unspotted faith towards you for *EveR*. God bless your Highness with long life, and prosper you to the end in all your kingly affairs. At Bedford, this Wednesday morning,[a] September 1580. Would God I were worthy to write

Your bounden slave,   CHR. HATTON.[b]

The surprise which is likely to be felt that Hatton should have written the following letter [c] to any one except to the Queen herself, or even to her unless he were as highly favoured as he is supposed to have been, will cease when it is remembered that Heneage was, as will appear from other letters, certainly the confidant of

[a] In September 1580, the 7th, 14th, 21st, and 28th, fell on a Wednesday. This letter was probably written on the 7th of that month.
[b] Autograph in the State Paper Office.
[c] This letter was first printed in the "Antiquarian Repertory," where it is said to have been addressed to Sir Thomas Smith, though he died in 1575. A few words are illegible, and the last figure of the date is obliterated, but it was certainly written in 1580.

their intimacy, and was often the transmitter of communications between them. Perhaps not the least remarkable part of this letter is the passage in which Hatton presumes to compare his love for the Queen with that of the Duke of Anjou, and which from any other of her Subjects, except perhaps Leicester, would have been perfectly ridiculous:—

TO SIR THOMAS HENEAGE.

MY GOOD SIR THOMAS, I thank you much for your happy letters, assuring our dear Mistress her present health unto me; pray God continue it for EVER. I have one servant yet free of infection, which I trust I may use to deliver my care and duty, to my singular comfort and satisfaction. I have presumed to send him, that I may daily know either by my own or yours the true state of our* Mistress, whom through choice I love no less than he that by the greatness of a kingly birth and fortune is most fit to have her. I am likewise bold to commend my most humble duty by this letter and ring, which hath the virtue to expel infectious airs, and is, as is telled to me, to be wearen betwixt the sweet dugs,—the chaste nest of most pure constancy. I trust, Sir, when the virtue is known, it shall not be refused for the value.

Since my coming to this town, two other of my poor servants are fallen sick; what their disease will prove is not yet discerned, but the physician feareth the small-pox. By this occasion I am determined to disperse my little company, and to take my way to Sir Ed. Bricknell's,[b] to view my house of Kirby, which I yet never surveyed; leaving my other shrine, I mean Holdenby, still unseen until that holy saint[c] may sit in it, to whom it is dedicated. I beseech you, Sir, acquaint her Highness herewith. I will be gone in the morning betimes, and so pass on a solitary pilgrimage for my folk's health, until all peril of infection may with the open and . . . . . be thereby purged out of my disconsolate body. Within

---

* Query.　　　　　[b] Sic.　　　　[c] The Queen.

six days I will return to Eltham, and there abide the good
call in time opportune.

My commendations to yourself are most abundant in
good-will. I pray you therefore impart of them to such of
my friends as you shall think worthy of them. And so a
thousand times farewell, my good noble friend. September
11th, 158 , [1580.] Yours most assured, CHR. HATTON.*

The receipt of a gracious letter from the Queen produced a reply much more like his correspondence from
Germany six years before, than his letter of the 7th of
September. He now again mentions himself by her
familiar appellations for him of "Lids" and "Sheep."
It is evident that Elizabeth also used a significant mono-
gram or cypher when writing to him; and, though some
of the passages are very obscure, her intended marriage
with the Duke of Anjou is obviously alluded to.   His
remark that "against love" as well as against "ambition," those "violent affections that encumber the hearts
of men,"—the Queen had held "a long war," is some
evidence that her favour to himself had never been in-
consistent with her honour:—

TO THE QUEEN'S MOST ROYAL MAJESTY.

$$\triangle \quad \triangle$$

THE gracious assurance which your Highness's grave letters
do most liberally give me of your singular favour and inestimable goodness, I have received on my knees with such reverence as becometh your most obliged bondman; and with like
humility, in my most dutiful and grateful manner, I do offer
in God's presence myself, my life, and all that I am or is me,
to be disposed to the end, and my death to do your service,
in inviolable faith and sincerity.

* Autograph in the Harleian MSS. 416, f. 200.

The cunning of your Highness' style of writing, with the conveyance of your rare sentence and matter, is exceedingly to be liked of; but the subject which it hath pleased your Majesty to endite for my particular, exceedeth all the eloquence, yea, all the eloquence of the world. Your words are sweet, your heart is full of rare and royal faith: the writing of your fair hand, directed by your constant and sacred heart, do raise in me joy unspeakable. Would God they did not rather puff up my dejected spirits with too much pride and hope. I most humbly thank God for these admirable gifts in your Majesty; they exceed and abound towards your Highness unequally in the measure of His graces amongst men, so far as, God knoweth, there is not your like. I crave most humbly your gracious favour and pardon for the offence I have made you. Frogs, near the friends where I then was, are much more plentiful, and of less value, than their fish is: and because I knew that poor beast* seasonable in your sight, I therefore blindly entered into that presumption, but *Misericordia tua super omnia opera tua.*

God bless your Highness in all your kingly affairs, and direct them through your wonted wisdom in that course that shall *EveR* succeed to your comfort. I find the gracious sign of your letters of most joyful signification, and the abbreviation of delays will breed a much more delightful hope in that great cause. Against love and ambition your Highness hath holden a long war; they are the violent affections that encumber the hearts of men : but now, my most dear Sovereign, it is more than time to yield, or else this love will leave you in war and disquietness of yourself and estate, and the ambition of the world will be most maliciously bent to encumber your sweet quiet, and the happy peace of this

---

* Among Queen Elizabeth's trinkets was "one little flower of gold with a *frog* thereon, and therein Monsieur's physiognomy, and a little pearl pendant." (Ellis' Royal Letters, first series, iii. 52.) Miss Strickland will probably think that her suggestion, " that this whimsical conceit was a love-token from the Duke of Alençon [query, Anjou ?] to his Royal *bel' amie*, and the frog designed, not as a ridiculous but a sentimental allusion to his country," is supported by Hatton's enigmatical remark.

most blessed Realm. I pray God bless your kingly resolutions what*Eve.R.* I trust your Highness will pardon this part of my presumption, because your little §ᵉ *siphere* hath proffered the occasion. And so your Highness' most humble Lydds,[b] a thousand times more happy in that you vouchsafe them yours, than in that they cover and conserve the poor eyes, most lowly do leave you in your kingly seat in God's most holy protection. This 19th of September 1580. Your Majesty's sheep and most bound vassal,

CHR. HATTON.[c]

On Hatton's return to London he expressed his opinion on public affairs to Walsingham, especially on the state of Ireland, and the dangers that beset this Country and the Protestant religion:—

TO SIR FRANCIS WALSINGHAM.

MY GOOD MR. SECRETARY, My zealous care over her Majesty's safety, now fearfully stirred up with this evil news of the affairs of Ireland, doth give me dutiful occasion in my absence to write some little of my simple opinion, though I know it needeth not, but only for my duty's sake. The long-expected mischief, maliciously conspired by the great and most dangerous enemies of her Majesty, and of her Royal estate, towards that Kingdom of Ireland, is now, I hear, in action: wherein, though that maxim of Kings, which containeth the counsel of Providence in this sentence, *Dubia pro certis debent timere reges*, hath been by our gracious Sovereign and her most politic foresight very gravely observed in sending out her ships to resist these intended treacherous attempts; yet that direction, by their untimely and unfortunate return contrary to order, having taken no place, we are again and again to prosecute our course, (as of necessity

* Part of Hatton's New-year's gift to the Queen in January following, was a pair of gold bracelets, with twelve *esses* of small diamonds, &c. Nichols' Progresses, ii. 300.

[b] Lids.

[c] Autograph in the State Paper Office.

we be violently urged,) with a resolute perseverance of her
Majesty's most noble beginning, wherein there remaineth
that her Highness, through her Kingly courage, should timely
and victoriously resist this rabble of rebels and traitors; and
to let nothing be spared, either of treasure, men, munition,
or whatsoever else, to save that Kingdom, being, as you know,
the principal key of this her Royal seat, by which means she
should crown this her most happy government with continuance of felicity over all her Dominions.   In which great
and important cause the best counsel is, according to the old
rule, to resist the beginning; and so, if it were possible, to
end this mischief before her other potent enemies might find
opportunity to work their malice upon us.   For when we
behold the great prosperity of Spain through her peaceable
possession of Portugal, we ought justly to fear, that, his
affairs being settled there in some good sort, he will then,
no doubt, with conjunct force assist this devilish Pope to
bring about their Romish purpose.   Let us not forget that
his sword is presently drawn, and then with what insolent
fury this his victory may inflame him against us, in whose
heart there is an ancient malice thoroughly rooted and rankly
grown for these many years, apparently known to all men
that do bend their eyes to behold the course of his actions;
and therefore we ought not only timely to foresee, but in
time most manfully to resist the same.   In all which proceedings God's cause and her Majesty's stand jointly to be defended; the consideration whereof persuadeth me that there
is no man that will spare travail or expense in any sort to reduce them to good end.   Cease not, good Mr. Secretary, to
put her Majesty in continual remembrance of these perils,
and with importunacy stir up her most earnest princely care
over God's cause and her own.   How that matter in Scotland
goeth, I do not well know; but this rule I hold in all certainty, that in Ireland and Scotland the entries and ways to
our destruction most aptly be found.   If there we safely shut
up the postern-gate, we are sure to repulse the peril; but, if
our enemy make himself the porter, it will be then too late

to wish we had the keys. Would God, some wise man were sent with the grave instruction of her Majesty to reclaim that country of Scotland unto us. The malice of France is there ever made up against us, and of those mischiefs they are ever the executioners. How they trouble us in Ireland we often see and feel; but if that King should be conveyed into France, and so governed and directed by the Guisians, I dare not remember, much less speak of, the dangers would ensue upon us. One thousand pounds employed now in time might haply not only buy her Majesty's present safety, but undoubt-edly save her the expense of threescore thousand before many years. With the disposition of France, which lieth now in her Majesty's arbitrament, I dare not meddle, for she only knoweth what shall become thereof; and so her judgment therein must needs be most sound, which in truth maketh much to all these matters before mentioned. But if her Highness mean to marry, I wonder she so delayeth it. If she do but temporize, and will leave it at the last, what may we look for then, but that the Pope, with Spain and France, will yoke themselves in all ireful revenge, according to their solemn combination so long ago concluded on against us? Now therefore, weighing the present accidents of the world together in an equal balance, how hurtful they may be to the safety of her Majesty's most Royal estate and preservation of her blessed government, first, the weak and broken estate of Ireland, then the uncertain, suspected amity of Scotland, the dangerous action of the French, tending to the subversion of the Protestant, the irrecoverable losses and overthrows re-ceived lately by the States of the Low Countries, and the fortunate and victorious success of the King of Spain in Por-tugal, I cannot but mourn in my heart to see us beset on all sides with so great and apparent dangers. I beseech God continue her Majesty's most careful and provident course to resist these so imminent evils in good time, and to make us ever thankful towards her for such her most gracious and in-estimable goodness conferred on us her poor subjects, through her most Kingly care over us. God bless you, Sir; and so, with a thousand thanks for your honourable letters, I bid you most friendly farewell.   From Hatton House, the 26th of Sept. 1580.   Your true poor friend,   CHR. HATTON.*

Thomas Norton, the busy informant of the following letter, was a stern Calvinist, and wrote many works against Popery. He was also the author of twenty-seven of the Psalms in Sternhold and Hopkins' collection, and of part of a tragedy called "Gorboduc," of which the remainder was written by his patron and friend Lord Buckhurst:—

TO SIR CHRISTOPHER HATTON.

MAY IT PLEASE YOUR HONOUR, Without all displeasant humour, and specially without the base disposition to afflict the afflicted, but only of true zeal to her Majesty's service, I am bold to inform you that long since I have seen a book written in French, intituled *Le Innocence de la tres illustre Royne*, &c.; in the end whereof is a treatise touching the cause of the Duke of Norfolk, written to the defamation of her Majesty and of his Peers, and of some special persons of her Highness' Council.   This book is there pretended to be written in French by a stranger, and to England, and not by an Englishman, for speaking of England he saith, *vostre paie*, and *vostre Roigne*, and such like; and yet in truth it is written by an Englishman, as by Robin Goodfellow and Goodman Gose, and an over-slipped title, and otherwise, as I am able to prove.   The whole course is very seditious, and defamatory to her Majesty, her Council, and Nobility.   He chargeth the Council with treason; and her Majesty with abandoning herself to be abused, to the disturbing of Christendom, to the maintenance of rebels, to the robbing of Princes. It may be that your Honour will think it good to inquire the author, and not unfit to examine the gentleman now in restraint.   The book is not only an Englishman's, but

* Additional MSS. 15891, f. 18.

also originally written in English and translated into French.
Mr. Doctor Hamond is well acquainted with his style, if it
please you to understand his opinion of it. Your Honour
may also send for Mr. Dalton, and ask him whether the same
party have not used at Mrs. Arundell's to maintain open disputations in defence of Papistry, and challenged Mr. Dalton
and others in that case upon wagers.   There goeth also underhand abroad an English treatise written, wherein her Majesty's ancestress is termed base in contempt, the Queen is
threatened with rebellion of Nobility, some great persons are
charged that under her Majesty's favour they have, as it
were, tyrannized over the people. If the book be his, it is
not good. Out of these books, great matters of charge may
be gathered to the author. It were pity he should be untruly
burthened with them; but greater pity that he or any should
carry such things clearly. And so I leave to trouble your
Honour any longer. At London, the 30th of December
1580. Your Honour's humbly,   THO. NORTON.*

A more convenient place cannot be found for an
undated letter, apparently to Lord Burghley, on the
subject of the French marriage. The writer was, no
doubt, a Puritan divine, and his sentiments are expressed with fervid eloquence:—

MY VERY GOOD LORD, Seeing my duty requireth it, and
your goodness hath so bound me, and the present dangers
now impending over the Church of God and this Commonwealth do constrain me, I trust your Lordship, of your accustomed clemency, will accept it well that at this time I
presume to take occasion to testify my dutiful remembrance
by these rude messengers. I hope you will not examine my
writing otherwise than by my simple meaning and your accustomed gentleness. For I protest before God and His holy
angels that stand as beholders of all men's actions, I do it
only in His fear, having first called upon His name; and

* Additional MSS. 15891, f. 75.

partly for the honour that I bear unto you, that the ill-success
of those dangers which all the world may see now not only
to hang over your head, but over the whole Realm, may,
through the gracious goodness of God, by doing our duties,
be wisely prevented, and, if it be His will, speedily turned
from us.   For, seeing the whole house is set on fire, why
should any man be suspected or misliked that bringeth water
to quench it?—seeing the city of God is assaulted, why
should our watchmen hold their peace?   O my Lord, I beseech you in the bowels of Christ, as you tender the Church
of God, love your Country, and honour her Majesty, so set
yourself, and as many as you can procure, to stop this devilish
device of her Majesty's untimely, unfit, and unseasonable
matching.   For if it be plain and manifest to be most dangerous to our Country in the regard only that he is a stranger,
what shall it be in respect of him that is unstayed and many
ways tainted, greatly dishonoured with a bloody race, with the
breach of faith, having drawn even from the teat the milk
of cursed treachery, and having been schooled up in the continual practice of godless policy grounded upon that incarnate
devil Machiavel, even yet witnessed in the fresh bleeding
wounds of God's saints crying still for speedy vengeance
against the whole generation of cursed persecutors?   Be not
deceived, I beseech you, my good Lord, in this weighty
cause ; recompense the honour that God hath bestowed upon
you by means of her Majesty with this fidelity, to hold her
back from the gulph of her destruction.   The Lord give you
wisdom to quench the fire that is already kindled by this unhappy attempt, which already burneth in such sort as it
breaketh out into violent flames, and, unless the Lord stay it,
giveth evident signs of the general subversion of our whole
Country.   For as warmth giveth life to the cold, and starveth
the slowworm, so the likelihood of this mischievous attempt
hath made our cold-starved Papists to gather great life. They
begin now to threaten us by open libels, by setting signs
upon the doors of many professors of the Gospel in divers
places, by hanging and lowering countenances, as though our

summer were past, and their harvest come; as though our day of destruction were at hand, and their golden day, so long looked for, present. But this is our hope, that God reigneth and liveth; and though it be very likely that our great sins, and unthankfulness, and wretched profaning of holy things have drawn upon us His fearful judgments, yet He knoweth those that are His, and will keep them and will defend them for His name-sake, howsoever He may punish their sins in seasoning and purging them from their corruptions. O my Lord, never forget the lamentable effects of that unhappy contention in the days of King John, when those unfortunate Barons sought for aid into France, when our Country was wasted, the nobility dispersed, and had been utterly destroyed, had not God made the mouth of one of the conspirators themselves to detect that treasonable treachery. What should I speak of the miserable end of Richard the Second, through his doting love, when the blood, as I have said, is not yet dry that was shed by that cursed marriage devised to the overthrow of so many millions of innocents. Between the King of Navarre that now is, and the French King's sister, doth your Lordship think that they rather seek her Majesty than her Crown and Kingdom? and do you doubt but that they will spoil and impoverish our Country, if they seek for her Crown and Kingdom, and that, doing the one, they must not of necessity shed the blood of the other? Though all the world should speak the contrary, yet I hope we are not such blocks as to believe it. Was it thought unmeet that they should settle in Scotland when they began to nestle there? and by her Majesty's good means, to her immortal praise, were they driven from thence; and can it be good now that they be joined with us in marriage? These are quite contrary. Good my Lord, pardon me: I lay open myself the rather to your Lordship, because you are in place to do good, and by my mouth may learn the common opinion of the best, and I have no small confidence in your assurance and staidness towards them. I hope God hath given you wisdom to make you see the end whereunto this device tendeth. And I beseech you, seeing it is a matter of weight, which concerneth not only our lives and goods, but stands upon the hazarding of our souls, that you will wisely look about you, and look up to God in true repentance, that being reconciled to Him you may be assured of His protection and presence, for in vain is man's help without His assistance. Beware whom you trust; for, in your place, it can not be but many will follow you for another end than they pretend; their lucre is not your safety, but their own commodity. Treason is never committed but where there is trust: falsehood is always in friendship and fellowship: every fair beck is not a seal of a faithful heart: poisons are mingled and ministered with honey that they may be the less suspected. The fairer the colours are without, the more suspicious is the ground; and harlots use more painting and decking than sober and honest matrons. Crocodiles have their tears, and they are very dangerous. O my Lord, this platform cannot be but ·perilous, and specially to your Lordship and many others, the undoubted professors of His glorious Gospel. In which respect if you stand grounded, your strength is assured; and though Papists should not join with you, yet commonweal Papists, that is, such as are but civilly-wise, will not, for their own safety, in this cause leave you. Howsoever it be, one godly man shall be stronger than ten enemies. The Lord is with them that stand sincerely for His name and for a good cause; yea, the death of the righteous is with honour, and what death soever they die that stand for God, for their country, and for their Prince, they shall go to their grave with peace. Wherefore, my Lord, be of good courage; faint not; the time will come when you shall feel the fruit of constancy in this good cause, to your high honour and immortal fame. Good my Lord, remember them that are in bands, and mitigate as much as in you lieth the hard hand that is holden upon the best sort. I dare call them so in respect of their religion, zeal, fidelity, and truth; whom to touch is to touch the apple of God's own eye, that cannot but draw upon the whole land a terrible vengeance. Beware of these elbow-informers: I mean not those that suggest good things, but such as labour to bring into disgrace good men, that thereby they may the better establish their own credits, and build up their houses with other men's ruins. If either the one or the other tell you of present danger, hear them willingly; if of perils to come, wisely prevent them. I pray . God give your Lordship the spirit of wisdom and counsel, that you may stand stout and faithful to defend the peace of the Church, the preservation of this common-weal, and the safety of her Majesty's royal person, whom God ever maintain and continue to His glory and all our comforts!

Arthur Lord Grey of Wilton was appointed Lord Deputy of Ireland after the death of Sir William Drury in 1579, and several letters occur from him to Hatton on the affairs of that Country.

LORD GREY DE WILTON TO SIR CHRISTOPHER HATTON.

SIR, I hope you have understood at large, by my letters which I have sent unto my Lords, what composition of peace is taken with Turlogh Leinigh.* Since which time I have received advertisement that Thomas Nugent, brother to the Baron of Delvyn, hath banded himself with the O'Connors, and is newly revolted, being no doubt enticed and heartened thereunto by Thurlow; with whom, I am by secret intelligence informed, there was a messenger of his seen not many days before he withdrew himself from her Majesty's obedience: whereby it appeareth how dangerous a back he is unto all rebels and disordered Subjects which shall attempt anything against this State; beside the peril wherewith he threateneth us daily by bringing in the Scots in great numbers, and the preparation he maketh to strengthen himself by all means possible, which plainly argueth in him great intention of mischief. I beseech you therefore, for the speedy repress-

* Vide Camden's Annals, b. ii. p. 118.

ing of this man's insolency, that you will be pleased to help forward, through your honourable solicitation to her Majesty, with more forces, and to hasten them hither with all possible expedition: which being once well arrived, I hope they shall give an end to all this war; so we may be therewith relieved with a new supply, and such money and victuals as shall be needful, whereof we have exceeding great want at this present: and so I commit you to God. Dublin, the 14th of March 1580. [1581.] Your most assured friend and loving cousin.

A. GREY.*

In April, the Commissioners appointed by the King of France to treat for the Queen's marriage arrived in England; and Lord Burghley, the Earls of Lincoln, Sussex, Bedford, and Leicester, Sir Christopher Hatton, and Sir Francis Walsingham, were constituted her Majesty's Commissioners to confer with them.

Sir Thomas Wilson, the writer of the annexed letter, was made one of the Principal Secretaries of State, and sworn of the Privy Council, in 1577, on the same day that Hatton became a member of that body. He was also Dean of Durham: and died in 1581, leaving a son, Nicholas, and the two daughters of whom he speaks; namely, Mary, who married, first, Robert Burdett of Bramcote, and secondly, Sir Christopher Lowther; and Lucretia, who became the wife of George Belgrave, of Belgrave in Leicestershire.

TO SIR CHRISTOPHER HATTON.

SIR, I received upon Friday such a message from you by a gentleman your servant as was greatly to my comfort, and though you had sent me no such word, yet should I never have doubted of your friendship; for where I have once conceived a good impression, my nature is like iron and marble,

* Additional MSS. 15891.

that never changeth without altering the substance: and
though I have received hard measure of some, of whom in
truth I have best deserved, yet can I not alter my disposition;
and love, once offered in faithful manner, requireth love
again; and yet where it shall fail on either side, the party
grieved cannot but show that flesh and blood can hardly bear
it. I sent you word that I would have been yesterday at the
Court, but then I was ill, and am yet nothing amended; so
you see man purposeth, and God disposeth. As soon as
God shall make me able, I will not fail to see you. In the
meanwhile I have sent thither my two daughters, my only
treasure; which I write unto you as a bachelor, to whom
maidens cannot be unwelcome. And so I commit you to
God. From my house, the 23rd of April 1581. Your very
assured friend,   THO. WILSON.[a]

Of Charles Arundell, whom Strype[b] calls a "busy
man," the writer of the following and of several other
letters to Hatton, little is known, except that he was
one of those unfortunate Papists who were the constant
objects of persecution. He was arrested and imprisoned
for some offence, real or imaginary, and sought the Vice-
Chamberlain's interest to obtain a trial. In a letter
from Monsieur Mauvissière, the French Ambassador, to
his Sovereign, in December 1583, he says, speaking of a
conspiracy which had been discovered to take the
Queen's life, "Meanwhile I must not omit to tell you
that a great many persons are committed to prison on
account of this conspiracy; and that Lord Paget, Charles
Arundell, and several more noblemen and principal gentlemen of quality in this Kingdom, fled four or five days
ago, and embarked at night on board a vessel at
Arundell, which still more astonished the Queen and her

---

[a] Additional MSS. 15891, f. 79.   [b] Annals, iii. pt. 1. p. 273.

Council." On the 17th of January following, Mauvissière informed the King, that the Queen thought, that
" if his Majesty were even inclined to deliver up to her
Lord Paget, his brother Charles Arundell, and her other
subjects, whom she calls rebels, he (Mauvissière) would
prevent him from doing so." [a]

CHARLES ARUNDELL TO SIR CHRISTOPHER HATTON.

RIGHT HONOURABLE, As one no less willing to remember
you than mindful of your great goodness, I have stayed this
bearer by the sleeve to increase his burden by the weight of
this short letter, and to release myself of a greater debt than
ink and paper can acknowledge. My meaning is not to be
cumbersome, nor to trouble you with my cause till time may
serve; only, to exercise the duty I owe you, I have sent you
these few lines, and that the bearer should not return empty-
handed without some show where he had been. Touching
my affection to yourself, I crave no more (till time may yield
you better trial) but that your virtue may in this time of
distress both plead and promise for your poor friend, that
wanteth means, not will, to make his faith more evident.
And so with humble remembrance of my duty I end, wishing
the happy supply of your desires, and myself ability to do
you service. From Sutton, the 23rd of May 1581. Your
Honour's more faithful than fortunate, C. A.

The subject of this letter, from Sir Walter Mildmay,
is not mentioned :—

TO SIR CHRISTOPHER HATTON.

SIR, I did yesterday speak with my Lord Chancellor,[b] and
have satisfied him in such things as he was not rightly informed of. I found his usage towards me very good and

[a] "Letters of Mary Queen of Scots,"
by Agnes Strickland, vol. ii. p. 733.
The Editor of that collection has mis-
placed the Ambassador's letter of the
18th of January, as it was evidently
written in 1583-4, and should have
followed all Mauvissière's letters of
1583.
[b] Sir Thomas Bromley.

courteous, so as I trust the matter shall receive a reasonable conclusion; the rather if it please you to take knowledge of thus much to him, and to pray the continuance of his good favour. You see how ready I am to trouble you, for the which I have nothing to yield you but my thanks, and that I will do ever; and so leave you to the Lord Almighty. From London, the 27th of May 1581. Yours very assured, to my little power,   WA. MILDMAY.[a]

Unless the question between Sir Christopher Hatton and the City arose out of one of his monopolies, it is difficult to suggest, and there is nothing to show, what the matter was to which Sir Walter Mildmay alludes in the following letter:—

TO SIR CHRISTOPHER HATTON.

SIR, This afternoon there came unto me Mr. Recorder, Mr. Alderman Woodrooffe, and Mr. Alderman Martin, sent from my Lord Mayor and the City touching the matter in question between you and them. The sum of their message was, that by common consent they had agreed to submit themselves in that matter to the judgment of my Lord Chancellor, my Lord Treasurer, and me, who, taking the advices of some of the Judges, might fully determine the cause. To this end they required me to be a mediator unto you; but, lest I should either misconceive or misreport their message, I have thought it best they report it to you themselves; for which cause they are come unto you. What an answer you shall think fit to make them I must refer to your own consideration, but for my poor opinion I do not see but that this way the conclusion may be good enough for you. And therefore, as hitherto you have yielded very reasonably unto them (whereof I am a witness), so, if you hold that course still, the end will fall out well on your part, as I think. Thus, wishing unto you always as unto my very good friend, and

* Additional MSS. 15891, f. 85ᵇ.

ready for you in anything I can do, I leave you in the keeping of the Lord Almighty. From London, the 1st of June
1581. Your very assured to my little power,

WA. MILDMAY.*

Bishop Aylmer's report of his persecutions in this
year, are alike characteristic of himself and his times :—

TO THE QUEEN.

MOST GRACIOUS SOVEREIGN, I have thought it my bounden
duty both to God and to your Majesty to acquaint you with
the state of a part of your charge, committed unto you by
the Lord as His lieutenant in His Church and spiritual Government. So it is, most gracious Lady, that we have daily,
to our great grief, brought before us out of Gloucester diocess
certain men of strange, erroneous, and perilous opinions:
whereof some hold that Christ took no flesh of the Virgin,
of whom we have presently one in prison ; other some there
are which most shamefully and slanderously rail against the
authority of magistrates; and some other, which do assemble
conventicles, study only for innovations, and do deride and
jeer at all good orders, and drive their course to so licentious a liberty, as it is to be feared that without speedy
controlment (which can hardly be done by us who are so far
off) this canker will creep and spread itself so far, as it will
not only grow incurable there, but fall out in time to infect
other countries also next adjoining. I find the cause of this
corruption to be no other but *percusso pastore disperguntur
greges,* and as the Scripture said in one sense, *quia non est rex
in Israel,* so say I in the like sense, *quia non est pastor vel
Episcopus in Ecclesia,* men dare be bold with widows; and
that Church being so long a widow, who dare not insult upon
it ? Therefore even for the tender care that your Majesty
hath ever had over your Subjects, and for the princely zeal
that you bear to the unity of the Church, provide that see
of a Bishop, that flock of a pastor, and that decayed house

* Additional MSS. 15891, f. 75.

of some good architect, lest the ruin grow irreparable ; which will bring great dishonour to God, anxiety of mind to yourself, and much harm to your people and subjects. I most humbly beseech your Majesty, therefore, to remember it, and then undoubtedly God will remember you with the richest blessing of His providence ; which shall stand your Highness in more stead than all earthly treasure, politic counsel, and warlike provision, ever more to your own safety and our comforts, who live in you and look to die miserably without you. From my poor house at Fulham, the 13th of June 1581. Your Majesty's most humble and dutiful poor Chaplain,   JOHN LONDON.[a]

So little is known of the poet or rather versifier Churchyard's life, that no light can be thrown on some of the passages in the annexed letter; but a marginal note in the " Letter Book " thus explains one part of it :—" This Monsieur Mauvissière was then the French Ambassador resident in England, who used Churchyard as a spy for English news and advertisements of Court,[b] and entertained him with money to that end; and, to do him some service in that kind, he sent him into Scotland about some exploit agreed on between them two, which was the cause that Mr. Randall, the Queen's Ambassador at that time in Scotland, much disliked his being there, suspecting that he was there for no good to the State of England."   Churchyard's application to the Scottish Parliament is not noticed in its " Acts."

THOMAS CHURCHYARD TO SIR CHRISTOPHER HATTON.

SIR, Having tried my uttermost fortune, and passed the fire of affliction, through a perilous pilgrimage not void of many deadly dangers and imminent mischiefs, I am now come prostrate in mind, and falling devout on my knees be-

[a] Additional MSS. 15891, f. 83.   [b] Query.

fore my Lord Governor of Berwick, submitting myself to the
Queen's Majesty's mercy and my Lord's good favour, always
hoping that your Honour hath in mind the promise which I
made you for a piece of service that I meant with hazard of
my life to discover for the discharge of my duty to my Prince
and Country; leaving certain notes by word of mouth, and also
in paper, for that purpose with you, and yet hearing no
answer of sundry letters which I sent you after my great
misfortune, I remained three months in England, drawing
myself down towards Scotland (as I wrote unto you) by the
mean of Monsieur Mauvissiere, of whom I spake with you
many times before my departure. But when I was entered
Scotland, I found things fall out far otherwise than I looked
for. And so I must either swear to be true to the King in
that extremity, or else depart, I know not whither. If I had
practised with Mr. Randall,* it had been present death to me;
besides, he disgraced me all he could: and if I had written to
your Honour, I had surely smarted for it; so that sufferance
and silence were my only succour. All which notwithstanding, I obtained licence at length to make my supplication to
the noble Parliament house; but I could find no messengers till
Sir John Seton went, whom I importunated daily to obtain
me favour for my return home again. But God knoweth
every thing went awry, and I stuck fast in the stocks among
many wild wolves and cruel tigers in the shapes of men, who
would have worried and torn me in pieces had not the King's
goodness guarded me; such is their uncivil manner and
malice, and such cankered stomachs they bear to an Englishman. I gave the King a book before I departed thence,
which manifested much their rudeness. If I had tarried
there never so little longer, no doubt it had cost me my life;
but God be thanked for a fair escape, most miserable wretch
that I am. How cursed may I seem after all these storms
if I have lost her Majesty's favour. I desire not to live longer
than I may enjoy her good opinion. I crave no more for all
my service than her gracious countenance; and, that not
granted, I wish I were either buried quick, or that the seas

* Thomas Randolph.

had swallowed me. I never meant to offend her Highness willingly, I take God to witness; and when I was sworn at the Council-board of Scotland,* all the Lords can testify that I protested openly I would never be false to the Queen's Majesty and my Country. And so, with a true face and clear conscience, I have humbled my body and life to her mercy. Wherefore, as I have ever boldly reposed my hope only in your honourable goodness, so I beseech you vouchsafe me some comfort, who still prayeth for the increase of your good gifts of grace in preservation of honour. From Berwick, 23rd June 1581. Your Honour's humbly at commandment,

THO. CHURCHYARD.[b]

Lord Grey finding, like so many of Queen Elizabeth's servants, that his most zealous exertions did not satisfy her, he, like them, used his private influence to be removed from his employment, and for that purpose wrote to Hatton:—

TO SIR CHRISTOPHER HATTON.

SIR, Because I have certified my Lords in a general letter of the present estate of this Country, and of the fruit of my last journey, I have not thought good to trouble you further therewith at this instant, but to refer you wholly to that advertisement. Wherein perceiving, that, notwithstanding all my endeavour and continual pains which I have taken here to advance her Majesty's service, I can no way so well satisfy her Highness as I have dutifully sought and ever wished for, my most earnest desire is, to be now disburdened of so thankless a place, and that some other, that with better liking and more sufficiency can answer that expectation, may be called hither. I am moved herein to crave your furtherance, both in regard of her Majesty's service, which I wish might take as happy success as herself desireth, as also for her better contentation and my own quietness. And yet my conscience

---

* A marginal note says, "He   Scotland to be true to the King." was sworn at the Council-board of

[b] Additional MSS. 15891, f. 64.

in the comfortless impression of this disfavour will always bear me witness that I rest simply blameless herein towards her Majesty, whose service never forslowing, I have ever followed with all dutiful care and travail, as faithfully as the power of my body and mind would give me leave. If the sway have been beyond my strength, the blame is justly theirs whose choice was no better; and not mine, that did plainly and simply at the first reveal that little which I found in myself for so great a charge. In this cause, that toucheth me so dear, I am now forced to fly to your promised friendship for the removing of me from hence; whereof I make the more assured account, for that I have ever found it ready in my causes of less importance. And so, earnestly praying herein your honourable solicitation and good furtherance, I commit you to the grace of God. From Dublin, the 1st of July 1581. Your most assured friend and loving kinsman,   A. GREY.[a]

Churchyard, having it appears slain a man, was imprisoned, and, being nearly destitute, he made a very ingenious application to Hatton for relief. The " poor present," of which he speaks, was no doubt one of the innumerable effusions of his prolific pen:—

THOMAS CHURCHYARD TO SIR CHRISTOPHER HATTON.

SIR, Your honourable and courteous taking of my small pains, with the great regard which you had of my patience in these troubles, doth comfort me so much, as my happiness in sending unto you and your goodness in accepting my letters are at strife, the one with the other, which of them both do best deserve the victory. But finding it folly by late experience to depend on fortune, and resting wholly upon God's direction and on the goodness of my friends, your favourable acceptation of my poor present doth richly reward me for my work, and conquereth both my fortune and all other vain hope that my presumptuous pen might give me. God, that worketh all goodness by worthy instruments, hath offered me great

[a] Additional MSS. 15891, f. 64.

good hap, and wrought a perfect means to restore me to liberty. The man's wife whose husband I slew is contented to abandon her suit, and henceforth to surcease her malice, so that I hope I shall presently depart from prison, though not able (poor wretch as I am) to depart with any money. The divers occasions of expense in my restraint have taken from me the best part of my purse, and only left me the bare strings to play withal. I blush, being old, to beg; and yet not ashamed to crave, being a courtier. A soldier should rather snatch than stand at world's benevolence; but no man appoints his own portion, and men often fare the worse for snatching too boldly. Well! I want, and how to get requires a cunning reach; and then is simplicity but a very blunt hook to take that which may supply a man's necessity. Why fear I my feebleness? the fortune of Poets hath been ever poor and needy. Homer had but one eye, and knew not where to dine; Ovid had two eyes, and yet could see but few that did him good; Virgil, Petrarch, Dante, Marshall, Marot, and many more, were poor and rich, but not to continue; and may not I presume among them, as poor as the best, and a writer not always among the worst? Though not a Poet, yet one that hath used both pen and sword with Poet's fortune, as well as they, to my own hindrance. Your Honour seeth my defects, and may easily help them, when you please, with some small remembrance of your bounty and goodness. I write not this to crave, but only desire some means to enlarge me, the sooner to drive away this indigence. Your Honour's servants, or whosoever please you, may now be welcome and visit me when they will in this sweet comfort and expectation of present liberty, and bring that with them which a prisoner is glad to see, and will be ever most joyfully willing to receive, whatsoever shall proceed from your accustomed goodness, whom I commit to the grace of God. From the Palace of Repentance, the 10th of July 1581. Humbly at your Honour's commandment,

T. CHURCHYARD.*

---

* Additional MSS. 15891, f. 60ᵇ.

The Earl of Oxford's ill-treatment of his wife, who was Lord Burghley's daughter, has been already mentioned;* and, Hatton having interested the Queen in the lady's behalf, her father wrote to thank him for his exertions. The "disaster betwixt two great Planets" was no doubt a quarrel between the Earls of Leicester and Sussex :—

TO SIR CHRISTOPHER HATTON.

Sir, Though I cannot always pay my debts, yet I use to acknowledge them many times to move my creditors to accept my good-will in towardness of payment; and so at this time, though I know myself many ways indebted unto you for your good-will, except you will accept for acquittal my reciproque good-will, I shall not be able to pay you that I owe you. Yet yesterday, being advertised of your good and honourable dealing with her Majesty in the case of my daughter of Oxford, I could not suffer my thanks to grow above one day old; and therefore in these few lines I do presently thank you, and do pray you in any proceeding therein not to have the Earl dealt withal strainably, but only by way of advice, as good for himself; for otherwise he may suspect that I regard myself more for my daughter than he is regarded for his liberty. I know only the Queen's Majesty's motions shall further the cause, and more than her motions I wish not. You see, being a debtor, I prescribe my manner to increase the debt; but, if I cannot acquit it, I know it belongeth to Almighty God to do it. I am most sorry to hear of the disaster fallen out yesterday betwixt two great Planets; but I hear they know their Jupiter, and will obey her Majesty, rather to content her than to follow their own humours. It is far out of season to have these breaches; our adversaries are ever ready to make them greater, and to leap in also to our common harm. I am not yet fully recovered; this north-west

* Vide p. 17, *ante.*

wind keepeth me back from my port of health, which God
send you ever, with increase of honour. 13th July 1581.

Yours assuredly,   W. BURLEIGH.[a]

Sir Thomas Heneage also alludes to the quarrel of
Leicester and Sussex, in the following letter. Lady
Heneage was Ann, daughter of Sir Nicholas Poyntz,
and died in November 1593:—

TO SIR CHRISTOPHER HATTON.

SIR, My extreme pain of the stone will make me write
shorter than I would or should. For your buttons, which I
bought for you, and would never have worn if I had thought
you would after have used them, I refer to your own best
liking whether I shall return them, or pay for them; and,
how well soever they like me, I like better to please you than
myself in a greater matter than this, as you shall ever find.
For your favour in commending my duty to her Majesty,
which showeth the nobleness and goodness of your condition
towards them that dearliest love you, I think myself principally bound unto you; and though her Highness' liking as
well for myself as her service shall ever be a law to me, yet
my wife's leg, that still holdeth her in her bed, as well as my
own present and sudden sickness of the stone, will hold me
here longer than I meant. I leave to tell you my mind of
the matter of quarrel till my body be more quiet, taking it
most kindly that you will but some time wish him with you,
that will ever love you; and so I commend me all unto you,
and us both to the Lord Jesus. The 15th of July 1581.

Your own, sick and whole,   T. HENEAGE.[b]

When the next letter was written, Sir Francis Walsingham was at Bologne, on his way to Paris to assist Lord
Cobham and Mr. Sommers in persuading the French King
to agree to certain propositions respecting the Queen's

---

[a] Additional MSS. 15891, f. 73.   [b] Additional MSS. 15891, f. 73[b].

marriage, and to consent to a League offensive and defensive between England and France. Walsingham's instructions, and great part of his correspondence (but not his letters to Hatton), while on this mission, are printed in " The Compleat Ambassador." [a]

TO SIR CHRISTOPHER HATTON.

SIR, Upon better consideration of the request I made unto you before my departure, to have moved her Majesty for the stalment of my debt due unto her Majesty, (to which purpose it was resolved between us that I should have written a letter unto you to that effect, whereby you might have taken the better opportunity to have moved her therein,) I have now changed my opinion, meaning to stay until my return. In the mean time, notwithstanding, I cannot but most heartily thank you for your honourable offer made in that behalf. Hitherto my success, both by sea and by land, (I thank God for it,) hath been such as I could desire. But I fear in the end, when I shall come to the matter, I shall not perform that which is looked for by her Majesty; not for lack of care or due endeavour in me, but through the weak and slender direction I am sent withal: and yet, perhaps, if the success fall not out according to expectation, the blame will be laid upon the poor Minister. This my doubt is greatly relieved through the assurance I have of your honourable and friendly defence of your absent friend. And so I commit you to God. At Bologne, 17th of July 1581. Your assured friend,

FRAN. WALSINGHAM.[b]

Poor Churchyard's situation again compelled him to implore his patron's assistance. The importunity of all who were in distress, for on the same day Hatton received a similar letter from Charles Arundell, must have been extremely painful; but they justify an inference

---

[a] Edited by Sir Dudley Digges, folio, 1655.　[b] Additional MSS. 15891, f. 70.

highly favourable to his character, since the wretched rarely appeal to the obdurate or heartless.

TO SIR CHRISTOPHER HATTON.

My duty most humbly remembered. Your Honour knoweth my calamity—long letters purchase small benefit, as the weight of my sorrow showeth. God and good men must help; and, in the number of the good, yourself is one in my poor judgment that may and will do what may most relieve me. I beseech you then weigh my affliction, and so work as the world may behold your integrity and upright dealing, to God's glory and to your own immortal fame. I live in misery; stained in credit, cut off from the world, hated of some that loved me, holpen of none, and forsaken of all; for what just cause I know not. My distress is great, my calling simple, and not able to avail anything without the assistance of your goodness. For God's sake, bring me to my answer; and, as you shall see it fall out, my accusers can prove nothing against me. Vouchsafe me speedy remedy, or, at the least, the justice of the law and the benefit of my Country; and, if I have failed of my duty willingly, let me feel the price of it. I crave no pardon, but humbly sue for favourable expedition; for the which I appeal to your honourable judgment, and pray for your good success in all your desires. From the Marshalsea, the 20th of July 1581. Your Honour's in all faithful devotion,   T. CHURCHYARD.*

TO SIR CHRISTOPHER HATTON.

SIR, It is a fault in grief, that either it complaineth too much, or else saith nothing: and yet, for my own part, I seek as much as I can to shun extremities. I have largely unfolded my whole estate to this bearer, because I would not be cumbersome unto you; only craving of charity and justice that my trial, which hath been long promised, may

* Additional MSS. 15891, f. 63.

not be any longer deferred : for then shall my enemies sink with shame, and I depart out of the field with honour; and whatsoever either malice hath unjustly built, or a fool devised upon a false ground, must play castle-come-down, and dissolve to nothing. And all that I have said or set down shall be confirmed by the formal depositions and oaths of those who were present when he talked idly, and told wonders. I will say no more until either trial or liberty may be obtained, which I wish to enjoy by your mediation, whom I commit to the grace of God. From Sutton, the 20th of July 1581. Your Honour's fast and unfeigned friend,   CHA. ARUNDELL.[a]

Sir Thomas Heneage was Treasurer of the Chamber, from whose office payments for couriers and special messengers were made, which explains this letter :—

TO SIR CHRISTOPHER HATTON.

SIR, I understand Mr. Secretary goeth presently into France ; and therefore, both for her Majesty's service and mine own discharge, I have thought good to let you know that in his absence I can grant no allowance to any gentleman, or courier that shall carry letters to or from him, except they be signed with the hand of my Lord Treasurer, my Lord Chamberlain, or yourself. Wherefore, as occasion may fall out for her Majesty's service, I beseech you my servant may attend on you to inform you of the right order of these dispatches for my discharge. And so I pray God to bless you with health, and honour, and the happiness I would myself. From Copthall, the 23rd of July 1581. Your own bound to love you,   T. HENEAGE.[b]

When the manner in which the Queen was importuned by her Courtiers for grants of every kind is remembered, the fact stated by Walsingham when making a

---

[a] Additional MSS. 15891, f. 79b.   [b] Additional MSS. 15891, f. 63b.

request for his brother-in-law, Mr. St. Barbe, that he had never asked a favour during the eight years he had been in her service, is very remarkable; but it is consistent with the integrity of his character, and accounts for the honourable poverty in which he lived and died :—

SIR FRANCIS WALSINGHAM TO SIR CHRISTOPHER HATTON.

SIR, The Dean and Chapter of Winchester are content at the request of this gentleman, my wife's brother, to grant him a lease in reversion of their parsonage of Hursley in the county of Southampton for fifty years, in respect of the well-deserving of their house, as well of his father as of his elder brother deceased, who were both their Officers for the receiving of their rents; a matter usual and common among them to pleasure those gentlemen with such like grants that have any doings for them touching their lands. But they desire, for their more orderly granting of the same, that her Majesty, to whom the lease is to be passed to his use, would write her letter unto them in commendation of the suit; upon the receipt whereof they will not fail to grant it, being of themselves already very forward to pleasure him therein. My request unto you therefore is, that it would please you to favour the gentleman so much for my sake as to move her Majesty in the matter, and procure her hand to the letter to be directed to the Dean and Chapter, which I send you herewith inclosed ready for her signature; not doubting but that by your good means her Majesty will easily be drawn to yield to so reasonable a suit, being no way any loss or hindrance to herself; and the now tenant of the thing no old tenant, but one that bought it very lately, and otherwise of so great wealth and ability that he may well forbear the profit of it, without any such prejudice to his estate as may justly be drawn into consideration to move her Majesty to mislike of the suit; wherein I am besides persuaded she will the rather incline to do the gentleman good, for that he is brother to a gentlewoman of whom she seemeth to have a

good liking.   In the moving of the matter it may please you
to put her Majesty in mind, that, in eight years' time wherein
I have served her, I never yet troubled her for the benefiting
of any that belonged unto me, either by kindred or otherwise;
which I think never any other could say that served in the
like place.   And so, once again praying you that it will please
you to deal effectually in this cause, for your travail wherein
I shall think myself greatly beholding unto you, I commit
you to God's good keeping.   At Bologne, the 27th of July
1581.   Your very assured friend,

FRAN. WALSINGHAM.*

Dr. Mathew, then a candidate for the Deanery of
Durham, was the Dr. Toby Mathew from whom several
letters have been inserted.   Many others will be found
from him on this subject; and, though he succeeded in his
wishes, it was not until August 1583.   He was afterwards Bishop of that diocese, and in 1606 became
Archbishop of York:—

SIR THOMAS HENEAGE TO SIR CHRISTOPHER HATTON.

SIR, I received a message from you by Lee, my man, yesterday, that when I liked to come to the Court, if you might
know it, you would make my way to be presently welcome.
Surely, Sir, it is a place I do honour and esteem, and would
be glad to be welcome to; but to come thither before I should
be welcome accordeth little with reason, and less with my
liking, except it were to do service to such as I am bound
to love, which is yourself and a few others.   By letters which
my Lord of Leicester wrote unto me from Wanstead, (which
I have sent you to peruse,) it appeareth that her Majesty
is neither well pleased with my absence, nor in anywise contented I should come over soon.   My wife's sickness and
lameness, so as she could not stir out of her bed, was the
cause I could neither in reason nor honesty come out from

* Additional MSS. 15891, f. 70ᵇ.

my house till she were better amended. And now, to come before her Majesty thought it fit, you know it were very inconvenient; wherefore I beseech you let me know your mind how long or short my return may be with her Majesty's best expectations, and I shall appoint myself so as I may know from you how best to please her. Sir, by my entreaty, Mr. Secretary Walsingham hath been a mean to her Majesty for the Deanery of Durham for Mr. Doctor Mathew, and found her Highness well-disposed therein. He hath prayed me to be a means likewise unto you to further him, which he will deserve with his prayers and all thankful service towards you. A man of the Church more fit for the Church than himself I know not in all England, nor more worthy to be preferred. My most earnest desire therefore is, that it would please you to help him, as a man well deserving advancement, and one whom you may command. Besides, I am most humbly to pray you for a poor man of mine, John de Vique, (that useth with great diligence to carry the Queen's packet,) that it would please you to grant him the next dispatch to Mr. Secretary, or otherwise but your own letters of advertisements unto him, which he will carry with all speed and faithfulness; and they, with my Lord of Leicester's, which I will procure, may draw him some little allowance. Further I will not trouble you, but ever love and honour you. From my house at Copthall, 30th July 1581. Your own bound to you,

T. HENEAGE.[*]

The wardship, which led to the imprisonment of the person mentioned by the Chancellor of the Exchequer, seems to have been granted to his son, Mr. Mildmay; whose interests, under that iniquitous and tyrannical system, were in some way affected by the conduct of the lady's husband, most probably in defence of what would now be considered to have been his own property.

[*] Additional MSS. 15891, f. 63.

TO SIR CHRISTOPHER HATTON.

SIR, Being informed that Mrs. T. is an earnest suitor at the Court by means of her Majesty for the enlargement of her husband, committed by the Lord Treasurer in the Court of Wards for such a contempt against her Majesty's authority in that Court as none before this durst ever attempt, I have thought good to send up this bearer, my son, both to hearken to her doings and to impeach anything that she goeth about to work indirectly upon untrue surmises; and because my son in this matter from the beginning hath been much bound unto you, I am the rather bold to make you thus far acquainted, and therewith also to pray you to favour and further him as he shall have occasion to desire your aid. I trust her Majesty will be gracious herein, and not to incline to favour them that so unjustly have sought to benefit themselves to the manifest injury of others, and now seek to conceal the proceeding of that whereby they claim; the matter also toucheth her Majesty, for, if this may be suffered, it may reach to her prejudice in greater things. And so, recommending the cause to your friendly and good remembrance, I leave to trouble you any further; but with most hearty commendation do wish unto you all prosperity in God Almighty. From Apthorpe, the 6th of August 1581. Your assured loving friend,   W. MILDMAY.[a]

"Danger of infection," the constant bugbear of the time, was the principal theme of numerous letters :—

SIR THOMAS HENEAGE TO SIR CHRISTOPHER HATTON.

SIR, I perceive by your letter her Majesty's pleasure is, I should, ere I came to her presence, remove from my own house to some other air. To obey her Highness's liking, which I esteem as my life, as soon as I can conveniently I will get me hence, though I know not yet whither to wander. You

---

[a] Additional MSS. 15891, f. 80ᵇ.

shall still understand what becometh of me; and I most earnestly beseech you that I may know from you from time to time how her Majesty and yourself doth.   And so, wishing you in my banishment the company most contents you, and none that loved you worse than myself, I commend me humbly unto you; and so doth my wife, your poor friend, not yet all recovered. From Copthall, the 7th of August 1581.   Your own at commandment,

THO. HENEAGE.[a]

Upon the day on which Walsingham wrote the annexed private letter to Hatton, (if its date be correct,) he made two reports of his proceedings, one to the Queen, and the other to Lord Burghley,[b] but in neither did he mention the same facts.   His other letters from Paris are also silent about Monsieur's having relieved Cambray, which was besieged by the Prince of Parma; but on the 24th of August Lord Burghley informed Walsingham of the Queen's satisfaction that Monsieur had "entered Cambray according to his honourable intention and promise, so as her Majesty rejoiceth greatly with this his fruits of so great an enterprize."[c]

SIR FRANCIS WALSINGHAM TO SIR CHRISTOPHER HATTON.

SIR, The matter of the treaty of the League is now brought to this pass with Monsieur, that he hath wholly referred the same to the King, to be proceeded in without marriage if it shall so like him, so that there be nothing concluded in the said treaty that may anyways be prejudicial to the marriage; whereupon it will shortly appear what issue the matter is like to have.   There came news yesternight to this town, that Monsieur was entered into Cambray, which were very well welcome to all those that are sound and well affected to

---

[a] Additional MSS. 15891, f. 85.
[b] Compleat Ambassador, p. 392.   [c] Ibid. p. 397.

this State, but as ill-come to divers that are at the devotion
of Spain. This happy beginning was accompanied with the
mishap of the loss of the Viscount of Tureen, who, hazarding himself to have entered into the town with fourscore
and ten horse, or thereabouts, was charged and taken by the
enemy, and all his company (some very few only excepted
that got into the town) taken or slain. The loss is great of
the gentleman, being of that virtue and value that he was,
and one so earnestly devoted to her Majesty as no nobleman
in France more. And thus I commit you to God. At Paris,
the 10th of August 1581. Your very assured friend,

FRA. WALSINGHAM.*

Lord Grey gave Sir Christopher Hatton further information of his proceedings in Ireland, on the 12th of
August:—

TO SIR CHRISTOPHER HATTON.

Sir, As your manifold courtesies have given me cause,
so could I not choose, reputing you in the number of my
best friends there, but yield you my right hearty thanks
for the same; taking the opportunity of this messenger expressly to salute you. I forbear to trouble you with the
particulars of my late journey into the North parts, for because I know you shall be partaker of them by my letters
which I sent unto their Lordships. If her Majesty would
have been pleased to have granted my demands, I would
not have doubted, with the assistance of God, but to have
settled some better order in this journey, as well in suppressing the pride of Tirlough, as also in expulsing the
Scots. But being now tied to those directions, which were
set down by the table there, and her Majesty's disposition
to peace, I have done my best endeavour to follow the
one and to satisfy the other. I have, against my will,
concluded, or rather patched up, a peace with Tirlough;

* Additional MSS. 15891, f. 96.

being such, indeed, as I can neither repose any assurance
in the continuance of it, nor for the honour of it justly
commend it.   The best is, that by this occasion some time
may be won, to yield us the more liberty to deal with
the mountain rebels; against whom I purpose, with God's
help, to bend myself with all present speed.   I beseech
you to have in remembrance the gentleman whom, before
my departure thence, you so often commended unto me;
I mean Ned Denny; that through your honourable mediation he may find her Majesty gracious in his old suit,
without the which, his forwardness to countenance her Majesty's service will bring him to late repentance, and deeply
touch him in credit.   I most earnestly pray you, therefore,
to stand to him, and you shall no less increase my band
towards you through your good favour vouchsafed him
therein, than bind the gentleman himself to remain ever
yours in all faithful devotion.   And so I commit you to
God.   From Dublin, the 12th of August 1581.   Your
assured friend and most loving cousin,   A. GREY.*

Hatton seems, from the following letter, to have wished that his nephew, Mr. Newport, should make a cam-
paign under the Duke of Anjou in the Low Countries; but
Walsingham considered that his reception by the Prince
would depend upon the Queen's acceding to his Highness'
request for a loan.   Elizabeth's usual parsimony showed
itself about the expenses of Drake's voyage; and Lord
Burghley wrote to Walsingham on the 18th of August,
" Now that all things are ready, as ships, victuals, men,
&c., the charge whereof cometh to 12,000l., she hath been
moved to impart 2000l. more, as a thing needful for the
full furniture of this voyage; wherewith she is greatly
offended with Mr. Hawkins and Drake that the charges
are grown so great above that was said to her when the

* Additional MSS. 15891, f. 85.

5000*l.* was demanded of her." [a]   On the 24th of August Burghley informed him that "her Majesty seemeth resolutely bent not to exceed 5000*l.*, whereby your charge is the greater, which I have essayed to qualify as if it had been my own case." [b]

SIR FRANCIS WALSINGHAM TO SIR CHRISTOPHER HATTON.

SIR, After the closing up of my former, I received your letters by your servant Pyne, wherein you recommend your nephew unto my favour, and best advice for his preferment into Monsieur's service in this journey for the Low Countries. Concerning which matter I am to let you understand, that, at Mr. Sommers' late being with Monsieur, he proposed a motion for a loan of money to be granted him by her Majesty, for the better furnishing of his necessities in those actions he is entered into. If this request be hearkened unto by her Majesty with effect, then is it well to be thought that any English gentleman that shall come to serve him shall be well accepted; but if it happen otherwise, no doubt their entertainment will be cold, and not worthy the embracing. In which respect my advice is, that it were first best to attend how her Majesty will resolve that way; which falling out accordingly to the P   's[c] desire, I will then both advertize you what I think meet to be provided there, and send over for this gentleman; and further give him the best advice and direction how to carry himself there, and the best address to be well received, that I can. I hear that I stand in so hard terms with her Majesty as I fear any persuasion I can use in furtherance of Sir Francis Drake's voyage will rather hurt than help. I am blamed as a principal counsellor thereof; and though I did concur with the rest in matter of advice, yet I do assure myself that her Majesty shall, ere a few months come to an end, have more cause to allow of the authors

---

[a] Compleat Ambassador, p. 388.   [b] Ibid. p. 395.
[c] A cypher, rather than a word, occurs here.

of that council than of the dissuaders thereof. The mischief will be, that the remedy will not be allowed of until
it be too late to apply it.   And so, with my hearty thanks
for your friendly and courteous letters, I commit you to
God.   From Paris, the 20th of August 1581.   Your assured
loving friend,   FRA. WALSINGHAM.[*]

The learned and accomplished Lord Buckhurst, afterwards Earl of Dorset, in asking Hatton's patronage for
another, expresses the deepest sense of his own obligations to him:—

LORD BUCKHURST TO SIR CHRISTOPHER HATTON.

SIR, I know well enough, that, of your own good disposition towards this gentleman, you are forward of yourself to further his poor suit now in hand.   But I that do
haply see more than another how much it importeth him
to have a speedy end, and that delay and protraction of
time will easily consume both him and the benefit which,
with the help of your goodness, he is like to reap by the
same, cannot but earnestly intreat the continuance of your
favour toward him, and that you would be pleased to bind
for ever unto you so worthy a gentleman.   Good Mr. Vice-
Chamberlain, remember that without your help and honourable mediation he is like to sink in his adversity, and that
it is needful he should in some sort be relieved.   Yourself was first pleased to become the only mean to her
Majesty for him: there wanteth nothing now but that you
would effectually perfect so noble a work as you have vouchsafed to begin in his favour; for which God shall reward
you, the gentleman shall serve you, and I shall for ever,
as you have bound me, both love and honour you; adding
this to the great heap of the rest of your favours towards
me, which burden me so much, as, being unable to requite

* Additional MSS. 15891, f. 91.

them, I must be forced to sink and fall down underneath
them. And thus, resting ever your own, I forbear any more
to trouble you. 30th August 1581. Your own assured for
ever,   T. BUCKHURST.[*]

The Deanery of Durham became vacant by the death
of Sir Thomas Wilson, the late Secretary of State, in
1581; and Dr. Mathew, as has been already observed,
was a candidate for the appointment, which he obtained
in August 1583, when the office had been vacant two
years. His letter to Sir Thomas Heneage shows the
great competition there was for the Deanery, and the
natural indignation of the learned divine, that a physician, and "such a man, by such means," should have
had the least chance of success:—

DR. MATHEW TO SIR THOMAS HENEAGE.

SIR, I beseech you first accept my humble thanks for
that exceeding great care which I do hear it pleaseth you
to continue in my cause; very tedious, I am sure, to you,
and almost desperate to me, if that be true which is reported. It is said, great and mighty means are made for
one Mr. Bellamy a physician: I pray God, with all my
heart, that country stand more in need of physic than of
divinity; not that I wish the people sick in their bodies,
but saved in their souls. If _aurum potabile_ be so full and
effectual in operation, I can find no fault with so many
that have spent so much to make elixir, the philosopher's
stone, whereout is to be drawn _quidlibet ex quolibet:_ and
then that old paradox, _omnia sunt unum,_ is verified by a new
device. But, good Sir Thomas Heneage, is all your good
purpose, your great persuasions, your favourable letters,
your open and often speeches, come to this issue, that Doctor Bellamy, professed in physic, a stranger at Court, never
seen there yet, never heard of till now, and now spoken

* Additional MSS. 15891, f. 78[b].

of abroad, and broadly enough, shall run away with such
a room; I say not from me, that am less than the least,
but from all the chaplains her Majesty hath, from all the
learned known reputed preachers in Oxon, in Cambridge,
in all this realm? Have I (poor man) intreated my Lord,
mine old Master, chiefly by yourself, by my Lord of York's
grace, by my Lord of Sarum, by Mr. Captain Horsey,
Mr. Philip Sidney, &c.; hath my Lord of Warwick been
contented to stay his own suit for Mr. Griffin, in respect
of me, that a third man, and such a man, and by such
means, may prevent both us and all others? I humbly beseech you, Sir, continue forth your favour yet still, till the
success and event be seen. Hit I or miss I, I shall all one
most bounden unto you, though not able alike to be thankful unto you. There be good causes that move me to be
now more earnest than ever I was. I would before this
have been at the Court, but for your absence: if you be
now returned, and think my presence might lessen your
labour, or further the suit, I will, upon any the least word
from you, repair thither, and so expect Mr. Secretary's
arrival. And so I humbly commend you and the good virtuous lady to the Lord Jesus. Sarum, 7th September 1581.

Yours, humble and bounden,   TOBIAS MATHEW.*

Walsingham's and his colleagues' official report of his
last interview with the French King, as well as his
private letter, both written on the same day as the
following one to Hatton hitherto unprinted, are in the
" Compleat Ambassador":—

SIR FRANCIS WALSINGHAM TO SIR CHRISTOPHER HATTON.

SIR, I write the less unto you at this present, for that I
hope to see you shortly, having taken this day my leave of
the King and Queen Mother. The only comfort I can take
of this voyage is, that though I have done no good, yet have I

* Additional MSS. 15891, f. 87.

done no harm, otherwise than that I spent the King and Queen's money. I mean, in my way homeward to visit the Duke of Anjou; at what time I will not fail to recommend your nephew, as also your particular desire you have to do him honour and service. By a letter I received this day from him, I do find that he meaneth, notwithstanding that there are divers of his troops gone away from him, to continue in the field the space of six weeks; in which time your nephew shall taste the incommodities of the war, especially now that the winter approacheth. And so, hoping shortly to see you, I commit you in the meantime to the protection of Almighty God. From Paris, the 12th of September 1581. Yours, most assuredly,

Fra. Walsingham.[a]

Sir Francis Walsingham's letters to the Queen form a striking contrast to those of her other Ministers. Neither Burghley nor Leicester, nor even Hatton, ever presumed to remonstrance so firmly, nor to vindicate themselves so boldly, as Walsingham did, whenever he thought it was his duty to speak the truth either in relation to her interests or his own character. There is also an honest frankness in his style, which is quite refreshing after reading the vapid adulation of his contemporaries; and in no part of his correspondence is this more remarkable than in the following fine letter. Who but Walsingham would have dared to reproach Elizabeth for having condemned him unheard, or, after justifying his own conduct, have ventured to tell her plainly, that, if she really meant to marry at her " years," she had no time to lose; that her meanness about money ruined all her projects; that it had lost her Scotland, and that it was likely to lose her England; that no Foreign power valued her friendship, because whenever money was wanted,

[a] Additional MSS. 15891, f. 95ᵇ.

she would do nothing unless it were " underhand,"
and that her predecessors never acted in such a manner?
While on that subject, he adverted to her treatment
of the Earl of Shrewsbury, whose allowance for keeping
the Queen of Scots, whom Walsingham calls " the bosom
serpent," it was proposed to reduce, though the Earl
was then driven to such extremity as to have contemplated the sale of all his plate ;[*] and he concludes with
the emphatic declaration, that, if the Queen persisted in
such a course, every one of her true counsellors would
prefer being in the furthest part of Æthiopia, to the
enjoyment of the finest palace in England.   It was,
however, no small merit in Elizabeth to have appreciated
Walsingham's integrity of purpose, for, though rarely in
favour, she was fully conscious of his merits.

SIR FRANCIS WALSINGHAM TO THE QUEEN.

It may please your most excellent Majesty, the laws of
Æthiopia, my native soil, are very severe against those that
condemn a person unheard, but most sharp against such as do
judge amiss of those that sit in Princely chair, as Gods here on
earth.   To tell your Majesty what others conceive upon the
late stay here of our proceedings (who can not think that such
effects should grow upon naked and weak causes), I hope is
not to condemn, as by your letter, which it pleased your Majesty to vouchsafe to write unto me, it seemeth you conceive.
When I either look into your Highness's own princely judgment (who for your own honour's sake ought to have care to preserve your Minister's credit), or consider my own duty, which
teacheth me not to condemn those whom I am bound to defend, I should then be worthy to receive the sharpest punishment that either the Æthiopians' severity or Draco's laws
can yield, if I should wittingly by wrong supposal grow to

---

[*] See a Letter from the Earl of   February in this year, in Lodge's
Shrewsbury, dated on the 23rd of   Illustrations, ii. 196.

so hard a censure as to think that your Majesty should prefer
in a matter of trust a stranger, before a servant who in loyalty will give place to neither subject nor stranger.   I cannot
deny but I have been infinitely grieved to see the desire I have had to do your Majesty some acceptable service in
the present charge committed unto me, to be so greatly
crossed.   But I will leave to touch my particular, though I
have as great cause as any man that ever served in the place
I now unworthily supply; being at home always subject to
sundry strange jealousies, and in foreign service to displeasure, though I dare make the greatest enemy that I have the
censurer of my actions and proceedings in such foreign
charges as have been committed unto me.   But now to your
public, wherein if anything shall escape my pen that may
breed offence, I most humbly beseech your Majesty to ascribe
that it proceedeth of love, which can never bring forth ill-
effects, though sometime they may be subject to sharp cen-
sures.   And first for your Majesty's marriage; if you mean
it, and your proceeding therein doth give the world cause to
judge the contrary, remember then, I most humbly beseech
you, that by the delay your Highness useth therein you lose
the benefit of time, which (your years considered) is not the
least thing to be weighed; if you mean it not, then assure
yourself it is one of the worst remedies your Highness can
use, howsoever you conceive that it serveth your turn.   And
as for the League that we were in hand withal, if the King
would have assented that the same should have proceeded in
general terms according to such direction as we have lately
received from your Majesty, I am for sundry causes led to
think that it would have proved as unprofitable as general.   I
know that there is a precedent to confirm the same: but if in
that time a King of Scots, pretending title to the Crown of
England, were like, by matching with Spain, to have wrought
that peril toward your Majesty's father as he is towards you,
he would not then have stood upon generality, as your Majesty doth now; for in diseased bodies there is not always
like use of medicines.   Sometime, when your Majesty doth

behold in what doubtful terms you stand with Foreign Princes, then do you wish with great affection that opportunity offered had not been overslipped; but when they are offered unto you, then, if they be accompanied with charges, they are altogether neglected. Common experience teacheth that it is as hard in a politic body to prevent any mischief without charges, as in a natural body diseased to cure the same without pain. Remember, I humbly beseech your Majesty, that respect of charges hath lost Scotland; and I would to God I had no cause to think that it might put your Majesty in peril of the loss of England. I see it, and they here stick not to say it, that the only cause that moveth them not to weigh your Majesty's friendship is, for that they see you do fly charges otherwise than by doing somewhat underhand. It is strange, considering in what state your Majesty standeth, that, in all the directions that we have now received, we have special order not to yield to anything that may be accompanied with charges. The general league must be without any certain limitation of expense; the particular, with a voluntary, and no certain charge; as also that which is to be attempted in favour of Don Antonio.* The best is, that if they were, as they are not, inclined to deal in any of these points, then were they surely like to receive but small comfort for anything we have direction to assent unto. Heretofore your Majesty's predecessors in matter of peril did never look into charges; when their treasure was neither so great as your Majesty's is, nor their Subjects so wealthy nor so willing to contribute. A person that is diseased, if he look only upon the medicine, without regard of the pain he sustaineth, cannot but in reason and nature abhor the same: if there be no peril, then it is in vain to be at charges; but if there be peril, it is hard that charges should be preferred before imminent danger. I pray God the abating of charges towards the nobleman that hath the custody of the bosom serpent hath not lessened his care in keeping of her. To think that in a man of his birth and quality, after twelve years' travail in a

* King of Portugal; vide p. 202, *post*.

charge of so great weight, to have an abatement of allowance, and no recompense otherwise made, should not work some discontentment, no man that hath reason can so judge; and therefore to have so special a charge committed to a person discontented, everybody seeth that it standeth no way with policy. What dangerous effects this loose keeping hath bred, the taking away of Morton, the alteration of the King, and a general revolt in religion intended, wrought altogether by her policy, doth show; and therefore, nothing being done to help the same, is a manifest argument that the peril that is likely to grow thereby is so fatal as it can no way be prevented. I conclude, therefore, (be it spoken in zeal of duty, without offence to your Majesty,) if this sparing and unprovident course be holden on still, (the mischiefs approaching being so apparent as they are,) there is no one that serveth in place of a Counsellor, that either weigheth his own credit, or carrieth that sound affection to your Majesty that he ought to do, that would not wish himself rather in the furthest part of Æthiopia than to enjoy the fairest palace in England. The Lord God, therefore, direct your Majesty's heart to take that way of counsel that may be most for your honour and safety. From Paris, the 12th of September 1581. Your Majesty's most humble, obedient subject and servant,

F. WALSINGHAM.[a]

Another instance of persons being forced by the Court upon the City for appointments, and of the difficulties with which the authorities had to contend, is shown by the following letter from Sir John Branch, the Lord Mayor:—

TO SIR CHRISTOPHER HATTON.

MAY IT PLEASE YOUR HONOUR, Upon the receipt of your letters signifying her Majesty's commendation of William Parker's request to be an alnager, or surveyor of search of

[a] Additional MSS. 15891, f. 93. This letter, with some trifling variations is in the "Compleat Ambas- sador," p. 426, where it is said to have been dated on the 2nd of September.

cloth in this City, we did consider what we reasonably could
for the relieving of Parker, in such manner as might be convenient, without hurt of this City, and our market, and the
commonweal. Some difficulty we find in it, with some other
matters touching Parker as we thought meet to inform your
Honour toward her Majesty's satisfaction; and for that cause
we did appoint some of our brethren to attend upon you, by
whom we had report that they supposed your Honour to be satisfied; so as we hoped we should not have had further following thereof on his behalf, unless he could by agreement with
the other that came in by Parker's nomination have made
a place empty for him. Since that time we perceive that he
hath said that we would make him pay 160*l.* for the office, as
though we, for ourselves, or the City, would take money of
him for an office which we never meant; and therein he
offereth us wrong. Howbeit, because we have again received
your second letters in his favour, and the same thing also preferred to her Majesty, and commended to us by our right honourable the good Lord, the Lord Treasurer (as appeareth in
the postscript of your former letters), we have likewise appointed some of our brethren to attend upon his Lordship, to
inform him also of the state of the causes, as your Honour
hath been, to the intent that her Majesty may have the better
conceiving of our dutiful proceeding. We are therefore
humbly to beseech you to join with his Lordship therein for
satisfying of her Majesty. Nevertheless, we still retain at the
commendation of his Lordship, and specially for the consideration of her Majesty's favour, a purpose to do Parker any
good that we reasonably may; and therefore because, as our
brethren that attended on you have made report unto us,
your Honour, allowing their answer on our behalf to be reasonable, did require their private promises some other way to
relieve him; which because they had no warrant to grant, yet
they have promised to move it among us; we have been
contented, in respect of those from whom he is commended, to
give him at our common charge a pension of 30*l.* yearly during
his good demeanour, and so long as he shall not alien the

same, but keep it to his own use. And this we trust her
Majesty will take in gracious part, and your Honour think
well of our thankfulness towards you. And so we commit you
to the tuition of the Almighty. At London, the 20th of
September 1581. Your Honour's to command.

J. BRANCH.[a]

From Dr. Humphry's letter to Hatton's secretary
Mr. Cox, which seems to belong to this year, it appears
that Cox had, through his patron's influence, in an unu‑
sual manner obtained some piece of preferment in the
gift of Magdalen College, and that it was very unwillingly conferred.

DR. LAURENCE HUMFREY TO MR. SAMUEL COX.

SIR, I have hastened from Winton to Oxford about your
matter, and would before have moved it if I could; you
know that I must follow my course, and keep my time of residence. And now the thing in effect is yours, if by law it
may be conveyed unto you. My company desireth the
Queen's Majesty's letter, as usually is accustomed; best for
our warrant in such an extraordinary case, and most safe for
yourself. Mr. Dr. Bayly was in that piece of policy very
wise, with whom, if it please you, you may consult. We
have drawn all things according to the letter and motion of
my honourable friend Mr. Vice-Chamberlain; but yet we
could not seal it in the absence of others. I am sorry it was
your luck to find out this, which I have denied to my dearest
friends in that shire, being now in the occupation of one who
was my predecessor and president here. The rest you shall
hereafter, and that shortly, understand. God keep you!
Oxon, September 21. Your assured friend,

LAUR. HUMFREY.[b]

Though the Lord Mayor of London has still many

---

[a] Additional MSS. 15891, f. 80.   [b] Additional MSS. 15891, f. 83.

anomalous duties to perform, he is no longer expected to lecture the City clergy. It will be seen that the proceedings of Branch's successor on this subject called forth an indignant letter from the Bishop of London:—

SIR FRANCIS WALSINGHAM TO THE LORD MAYOR OF LONDON.

AFTER my hearty commendations to your good Lordship. Her Majesty being doubtful that certain of the preachers of the City under your charge, provoked perhaps thereunto by a lewd book lately published and seditiously scattered abroad, not only in the City, but in sundry other parts of this Realm, may be drawn to envy against the marriage now in treaty between the Duke of Anjou, the French King's brother, and her Highness, hath therefore thought meet that your Lordship should assemble them to-morrow, and severely to admonish them to have due consideration how they intermeddle in matters of State not incident to their profession and calling; putting them in mind, that, if they would call to their remembrance the most Christian and singular care her Majesty hath always had for the maintenance of true religion, having thereby exposed herself to the malice of the mightiest potentates in Christendom, as one that hath wholly depended upon God's protection, they should then have no cause to doubt that either this match now in treaty, or any other cause, can draw her to do anything that might tend to the prejudice of the same; as one that doth acknowledge that the happiness of her government hath proceeded only from the goodness of God, whom it hath pleased to make her a nurse to his Church; assuredly persuading herself, that, when she should any way decline from the faithful embracing thereof, she should then provoke God in justice to withdraw His merciful and fatherly protection from her. And as she doth think it agreeable to their duties that they forbear to intermeddle with any such matters, so is she pleased to say and conceive in her gracious wisdom that it is meet for men of their callings, in case they shall understand that either by the publishing of

this book, or otherwise by the sinister persuasions of such as
would be glad to breed some disquiet in this state, that any
of her subjects should be carried into some doubt of change
and alteration of religion, that they should seek by all good
and dutiful means to remove all such undutiful and lewd
attempts and conceits of their Prince and Sovereign, under
whom, through God's goodness and her provident care, they
have enjoyed so many peaceable days with liberty and freedom of conscience.   Thus much her Majesty hath willed me
to signify unto your Lordship, not doubting but the good
and godly preachers of that City, upon knowledge of her
Majesty's good-will and pleasure in this behalf, will bend
themselves, as in duty appertaineth, to do that which shall be
most to her Majesty's contentment.   And so I commit your
Lordship to the grace of God.   From Collier Row, by Rum-
ford, the 25th September 1581.   Your Lordship's very loving
friend,   FRA. WALSINGHAM.*

Mr. Newport did, it seems, join the Duke of Anjou's
army, in which Philip Sidney was also serving:—

SIR FRANCIS WALSINGHAM TO SIR CHRISTOPHER HATTON.

SIR, By the inclosed from Mr. Sidney, you may perceive
how desirous he is to return, and what is the impediment:
wherein I am to pray you on his behalf to procure her
Majesty's assent, for that without the same he doubteth he
should offend.   I send you also a letter from your nephew,
by the which you may perceive that the Duke was the 22nd
of this present at Pontdormi, but is now, as I am otherwise
informed, departed from thence to a place called Blangy,
in the way to go to Dieppe; which maketh me to conjecture
that his determination for the Low Countries holdeth not.
I fear that a letter which her Majesty wrote unto him about
ten days past hath wrought that alteration in him; and, if it
fall out so, it will breed a great change in the Low Countries,
such as cannot be but very perilous to her Majesty: so

* Additional MSS. 15891, f. 57.

that it is apparent that danger on all sides groweth fast upon us; which, if it grew not through our own default and lack of providence, I should fear the less. The haste this bearer maketh, forceth me to make an end. At Barn Elms, the 26th of September 1581. Yours most assuredly,

FRA. WALSINGHAM.[a]

"The King," upon whom Philip Sidney describes himself to have been in attendance at Dover in November in this year, must have been Don Antonio, who had been elected King of Portugal by the people; but, being driven out of his dominions by the Spaniards, came to France and thence to England in this year. According to Camden, Elizabeth received him with kindness, and "bountifully relieved him as a kinsman descended from the House of Lancaster;" but this statement does not agree with the account given of the unfortunate Prince's condition by one of his English servants in 1582, who writing to Burghley said, "The King, my master, lies in London in the greatest misery that ever any man lay, desolate not only of necessaries, but of comfort: for he, feeling extreme sick at Uxbridge, sent hither to have the help of one of her Majesty's physicians." No one came however; and he adds, that, if the French Ambassador had not supplied him daily, "the poor Prince had remained altogether without any comfort." Though the Queen had ordered two rooms to be furnished for him, he was then living "between four bare walls, void of all good comfort."[b] Don Antonio was in England several years, and many letters are preserved about his affairs, but it appears

[a] Additional MSS. 15891, f. 83[b].
[b] Wright's Queen Elizabeth and her Times, ii. 176. Other letters relating to Don Antonio are in the same volume, and in the Lansdowne MSS.

from Sidney's letter that in September of this year he was at Dover waiting for his ships from the Thames. It was intended that Sir Francis Drake should assist the Prince in taking the Azores.[a]

MR. PHILIP SIDNEY TO SIR CHRISTOPHER HATTON.

SIR, The delay of this Prince's departure is so long, as truly I grow very weary of it, having divers businesses of mine own and my father's that something import me; and, to deal plainly with you, being grown almost to the bottom of my purse. Therefore your Honour shall do me a singular favour if you can find means to send for me away; the King himself being desirous I should be at the Court to remember him unto her Majesty, where I had been ere this time, but, being sent hither by her Highness, I durst not depart without her especial revocation and commandment. The Queen means, I think, that I should go over with him; which at this present might hinder me greatly, and nothing avail the King for any service I should be able to do him. I find, by him, he will see all his ships out of Thames before he will remove. They are all wind-bound, and the other that came hither, the wind being strainable at the east, hath driven them toward the Isle of Wight, being no safe harbour here to receive them; so that he is constrained to make the longer abode, if it were but to be wafted over. I beseech you, Sir, do me this favour; for which I can promise nothing, seeing all is yours already. At Dover, the 26th September 1581.   Your Honour's humbly at commandment,   P. SIDNEY.[b]

In appearances at least Hatton and Leicester lived on good terms with each other; and every letter that passed between them was, like the annexed, full of expressions of courtesy and good-will:—

[a] Lansdowne MSS. 31, art. 81, 82, 83.   [b] Additional MSS. 15891, f. 61.

THE EARL OF LEICESTER TO SIR CHRISTOPHER HATTON.

MR. CAPTAIN, I have received both your letters at one time, and touching your request in the one for your servant, albeit I did move her Majesty long ago for a very tall and good footman that is my own servant, and one her Majesty did very well allow of, yet for your sake, knowing how far you may dispose of anything in my power, you shall command and be sure of my furtherance for your man before all men. I trust her Highness will give me leave, as all other my predecessors in this office have done, to place these rooms with such persons as I shall prefer; and, if I place any unfit men, let me have blame with their removal: and so, Sir, make your reckoning for your man as far as I have power. I thank you for the comfort you sent me that her Majesty remaineth in her gracious disposition; I will pray for no life to give just cause to the contrary. So, commending me to you as heartily as I can, I bid you as myself farewell, in some haste, greatly occupied with affairs such as you may guess at about this poor house. This 27th September 1581. Yours always assured,   R. LEICESTER.[a]

If success be the proper reward of perseverance and assiduity, Dr. Mathew well deserved the Deanery of Durham. His letter on this subject to Hatton's Secretary explains his motives for so earnestly seeking the appointment:—

DR. MATHEW TO MR. SAMUEL COX.

SIR, For your good friendship I have greatly to thank you already, which if you in my absence continue towards me, you shall doubly make me beholding unto you; in hope whereof, now going to Oxon for a week or more, I think it necessary to put you in remembrance by these few notes. The causes that move me to desire Durham be these, as I have imparted to you, and pray you to inforce them, as you

[a] Additional MSS. 15891, f. 63[b].

can right well, to Mr. Vice-Chamberlain at his good leisure.
First, I seek it not in any ambitious or covetous respect, as
being in degree a place of no greater name than I have
already, and assuredly promising to resign for that alone all
the promotions I have; but rather to deliver myself of a
troublesome room in Oxon full of contention, a kind of life
far from my disposition and further from my profession.
Secondly, the Livings I presently possess, though they be not
so great as they are reported, yet be they more than I would
they were, whereby my body is overtoiled in travailing up
and down, my conscience less quieted, and duty less done in
many than it might in that one.   Thirdly, my good friends
have persuaded me, whom I credit well, it is no small touch
to my poor reputation among men best given in religion, and
to myself not worst affected, that I keep Livings ecclesiastical
so far distant; that albeit I have, nor never had, but one
benefice with cure of souls, yet those other things I have,
being so far distracted, make me more than almost infamous,
especially in their eyes who look not upon the nature but
into the number of them.   Hereto may be added, if you so
think it good, that if to seek and not find be either a folly in
the beginning or a misfortune in the end, or rather both, as
the wiser sort esteem it, I must reckon myself not singly
disgraced to see a physician preferred before a divine; a
mere stranger before an old servant; one that will depart
from all he hath, rejected for him that hath nought to leave;
one by whose preferment many may be gratified, for him
by whose preferment none can be pleasured but himself
alone.   This minute if you will enlarge, and descant with
your cunning upon my plain song, you may make this of mine
with more of your own well serve the turn.   What shall I
further say? Though there be no cause why I should importune Mr. Vice-Chamberlain but his own honourable and
favourable goodness, whereof no man hath tasted more deeply
than myself, (he hath my daily service and prayer to God
for it, and shall have while I live, however this succeed,) yet,
that I cannot with modesty say by word to his Honour I

am bold to crave you to discourse as opportunity will serve. Sir Thomas Heneage I hope will once again debate it with him; and that Mr. Vice-Chamberlain be not alone, and so wax the wearier, I trust my Lord of Leicester and Mr. Secretary will bear the burden with them, or the one of them at the least. Well, good Mr. C., want not you for your part, but make me ever beholding to you and ever bounden to your Master. And even so now and ever I wish you to fare well in the Lord. At London, the last of September 1581. Your assured friend,

TOBYE MATHEWE.[a]

Philip Sidney appears in his next letter as a suitor for the lands of Powerscourt in Ireland for a friend. Nothing could more strongly mark the contempt which was then felt for the Irish than his saying that the man of whom he speaks was "indeed a good honest fellow according to the brood of that nation!"

MR. PHILIP SIDNEY TO SIR CHRISTOPHER HATTON.

RIGHT HONOURABLE, I have spoken with my father touching Powerscourt, which Mr. Denny sueth for. He tells me assuredly that it is most necessary some Englishman should have it, being a place of great importance, and fallen to her Majesty by the rebellion of the owner. As for him that sueth for it in the Court, he is indeed a good honest fellow, according to the brood of that nation; but, being a bastard, he hath no law to recover it, and he is much too weak to keep it. So that your Honour may do well, if it please you, to follow this good turn for Mr. Denny, who can and will endeavour to deserve it of her Majesty, and do you service for it in all faithful good-will whensoever you shall command him. And so I humbly take my leave, and rest at your devotion. From the Court, the 17th of October 1581. Your Honour's humbly at commandment, as you have bound me,   P. SIDNEY.[b]

[a] Additional MSS. 15891, f. 94[b].   [b] Ibid.

Mr. Tremayne, the writer of the following letter, has been before mentioned.[a] The particulars of the suit are not stated.

MR. EDMUND TREMAYNE TO SIR CHRISTOPHER HATTON.

Sir, Upon an opinion that my poor credit in Court may do some good in the reasonable suit of a country gentleman, there is occasion taken, through some former friendly acquaintance that the party hath had with me, but especially by the near neighbourhood, and consequently the loving intercourse of friendship daily practised with my brother, the Treasurer of the Church of Exeter,[b] to desire my advice and help for the procuring of a quiet end in a cause very vehemently followed in your Honour's name; the course and state whereof I am bold to send you herein inclosed. When I was told this matter was carried and prosecuted principally under the countenance of your favour, to whom I am both especially bound in duty, as also for many loving and favourable usages towards me; and that the forfeitures (if any grow) do appertain to the executors of Mr. Colshill, deceased, and to Mr. Mackwilliam, my especial good friend, that hath always, and upon all occasions, showed himself desirous of my well-doing; I have been in mind in this case to leave both friend and brother, and in country manner to attend to my own quietness, or, at the least, not to busy myself with that wherewith I need to have little or nothing to do. Considering, nevertheless, with better advice of the discourse of the matter as it was laid down before me, and imagining that you might be otherwise than rightly informed, or haply than the truth will fall out upon due and indifferent proof; and holding such opinion of your integrity, and likewise of the good conscience of Mr. Mackwilliam, as no respect of gain to your friend can be able to draw you from justice; I have not thought it imper-

---

[a] Vide p. 95, ante.
[b] Richard Tremayne, who was installed in 1561, and died in 1584.

tinent to my duty towards your Honour, much less to pass
the bonds of an honest friend to Mr. Mackwilliam, to send
the case unto you as it was delivered unto me, desiring
nothing for the party but justice with indifferency; a matter
due to every Subject, and the more aptly to be ministered
when both parties are heard.   And thus, though I hold the
gentleman as wise a man as any in this country, a good Justice, and well liked of the better sort that be best inclined to
the State and to true religion, and is besides a friend to me
and to my nearest friends; yet I protest unto you, as I am a
true man, that no respect doth so much move me thus to
trouble you as the zealous regard that I have of your Honour, of whom I desire so good a fame to be spread, and so
much advancement in all happiness, as to him that I am most
bound to honour and love in all faithful devotion.   And so,
beseeching you to accept of my true and plain meaning
herein, I shall ever pray to God to prosper you according to
your noble heart's desire.   From my poor house at Collo-
cumb, the 27th of October 1581.   Your Honour's most
bounden and assured at commandment.   E. TREMAYNE.[a]

Mr. Dyer, for whom Sir Christopher Hatton interested himself with Winchester College, was no doubt his
intimate friend Edward Dyer, from whom a remarkable letter has been given.[b]   On the 1st of December in
this year, Edmund Campion, a celebrated Jesuit, and two
other Priests, were executed for high treason.   Dr. Humfrey's reply to Campion, of which he speaks, was his
" Jesuitismi Pars Prima, " which appeared in 1582.

DR. HUMFREY TO SIR CHRISTOPHER HATTON.

MY duty in humble wise remembered to your Honour.
Receiving a letter from your Honour at Winchester, to me,
and the Fellowship being then tied there by residency, I
returned with as much convenient speed as I could to Ox-

---

[a] Additional MSS. 15891, f. 89.   [b] Vide page 17, *ante*.

ford, and have so dealt for Mr. Dyer that I trust he is satisfied, and the party the farmer well contented. I thought the
way which is taken most commodious for all parties, and so I
hope your Honour will accept it. The circumstances were
such by the provision of corn set down in statute, and by
space of years which the old tenant hath, and by the small time
by our statute received to the next incumbent, that a present
payment in my mind was better than a long expectation
and an uncertain event. And so it is concluded, except
your Honour will otherwise advertise me; wherein I shall
be always ready as much as shall lie in me to accomplish
your commandment. I have written long since to your
Secretary Mr. Cox, unwilling to trouble your Honour until some reasonable conclusion did appear, and therefore
humbly request pardon for my long silence; the rather for
that I have been of late occupied in making a reply to Campion and his accomplices, whose case I lament, and crave of
God his reformation; and would beg further mercy here, if I
durst, upon repentanee, if it might be wrought in him. The
Lord Jesus be merciful to us all, direct us in His ways, preserve her Majesty from all privy and apert practices, and
keep your Honour for ever in all felicity. Oxon, November
13th. Your Honour's always most bounden,

LAUR. HUMFREY.[a]

All the printed accounts of the Lords Montjoy state,
erroneously, that James the sixth Lord died in the
thirty-fifth year of the reign of Queen Elizabeth, 1592-3,
and the manuscript pedigrees are silent on the subject;
but it appears[b] that he died in 1581, to which date the
following letter may be referred. The wardship of his
son, William the seventh Lord Montjoy, was of short

---

[a] Additional MSS. 15891, f. 69[b].
[b] Letters of administration were
granted to his son, William Lord
Montjoy, on the 9th of November
1581.

duration, as he was of full age in the ensuing year,[a] and died unmarried in 1594 :—

F. A. TO SIR CHRISTOPHER HATTON.

Sir, I am now to address myself as a suitor unto you, out of the conceit I hold of your just and plain dealing with such as have cause to use you : in so much as, being so sick myself at this present of an ague as I durst not go to the Court to speak with you, I determined more willingly to take a plain denial from you than a fair unsound promise from any other. My suit is this : My Lord Montjoy being lately dead, his son is thereby, as I take it, become her Majesty's ward. If it might now please her Majesty, of her favour, to vouchsafe the same in gift on me by your honourable mediation, for the preferment of a niece of mine that I love and greatly care for, I should acknowledge myself infinitely bound to her Highness, and greatly indebted to your goodness, whom I earnestly beseech to afford me your favour in moving it to her Majesty ; and, whatsoever the success shall fall out to be, to conceal it from all others, as a thing never spoken of to any but to yourself, whose honourable happiness I wish most heartily may accompany all your actions.

Your assured friend,　　F. A.[b]

It ill accords with the popular idea of the chivalrous Philip Sidney, to find him, like the shoals of obscure Courtiers, whose names are either totally forgotten or remembered only to their discredit, saying that " need obeys no law and forgets blushing," confessing himself, like them, overwhelmed with debt, and beseeching Hatton to obtain the Queen's signature to some grant by which he might extricate himself from his difficulties :—

TO SIR CHRISTOPHER HATTON.

Sir, I do here send you my book ready drawn and prepared

---

[a] Inquisition on the death of his grandmother, Anne Lady Montjoy, in October 1582.　　[b] Additional MSS. 15891, f. 86[b].

for her Majesty's signature, in such order as it should be; which I humbly beseech you to get signed accordingly with so much speed as you may conveniently. For the thing of itself in many respects requireth haste; and I find my present case more pitied now than perchance it would be hereafter, when haply resolution either way will be hard to get, and make my suit the more tedious. Mr. Popham thought it would be little or nothing worth unto me, because so many have oftentimes so fruitlessly laboured in it; and this is the general opinion of all men, which I hope will make it have the easier passage. But indeed I am assured the thing is of good value; and therefore, if it shall please you to pass anything in my book, you shall command it as your own for as much or as little as yourself shall resolve of: it will do me no hurt, that seek only to be delivered out of this cumber of debts; and if it may do your Honour pleasure in anything of importance, I shall be heartily glad of it. I pass nothing by any other instrument than by your own servant, and it shall greatly content me that the fruit is of such nature as I may have means at the least to show how ready I am to requite some part of your favours towards me. If it be not done before this day sevennight, I shall be in great fear of it; for, being once known, it will be surely crossed; and perhaps the time will not be so good as it is at this present, which, of all other things, putteth me in greatest confidence of good success, with the help of your honourable favour. If you find you cannot prevail, I beseech you let me know it as soon as may be, for I will even shamelessly once in my life bring it her Majesty myself. Need obeys no law, and forgets blushing: nevertheless, I shall be much the more happy if it please you indeed to bind me for ever by helping me in these cumbers. And so, praying for your good success in everything, and in this especially, my greatest hope of comfort, I humbly take my leave. From Baynard's Castle, the 14th of November 1581. Your Honour's humbly at commandment,

P. SIDNEY.[a]

---

[a] Additional MSS. 15891, f. 60.

In November the Duke of Anjou arrived in England, and was received with every mark of confidence and honour. The Queen's conduct towards him, especially her having publicly taken a ring from off her own finger and placed it on one of his, " upon certain conditions betwixt them two,"* convinced her Courtiers that she really intended to make him her husband. " At home," says Camden, " the Courtiers' minds were diversely affected; some were astonished, and some were cast down with sorrow." Though Leicester, Hatton, and Walsingham were commissioners for the treaty, and though Hatton had often alluded to, even if he did not urge, the alliance, yet, according to Camden, when they thought it would actually take place, " Leicester, who had begun to enter into a secret conspiracy to cross the marriage, Hatton Vice-Chamberlain, and Walsingham, fretted as if the Queen, the Realm, and religion were now undone." Moved by the wailings and weeping of her women, as well as by their representations, the Queen passed a sleepless night, and the next day, sending for the Duke, a private conversation ensued; after which, retiring to his apartments, " he cast the ring from him, and soon took it again, taxing with one or two quips the lightness of women and the inconstancy of Islanders." The sequel is too well known to be here repeated. After dallying for three months in uncertainty, the Duke of Anjou quitted England for ever; and the Country was spared a most unpopular alliance.

Sir George Bourchier, thus flatteringly recommended to the Queen by the Lord Deputy of Ireland, was the son of John second Earl of Bath, and had com-

* Camden's Annals.

manded the Queen's troops in Munster before Lord
Grey's arrival :—

ARTHUR LORD GREY DE WILTON TO QUEEN ELIZABETH.

MAY IT PLEASE YOUR MOST EXCELLENT MAJESTY, Sir
George Bourchier, upon advertisement received from some of
his friends out of England, of a conveyance intended by my
Lord of Bath for the inheritance of his lands, whereof he
formerly passed a promise to this gentleman before his coming
over, hath craved license of me to repair into England for the
space of three months ; which I was the more willing to grant
him, both for that the cause concerneth him deeply, and
chiefly for that the heat of this service beginneth now
somewhat to be assuaged.   Nevertheless I could not let him
pass without delivering to your Highness such commendation of him as, by his good service in this country, and
ready forwardness in all occasions of employment, he hath
well deserved : humbly beseeching your Majesty hereby to
take knowledge thereof, and to show him such gracious favour and countenance as he may be confirmed in his well-
doing, and others thereby encouraged by the like means to
deserve your Majesty's good opinion.   And so, with most
humble remembrance of my bounden duty, praying God for
your Highness' long health and happy prosperity, I humbly
take my leave.   Dublin, the 28th of November 1581.   Your
Highness' most humble servant and faithful subject.

A. GREY.*

Sir Henry Cheke's letter from York may be inserted
without comment :—

SIR HENRY CHEKE TO SIR CHRISTOPHER HATTON.

SIR, I have ever since my coming to York been entertained
in such sort between sickness and business as I have not had

---

* Additional MSS. 15891.

any good opportunity to write unto your Honour, unto whom I must confess I have ever desired, as I am bound, to show myself dutifully thankful; and, as the present time falleth out, I have now more good-will to write unto you than matter worthy wherewith to trouble you. The country here yieldeth few occurrences, and I find they are blown hither from other places with a scant wind. I had some news not long sithence which were strange unto me and unexpected; but I hope God will direct all things to the best, and make your Honour a good instrument thereof, according to the expectation generally conceived of you. I will not cease continually to remember your Honour in my prayers, nor forbear to do you any other service I may; unto whom wishing most happy success in everything, and, above all, the grace of the Highest, I humbly take my leave. From York, the 15th of December 1581. Your Honour's most assured to command,   HENRY CHEKE.[a]

Philip Sidney appears in the following letter in a character perfectly consistent with his reputation; declining, as when he received his death-wound, to allow his own necessities to be relieved at the expense of others, still less to become the instrument of impeding the Queen's mercy to the unfortunate:—

PHILIP SIDNEY TO SIR CHRISTOPHER HATTON.

RIGHT HONOURABLE, I must ever continue to thank you, because you always continue to bind me, and for that I have no other mean to acknowledge the band but my humble thanks. Some of my friends counsel me to stand upon her Majesty's offer touching the forfeiture of Papists' goods: truly, Sir, I know not how to be more sure of her Highness in that than I thought myself in this; but, though I were, in truth it goeth against my heart to prevent a Prince's mercy.

[a] Additional MSS. 15891, f. 74[b].

My necessity is great; I beseech you vouchsafe me your honourable care and good advice; you shall hold a heart from falling that shall be ever yours; and so I humbly take my leave. At Salisbury, the 18th of December 1581. Your Honour's humbly at commandment,

P. SIDNEY.[a]

Mr. Davison had, by Katherine, sister of Francis Spelman, of Bolebrook in Sussex, several sons, of whom Francis Davison, the eldest, was the editor of the " Poetical Rhapsody;" to which work he and his brothers, Christopher, who, it now appears, was Sir Christopher Hatton's godson, and Walter,[b] were contributors :—

TO SIR CHRISTOPHER HATTON.

SIR, I have received many favours at your Honour's hands, which have already infinitely bound me unto you: amongst which this is not the least, that it hath pleased you to send down this gentleman expressly, in your behalf, to give the name to my young son; whom, as a testimony of my own devotion, I have desired to offer and dedicate to your service. And because I know your Honour is both an enemy to ceremonies, and of judgment sufficient to discern the affection of such as your deserts have bound unto you, I do forbear in these any other testification of my thankfulness than that which I trust your Honour doubteth not of, which in a word is a faithful and dutiful offer of myself and all that I have, to be, whilst I live, at your Honour's good devotion; whom beseeching God to bless with all increase of happiness, I most humbly commend to His good providence. From my poor house at Bolebrook, this 28th of December 1581. Your Honour's most humbly bounden,   WILL. DAVISON.

---

[a] Additional MSS. 15891, f. 74[b].

[b] Memoirs of these sons, and of the other contributors, are prefixed to the last edition of the " Poetical Rhapsody."

Postscript.—Though the suddenness of this gentleman's departure from me hath half broken my charity, yet acknowledging myself greatly bound unto him in taking so foul a journey to do me this pleasure, and not able otherwise to deserve it, I must beseech your Honour to supply my want in giving him thanks, till I may myself in some sort be able to make him the amends.*

Of the numerous undated letters, the following appear to belong to this or to the early part of the next year, though with respect to some of them the date is very uncertain. The first four are from Charles Arundell, from whom two letters on the same subject have been already inserted:—

CHARLES ARUNDELL TO SIR CHRISTOPHER HATTON.

Sir, I have conceived such comfort of your last message sent me by this bearer, as I am emboldened thereby most humbly to crave your honourable aid and good favour in my cause ; and, of your goodness, either to procure me trial, that I am sure will acquit me, or to release me of my bands, with free enlargement, that would greatly ease and relieve me. If her Majesty shall pretend to take a pause upon your motion, or require time to be advised, as she hath done all this while without fruit, it may please you to do me the favour (if in your wisdom you shall think it meet) to answer that excuse by alleging unto her my eight months' imprisonment, a more grievous punishment to him that either regardeth the comfort of her Majesty's favour, or his own poor reputation, than an honest mind is able to bear without many tears and continual affliction. I hope her Majesty will not deny you the sweetness of her princely goodness in the behalf of me her poor distressed servant, lightly suspected, nothing faulty, and never offending her so much as in thought, I take God

* Additional MSS. 15891, f. 71.

to witness; seeing she hath lately vouchsafed the same to some others in the favour of my most hateful and wretched adversary, a person convicted, as you know, of great abomination, and notably detested of all men for his wickedness. Well, I must and will ever rest obedient in all lowliness of duty, as becometh me, to her Majesty's commandment; and what in her wisdom she shall think most reasonable, I will always repute most just and full of princely goodness. And so, expecting still, as I have done long, the happy hour of my deliverance through your honourable mediation, I humbly take my leave, and commit you to God. Your Honour's wholly to command and dispose at your pleasure,

CHARLES ARUNDELL.[a]

CHARLES ARUNDELL TO SIR CHRISTOPHER HATTON.

RIGHT HONOURABLE, I may not forget my humble duty, but let it always occupy the chiefest place in my letters, as a thing most fit for me, and most due to your Honour. I was glad to understand by this bearer of your good acceptation of my last, but so much comforted by your honourable message as this paper sufficeth not to let you understand at full. And my hope is, that my innocent cause, that hath long lain asleep, shall be shortly awakened and remembered by your Honour as convenient opportunity shall serve you. Because I would not be cumbersome unto you, I have requested this gentleman to unfold unto you my poor estate, and how I live, which is much harder I assure you than I complain of. But God and truth being on my side, is all my comfort; and I now know well, that whatsoever the devil or his ministers could devise against me was not wanting, and, if there had been any probability in my enemies' accusations, I had been ere this time past *laudate*. What I know, and of whom, I will say more unto you, when time shall serve, than to any person living. In the mean while I humbly take my leave, and commit you to God. Your Honour's most assured,

CHARLES ARUNDELL.[b]

[a] Additional MSS. 15891, f. 58.   [b] Additional MSS. 15891, f. 73[b].

CHARLES ARUNDELL TO SIR CHRISTOPHER HATTON.

SIR, Though hitherto I have had small means to declare my good affection towards you, yet hath there not wanted good-will to wish well with the best; and so wishing as with effect I might express it, and leave you satisfied of my good meaning. I speak not this to merit the more, but only for the due respects I owe you, by whose aid only I have been enabled to live the better; praying you to esteem of me as truth shall try me, and as hereafter upon better proof you shall find me. The hope I had to see you here hath stayed me thus long from writing; my case requireth your favour, and myself your comfort. I have most plainly unfolded before you my knowledge in all points, not concealing anything to excuse myself, nor adding more than is truth to harm others. I therefore humbly crave your favour in this my perplext estate. My restraint of liberty troubleth me nothing; but the disfavour of her Majesty grieveth me so much, as I would rather choose to die, than thus to continue my lingering sorrows in suspense, without assurance of any certain remedy. God I take to witness I never faulted against her Majesty's person; and as no man hath more cause to honour and serve her than I, so hath no man held her virtues in more admiration, nor defended them further when some other have not been so forward to perform that towards her Highness which in duty they ought to have done. As this is true, so God deal with me, and dispose your mind to do me good, who resteth more yours than I am able to express. Your Honour's humbly to dispose and command,   C. ARUNDELL.*

CHARLES ARUNDELL TO SIR CHRISTOPHER HATTON.

SIR, Your desire to do me good can do no more than confirm my former intent and readiness to deserve as well as I can of you and your friends. My case requiring indifferency will abide any trial, and I account it not my least

* Additional MSS. 15891, f. 95.

good hap that you shall have the hearing of my cause. As
I have already most plainly and sincerely betrayed my knowledge in all points of my examination, so I beseech you with
all humility to be the mean to restore me to my former
liberty, and to her Majesty's good favour, without the which
I desire not life ; and, if plain and open confession may purchase pardon for my former offences to the law, I will, as I
have begun, unfold unto you what I meant to impart to her
Majesty; and, because the offence was not committed wilfully,
I presume of pardon through your mediation easily. And so,
recommending myself and cause to your honourable direction,
I humbly take my leave, with full and faithful vow to be
yours in all service. Yours more bound than I have mean
to acknowledge,   CHARLES ARUNDELL.*

The name of the writer of the following letter, to
whom Hatton had given permission to state his opinions
on public affairs, has not been discovered :—

TO SIR CHRISTOPHER HATTON.

SIR, Being so much bound unto you as I am, I were much
to blame to be slack in obeying your commandment, especially at this present, when, in respect of your singular
favour to me and mine, I must confess my band to be greater
towards you than ever it was at any time, and my debt much
increased by your late goodness. It is no small grief unto
me, that, beholding your virtuous and godly disposition, I
am not any way able by my poor service to further it; nevertheless, seeing you were pleased to give me leave, whensoever
occasion should occur, to deliver my simple opinion, I will
humbly obey your direction, and beseech you to excuse my
presumption with the authority of your own commandment,
which I embrace with that reverence and regard of duty, as
to neglect it were a manifest argument that I little respected

* Additional MSS. 15891, f. 90.

my own comfort. I will not, for all that, be so bold as to
take upon me to judge what were needful and convenient for
you to do in the consideration of these great causes, though
your courtesy hath vouchsafed me that liberty, and greatly
encouraged me to that end. It shall suffice that I presume
no further than to declare what reasons induce me to hope
of some good conclusion of peace between her Majesty and
the French King; which, how simple or weak soever they
may seem, shall argue notwithstanding an honest desire of
a good effect, and such cannot but greatly redound to the
general quiet and preservation of the state of Christendom.
It is not likely that (the state of France being such as it is
now) the King will be brought to yield and conform himself
to peace, unless he may have Milan; and to make them abandon the wars of Italy by force, were a hard course, and such
as they themselves (who always make their hope a certainty)
will sooner wilfully perish than endure. Experience hath
already taught us that it is no easy matter for her Majesty to
draw that people by violence to forsake their right. And
though it were, yet it is not to be wished that her Highness
should build up her own estate with the ruins of so mighty
a Prince, who hath both power and will to do what he can,
and as much as any King in Christendom is able to do,
against the Turk, our common enemy; whose forces he
would never cease to oppugn by continual war, if he found
not all other Princes so contrarily addicted as that they will
rather (to wreak their malice against him) choose to stand to
the mercy of the Turk, than suffer him to recover his right,
which they cannot detain from him in justice. Her Majesty
hath already given him sufficient cause to fear her; and
though there be no warrant to be assured of the insolency of
that nation, yet may I boldly say, that, being so much
afflicted and broken with troubles as they have been lately,
they will have now the more reason to make account of those
that have power to hurt them. And of this (if I may speak
it without offence) I dare adventure my life, if it were worth
the least part of her Majesty's favour. If I should speak all

that I think, and that needfully occurreth to be considered of,
I should hold you too long, and yet say nothing that you do
not see much better than I am able to imagine. I will therefore here conclude; only beseeching you to pardon my boldness, and to vouchsafe me the favour to think that my desire
of her Majesty's quiet and greatness, and not any trans-
portation of passion, hath moved me to make this motion.
And so I commit you to God.*

Nothing can be stated in illustration of the two following letters :—

TO . . . .

SIR, I have taken no small comfort to understand that the
State of Venice hath called you to so honourable a degree,
with such fame and reputation as your faithful service hath
worthily deserved. To express my joy and gladness for this
fortune which your virtue hath laid upon you, I have presumed to send you these few lines, which shall testify unto
you as much as paper and ink can specify for my hearty
good-will towards you. I rejoice even in my soul, that in
your most tender years your virtue, accompanied with fortune,
hath brought you to that good state of credit and favourable
opinion with the world, which many men, even in their
ripest age, have laboured to get with long study, and could
never attain to. I do not doubt but that the effects of your
actions will correspondently answer the expectation which
your value promiseth. One thing I will be bold to tell you
for the especial love I bear you, which is such as can suffer
no increase; and this it is: that the same Glory, with whose
beauty you were in your youth and tender years so greatly
enamoured, may purchase you perpetual fame and comfort, if
with your study and painful industry you will now carefully
follow and continue it; whereby myself, with the rest of

* Additional MSS. 15891, f. 52b.

your friends and servants, which are infinite, shall rejoice to be partakers of your honour and well-doing. God keep you in health, that you may be always an instrument to minister good to many men, as you have done hitherto by your gravity and virtue. Your loving friend.

TO SIR CHRISTOPHER HATTON.

Sir, I will not violate the law of our ancient familiarity and friendship by recommending this gentleman, my friend, unto you with long and ceremonious letters, for so should I do injury both to your grave judgment and goodness; the party being a man of quality as he is, and accompanied with such rare and singular conditions. I shall not need to say any more but that he is my friend, and worthy of your favour and acquaintance. The rest you shall gather of yourself; which when you have done upon further trial and proof of his desert, I am assured you will not only love him, but likewise embrace and accept his faithful devotion towards you in most thankful part. He is now come from Venice upon the occasion of some private business of his own, for the expedition whereof he shall stand in need of your good favour and assistance. I know your gentle nature, being so officiously disposed to do good as it is, will work as much readiness in you as I wish for; and so will the merit of the gentleman, not so much in respect of my entreaty, as by the instigation of your own virtue and of his desert. I shall be glad that he may know you by this occasion to be a free and liberal steward of the benefits of courtesy and wisdom that God hath given you, and you him to be a grateful and kind receiver in requiting you with the like, as his poor ability will suffer him; in which respect, to be plain with you, I think you to be as much beholding to me in acquainting you with a gentleman of so rare virtue, as he is unto you for enjoying of the possession of your friendship, and in receiving this pleasure at your hands by my mediation. God prosper you in the highest degree of happiness; whom I beseech so to direct your mind as that I may always have place in the bosom of your love and good favour, so far forth as yourself doth desire it, and I may deserve it.   Your vowed true friend.

The lady who solicits Hatton to prevent, if possible, the inconvenient and expensive honour of a visit from the Queen, was, no doubt, the Lady Anne Askewe who presented the Queen with a gold anchor ornamented with diamonds, hanging to a gold bodkin, as a New-year's gift in 1581 :—

TO SIR CHRISTOPHER HATTON.

SIR, This short warning, and my unfurnished house, do ill agree; for, besides her Majesty's diet, there be many things which I know to be fit for her ease that I want: wherefore, if her Majesty's pleasure would otherwise determine, my shame were the less, and my band to you the greater.   Nevertheless, if it be her Highness's direction, I with my little might will do all with the best will I can, and pray you, my honourable friend, to help by your commandment that otherwise is beyond my reach.   And so, expecting her Majesty's pleasure, I beseech God to bless you with all happiness.   Your true friend in her ability,   A. ASKEWE.

Post.—I would gladly Mr. Killigrew would take the pains to come to-day and appoint what were fittest for her places of ease, and how they should be ordered.[*]

None of the following undated letters can be illustrated, either by identifying the writers, or by explaining the several matters mentioned in them :—

---

[*] Additional MSS. 15891, f. 87ᵇ. A letter from Lady Anne Askewe to Lord Burghley in September 1577, asking for some concealed lands for her husband, is in the Lansdowne MS. 25; and two other letters from her, written in October and December 1582, are in the Lansdowne MS. 36.

WRITER UNKNOWN, TO SIR CHRISTOPHER HATTON.

SIR, It is thought by those that know us that I may do much with you; which is an opinion rather grounded upon the reciprocal good-will which we bear to each other, than either upon any merit on my part, or any duty other than of love and kindness on yours.   Howsoever it be, I may boldly assume thus much to myself, that the sincereness of my good meaning towards you deserveth your friendly acceptation, which is enough to make me think that I may do somewhat more with you than commonly other men can do. Pardon me, I pray you, if I trouble you oftener than I would; it is only my earnest desire to benefit and pleasure my friends in their honest causes that moveth me thus to importune you.   My good affection to this party makes me most careful in commending him to your favourable and good opinion; wherein if I should use but my wonted and ordinary words of entreaty, I should neither satisfy his need nor my own desire. The gentleman meriteth much, and reposeth great confidence in my poor furtherance; therefore I pray you, whatsoever you shall find wanting in my letters to express my earnestness to pleasure him, let your goodness supply it with your own benignity and wisdom in vouchsafing him courtesy, whose virtue is worthy of all favour and advancement. Himself shall deliver his own careful cause and complaint unto you. Let me be so much beholding to you as to make him know that his hope which he conceiveth of me is not deceived, and that I may assure myself of the comfort which your love hath always promised me; so shall he have cause to acknowledge a perfect obligation unto me, and I yield you infinite thanks in his behalf, as you have bound me.   God give you all good effects of your honourable desires, and the due reward belonging to your virtue !

Your friend, ever one and all your own.[a]

[a] Additional MSS. 15891, f. 102.

SIR, If the malice of men were not sooner supplanted by silence than by words, I should be as forward to speak as I am now willing to hold my peace. But seeing most men in Princes' courts are subject to slander; to be passionate with those and such other abuses, were but to complain without remedy, and to call your wisdom and grave judgment into doubt, which I will not do. I will shut up my lips, therefore, to avoid all further danger; and rather endeavour with patience to suffer wrong, than give them cause to exasperate their malice by answering to their reproachful speeches. As near as I can, I will have care of my own reputation, howsoever other men's tongues are led to report of me; neither will I much regard the opinion of such persons, whose commendations cannot greatly increase my credit, and whose discommendations cannot turn me to imputation of blame by their obloquy and infamous reports. It was never the office of ill-will to speak well; and such is the condition of malice, that it ever worketh trouble where it is least deserved. I am content they shall excel me in ill words, so I may be able by good deeds to keep myself harmless. It is enough for me they know that I hold not my peace for fear; and that, if they have their tongues prompt and prepared to utter evil, I have my pen as ready as they when wisdom will so command me. But wise men are of opinion that words should not pass the circuit of a parlour or a chamber, and man's talk is the image of his mind; I will therefore use my ears, and forbear my tongue. Wishing you health and all other happiness now and ever. Your poor, oppressed, unfortunate friend.*

It would be vain to attempt to explain the following well-written letter of counsel to some one who had entered a foreign service:—

* Additional MSS. 15891, f. 103.

UNKNOWN TO UNKNOWN.

SIR, You do wrong to the love I bear you to pray me to do that which in duty I am bound to do without any entreaty. The only remembrance of your goodness had been a sufficient commandment of itself to move me to do anything that concerneth your service. The trust which you seem to repose in me is my greatest comfort in this world; and I hope I shall so well discharge it, as, what fortune soever shall befal you, you shall never have cause to change your opinion of me, or repent you of the favour which you have thought me worthy of. Because you ask my advice, I will be bold in the sincereness of my good-will to give it you; but with entreaty of pardon that my dutiful thankfulness, and your own courteous disposition, may excuse me if, in saying freely what I think, I shall happen to give occasion of offence in doing that which yourself hath commanded me. To flatter or dissemble with you in a matter that so much importeth you were plain treachery, and a course of dealing as unpleasant unto me as it is unworthy of your virtue and wisdom. It may please you therefore in direct terms to give me leave to tell you that your departing from the service of this State is like to prove most prejudicial unto you, as well in respect of the bounty and goodness which you had cause to hope for in regard of your merit, as for the singular satisfaction which all men reaped through your wise and discreet government in the place you served. In few words, you have done yourself injury, and forsaken the flesh to take the shadow, in preferring the service of this King before that famous Commonwealth that hath so liberally rewarded your virtue, to the increase of your reputation and fortune. If he were such a Prince as loved our Nation, or his people such as would be content in the justice of our deserts to give us our due, there were no cause I should dislike your determination; but finding that he maketh a virtue of necessity, and only to serve his turn by your service, it moveth me to think that you will soon repent you. I know there is reason you should hope to win the love of one much sooner than of many; and that where there are many linked in society together, they are neither always all virtuous, nor equally disposed to remunerate and advance those which in all duty of faithful service have well deserved. But when I consider that as your merit increaseth, so the envy of the Prince will be every day more eagerly bent against you to overthrow and supplant your reputation and credit in the midst of your best endeavours, I cannot imagine how you might better your fortune without manifest peril of your own decay and disgrace, by serving this King, as you have undertaken. It is not the least reproof that our Nation sustaineth, to become servants and tributaries, as we do daily, to strange and barbarous people; even to such as our predecessors were wont many ages since to lead bound and captive before their chariots, fraught with chains and fetters, in their victorious triumphs. Your own wisdom can consider that Kings are mortal, and though their sons are heirs to their paternal estates and inheritances, yet are they not commonly successors in the distribution of virtue and love to their fathers by favouring and affecting their ancient servants; but a popular estate, which is perpetual and never dieth, because there reigneth no King, always thankfully remembereth and bountifully rewardeth those that have truly and faithfully served, and will acknowledge it both in the father, in the son, and in all their posterity. It is superfluous that I trouble you so long in showing you my poor opinion of a matter which you may govern as please yourself, and see much better in the glass of your own wisdom than I can be able to imagine. It is my good-will, and the earnest desire which I have to increase your reputation, that makes me thus bold; which it may please you to pardon and accept in good part, vouchsafing me that favourable opinion of my service which I hold of your virtue and kindness.   Your assured friend.[*]

* Additional MSS. 15891, f. 103[b].

Elizabeth Lady Leighton, the writer of the annexed letter, was the wife of Sir Thomas Leighton, Captain of Guernsey; and was a distant kinswoman of the Queen, being the daughter of Sir Francis Knollys by Katherine Carey, whose mother was the sister of Queen Anne Boleyn. Except the little compliment to the Queen's attractions, there is nothing so remarkable in this letter as to account for its having found a place in Hatton's "Letter Book:"—

LADY LEIGHTON TO SIR THOMAS LEIGHTON.

My most worthy Husband, Though I feared you had forgot me, (for which I must crave your pardon,) seeing as they say such effects proceed from the greatest love, yet I perceive you will always be yourself in keeping that constant course as not to cast off your poorest friend, whom you have once well thought of; which indeed is none of the smallest of your commendations. And so kindly do I now take your careful inquiry of my well-doing, witnessed by your friendly letter, as I must tell you my love is great towards you; and though it be fruitless, and unaccompanied with such pains as I have lately felt, yet shall it be such as shall ever joy in your contentment, and desire you may increase in all happiness. These be the poor acquittals, my dear Husband, that my good-will can yield you for all your honourable favours; but I hope you will accept the mind from me, whensoever you receive the effects, and persuade yourself that nothing you can wish to be added to your fortune shall want my consent, though it were for the favour of her Majesty, which is much for a wife to agree unto. Notwithstanding, I leave you to her good grace, and myself to your wonted good opinion.

Your faithful Wife, and well-wishing friend,

E^h. LEYGHTON.*

* Additional MSS. 15891, f. 78.

Two letters from Mr. Davison to Hatton, the one written while on one of his missions, and the other soliciting his interest to obtain some favour from the Queen, as well as a letter from Sir Henry Cheke, need no observations:—

TO SIR CHRISTOPHER HATTON.

SIR, I wrote nothing unto your Honour by the last post, by reason of his sudden departure; and though I doubt not but that want of mine was otherwise supplied, yet I beseech you to excuse the same. Now what doth occur in the broken and confused estate of things here you may perceive by the particulars herewith sent; to the which referring your Honour, and beseeching the same to reckon me in the number of those whom your favours have faithfully devoted to you, I most humbly take my leave.   Your Honour's humbly bounden to do you service.   W. DAVISON.[a]

SIR, You know my modesty in pressing the favour of my friends in my own particular; I beseech you, Sir, let it not hinder that disposition you have ever had to do me good. My state I have oft laid open to you, which to renew in these were needless.   It is enough that the common report of my best friends do testify of it as worthy her Majesty's gracious consideration, since neither my purse, my body, nor my time hath been spared for her service; my experience of whose gracious bounty to others and favour to myself doth assure me that there wanteth but good offices from my friends; which as your Honour hath not hitherto been spare of in my behalf, so do I beseech you to continue it till I may gather some fruit thereof, to my perpetual obligation and your own honour.   W. DAVISON.[b]

SIR HENRY CHEKE TO SIR CHRISTOPHER HATTON.

SIR, The aptness of this bearer hath very easily enticed me to write these few lines unto your Honour, rather for a tes-

---

[a] Additional MSS. 15891, f. 108[b].   [b] Ibid. f. 101.

timony of my duty towards you than for any good advertisement I have to send you, wherein I hope the barrenness of this country shall excuse me. The latest thing which hath happened here of any moment is the death of Sir Thomas Boynton, old Mr. Gooderick, and divers other gentlemen, who have been taken away on the sudden; wherein her Majesty in my opinion hath received great loss, the most part of them being very sound in religion, and well affected to her Highness' service. For myself, I hope I have escaped for this year, and shall live a while to do your Honour some service, either here or wheresoever else it shall please you to command me. And so, recommending the good and happy success of all your actions to the Highest, I humbly take my leave. From York, the 15th of January 1581 [1582]. Your Honour's most assured at commandment,   H. CHEKE.[a]

Dr. Bartholomew Clark, Dean of the Arches, was, it seems, a suitor to Hatton for the Archdeaconry of Wells, which fell vacant by the death of John Rugge in 1581; but, as the register is defective[b] until the appointment of Dr. Langworth in February 1588, the result of his application is unknown. The learned civilian's remark, that though he had not performed any services to entitle him to the Queen's favour, yet that he was always ready, and that if he obtained this preferment he should be the better able to do so, is ingenious:—

TO SIR CHRISTOPHER HATTON.

RIGHT HONOURABLE, It may please you to understand that one Mr. Upton of Wells, who exerciseth the ecclesiastical jurisdiction under the Archdeacon there, hath written to my good Lord of Buckhurst that Mr. Rugg lay speechless and at the point of death the first of this present month of February; whereof I am now bold the rather to advertise your

[a] Additional MSS. 15891, f. 96.
[b] Le Neve's Fasti Ecclesiæ Anglicanæ, p. 44.

Honour, lest haply any man (not knowing of my advowson) should make suit unto her Majesty for the Archdeaconry before the breath were out of his body, and so breed me great vexation and trouble in law by opposing her Highness' prerogative against my former right. If her Majesty shall find it strange that any man that hath not served her in greater causes than myself should enjoy spiritual Livings, it may please your Honour to remember that I am not only as ready as ·any man to serve her Highness to my small power, but shall be made the more able by this accession of living to serve, either in these places or otherwise, as shall be best pleasing to her most excellent Majesty. And as the statutes of the Realm do make especial and express mention of the Master of the Rolls and the Dean of the Arches, touching the retaining of ecclesiastical livings, so hath it been a continual use from time to time that the Deans of the Arches (myself only excepted) have been furnished with many spiritual promotions; for that they have invested in them, by the statutes of this Realm, spiritual jurisdiction, which is a far greater matter than an ecclesiastical living without cure of soul thereunto annexed, as an Archdeaconry is by the common laws. To end: that all our whole profession may ever acknowledge you their honourable patron, it may please you, as occasion shall serve, to take notice that by the statute of 31 of King Henry the Eighth a Doctor of Law is qualified for two benefices with cure of soul, much more without cure and so great a charge; which argueth that those times thought always the men of that profession to be very necessary members of our Commonwealth, and worthy by all good means to be cherished and supported: which opinion if your Honour do likewise conceive of us, you shall bind both myself and all the rest to be ever thankfully ready in all faithful devotion to do you service. And so I beseech God to prosper you in all your honourable actions. From the Arches, the 4th of February 1581 [1582]. Your Honour's ever to command,   B. CLARK.*

* Additional MSS. 15891, f. 59ᵇ.

SIR FRANCIS WALSINGHAM TO SIR CHRISTOPHER HATTON.

I THOUGHT good to send you the enclosed, which I received sithence my return unto my lodging, to the end you may send the same unto her Majesty, by the which she may perceive that the advertisements given of the accord between certain of the towns in Flanders and the malcontents are untrue. It is likely that, if the Duke had not repaired thither, there might have fallen out there some strange alteration, having settled their hope altogether on him. God bless her Majesty, and send you well to do. At my lodging, the 8th of February 1581 [1582]. Yours most assuredly,

FRA. WALSINGHAM.*

Another letter was written in February by the persevering Dr. Mathew to Mr. Cox, Hatton's secretary, about the Deanery of Durham: nor is it the last by many from him on the subject:—

TO MR. SAMUEL COX.

MR. Cox, Were it now possible, *post multa tandem sæcula*, to hear a comfortable word or two from the Court, of a suit so long forlorn as that of Durham hath been? Hath Monsieur's departure brought on any more seasonable times than during his abode such as poor I did find? Could Dr. Bellamy's friend steal occasion to get a new grant, and cannot anybody for me have opportunity to satisfy her Majesty's former promise? Good Mr. Cox, let me boldly desire you to learn as you can what the terms were her Highness gave my Lord of Hunsdon in the cause. The comfortable words Mr. Vice-Chamberlain vouchsafed me at my departure from the Court (which if you remember I did impart unto you) were, methought, sufficient to assure me of the place. I cannot as yet persuade myself her Majesty would so revoke or could so forget her word; or if her Highness, so many ways affaired,

---

* Additional MSS. 15891, f. 63ᵇ.

hath past unawares any such half-allowance of my Lord of Hunsdon's petition, I trust upon good instruction I may be restored to my former possibility. Little thought I (God wot), when I came up hither, but I should with the first have been dispatched, not from it, but with it. And my heart yet serveth me, that all Mr. Bellamy giveth out by reports are but rumours, rather of crack than of cause. I pray you, Sir, take some time with Mr. Vice-Chamberlain to consider of me. I have great hope in his Honour to her Majesty, and in you to him. As hitherto you have especially friended me, so I trust you will earnestly further me now at a pinch; for although I doubt not but it liveth and will recover, yet I fear it bleedeth and lieth in danger. If I wist the Court would have any long continuance in those parts, and that my presence would further the expedition or assurance of the matter, I should upon your direction soon be there. But howsoever, I heartily request to receive a few lines from you by the next. If her Majesty be disposed hitherward, I hope we shall the better and sooner meet, and further confer in more particular. And so I recommend me to your remembrance, and you as myself to God. London, 12th of February 1581 [1582]. Your debtor and friend assured,   TOBIE MATHEW.[a]

SIR WALTER MILDMAY TO SIR CHRISTOPHER HATTON.

SIR, Understanding by this bearer, my cousin Wiseman, that he hath made suit unto you to move her Majesty for him, I am bold, by these few lines, to recommend his cause unto you; praying you heartily, as time and opportunity may serve you, that it will like you to remember it, and to further him so far as you may. For the which he shall be greatly bound unto you, and I be ready with my poor good-will to be thankful unto you for your good favour towards him. So, praying you to bear with me in troubling you in such matters, I leave both the gentleman and his suit to your good consideration; wishing you ever all felicity in the Lord

[a] Additional MSS. 15891, f. 119.

Almighty. From London, the 20th of February 1581
[1582]. Your assured in all that I may for ever,

WA. MILDMAY.*

Even a prison did not restrain the controversial spirit
of the Puritans; and Norton, who has been before mentioned, though in disgrace for his dangerous zeal, writes
to Hatton, that though he lay " on the ground and cried
on his knees to his Sovereign," if he were only per-
mitted to do so, he would let the Papists know, " that
yet Norton, with a true man's heart and face, can and
dare speak on tiptoe!"—

MR. THOMAS NORTON TO SIR CHRISTOPHER HATTON.

IT may please your Honour before any answer to your
letter to receive answer to your goodness, and that is nothing
but thanks unto your virtue and my prayer to God for your
prosperity; beseeching you to be assured that I am still, as
you have ever known me, a true fool at the worst. For the
matter of your letter, I am so thrown down in heart, and in
loathing of mine arrogance in offending Her whom I least
should, and never wittingly would, I take God to witness
that since my last check I never durst enter into any matter
of State uncommanded; and I do so flee the peril of offence
that way, that I have not conceived the hardiness once to go
about any such work. I fear lest the Queen's old enemies
and mine, the Papists, have spread this rumour of me to
increase my trouble, as of one that even in restraint cannot
have grace or patience to be silent. Nevertheless, if I were
commanded by my Lord Treasurer, my singular good Lord,
to deal in it, whom it toucheth especially, and who by employment in her Majesty's service that way hath some understanding of this case, the Papists should know, that howsoever I lie on the ground, and cry on my knees to my Sove-

* Additional MSS. 15891, f. 84.

reign Lord and Lady, God and the Queen, that yet Norton, with a true man's heart and face, can and dare speak on tiptoe. And though I desire not to undertake any such work, but do shun it as storms in a broad sea for a weak vessel; yet at commandment I will refuse no adventure, and, having once performed it, I will then offer it to my Lord Treasurer and your Honour to be done withal as they shall think best. And, for the printing, I must not forget that I have your Honour's letters. In the mean time I commend you to the Almighty, and myself under Him to your goodness; beseeching you to give me your good testimony to my Lord Treasurer of my obsequiousness in her Majesty's service. At my close prison-house in London, the 28th of February 1581 [1582]. Your Honour's most humbly bounden,

THOMAS NORTON.[a]

Scarcely any letter in this work is so curious as the Bishop of London's remonstrance with Sir James Harvey, the Lord Mayor. It will be remembered, that his predecessor, Sir John Branch, was commanded to reprimand the City clergy for their sermons about the Queen's marriage; and his successor seems to have obeyed the injunction with singular pleasure, adding personal reproaches and abuse to his admonitions. Harvey in his zeal spared neither his own diocesan, the fiery Aylmer, nor Horne, late Bishop of Winchester[b]; and it is amusing to find a Lord Mayor calling a scholar "lack-Latin," and somewhat natural that Aylmer's want of hospitality in not entertaining the City functionaries should be a sin in the eyes of the citizens. Though the Bishop of London says he is obliged to submit to part of the Lord Mayor's offensive conduct so long as he remained in office, yet he promised to remember it in the ensuing year when he

---

[a] Additional MSS. 15891, f. 81ᵇ.   [b] Bishop Horne died in June 1580.

should still be as he was, but when Harvey would be somewhat inferior. The threat to teach the Lord Mayor his duty in a sermon at Paul's Cross, when he would be obliged to listen without being able to reply, was, in those days, more than a *brutum fulmen ;* and, coming from such a man as Aylmer, was not to be despised :—

BISHOP AYLMER'S LETTER TO THE LORD MAYOR.

MY LORD MAYOR, I hear that you deal very hardly with the preachers and clergy of whom the charge and oversight is committed unto me by God and her Majesty's gracious direction. I must therefore needs foresee, as chief Pastor both to you and them, that in their function they suffer no injury ; in which respect I am to desire you to use them as the Ministers of God, and as the keepers and rulers of your souls, which I hope you esteem to be the better part of you : of whom the Holy Ghost hath said, that they are worthy of double honour, the like whereof cannot be found spoken of you. And yet I hear (whether it be true or not I know not,) that you *thou* them, and taunt them as base, contemptible, and abject persons : yea, such as by calling are Archdeacons, and in quality, justice, and desert nothing inferior to yourself when you are out of your office, your son raileth and rageth at them with all reproachful and uncomely speeches ; which he is like to answer, haply little to your comfort, and less to his own credit, if any complaint be presented against him. You are not only content thus indiscreetly to triumph over the meaner sort, but you presume farther to reach at those which are always as good as yourself, even now in your Mayoralty when your reputation is at the highest, and somewhat your superiors when you are out of office. 'That Horne' (as you term him), a worthy grave Prelate, you call him 'hypocrite and lack-Latin' with many other unreverent and disdainful speeches, no less untrue and shameless for you to utter than slanderous for him to receive ; whose virtue, learning, wisdom, and good government hath, in the general opinion of the

world, deserved as great fame and commendation as ever
did any man in this age ; and therefore not to be maligned
after his death (especially by a man of your place), having
in his life-time been so well loved and embraced of all men
for his integrity, that had either judgment or justice to give
every man his right. Her Highness, whose person you do represent (the Lord preserve her Majesty) would not so speak
of him, nor of any other Prelate within this Realm.   I pass
over myself, whom it hath pleased you of your goodness to
term familiarly by the name of Aylmer, as unreverently as if I
should omit the title of your office and call you Harvey ;
which, to teach you good manners and what you ought to do,
I mean not to do, God willing.   You say, that, when Aylmer
was in Zurich, he thought a 100*l.* was enough for any Minister.   Admit he said so : so thought you, peradventure, in
your prenticehood that 100*l.* by year had been enough for a
Merchant.   It pleaseth you, as a curious censor of other
men's faults, to glance at my poor housekeeping, objecting
that the Bishop of London was wont to feast the Lord Mayor
and his brethren.   Your Lordship in your wisdom ignorantly
mistaketh the nature of a custom.   This wont was but once,
and not usual ; neither convenient nor necessary for me to
follow it as a precedent.   And yet, as little as you make of
Aylmer's hospitality, if you compare five years of yours with
five of his, his may chance to overreach you 4000*l.* thick.
My Lord, I have never spoken nor so much as thought
unreverently at any time of your Lordship, neither have I
been so used at any of your predecessors' hands ; and therefore I must needs say, that this is a great forgetfulness in you
of that dutiful goodness, that, both by the law of God and
man, you owe to your Bishop and Ordinary ; the lack whereof though I bear it now for your office sake (which I need
not unless I will), yet the next year I may haply remember
it when by God's grace I am like to be as I am, and you somewhat inferior to what you are now.   Well, to end as I begun :
I pray you use the Ministers according to their calling ;
though not for their own sakes, nor His whom they serve, yet

for the laws of the Realm, which do provide for their safety; and in respect of her Majesty's commission, which is chiefly committed to our charge to the end we might see that they be not misused; and think that the meanest of them is richer than you in that sort of wealth which in God's sight shall shine as gold, when yours shall be accounted as dross. I could not but as one that hath the chief charge of your soul admonish you, that, by the despising of His Ministers, and so consequently of Him that sent them, you provoke not His wrath and offend her Majesty, who would have them reverenced and well used; making, besides, all wise men think that there is some want in you of that gravity and discretion that should be in him that hath the Royal sword carried before him. If you take this in good part, as coming from him that hath charge over you, I am glad of it; if not, I must then tell you your duty out of my chair, which is the pulpit at Paul's Cross, where you must sit, not as a judge to control, but as a scholar to learn; and I, not as John Aylmer to be taunted, but as John London to teach you and all that City, and, if you use not yourself as an humble scholar, then to discipline you as your chief Pastor and Prelate. And so I bid your Lordship heartily farewell. 1st March 1581 [1582]. Your Lordship's loving friend and Bishop,

JOHN LONDON.[a]

Mr. Egerton, to whom the following letter was addressed as the Queen's Solicitor-General, was afterwards the celebrated Lord Ellesmere:—

TO MR. EGERTON, HER MAJESTY'S SOLICITOR.

SIR, Where it hath heretofore pleased her Majesty to grant a warrant for the revealing and finding out concealed lands to the value of 100l. per annum, by virtue whereof there have been found out and discovered certain other lands to be concealed, over and beside the said 100l. per

---

[a] Additional MSS. 15891, f. 58b.

annum, to the yearly value of 40*l.* or thereabout, which it
hath pleased her Majesty, at my humble suit and petition, to
grant unto Theophilus Adams my servant, and James Wood-
shaw, in fee-farm; I have therefore thought good to desire
you, that, according to her Majesty's gracious pleasure, you
will have care to make a Book thereof with what speed you
may conveniently, that it may be ready for her Highness'
signature wheresoever it shall please her to call for it.   You
shall receive the particulars of the grant by this bearer,
whom I have sent unto you expressly to satisfy you in any
thing that you shall doubt touching this matter.   And so
I commit you to God.   From the Court at Greenwich, this
17th of March 1581 [1582].   Your very loving assured friend,
                                        CHR. HATTON.

Postscript.— Sir, Her Majesty is pleased to grant the
averages of these concealed lands.   I pray you draw the Book
accordingly, for such is her pleasure.[a]

According to a marginal note in the " Letter Book,"
the object of Bishop Aylmer's next letter to Sir Christopher Hatton was the Bishoprick of Ely, and the " old
tired father" whom he wished "eased of his place," was
Dr. Cox; but the accuracy of these marginal notes cannot always be depended upon.   As this letter is dated
on the 20th of March 1581, it was presumed to have
been in fact written in 1582; but, if Le Neve be
correct in saying that Bishop Cox died in July 1581,
Bishop Aylmer or the copyist must, however unlikely,
have used the historical instead of the ecclesiastical or
civil computation.   The style of this letter from Hatton's
" own creature," as he disgustingly calls himself, and,
indeed, the whole of Bishop Aylmer's correspondence,
makes it satisfactory to know, that though the Bishoprick of Ely was vacant more than eighteen years, it was

---

[a] From the Egerton Papers, ed. Collier, p. 87.

never held *in commendam* by the grasping Bishop of
London.

BISHOP AYLMER TO SIR CHRISTOPHER HATTON.

RIGHT HONOURABLE, The time draweth nigh for you to
remember your honourable promise unto me, that I may likewise perform mine unto you; wherein if you should show
any remissness, it may haply hurt us more than either of us
is like to gain by the bargain.   I pray you be as earnest
now in taking the burthen on yourself as you were willing at
the first to lay it upon me.   I beseech you send me word
whether you mind to deal in it, or no; and what hope or despair you find to speed.   You may use divers arguments to
help forward the matter: as, the crookedness of the old tired
father, whom if her Majesty do not soon ease him of this
place of service, she must shortly lose him, either by death,
where she can have but the bones, or by unableness of service; in which case she shall be sure deceived, and I by
weariness compelled, not as the common saying is, to hang
up my hatchet, but as infirmity, and not lack of duty, will
force me, to yield up my rochet.   Sir, if you will have her
Majesty well served, your own creature somewhat in life preserved, and your credit kept uncracked for commending me
first, and now retaining me still in state of reputation by this
increase of advancement, put to your hand resolutely; pro-
tract no time, lest danger ensue delay ; forget not yourself in
failing your friend, that liveth unfeignedly at your devotion,
whom I commit to God's good providence.   At Fulham, the
20th of March 1581 [1582?].   Your Honour's in the best, the
surest, and humblest manner,   JOHN LONDON.[a]

The "Lord Dyer," whose death Sir Walter Mildmay
speaks of, was Sir James Dyer, Lord Chief Justice of
the Common Pleas, to which office he was appointed in
January 1560.   He was succeeded on the 2nd of May
1582 by Sir Edmund Anderson:—

[a] Additional MSS. 15891, f. 71[b].

SIR WALTER MILDMAY TO SIR CHRISTOPHER HATTON.

SIR, I am credibly informed this morning that my Lord
Dyer is dead, and therefore I have entreated my brother Cary
to take so much pains as to let you know it if you have not
heard it before, and therewith to say unto you a few words
from me what I would desire that it might like you to do in
that matter, which, nevertheless, I refer to your own consideration, who seeth better what is to be done there than
I can. And so, praying you to bear with me in troubling
you thus much, I wish unto you all felicity in God Almighty.
From London, the 26th of March 1582.   Your assured to
use as your own,   WA. MILDMAY.[a]

Nothing more is known about Don Antonio's ring
than is stated in the following letter and in the marginal note:—" Don Antonio was the banished King of
Portugal, who impawned this ring to her Majesty while
he was in England for a lack of money;—"

SIR FRANCIS WALSINGHAM TO THE EARL OF LEICESTER.

MY VERY GOOD LORD, For that it is doubtful whether
the ring may be sold in France, it were very convenient that
Don Antonio's agent were dealt withal to send to the
King's Majesty to procure means for the redeeming of
the said ring, who, considering the value thereof, (being of
far greater price than it is impawned for,) when he shall see
that it is determined to be put to sale, will strain himself to
redeem the same.   Herein it shall be requisite that the said
Agent be pressed to use expedition, for that the time will
draw fast on, and the King is now in the furtherest parts of
France.   And so, referring the ordering of this cause to your
Lordship's best direction, I most humbly take my leave. The
4th of April 1582.   Your Lordship's to command,

FRA. WALSINGHAM.[b]

[a] Additional MSS. 15891, f. 72b.   [b] Additional MSS. 15891, f 95b.

R

Hatton again appears in the amiable light of aiding the unfortunate; and it seems that it was mainly to his influence that Norton owed his liberation :—

MR. THOMAS NORTON TO SIR CHRISTOPHER HATTON.

MY DUTY HUMBLY DONE TO YOUR HONOUR, I beseech you pardon this boldness that I write unto you, which I am forced to do, for that you are in her Majesty's Court, a place where I, a wretched publican, dare not presume to enter, and lift up my eyes; and yet must I take hardiness to open unto you my heart one way or other, or else to fall into a much greater fault of unthankfulness. My heart always assured me that your Honour did bear me a charitable mind, for so you ever made appearance; and I am well acquainted with the nobleness of your nature not to seem other than you are, specially that affection that you have borne openly towards me, being grounded upon your persuasion of my fidelity to her Majesty : yet how much and in what sort particularly in my late wretchedness I have been bounden unto you I had no mean to understand by the closeness of my restraint, whereunto I beseech you impute my silence. Now, since her Majesty hath extended to me her merciful grace for my enlargement, I have attained to hear some part of your great pity towards me, beside the comfort that my poor wife received of your gracious speeches in her heavy extremity. I have no mean to acknowledge it to you but by my prayer, and that can be no more hearty for you than it was before; and so you have obtained of me no more but to be the more indebted. But of honest esteemers in the world you have won a more knowledge of your nobleness; and with God, I trust, a blessed acceptation of your goodness done to me for His sake. Now, Sir, see again the hardness of my case; I so over-bound must yet be ever bold, not only to pray you to vouchsafe the taking of my most lowly thanks to yourself, but also to help me yet more to give thanks for me to my Lord Treasurer, to whom I am most highly bounden for my delivery by his mediation; God render it in mercy to him

and his.   O noble Sir, if the heaviness of my case in respect
of her Majesty's displeasure (which I could never lightly
esteem, regarding her so highly and dearly) had been known
unto you, and the sorrow of my soul for giving triumph to
the enemies of God, speaking little of so great loss to so
poor a man, so burthened with charge as I am; and the lamentable estate of my poor wife, whereof I am not yet in
full hope of recovery (and her loss were my utter worldly
destruction); your honourable nature would in pity soon record my misery, and therewith see what cause I have both to
thank you and to beseech you, and all those that have been
good unto me, to help me, that my Lord Treasurer may know
how deeply the thankful remembrance of his goodness sit-
teth in a poor man's heart, that daily shall pray to God for
her Majesty, his Lordship, and for your Honour, whom I
forbear to trouble any longer.   At London, the 10th of April
1582.   Your Honour's most humble and bounden,

THO. NORTON.[a]

The Bishop of London's letter to the Queen, about
April or May 1582, is deserving of attention.   A person of the name of Rich, accused of having favoured
Stubbes and of keeping his book contrary to the proclamation, was committed to prison, but was admitted to
bail by Bishop Aylmer, for which he incurred the
Queen's displeasure.   In his defence Aylmer needlessly
states that he would not have released Rich if he could
lawfully have kept him longer in prison; and the ac
count which the prelate gives of himself is not a little
curious:[b]—

BISHOP AYLMER TO THE QUEEN.

MOST GRACIOUS PRINCE, God hath placed you in His
own throne of justice to deliver unto His people equal mea-

---

[a] Additional MSS. 15891, f. 92.   213, 214. Life of Bishop Aylmer,
[b] Strype's Annals, III. pt. i. pp.   pp. 56—60.

sure of indifferent judgment, as He doeth unto you; wherein
you have hitherto so honourably carried yourself, as I doubt
not but you shall be to all posterity a mirror of magistrates, a
pearl of princes, and a true pattern of princely virtue, to be
followed of many, and attained of few. Whereof as all sorts
of men have most plentifully tasted, so I beseech you in the
bowels of Jesus Christ to vouchsafe the favour to me, your
most humble chaplain, God's poor minister, and your Majesty's faithful subject, that you will be pleased to hear me,
and to read these my letters, as yourself would be heard at
His hand who is much more above you than your princely
Majesty is above me. Your Highness is persuaded by my
ill-willers (for it cannot proceed from your own gracious nature) that my service is all in words, and nothing performed
in deeds. I let pass my words; my deeds are these: While I
was a private man in Lincolnshire and Leicestershire, I thank
God there was none whom, either by rigour of law, by gentle
persuasion, or weight of argument, I brought not to the
Church, and to the level of God's obedience and your Majesty's devotion. Since my departure from thence and my
coming to the *Sea* of London (for so I may justly call it in regard of the tempests that continually afflict it) things are
much altered and fallen to ruin. I suppressed the private
conventicles, which were very rife; and the deformed, or, as
they termed them, reformed churches, which were many,
and far out of order, I reduced them to conformity, agreeable to the establishment of your Majesty's proceedings. In
the country where I lived I brought the greatest towns to
unity; I made the ringleaders and guides of those seditious
sects build up that which their disobedience had destroyed; I
made them to gather where they had dispersed, and sow the
seeds of obedience where they had trodden down the corn; I
have had ever such watch upon Paul's Cross, that in my time
there came never any Puritan in that place. The ministers
and preachers in London are brought to that pass, that at
this day they be the most staid men that commonly live in
your Kingdom. To speak of punishment for disorders and

corrupt opinions, was it ever heard of that any of my predecessors did either deprive, imprison, or banish so many as I
have done?   Did ever any man stand so much with them in
disputation, or sustain by them and for them so great malice, so many slanders, yea, or so great dangers as I have
done?   These be deeds, with your Majesty's favour, and no
words.   Is there any man in England whom they take to be
so professed an enemy unto them as they hold me to be?
Whom ever have I preferred of that faction, either by myself
or by my friends on that side?   I am called a Papist, a tor-
mentor of God's children, a Bonner and butcher, a clawback,
a man-pleaser; and I am reported to your Majesty to be a
favourer of them, a milksop, and to fear such as be their
friends above the reverence and fear that I owe unto you.
No, no, most gracious Sovereign; I have learned to have but
one king, one faith, and one law, and that only will I fear.
And, for those which your Majesty thinketh do carry me in
their sleeve, I thank God the case standeth so with me, that
of a good time they have had, and yet have, a contrary
opinion of me; they know I am too inforceable, and not
easily to bend or stoop to their unlawful requests.   But if I
did fear such as be of so great power, have I not great cause to
do it, when other much meaner than they shall carry your
noble and princely nature so far from itself as what they report that you believe, and what I answer in truth that you
cannot credit?   If the meaner sort can thus much prevail
against us, what may we fear of such as your Highness hath
made so great?   But if God would breed in your sacred
breast such a princely inclination as that you would be
pleased to hear us and them alike, their accusation and our
defence, then your Majesty should see whom we would be
afraid of, when we might hold ourselves assured that we shall
come to our answer before such a Princess and so loving a
mother as will in justice hear the parties before she pronounce judgment of either.   This Rich, for whom I suffer
this heavy displeasure of your Majesty, is he not my deadly
enemy? doth he not doggedly bark against me wheresoever

he comes? What should move me to bail him, if with any
lawful regard I might have justly detained him prisoner any
longer? But admit (with your Majesty's gracious favour)
that I had erred; is there any Judge under your Highness
that walketh so uprightly as at some time or other he may
not be thought to trip or stumble? Shall all men taste
of your mercy save I? Have I not sustained these five
years the importable burden of both the Sees of Canterbury* and London, behaving myself so in that charge
as I dare justify my service before God and man? If in all
this time I have stumbled but once (if it were so), shall all
my former service be so soon forgotten, and this peccadillo
written in marble? Your Highness thinketh that the Bishop
of London may do what he will, and see everything reformed
as he listeth in the government of the Church; wherein I
beseech your Majesty to inform yourself better, and not to
suppose my authority under you greater than it is, thereby to
aggravate and make greater your indignation against me. I
can do nothing by your commission without two more, and in
these odious matters every man is commonly wont to shrink
from me. And we Bishops, what can we do? Only ex-
communicate them, and that they hold for an advantage to
keep them from the Church. If we do imprison them, or fine
them, it is a premunire, or an action of false imprisonment
may be brought against us. If we do anything in the commission, or leave anything undone, who bears the burden but
I only? when other men are at the doing of it, and have as
great authority as myself. There is nothing grieveth me
more than to see you unquieted with these sinister reports,
whereby your good blood is dried up that should water your
life in your old years, which I trust to see many, and pray
God that they may be many more than by me I am like to
see. I take God to witness, I had rather spend ten ounces of
my own than one drop of yours should be dried up by any
defect of mine. God grant your Highness may see men's
faithful service with your own eyes, and not by others, who

* In consequence of Archbishop Grindall's suspension.

commonly use such insinuations as they think you like to
hear, to further such suits of theirs as they desire to obtain;
against whom and against all men I stand thus resolute, that
I will always justify my doings, and for that I crave no mercy,
but justice. Consider, I most humbly beseech you, what
service I can be able to do you without your gracious countenance; how little my sentence shall be regarded; how those
that you will have bridled will insult, if you turn from me
your favour and countenance. Then turn me out of my place,
take again your commission, let me lead a private life, continually to pray for you; seeing it is not my good hap, with
your good liking, publicly to serve you. And thus I beseech
God, who directeth Princes' hearts *ut rivos aquarum,* ever
abundantly with His grace to bless and preserve your Majesty, and to frame your princely heart to read these my
follies without offence.   JOHN LONDON.[a]

Lord Burghley's servant, Henry Maynard, whose suit
he requests Hatton to support, was one of his Secretaries. He was afterwards knighted, and his son was
raised to the peerage:—

LORD BURGHLEY TO SIR CHRISTOPHER HATTON.

SIR, As I meant by my speech to have recommended unto
your favour this bearer, my servant Henry Maynard, in a
suit that he hath conceived, which he will declare to you, to
have the same of her Majesty's grant, being no charge to her
Highness' coffers or revenue; so being tied here by my accustomed adversary, the gout, in such sort as I durst not irritate his further malice by journeying to the Court, I do, as
you see by my writing, trouble you with my earnest request
unto you, that, if you shall not mislike his suit, you will the
rather for my sake, and so much the more as indeed his service under me is specially and only for causes appertaining to
her Majesty, and in no part appertaining to myself, show

[a] Additional MSS. 15891, f. 76.

your favour to prefer his suit to her Majesty; and in your so
doing you shall bind both me in friendship, and him in service, to be mindful to requite your goodness. From my
house at the Strand in Westminster, the 5th of May 1582.
Your most assured, loving friend,   W. BURGHLEY.[a]

Mr. Yelverton was probably Christopher Yelverton,
of Northamptonshire, an eminent lawyer, afterwards
Queen's Serjeant, Speaker of the House of Commons,
and a Justice of the King's Bench:—

SIR WALTER MILDMAY TO SIR CHRISTOPHER HATTON.

SIR, Upon some things conferred of between you and me
yesterday, I did this morning speak with Mr. Yelverton, who
at your next repair to this town will attend upon you. In
the meantime he doth assure me that he is utterly guiltless of
any of those matters whereof her Majesty hath been informed against him, and doubteth not fully to satisfy you
when it shall like you to hear him, which my request to you
is that you will vouchsafe to do; for it will be grievous unto
him that her Highness should retain any such opinion of
him, whereof he hath given no just cause. Touching the
matter I wrote of to you for him, I assure you it was altogether without his knowledge or privity. I remain of opinion as I was, that there is not a fitter man; and, these impediments being removed, I trust her Majesty will be his
gracious Lady. And so, without troubling you any further, I
leave all to be ordered as you think best, and commend you
to the Lord Almighty. From London, the 12th of May
1582. Yours for ever most assured to my power,
WA. MYLDMAY.[b]

The desire of Sir James Harvey, the Lord Mayor, to
stand well with Hatton, and the Vice-Chamberlain's

[a] Additional MSS. 15891, f. 89[b].   [b] Additional MSS. 15891, f. 85[b].

jealousy that the City should apply to any other person at Court than himself, are shown by the following letter :—

SIR JAMES HARVEY, LORD MAYOR, TO SIR CHRISTOPHER HATTON.

MAY IT PLEASE YOUR HONOUR, It is to my great grief informed me that your Honour hath conceived, that where a letter was directed unto you, praying your favour according to your accustomed goodness to this City, before any suit made to any other of the most honourable Council, and that the same was stayed by me, whereupon have proceeded such solicitations of the matter as I hear have been offensive unto you: for my own part, I am not privately so interested in the cause as that I could have any reasonable occasion to draw your displeasure upon me; and the letter that was written to sue for your favour was subscribed and sealed by me only, which could not be without intention to be a suitor unto you. The complaint was made to me by the Companies, and is a thing that concerneth not the general Corporation of the City, and Mayor and Aldermen, but the Mysteries, praying the aid of me and my brethren. Now in their own suit it was reason to hearken to themselves; and, being informed that it was their own advice among them to stay the sending of that letter, I followed their own opinions in their own matter, thinking it reasonable not to make any other suit for them, nor in other manner than I understood themselves to desire. Which being so, as it was told me that it was, I beseech your Honour to retain good opinion of me, as one greatly beholden unto you, and desirous in what I may to deserve your good favour. And so I commit your Honour to the tuition of the Almighty. From London, the 3rd of June 1582. Your Honour's to command, JAMES HARVEY, Mayor.[*]

* Additional MSS. 15891, f. 63.

Mr. Swale, the person thus warmly recommended by Hatton to the head of his College to be elected Proctor of the University of Cambridge, seems to have been the eminent civilian before mentioned:—

SIR CHRISTOPHER HATTON TO . . . .

AFTER my very hearty commendations. Understanding that one of the Proctors of the University, to be chosen to supply that place this next year, is to be nominated and appointed out of your House; and being informed by some of my good friends, and partly by mine own knowledge, that Mr. Swale is the next that, both in seniority and by the statutes of your College, ought to be elected before any other to exercise that office; I have thought good to commend him in that respect to your good favours: not for that I have any way cause to doubt that any of you, by occasion of faction or any other private regard, will be moved therein to offer him any wrong, or to keep him from his right; but especially for the good opinion which I have conceived myself of his great sufficiency, gravity, and good government, which I must justly say is such, and so well to be accepted of all those that will do him justice, as no man in your House, of his time, can deserve more commendation. In consideration whereof, I have the rather taken this course to intreat you to have due regard of his right in this behalf, that (without making any further moans to her Majesty to move you to that which otherwise you ought of your own good disposition willingly to yield unto) he may enjoy the place, according to the statutes of your College ordained directly in that behalf; wherein not doubting of your careful and friendly accomplishing, I bid you right heartily farewell. From the Court at Greenwich, the 6th of June 1582. Your very loving assured friend,

CHR. HATTON.

I am the rather bound to move you earnestly in Mr. Swale's behalf, because he is towards me, and a man in truth in whom

I repose great confidence : I pray you, therefore, do him all right with your good favours.*

Sir Robert Stapleton, whose disgraceful conduct will cause him to be again mentioned, married to his second wife Olive, daughter and coheiress of Sir Henry Shering-ton, of Lacock in Wiltshire, and widow of John Talbot, of Salwarp in Worcestershire, the " Mrs. T." of this letter from Sir Walter Mildmay :—

SIR WALTER MILDMAY TO SIR CHRISTOPHER HATTON.

SIR, I have great cause, and so I do most heartily thank you for the care I find you have of me and mine. And, for this matter of Sir Robert Stapleton's suit, it is true that he is a gentleman whom I have and do love and like of as well as of any in the North parties, whereof I trust he hath no cause to doubt; and therefore, seeing Mrs. T. is a woman very likely to marry again, I can wish her rather to light in the hands of my good friend, such a one as I take him to be, hoping surely, that, the rather by his promise made unto you, he will be a constant mediator to bring all these unnatural quarrels to a quiet end, which is the thing that I have desired from the beginning: and therefore any favour that it shall please you to procure for his furtherance at her Majesty's hands shall not discontent me; so as to yourself, and if you think good to my Lord of Huntington also, he will again confirm that which he hath so faithfully promised touching my daughter and those causes. If it would please her Majesty to show herself likewise desirous that a reasonable end might be made, I think the same would take the better success; and I and mine should be most bounden unto her Highness for so much favour in so just a matter. I am greatly beholding unto you for this most courteous and friendly dealing toward me, which, to my power, I will be

* Autograph in the Lansdowne MSS. 36 art. 38.

senting unto you his serviceable labours; humbly praying
your Honour to receive in good part his small gift which he
sendeth you, and hereafter to know and accept of his offered
good-will, according to the honourable fame which all men
give you for your courtesy. And so I beseech God to increase His grace in your worthy person. From the Marshalsea, the 10th of July 1582. Your Honour's humbly
during life, T. CHURCHYARDE.[a]

The election of Mr. Swale to the Proctorship of the
University of Cambridge was the subject of many letters, part of which are printed in this work, and others
are in the Lansdowne manuscripts in the British Museum :—

SIR CHRISTOPHER HATTON TO MR. DOCTOR NORGALL, MR. D. HARVEY, AND MR. D. HATCHER.

AFTER my very hearty commendations. Understanding that
the Master and Fellows of Caius College in Cambridge have,
by the consent and good liking of the greatest part of them,
made choice of my servant Swale, according to the statutes
of their College, and partly for his sufficiency and great forwardness in virtue and learning, as one of the meetest men
among them to supply the place of Proctorship in the University this next year; and being credibly informed, that, notwithstanding all good order hath been observed in that election, and nothing done therein which hath not been in all
respects agreeable to the true meaning of the statutes of
that house, there have been some of the Fellows there, which,
either for ill-will or other private regard, do oppose themselves against it, intending to bring the matter again into
question, which seemeth in itself so plain and apparent
as it needeth not further consideration; I have therefore
thought good, in case it shall be further urged and referred
unto you, who are the Visitors appointed in this behalf, to

* Additional MSS. 15891, f. 61[b].

commend the right of my servant in this case to your good and lawful favours; desiring you that (as I would be loath for my own part that any man should be hindered or injured by his advancement otherwise than as the order of that College shall justly allow of), so that you will be likewise pleased, the rather for my sake, to afford him indifference and justice, and not to suffer him wrongfully to be troubled, or the late election to be frustrated or overthrown, if there appear sufficient and good cause unto you to approve and confirm it; which referring to your good considerations, I bid you right heartily farewell. From the Court at Nonsuch, the 14th of July 1582. Your very loving assured friend,

CHR. HATTON.[*]

It appears that Ann Countess of Warwick (the daughter of Francis Earl of Bedford, and third wife of Ambrose Earl of Warwick, the brother of the Earl of Leicester,) had greatly interested herself for Dr. Mathew:—

DR. MATHEW TO THE COUNTESS OF WARWICK.

RIGHT HONOURABLE AND MY SINGULAR GOOD LADY, What words may I use to give your good Ladyship sufficient thanks for your so careful and honourable furtherance of my suit? But, what pen or tongue cannot express, that my faithful and dutiful heart shall perform, as during my life I am most bounden. The while, presuming upon the continuance of your Ladyship's favour, I am so bold as to send you these inclosed, which are my Lord of Hunsdon's letters to Mr. Vice-Chamberlain, to signify unto him, that as her Majesty, long sithence, did answer him, as touching Dr. Bellamy, that she liked not to bestow the Deanery of Durham upon him, so he hath utterly surceased his suit, and is well content that my friends shall, without any let of his Lordship's part, proceed in obtaining the same for me; which himself also, he

---

[*] Autograph in the Lansdowne MSS. 36.

saith, would do, but that he hath already named Dr. Bellamy unto her Highness, and therefore cannot well deal for any other. Truly, Madam, I find, that if my Lord of Hunsdon had been entreated by anybody to my behoof heretofore, he would have easily yielded me his consent, especially sithence he had received his answer against Dr. Bellamy. And I assure your Ladyship his Honour in talk giveth me just cause to suspect lest I have been, and may be, most abused where a great while I best trusted. Wherefore it may please your good Ladyship so to bestow my Lord's letters, and your favourable speeches withal, as now no longer delay be made, this only hindrance all this while pretended being thus removed. And thus humbly referring both my suit to your wisdom and experience, as also myself to your direction and commandment, I betake your Ladyship to all the good blessings of Almighty God. Christ-Church in Oxon, 23rd of July 1582. Your Ladyship's most humble and most bounden,

TOBYE MATHEWE.[*]

No other information has been found on the subject of the next letter than this marginal note:—" Mr. Knyvett had slain a man of the Earl of Oxford's in fight." Thomas Knyvett, the person in question, was a Groom of the Privy Chamber; and the interest which the Queen took in the matter was shown, in what would now be considered an unconstitutional manner, by Hatton's letter to the Lord Chancellor. It will afterwards be seen that this affair led to a quarrel between the Earl of Oxford and Knyvett in the following year, in which another man was killed:—

SIR CHRISTOPHER HATTON TO LORD CHANCELLOR BROMLEY.

MY VERY GOOD LORD, Mr. Knyvett hath informed her Majesty of his desire to have his cause of *se defendendo* determined by a privy sessions in this vacation-time. It seemeth

---

[*] Additional MSS. 15891, f. 105.

he hath found your Lordship not to like of that manner of proceeding, in which respect your Lordship hath refused to grant forth the commission. Her Majesty, in that she thinketh Mr. Knyvet's request to stand in ordinary course, marvelleth not a little that your Lordship should deny her servant the same that is usual, and that every other subject may ask. It hath pleased her, therefore, to command me to signify unto you that she looked for justice, with favour at your hands, towards this gentleman. 'You know,' saith she, 'who he is, and where he serveth; and therefore, in a cause so little important as this, you might have restrained the malice of his enemies well enough.' Haply, she thinketh, they would have his trial at Newgate amongst common thieves, or in the Bench in like sort, of purpose to make him suffer as much public reproach as they could lay on him. In this, without defrauding the law, her Highness supposeth, and is persuaded, he might be better dealt withal, and find ordinary favour, without just offence of any. It may, therefore, please your good Lordship to return by your letters the cause that moved you to stay the commission, and what way you can best devise for the help of the gentleman, to her Majesty's better satisfaction. It is her pleasure to have your answer in these two points. Mr. Knyvet likewise requireth bonds, which he and his friends, as it seemeth, have acknowledged before your Lordship of some very great sums; he is earnest to have them redelivered, and hath alleged his reasons to your Lordship therefore, wherein I have no doubt but you will deal with him according to your goodness. My good Lord, it is very necessary you take care to please the Queen in this case, for, in truth, she taketh it unkindly at your hands that she should be strained to meddle and be seen in this matter. At our meeting I will tell you more of her Highness' conceit; and so God bless you for ever, and command my service, for it is due to your Lordship. Haste; this 27th of July 1582. Your good Lordship's most bound poor friend,

CHR. HATTON.[a]

[a] Additional MSS. 15891, f. 65[b].

The Lord Chancellor's reply was not discreditable to him :—

SIR THOMAS BROMLEY TO SIR CHRISTOPHER HATTON.

Good Mr. Vice-Chamberlain, I received this 28th of July your letters dated the 27th of the same ; by the which I do perceive that Mr. Knyvet hath informed her Majesty of his desire to have his cause of *se defendendo* determined by a privy sessions in this vacation-time ; and that he found me not to like of this manner of proceeding, and therefore that I refused to grant forth the commission. True it is that I misliked of his suit ; but, that I did expressly refuse to grant the commission, that is not so. Marry, not finding his suit in my opinion reasonable, nor fit for me upon his bare request, being the party, to yield unto without further commandment, I asked him what counsel he had that so advised him ; he answered me that Mr. Recorder of London gave him that counsel. I prayed him, therefore, that he would cause Mr. Recorder to come and confer with me ; and that which in justice and conveniency I might do I would be ready to perform. Since which time I neither heard of Mr. Recorder, nor of any other of his counsel, nor of himself, touching his cause. It seemeth further, that her Highness should be informed that Mr. Knyvet's request should be a matter of ordinary course, and therefore marvelleth that I should deny unto her servant that which is usual, and every other subject may ask. This suggestion to her Majesty riseth, as I think, of ignorance ; I will not say of untruth, though indeed the matter be not true. I never knew, nor I never heard, that any party supposed to be an offender might of ordinary course have a special commission at his proper suit ; neither is it reason it should be so, for that were to open a gap to let offenders pass through without due punishment : for this commission being secretly awarded, haply to commissioners not indifferent, may sit, touching the execution of their commission, without the notice or knowledge of the adverse party; without which it is impossible to produce the proofs against the offender, and for lack of proof he must necessarily be acquitted. Indeed, in case some great or notable robbery, murder, or other offence be committed, at the suit of the parties that seek the punishment thereof, then upon advertisement from the Justices of Assize in the county where the fact is committed, or at the complaint of the Justices of the country, or by commandment from higher authority, sometimes such commissions be granted for the speedy punishment of the offence. But, at the suit of the party who is supposed the offender, I have not known any such commission granted, neither did I think it fit to be granted, until I were further satisfied by his counsel, or were otherwise commanded; the rather for that I well knew I was greatly suspected by the adverse party and his friends of favour and friendship to Mr. Knyvet; which whether I did bear and show unto him before the Coroner's inquest gave up their verdict, or not, I leave to his own conscience and report, and to the testimony of others, his friends, who were travailers in his cause; the regard and respect whereof, lest I should incur some further note, made me the more advised and circumspect touching Mr. Knyvet's desire. Lastly, in my own opinion, I could not understand how his suit for a special commission could in anywise have satisfied that which he sought for, to wit, the clearing of himself; because he standeth subject to the appeal which the brother of him that was slain may bring at any time within the year and day after the fact, notwithstanding any trial that might have ensued upon that special commission. If Mr. Knyvet were loath to be brought in public to plead his pardon, which he may have of course, touching the indictment before the Coroner that findeth it *se defendendo*, that small matter I could have devised easily to have holpen, without special commission. If he were afraid of any other indictment to have ensued by the procurement of his enemies, her Majesty's pardon, or else her warrant to her Attorney-General, would easily have cleared him of all those troubles which might have grown by any such indictment. And thus I have briefly touched unto you the causes that moved me to defer and respite Mr. Knyvet's suit. Touching the granting of any special commission, far be it from me that I should so much forget myself as to deny any of her Majesty's servants that which is ordinary or of course for every common Subject to ask: I should thereby leave my duty to her Highness, forget that which belongeth to my office, and be injurious to the party, which faults by the grace of God I will never willingly commit; and in this case now in question I am well assured I have not offended in anywise. It is happy that we serve and live under a Prince of that wisdom and bounty of nature as is not easily carried with such surmises and suggestions, otherwise the time were too miserable to serve in. For the clearing of the state of the gentleman against all that may seek his peril in this matter, I see no other way but to quit himself, and to expect whether the brother of the party slain will commence his appeal within the year and day; which I think in respect of the verdict already given before the Coroner, and the truth of the case, he never will. If he do not, then, to be out of all danger of malicious practices of his enemies, her Majesty's pardon shall be needful, though the matter of itself require it not. If the brother be disposed to sue his appeal, there is no device (to my understanding) to keep him from it; if Mr. Knyvet's counsel know therein more than I do (as they easily may), I would gladly confer with some of them, and be ready to do all the good for him that conveniently I may. Concerning Mr. Knyvet's bond true it is he required me to deliver the same. I prayed him to content himself till the whole cause were ended, and I would in the meantime keep the bond from enrolment, as I still intend to do, whereby he should not fear any danger; which answer might well have contented him without troubling of her Majesty. It had been some rashness in me to have delivered his bond, the cause not ended. And thus, heartily praying you to acquaint her Majesty with this my answer, whom I would be loath to offend in the smallest point that may be, I commit you to God.   From Weld Hall in Essex, the 28th of July 1582.   Your loving and assured friend in all I can,   T. BROMLEY, CANC.*

Former letters from Sir Christopher Hatton show the interest he took in the affairs of the University of Cambridge, especially with relation to Dr. Swale; and it now appears that Lord Burghley found it necessary, as its Chancellor, to interfere:—

LORD BURGHLEY TO SIR CHRISTOPHER HATTON.

SIR, After my hearty manner I did yesterday, lacking leisure, send to my wife, then being at the Court, that she should do a message to you, being a request that you would forbear to deal in a cause whereof I made you privy concerning some disorder in Gonvill and Caius College in Cambridge; but for that by her report of your answer (the conclusion whereof was that you would forbear, as I desired,) you did explicate to her, as she saith, being ignorant, the state of the case otherwise than I and the University take it to be, which I know is, by the information of Swale the President, contrary to the manifest truth.   I have thought good at this time briefly to inform you, that as both Doctor Legge the Master, and this Swale, hath, for my courtesy showed to them (they both deserving correction), abused me many ways, and specially have maintained covertly in the College a faction against the true religion received, corrupting the youth there with corrupt opinions of Popery; and for that I doubt that Swale and his partners will (to colour their dissimulation) inform you otherwise than truth, I do send you my servant, Vincent Skinner, who is a member of that University, to show you briefly the state of the case, and to declare unto you the proofs thereof, and consequently the true judgments against these men, one by the Visitors and superintendents of the College, the other by all the Heads of the University; so as I am

* Additional MSS. 15891.

bound to oppugn these two men's crooked proceedings, and yet therein mean no way to proceed but according to the statutes of the University and College. And at this time I have more cause to mislike them, for that they would never vouchsafe to come to me, although they have been in the City; and Swale, who is, as I perceive, now your man, (though I think he was not when he was called before me,) hath two or three times posted to this city within these few days, and that twice since I spake with you at the Court; whereby they seem to mistrust their cause, or else do presume to find some indirect favour against me, who am their principal Officer. Whereof I trust they shall be deceived, and specially at your hands, now that you are by me thus informed, according to your friendly answer given me at the Court. And so to end, I do send you the warrant for yourself signed, according to which I had subscribed your book; and pray you to procure Mr. Secretary to seal it with the signet, and to return it to me by this bearer. From my house, 30th July 1582. Your assured loving friend,   W. BURGHLEY.[a]

The following short letter from the Earl of Leicester was accompanied by a buck, which Hatton was to present to the Queen:—

THE EARL OF LEICESTER TO SIR CHRISTOPHER HATTON.

MR. CAPTAIN, I am most humbly bold to send to her sacred Majesty a poor beast bred in this soil, because it was the first was killed, and yet not the greatest I meant should have been killed; but being well killed, and the first, I sent him now to her Highness. I beseech you, Sir, present him, if he come in good order, to her Majesty, whom I trust to see kill forty of his fellows in this place; which are, and shall be preserved for her Majesty's best pleasure as long as I live, with my continual prayer for her most blessed preservation. I do mean very shortly to send again, and therefore to take

[a] Additional MSS. 15891, f. 65.

leave of you now, with my most hearty commendations.
Fare you well. This 2nd of August 1582. Your assured
friend,   R. LEICESTER.[a]

Sir Christopher Hatton's letter to the Lord Chancellor respecting Mr. Knyvet, in a former page,[b] and
his Lordship's reply, sufficiently explain the following
letters :—

SIR CHRISTOPHER HATTON TO LORD CHANCELLOR BROMLEY.

MY VERY GOOD LORD, I have showed unto her Majesty
your honourable and grave letters in answer of those which
by her Highness' direction I sent unto you of late touching
Mr. Knyvet, which were in all respects so acceptable, and
amply satisfying her expectations, as it pleased her very graciously to commend them ; allowing your judgment for the stay
and respite of the special commission to be no less considerate and agreeable to justice than this answer of yours importing the same effect to be wise and full of all honourable and orderly dealing ; wherein her Majesty, with her
great good liking, taketh especial notice of your Lordship's most discreet and careful service, for the which she
yieldeth you her most princely thanks. When I had
showed her Majesty your letters, she commanded me to
make Mr. Knyvet privy to them, who, finding them written with all honourable care and declaration of the due
course of justice, resteth likewise exceedingly well satisfied
in all respects ; saving only in the error which I had committed in my former letters to your Lordship, wherein I
termed and mistook the fact to be manslaughter, which in
very truth was found by the Coroner's inquest to be *se defendendo.* In which case he was advised by his learned Counsel
to be an humble suitor to her Highness for her gracious
favour in requesting your Lordship by letter, or otherwise,
to vouchsafe him a special commission, whereby he might in
ordinary course plead the statute, and without any suit of

pardon or further trouble be forthwith delivered and relieved
by virtue thereof. According to which direction he made
her Highness privy to the state of his cause, and humbly besought her princely goodness to signify her pleasure to this
effect to your Lordship, by whose favour he might the rather
obtain the commission which he sued for: wherein if her
Majesty have proceeded more roundly than the cause required on your Lordship's behalf, he is sorry for it, and
humbly beseecheth you not to impute it to any complaint or
want of duty in himself, but to her Majesty's own direction
and most gracious care of the good success of his troubles; in
the which as he confesseth that your Lordship hath dealt
very honourably with him in affording him the comfort of
your good favour from time to time, so doth he protest, and
for my own part I may boldly affirm as much unto you, that
he never uttered any word, either by himself or any other,
to irritate her Majesty's displeasure in any respect against
your Lordship, but thinketh himself so greatly bound unto
you, as, he saith, he must and will make known the goodness
you have showed him unto her Majesty, and endeavour in all
faithful service and good-will to deserve it. And so, most
earnestly craving that anything passed in this action may not
diminish your Lordship's good opinion of the gentleman, who,
in truth, resteth clear from any such suspicion of ill-deserv-
ing, I commit your Lordship to the grace of God. From the
Court at Nonsuch, the 2nd of August 1582. Your good
Lordship's most bound assured poor friend,

CHR. HATTON.[a]

The writer of the next letter was Anne, wife of Philip
Howard Earl of Arundell, whose father, Thomas Duke
of Norfolk, had particularly recommended him to culti-
vate Hatton's friendship.[b] The Countess of Arundell
was the sister and coheiress of George Lord Dacre of
Gillesland.

[a] Additional MSS. 15891, f. 67.   [b] Vide page 9, *ante.*

TO SIR CHRISTOPHER HATTON.

GOOD MR. VICE-CHAMBERLAIN, Having at this time so
convenient a messenger, and never wanting at any time cause
to remember how much I have been beholding unto you, I was
loath either to omit the opportunity of the one, or to show
myself unthankful for the other; and therefore, since I found
that writing was the best mean to satisfy me in either, I desired to recommend my letters to this bearer, and myself by
them to your good opinion; which, as I have often said, and
now must needs repeat, is one of the greatest comforts I have,
and the greater, because I rest assured that the constancy of
your friendship, and the goodness of your nature, is such as I
shall never lose it without desert; and I know myself so well,
as, by the Grace of God, I never mean willingly in the least
respect to deserve the contrary. I am loath to trouble you
with long letters, and the less careful to enlarge the good-will
I owe you, because, as I hope, it is sufficiently known unto
you; and therefore will here conclude, wishing you all good
hap. From Arundell Castle, the 20th of August 1582. Your
most assuredly ever,   A. ARUNDELL.[a]

LORD BURGHLEY TO SIR CHRISTOPHER HATTON.

WHEREAS her Majesty, as I understand by your letter,
would be advertised from me of the circumstances and rea-
sonableness of a suit of a certain number of her poor tenants
in Huntingdonshire being copyholders, who, seeking to have
purchased their several poor tenements from her Majesty,
upon the exchange passed to Sir Henry Darcy, wherein her
Highness had a beneficial bargain; so it is, that, though the
greatest number of these tenants held their tenements under
twenty shillings by year, as some at seven pence, some at
twelve pence, fourteen pence, twenty pence, and so at very
small values under ten shillings, yet, their small rents being
cast up altogether, there arose in one hamlet a sum of seven-

[a] Additional MSS. 15891, f. 63.

teen pounds' rent by year, and another of twenty-seven pounds, and the third to twenty-eight pounds; whereby, having regard to those of three entire values certified by the auditor, without knowing how the same did grow of such small parcels, the same tenements in one total sum were rated to be holden of her Majesty *in capite*, which otherwise, if the parcels had been expressed and severally purchased, should have been only socage, for that there is never reservation of any tenure *in capite* upon any lands but where the parcel purchased is of the value of ten pounds and upwards. But now, whereas these poor silly souls sought to purchase their several tenancies by purchases alone to every of them, they took themselves to be abused, having paid their money, and yet to be charged with a tenure *in capite*, a thing unknown to them; whereas they were as good, or rather better, to give up all their tenements freely to her Majesty, than for so small values to be charged upon every licence of alienation, and upon every death of the tenant, with so much as may extend at every time to ten pounds of fifty years' purchase, yea, to make all the rest of their lands subject to like charge; which is a thing to be pitied, and against all good meaning and conscience, as I take it. And therefore I doubt not but her Majesty will be pleased to relieve them of this their burthen by changing their tenures into socage, whereby her Majesty shall not lose anything which she had before; for none of all those tenements were ever otherwise holden but by base tenure in socage, neither will any man take them at that burthen of free gift. And so I leave to trouble you, although the poor tenants trouble me daily with their continual pitiful complaints, as being deceived in their opinions in laying out their money to have purchased their quietness, where, by this accident, they are with their own made subject to a charge unreasonable. From my house at Theobald's, this 1st of September 1582. Your assured loving friend,

W. BURGHLEY.[a]

<hr>

[a] Additional MSS. 15891, f. 61b.

The " Peerages " do not give the exact date of the death of the young nobleman upon whose decease the Queen wrote the annexed consolatory letter to his father, the Earl of Shrewsbury; but a letter from the Earl of Leicester* on the same subject, written on the 5th of September 1582, shows it had taken place shortly before that day :—

BY THE QUEEN.

RIGHT trusty and right well-beloved Cousin and Counsellor, we greet you well. We had thought, immediately upon understanding of the death of the Lord Talbot your son, to have sent you our letters of comfort, but that we were loath that they should have been the first messengers unto you of so unpleasant matter as the loss of a son of so great hope and towardness, that might have served to have been a comfortable staff unto you in your old years, and a profitable pillar unto this our estate in time to come, whereof he gave as great hope as any one of his calling within this our Realm; which we know, in respect of the love you bear us, cannot but greatly increase your grief. But herein, We, as his Prince and Sovereign, and you as a loving and natural father, for that we both be interested in the loss, (though for several respects,) are to lay aside our particular causes of grief, and to remember that God, who hath been the worker thereof, and doeth all things for the best, is not to be controlled. Besides, if we do duly look into the matter in true course of Christianity, we shall then see that the loss hath wrought so great a gain to the gentleman whom we now lack, as we have rather cause to rejoice than lament; for if the imperfections of this declining age we live in be truly weighed, and the sundry miseries that we are daily subject unto be duly looked into, we shall then find more cause to judge them unhappy that live, than to bewail those as unfortunate that are dead. But,

* Lodge's Illustrations, II. 235.

for that the weakness of frail flesh cannot so rest upon that comfort which the happy estate of his change hath wrought but that nature will have her force, We cannot therefore but put you in mind how well God in His singular goodness hath dealt with you, in that He left you behind other sons of great hope, who through the good education that you have carefully given them, and the good gifts of nature they are plentifully endowed withal, are like to prove no less comfortable unto you than serviceable unto us. And, therefore, for your comfort you are to remember, that, of four sons that He hath given you, He hath taken only one to Himself. These reasons, which we have thought on and used with good fruit as means to lessen our own grief, we have thought meet to impart them unto you, and do hope they shall work no less effect in you, whose case we tender as much as our own, having made as great trial of your care and fidelity towards us as ever Prince hath made of servant. And, therefore, we do assure ourself that in this discomfort there is no earthly thing can yield you more comfort than the assurance of our gracious favour towards you; whereof you may make full account to receive the same from us in as full measure as a well-deserving servant and subject may in true gratuity look for at a gracious and thankful Prince's hands. Given under our signet.[a]

Walsingham seems to have neglected no opportunity of recommending that acts of courtesy should be shewn to the Earl of Shrewsbury, while the Queen of Scots was in his custody :—

SIR FRANCIS WALSINGHAM TO SIR CHRISTOPHER HATTON.

Sir, I send you herewithal a letter directed to the Earl of Shrewsbury from her Majesty, containing such points as were prescribed by your letter. I pray you help to excuse such defects as are fallen out in penning of the same, which may work, without your good and friendly endeavour therein,

---

[a] Additional MSS. 15891, f. 88[b].

some dislike in her Majesty. I could wish that this letter were sent by an express messenger. The Earl is a great personage, and employed in service of greatest trust, wherein he hath both honourably and faithfully acquitted himself, and therefore deserveth some extraordinary regard to be had of him. In such a time of discomfort, such an unwonted kind of favour doth work a singular contentment in one of my Lord's birth and desert. Now, having delivered my opinion unto you, I refer the use thereof to your good consideration, and so commit you to God. At Barn Elms, the 6th of September 1582. Yours most assured,

FRA. WALSINGHAM.*

The "hearty noble couple," from whose house Leicester wrote the following letter, were Henry first Lord Norris of Rycot, and his wife, Margery, daughter and coheiress of John Lord Williams of Thame. It appears that they expected to have been honoured with a visit from the Queen :—

THE EARL OF LEICESTER TO SIR CHRISTOPHER HATTON.

GOOD MR. CAPTAIN, Having so convenient a messenger I thought good to salute you, and withal to let you know I found a very hard journey yesterday after I departed from you. It was ten of the clock at night ere I came here, and a more foul and ragged way I never travelled in my life. The best was, at my arrival I met with a piece of cold entertainment at the Lady's hands of the house here; and so had you done too, if you had been in my place; for she was well informed ere I came that I and you were the chief hinderers of her Majesty's coming hither, which they took more unkindly than there was cause indeed. But I was fain to stand to it that I was one of the dissuaders, and would not for anything, for the little proof I had of this day's journey, that her Ma-

* Additional MSS. 15891, f. 94.

jesty had been in it; being, indeed, the very same day her Highness should have come hither, which I remembered not till this question grew. Well, I did, I trust, satisfy my Lady, albeit she saith she cannot be quiet till you have part of her little stomach too. Trust me, if it had not been so late, I think I should have sought me another lodging, my welcome awhile was so ill; and almost no reason could persuade but that it was some device to keep her Highness from her own gracious disposition to come hither. But I dealt plainly with her, that I knew she would have been sorry afterwards to have had her Majesty come at this time of the year to this place. I assure you, you should find it winter already. Thus much I thought good to tell you, that, when my Lady comes thither, you may satisfy her, as I hope I have done; but her Majesty must especially help somewhat, or else have we more than half lost this lady. To help to make amends, I offered her my lodging there, if her Majesty stayed at Oatlands. They had put the house here in very good order to receive her Majesty, and a hearty noble couple are they as ever I saw towards her Highness. I rest here this Sabbath-day to make peace for us both ; what remains you shall do at their next charge upon you. God grant I find her Majesty no worse than I left her, and you as well to do as myself. From Rycott, the 11th of September 1582. Your old assured friend,   Roᵗ. LEICESTER.*

The Earl of Sussex was long afflicted with a painful disease, and died at Bermondsey, in Southwark, on the 9th of June 1583. His Countess, who so affectingly describes his sufferings, was his second wife, Frances, daughter of Sir William, and sister of Sir Henry Sidney, K. G., and the foundress of Sidney-Sussex College, Cambridge ;—

* Additional MSS. 15891, f. 58ᵇ.

FRANCES COUNTESS OF SUSSEX TO SIR CHRISTOPHER
HATTON.

GOOD MR. VICE-CHAMBERLAIN, I heartily thank you for
your friendly letter, wherein you do as well bemoan my
Lord's painful sickness as comfort my grieved mind. I would
I saw cause to write to you that either the consultation of
the physicians about his estate, or their medicines applied to
his feeble body, did procure him any ease; but, to be plain
with you, as with one that I presume loveth my Lord much
and wisheth his well-doing, with heart's grief I must briefly
advertise you that his strength generally is decayed, his pain
greatly increased, and his physic hath offered him rather torment than remedy; so as he is at this present determined for
a few days to forbear medicines, and to see what good office
nature is able to work for his ease. I suppose no man be
more grieved than my sick Lord; nevertheless he armeth his
mind in that resolute manner, that with all humility he
thanketh God for his visitation, and with all patience he endureth the painful torments of his disease. God, I humbly
beseech Him to send him shortly to recover, and me some occasion to requite the great courtesy that you have now showed me. And so I commend me heartily unto you. From
Newhall, the 16th of September 1582. Your loving friend,

FRA. SUSSEX.[a]

A marginal note states that the following letter, to
which there is no signature, was written by "the old
Countess of Bedford," meaning Bridget, daughter of John
Lord Hussey, and widow of Sir Richard Morison. She
was the second wife of Francis second Earl of Bedford,
and died without issue by him in January 1600. The
interest she manifests about the Lord Deputy of Ireland, Arthur Lord Grey of Wilton, is explained by his

[a] Additional MSS. 15891, f. 77b.

having married her daughter, Jane Sybilla Morison, widow of her step-son, Edward Lord Russell, the son and heir-apparent of the Earl of Bedford, by his first wife Margaret, daughter of Sir John St. John of Bletshoe;—

ANNE COUNTESS OF BEDFORD TO SIR CHRISTOPHER HATTON.

GOOD COUSIN, I have by many experiences approved that such is the nature of envy as it ceaseth not by all endeavours to darken the worthy actions and services of those that have dutifully and faithfully with their great perils and exceeding toil performed all good offices in their callings, and in those affairs wherein they were employed for their Prince and Country.   And therefore, though my conscience persuadeth me that my Lord Grey hath by his travails in Ireland done as well, and governed those parts as painfully, carefully, and justly as any man that ever exercised that place before him ; yet, I fear me there hath not wanted some such as have extenuated his Lordship's good services : for this cause I could not but earnestly recommend unto you the preservation of his Lordship's well-deserved honour and credit with her Majesty against such as have, or may seek to impair the same. I am loath often to trouble any of my best friends (in which number I reckon yourself); but, when I have cause, I make full account they will not be slack to further such reasonable requests as I make unto them : and both the party, (who particularly is very dear unto me,) and the matter, assureth me of your best favour herein towards the one and the other ; and though I be not ignorant of your special affection to his Lordship, many ways witnessed by your friendship, nevertheless I might not be satisfied unless I had said somewhat for him : neither could I bethink or make choice of any to whom to write, that for both our sakes would be more willing to yield furtherance to all his Lordship's actions than yourself. And so I pray God to increase in you all true honour and happiness.   1st October 1582.   Your assured friend.*

* Additional MSS. 15891, f. 97.

No clue exists to the name of the writer, nor to the subject of the following letter:—

TO SIR CHRISTOPHER HATTON.

SIR, I have briefly set down, as you may see in this paper herein inclosed, the state of the note which I gave you intelligence of at my last being in Court; wherein, considering the great conscience and reason that the case carrieth with it, in all appearance there may easily some good be obtained in my poor opinion. But if it should happen otherwise, and that the success should not fall out to be so fortunate, either in this or in any thing else that I should give you notice of, as I would wish for, yet I hope that of your wonted noble mind and great wisdom you will not make it my fault, nor measure my good meaning and faithful heart by any unhappy event, much less by any undeserved gall that fortune may mingle with your honourable actions, whom I know to be far more wise to judge, and better able to compass, than I am or ever shall be; assuring you, that if either well wishing, or a poor man's earnest devout prayer might do you service, your noble heart (that hath so often wrought my good) should never fail of that which it most desireth. Whom I commit to God's providence. 3rd October 1582. Your Honour's most bound.*

The name of Theodore Beza, one of the most celebrated of the Reformers of Germany, is well known. When the following letter to Hatton, requesting aid from England, was written, Beza was Chief of the College at Geneva, founded by Calvin.

THEODORE BEZA.

GRATIAM ET PACEM A DOMINO.

QUOD ipsa necessitas, tentare nos cogit, minime tamen auderemus, nisi nobis ad te illustrissime Domine aditum

---

* Additional MSS. 15891, f. 97ᵇ.

patefaceret illa singularis tua, sermonibus omnium celebrata, humanitas; qua non tuæ tantum gentis homines sed etiam peregrinos, et procul natos comiter excipere atque adeo laborantes sublevare consuevisti; facile igitur ut spero excusationem apud te, hæc audatia nostra inveniet. Quod autem, cogente summa necessitate petimus partim ex ipso hujus reipublicæ legato nisi molestum est cognoscere, te velim; partim etiam, illustri tuæ amplitudini brevibus exponam. Veteres Sabaudicie domus, cum hac civitate, intra ipsius ditionem sitæ, inimicitias quales nimirum Philippus cum Atheniensibus et reliquis Græciæ civitatibus, tantisper exercuit dum illarum libertatem opprimeret, juvenis hic princeps, quorundam conciliis usus, violatis pactis quæ pater ipsius nobiscum adhibito jurejurando, sanciverat, renovavit, nobis proditione primum multiplici, tentatis, mox etiam aperta vi ætate superiori, impetitis, proditiones dominus admirabili prorsus ratione patefecit, et sapientissimi magistratus manu vindicavit. Vim illatam, patientia fregimus; civitatem communire contenti et præsidium intra urbem continere tantisper dum copias justas, partim ex Helvetiis quorum ille tamen partem sibi conciliarat, partim ex Gallicis ecclesiis colligeremus: Ecce vero, cum jam jam, ad irruptionem, una cum sociis Bernensibus faciendam parati essemus, factum est Helveticarum septem civitatum interventu, ut data utrimque fide, futurum est (quod unum semper cupivimus) omnes controversiæ jure, non vi, coram Helvetiorum concessu, decidantur arma deponerentur. Et hic quidem est, presens nostrarum status quo nihil sane optabilius contingere nobis potuit, si modo convenire de sessuris minime suspectis judicibus inter nos possit; qua de re hoc ipso tempore apud Thermopilas, Helveticas disceptatur. Sed dum, quod sit hostium ingenium, quod sit verum illorum consilium, consideramus Tridentini videlicet conciliabuli executionem in his regionibus a civitatis Genevensis hac deinceps quatuor Evangelicarum Helvetiæ civitatum oppressione, Sabaudicarum licet vix . . . . . . spetiem preferentium, controversiarum, prætextu . . . . . . quid aliud, nisi longe quam . . . . . .* tates

* Sic.

possimus expectare. Ne dum. Ut quicquam sermi possimus ex ista juridicæ cognitionis simulatione, quam ab hoste necessitas extorsit polliceri: ad hoc malum accedit et aliud, quod videlicet ita jam sit exhaustum hujus reipublicæ ærarium quæ publicum longe, maxima ex parte, proventum, consueverat ecclesiæ impendere ut nisi aliunde fulciatur coactura sit illam necessitas maximo cum plurimarum ecclesiarum detrimento curam illam si non totam abjicere (absit enim illud) tamen non minima ex parte, abrumpere, quod sese nimirum tutari et tantis in res illas, sumptibus, sufficere non possit. Hæc sunt illustrissime mi Domine, quæ nos cogunt, tam procul subsidium aliquod ab his petere, quorum pietatem et caritatem scimus nunquam afflictis piis desuisse. A vobis inquam Anglis quibus cum nobis peculiaris quædam veteris hospitii necessitudo intercedit, petitione nostra ut speramus, licet in verecunda tamen propter periculi saltem magnitudinem facile excusationis locum inventura. Bene vale illustrissime mi Domine. Dominus Jesus Deus et Servator ille noster exaudit suorum gemitibus, rabiem Satanæ coerceat, suas ecclesias adversus exteros et domesticos omnes hostes quam diutissime tueatur. Genevæ, decimo Octobris 1582. Amplitudini tuæ addictissimus,

THEODORUS BEZA.

Post.—Oro te mi domine, ut quod aliena manu ad te scribam, tremulæ meæ vaccillationi tribuas.*

The annexed mysterious letter from Sir Thomas Heneage to Hatton may, with the assistance of two marginal notes,—the one stating that by "water" Sir Walter Raleigh was indicated, and the other, that the Queen sometimes called Hatton her "bell-wether," and "pecora campi,"—be fully explained. It appears that Hatton, jealous of being superseded in the Queen's favour by Raleigh, had sent her a letter expressing his fears on the

* Additional MSS. 15891, f. 113ᵇ.

T 2

subject, accompanied by three "tokens," namely, a diminutive bucket, (typical of his rival,) a bodkin, and a book. These were committed to Heneage to deliver to the Queen, who found her going into the park to kill a doe. Expecting that Raleigh would soon approach, Heneage immediately presented the tokens and letter. On seeing the bucket she perfectly understood its import, and exclaimed "There never was such another!" Elizabeth then tried to place the bodkin in her hair, but failing, gave it back, with the letter unread, to Heneage. After walking a little distance, the Queen asked for the letter, which she perused "with blushing cheeks," and said many things, as if doubtful "whether she should be angry or well-pleased;" but she at last expressed "her settled opinion of the fidelity and fastness of his affection, and her determination always to give him good cause not to doubt her favour." Heneage was then commanded to inform Hatton that she was so ill pleased with his letter, that she had little desire to look at his tokens ; that Princes should be like Gods, and suffer no element so to abound as to breed confusion, meaning that Raleigh's influence would have no undue effect; that "*pecora campi* was so dear to her that she had bounded her banks so sure as no water or floods could overflow them," *i. e.* that she loved him too firmly for Raleigh to supersede him in her regard: and to prove that he need not fear "drowning," she sent him a dove, "the bird that, together with the rainbow, brought the good tidings and the covenant that there should be no more destruction by water." She moreover bids him remember how dear her "sheep" was to her, and sends Mr. Killigrew specially to carry this token and Heneage's letter to him, with directions to bring her word how he did:—

SIR THOMAS HENEAGE TO SIR CHRISTOPHER HATTON.

SIR, Your knowledge of my love shall suffice, I trust, to satisfy you of my best endeavour to do that which may best content you. I received your letters, with your token to her Majesty, before ten of the clock this morning, which I carried up immediately to her Highness, then ready to ride abroad to kill a doe in the parrock of the great park; and desiring to furnish her Majesty with the bucket, because I thought (as it happened) water should be so nigh her as soon as she came out of her drawing chamber, I presented her withal together with the letter you wrote, which she took in her hand, and smiling said 'there was never such another.' And seeking to put the bodkin in her head, where it could not well abide, she gave it me again, and the letter withal; which when she came into the standing in the parrock she took of me and read, and with blushing cheeks uttered many speeches (which I refer till I see you), the most of them tending to the discovery of a doubtful mind, whether she should be angry or well pleased; in the end showing upon conference her settled opinion of the fidelity and fastness of your affection, and her determination ever to give you good cause nothing to doubt her favour. That which I was willed to write unto you is this: that she liked your preamble so ill, as she had little list to look on the bucket or the book; and that if Princes were like Gods, (as they should be,) they would suffer no element so to abound as to breed confusion. And that *pecora campi* was so dear unto her that she had bounded her banks so sure as no water nor floods could be able ever to overthrow them. And, for better assurance unto you that you should fear no drowning, she hath sent you a bird, that (together with the rainbow) brought the good tidings and the covenant that there should be no more destruction by water. And further she willed me to send you word, with her commendations, that you should remember she was a Shepherd, and then you might think how dear her Sheep was unto her. This was all that I was willed to write, which she commanded me with her token to deliver to Mr. Killigrew, whom she meant to send to bring her word how you did. Since you went, her Majesty hath had very sharp disposition, as it appeared to Sir Thomas Leighton and my Lady Tailboys. Yesterday all the afternoon Stanhope was drawn in to be with her in private, and the Ladies shut out of the Privy chamber. To conclude, water hath been more welcome than were fit for so cold a season. But so her Majesty find no hurt by it, I care the less, for I trust it shall make neither me nor my friend wetshod: with which hope I commend me wholly to your taking pity of Jacques' long and late journey. From the Court, hastily, this 25th of October 1582. Your own so bound ever,

THOMAS HENEAGE.[*]

Dr. Mathew, and his suit about the Deanery of Durham, again appear in November of this year:—

DOCTOR MATHEW TO MR. SAMUEL COX.

MR. Cox, For your direct and loving letter in answer to mine I am far in your debt. But, under the reformation of his Honour, I think it will not appear by any note of my hand that ever I meant to withdraw my suit for Durham. Only it may seem how great lack I should sustain by dependence of the suit till Michaelmas was past, whereby the former years' fruits must grow rather to the Residentiaries of that Church than to the next Dean, and so he be the less able a good while after to keep that hospitality which would be expected. Howbeit, since a man cannot have as he would, I would as I can. It may please you to peruse my note again, if it be kept. I dare assure you it will be found none other in effect than I have now declared, for it were hard I should write that I never thought. But now that Mr. Vice-Chamberlain resteth already, by your good persuasion, satisfied in the point, and signifieth unto me by you the full continuance with increase of his honourable disposition to my preferment unto that place before all other, with a careful

<hr>

* Additional MSS. 15891, f. 97ᵇ.

regard to be mindful of so poor man, I beseech you, Sir, do me this favour to return his Honour, with my bounden duty, most humble thanks, and re-assure him in your best and truest manner you can possible, that as my good success hath and doeth depend upon his favour in the furtherance thereof, so shall I never omit any occasion to do his Honour all duty and service.   To yourself, for the pain you take therein to do me this pleasure, I shall be more and more beholden, and accordingly bounden to requite your friendship.   And so, waiting a good hour, not of death yet, but of despatch at last, I most heartily recommend you, as my very self, to the grace of God.   Sarum, 2 Novembris 1582.   Your assured loving friend,   TOBIE MATHEW.[a]

On the 7th of November 1582, Lord Burghley lost his son-in-law, Mr. William Wentworth, eldest son of Lord Wentworth, who had married Elizabeth Cecil, Queen Elizabeth's god-daughter;[b] and it is to this event that Sir Francis Walsingham alludes in the following letter.   Burghley's other son-in-law, the Earl of Oxford, had for some time been in disgrace; and this was thought a favourable opportunity to move the Queen to restore him to her favour:—

SIR FRANCIS WALSINGHAM TO SIR CHRISTOPHER HATTON.

SIR, At my arrival at my poor cottage, I met with this woeful letter, and because I cannot perform his request of excuse touching his lady, nor repair to Hertford, by reason of my absence from Court, I have thought good to lay the burden upon you.   It would be some comfort to his Lady, if it might please you so to work with her Majesty as his other son-in-law, that hath long dwelt in her Majesty's displeasure, might be restored to her Highness' good favour.   I leave this to your best consideration.   Besides my particular

---

[a] Additional MSS. 15891, f. 26[b].
[b] Murdin's State Papers, pp. 746, 755, 756.

grief for the loss of that virtuous young gentleman, I am sorry, for her Majesty and the Realm's sake, that so towardly a member should be taken away. 7th November 1582. Your most assured friend, FRA. WALSINGHAM.[a]

The following are Hatton's letter of consolation to Lord Burghley on Mr. Wentworth's death, and his Lordship's reply:—

SIR CHRISTOPHER HATTON TO LORD BURGHLEY.

MY SINGULAR GOOD LORD, Her Majesty standeth so much moved with your sorrowful letters, as she findeth herself more fit to accompany you in your grief than to comfort you in this your irrecoverable loss. Your Lordship so well and holily instructed in God's fear, and so well exercised with the mutable accidents of this wretched world, will call reason to your relief, with thankfulness that God the Creator of us all hath called this His virtuous and zealous creature to the participation of His heavenly inheritance. We should lack of duty towards our Redeemer in resisting His will, and show a kind of envy in lamenting his most glorious exchange out of a frail and sinful life to an everlasting mansion and Heaven of joys. My good Lord, cast off this woe; let it not touch your heart, in which the wisdom of this world and state hath found her seat for many years, to God's glory, the Realm's safety, and your mortal renown. Her Majesty sendeth your good noble friend, Mr. Minors, to you, who will more largely impart her pleasure unto you; and so, with my humble prayers to God for your long life and comfortable being, I most humbly take my leave. In haste, this 8th day of November 1582. Your good Lordship's most bound poor friend, CHR. HATTON.[b]

LORD BURGHLEY TO SIR CHRISTOPHER HATTON.

GOOD MR. VICE-CHAMBERLAIN, I have great cause to thank you for your letter, full of good counsel and godly advice,

[a] Additional MSS. 15891.
[b] Autograph in the Lansdowne MS. 36, art. 7.

which God give me grace to follow, knowing it necessary for
me to obey His will in all things; but yet a hard lesson for
flesh to learn, and herein my case differeth from all others.
For though I know I ought to thank you, yet, contrarywise
to all other causes that require thanks, which are given with
joy from the heart, in this I cannot but sprinkle my thanks
with tears and sobbings; and yet from my heart. I will not
defend my passions, but beseech God to be my comfort, as in
some part I feel thereof, by the comfortable messages sent to
me and mine by His principal minister, my Sovereign sweet
Lady the Queen's Majesty, whom I pray God to preserve
from all grief of mind and body, whereby her poor people
may long enjoy her, as a mother and a nurse of general peace,
both worldly and heavenly, by the free teaching of God's will
out of His holy word. And so abruptly I end, without end
of quietness. And truly, Mr. Vice-Chamberlain, I do not
lament so much the loss of a son-in-law, (which was very
good,) but of a virtuous gentleman, in whom I took so great
delight as now my grief is the more increased. From my
poor house at Theobalds, the 9th of November 1582. Yours
and yours,   Wm. Burghley.*

The two following letters do not require any remarks :—

WRITER UNKNOWN, TO MR. SAMUEL COX.

If you were as careful to perform as you are ready to
promise, you had long ere this time tasted of our sweet and
pleasant air; and your poor friends here had enjoyed your
company, which they have so often wished for. Seeing it
will not please you to come upon the motion of your own
desire, do me the favour, I pray you, to come at my entreaty;
and so shall you make me the more beholding unto you, in
respect that you have done me this pleasure, to take this
pains rather to satisfy my contentment than your own liking,
especially in a time when your coming can yield you no other
delight than the only sight and hearty entertainment that

* Additional MSS. 15891, f. 26ᵇ.

your faithful true friend can give you, whose comfort shall be
greatly increased by your presence. Let me put you in mind,
therefore, as I have done often, to be careful of your promise,
and endeavour somewhat, as you may, to answer my expectation, and to satisfy the debt which you owe me in respect
of the love I bear you; otherwise you shall make me challenge the commendation of courtesy and good-will before
you, which neither my desert can in truth attain unto, nor
your gentleness and wisdom suffer without apparent note of
injury. If you will make me worthy of this favour, then, to
increase my debt, let me intreat you to bring your brother
with you. So shall I acknowledge myself doubly beholding
unto you, first for your own coming, and then for his company, unto whom I wish all happiness, as I do to you the
fortunate supply of all your desires. From the Court at
Windsor, the 20th of November 1582. Your assured friend.[*]

SIR THOMAS HENEAGE TO SIR CHRISTOPHER HATTON.

MY DEAR AND MOST HONOURABLE KNIGHT, Your letters
declaring your noble kindness and remembrance of me,
together with the notice of her Majesty's but once thinking
graciously of so poor a man as myself, doth bring especial
comfort unto me, that otherwise, in this unthankful and forgetful age, should be very little displeased to be both forgotten and contemned, which the high and great minds of the
world so much scorn and hate. Yet this same base contempt
and withdrawn life is found full oft to be no unsafe shadow
from very great displeasures, which the pride and disdain that
accompanieth praise, and the business of much action and
greatness of place, doth bring unto men. And sure, Sir, this
earthly mind of ours, entangled with pleasures which all
flesh delights in, and entrapped with great hopes of honour
and praise which the best wits are caught with, can seldom
have leisure to look into itself, much less up to Heaven,
whither till he come, none can be happy. Then, to miss our
desires, to fail in our expectations, to be forgotten of our

[*] Additional MSS. 15891, f. 98[b].

friends, to be left of the world, and so to be carried home to look up to God, what loss is in this reckoning? And if it be, as it is said, that the way to Heaven is rather upon crosses than carpets, what cross can be so light as this, (both without shame or pain,) not to be cared for, specially when we see that God, of His unspeakable goodness, is most ready to take them to His favour and care that the world hath cast off, yea, and that care not for themselves? But whither run I out of Seneca's school, where I learn, 'to speak well is easy, to do well is hard, but to be well is happy,' which God grant you long on earth with honour, and at last in Heaven with glory. From Copthall, 26th November 1582. Your own ever bound, &c.   T. HENEAGE.[a]

Were it not the plan of this work to give the whole contents of Sir Christopher Hatton's " Letter Book," the fact that the following memorable remonstrance of Mary Queen of Scots has been often published, as well in the original French as translations, together with its great length, might have made it doubtful whether it should be now reprinted, even though this is a contemporary translation, and differs from all the others. But no one, who peruses this beautiful letter, could wish it excluded from any collection in which it once found a place. Its touching eloquence; its solemn admonitions; its pathetic description of the feelings of an imprisoned Queen debarred from her rights, and of the yearnings of a mother for her only son; its imperative demand for justice; its bold, if not convincing, assertion of innocence, and its burning reflections upon her oppressor, impart to this document an interest which it is as impossible to describe as to exaggerate:[b]—

[a] Additional MSS. 15891, f. 29.
[b] The original letter is preserved in the Cottonian MSS. Caligula C. vii. f. 54. An abstract was printed by Camden, in his "Annals of Queen Elizabeth," and it is given at length

MARY QUEEN OF SCOTS TO QUEEN ELIZABETH.

MADAM, Upon the intelligence I have received of the late conspiracies executed in Scotland upon my poor son, and being occasioned to fear the consequence thereof by mine own example, it behoveth me to employ that small part of my life and power that I have remaining, in disburthening my heart, before I die, of my just and lamentable complaints; whereof my desire is, that this my letter may remain unto you, as long as you live after my death, as a perpetual witness and imprinted seal in your conscience, as well for my discharge to all posterity, as to the shame and confusion of all them that by your privity have so cruelly and unworthily intreated me unto this day, and brought me to that extremity where now I am. But because their purposes, practices, actions, and proceedings, how detestable soever they were, did always prevail with you against my most just defences and sincere behaviour; and because the power which you have in your own hands hath carried away credit amongst men, I will have recourse to the living God, our only Judge, who hath equally and immediately established us under Him over His people to govern them. I will call upon Him in this extremity of my most urgent afflictions to render to you and me, as He will do in the Last Day, the portion of our merits and deserts, the one as well as the other. And remember, Madam, that no masks, nor paintings, nor policies of this world will help us before Him; though mine enemies under you may for a season cover their subtle and malicious inventions and godless sleights from the eyes of men, and peradventure from yours. In His name, therefore, and as before Him sitting as Judge betwixt us both, I will call unto your remembrance, first, how by the agents, spies, and secret messengers sent under

in Adam Blackwood's " Martyre de Marie Stuart, Reyne d'Escosse." It is in Jebb and Whitaker, and of course in Prince Labanoff's collection, in Miss Strickland's "Letters of Queen Mary," and in some other works.

your name into Scotland whilst I was there, my Subjects
were corrupted, practised withal, and stirred up to rebellion
against me to seek the destruction of my person; and, to
be short, to do, enterprise, and execute all that was done
in that country during the troubles: whereof I will make
no particular recital more than of that which I drew out
by the confession of one of them that was most advanced
afterwards in respect of that his good service, and by witnesses brought face to face unto him, whom if I had at that
time executed, as in justice I should have done, he had not
afterwards by means of his old intelligences renewed the
self-same practices against my son, neither had he been a
mediator unto you for my traitorous and rebellious Subjects
for aid and support to be yielded them from hence, as they
had ever since my imprisonment here; without which support I think the said traitors could not have prevailed
then, nor afterwards have made their part good so long as
they did.   During my imprisonment at Lochleven, Throckmorton, that dead is, counselled me in your name to sign
this release, which he told me should be offered me, assuring me that it would not be good.   And since that time
there is no place in all Christendom where it hath been so
reputed and taken, but only here, where the authors of it
have been assisted with open force.   In conscience, Madam,
would you acknowledge such like liberty and power in
your Subjects?   And yet, notwithstanding, my authority
hath been by my Subjects cast upon my son at these years
when he was not able to execute it; and since, when I
would have established him lawfully in it, being of age to
help himself for his own good, it was upon a sudden plucked
out of his hands, and given to two or three traitors that
have already taken away the effect of it, and will in fine
take away the name and title, as they have done from me,
if he gainsay them never so little; yea, and his life too,
if God be not watchful to preserve him.   And as soon as
I had escaped out of Lochleven, and was ready to give my
rebels battle, I sent unto you by an express gentleman a

diamond which before you had sent me for a token, and
to assure me that you would aid me against my rebels; and,
that more is, in case I would withdraw myself from thence,
you would come to the borders to assist me in person: and
this was confirmed unto me by divers other messengers.
This promise coming from your own mouth, and often repeated, (though I had been oftentimes abused by your
Ministers,) caused me to put such trust in the effect thereof
as that, when my camp was broken, I came straight to cast
myself into your arms, if I might have come unto you as
well as my rebels did.   But, as I purposed to repair unto
you, I was taken by the way, and delivered up to a guard,
and shut up in divers castles, and, in fine, brought past
all shame into that captivity wherein I stand at this day,
languishing with the sufferance of a thousand deaths.   I
know you will object against me the matter that passed
between the Duke of Norfolk, that dead is, and me.   But
I will stand in it and make it good, that there was nothing
done therein to your prejudice, nor against the good estate
of this Realm.   And the treaty was first allowed of by the
advice and seals, yet extant, of the chiefest that were then
of your Council, assuring us that they would procure your
favour and good liking to it.   How durst such personages
enterprise to have made you consent to the taking away of
your life, honour, and crown? for so you make semblance,
to all Ambassadors and others that talk with you of me,
that you are persuaded.   In the mean season, (my rebels
perceiving that their outrageous headiness carried them further than they purposed, and the truth of those slanders
that they spread of me appearing to the world by that
conference whereunto I submitted myself voluntarily in this
country to discharge myself publicly in the full assembly of
your deputies and mine,) behold the chiefest among them,
being now reclaimed and sorry for their former error, pur-
sued by your forces, and besieged in the castle of Edinburgh, with others that held with me; and one of the
chiefest amongst them imprisoned; another, less guilty than

any, most cruelly hanged; after that I had twice caused
them to disarm themselves at your request, upon assurance
of accord and agreement, which God knoweth whether my
enemies ever meant.   I resolved a long time by experience
to try if patience would amend the rigour and ill entreaty
which had been used towards me, especially the space of
ten years, conforming myself exactly to the order that was
prescribed me for my captivity in this house, as well in
respect of the number and quality of my servants which I
keep, having dismissed the other, as for my diet and necessary exercise for my health.   I have lived hitherto more
peaceably and quietly than any one of much baser quality
than I am, and more bound than by such entreaty I ought
to be, forbearing to make request to have any intelligence
with my son and Country, and only because I would minister
no occasion of suspicion or mistrust unto you; a matter
that by no right or reason could be denied me, especially
against my son, who against reason and nature was by all
means possible persuaded against me, to the end that by
our division we might be weakened.   But you will say
that I was licensed to visit him above three years ago:
his captivity at that time, under the tyranny of Morton,
was the cause of it, as his liberty since was of your refusal to give me leave to visit him in like sort all this
year past.   I did oftentimes make motions for an establishment of good amity betwixt us, and a sure intelligence betwixt these two Realms for the time to come.   At
Chatsworth, about eleven years since, there were certain
Commissioners sent unto me for that purpose.   The matter was dealt in with yourself by the Ambassadors of
France and mine.   I myself, the last winter, offered by
Beale as large conditions as possibly I could.   And what
is come of it?—My good meaning despised; the sincerity
of my behaviour neglected and misreported; the state of
my business thwarted by delays, surmises, and such other
sleights; and, to be short, worse and more unworthy usage
from day to day, whatsoever I could do to deserve the

contrary: my too long unprofitable and hurtful patience
having brought me to this point, that mine enemies, through
their wonted custom to do me ill, may now by right of pre-
scription use me, not as prisoner, (as in reason I ought
not to be,) but as a slave, whose life and death, without all
respect either of God's laws or of man's, dependeth upon
their only tyrants. I cannot suffer it any longer, Madam,
but must needs, being in way of death, discover the causes
of my death; or if I live, as God shall give me any longer
respite, assay under your protection to extinguish by what
means soever the cruelty, slanderous reports, and traitorous
purposes of my foresaid enemies, to the end I may purchase
myself some little better rest for the small time I have to
live. And therefore, first of all, to clear the pretended
occasions of all differents that are betwixt us, rip up and
unfold, I beseech you, if you please, whatsoever hath been
reported unto you of my behaviour towards you, cause
the depositions of the strangers taken in Ireland to be
perused, let the examinations of the Jesuits lately executed
be laid open before you, give all men liberty that will to
charge me openly, and suffer me likewise to answer for
myself. If I be found guilty, let me suffer for it; which
I shall more patiently abide when I know the occasion. If
I be guiltless, cloak it not any longer; and suffer me not
to be so evil recompensed any more, to your great burthen
both before God and man. The vilest malefactors that are
in your prisons, and born under your obedience, are brought
to their trial; and their accusers, and matters wherewith
they are charged, always brought before them. And why
cannot I, in like order, be proceeded with; being a Sovereign Queen, nearest of your blood, and your lawful heir?
I think that this last quality hath been hitherto the principal cause of mine enemies, and of all the slanderous
speeches that have been cast out of me, to the end to set
us at variance and to cover their unjust pretences withal.
But alas, they have now small reason and less need to
torment me any longer in this respect; for I protest unto

you upon my honour, that, at this day, I look for no other
Kingdom but the Kingdom of my God, which I see prepared for me, for the better end of all my afflictions and
adversities by-past. It shall behove you to discharge your
conscience towards my son for that in this behalf shall
belong to him after my death; and in the mean season
not to suffer the continual practices and secret drifts, which
our enemies in this Realm daily go about for the advancement of their pretensions, to prevail to his prejudice, labouring on the other side with our traitorous Subjects in Scotland by all the means they can to hasten his ruin. Whereof I require no better proof than the charge given by your
late Ministers and Deputies sent into Scotland, and that
they have treated and seditiously practised there, without
your privity as I will believe, but with good and earnest
solicitation of the Earl my good neighbour of York. And
to this purpose, Madam, by what law can it be maintained
and made good, that I, a mother, should utterly be forbidden, not only to help my son in this so extreme necessity
wherein he is, but also to be made acquainted with his
state? Who can be more dutifully and sincerely careful for
him than I? Who can be more near him than I? At the
least, if by sending to him to provide for his safety, as the
Earl of Shrewsbury gave me to understand of late from you,
it had pleased you to have received therein my advice, you
might with better occasion, me thinketh, and with greater
bond of my part, have dealt in the matter. But consider
what you have given me occasion to think, when, upon such
a sudden forgetting of the offence that you pretend against
my son, even then, when I prayed you that we might send
to him together, you despatched a messenger to him where
he was prisoner, not only not making me privy to it, but
also restraining me at the same time from all liberty, to the
end I might in no sort have any news of him. But if their
meaning which persuaded you thus suddenly to visit my son,
was for the preservation of the quiet state of that Country,
they needed not to have been so careful to have kept it secret

U

from me, as though it had been a matter wherein I would
not have concurred with him; and they have caused you to
lose the thanks that I would in that behalf have given you.
And, to speak more plainly unto you, I pray you, use no
more such means nor persons. For although I make this account of Sir George Carey, in respect of the place whence
he cometh, that he will not engage his honour in any vil-
lainous act, yet had he an assistant, a sworn partisan of the
Earl of Huntingdon, by whose ill-offices so wicked an account
could not but bring forth answerable effect. So that this
only shall suffice me, that you would not suffer my son to receive any hurt out of this Country, (which was all that I ever
required of you heretofore, especially at such time as an army
was sent to the frontiers to stay justice that was executed
upon that detestable Morton,) nor that any of your Subjects
either directly or indirectly do meddle with the affairs of
Scotland without my privity, to whom only the authority of
those matters belongeth, or without the assistance of some
one from the French King, my good brother, whom, as our
principal confederate, I desire to make partaker of all this
cause, notwithstanding the small credit that happily he hath
with the traitors that at this present have my son in prison
amongst them. In the mean season, I tell you plainly that
I esteem and account this last conspiracy and innovation as
mere treason against the life of my son, the good estate of his
affairs and of his Country; and that, as long as he shall remain in this estate, (whereof you are privy,) I will never
repute and take any word, writing, or any other act that
cometh from him or passeth under his name, to proceed from
his free and voluntary disposition, but only from the foresaid
conspirators, who, with the hazard of his life, make their
profit of him to serve their own turns. But, Madam, besides
all this liberty of speech, which I foresee may haply displease
you in some part, although it be nothing but a truth; you
will take, I am sure, more strange that I come to importune
you with a request much more important, but yet very easy
for you to grant, and this it is: that whereas I could not

hitherunto, by accommodating myself patiently so long a time to the rigorous entertainment of this captivity, and carrying myself most sincerely in all things, even to the least, that might any ways concern you, purchase myself any assurance of your good favour towards me, nor give you any of my sincere affection towards you, whereby I am out of all hope to be anything better used the rest of the small time I have to live; it would therefore please you for the honour of the painful passion of our Saviour and Redeemer, Jesus Christ, to give me leave to withdraw myself out of this Kingdom into some place of rest, where I may seek some comfort for my poor body so much tormented with continual grief, and with liberty of my conscience prepare myself to God who daily calleth for it. Believe me, Madam, (as the physicians also which you sent me the last summer be of like opinion,) I am not like to live long, so that you can have no just ground of any jealousy or distrust on my part, and yet, notwithstanding, take of me such assurances, and conditions so just and reasonable, as you shall please, which you may enforce me always to keep by reason of the great ability and power you have, though I would not break them for any thing in the world. You have sufficient experience of the keeping of my simple promises, though sometimes prejudicial to me, as in this behalf I showed you about two years since. It may please you to remember what I wrote unto you at that time, how that you could by no means, save only by gentleness and by a mild course, bind my heart firmly unto you, though you would confine my poor languishing body for ever between two walls; considering that those of my quality and nature cannot be forced by any rigour. Your wrongful prisons, void of all rightful ground, have already destroyed my body, which you cannot but shortly see brought to an end in case you continue it there but a little longer, and mine enemies shall not have much time to satisfy their cruelties upon me. I have nothing but the soul left, which cannot be captivate by any power you have. Give it leave, therefore, freely to breathe a little after her safety, which she

only seeketh at this day more than all worldly honours. Me
thinketh it should be no great satisfaction and advantage unto
you to have mine enemies tread my life under their feet,
and to stifle me before your eyes; whereas, if in this extremity, though too late, you have delivered me out of their
hands, you should make me greatly beholding to you, and all
that belong unto me, and especially my son, whom peradventure by this means you might make assured to you. I will
not cease to make this request unto you continually until
you have granted it me. And, therefore, I pray you that I
may understand your pleasure herein; having for your better
satisfaction attended this two years' space until this day, and
forborne to refresh the same, whereunto the miserable estate
of my health presseth me more than you can conceive. In
the mean season provide, I beseech you, that my entertainment here may be amended, which I can no longer bear; and
put me not off to the discretion of any other but to your own,
to whom alone, as I wrote of late unto you, I will hence-
forward take myself beholding, and impute the good or evil
that I shall receive in this Country. Do me this favour,
that I may have your pleasure in writing, or the Ambassador of France for me; for to trust to that that the Earl
of Shrewsbury, or any other, shall say or write to me in
your behalf, I find by experience it will be no assurance
for me : the least occasion in the world that they can devise
will be sufficient to alter the whole between this night and
to-morrow in the morning. Moreover and besides, when I
wrote last to your Council, you willed me that I should
not refer myself to them, but to you only. And, therefore,
to extend their credit and authority only to do me hurt, it
were no reason; as it fell out in this my last restraint, where,
against your meaning, I was too unworthily used. Which
thing causeth me to doubt lest that some of mine enemies in
your Council have an eye to beware and take heed that
other of your Council be not partakers of my just complaints, seeing haply that some of their companions like not
of their wicked attempts against my life, or, in case that they

should come to the knowledge of them, they would oppose themselves both for your honour and for their duty towards you. Two things, in fine, I am principally to require of you: the first, that, as I am ready to depart out of this world, I may have with me for my comfort some honourable church-man daily, to put me in mind of the way that I am to make an end of, and to instruct me to finish it according to my religion, wherein I am resolutely bent both to live and to die. This is the last duty, that cannot be denied to the veriest caitiff that goeth upon the earth. It is a liberty that you give to all Ambassadors of foreign nations, as in like sort all Princes catholic do give to yours,—exercise of their religion;—and I myself never forced my own Subjects to do anything contrary to their religion, although I had Sovereign authority over them. And if I should in this extremity be deprived of this liberty,—you cannot justly do it, (and what should it profit you to deny it me?)—I hope that God will excuse me, if, being oppressed in this sort by you, I render him that duty in heart which is only left me. But you shall give a very ill example to other Princes of Christendom to use the like rigour towards their Subjects as you use towards me, being a Sovereign Princess and the next of your blood, as I am and will be as long as I live, in despite of all mine enemies. I will not be troublesome unto you at this present for the increase of my household, which I shall not have so great need of during my time I have to live here. I only pray you that I may have two chamber-maidens to help me in my sickness, assuring you that I could not be without them if I were the poorest creature that goeth upon the earth. I beseech you grant me so much even for God's sake, and that mine enemies may know that they have not so much credit about you against me as to wreak their vengeance and cruelty in a matter of so small consequence, and depending upon a simple office of humanity.

I come now to that wherewith the Earl of Shrewsbury did charge me, to wit, that against my promise made to Beale, and without your privity, there hath·been some dealing be-

twixt my son and me to surrender to him my title of the
Crown of Scotland, having bound myself not to proceed
therein without your advice and by one of my servants, who
was to be directed by one of yours, in whose company he was
to go.   These be the very words, if I be not deceived, of
the said Earl.   Touching this matter, I will tell you, Madam,
that Beale had never any simple or absolute promise of me,
but only certain conditions of motions, which I am not in
anywise to be bound unto unless the conditions be first performed which I joined with them.   To which conditions I am
so far from having received any satisfaction, that contrarywise
I never had any answer to them, neither yet any mention
of them from you.   And to this effect I remember very well,
that when the said Earl of Shrewsbury, since Easter last,
would have had me to confirm that that I said to Beale, I
answered him plainly, that it was only upon condition that
the said conditions should be granted me, and thoroughly performed.   They are yet both alive to witness the truth of the
matter, in case they will deliver the truth.   Since that time,
seeing I could receive no answer, and contrarywise that mine
enemies did by delays and surmises continue, more licenti-
ously than ever they did before, these practices, built from
the time that Beale was with me, to traverse my good meaning in Scotland, as by effects hath well appeared—that by
these means the gate lay still open to the destruction of my
son and me ; I took your silence for a denial, and discharged
myself by express letters both to yourself and to your Council of all that that had passed betwixt me and Beale.   I acquainted you with that that the King my brother, and the
Queen my mother-in-law, wrote unto me with their own
hands touching this matter, and plainly requested your advice, which is yet to come: by direction whereof, in truth,
I meant to have proceeded, if you had thought good to have
let me known it in time ; and would have suffered me to have
sent to my son, assisting me with those motions which I had
acquainted you withal for the establishing of a good amity
and perfect intelligence in time to come between these two

Kingdoms. But to bind myself barely to follow your advice before I knew what it would be, and to submit my minister for the voyage to the direction of yours, especially within my own Country, I was never so simple as once to think of it. Now I will refer to your consideration, in case you have been acquainted with the false play that my enemies on this side have played in Scotland to bring their purposes to that pass they are at, whether of us two went the soundest way to work? Let God be judge betwixt them and me, and turn from this Island the just punishment for their deserts. Look over once again the advertisements that my traitorous Subjects of Scotland may haply have sent you, you shall not find amongst them,—which I will maintain before all Princes christian,—that there hath passed anything from me sounding to your prejudice or against the quiet estate of this Kingdom, which I affect as greatly as any Counsellor or Subject you have, having greater interest in it than any of them. There was speech to gratify my son with the title and name of King, and to assure him in that title, and the rebels of free pardon of their former offences, and to set all things in good quiet and peace for the time to come, without any alteration or change of anything. And was this to take away the Crown from my son? I think mine enemies would not have him established in it, and therefore are very well content that he should hold it by the unlawful violence of certain traitors, ancient enemies to our whole race. And was this to seek to punish the former offences of the said traitors, which my clemency did always surmount? But an ill conscience can never be at rest, carrying always about with it fear and trouble. Was the seeking and procurement of a general reconciliation betwixt our Subjects by a merciful forgetting of all former things, a means and purpose to alter the quiet estate of the whole Country? What prejudice had this been unto you? Tell me, then, and let me plainly understand, if you please, wherein you will have me answer upon my honour. Oh, Madame, will you suffer yourself to be so much blinded with the cunning sleights of mine enemies as to establish after you, and 'peradventure against yourself, their unjust pretensions to this Crown ? Wil you suffer them wittingly and willingly to ruinate and cruelly seek the destruction of them that are so near you both in heart and blood? Can it ever be any honour to you, or profit, that by their means my son and I should be separate so long the one from the other, and we both from you ? Lay hold upon the old earnests and pledges of your good nature; bind your own unto you: give me this contentment before I die, that I may see sound good-will and amity betwixt us; that, when my soul shall depart from this body, it be not constrained to pour forth sighs and sobs to God for the wrong that you have suffered to be done us here on earth; but contrarywise, departing in peace and concord with you out of this captivity, it may go to Him, whom I pray to inspire you aright with due compassion of my foresaid most just and more than reasonable complaints and grievances. At Sheffield, this 28th of November,[a] 1582.

Your very disconsolate nearest relation and cousin,

MARIE R.[b]

Walsingham seems to have been more exposed to mis-representation than any of his colleagues, possibly be-cause it was well known that the Queen always disliked him :—

SIR FRANCIS WALSINGHAM TO SIR CHRISTOPHER HATTON.

SIR, In men's absence from Court envy oftentimes doth work most malicious effects; and therefore I am to pray you, as my honourable good friend, to procure that I may enjoy the ordinary course of justice, not to be condemned un-heard. I trust there will be no fault found with my absence, for that I see no use for the present of my service. And, if

---

[a] The date of this letter in the original is the *eighth* of November 1582; but in Hatton's " Letter Book," and in Blackwood, and other places, it is dated on the *twenty-eighth* of that month.

[b] Additional MSS. 15891, f. 9.

there were, I hope as it hath not been hitherto, so shall it never be found that I shall prefer my particular before the public.   This day the Earl of Leicester took my poor house (where he dined) in his way to London; where, as I gathered by him, he is to be occupied about the provision of New-year's gifts.   He desireth, that, if there be any fault found with his absence in this present nakedness of your Court, you will excuse him.   And so, Sir, praying you to have us both in your protection, I end.   At Barn Elms, the 22nd of December 1582.   Your assured friend to command,

FRA. WALSINGHAM.*

Sir Thomas Heneage's next letter relates to a similar proceeding, and contains the same allusions as those in his letter of the 25th of October.   Still jealous of Raleigh, Hatton intimated his feelings this time by a jewel or token, in the form of a "fish prison," instead of a "bucket;" on receiving which, with his letter, the Queen again expressed her preference of him to his rival, by the same silly conceits about "water," "fish," "flesh," and "sheep," as on the former occasion:—

SIR THOMAS HENEAGE TO SIR CHRISTOPHER HATTON.

SIR, There is no office I more willingly execute than to satisfy your desire, or to testify unto you the service of my best good-will.   The fine fish prison, together with your letter this bearer brought me, I presented immediately to the delightful hands of her sacred Majesty, who read it, well pleased to see you a little raised from your sour humour; and hath willed me to write unto you that the water, and the creatures therein, do content her nothing so well as you ween, her food having been ever more of flesh than of fish, and her opinion steadfast that flesh is more wholesome; and further, that if you think not *pecora campi* be more cared for of her

* Additional MSS. 15891, f. 37.

both abroad and at home, and more contenting to her than
any waterish creatures, such a beast is well worthy of being
put in the pound.   Besides, but for stirring choler in you,
that for the most part carrieth men too far, her Highness
told me she would have returned to you your token; but
worn it is with best acceptance.   And to conclude: to please
you and not to play with you, by her looks and words, which
be no charms of guile, but the charters of truth, I am fully
persuaded you are so sure of her blessed favour as may comfort your life, content your heart, and conclude you to be
most happy.   In which estate God long hold you till He take
you to Himself.   From the Court, 29th of December 1582.
Your own, whilst I am anything,   T. HENEAGE.*

Several undated and not very important letters occur
in the "Letter Book," among those of this period;
and, it being impossible to assign them to their exact
places, they will be added to the correspondence of
this year.   As all the writers and the subjects of their
letters, where material, have been before mentioned, no
illustrations are necessary.

DR. MATHEW TO SIR CHRISTOPHER HATTON.

RIGHT HONOURABLE, What furtherance I have found by
your especial favour in my suit for the Deanery of Durham,
I shall never forget while I live, but ever acknowledge
with all the thankfulness and service I may possibly show.
Howbeit, as I have divers times and divers ways been sounded
so deeply, as some could reach to my shallow bottom, what
assistance therein I have found at your hands; so, the more
curious they were to understand thereof, the more was I still
fain and forced to suppress how singularly I have been
bounden to your Honour, and thereupon constrained in sort
(not without grief of mind and danger of your evil opinion)
to withdraw myself, both further than I would and longer

* Additional MSS. 15891, f. 30.

than was meet, from presenting to your Honour my humble
due thanks for your secret and assured favour. But such is
your experience in this place, and your wisdom such in
causes of weight, as, all circumstances considered, I trust
you will make an honourable and favourable construction
both of mine absence and of my silence: and give me leave
withal to beseech your Honour, as well to continue her Majesty's resolution upon me, as also to further my more
speedy despatch, to my more credit here and my less loss at
Durham; whence I am credibly informed that many things
there (besides the government of the Church) go daily to
rack; the mansion-houses decayed, the woods wasted, the
game spoiled, and the grounds unlet, but not uneaten, and
as much havoc made as may be of all that might be beneficial unto me.   To this if the season be added, which now
more and more hasteth on, as well for carriages as for other
provisions necessary to be made for the whole year ensuing,
it may partly move her Majesty to the more tender consideration of the poor estate of her humble servant, leaving behind him all the living he hath, and departing so far off, as
it were, into another world; and although it may seem to
savour of presumption both to crave the benefit and to
assign the time, yet verily, Sir, I am nothing so importune
with your Honour to be gone, as many good men of that
country and Church been earnest with me to be there, who
suppose the delay rather to grow upon some slackness in
myself, than of any slowness in my good friends and honourable intercessors: among whom as I have to reckon you, Sir,
for one of the chiefest of all in many respects; so, might it
please you to expedite the matter, as I know you may, I
should not only be double bounden unto you, both for my
happy success in the end and for my good speed the while,
but accordingly be both directed and commanded by your
Honour, whom I thus humbly recommend to the grace of
God. Your Honour's at commandment, humble and bounden,

                          TOBIE MATHEW.[a]

[a] Additional MSS. 15891, f. 91b.

DR. MATHEW TO MR. SAMUEL COX.

SIR, Although, either by your absence from the Court or lack of leisure, I receive no news from you of my bill signed, yet, knowing how much you have steaded me therein from time to time, I cannot but remember you with letter thanks until I may see you at the Court, which I hope to do the end of the next week; for by that time I hope to be delivered of an impediment I am letted withal, as this bearer may better tell you than this ink and paper will well bear. The while, I pray you deliver these enclosed, and furnish out their defects with the supply of your accustomed friendly words. And so, for this time, I most heartily betake you to the grace of God. Your ever assured friend,

TOBIE MATHEW.[a]

LORD BURGHLEY TO SIR CHRISTOPHER HATTON.

SIR, I have read your letters of the 17th, by which you declare her Majesty's gracious conceiving of the good service of her servant, Mr. Middlemore, to be such as she vouchsafeth him the Searcher's office void by the death of Gray; and to that end she willed you so to advertise me, and therewith to let me understand, that herein having (as your words are) partly encroached upon me to do her servant good, I shall find her Majesty graciously willing to pleasure any man of mine to whom I intended the same. For answer to thus much, I know my duty is to obey anything that her Majesty shall command, as well in any other thing as in this; specially considering the disposition of this Office dependeth upon the Office which I hold but at her pleasure, and thereof I confess myself unworthy for all respects but for good-will, wherein I may as a gnat compare with a camel. True it is, that as my predecessor disposed of this to a man of his own, so I had a meaning to have done the like upon one that serveth under me, but not principally for myself; and yet, now her Majesty

[a] Additional MSS. 15891.

knowing this my intention, minding it otherwise, I shall withdraw my own mind therein, and conform myself to her Majesty's pleasure, neither regarding the relief of my servant
that hath lived long in expectation, nor yet any small scrupulous point of my own estimation, not doubting of any meaning
in her Majesty hereby to diminish my poor credit. And, so to
conclude, I will presently, as once already I have done, give
strait charge to all the inferior Officers to have good regard to
this charge.   And for Middlemore's placing, at my coming to
the Court, (which shall be very shortly,) I will do that which
shall serve to the execution of her Majesty's commandment;
and so have I told Mr. Middlemore, the bringer hereof.
Praying you, Sir, to interpret my writing to the best sense to
content her Majesty, whom to please I know it my bounden
duty, and that simply, even both for God's cause, (whose
image to me she is,) as also for her own particular goodness
showed largelier to me than I can deserve : and yet without
hypocrisy, I dare say, there is no servant, from her Porter's
lodge to her Chamber door, hath more care in conscience and
in deeds to serve her than I.   You see my cogitations are
somewhat stirred, to enlarge thus much to you my good friend.
Your assured loving friend,   W. BURGHLEY.[*]

THOMAS CARTWRIGHT TO SIR CHRISTOPHER HATTON.

YOUR Honour's love to the doctrine of the Gospel, with
hatred of Foreign power and Popery, whereof I have conceived
opinion by report of some persons of right good credit, (your
sincere proceeding wherein I beseech God may make you
truly and perfectly honourable,) hath put my pen in my hand
to write unto you for the obtaining of some of that grace of
which you have so great store with her Majesty, to my especial relief in a cause, the equity whereof I leave to your
Honour's judgment after it shall please you to inform yourself
of the same. For, seeing all Godly truth is so near of kin one
to the other as no sisterly bond is to be compared therewith,

[*] Additional MSS. 15891, f. 90[b].

the door of your harbour being open to the one, I trust shall
not be shut up against the other.   Having laid hereupon the
principal ground of my encouragement, there came to my
mind for my further confirmation therein, that, if it be of
honourable report to do good to many, it is much more that
your goodness should light upon those that are trodden underneath the foot: which is so much the more acceptable to God,
as He hath more especially commanded the care of those than
of any other; and so much the more welcome unto men, as
every one hath a nearer sense and greater gladness of his
change from a troublesome estate unto a quiet, than from a
quiet unto a more commodious.   My trouble, if it like your
Honour, is not only the restraint of my liberty these six
years, but especially, as that which lieth much heavier upon
me, the suspicion of disloyalty whereof I stand accused to her
Majesty.   The matter is this: First, I do with most humble
thanks, chiefly unto the Lord our God, and then to her Majesty, which is His good hand towards us, acknowledge the
estimable treasure of the doctrine of the Gospel that shineth
amongst us.   Then, I cannot deny but that I have written
some things which run into the evil speeches of divers otherwise well-disposed; the cause whereof is the clamorous and
unconscionable reports of certain which love themselves too
much; who have learned too well this point of husbandry, to
sow their seed of slanderous speeches thick and threefold, to
the end that some at the least may take.   For I am charged
with things which not only I did never write, but which never
entered so much as into my thought.   As, to give the attempt
of the overthrow of all good government in the commonwealth; to mislike of Magistrates, and especially of Monarchs;
to like of equality of all Estates, and of a headless ruling of
the unruly multitude.   In the Church, to persuade the same
disorder of setting no difference between the people and their
governors; in their governors to leave no degrees; to give to
the Ministers in their several charges an absolute power of
doing what them liketh best, without controulment of either
civil or ecclesiastical authority; and, for the present estate of

our Church, that I carry such an opinion of it as in the mis-
·like thereof I dissuade the Ministers from their charges, and
the people from hearing the word and receiving the sacraments at their hands, unless it might be in such sort as I myself would have it.   All which judgments as I utterly detest,
so for the maintenance of them there shall not be found,
without open and violent wresting, so much as one sentence
in any of my books that have been published: whereas to the
contrary there are divers sentences of that clearness that none
can deny but he will say that it is not light at noon-day.   If
haply your Honour will ask after proof, it cannot be more
certainly had than of my books written in this behalf.   If
that may seem too long, let the trial be by the Ecclesiastical
Discipline* written in Latin, which as it handleth the same
matter, so, by a preface set before it, I have testified my agreement therewith.   If yet a shorter way be sought, the prefaces
to my several books, containing the sum of the matter in demand, will answer of my dutiful meaning in these causes.   If
any other more reasonable way may be advised of, I will thereunto most willingly submit myself.   Only my humble suit is,
that I be not condemned in silence, but there may be a time
of trial, as there hath been of accusation.   Her Majesty hath
an ear open to her poorest Subjects : I am one of that number; in humble submission with the poorest, in affectioned
good-will towards her long reign and heaped felicity with the
richest, as that which I have daily most humbly commended
unto the Lord from the first time that ever I had any feeling
knowledge of the Gospel until this present.   Others have
audience at her Majesty's hands when their goods are but
touched; my name, which is a much more precious possession, is rent asunder: their causes concern but themselves;
mine reach unto many and divers persons: theirs is in earthly
matters; mine is in heavenly.   Being, therefore, in dutiful al-

---

* "A full and plain Declaration of
Ecclesiastical Discipline out of the
Word of God, and of the declining
of the Church of England from the
same ; with a Preface by Cartwright," 4to., 1574. A Reply to
this work, by Dr. Bridges, was published in 1584 ; and a Defence of it,
in answer to the Reply, in 1588.

legiance equal, and in a matter which I complain myself of
above others, my humble suit is, that in indifferent hearing
and information of the cause I may not be inferior unto them
all. I desire nothing more than that the cause itself, so far
as it shall be proved good, might so appear unto her Majesty.
My next desire is, that, if I must needs remain in her Highness' suspicion, (the grievous sorrow whereof I shall not lay
down but with my life,) yet that it may be according to that
which I have written, and not according to that which I am
reported of; so shall I be sure to be eased of the slanderous
surmise of my disloyalty to her Majesty's estate and to the
Commonwealth, likewise of my love to Puritanism and
Church confusion; the contrary of both which I do most earnestly protest, with this offer, that if either be proved against
me, I will refuse no extremity to be practised upon me. This
is my humble suit; wherein whatsoever your Honour shall
bring to pass, for that you shall not have me alone, but numbers of others favouring the truth, bound unto you. And
thus I humbly commend your Honour to the Lord's gracious
keeping, whom I beseech daily to increase in you all godliness
and honour to His glory. Your Honour's humbly to command,   THOMAS CARTWRIGHT.[a]

THOMAS CHURCHYARD TO SIR CHRISTOPHER HATTON.

SIR, Though I am over-bold so often to write, yet having
ill hap by God's visitations, and hoping your honourable
favour will excuse this my hardiness, I have presumed, as you
see, to trouble you with these few lines. I trust now my long
suit will shortly be answered to my desire, and I believe
assuredly that order was taken for my release before I fell
sick; but, as I have ever seen and found, some takes the
wood from the fire when I seek most to be warmed; and
yet all these hinderers of hap cannot take away the love
which I bear unto my dear friends, nor appal no part of my
honest mind. I know it is miserable to crave, servitude to

[a] Additional MSS. 15891, f. 22.

receive, and beggarly to want; which three afflictions my betters are visited with, and my inferiors cannot avoid : but yet I would it might have pleased God that I had never known them.   My late imprisonment is cause presently both of my necessity and gout; God forgive them that clipped my feathers, and hindered my health, when I might have flown where I had listed.   To come home for mercy, and have imprisonment presented to me; to serve truly, and to be coldly considered; to lie sick, and not visited, is a strange destiny; but yet much more strange to live long in liberty, and no one man living to help me.   Thus do I, poor abandoned wretched creature, bear the insupportable burthen of all sorrowful imaginations, as God Himself knoweth best, who send me health and increase your Honour.

THOMAS CHURCHYARD.[a]

The " Company " mentioned in a letter from Norton to Sir Christopher Hatton, was clearly the Stationers' Company, whose privileges a printer called Bynneman, " his servant," had infringed :—

MR. THOMAS NORTON TO SIR CHRISTOPHER HATTON.

It may please your Honour, your servant Henry Bynneman, being charged by complaints of some of his Company for obtaining her Majesty's privilege for printing of certain books, hath in his defence exhibited her Majesty's letters patents under the Great Seal of England, to which it becometh every good Subject to yield due reverence and obedience.   And, for my own part, I would be loath not to be found an obsequious acknowledger of her prerogative and authority.   He hath yet, upon charitable motions, for relief of poor men of that Company, yielded some good part of his right; and the rather, that your Honour may have cause to think him an honest man and worthy of your favour.   This being true, and he desirous that you may know that for your

<hr>

[a] Additional MSS. 15891.

X

Honour whom he serveth he would do what becometh an
honest man, I am bold to signify it unto you, that you may
find yourself in your honourable disposition to have the more
cause to continue to him your accustomed goodness in defence of that right whereunto her Majesty by your mediation hath entitled him, and which he so reasonably offereth
to use. And thus, humbly commending you to the grace of
God, I forbear any more to trouble your Honour. At London, the 5th of January 1582 [1583]. Your Honour's
humble at commandment,   THO. NORTON.[a]

All that Camden says of the affair of which Sir John
Norris gives so full an account in the following report to
the Queen, is that, when the Duke of Anjou "had spent
in the Netherlands a great mass of money supplied
out of England, and that with no success, and found
that there were bestowed on him bare and idle titles
only, and that the government and managing of matters
rested in the Estates' hands, he attempted, with a rash
design, to force Antwerp and other Cities, but all in vain,
and not without loss of his own men; and shortly after
left the Netherlands with dishonour :" [b]—

TO THE QUEEN.

MOST GRACIOUS SOVEREIGN, It may please your most
excellent Majesty to understand that on Saturday night last
past, being the sixth of this present, the burghers of this town
of Antwerp being in some jealousy of the French, who were
lodged in the town in great numbers, increased their watch
to the double number they were ordinarily accustomed,
causing every household to hang out lights into the streets,
and withal in the evening gave warning at the Court to such
gentlemen as were lodged in the town to repair to their
lodgings by nine of the clock. The Duke took not this

---

[a] Additional MSS. 15891, f. 42.   [b] Annals, b. iii. p. 13.

dealing in good part, but seemed much discontented that any
jealousy should be conceived of those of his train; and the
next morning about nine of the clock, repairing to the
Castle, had conference with the Prince touching that matter,
which was executed in as good sort as might be, and the
occasion thereof imputed to some light dealings and indiscreet
speeches lately let fall by some of the French; and, that all
might be appeased, proclamation was presently made that
all those of the French which belonged to the army should
forthwith repair to the troops at Burgherhault, whither the
Duke determined to go after dinner to take a view of the
whole forces between one and two of the clock, accompanied
with the most of the gentlemen of his Court. His Highness
passing through the gate that leadeth to Burgherhault, suddenly those of his train which came after began to seize the
gate, and fell to some blows with the burghers which that day
guarded the port; having caused eight ensigns of the French
to be in a readiness and to come forward, who also entered the
gate, and had advanced themselves within the town as far as
St. Jaques Church and near to the Great Bourse. The alarm
being given throughout the town, the Burghers immediately
took arms, and so well acquitted themselves, that in somewhat less than three quarters of an hour the gate was recovered, and the French caused to retire with the loss of
eight or nine hundred at the least, besides Messieurs De
Fervaques, Chamount, De Fargie, L'Averne, Beaupre, La
Ferte, La Rasseliere, and some others, whose names I have
not learned, which, being dismounted from their horses, were
brought into the town by the Burghers, and remain under
guard in several houses. The Marshal Biron was the night
before gone out of the town to set all things in order against
the Duke's coming to Burgherhault; the Duke of Mont-
pensier accompanied his Highness, and so did the Count De
a Vall. The Count De la Marshe, not thinking of any
such matter, was playing at tennis, and from thence conducted by the Burghers safely to his lodging. In this tumult
hath been slain men of name: the Count Chasteaureux'

son; the Count St. Aignon and his son; Monsieur De Tyan, governor of Alost; a son of the Marshal Biron's; Secevalle; Biragues; and many others of good account. The Duke went straight to Berckham to a castle one mile from Antwerp, where he yet remaineth; from whence this day he sent letters to the Prince excusing the attempt of the soldiers, being driven thereunto, as he saith, by the great misery and extremity they had long endured; offering to employ himself, and such means he had, to the benefit and defence of their country if they should think good to accept thereof. The messenger, being a Maister d'hostell to his Highness, with a Colonel of the town, are returned back again with answer, the effect whereof I cannot yet understand. About the same time of this attempt in Antwerp, the French possessed themselves of Dermound, Dixmuyde, Dunkirk, and Vilvorden; and, attempting to do the like at Bruges, it is said the Burghers of the town have cut all the French in pieces. Letters were immediately sent from the Prince and the States here to others their towns of garrison, advising them to stand upon their sure guard for the better preventing of any French practice against them. There was slain of the Burghers in this tumult between forty and fifty persons, and some few hurt; and of the French better than a thousand; as it is judged, besides three or four score hurt, which have been found alive under the dead bodies when they were carried to their burial. This being as much as I can presently advertize your Majesty touching this late accident, it may please you to give me leave to end with my most humble and hearty prayers to Almighty God to defend and keep your most excellent Majesty against the practices of your enemies, to bless your estate, and to grant you a long and prosperous reign amongst us. From Antwerp, the 9th of January 1582 [1583]. Your Majesty's most dutiful subject,

J. Norris.*

* Additional MSS. 15891, f. 48.

Another proof of Hatton's amiable disposition is afforded by the following letter :—

TO THE EARL OF DERBY AND THE BISHOP OF CHESTER.

MY VERY GOOD LORDS, Whereas the Lady Egerton of Ridley standeth bounden for her appearance before your Lordships to answer such matter as she is charged with touching her disposition in religion, I am credibly given to understand, that albeit she hath not hitherto conformed herself to her Majesty's proceedings, upon a certain preciseness of conscience incident to divers of her sex, without reason or measure oftentimes ; yet in other respects she hath always showed herself very dutiful and of a good behaviour, so far forth as she continually entertaineth a chaplain in her house, who usually says the service both for her household and neighbours according to her Majesty's laws.   I am further informed the gentlewoman is very aged, and in very weak disposition of health, troubled oftentimes with sundry infirmities, the which of late are much increased upon her; in consideration whereof I think her case rather to be pitied, and that haply it may fall to better purpose to seek to reduce her by a mild and gentle course, than to endanger her health by imprisonment or other of the said proceedings against her. I am therefore to recommend her to your Lordships' favourable considerations, and to desire you (if in your wisdoms it may be thought convenient) to be pleased to give her a further time of toleration until Michaelmas next, in hope that, by such convenient means as in that space may be wrought, she may be easily brought to better conformity. Wherein what course it shall please your Lordships to take, together with the grant of this her humble request (wherein I am earnestly pressed by special friends), I shall think myself much beholden to your Lordships for it, and be ready to requite the same in what I may, as it shall please your Lordships to use me.   And so, wishing to you, my Lords, most happy fortune, I take my leave.   From the Court at Wind-

sor, the 10th of January 1582 [1583].   Your Lordships'
poor friend, most assured,

Chr. Hatton.[a]

La Motte Fenelon and Manninville were sent to
Scotland by the King of France in 1582, to endeavour
to deliver the young King out of the hands of the Earl
of Gowrie and the other conspirators, and to confirm
him in the French interests.   The article proposed by
La Motte is mentioned by Camden :—

THE COPY OF AN ARTICLE PROPOUNDED THE 20TH OF
    JANUARY 1582 [1583] BY LA MOTTE, TRANSLATED
    INTO ENGLISH.

To congratulate greatly with him on their parts, in that
the Queen of Scots, Dowager of France, his mother, which is
sister-in-law and daughter-in-law to their most Christian Ma-
jesties, after many obstacles and difficulties presented, hath,
with a good and motherly affection, most willingly declared
that she will that her said son be called by the title of King
in her life-time, and associate with her in this Crown ; a thing
which maketh far more lawful, and out of all contradiction,
and well approved of all other Christian Princes, the happy
reign of the said most noble King her son: which is a matter
that ought to be published throughout this Realm, according
to the form of the declaration, to the intent to remove the
partialities and divisions that might be in the same.[b]

La Motte's and his Colleague's proceedings in Scotland
are thus described in a letter to Sir Christopher Hatton
by Mr. Davison, who was sent on a mission to the King
of Scots in December 1582, with the object of counter-
acting the French Ambassadors :—

---

[a] Peck's Desiderata Curiosa, p. 130.   [b] Additional MSS. 15891, f. 100.

MR. DAVISON TO SIR CHRISTOPHER HATTON.

Sir, I shall not need to excuse unto your Honour my silence used towards you since my coming hither, because your own good-nature, and experience of the honest devotion I bear you, will not, I am sure, impute it to my want or forgetfulness of my duty towards you. It shall be enough that the sufficiency and diligence of my good friend Mr. Bowes, who I know faileth not to visit your Honour often with his letters, and my own rawness yet in matters of this State, do therein purge and excuse me. Now, presuming your Honour is there particularly acquainted with that I have written hitherto since La Motte's entry and mine, I will in these only discharge some piece of my duty with such matters as hath happened since our last to Mr. Secretary. Upon Manninville's arrival and receipt of some letters from him, La Motte began to speak more frankly than before, and the very next morning delivered in a new article in writing, containing a congratulation with this King touching his mother's consent that his Highness should be called by the title of King in her lifetime, and associate with her in the Government, &c.; a thing to be published according to the form of the declaration (which yet is not come to our sight) for avoiding of the inconveniences might otherwise happen, &c. The copy of which article I herewith send your Honour, that by their own acts you may the better aim at their scope and intent. Yesterday he followed the King on hunting, and on the fields had large conference with him of many things, where, pressing the King to deal plainly and frankly with him touching his private estate and liberty, he let fall many speeches both of his Council and Guard; showing him that he understood this Guard and the commanders thereof were entertained at the Queen's our Sovereign's charge, which being, as he said, a thing perilous and of rare example among Princes, made him the more suspicious that his Highness was not in that free condition and liberty which became his estate of a King; offering him, if he had any mislike thereof, and would

deal plainly with him, there should be remedy enough found
for his relief. Which the King answered in like terms as he
had before, that there was no cause to suspect either his
Council or his Guard (being of his own choice and approbation) of any indirect dealing against the freedom either of his
person or government; assuring him he was abused in his
information thereof, as also in that point concerning her Majesty, which he excused to have grown only of some particular dealing between his treasurer and Mr. Bowes, of
whom (without her Majesty's privity) Gowry upon a sudden
necessity had borrowed some little matter, for which he had
given his own particular bond, and remained his debtor;
which being afterward employed in his Highness' service, he
had taken order with Gowry to see Mr. Bowes answered, so
as the charge was his own, and not her Majesty's. Many
other things to like purpose passed between them, in all
which La Motte, plucking down his vizard by degrees,
makes sufficiently appear to such as are anything clearly-
sighted the concurrency of their negotiations here with the
doings in Flanders, though that poor Country hath at this
time played the first part in this common tragedy; which I
pray God that her Majesty, and others whom it specially
concerns, may give that heed and regard unto that appertaineth. Manninville, landing at Leith on Sunday night,
came yesterday to this town. His train is to the number of
twenty-two or twenty-three persons; amongst which is one
Dormes, a gentleman reported to be of the house of Lor-
raine, and of the French King's chamber, (a gallant at all
sports to entertain this young King withal,) who, whilst Manninville attends his business here, being sent, as his men give
out, to remain Ambassador resident for his Majesty, is appointed to make a progress into every part of the Country;
but the scope of that journey well enough foreseen will, I
think, be otherwise met withal than he looks for. They have
brought with them a massing priest; which, known in the
town, hath greatly moved the common people, whose fury it
will be hard for him to escape if he be taken abroad: which

the King understanding, hath forewarned La Motte and the other to look unto it, as a thing very hard for himself otherwise to provide for; whereupon they have all this day kept close their doors, standing on their guards with as much fear as discontentedness. There is some order given for La Motte's dispatch, but his departure is yet uncertain. Gowry is come this evening to this town; the rest of the Lords written for at La Motte's request have excused themselves. The Lord Harris died here on Sunday last very suddenly of an apoplexy (as some think), which he had fallen into once or twice before. To-morrow afternoon is Manninville appointed his audience; his charge, as La Motte pretends unto us, is none other than his own, which appears ill enough, if he may have time and means to execute it. What I shall further learn of these things I will not long conceal from your Honour, whom in this meantime I beseech the Almighty long to preserve, with much increase of honour and health. At Edinburgh, the 22nd of January 1582 [1583]. Your Honour's most humble at commandment,   W. DAVISON.*

It appears that Davison had urged some private suit in a postscript to the preceding letter, but it was not copied into the "Letter Book;" on which subject he also wrote to Hatton's secretary:—

MR. DAVISON TO MR. SAMUEL COX.

MR. Cox, I pray you let my business excuse at this time the shortness of these to yourself, whom I would not leave unvisited with a line or two, having some occasion to write to my honourable good friend Mr. Vice-Chamberlain. For public things I refer you to his; and herein will only put you in mind of my particular, which I trust you are no less mindful to commend and further to his Honour, than I am willing to be thankful for any courtesy you shall do me. I have, in a postscript to his Honour, touched it somewhat generally, which you may help and supply with such particulars as you think agreeable to the matter, and answerable to our friend-

* Additional MSS. 15891, f. 100.

ship. The sum and place (I mean the Duchy) last resolved
on I pray may be followed; other direction you need not,
that can better skill thereof than myself, on whose care and
friendly travail reposing myself in this behalf I do heartily
commend you for this time to the grace of God.   Edinburgh,
22nd January 1582 [1583].   Your own assured,

W. DAVISON.[a]

The three following letters relate to one of the most
disgraceful transactions of Elizabeth's reign. Sir Robert
Stapleton, of Wighill, in Yorkshire, the representative
of an ancient and affluent family, and who is described by
a contemporary " as a man well spoken; properly seen in
languages; a comely and good personage; had scarce an
equal, and, next to Sir Philip Sidney, no superior in England," basely conspired with an innkeeper, called Sysson,
and his wife, to extort money from Dr. Sandys, Archbishop
of York, by accusing him of adultery. The circumstance is thus related by Strype:—" In May 1581,
while the Archbishop lodged at Doncaster, on his journey, one Sysson, the host, caused his wife to go by night
into the Archbishop's bed to him, and he, presently
after, followed, with his dagger in his hand, into the
chamber, which he put to the Archbishop's breast,
with Alexander his man, and Maud, that had been the
Archbishop's servant, saying, ' God's precious life, I will
mark a whore and a thief.'   Stapleton then made his
appearance, and after requiring 800*l.*, the Archbishop
agreed to give 600*l.* and a lease of some lands to hush
the matter up; but afterwards, when they proceeded to
demand more lands, manors, and benefits, the Archbishop
refused to go any further, but resolved to send the whole

[a] Additional MSS. 15891, f. 47[b].

case, with all their horrible dealings, to Burghley, and through him to the Queen."

Proceedings being instituted against Stapleton and his accomplices, he was heavily fined and committed to prison; and he continued in confinement until the following year :—

LORD BURGHLEY TO SIR CHRISTOPHER HATTON.

SIR, My servant shall show you why I must write so evil and so little. Sir Robert Stapleton required to come to me, and so the Examiners thought good; afore whom charging him with Sysson's confession, he protested against Sysson as against a bankrupt and a beggar. Yea, he could tell of the late intent to have had a preacher treacherously used; he rested upon Maude and Mallory as gentlemen. But now, coming to me, he yieldeth to his offence, and asked God mercy; and thus far he yieldeth, that Sysson first, and afterward also his wife, opened to him the device to have the Bishop entrapped, she pretending that the Bishop had moved her to evil: the same was also imparted to Mallory and Maude. And Sir Robert, having conceived displeasure against the Bishop, confesseth he yielded hereto, as thereby to have the Bishop under his girdle. He denied not to have had £200 of Sysson by way of loan, which, he saith, Maude procured to be repaid to Sysson, which he now thinketh was the £200 that Maude had last of the Bishop. To conclude: he penitently asketh God mercy for exercising his malice in this sort; but yet he termeth his offence but a sufferance of the practices begun by Sysson and his wife to proceed as it did. He desireth pardon of her Majesty, offering his life in service to redeem it; he also desireth that he may be used so as Mrs. Talbot* may continue her affection, by whom, he saith, he is to have £1200 by year for thirteen years. I have quieted him, that there is no cause to doubt of his fleeing; and truly his tears do move me to have compassion of him, being myself well sa-

* Vide a former Letter.

tisfied with the purgation of the Bishop. His further examinations do stay ; he confesseth the combination at York
with all the parties to agree upon one compounded tale.
Sysson saith, his speeches of looking in at the keyhole were
false, and of the Bishop kissing of his wife. Yours assuredly,   W. BURGHLEY.[a]

TO LORD BURGHLEY.

MY SINGULAR GOOD LORD, Her Majesty yieldeth her
most kind and gracious thanks unto you for your grave and
wise handling of this great cause ; only she resteth not satisfied that Sir Robert Stapleton is not more straitly looked
unto than hitherto he hath been. Her good pleasure is, that
your Lordship send for the Master of the Rolls, and give him
most earnest charge, upon peril of her Highness' uttermost
displeasure, to intend to his safe keeping; the rather because
her Majesty pretendeth to know more than hitherto she will
be pleased to speak of. There will no favour be found as
yet in the accommodating of his cause with Mrs. Talbot, but
through your goodness hereafter haply somewhat may be
wrought; but surely he cannot escape without public note
and severe punishment, for such is her Majesty's censure
moved for justice sake both for the man and matter. My
Lord of Leicester will be at London the morrow, when I
think the Queen will direct him to speak with you. Thus,
with all humble duty, I pray God for your health, and commend my service unto you. Haste, at Richmond, this 24th
of February 1582 [1583]. Your good Lordship's most bound,
                                           CHR. HATTON.[b]

TO LORD BURGHLEY.

MY VERY GOOD LORD, I thank God from my heart that
your travail in this great cause hath brought forth so blessed
effects. Innocency is delivered, and truth hath prevailed, to
God's glory, and the due commendation of your wisdom and
goodness. Her Majesty rejoiceth exceedingly in it, and

---

[a] Additional MSS. 15891, f. 104.   [b] Autograph in the State Paper Office.

yieldeth her most gracious thanks to your Lordship for your
so great and wise proceeding in it. My Lord of Leicester
hath her Majesty's directions to signify thus much of her
pleasure, with further matter unto your Lordship, as I suppose. And, for present answer to these your last letters, (considering this and her Majesty's business in receiving La
Motte, and after in the sermon, in which my duty of attendance is of necessity,) I cannot deliver as I dutifully would;
but, so soon as is possible, your Lordship shall receive her
Majesty's further pleasure. I pray God restore your health,
and bless your Lordship with a long and happy life. The
24th of February 1582 [1583]. Your good Lordship's most
bound,   CHR. HATTON.[*]

Lord Burghley's answer to Hatton's letters respecting
the Archbishop of York is preserved:—

LORD BURGHLEY TO SIR CHRISTOPHER HATTON.

SIR, For answer to your two letters of this day, I pray
you in my behalf to render my recognition to her Majesty of
my comfortable acceptance of her gracious and favourable
allowance of my careful proceeding to the discussing of the
truth in the Archbishop's cause, which was very cunningly
covered, and made almost desperate to have been disclosed:
but, in the end, God, the father of truth, left the adversaries in
fear to be otherwise convinced by the contrarieties of their
own answers; for so indeed it has fallen out by discrepance in
their own answers, that, if none of them had confessed their
offences, the comparing of their contrarieties would have
condemned them in any ordinary place of judgment. But
now, Sir, considering that truth hath the victory, her Majesty's honour is advanced by her princely care taken to have
her Prelate protected; and the Bishop himself, a churchman
and preacher of mercy, following the example of Christ his

---

[*] Autograph in the Lansdowne MS. 32, art. 22; and partly printed in
Strype's Annals, vol. III. pt. i. p. 148.

Master, that forgave all offences without revenge. I wish that some such course might be taken by her Majesty in clemency, as truth may enjoy the victory, her Majesty dilate her honour, and the Bishop that hath suffered the wrong may give an example for the place he holdeth, rather of remission than of revenge. And how all these things might be done without the utter ruin of Sir Robert Stapleton, a man of good service in his country, and never to my understanding touched with any dishonest action, I leave to be further considered by her Majesty's wisdom, whereunto I humbly submit this project of mine as becometh me, forbearing further to trouble you at this time, in respect of my present feebleness not able myself to write unto you; for which cause I have been bold to use the hand of one at my commandment, derived as it were by propagation out of mine own, making him now my scribe, whom I wish hereafter to do her Majesty some service, as a remembrancer of mine, when both my hands shall be under the earth. From my bed in my house at Westminster, the 28th of February 1583.

W. Burghley.[a]

Davison wrote several letters to Hatton detailing his proceedings in Scotland, where, notwithstanding his request to be recalled, he continued until about September 1584 :—

MR. DAVISON TO SIR CHRISTOPHER HATTON.

It may please your Honour, I have by every post of late looked for my revocation, finding no great cause of my particular stay here, to the increase of her Majesty's charge, and some incommodity to myself; but, because your Honour hath yet rather given me hope than assurance thereof, I must beseech you that in your next I may fully understand her Majesty's good pleasure in that behalf. Mr. Bowes's experience and acquaintance with the affairs of this State enableth him sufficiently alone to go through with any ser-

[a] Additional MSS. 15891, f. 51.[b]

vice is to be done here, without any great want of language
for any negotiation between us and Manninville; whose stay
we hope will not be long here if things frame not all the
sooner to his full contentment, which will appear shortly
after the coming of the rest of the Lords looked for this
week. In the mean time the people here have much to do
to contain themselves from hastening his departure by some
rude entreaty, which they have been willing to offer him ere
this, and had surely done it, had not the masters and some
discreet Burgesses hitherto stayed them, so great is the
prejudice they have of his traffic here to the hurt of religion
and disquiet of their State; and now forbear only in expectation of his despatch upon the coming of these Lords,
according to the promise made unto them by such as were
intercessors to the King for them in that behalf: and yet
it seemeth that himself is determined to ride out here, if he
may, till he hear further out of France. By our common
letter your Honour shall understand all these things more
particularly; as also of our apprehension of one William
Holte, a Jesuit, entertained secretly here by the Lord Seton,
and appointed to a voyage into France and from thence to
Rome, who, being ready to take passage with the first fair
wind, we caused to be apprehended at Leith. About him we
found divers ciphers and some two or three letters, whereof
(the originals being delivered to the King) we send you herewith the copies: divers other letters he had and should have
received here, but where he hath bestowed them we cannot
yet learn. By these we send your Honour you may pick
out English enough touching the doings and employments of
himself and others of that crew, but in his examination we
cannot yet draw him to any further particularities. In general
only he confesseth to Mr. Bowes and myself, that he thinketh there is some purpose in hand by the Pope and divers
Princes Catholics for a war against England, and that they
have a party strong at home; that the pretext will be religion, and liberty of the Queen of Scots; that they hold
the enterprize easy, considering their own preparations and

the factions at home; that the Pope hath gathered a great mass of money, and collecteth daily, as he heareth, to the same use; that the King of Spain, as appeareth by the letter deciphered, is also to furnish a part; but of the time, the instruments to be used, and other particularities, he can say nothing, as he pretendeth. This day my Lord of Dunfermling and others (who have been with us to the same end once or twice already) are appointed to be with us again, with some special articles of his more formal and precise examination, of the proceeding wherein your Honour shall hear more by the next. Manninville doth storm at his apprehension and detaining with us, and hath been earnest with the King to remove him out of our hands; both he, Seton, and the rest of that part, fearing lest their doings by this means may come to light. Alexander Seton, Prior of Pluskett,[b] and third son to the Lord, author of one of these letters, is sent for, and to be examined thereupon before his Majesty and the Council, who is able to discover more than I think they shall easily get from him. With this Holte we took two others; the one a Scottishman, his servant, whom we have delivered over to the Colonel Stuart; the other an Englishman lately come hither, whom, after his first apprehension, we used as a stale to entrap the other, wherein he served us to great purpose. His name is Roger Almond, one that was taken about two years past at Dover, and examined before your Honour at the Court, and afterwards sent down to my Lord of Huntingdon to York, and hath, as he saith, been an instrument to decipher and discover divers of that party; howsoever it be, his doings in this deserveth favour. Thus, referring your Honour's more particular satisfaction to our general letters, and that you shall else receive from Mr. Bowes, I do most humbly take my leave. At Edinburgh, the 4th of March 1582 [1583]. Your Honour's most humble at commandment,   W. DAVISON.[a]

[a] Additional MSS. 15891, f. 49.
[b] Alexander Seton, younger son of George fifth Lord Seton, was Prior of Pluscardine: he was afterwards High Chancellor of Scotland, and Earl of Dunfermling.

The Earl of Oxford had, as has been before said, incurred the Queen's serious displeasure; and he now appears to have been involved in a fray with Mr. Knyvet, in which a man was slain.   It does seem extraordinary, as Burghley naturally thought, that his intercession for his son-in-law should be unsuccessful:—

LORD BURGHLEY TO SIR CHRISTOPHER HATTON.

Good Mr. Vice-Chamberlain, My lack of health and strength serveth me not to write as much as I have cause; but yet many urgent necessities constrain me to write somewhat for ease of my mind, which I pray you to intèrpret after your friendly manner.   I perceived yesterday by my Lord of Leicester that you had very friendly delivered speeches to her Majesty tending to bring some good end to these troublesome matters betwixt my Lord of Oxford and Mr. Thomas Knyvet; for the which your doings I do heartily thank you, and beseech you to continue your former good meaning, though the event expected and desired hath not followed.   And now perceiving by my Lord of Leicester some increase of her Majesty's offence towards my Lord of Oxford, and finding by Mr. Thomas Knyvet that he only being called and demanded of her Majesty what he would say herein, he did, as served his turn, declare to her Majesty that his men were evil used by my Lord of Oxford's men, and namely that one of his men was killed by a man of my Lord of Oxford's, and no redress had, I cannot but think that her Majesty had just occasion given by such an information to be offended towards my Lord of Oxford, or his man, and did therefore, like a Prince of justice and God's minister, command the matter to be examined, which was done yesterday at great length by my Lord of Leicester, to his trouble and my grief; and I doubt not but my Lord of Leicester will honourably declare to her Majesty how my Lord of Oxford resteth untouched, or at least unblotted, in any kind of matter objected by Mr. Knyvet,

Y

whom we heard at great length, and his men also. But because Mr. Knyvet's man, called Long Tom, that once served and was maintained by my Lord of Oxford, a bad fellow to serve any honest man, came to his death, I am bold to send to you the inquisition before the Coroner of London, with the verdict of the jury and the depositions of the ocular witnesses; by all which, and by a new acquittal at Newgate, Gastrell, the party named my Lord of Oxford's man, and yet was not then his man, nor yet is, though Mr. Knyvet report him so to be, was and standeth acquitted of the death of the said Long Thomas; so as, where her Majesty had just cause to conceive somewhat hardly of my Lord of Oxford, I doubt not but when her Majesty shall be informed by my Lord of Leicester of the truth which he hath seen and not disproved, her Majesty will diminish her offensive opinion: and I trust also, after you shall have read these writings, which I will on my credit avow to be true, you will be of the same mind, and, as opportunity may serve, will also move her Majesty in this case to think otherwise hereof than the informer meant to induce her to think. As to the rest of the brabbles and frays, my Lord of Leicester can also declare upon what small occasions of repute and light carriages of tales, whereof my Lord of Oxford is nowise touched, these brabbles are risen. And for the quarrel of one Roper, of the Guards, against Gastrell, my Lord of Oxford's man, it is confessed that Roper challenged Gastrell that he had complained of him; whereas in truth yourself knoweth it was my Lord of Oxford that did complain to you of Roper and of one Hall, so as Roper was therein too busy. And hereupon he wrote a long epistle to Gastrell to challenge him to fight, and so also Costock made the like challenge, whereby appeareth that these frays grow by challenges made to my Lord of Oxford's men: and yet it must be informed that my Lord of Oxford's men do offer these frays. Good Mr. Vice-Chamberlain, these things are hardly carried, and these advantages are easily gotten, where some may say what they will against my Lord of Oxford, and have presence to utter their humours; and

my Lord of Oxford is neither heard, nor hath presence
either to complain or defend himself: and so long as he shall
be subject to the disgrace of her Majesty (from which God
deliver him), I see it apparently, that, how innocent soever he
shall be, the advantages will fall out for his adversaries; and
so I hear they do prognosticate.   It hath been also informed
her Majesty that he hath had fifteen or sixteen pages in a
livery going before him in Cheapside; but, if these tongues
that uttered this were so much lessened by measure in their
mouths as they have enlarged in their number, they would
never be touched hereafter with making any verbal lie.   Indeed I would he had less than he hath, and yet in all his
house are, nor were at any time, but four: one of them waiteth
upon his wife, my daughter; another in my house, upon his
daughter Bess; a third is a kind of a tumbling-boy; and the
fourth is the son of a brother of Sir John Cutts, lately
put to him.   By this false, large, lying report, if her Majesty
would cause it to be tried, she should find upon what roots
these blasphemous branches do grow.   But I submit all these
things to God's will, who knoweth best why it pleaseth Him
to afflict my Lord of Oxford in this sort, who hath, I confess, forgotten his duty to God, and yet I hope he may be
made a good servant to her Majesty, if it please her of her
clemency to remit her displeasure; for his fall in her Court,
which is now twice yeared, and he punished as far or farther
than any like crime hath been, first by her Majesty, and then
by the drab's friend in revenge to the peril of his life.   And
if his own punishment past, and his humble seeking of forgiveness, cannot recover her Majesty's favour, yet some, yea
many, may think that the intercession of me and my poor
wife, so long and importunately continued, might have obtained some spark of favour of her Majesty; but hereof I
will in nowise complain of too much hardness, but to myself.
I would I could not, in *amaritudine animæ*, lament my
wife's oppressing of her heart for the opinion she imprinteth
therein of her misfortune, a matter not to be expressed
without mistaking: and therefore both I and she are deter-

mined to suffer and lament our misfortune, that, when our
son-in-law was in prosperity, he was cause of our adversity
by his unkind usage of us and ours; and now that he is
ruined and in adversity, we only are made partakers thereof,
and by no means, no, not by bitter tears of my wife, can
obtain a spark of favour for him, that hath satisfied his offence
with punishment, and seeketh mercy by submission; but
contrariwise, whilst we seek for favour, all crosses are laid
against him, and by untruths sought to be kept in disgrace.
But, good Mr. Vice-Chamberlain, pardon me herein, for my
heart too full to stay my pen, and yet I will end, because
I will no further trouble you with my troubles, which are ordained of God for myself; and so I will patiently take them
and lap them up to carry with me to the grave, where, when
I shall be, I am sure they shall not follow me. When I
began to write, I neither meant nor thought I could have
scribbled thus much; but the matter hath ministered me the
cause, for I take no pleasure therein. God preserve her Majesty, and grant her only to understand the true hearts of my
poor wife and me, and then I doubt not the sequel of her
gracious favours in far greater matters than we have required.
We have not many years to live, perchance not many days,
and the fewer I am sure to find lack of her favours, of whom
we seek to deserve well by our daily services. From my
house in Westminster, this 12th of March 1582 [1583].
Yours assuredly, as you see, very bold,   W. BURGHLEY.[a]

Albertus Alasco, free Baron of Lasco, Palatine of
Saradia in Poland, arrived at Harwich, and proceeded
on the 30th of April to Winchester House, in Southwark, where he mostly resided while in England.[b] Camden says he was " a learned man, of a good feature of
body, a very long beard, and very comely and decent
apparel, who, being graciously welcomed by the Queen,
and entertained by the nobility with great honour and

[a] Additional MSS   91, f. 50.   [b] Stow's Annals.

feastings, and by the University of Oxford with learned delights and sundry pageants, after four months' abode here, withdrew himself secretly, being run far in debt."

LORD BURGHLEY TO SIR CHRISTOPHER HATTON.

SIR, Upon my Lord of Leicester's speeches with me this day of some things, I have thought meet to write to you my mind thereof, only to remit the use of them to your own consideration. I perceive that a Count of Polonia, named the Palatine Laschi, is either arrived, or shortly will, at Harwich to come to her Majesty; and if he be the very Count Palatine of that House of Laschi, he is a personage of great estimation, such as few are subjects to any Monarch in Christendom, few in the Empire of the greatest exceeding him in sovereignty and power: and he is also one that, as I find by late observations since this King Stephanus' reign, hath carried great authority; and before his time, in the interreign, none that had greater than he, but only the great Palatine of Lineland. This I write unto you, wishing that her Majesty might please to command some nobleman in Essex, as my Lord Rich or Lord Darcy, with the attendance of some gentlemen, to conduct him to the City, where it were good he had some lodging on the water-side, as Baynard's Castle, whereunto my Lord of Leicester doth assent; but you may say *actum ago*, for this and more is foreseen; yet, Sir, I pray you mislike not a poor remembrancer. Another matter is, that I find by my Lord of Leicester that her Majesty hath a disposition to leave her own stately palaces, and to vouchsafe to survey my poor house after Easter; which, I am sure, if it had sense as the Master hath, would stoop down with so much pride to be possessed of her Majesty, as hereafter it would scantly know the Master. I confess it is my comfort to have anything that may like her Majesty, but in very truth I know there is nothing worthy of her steps but only the goodwill of the owner, who will yield both soil, house, and all appurtenants to be serviceable to her Majesty. And lastly, my grief is, that neither my health and strength,

nor my wife's presence, can serve to supply the wants that
will be there, but they must be all covered with the serenity
of her Majesty's countenance. A last matter whereof my
Lord spake was a divers answer to my expectation for my
Lord of Oxford, whose infortunes increase my wife's griefs
and mine more than I will mention, because I see not the
way to remedy them, otherwise than by continuing in the
beaten heavy ways of forced patience. And now I end my
scribbling with my hearty commendations. From my house
in Westminster, the 18th of March 1582 [1583]. Yours assured at commandment,   W. BURGHLEY.*

Hatton's reply to Lord Burghley's letter shows that
there was some uncertainty at Court respecting the
Palatine's rank :—

TO LORD BURGHLEY.

I MOST humbly thank your Lordship for your honourable
advertisement touching the coming in of this great Personage. Her Majesty deferreth all her direction for order to
receive him, until she be more fully informed both of his
quality and occasion of access. She seemeth to doubt that
he departeth from his Prince as a man in displeasure, because
in one sentence of his letter to her Majesty he calleth her
the refuge of the disconsolate and afflicted, &c. Worthe,
my man, that brought these letters, is not here, neither do I
know where to find him, so as I know not how to learn what
information I might give the Queen in this matter; only I
must stay until the return of my Lord of Leicester, and then
I hope her Majesty will resolve. Her Majesty accepteth in
most gracious and good kind part the offer of your Lordship's
house, unto the which, (although yet she will give us no order
to lay in her provisions,) I assuredly think she will come in the
Easter week ; but as I learn the more certainty, so will I
readily advertise your good Lordship. My Lord of Oxford's

* Additional MSS. 15891, f. 52.

cause standeth but in slow course of proceeding to his satisfaction; but yet, for my own part, I have some better hope than heretofore, wherein as a preservative you must all use patience for a while. His Lordship wrote to me a very wise letter in this case of his, the report whereof her Majesty took in reasonable good gracious part. By the next messenger I will briefly write . . . . the answer. I pray God bless your Lordship with all His heavenly graces. Haste, from the Court at Richmond, this 19th of March 1582 [1583]. Your good Lordship's most bounden   CHR. HATTON.[a]

In 1583, Philip Sidney married Frances, the only child of Sir Francis Walsingham; and it appears from Walsingham's letter to Hatton, that the Queen had opposed the match:—

SIR FRANCIS WALSINGHAM TO SIR CHRISTOPHER HATTON.

SIR, As I think myself infinitely bound unto you for your honourable and friendly defence of the intended match between my daughter and Mr. Sidney, so do I find it strange that her Majesty should be offended withal. It is either to proceed of the matter or of the manner. For the matter, I hope, when her Majesty shall weigh the due circumstances of place, person, and quality, there can grow no just cause of offence. If the manner be misliked for that her Majesty is not made acquainted withal, I am no person of that state but that it may be thought a presumption for me to trouble her Majesty with a private marriage between a free gentleman of equal calling with my daughter. I had well hoped that my painful and faithful service done unto her Majesty had merited that grace and favour at her hands as that she would have countenanced this match with her gracious and princely good-liking thereof, that thereby the world might have been a witness of her goodness towards me. As I thought it always unfit for me to acquaint her Majesty with

[b] Additional MSS. 15891.

a matter of so base a subject as this poor match, so did
I never seek to have the matter concealed from her Majesty,
seeing no reason why there should grow any offence thereby.
I pray you, Sir, therefore, if she enter into any further
speech of the matter, let her understand that you learn generally that the match is held for concluded, and withal to
let her know how just cause I shall have to find myself ag-
grieved if her Majesty shall show her mislike thereof.   And
so, committing the cause to your friendly and considerate
holding, I leave you to the protection of the Almighty.   At
Barn Elms, the 19th of March 1582 [1583].   Your most assuredly to command,   FRA. WALSINGHAM.

Postscript.—I will give order that my cousin Sidney shall
be forewarned of the matter, who, as I suppose, will not be
at the Court before the next week.   If her Majesty's mislike
should continue, then would I be glad, if I might take knowledge thereof, to express my grief unto her by letter, for that
I am forced, in respect of the indisposition of my body, to be
absent until the end of this next week, whereof I made her
Majesty privy.*

Dr. Mathew was, it seems, deputed to convey the
Archbishop of York's thanks to Hatton, for having so
zealously defended him against Sir Robert Stapleton's
accusation ; but the candidate for the Deanery of Durham did not fail to press his own suit on the same occasion.

DR. MATHEW TO SIR CHRISTOPHER HATTON.

RIGHT HONOURABLE SIR, Now that your greatest businesses of this term are well over-blown, I beseech your Honour give me leave among other to present you mine humble
thanks in my Lord Archbishop's behalf, who as he was and
shall be much bounden to the rest, so to none more than to
yourself; specially for that excellent oration of yours (for it

* Additional MSS. 15891, f. 101.

was no less) in his purgation and punishment of his accusers,
to the glory of God, the honour of her Majesty, the credit of
our calling, the furtherance of the Gospel, the confusion of
our adversaries, the comfort of all true professors, and perpetual testimony of your zeal to religion, justice, and innocency.   If he should be unthankful, or we unmindful, of that
day's word or work of yours, yet God shall both regard you
and reward you for it.   I presume thus far to be bold to
write, for that your Honour vouchsafed to impart with me of
the matter when it stood most suspicious, which now Truth,
the daughter of Time, hath discovered to be but slanderous.
Whereof, suspicion I mean, and slander touching our fame or
infamy, such is the condition, as, although we may be glad
when it is dead, yet might we rejoice more if it had never
been born.   But how happy a man (of a man most unhappy)
had he been, had he never been drawn into the danger of this
discredit.   Howbeit, sithence God the author of all good
things, and the sufferer of all wicked practices, would needs
permit that so it should be for causes best known unto Him
and least unto us, amidst so many mishaps, what happiness
had he to light upon so gracious a Prince as is our Sovereign,
so sacred a Senate as is that board, so plain, so dear, so honourable a friend and advocate as was your Honour.   Truly, Sir,
I can hardly hold mine idle pen from further enlarging in this
behalf your goodness towards him, and his debt to you.   But
what speak I of his debt, being, if that may be, myself much
further indebted to your Honour? which yet I am forced
now to increase against good manner, but more against my
will, for that my competitor, after he hath fled the field, doth
begin to give a fresh assault, as by this bearer it may appear
unto your Honour.   Wherefore I humbly beseech you, Sir,
to work my dispatch; the rather, for that the more delay is
made, the more danger is mine, the more trouble yours.   So
shall you more favour, more bind me to do you all honour,
duty, and service, besides my daily prayers for your prosperous estate.   From the Savoy, the 11th of May 1583.   Your
Honour's most bounden,   TOBIE MATHEW.*

* Additional MSS. 15891, f. 106.

Camden * says, as soon as the French Ambassadors left Scotland, " the King offered all kindness to the Queen of England by Colonel William Stuart and John Colville, and asked her counsel and advice for compounding the commotions and contracting of marriage :"

THE SCOTTISH AMBASSADORS TO SIR CHRISTOPHER HATTON.

SIR, It hath been always our great mishap, since our arrival in this Country, to find your Honour ever occupied when we have thought to deliver unto you his Highness' letters, with the credit committed unto us in the same. This day it was our purpose to have given ourselves wholly to have attended on your leisure; but, being called to dinner by my Lord of Leicester, certain of the Lords of her Highness' Council being met there, detained us with them all this afternoon, advising and conferring with us upon the heads given in by us in writing on Thursday last: where, having given us some feeling of our answer by a plot and project thereof, wherewith it was their pleasures to let us be acquainted, we found it so far disagreeable to his Majesty's expectation of our success, and to the towardliness of good hope which we have always had since our coming, that, if they should be given us as they are projected, it should not be without great prejudice and apparent alteration of the good course which his Majesty, by the earnest travails of faithful and good instruments in both the Realms, hath with no small difficulty been persuaded to like of and follow as his best. The only comfort which armeth us against this wound resteth in her Majesty's better disposition towards his Highness, with some more amiable kind of dealing than this giveth us appearance of: which, if her Highness' other occupations might give her leisure, we would be very glad to move unto her ourselves this afternoon, praying your Honour very heartily that we may have her audience, and therewith to yield us at this time your wonted

* Annals, A. D. 1583.

favour and good disposition, which you have ever professed, to the furtherance of the wished effects of these good overtures, which we have partly already, and do mean to move more plainly to her Majesty; the good success whereof, as it will give likelihood of an unspeakable benefit to the prosperous estate of both the Realms, so is it very difficile to conjecture what may fall out upon the contrary. But, praying God to inspire her Majesty and her grave Councillors otherwise for the better preservation of the common benefit and tranquillity of both Kingdoms, we take our leaves, committing your Honour to God's good protection. From London, the 12th of May 1583. Your Honour's assured faithful friends,

WM. STUART.   JOHN COLVILL.*

Mr. Herle, who informs Hatton that the Count Palatine had visited the library of Dr. Dee, the celebrated mathematician and astrologer, at Mortlake, and reports the Count's answer to some communications made to him, was frequently employed in the public service, and was, on several occasions, an Agent for conducting business abroad. The Count, like Dr. Dee, was a professor of the magic art; and Dee accompanied him to Poland, where their proceedings excited so much attention, that the Queen ordered Dee to return to England :—

MR. WILLIAM HERLE TO SIR CHRISTOPHER HATTON.

RIGHT HONOURABLE, May it please you to understand, that yesternight, upon my return to Winchester House, I found the Count Palatine Laschy absent, who, in the morning before, was privately gone to Mr. Dee's to recreate himself with the sight of his library, so as it was past ten of the clock before he came back to his house. And I being careful this day how to break with him discreetly for the under-

* Additional MSS. 15891, f.   .

standing what course he would hold in his journeys, Mr.
Athye came opportunely with a message from her Majesty
about the same; touching the which, he is determined to
morrow to advertise my Lord of Leicester of his whole intention, taking her Majesty's gracious care had of him in
very good part; but withal he knows of no Parliament, he
saith, to be holden shortly in Poland, neither concerns it him
much in business or duty whether any be holden or no before his own pretended return; which I thought my part to
certify your Honour of, reserving somewhat to impart with
you herein by mouth at my next attendance on you.   In the
mean time, I do very humbly pray your Honour to join with
you Mr. Secretary, and some other of the Council, (if you
think good,) for the stay of the outlawry in Oxfordshire that
will otherwise be pronounced on Tuesday next against my
kinsman John Herle: his fact not great, but the harm and
stain much, if your Honour of especial goodness do not
vouchsafe to assist him at this pinch.   You shall find the
man to have valuable parts in him, which he shall employ
from henceforth in service of her Majesty, and in all thankful duty to acknowledge his preservation to proceed from
your only mean; and me your Honour shall bind (in regard
I have of the party and of my name) as for a benefit merely
bestowed upon myself.   I would have waited on you to-day,
but that I was constrained to take physic; but by this bearer,
my servant, I recommend the cause and myself to your honourable consideration and dispatch, for it requireth speed,
as your wisdom seeth, meaning to send one down in post with
the letter procured touching the premises. Herewith finish-
ing, I crave most truly pardon for this bold presumption
of mine, grounded upon the favour I hope you bear me: and
so the Almighty God have you ever in his tuition.   From
my lodging, the 20th of May 1583.   Your Honour's ever to
command,   W. HERLE.[*]

[*] Additional MSS. 15891, f. 109.

Towards the end of May, the Queen, attended by the Marchioness of Winchester, the Ladies Cobham, and Stafford, the Earls of Leicester and Warwick, the Lord Admirals, Lords Howard and Hunsdon, Sir Christopher Hatton, and a large retinue, visited the Lord Treasurer at Theobald's, and remained there five days. Lord Burghley has left, in his own hand, a description of the arrangement of the lodgings of his guests, whence it appears that the Queen's apartments were at the north-west end of the gallery; and that the gentlewomen of the bedchamber, Mrs. Blanch Parry, and Hatton, probably from his office as Vice-Chamberlain, occupied rooms near to her.[a]

Sir Thomas Heneage's description of Holdenby agrees with that of Lord Burghley some years before, and raises a high opinion of its magnificence:—

SIR THOMAS HENEAGE TO SIR CHRISTOPHER HATTON.

Sir, Being neither Momus nor Aristippus, but a poor true friend of yours, having seen your fair house with great desire, I send you word hereby with best contentment. For my own opinion, Holdenby is altogether even the best house that hath been built in this age; and it more showeth the good judgment and honour of the builder than all the charge that hath been bestowed upon stones by the greatest persons and the best purses that hath been in my time. Shortly, if the praise of a house consist in the seat, beauty, and use, both within and without, (howsoever it may be cavilled with,) Holdenby shall hold the pre-eminence of all the modern houses I have known or heard of in England. This is all I will say of it; saving, your out-houses make me remember my noble old master the Earl of Arundell, that made his gar-

---

[a] Nichols' Progresses, vol. II. p. 403.

ments most beautiful and rich where the common sort least looked for it.   There is nothing better pleaseth me than your park, which you dispraised; your green and base court, that you devised: and your garden, which is most rare; but all the steps of descent must be of stone, which it lacketh. The honourable entertainment it hath pleased you I should receive here, with excessive cheer, (fit for the best man of England,) together with the diligent attendance of your good servants, deserveth more than my thanks, but can receive no more but my love, and that have you as great an interest in as any man alive, and withal my prayers to the Lord of all that with God's best blessings, her Majesty's best favour, your friends' most joy, and your own most honour and comfort, you may be longest owner of this earthly noble house, and after possess perpetually the most happy habitation in heaven. From your Holdenby, very late this 5th of July 1583.   Your own more and more bound unto you,   T. HENEAGE.[a]

SIR THOMAS HENEAGE TO SIR CHRISTOPHER HATTON.

SIR, This second of August I have received your letters of the 23rd of July, wherein I find your most honourable and kind remembrance of your poor true friend, that, when he seeth you not, desireth nothing more than to hear from you. As for your best built house of Holdenby, which I particularly affect, not for the partial love I bear to the owner, whom I will ever honour and hold dear, but for the many just causes I find to like it, I will say, as I think, that for a gentleman's dwelling of most honour and estimation it is the best and most considerate built house that yet mine eyes have ever seen.   The Lord Jesus, whose the earth is and the fulness thereof, make you long to enjoy it with most honour and comfort.   For the news you sent me of Scotland, I humbly thank you; though in very troth I take them to be the heralds of our greatest harms without timely prevention. The manner of Sir Robert Stapleton's behaviour and sub-

---

[a] Additional MSS. 15891, f. 109[b].

mission at York, as it was even now sent unto me, I send
you here inclosed, which for my own poor opinion I see no
cause to like of : of this matter and of that country, when we
meet, I shall tell you my mind. The whilst, and ever, I will
love and honour you, as I have cause ; and having no more
leisure to write unto you, through the hasty departure of this
bearer who is a stranger unto me, I do commend myself all
humbly unto you. From Hatfield, where the only princely
game of red deer is that ever I saw, this 2nd of August 1583.
Your own so bound for ever, THO. HENEAGE.[a]

On the 4th of August Sir Christopher Hatton wrote
to Sir William More, of Loseley Hall, in Surrey, that " in
ten or twelve days the Queen intended to go to Loseley
for four or five days, and desired that every thing might
be got in order, and the house kept clean and sweet."[b]

FROM THE LORDS OF THE COUNCIL TO THE SHERIFF OF OXFORDSHIRE.

AFTER our hearty commendations. These are to give you to
understand that her Majesty, having partly by her own hearing, and partly by report of others of credit, considered of a
cause of long time depending in controversy and suit between
John Croker, Esq., plaintiff, the son and heir of Sir Gerard
Croker, deceased, and Richard Lee, Esq., defendant, late
husband of the Lady Croker, late wife of the said Sir Gerard,
concerning certain leases of divers manors, parks, rectories,
tithes, lands, and hereditaments in Hocknorton in the county
of Oxford ; and finding the said cause somewhat doubtful
without some further proceeding, to be resolved directly, for
any of the said parties ; hath thought good to have the profits
thereof growing to be sequestered from both the said parties
until the end of Michaelmas term next, and therewith also
mindeth and hopeth to have the same controversy determined
before that time, either by way of arbitrament of friends, or

[a] Additional MSS. 15891, f. 112[b]. [b] Nichols' Progresses, II. 412.

otherwise by some ordinary course of the law. And for this purpose her Majesty hath straitly commanded us by her own speech to take order in her name that the profits of all the said lands, tenements, tithes, rectories, and hereditaments should be sequestered. And therefore, in her Majesty's name, and by her express commandment, we do will and require you, and by these presents do authorize you, being her Majesty's High Sheriff in the County of Oxford, to repair to the foresaid manors, lands, rectories, tithes, tenements, and hereditaments so held on lease by the said Sir Gerard in Hocknorton aforesaid, and there to enquire by all good means what persons do hold and possess any such houses, manors, parks, parsonages, tithes or tenements, or any other hereditaments in Hocknorton, which the said Sir Gerard Croker held by leases, and which after his death the Lady Croker his wife held during her widowhood, which after her death the said Richard Lee hath also held and possessed or takes the profits thereof, and to charge all manner of persons that do now hold, occupy, or possess any part thereof to pay unto you as by way of sequestration all manner of rates that shall be due or payable by them betwixt the feasts of Michaelmas and All Saints next, and the same to retain with yourself. And if any persons be charged with the payment of any tithe which heretofore was answerable to the said Sir Gerard, that you first cause a valuation to be made thereof, and then to charge them to retain the same in their own hands, without rendering the same either to the plaintiff or defendant, or to any other claiming any title to them, so as every one be answerable to render the same, or the just value thereof, to such as hereafter by law or order it shall be determined to be restored. And if any of the said persons so answerable for any tithe shall appear to you to be of disability hereafter to answer the same, or the value thereof, you shall then order the same to be sequestered from their possession, and to be put into the custody of such other able and indifferent persons as shall be now able to answer for the same; and of your doings you shall make certificate unto us

as soon as you can conveniently execute the premises. And
if any person, being not the tenant and occupier, have since
Midsummer last taken any such tithes from the occupiers of
the grounds, you shall view the same and make thereof a just
value, and in her Majesty's name charge the parties to be
answerable for the same. And because there are rents to be
paid for the said lands, leased to such as have the reversion
thereof, our meaning is, that you shall enquire to whom any
such rents are due, and thereupon to give order that tenants
and occupiers shall pay so much as the rents shall amount
unto; and, if need be, you shall make sale of so much of the
tithes as shall be requisite to pay the rents. And if any person shall charge for payment of any debt wherewith the said
leases are charged, you shall advertise us thereof, whereby
you may have our direction how to pay the same as the case
shall require. Furthermore, if there shall appear to you that
there be any houses or grounds, parcel of the premises, not
granted out for any rent, you shall commit the same to the
custody of such fit persons as will answer a yearly rent to the
most advantage. And also you shall demand and receive of
the tenants which have any in their hands already not paid,
and the same also you shall safely keep in your hands. And
whereas we are informed of some suits depending betwixt
some tenants of Richard Lee and some belonging to John
Croker, for which there is to be some inquisition at a sessions
now shortly to be holden, you shall also cause a stay to be
made of any proceedings at the said sessions; and generally
you shall on your part, and therewith also you shall in her
Majesty's name, move the Justices of Peace that care be had
for conservation of her Majesty's peace betwixt the said
parties, their servants and tenants. So fare you well. From
the Court at Oatlands, the 16th of August 1583. Your loving friend.*

It appears from Archbishop Sandys' letter to Hatton,
that he was greatly dissatisfied with the termination of

* Additional MSS. 15891, f. 113.

Z

the affair with Sir Robert Stapleton and his confederates ;
and that, though they had made a "submission," yet
that it was done in terms which tended more to their
justification than his own innocence:—

ARCHBISHOP SANDYS TO SIR CHRISTOPHER HATTON.

SIR, I had in mind to have imparted unto you, ere this, the
disordered and scornful submission made here at York by the
insolent Knight and his godless confederates; but I forbear
so to do, for fear lest I should be over-troublesome unto you.
Yet now this bringer, my son, passing by London to Oxford,
who was *auritus testis*, I have commanded him to attend upon
you, and to declare unto you how the matter was here used,
if it shall please you to hear him.   The submission was made
in such sort as tended only to my condemnation and their
justification; but I doubt not that this their disordered doing
will be looked into, if it be but in respect of the common
cause.   My state and condition here standeth hard; but I will
fly to my good God for help, comforting myself that the
Queen's Majesty is my most gracious Sovereign, and will not
suffer my enemies to triumph over me.   And how much I am
bound unto you for the greatest favour I have received at
your hands, I can better remember than requite; yet will I
never be found unthankful.   And so I commend you to the
good direction of God's Holy Spirit.   From Bishopsthorp,
the 17th of August 1583.   Yours in Christ, ever to use,

E. EBORICENSIS.[*]

In August Sir Francis Walsingham was sent by the
Queen to the King of Scots, "out of her kind care lest
he should," says Camden, "by corrupt counsels, in the
very flexibility of his age, be alienated from the amity
of England, to the damage of both Kingdoms."   On his
arrival at Newcastle he made a report of what he had
heard, apparently to Lord Burghley:—

[*] Additional MSS. 15891, f. 113.

MY VERY GOOD LORD, The letter you sent me, directed
unto Colonel Stuart, is written to singular good purpose;
but I fear he hath made shipwreck both of conscience and
honesty. He guideth altogether the King his Master, (as it is
now reported,) and therefore there is small hope of his recovery when misrulers become guiders. As I pass through
these parts, I learn that the ill-affected are altogether inclined
to that King, being now resolved that his Mother cannot live
long. They defend his proceedings, and wish no good friendship between the two Crowns, which I fear will fall out according to their desire. Mar, as your Lordship will find by
the last from Mr. Bowes, showeth himself to be a very constant gentleman; and the deputies for the Church, that have
been lately with the King, have taken a wise and a Christian
resolution. If such Ministers as are employed were well
backed by her Majesty, there might be more good done than
I can now hope after; and yet am I persuaded that this dis-
sembling King, both with God and man, will not long stand,
though, before his ruin, he . . . . . . some trouble unto her
Majesty. I hope, within a few days now, to give your Lordship some taste what is to be looked for in that Realm. And
so, in the mean time, I most humbly take my leave. At
Newcastle, the 26th of August 1583. Your Lordship's to
command,   F. WALSINGHAM.[a]

On the 24th of August the Vice-Chamberlain wrote
again to Sir William More, stating that " the Queen intended to dine at Woking on the 27th, and to go to bed
at his house; that he should have everything made
sweet and meet to receive her; remove his family, and
have everything ready; that the Sheriff need not attend,
but that he, Mr. Lyfield, and some other gentlemen
should meet her at Guildford."[b] The annexed letter was

---

[a] Additional MSS. 15891, f. 117 [b].   [b] Nichols' Progresses, II. 412.

probably written a few days after Walsingham had left
the Court for Scotland, and possibly before the letter
just inserted :—

SIR FRANCIS WALSINGHAM TO SIR CHRISTOPHER HATTON.

Sir, You have rightly conceived her Majesty's meaning,
for that it agreeth with the charge she gave me herself. It
may please you to let her Majesty understand, that, within an
hour after I departed from her, I despatched letters unto
Mr. Bowes to the effect she commanded, which I pray God
may arrive at a good season. This last night I was troubled
with an extreme pain in my right side, which did bereave me
of my sleep; it continueth with me still, and therefore I
mean to use both Gifford's and Hector's advice. I find the
pain accompanied with an unaccustomed faintness, and a disposition altogether subject to melancholy. I hope I shall
enjoy more ease in another world than I do in this. And so,
forbearing further to trouble you, I commit you to the protection of the Almighty. [August] 1583. Yours most assuredly to command,   Fra. Walsingham.[*]

By Statute of the 27th Hen. VIII. c. 6, the owners of
parks were bound to keep brood mares; and in the 33rd
Hen. VIII. an Act was passed that all Peers and other
owners of lands should be obliged to keep a certain number of horses of a prescribed height; and it was enacted
that every other person whose wife wore any French hood,
or velvet bonnet, or any ornaments of gold or jewellery
on their dress, should maintain one stone trotting horse,
upon pain of forfeiting ten pounds. The exportation of
horses was prohibited by several statutes :—

FROM THE LORDS OF THE COUNCIL.

After our right hearty commendations. Whereas, by
virtue of the Queen's Majesty's commission to us and others

* Additional MSS. 15891, f. 110.

directed, we deputed you to rate as well yourselves as all other persons within the County of . . . . . . that ought to keep horses or geldings for service, according as their livings be indeed in yearly value, which is the law provided for this case, and not to be abused by a pretence of such values as are accustomably taxed in the times of assessments for subsidies, which how far under the full they may be is most manifest, whereof we do not at this time make any certain account, which rates you have also set down and certified hither, although in some parts not so full as was required and expected of you; yet, to the intent her Majesty may be truly informed how that rate, so by your last letter certified, is observed, and how sufficiently the mares and horses set down therein are appointed and furnished, as by some former instructions you are directed, if present occasion of service at any time should so require, it hath pleased her Majesty at this time to will us to signify unto you (which we do by these presents), that her Highness' pleasure and strait commandment is, that upon the 20th day of September next you do cause a general muster to be made at . . . . . . of all the lances and light horsemen within the County of . . . . , according to the last rate you certified hither. And for that it may happen that some persons lastly by you certified and rated to have horses or geldings be since that time departed out of this life, or otherwise removed and not resident in the Country, whereby there may be want of the said horses or geldings at this your muster, we will and require you that you have due consideration hereof beforehand; and, in place of them that are dead, to devise how the heirs and wives of the parties deceased, or any other possessing the lands of the deceased, may be rateably by you assessed to supply the want, and in her Majesty's name to signify to them how far forth you shall think it convenient to charge them; and therewith to give them commandment to send such horses or geldings, with able men, to the musters, and of your doings herein to certify us. And if any persons be removed from their dwelling to some other habitation unto any Shire near unto you, we will that by your letters you shall certify the Commissioners of that County how far forth that same person was charged, and to will them to warn the party to appear afore them at their musters with the furniture requisite. And so also, if any other Commissioners shall certify you of the like, you shall summon the party to do his duty therein. And if any person heretofore rated and certified, or any person now to be newly rated by you for supply of such as are deceased, shall make default, we will that you command the same parties in her Majesty's name, on pain of one hundred pounds and further punishment, that the same persons appear before us the seventh of October next. Finally, if it shall seem to you that by the largeness of the Shire it will be difficult to have all persons appear at one place and at one day, we leave to your consideration that you appoint several places for the said musters, so as nevertheless the day by us fixed be straitly kept; and to that end you may divide yourselves, so as at every place there may be a convenient number of you to be present to view and to take the same musters, except some of us that are in commission shall give you knowledge, ... days before, that we will be there present at the same musters. We require you, also, to have in remembrance to certify us the number of parks and enclosures within that County, and how many horses and mares for breed are kept in every of them according to the statute, and, according to our former instructions, to give order for the manner of the impress of horses and stallions upon commons, so as, against the next spring, all persons chargeable to provide stallions for that purpose may have them against that time in a readiness, as by the laws is prescribed : and if there be any newly come to inhabit the County, being able by their possessions to find horse or gelding, whereof at the time of the former musters there was no mention made, that you by your discretion consider thereof, and make some reasonable rate for horses or geldings, and to charge them to show and prefer the same at these next musters; and if they shall refuse, then to advertise your opinions, and to command such recusants to appear afore us the 7th of

October next. And so we bid you heartily farewell. Your very loving friends.[a]

At last Dr. Mathew succeeded in obtaining the Deanery of Durham; and his letter of thanks to Sir Christopher Hatton was probably written about August, as he was installed on the 31st of that month;—

DR. MATHEW TO SIR CHRISTOPHER HATTON.

RIGHT HONOURABLE SIR, Having such present impediment as I conveniently may not travel to yield her Majesty and your Honour my manifold and most humble thanks for my dispatch to Durham, (according to my bounden duty and just desire,) I presume upon your accustomed good favour to do that by writing which by word I cannot yet; that is, to acknowledge how much I know myself in that bill of mine indebted double and treble to your Honour, as without whose plain importunity (for so I am informed) it could not pass to signing, so many sundry turns and thwarts it suffered. But it cometh soon enough now, and well enough too, for that it cometh with her Majesty's gracious liking and good contentment, which I am to hold at an higher price than all the profits and promotions of this world. I beseech God I may so there bestow my time and behave myself as I may discharge my duty in glorifying of Him, in serving of her, in profiting of that people, and in verifying some part of those good speeches it hath ever pleased your Honour to bestow upon me; which I hope in Christ I shall endeavour to do to the uttermost of my small power, as well in conversation and hospitality as in doctrine and government. And so, with an unfeigned profession of my thankfulness to your Honour, together with my readiness at your commandment, I humbly betake you for this time and for ever to the grace of Almighty God. Your Honour's humble and bounden,

TOBIE MATHEW.[b]

[a] Additional MSS. 15891, f. 114.   [b] Additional MSS. 15891, f. 110.

A remarkable fact in the life of the Earl of Sussex is brought to light by the following letters from his widow to Hatton and to the Queen, written in September 1583,* namely, that some malicious persons had, in his last illness, alienated his affections from his wife:—

THE COUNTESS OF SUSSEX TO SIR CHRISTOPHER HATTON.

SIR, Knowing the great good-will that it pleased you to profess unto my dear Lord deceased, together with the great courtesies and honourable speeches which you have often vouchsafed me; and now finding myself in an unfortunate estate, trodden down on all sides by cunning adversaries, and most wrongfully disgraced as undutiful to her Majesty; for that I know right well your aptness to do good to everybody, and of what value your friendship is amongst all others where you promise and profess, I have thought good to commit myself and my whole credit to your defence and protection. And albeit I neither have nor ever am likely to be able to deserve that favour and goodness which I now require of you, yet assure yourself that, if God spare me life, I will be most thankful for it, both to you and yours, to the utmost reach of my small power. In the mean time let this be a sufficient testimony and reward of your virtue, that they who know no cause nor desert had rather put themselves in their estimation into your hands, than into theirs of whom they have much deserved. I have herein inclosed a letter to her Majesty for the clearing of my undutifulness, the which I pray you read, to the end you may be the better acquainted with my cause; and at your best opportunity I earnestly desire you, with my true and humble duty, to deliver it, with your best assurance of my vowed faith and loyalty to her Highness; and, if it please you any further to know the particularities of my unhappy estate, this bearer, my dear friend, and one that much honoureth you, shall let you understand

* Vide a former page.

it at large. Thus, only intreating your protection as far as
truth and justice shall bear, for which I will never be proved
unthankful or ungratefully-minded towards you, I commit
you to the merciful goodness of God Almighty. From my
desolate close at Bermondsey, the 18th of September 1583.
Your poor friend to be made most bound to you,

F. Sussex.[a]

TO THE QUEEN.

Most gracious and most merciful Queen, I most
humbly beseech your Majesty to view these few lines, written
with many tears, and even in the bitterness of my soul, with
that pitiful regard wherewith God hath viewed your Majesty
at all times and in all cases. And albeit I am now beaten
down with many afflictions and calamities hardly to be borne
of flesh and blood, yet is there no grief that pierceth me so
deeply as that by sinister suggestion I should be defamed
to be undutiful to your most excellent Majesty, and injurious
to the honour of my dear Lord lately deceased. For the first,
I appeal to God himself, the searcher of hearts, and revenger
of all disloyalties: for the second, I appeal to none but unto
my most gracious Queen, whether I have not from time to
time been more careful of his health, honour, and well-doing
than of mine own soul and safety; refusing all friends and
friendships in this world for so dear a Lord, whom I followed
in health and sickness, in wealth and woe, with more care than
becomed a true Christian to owe unto any worldly creature.
The which if it be true, (as I trust your Majesty in my right
and your justice doth acknowledge it is,) marvel not, most
dread Sovereign, if the vigilant malice of those who have long
complotted my ruin, who espied their time, when my Lord
through anguish and torments was brought to his utmost
weakness, to break the perfect band and love of twenty-eight
years' continuance, have also, by cunning sleights devised, and
by slanderous speeches, instilled into your Majesty's ears the
want of that duty, the which I pray God may sooner fail by

<hr>

[a] Additional MSS. 15891, f. 112.

lack of life than want of loyalty.   And thus, most noble Princess, am I trodden down by my inferiors, not only in worldly
maintenance, which I nothing esteem (having far more, by
God's goodness, than I deserve), but also am touched in the
chiefest point of honour, and the highest degree of duty,
which bringeth on every side such a sea of sorrows as, were it
not for the fear of God's revenge, I could, with all my heart,
redeem them with the sacrifice of my life.   Wherefore, most
gracious Lady, even for the pity which ever hath been engrafted in your Princely heart, I most humbly beseech you,
see not your Majesty's poor servant trodden down by the malicious speeches and unconscionable extremities of those who
take the advantage of my Lord's painful weakness to work my
disgrace, nor increase my just and perpetual griefs with your
heavy displeasure ; praying God that I may rather presently
die while I write these lines, than that I may live wittingly to
deserve your Majesty's just dislike.   In the meantime, I will
not cease to pray to the Almighty for your Majesty's life,
health, and prosperity.   From the poor careful close of Bermondsey.   Your Majesty's poor, but true faithful servant, to
die at your feet,   F. Sussex.[a]

The rigour of the Queen's displeasure towards the
Countess of Derby seems to have been at last somewhat softened :—

COUNTESS OF DERBY TO SIR CHRISTOPHER HATTON.

My dear and noble good Friend, Having, by means
of your honourable favour, obtained that grace as to present
myself to the view of her Majesty at what time her Highness
removed from her house of Sion to Oatlands, my humble suit
is now, you would happily find that good leisure and opportunity as to let it be known unto her Majesty that thereby I
received that hope of her gracious farther good-liking, which
since hath not only kept life in me, but also embolden me
more and more to prostrate myself as a loyal and faithful Sub-

[a] Additional MSS. 15891.

ject unto my so good and gracious a Princess. Wherefore,
that I may at length desist and leave off, (though ever most
bound unto your noble courtesies,) my request at this instant
once again is, that by means of your happy motion I may
come to the kissing of her Highness' hand, which would yield
me that comfort as no earthly thing the like. Good Mr.
Vice-Chamberlain, let me not seem tedious (though so indeed) unto you; for were it that I possessed all things, yet in
this her Majesty's disgrace I esteem myself as possessing
nothing, insomuch as I take her Highness unto me as life
with her gracious favour, but as death with her heavy displeasure. Thus, holding you as my surest hold, and most honourable good friend, from whom must proceed my chiefest good,
I humbly take my leave. From Clerkenwell, the 26th of
September 1583. Your assured and most bounden poor
friend,   MARGARET DERBY.[a]

It may be inferred from the Countess of Sussex's
next letter to Sir Christopher Hatton, that she had
been involved in a lawsuit with her husband's executors, and that her proceedings were disapproved of by
the Queen, whose displeasure her former letters show
she had incurred:—

THE COUNTESS OF SUSSEX TO SIR CHRISTOPHER HATTON.

RIGHT HONOURABLE, I understand by my dear friend
Mr. Dean of the Arches, how much I am bounden unto
you, and how honourably you have satisfied mine expectation
and the true opinion that the world conceiveth of you. And
although I confess there is no reason to trouble you in this
action any farther, yet will I not cease by all good ways and
means to seek and crave her Majesty's favour, even with as
much duty and humility as the poorest creature that ever lay
at her Highness' feet. And if her Majesty did indeed know
how far undutifulness was ever from my heart, or how little I

* Additional MSS. 15891.

suspected her Highness' heavy displeasure, knowing mine
own innocency, or how far my thoughts are from law and
trouble, if I might find any indifferency and courtesy in my
Lord's executors, truly her merciful heart would never have
refused my letters written with so many tears, nor mine
humble duty so unfeignedly tendered; which albeit her Majesty hath done, yet will I not omit eftsoons to do the part
of a true servant and humble subject: the which I beseech
you most heartily, upon every good occasion, to signify unto
her Highness; of whose grace if I only am born to fail, without my desert to my knowledge, I can do no more but pray
unto God that it be His holy pleasure to shorten my unhappy
days, wrapped and overwhelmed with many sorrows, but especially with the heavy indignation of my Prince, whom I
beseech God long to prosper to His goodwill and pleasure.
And so, eftsoons thanking you of your great goodness, I
commit you to the mercy of the Almighty. This 10th of
October 1583. Your friend most bound,   F. Sussex.[a]

In what manner Bishop Aylmer gave offence to Leicester has not been discovered; but the following letter
shows his habitual subserviency :—

BISHOP AYLMER TO THE EARL OF LEICESTER.

My singular good Lord, It grieveth me not a little that
this mischance should happen between you and me, considering that I ever meant to stay myself upon your good and
honourable favour in all manner of office and duty belonging
to such a personage.   I have always found you my very good
Lord till this unhappy paroxysm so shook the former sound
state of your honourable friendship that I might half despair
of the full recovering thereof, but that I have ever observed
in you such a mild, courteous, and amiable nature, that you
never kept as grave in marble, but written in sand, the
greatest displeasure that ever you conceived against any man.

[a] Additional MSS. 15891, f. 17.

I fear not, therefore, my good Lord, in this strait that I am in, to appeal from this Lord of Leicester, whom either my oversight, or other mistaking and misreport of messengers, or both, have incensed with displeasure, unto mine old Lord of Leicester, who in his virtue of mildness and of softness (which the Apostle so commendeth) hath carried away the praise from all men. Admit, I pray your Lordship, this poor appeal of mine, seeing it is but to yourself who in former time have bound many unto you with the golden chain of love, rather than carried or driven any with the boisterous tempests of terror, wherein, my good Lord, is hidden this danger, as oft is said, *quem metuunt oderunt*, &c. You hate ingratitude, I cannot blame you; for I assure you, if I found it in myself, I would not spare to hate myself; for *qui ingratum dicit, omnia dicit.* Let not (my good Lord) the Bishop of London in his old age (when, though he is not the happiest, yet ought to be the wisest) lose that good Earl whom he so comfortably enjoyed in his younger years. I hope these two arguments will forcibly move you to reconciliation. The good and kind nature of our God, who loved us His enemies, and daily forgiveth us our offences, without any reliques of remembrance or desire of revenge. Our gracious Queen, when she was highly displeased with me for Mr. Rich, yet the beams of her grace, soon upon my humble writing to her Majesty, as it were dispersed the clouds of her indignation. Oh, my Lord! will God forgive and her Majesty forget, and my Lord of Leicester retain and keep that which is not worth the keeping, I mean the remembrance of offences? I believe you will not; I know you cannot; and I assure you in this profession you may not. To end: if it may please your Lordship to appoint me any time, I will attend upon you, if I may better satisfy you, whom God bless now and ever with His gracious goodness. 2nd November 1583. Your Lordship's to command assuredly,   JOHN LONDON.*

* Additional MSS. 15891, f. 118.

TO JOHN DUTTON OF DUTTON, ESQ.

Sir, The return of my cousin and servant, your son Peter
Dutton, after his long and dangerous travel abroad, hath been
cause of exceeding comfort unto me, both for the good affection which I bear him, and for the virtuous disposition which
I have always noted in him; the which being now much confirmed in him both by judgment and staidness of behaviour,
I cannot but earnestly recommend him to your goodness upon
occasion of this present repair unto you, and heartily entreat
you to receive him with the regard of good and fatherly affection, which I trust you will judge him very well worthy of,
both in respect of his dutiful disposition towards you, and
also for many other good parts which justly crave the continuance of your good favour towards him. Her Majesty
doth very graciously accept of the gentleman's travel, liking
also very well of his return, with assurance that he will prove
a man meet to be hereafter employed in service to the benefit
of his Country. In which respect, Sir, I must entreat you
to make much of him, and to encourage him to hold in that
good course which he hath already begun, to the great contentment of his friends; whose expectation I doubt not he
will perform honestly in every point to his own credit and
commendation, and in time do much honour and reputation
to the House he cometh of. I have always thought myself
beholden unto you in that it pleased you (upon very good
will, I take it,) to bestow him in my service; for which your
kindness I very heartily thank you. And even so I do assure
you that he shall not want my best friendship and favour
wherein I may do him good, or any way further the towardness of virtue which I find in him to due perfection.

After he hath been with you a while, and discharged some
part of his duty by presence towards you, in case I may perceive any desire in him to follow the life of a courtier yet
for a time, he shall have my best furtherance for his preferment, doubt you not, as occasion shall be offered; accounting
that whatsoever I shall do for him I shall do for one of my

best friends and kinsmen. I pray you, Sir, once again,
cherish him and make much of him for my sake. And even
so, offering my like readiness to yourself to pleasure you in
what I may, with my heartiest commendations I commit you
to God. From the Court at St. James's, the 16th of December 1583. Your very loving assured friend and cousin,

CHR. HATTON.[a]

About the end of April 1582, Sir Thomas Tresham,
the brother of Dr. William Tresham, the writer of the
following eloquent letter, heard mass said by a seminary
priest, called Osborne, in Lord Vaux's chamber in the
Fleet prison,[b] and was convicted of recusancy in January following.[c] It is without date, but may be assigned
to this year. The warning he gives Hatton of the Earl
of Leicester is remarkable:—

WILLIAM TRESHAM TO SIR CHRISTOPHER HATTON.

IF there be no greater grief to the heart of man than unkindness offered where it was never deserved, and where assured friendship hath been looked for, then, Sir, marvel not
at me if I be fraught with infinite woe and full of heaviness;
for I am persuaded that in all the world there was never
any man that bare more perfect affection to another than
William Tresham to Sir Christopher Hatton long and faithfully before he was a Counsellor, and never ceased (oh that I
am inforced to declare it!) until so strangely I was rejected.
It was not my own desert, I take God to witness. My heart
was too much devoted yours, not so much as in thought to
wish amiss. There was never any man's good-will purchased
at so dear a price as I bought the favour of Mr. Vice-Chamberlain: and however, not with the benefit of giving much,
(yet greatly pleasuring you as any man that hath gained most

---

[a] Desiderata Curiosa, I. 142.
[b] Ellis' Original Letters, 2nd series, vol. III. p. 88.
[c] Wright's Queen Elizabeth and
her Times, II. 187. Strype says that

Sir Thomas Tresham was committed
and fined for having harboured Campion, and been privy to his treasonable designs. Annals, III. pt. I. pp.
180-181.

by you,) but by often and serious protestations, with many
humble and earnest requests, with much sincerity of mind,
great integrity of heart, with resolute avowing not to tarry in
Court if you once disliked my continuing there; yea, and
more than all that, lamenting with many grievous tears whensoever upon any small occasion or simple surmise you had
conceived any displeasure against me: such was my grief
to have your ill-will, and my care to entertain your good
liking. Ah Sir, you have often sought to cast me off when
I would not see it, so faithfully dear were you always to me
in all fortunes. But oh blind affection that never deceiveth
but with late repentance! How may it be thought that ever
you would have rejected me, your devoted poor friend, for
the sole pleasure of the Earl of Leicester, without any occasion or small suspicion given on my part to yourself, knowing
especially, as you do, that he affecteth you only to serve his
own turn? Take heed of him in time! I speak it for good-
will; and all the harm I wish you is, that you will with the
eyes of wisdom look into him thoroughly; and then you
shall find that he knoweth only to gain friends, and hath not
the good regard or grace to keep them. I pray you, Sir,
deceive not yourself so far as to think that Counsellors only
are wise; for there are many other men of great judgment
and understanding, whom fortune never advanced to so high
degree, *sapientissimus enim ipse qui discrete seipsum videt,*
and deemeth not vainly or passionately of others. I make
small account in what sort you scorn my letters now in my
absence, considering how little grace my speeches had in your
ears when I was present with you. For myself, I know,
being a banished man, you can pleasure me little; but my
poor brother, detained now in prison for the remorse and
liberty of conscience, may haply fare the better if he find
favour in your sight; which if it shall please you to vouchsafe
him in this discomfort and heaviness of affliction that he now
lieth in, you shall both requite with courtesy a friend that
hath ever loved you with constancy, and bind me with my
devote prayers to God to be thankful unto you for it. I

pray you, Sir, remember, that the bee gathereth honey of every flower, and of many travails frameth a sweet and comfortable being for herself and young ones all the cold winter; but the grasshopper all the summer-time joyeth with gallantry in the pleasant meadows, and dieth commonly with the cold dew of Bartholomew. You know that the high cedar-trees on the tops of huge mountains are most subject to the danger of storms, and therefore have most need of many and sure roots. We are all in God's hands, to be raised or pulled down as it shall please Him; and there is none so high now, but may one day, through affliction, stand in as great need of comfort as now my poor brother and your dear friend doth. I beseech you think of him, and vouchsafe to bind us and our posterity unto you by the goodness that you may now afford him in furthering his enlargement. The day may come that you may find either him, or his, better able than now they are to acknowledge in all good sort, and thankfully to requite your kindness. God bless you with all good favour, and grant you the happiness to love your friends with that faithfulness which is due unto them, and without the which you cannot keep them! Your Honour's to command,

WILLM. TRESHAM.*

No light can be thrown upon the following letter, which is without either signature or date:—

UNKNOWN, TO THE QUEEN.

MAY IT PLEASE YOUR MOST EXCELLENT MAJESTY to vouchsafe with your gracious and pitiful eyes the reading of these few lines, and by them to understand the unhappy estate of me your Majesty's most humble and loyal Subject, who was long in debating with myself what course I might devise which was most agreeable to express the duty which I did owe unto your Majesty, and most likely to relieve the misery which I did feel within myself. And, at the last, calling to mind how ready your sacred hands have been to receive

---

* Additional MSS. 15891, f. 81.

A A

the supplications of the poor, and how rightly noble your
princely heart hath ever showed itself in pitying the state of
the miserable; nay, remembering what undeserved clemency
you have sometimes showed to those which have offended,
and what unspeakable favour you have ever used to such as
have been innocent, I was emboldened (though mine own unworthiness dissuaded me), lying prostrate at your Majesty's
feet, to present this humble supplication of mine, and in it
neither to protest further than I can with a good and sound
conscience warrant, nor to desire more than your Majesty
shall in your grave and deep judgment think me worthy.
And because that which is past and known is sometime a
mean to explain that which is present and not manifest,
I most humbly beseech your Majesty to consider, how, at my
first entrance into the world, I was laid open to all danger
and only protected by you; how I was assaulted by malice
and defended by you; how I was overthrown by misfortune
and upholden by you; how I must acknowledge all that I
have to proceed from your goodness, and how I do confess
that which I am to be by your favour. And if your Majesty
do consider this, I know the gracious disposition of yours
(which is easily moved to believe the best though it be doubtful, and hardly drawn to conceive the worst though it be
manifest) will not suffer you without open and evident proof
to condemn me of so great and horrible ingratitude as that I
should think a thought which might displease you, much less
do a thing which should offend you. Wherefore, seeing I am
not only bound to your Majesty in that universal and highest
band which is common to me with all your other subjects,
but in this special and particular band which is peculiar to
myself alone, as I must acknowledge myself unworthy to
live if I have willingly offended your Majesty in the smallest
matter, so, if it may be lawful for me with all humility to
sue for so much favour at your Majesty's hands as that I
might, with your gracious licence, speak unto yourself, I
doubt not but so to lay open the sincerity of my mind and
the integrity of my dealing from time to time in anything

which concerned my duty to your Majesty, that I shall appear far different from that which, peradventure, the malice of some would have made me. And in the mean time I most humbly beseech your Majesty that I may protest with your favour thus much; and, for confirmation of it, I will call God to witness that mine own thoughts cannot accuse me of the least undutifulness to your Majesty; that I am ready and willing to hazard my life, whensoever, howsoever, or wheresoever it pleaseth your Majesty to command to employ me; that the whole course of my life is bent to serve you; that it is my daily study how to please you, and my only desire by any mean to content you; that I have no comfort in this world but your favour, and that no earthly thing either doth or can grieve me so much as your displeasure. To conclude all in a word, that I desire God so to prosper me in this world, and to bless me in the next, as I have been in all my words, intents and actions, true, faithful, and dutiful unto your Majesty. And thus, craving pardon with all humility if either I have been in this supplication more tedious than becomes me, or have done in anything otherwise than agreed with your Majesty's liking and pleasure, I beseech God from the bottom of my heart ever to send your Majesty that happiness which your most incomparable virtues do deserve, and your most affectionate subjects do desire.[a]

Dr. Mathew never appears except as an importunate suitor; but the precise nature of this application is not stated:—

DR. MATHEW TO MR. SAMUEL COX.

MR. Cox, I never call upon you but when I have need to use your friendship; and, when I need it, I ever find it. I thank you for it. My good friend Mr. Doctor Lougher will let you know the cause, and let you see the letter that now doth move me to solicit Mr. Vice-Chamberlain. I pray, Sir, most instantly direct Mr. Doctor what course he shall take in

[a] Additional MSS. 15891, f. 118[b].

A A 2

discoursing with him, which I have entreated him to do ; for that I dare not come to the Court, as well lest I should exasperate mine adversaries, as also being in this place so subject to the sickness as I know not with what safety or duty I may approach unto his Honour. My especial affiance, you know where it is, and I beseech you answer my expectations once for all. I do more than marvel that we have no word of answer to the letter written to the Prebendaries of Durham, in her Majesty's name, from my Lord of Leicester and Mr. Vice-Chamberlain. If you understand anything thereof, I pray you iinpart it to this bearer, as all other things that you would to myself. So fare you most heartily and friendly well. Your assured friend,   TOBIE MATHEW.[a]

TO SIR CHRISTOPHER HATTON.

GOOD MR. VICE-CHAMBERLAIN, This messenger your servant having given me some little warning to wait on you, I have adventured to trouble you with my ill-written letter, false English, and matter as little to be regarded as the profession of her good-will who wrote it, who is herself little or nothing worth. Nevertheless, when I remember your courtesy offered even then when Fortune most showed her despite against me, I am persuaded a certain planet reigned that then assured me, and so doeth still, that I should receive some good of you, though the storms of my ill-fortune have shed since many drops untimely for me to gather fruit of your favour. I have nothing to present you with but the thought of the heart by the pen's description, in what thankful manner I take your good and kindly offer to do me pleasure ; holding that opinion of your great virtue that I have ever conceived, which is, that you love faithful plain-dealing, and hate dissimulation. I am grievously sorry for her Majesty's heavy displeasure so kindled against me, as I fear it is. If God will make my prayers worthy to enter into His ears, I will with all lowliness of mind incessantly beseech Him to prosper her estate ; and for my offence, which she

* Additional MSS. 15891, f. 105.

supposeth to be heinous in her judgment and justly deserving her disfavour, I appeal to the Highest, that is best able to look into the bottom of my heart, whether my innocency have not always dreaded only to conceive so much as an ill thought of her. God bless her! and give me grace to serve Him, that by His goodness it may plainly appear unto her how unjustly I am afflicted with her disgrace and indignation. It shall make me less careful than I have been (but only for duty sake) for that life of courting. But, country-woman or courtier, as long as Mr. Vice-Chamberlain will do me the honour to judge me worthy to be esteemed an honest poor friend, I will ever, with all honour that any tongue can express, think I do right to myself in giving you that which your virtue deserveth. Yours, as ever vowed during life,

ELIZABETH . . . . . .

Post.—I hope, Sir, that if a poor pilgrim, wandering in the Park with a long bow, shoot at rovers, and hit a buck where the sign is, and die of it, you will not make it a pretended murder.*

The following letter, relating to some proposed changes in the Church of St. Patrick, which will be again noticed, was written by Adam Loftus, Archbishop of Dublin from 1567 to 1605: but the date is not given, and it may have been written in 1584, or even in 1585:—

ARCHBISHOP OF DUBLIN TO LORD BURGHLEY.

May it please your Lordship, Upon the return hither of the Archdeacon of Dublin, with report of his success in the humble suit exhibited in his behalf of the Church of St. Patrick, I did not only find the gracious resolution that was set down there by the Lords and others of her Majesty's Privy Council, but the especial favour showed by your Lordship, so honourable and conscionably vouchsafed as deserveth the perpetual prayers of my brethren and me; the same resolution tending to this end, that nothing should be done in the

* Additional MSS. 15891, f. 62.

dissolution of the Church without a conference between the
Lord Deputy and me, and a consent in me (as I take it), is now
brought over, as I hear, by Sir Lucas Dillon, but is not
hitherto, neither I think shall be, imparted to me by his
Lordship.   I know, my good Lord, that nothing but zeal and
care of the common good doth carry my Lord Deputy into
the settled purpose to change the ancient institution into such
an alteration as he conceiveth to be more beneficial to the
Commonwealth, by establishing public lectures in several
studies and sciences; which if it might be without overthrow-
ing the great for the less, or with the expense and diminish-
ing only of mine own private, and not with the ruin in manner of all the Professors of Divinity in the land, I would not
stand against his Lordship (whom I honour and love) in a
cause that hath so good appearance for the public wealth.
But this, my good Lord, is the case: My church standeth not
upon temporalities, as all churches in England do, but every
dignity and every prebend is a parsonage with cure of souls,
saving a little demesne land in the country for the dean and
the chaunter; no impropriation belonging to all St. Patrick's;
but the dean, the two archdeacons, chaunter, treasurer and
prebends are all persons without vicars endowed, and ought
to be all divines, for so the foundation requireth.   The
church of Christchurch neither hath, nor is able to maintain,
one preacher.   Then, my Lord, behold the state of this
wretched Country; in all the whole Realm there is not one
preacher (three bishops excepted, of whom two were preferred out of this church, but only in St. Patrick's.)   These
preachers must be removed, and as it were banished, in hope
that, twenty years hence, some divines may spring out of a
lecture to be instituted out of this intended college.   In the
mean season, the several cures of the incumbents of the
church must be left to unlearned stipendiaries.   The arch-
bishoprick must neither have archdeacon to visit, (for Christ-
church hath none,) neither hath he one church in the Realm
whereunto to present a learned man; a perpetual indignity
to all my successors, Archbishops, which since the Conquest

have been all Englishmen (one only excepted), and all in more than ordinary credit here with their Sovereigns. Now your Lordship in all godly wisdom looking into these things may see my estate: either I must contend with him, whom I highly esteem, and ought in all dutiful love to obey, or else I must neglect my personal charge, or leave myself to all my successors a perpetual blot and infamy, that the endowments of the church, founded by noble Princes, and continued in so many ages, should determine in my time, and a present evil to grow upon hope of a future good. I might say, schools are provided for in every country here; Oxford and Cambridge are not far off, all under one dominion; but this will not satisfy. Therefore, my dear Lord, I conclude, that if her Majesty by her private letters do not expressly forbid this dissolution to be talked of in Parliament, I foresee (as things are like to be wrought) the ruin both of this See and of this Church, with a general discontentment of the people, her Majesty having never given the like example. And therefore, if that letter may not by your only favour be procured, it shall be best for me (being old, and not suffered longer to do good,) to avoid the present evil, and to resign the bishoprick with all duty and humility to one more worthy than myself, that can frame reason for the time; which is my determinate purpose with your Lordship's good advice and favour, whereupon I depend more than any worldly man. I have given order to Mr. Bancroft, the bearer hereof, and one of the prebendaries of my church, not only to deliver these letters to your Lordship, but also to attend on you for this cause, in such sort and at such time as it shall please you to command him. And so, commending your Lordship to God's gracious favour in my humble prayers, I forbear to trouble you any longer.[a]

The Bishop of St. David's, to whom Dr. Mathew compares himself in this letter on the old subject, was Marmaduke Middleton, who was translated from the See of Waterford in December 1582;—

[a] Additional MSS. 15891; f. 143.

DR. MATHEW TO MR. SAMUEL COX.

MR. SAMUEL COX, I trust you will license me with good leave to challenge your promise at my departure, not only to have consideration, but care, of my suit. I cannot but remember your words full of friendship and good affection; and by this time, it may be, you can beyond conjecture send me some good hope of better expedition than I found at my last being there, yet too soon methought by so sudden an alteration as seemed very strange, no more to myself than to sundry others. But all things have their times, and that time was not the time of that thing. But will it be in any time, trow you? Can Mr. Michael Stanhope win the time to write two letters to Doctor Sprint my friend and countryman, and assure him that he shall have the Deanery of Durham if he will come, or send his brother to enter as one authorized for such a matter, and so to carry it away without delay; and cannot Mr. Cox see, or foresee, or aftersee what cause or colour might work such alteration? Am not I an old man? —he is younger. Am I married?—he is once more married than I. But what speak I of age, or marriage? when, to let all other answers pass, her Majesty was pleased amidst those exceptions to advance, I say not to a Deanery, but to the Bishoprick of St. David's, as young a man as myself and married; wherefore, some other matter of stay there must needs be than these. I pray you, Sir, do me the friendship to learn it, and write it, or say it to this bearer as to myself. Be as good to me towards Mr. Vice-Chamberlain as his Honour hath been towards her Majesty for me. If there be any secret, desire it may be discovered, that so you may the less trouble him, and he her Majesty, and I my friends. Howsoever this fall, I trust you will love us as we like you. Your assured loving friend,   TOBIE MATHEW.[*]

Another letter from Dr. Mathew, expressing his gratitude to Hatton, without any date, may also have been written about this period :—

[*] Additional MSS. 15891.

DR. MATHEW TO SIR CHRISTOPHER HATTON.

RIGHT HONOURABLE, Your special favour towards me hath many ways appeared, but most singularly of late, to my great comfort, amidst my sickness; for the which your goodness and bounty albeit no length of words or writing would suffice me to be worthily thankful to your Honour, yet such is, you know, my present occasion, as I must think the rest, and only say, that, if ever such a one as I were most bounden to such a person as yourself, I am the man, both sick and whole, both in your presence and in your absence, as finding your Honour my best physician, and your cook my best apothecary. Now would to God, Sir, I were as worthy to enjoy my health as you may be assured to command my life. And even so, with my humble thanks unto you, and mine unfeigned prayers for you that God will increase your Honour to His glory, I take my leave. Your Honour's most bounden in all duty,

TOBIE MATHEW.[a]

The earliest letter in 1584 relates to the persecution of some unhappy Roman Catholic:—

SIR FRANCIS WALSINGHAM TO SIR CHRISTOPHER HATTON.

SIR, Though for my own part I do very well allow of the course you were entered into touching the examining of Keeper, yet, seeing the Earl of Leicester doth not hold it best, I think it best forborne until we may confer with him to-morrow what way he shall think meet to be taken with the said party. In the mean time, I doubt not but that you will have care, both that he may be forthcoming, as also that he may be kept from intelligence. They that have given advertisement that he is a priest do take upon them to be most assured of it, as the Lord of Hunsdon telleth me; and therefore I find it strange that his answers be so peremptory. It may be, when he shall be pressed with oath, he will yield another

[a] Additional MSS. 15891.

answer.   If he prove to be a priest (as is reported), then will
he not greatly weigh his allegiance, having, as the rest of his
associates have, a very unreverent opinion of her Majesty's
authority.   Thus, Sir, I am bold to scribble some more lines
than were necessary, and so do commit you to the tuition of
the Almighty.   At Seething Lane, the 30th of January 1583
[1584].   Yours most assuredly to command,

FRA. WALSINGHAM.[a]

A marginal note gives this account of the writer of
the following letter, who was, he says, " a sworn officer
touching the Queen's revenue:"—" This was that William Dodington, that wilfully brake his neck by casting
himself down headlong from the battlements of St.
Sepulchre's steeple, upon the sight of certain depositions
touching a cause in controversy between him and one
Brunker in Chancery."   And a letter is preserved, entitled " A lamentable ejaculation of W. Dodington's
distressed soul;"[b] intimating his intention to commit
suicide.

MR. WILLIAM DODINGTON TO SIR CHRISTOPHER HATTON.

. MAY IT PLEASE YOUR HONOUR, The morrow after my
departure from you my late Master sent for me, and showed
me the order devised by Mr. Manners, being the same which
I had read to you the day before.   He told me that he
received it of the Lord Treasurer, with earnest desire to have
the cause so laid as the lands might come again to her Majesty, and so to Mr. Manners' hands.   I prayed him not to
deal with you to that effect; I told him the harm and shame
would grow to me thereby, and that for my part I would
never agree to it whilst I lived.   He wished me not to labour you to the contrary, and said he knew what he would
do therein; and this was all our talk: sithence I hear by
Mr. Carey that your Honour is drawn to that course, as a

---

[a] Additional MSS. 15891.   [b] Lansdowne MSS. 99, art. 32.

thing whereunto I should have also yielded my consent. I
most humbly beseech you to weigh my hard case. Mr. Manners hath of record accused me (her Highness' sworn Officer
touching her revenue), first of fraud, of deceit, of cunningly
and closely inserting and shifting into a bill, to be signed by
her Majesty, matter to her great loss and hindrance in the same
revenue: this is in his bill. In his replication he particularly entertaineth his slander, and not obscurely in the end
chargeth me with perjury, to make me amends withal. But
I am in a sort discharged of all this matter, saving the perjury; and now Mr. Manners must have the land again by William Dodington's consent. But whether I consented to re-
assure the lands to the intent to be discharged of the fraud,
or were discharged without consent, that must remain for
ever a question; and, make the best of it that may be made,
the conclusion is, if I be washed at all, it shall be yet, Sir, (as
the proverb is,) but with Sowler's ink. Touching the land,
it is your Honour's now, and you may do with it as it
pleaseth you, always reserved that my consent shall never be
that Mr. Manners shall have it; and be it spoken without
offence, I take it not convenient that your Honour should
yield to no good friend of yours such a favour, for hurting of
him that would, if he might, be your good servant. Your
Honour did once friendly for him, as much as he now requireth, and it liked him not to have it that way. Be you
sure, that, when he hath it, he will neither esteem you nor
care for me; and that which he could not hitherto win of me
by other means I shall now be forced to yield by your precedent. This I say, Sir, over boldly, as I am wont in your gallery at London; and, if I were afore you in place of judgment, I would then challenge you to do me justice, and to
grant me damages at my accusers' hands. Marry, this is
another course not fit for that place; for now the party that
hath done the injury shall be benefited, and he that is already
wronged shall be further punished. But, Sir, God's will be
done and yours, and follow that which is best for yourself.
As for me, it is no great matter; and it would be more grief

unto me to have your Honour disquieted, than pleasure to see
mine enemy requited. If the worst befal me, I shall fly to
Chaucer's borrow, sit down and sigh, and drink mine own
sorrow. Having troubled your Honour too long, I humbly
pray you to forgive me, if I have said anything amiss: in
truth, in this case I am not mine own man. God evermore
prosper you; and so I make an end. From Brearmore, in
the New Forest, the 4th of March 1583 [1584]. Your
Honour's, as I am bound, WILLIAM DODINGTON.[a]

Mr. Cox, Hatton's Secretary, seems to have prided
himself upon his epistolary talents, for several letters[b]
from him occur in the "Letter Book," which, like the
following, are remarkable for nothing but their style:—

MR. SAMUEL COX TO . . . .

SIR, I am sorry to hear of the heavy news of your father's
departure out of this life, a gentleman to whom I was in many
respects much beholding, and one whom I have ever especially honoured for his integrity and virtue; the lack whereof is
the chiefest cause that now justly moveth me, as much as any
man, to lament the loss of so rare and faithful a friend. But,
seeing God hath thought good in His high wisdom to take him
from the earthly tabernacle of this worldly mansion, as fitter
to be placed with Him in the heavenly inheritance of His
glorious Kingdom, where he remaineth eternally happy, than
to dwell here any longer amongst us in this vale of worldly
vanities, there is no cause, in the true course of Christianity,
why we should mourn so much for his death, as we should take
comfort and rejoice for his happy change; neither ought we to
murmur at the divine pleasure of God, who hath so ordained
it. I understand, by the report of such as seem to know
much, that he died intestate, whereof is like to ensue some
dissension and unkind debate between you and your brethren; which I should be sorry were true, as well for the slan-

---

[a] Additional MSS. 15891, f. 120[b].
[b] Most of these Letters, with a few others of a miscellaneous nature, will be found in the APPENDIX.

der which by this means might be raised against your dead
father, (whom the world might judge, through this lack of
providence, to be inconsiderate in his death, though grave
and wise in his life,) as also for the particular love I bear
you, both for his sake and your own; in which respect I
wish that these unnatural quarrels might be far from you.
It is said he made a will, but not orderly and perfect; because therein some part of the solemnity of law was omitted,
the intervention whereof was necessary.   It was written
plain and at large, with the subscription of his hand, but
there wanted the seal and witnesses; for which cause, in the
strict censure of law, he is in truth judged to die intestate:
*paria enim sunt, aliquid omnino non fieri aut minus rite
fieri.*   Other some say that he left a direct and a perfect will
behind him; but *pronuntiabatur irritum et injustum, propter secundi testamenti factionem;* in which case the law findeth him likewise to die intestate, *idem enim est . . . . . .
mentum omnino non facere vel . . . . . facere quod . . . . .
pronuntietur.*   But, this day, a friend of mine advertised me,
a man of good learning and judgment, that he made a will,
but did not nominate therein any certain executor; which
being true, the law is directly apparent, in the opinion of all
men, that he died intestate: *nam intestatus est cujus hære-
ditas adita non est.*   It is the executor that giveth consum-
mation and effect to the will, without the which the true
meaning of the testator cannot be observed; and therefore
the law esteemeth it to be a vain and frivolous will, and no
will at all indeed, where the executor to the testator is not
expressly mentioned, wherein I would wish you to take good
advice, with the best endeavour and expedition.   The greatest scruple that might justly trouble you most, if it were
true, is the report that he died distracted and furious; and
that there was a will readily made and framed by some about
him, without his privity or direction, who afterward brought
it unto him, and, putting the pen in his hand, constrained
him to subscribe it by leading and guiding the same, according to their own corrupt fancies.   If this should fall out to

be proved by witnesses, it is indubitable also, in my poor
opinion, that he died intestate, *nam furiosus, pupillus et
prodigus testamenti faciendi jus non habent;* and so he will
be found to make no will, though in this case he be not
proprie intestatus, but *intestabilis, cum nullus testandi præ-
cesserit habitus.* Thus you see how my good-will hath made
me bold to deliver you my rude and simple advice; which,
though it be not worthy of your notice, yet, I pray you,
accept of it well, because it was well meant to do you
good in that which might best satisfy the effect of your
virtuous desires; the increase whereof, and of all other
prosperity, wishing ever to you as to myself, I remain yours
unfeignedly at commandment. In haste; from the Court
at Greenwich, the 29th of March 1584. Your poor fast
true friend,   SAMUEL COX.[a]

The following letter from Hatton to the Queen shows
that in April of this year he had taken offence at her
Majesty's proceedings, and withdrawn from the Court;
the cause of which is thus stated in a marginal note:
" A man of his, Mr. George Best, was slain in fight a
little before by one Mr. Oliver St. John, and, as it was
suspected, scarce manfully and in good fight, which Mr.
Vice-Chamberlain took very grievously; and finding the
Queen unwilling that he should prosecute the offender
in course of justice, but rather desirous to save him,
Mr. Vice-Chamberlain took this, and some other hard
measure offered by the Queen, very unkindly, and therefore forbore his wonted access and attendance, and
withdrew himself from the Court to his house at Holdenby, in Northamptonshire, where he remained in great
sorrow and perplexity many days, until at the length
she was pleased to take some pity of his grief, and to

[a] Additional MSS. 15891, f. 134.

send for him." It is remarkable, that, though his letter is full of humility and contrition, and though he admits his "too high presumptions" towards her Majesty, yet he prays of her to remember the "causes," which were, he says, as "unfit for him as unworthy of her";—

SIR CHRISTOPHER HATTON TO QUEEN ELIZABETH.

On the knees of my heart, most dear and dread Sovereign Majesty, I beseech pardon and goodness at your princely hands. I fear I offend you in lack of attendance on your princely presence, wherein, before our God, frowardness and obstinacy of mind are as far from me as love and duty would have them; but that the griefs and sorrows of my soul so oppress me as I cannot express unto you, and so entangle my spirits that they turn me out of myself, and thereby making me unfit to be seen of you, is the true cause that I forbear access. I most humbly thank your sacred Majesty for your two late recomfortations. Would God I had deserved your former goodness; for, God knoweth, your good favour hath not been ever, or at any time, evil employed on me your poor disconsolate wretch. I will leave all former protestations of merit or meanings; only I affirm, in the presence of God, that I have followed and loved the footsteps of your most princely person with all faith and sincerity, with a mind most single, and free from all ambition or any other private respects. And though, towards God and Kings, men cannot be free of faults, yet, wilfully or wittingly, He knoweth that made me, I never offended your most sacred Majesty. My negligence towards God, and too high presumptions towards your Majesty, have been sins worthily deserving more punishments than these. But, Madam, towards yourself leave not the causes of my presumptions unremembered; and, though you find them as unfit for me as unworthy of you, yet, in their nature, of a good mind they are not hatefully to be despised. I humbly prostrate myself at your gracious feet, and do most heartily recognize that all God's punishments laid on me by your princely censure are taken by me with singular humility; wherein I stand as free from grudging of heart as I am full of intolerable and vain perplexity. God in Heaven bless your Royal Majesty with a long life, a joyful heart, a prosperous reign, and with Heaven at the last. April the 3rd, 1584. Your Majesty's most lowly subject and most unworthy servant,   CH. HATTON.[a]

Philip Earl of Arundell, the head, and many members of the House of Howard, were supposed to have been implicated in Throckmorton's treason; and, though Camden mentions that Mr. Henry Howard, whom he describes as " a man of most noble blood, a bachelor, passing Popish, and in very great favour amongst the Papists, afterwards Earl of Northampton, was often examined on the subject," neither he nor Howard's biographers notice his sufferings and imprisonment, as described in this and in other letters to Hatton. He was, however, suspected of a design to marry the Queen of Scots, and of being elected King of England by the English Catholics[b];—

HENRY HOWARD TO SIR CHRISTOPHER HATTON.

THOUGH you were none of those, good Mr. Vice-Chamberlain, to whom it pleased her Majesty to recommend the trial and examination of my cause, yet now that my Lord of Leicester, mine especial good Lord, and Mr. Secretary, my most assured friend, have given their faithful and honourable promise to deal for my liberty, I cannot omit your Honour in the number of my constant friends, whom during my last suit I found so willing to do me good, and so favourably bent to recommend and further my petition. Six months complete I have endured all kinds of sifting and examining, with

_____

[a] Additional MSS. 15801, f. 121[b].   [b] Camden's Annals, B. iii. pp. 34, 41.

what integrity I could rather wish you should receive at their
mouths (as I doubt not but you have done already) who were
acquainted with the matter from the first beginning, than by
mine own report, who may be deemed over-partial in mine
own particular.   Only thus much I will note, that neither I
spake ever with one Throckmorton (with whose familiar
acquaintance I was charged) more than once, and then of
nothing otherwise than fell out by chance, without offence to
any man alive; neither did I ever receive any ring from the
Queen of Scots, whereof I was accused.   This long and close
endurance hath already brought me to that extremity of the
stone, as, I protest to God, I had rather yield my life in the favour of Almighty God to any sudden stroke of fortune whatsoever, than languish in this endless maze of pain and misery.
Wherefore I most humbly beseech you, good Mr. Vice-Chamberlain, first for charity, and then for the pity and compassion which is engrafted in your honourable mind, and, last of
all, for that favour to myself whereof (to my inestimable comfort) your own mouth assured me, that it will please you to
adjoin your favourable help to the rest of my good friends
for the procurement of my liberty.   You shall by this mean
bind a gentleman to rest at your commandment during life,
who no less earnestly calleth on you for your assistance in
this cause, than he esteemeth you most worthy of all service
and honour.   Thus, beseeching God to increase and prosper
you in all good haps that your own honest and honourable
heart can desire, I most humbly take my leave, this 27th of
April 1584. Your Honour's most humble and assured at
commandment during life,   HENRY HOWARD.*

The annexed letter from John Whitgift, who was
translated from Worcester to the Archiepiscopal See
of Canterbury on the death of Archbishop Grindall,
is elucidated by a passage from Camden's Annals:—

* Additional MSS. 15891, f. 122ᵇ.

BB

To him [Whitgift,] the Queen (who as in civil matters, so also in the ecclesiastical laws, thought that no relenting was to be used) gave in charge, that before all things he should restore the discipline of the Church of England, and the uniformity in the service of God, established by authority of Parliament, which, through the connivance of the prelates, the obstinacy of the Puritans, and the power of certain noblemen, was run out of square, while some of the ministers covertly impugned the Queen's authority in ecclesiastical matters, separated the administration of the sacraments from the preaching of the word, usurped new rites and ceremonies at their pleasure in private houses, utterly condemned the liturgy and the administration of the sacraments established, as contrary in some points to the Holy Scriptures, as also the vocation of Bishops, and therefore refused to come to Church, and made a flat schism, while the Papists stood at pleasure, and drew many to their side, as if there were no unity in the Church of England.   To take away these inconveniences, and restore unity, he propounded these articles to be subscribed unto by the ministers :—First, that the Queen had the highest and supreme power over all persons born within her Realms, of what condition soever they were ; and that no other Foreign Prince or Prelate had, or ought to have had, any civil or ecclesiastical power in her Realms or Dominions. Secondly, that the Book of Common Prayer, and another Book of ordaining of Bishops and Priests, contained nothing contrary to God's word, but might lawfully be used; and that they should use that, and no other form either of prayer or administration of the sacraments.   Thirdly, that they approved the Articles of the Synod at London, published by the Queen's authority in the year 1562, and believed the same to be consonant to God's word.   By occasion hereof, incredible it is what controversies and disputations arose, and what hatred, what reproachful speeches he endured at the hands of factious ministers, and what troubles, yea and injuries also, at the hands of noblemen, who, by promoting unmeet and unworthy men, raised trouble in the Church, or else hoped after the Livings of the Church; nevertheless through constancy, fortitude and patience he overcame at last, and restored peace to the Church, so as not without good advisement he may seem to have usurped that motto, *Vincit qui patitur*, that is, He overcometh which suffereth with patience." [a]

The Archbishop " in his weighty business," observes Strype, " had the encouragement and cordial friendship of Sir Christopher Hatton, who had sent to the Archbishop a paper of notes, containing, as it seems, the sum of those petitions for reformation that were to be brought into the Parliament house now ere long to sit, that so the Archbishop might the better understand the import of them, and get replies ready upon occasion. The Archbishop made use of Mr. Bancroft, his faithful Chaplain, as his messenger to Sir Christopher."[b]   In a letter from Dr. Bancroft to Hatton, on the 4th of November 1584, subscribed " your honour's most bounden and dutiful Chaplain," he says " I have been with my Lord's Grace as your pleasure was, and have returned your notes according to your commandment";—

ARCHBISHOP WHITGIFT TO SIR CHRISTOPHER HATTON.

RIGHT HONOURABLE, I am bold to use that great friendship and courtesy which you most honourably offered unto me, especially at this time in the public cause of the Church and State.   Yesterday certain gentlemen of Kent were with me to entreat release of some of the Ministers whom I had suspended for not subscribing to the Articles according to the order taken; and because, upon great and weighty considerations then declared unto them, I refused to grant their request, they said they would make their petition to her Majesty, or to the Lords of her Highness' most honourable Privy Council; some of them also after a sort

[a] Camden's Annals, B. iii. p. 27.   [b] Strype's Annals, III. pt. i. p. 333.

threatening me otherwise than they durst have done in times past to men of my calling. I have in my diocese in Kent one hundred preachers and more, whereof ten only, or thereabouts, have refused to subscribe, and eight of them never licensed to preach by any lawful authority; who besides their refusing to subscribe, have spread abroad and published certain articles tending not only to the defacing of the Book of Common Prayer by law established, but also to the altering and changing of the whole state of government in matters ecclesiastical, to the discrediting of the religion now professed, and disturbing of this most happy and quiet regiment: wherefore I heartily beseech your Honour to foresee (as much as in you lieth) that these men receive no encouragement from thence, and (if need require) to signify this my petition to her Majesty. If these few, being of none account either for years, learning, or degree, (which I speak of knowledge, whatsoever the gentlemen in their favour shall report to the contrary,) shall be countenanced against the law, against me, and against all the rest of the preachers in my diocese, it will not be possible for me either there or anywhere else to do that good in procuring the peace of the Church, obedience and observation of good orders, which I am assured I shall bring to pass, if I be suffered without such overthwarts to proceed as I have begun. Unless such contentious persons were some way animated and backed, they would not stand out as they do. And yet, (God be thanked) the number of them in this province is not great, and indeed of no account in comparison of the rest, wherefore my hope is, the rather by your Honour's good means, that nothing shall be done prejudicial to the order set down by her Majesty's consent and according to the laws established, which I most heartily desire you by all ways and means you can to procure. And so, remaining yours most assuredly in anything that shall lie in my power, I commit your Honour to the tuition of Almighty God. From Lambeth, the 9th of May 1584. Your Honour's as his own, JOHN CANTUAR.[*]

[*] Additional MSS. 15891, f. 123.

The name of this supplicant to Hatton is unknown :—

TO SIR CHRISTOPHER HATTON.

IT MAY PLEASE YOUR HONOUR, Such hath been your goodness towards me as I must acknowledge for due the offer of my life in your service. I presented unto Mr. Secretary on Sunday last my petition to your Honour and the rest of my Lords for my liberty and mitigation of fine, together with the reasons that constrained me to that boldness. I humbly beseech you, even for God's cause, to prevent my ruin and utter overthrow, with your honourable furtherance for the safety of my goods. The Lord of Heaven knoweth I entreat not for the ease of my person, but for the preservation of my poor house and children. Alas, Sir! in reason I can say nothing for myself, having so highly offended such a gracious Prince and so honourable a Government, but do simply appeal to her Majesty's mercy and your favourable goodness. I dare not crave according to the measure of my necessities, but do commend my humble suit, my service, and life, to your honourable favour; and so do take my leave, beseeching God to preserve you in all happiness. From the Fleet, the 10th of May 1584. Your Honour's in all duty.[*]

Mr. Cox might well suppose that his learned disquisition on the difference between Deputies and Ambassadors would "offend by tediousness." He says nothing to show in what manner Calveley had given offence, nor has any information on the point been found elsewhere :—

MR. SAMUEL COX TO SIR CHRISTOPHER HATTON.

SIR, I am sorry you have conceived so great offence and displeasure against my poor kinsman, Robin Calveley, for dealing in a just cause more roundly with the Deputies of the Low Countries than was expedient he should have done,

---

[*] Additional MSS. 15891, f. 124.

in respect of their place and calling. I confess it was an error in him to use violence, or any such rigorous course, against personages whom we ought in common duty to regard and reverence; but, where it pleaseth you to call them Ambassadors, and to privilege them under the protection of so honourable a title, and so to make his fault the greater, I am of opinion, under your favourable correction, that they ought not justly to be so esteemed, nor aptly to be so termed, considering what they are and from whom they come. I say not this to extenuate vainly the error of the offender, but to let you know, that, not taking them for Ambassadors, but for Deputies, himself was the rather induced to think he might the more boldly proceed with them as he did. They are not all Ambassadors that are sent to any Prince or people to deal with them in matter of state; neither ought they to enjoy the privileges of Ambassadors. Subjects in time of rebellion, revolted from their natural Sovereign King, may authorize and send Commissioners unto him to treat of peace, whom we cannot properly call Ambassadors, but Deputies; for no Prince or State can, in the justice of law, assume unto himself the right of legation unless he be absolute and Sovereign of himself, not depending upon the Imperial authority of any other, or any way tied by any oath of fidelity or obedience to any other Prince or superior power whatsoever. Subjects cannot constitute or send Ambassadors to their own Prince, for the law will not give them any such authority; neither can they send any to a Foreign Prince, without peril of treason : *populi et civitates quæ alterius imperio parent suis auspitiis legatos mittere non possunt.* When the great sedition, *ob leges agrarias* . . . . Rome, Fulvius Flaccus and Lucius Craccus, the authors thereof, sent the son of Flaccus as Ambassador to treat with the people and Senate for a composition of peace. As soon as Opimius the Consul heard he was come, he was so far from entertaining him as an Ambassador, that, by the decree and order of the Senate, he caused him to be committed to prison. The Romans would not receive those men as Ambassadors

whom Spartacus sent unto them, a man famous, as you know,
for the fortune of three notable victories. Tiberius rejected
likewise, and would by no means give them the reputation
of Ambassadors, which Talpharinus sent unto him, a man
so mighty and potent that he possessed almost all Africa
with his infinite huge host which he had of bondmen. When
John, who usurped the Empire of the West parts, did send his
Commissioners to Theodosius, Emperor of the East, Theodosius would not receive them as Ambassadors, but cast them
into prison; whereby it is manifest that the Romans would
not allow them for Ambassadors which were sent unto them
from their rebellious subjects; they were not reputed legate,
but *selecti*, whom the Subject sent to their Prince, and therefore not to be accounted *sacrosancti*, or *inviolabiles*, because
they came not from any Sovereign, Kingly state, or absolute
Commonwealth. *Legati enim a Regibus, imperatoribus, rebus-
ve pub. quæ superiorem Cæsarem non agnoscunt mittuntur,
atque, ob id, sacrosancti et inviolabiles sunt.* Neither are they
properly called Ambassadors, whom the Prince sendeth to the
Subject, but *missatici, juridici*, or *delegati;* and yet we read,
that when Marcus Antoninus was condemned of treason, the
Romans, considering how many legions he had under his commandment, sent Servius Sulpitius and many other Ambassadors of quality and honour unto him, fearing lest they might
otherwise have provoked him to take up arms: but Tully will
not admit this for a legation, but for a denuntiation, *quoniam
paratum erat illi exitium nisi Senatui paruisset.* Thus you
see how my honest meaning and defence of my friend maketh
me offend by tediousness, where I least should and would.
Unless it please you, therefore, to use your accustomed benignity . . . . in good part, I fear my long vain letters, which
are written to entreat pardon for him, will be accusations
against myself to declare my unworthiness to speak for another. I must refer all to your goodness, without the which
my friend and I both are like to fall into the peril of your disfavour, which would grieve me more than I will now mention.
And so I commit you to God's eternal providence and best

direction. From the Court at Greenwich, the 20th of May 1584. Your assured poor friend,   SAMUEL COX.[*]

In his letter of the 27th of April, in a subsequent page, Mr. Howard says he had then been subjected to six months' confinement; and as in the following one, which has no date, he states that he had "lain seven months in prison," it was probably written about the end of May or beginning of June in this year:—

HENRY HOWARD TO SIR CHRISTOPHER HATTON.

IT was no small comfort unto me, good Mr. Vice-Chamberlain, to understand by Mr. Tresham of your favourable acceptance of my letter; hoping rather by plain deeds than words, if ever it may lie in my power, to make good my meaning. And where I perceive by the same friend that some have sought to put into your head (as I heard before) some jealousy of my devotion towards you, I can say no more than that their tales are both false and slanderous; desiring thus much only for my further trial, that, whosoever hath been author or inventor of the same, he will take the pain to avow them in this quarter, and, as we can agree upon the price, so you will vouchsafe to settle and to frame your judgment. I protest that never doubtful thought against you lodged in my heart; but if you found me not so forward in appearance or following, (as I know myself most clear and innocent from harm,) impute the same rather to the plainness of my nature, which could not serve in divers camps, nor look one way (like a cunning bargeman) when I stretch mine arms another, than to the malice of my meaning. God can witness mine upright conceit of yourself, and of your plain and honourable dealing, when I swerved furthest from your course; and often would I wish but one such friend as you, when I found scant answerable offices to my devotion. I am not ignorant that some, which promise great good-will to you, were ever

* Additional MSS. 15891, f. 136.

opposite in private inclination against me, and would never suffer any sound conceit of my good-will to settle in your judgment. But if none dare avow such prefye fancies as they have suggested by report, then credit simple truth, that hath none other armour than good faith; and think my mind to be so great, howsoever fortune bear me down, that, if I carried any spark of grudge to you, I would not seek to be beholding to you for one dram of favour. I pray God you may live as happily as yourself can wish, till I ever stoop to seek for favour of mine enemy, or with a servile shadow cover an unfaithful meaning. I have lain seven months in prison, and yet am not privy to the least offence either to my Prince or country. All the world acquitteth me from sight of any gewgaw. Stevens is not yet a Jesuit, much less he was then. My Lord of Southampton can avow upon his honour that I never heard mass with him, and yet I must be kept in prison. Good Mr. Vice-Chamberlain, according to my trust reposed in your friendship, rid me from these manacles which I never merited. You know my case, and therefore I will urge no further, but desire you to conceive, that as I have received wrong concerning public causes, so have I done by private whisperings, to drive matters nearer to the quick. I rest yours, and so will do, in spite of those that labour to imprint another fancy in your favourable judgment. And so, with as many wishes of good success as my pen can utter or yourself desire, I end in haste, this Saturday morning. Your poor friend most assured at commandment,

HENRY HOWARD.[a]

Lady Leighton has been already mentioned. Her present letter is only remarkable for what she says of the Queen's " grief and solitariness," which agrees with Camden's statement that Elizabeth was greatly affected by the death of the Duke of Anjou, which took place on the 10th of June, seven days before the date of this letter :—

[a] Additional MSS. 15891, f. 119ᵇ.

LADY LEIGHTON TO SIR CHRISTOPHER HATTON.

SIR, I am sorry, for mine own sake, you are any way hindered of your honourable proceeding in my suit, but specially that it should happen by so ill an accident as the grief and solitariness I hear her Majesty gives herself to of late. But I hope that time and her wisdom will overcome that which is both so harmful to herself, and helpless to the cause that procures it. And as the extremity of her sorrow decreaseth, so I hope you shall have your wonted opportunity to do good to those that have their affiance in you; as myself, for one, that will ever ground my assurance upon your faithful promise. And I beseech you think, that my often troubling of you with my scribbling riseth not of any mistrust I have in the performance of your word, but to show myself thankful for your favour, howsoever I speed. And so I leave you to as great honour and happiness as my opinion thinks you worthy of. Charter-house, this 17th of June 1584. Your poor friend, if it please you,   E. LEIGHTON.[a]

When it was resolved to destroy a theatre, in June 1584, Hatton, as well as the Lord Chamberlain, vainly endeavoured to befriend the poor players. Serjeant Fleetwood, Recorder of London, in one of his gossipping letters to Lord Burghley, dated on the 18th of that month, says, "Upon Sunday, my Lord" (apparently the Lord Chief Justice Anderson) "sent two Aldermen to the Court for the suppressing and pulling down of the theatre and curtain; for all the Lords agreed thereunto saving my Lord Chamberlain and Mr. Vice-Chamberlain: but we obtained a letter to suppress them all. Upon the same night I sent for the Queen's players and my Lord of Arundell's players, and they all well nigh obeyed the Lords' letters. The chiefest of her

[a] Additional MSS. 15891, f. 135[b].

Highness's players advised me to send for the owner of the theatre, who was a stubborn fellow, to bind him. I did so." In the same letter, Mr. Fleetwood said, " The eldest son of Mr. Henry, I hear, upon Monday, being yesterday, fought in Cheapside with one Boat,ᵃ that is, or lately was, Mr. Vice-Chamberlain's man; and all was, which of them was the better gentleman, and for taking of the wall."ᵇ

Hatton again appears as an intercessor :—

TO THE EARL OF DERBY AND THE BISHOP OF CHESTER.

MY VERY GOOD LORDS, Whereas I am informed that your Lordships have taken bonds of Richard Massy, of the County of Chester, gentleman, to appear before you concerning matters Ecclesiastical at the feast of St. Bartholomew next, I am moved (upon some consideration, but specially in hope of his conformity and better disposition to her Majesty's proceedings hereafter than he hath showed heretofore,) to intreat your Lordships to be pleased once again to extend your favour towards him; as namely, upon the removing of his bonds to forbear his appearance before you till Candlemas next; by which time I am persuaded your Lordships shall find such token of reformation in him as, I trust, you shall think your goodness herein well bestowed on him, and be glad of this course of lenity taken presently with him in hope of his amendment. Wherein praying your Lordships' favourable acceptance of this my request, I commend you, as myself, to the grace of Almighty God. From the Court at Richmond, the 23rd of June 1584. Your good Lordships' very loving assured friend,

CHR. HATTON.ᶜ

ARCHBISHOP WHITGIFT TO SIR CHRISTOPHER HATTON.

RIGHT HONOURABLE, I give you most hearty thanks for that most friendly message which you sent unto me by your

ᵃ Sic.
ᵇ Wright's Queen Elizabeth and her Times, ii. 229, 230.

ᶜ Desiderata Curiosa, I. p. 150.

man, Mr. Kemp. I shall think myself bound to you for it as long as I live. It hath not a little comforted me in respect of some unkind speeches lately received from those who, I little thought, of all others would have taken offence against me only for doing my duty in this most necessary business which I have now in hand. I marvel how it should come to pass that the self-same persons which will seem to wish peace and uniformity in the Church, and to mislike of the contentious and disobedient sort, cannot abide that anything should be done against them; wishing rather that the whole ministry of this land should be discountenanced and discouraged, than a few wayward persons, of no account in comparison, should be suppressed and punished. Men, in executing of laws according to their duties, were wont to be encouraged and backed by such as now, in this weighty service, do partly impugn the due course of justice. It falleth out in these days clean contrary. Disobedient and wilful persons (I will term them no worse) are animated, laws contemned, her Majesty's will and pleasure not regarded, and the executors thereof, in word and deed, abused. Howbeit, though these thwarts something grieve me, yet I thank God they cannot withdraw me from doing that duty in this cause which, I am persuaded, God himself, her Majesty, the laws, and the state of the Church and Commonwealth do require of me. In respect whereof I am content to sustain all their displeasures, and am fully resolved to depend upon none but upon God and her Majesty. And therefore your Honour, in offering unto me that curacy, offereth me as great a pleasure as I can desire. Her Majesty must be my refuge; and I beseech you that I may use you as a mean, when occasion shall serve. Whereof assuring myself, I commit you to the grace and favour of God, to whom you shall ever have my most hearty prayers for your health and prosperity. From Lambeth, the 17th of July 1584. Your Honour's assuredly,   JOHN CANTUAR.*

* Additional MSS. 15891, f. 124.

The Earl of Leicester's only legitimate child, Robert Lord Denbigh, died at Wanstead on the 19th of July 1584; and the following admirable letter from Hatton on his loss, with Leicester's reply, form additional evidence of their having lived on terms of friendship with each other:—

SIR CHRISTOPHER HATTON TO THE EARL OF LEICESTER.

MY SINGULAR GOOD LORD, Your excellent wisdom, made perfect in the school of our eternal God, will, in the rule of Christian reason, I trust, subdue these kind and natural affections which now oppress your own loving heart. What God hath given you, that hath He chosen and taken to Himself, whereat I hope you will not grudge; as well for that it is the executor of His divine will, as also for that He hath made him co-heir of His heavenly Kingdom. When in the meditation of your religious conceits it shall please you to weigh the singular blessings and benefits which God hath conferred on you in this world, I nothing doubt you will be joyfully thankful; and accept this cross as the sign of His holy love, whereby you shall become happy and blessed for ever. Unto the Gospel of Christ His poor flock do find you a most faithful and mighty supporter; in the State and Government of this Realm, a grave and faithful Councillor; a pillar of our long-continued peace; a happy nourisher of our most happy Commonwealth; flourishing in the stirp of true Nobility abundantly in all virtuous actions towards God and men; all which are the high gifts of the High God. Leave not yourself, therefore, my dear Lord, for God's sake and ours. Go on in your high and noble labours in the comfort of Christ, which no man can diminish nor take from you; cherish yourself while it shall please God to let you dwell on earth; call joy to dwell in your heart, and know for certain, that if the love of a child be dear, which is now taken from you, the love of God is ten thousand times more dear, which you can never lack nor lose. Of men's hearts you enjoy more than millions, which, on my soul, do love you no less than children or brethren. Leave sorrow, therefore, my good Lord, and be glad with us, which much rejoice in you. I have told her Majesty of this unfortunate and untimely cause which constrained your sudden journey to London, whereof I assure your Lordship I find her very sorry, and wisheth your comfort, even from the bottom of her heart. It pleased her to tell me that she would write to you, and send to visit you according to her wonted goodness ; and therefore she held no longer speech with me of the matter. Thus, remaining humbly at your Lordship's commandment, I forbear any longer to trouble you; beseeching God to comfort you, in your lamentation and grief, with the remembrance of His gracious goodness. From the Court at Nonsuch, the 21st of July 1584. Your good Lordship's humbly to command,

CHR. HATTON.*

THE EARL OF LEICESTER TO SIR CHRISTOPHER HATTON.

MR. VICE-CHAMBERLAIN, I do most heartily thank you for your careful and most godly advice at this time. Your good friendship never wanteth. I must confess I have received many afflictions within these few years, but not a greater, next her Majesty's displeasure: and, if it pleased God, I would the sacrifice of this poor innocent might satisfy; I mean not towards God (for all are sinful and most wretched in His sight, and therefore He sent a most innocent lamb to help us all that are faithful), but for the world. The afflictions I have suffered may satisfy such as are offended, at least appease their long hard conceits: if not, yet I know there is a blessing for such as suffer; and so is there for those that be merciful. Princes (who feel not the heavy estate of the poor afflicted that only are to receive relief from themselves) seldom do pity according to the true rules of charity, and therefore men fly to the mighty God in time of distress for comfort; for we are sure, though He doth chastise, yet He forsaketh not, neither will He see them unrewarded with the

* Additional MSS. 15891, f. 128.

highest blessing. I beseech the same God to grant me patience in all these worldly things, and to forgive me the negligences of my former time, that have not been more careful
to please Him, but have run the race of the world.   In the
same sort I commend you, and pray for His grace for you as
for myself; and, before all this world, to preserve her Majesty
for ever, whom on my knees I most humbly thank for her
gracious visitation by Killigrew. She shall never comfort a
more true and faithful man to her, for I have lived and so
will die only hers'. 23rd July 1584. Your poor but assured
friend,   ROBT. LEICESTER.*

The Mr. Drake to whose son Hatton was god-father
was Richard Drake, Equerry of the Queen's stable,
ancestor of the family of that name, which was long
seated at Shardeloes, in Buckinghamshire ;—

SIR CHRISTOPHER HATTON TO . . . .

SIR, It hath pleased God to bless my good friend Mr.
Drake with the birth and comfort of a young son, and he
hath earnestly entreated me to christen him ; which being a
holy office and full of piety in itself, hath easily persuaded
me to satisfy his desire, but much the rather for the love and
good-will I bear him.   And because among many friends of
mine in those parts which wish me well, and with whom I
may be bold, I know none more zealous, kind, or fitter than
yourself to testify so sacred an action, I have been moved
before all others to request your favour and presence in sup-
plying my place in this Christian and religious office:
wherein as you shall do an acceptable deed to God, and to
the parents of the child, in witnessing and receiving of him
into the congregation of the faithful by the apposition of
that gracious seal of God's promised mercy, so shall you
particularly make me much beholding to you as one whom
you shall find thankfully willing to requite this kindness with

* Additional MSS. 15891, f. 129.

the like courtesy in any occasion wherein you shall think good to use me. And so I commit you to God. From the Court at Nonsuch, the 4th of August 1584. Your very assured friend, CHR. HATTON.[a]

Sir Christopher Hatton's chaplain, Dr. Richard Bancroft, afterwards Bishop of London and Archbishop of Canterbury, was a candidate for the Rectory of St. Andrew's, Holborn;—

LORD BURGHLEY TO SIR CHRISTOPHER HATTON.

SIR, I perceive by your courteous letters your desire to procure your Chaplain, Mr. Bancroft, to succeed in the place of the parson of St. Andrew's, lately deceased, the patronage whereof is belonging to the Earl of Southampton, now in wardship, and so, as you suppose, to be disposed of by us. Herein I am very willing, both for your own sake and for Mr. Bancroft, being very meet for the place, to do what in me lieth. The doubt I have is, that the patronage appertaineth to the Earl in right of his house in Holborn, that was aforetime the Bishop of Lincoln's; and then the right of presentation belongeth to the executors, whereof one of the heirs is principal, and Edward Caye another, and one Wells another, with whom you may do well to deal; and, if it be not in them, you shall have my assent. And for better knowledge hereof I have given your Chaplain my letter to the Auditor of the Wards, who can best inform whether it remains to the Queen or to the executors. From my house at Theobald's, the 6th of August 1584. Yours assuredly as any,

W. BURGHLEY.[b]

The " young child" mentioned in this letter was one of the numerous children of Sir Richard Knightley of Fawsley, in Northamptonshire, by his second wife, Elizabeth,

[a] Additional MSS. 15891, f. 126.   [b] Additional MSS. 15891, f. 270.

daughter of Edward Seymour, Duke of Somerset, the
Protector, whose widow was one of the other sponsors:—

SIR CHRISTOPHER HATTON TO THE EARL OF HERTFORD.

MY VERY GOOD LORD, I have been requested by my dear
friend Sir Richard Knightley to christen his young child, which
it hath lately pleased God to send him; an office godly and
full of piety in itself, and such as I could have been right glad
to perform in person, if her Majesty's services here did not
otherwise dispose of me by her own commandment. I have
therefore made bold (not finding any nobleman in Court at
this present fit to accompany my Lady's grace, your mother,
in that holy action) to entreat you to supply the place for
me, and to do me the favour to be a witness, in baptism, of
God's goodness participated through that holy Sacrament
to this young infant, of whom I hope another day you shall
receive both thanks and comfort for it; and, in the mean
while, of myself a grateful acknowledgment of this honourable courtesy, which I will be ready to requite with all faithful good-will in anything I am able. I will send a gentleman
unto you to-morrow, at one of the clock, to wait on you with
such duty as is fit and belonging to the ceremony of this action; which commending to your honourable regard, I wish
ever to your Lordship, as to myself, the gracious favour of the
Almighty. From the Court at Nonsuch, the 7th of August
1584.   Your Lordship's very loving assured friend,

                                    CH. HATTON.*

Lord Grey of Wilton, from whom several letters have
been inserted while he was Deputy of Ireland, had been
superseded by Sir John Perrot:—

ARTHUR LORD GREY DE WILTON TO SIR CHRISTOPHER
HATTON.

SIR, If convenience of a messenger had been as ready as
cause and good-will, you had not been so long without re-

* Additional MSS. 15891, f. 126.

C C

ceiving from me the due thanks that your great courtesy hath
merited of me. I have found, by your officers and keepers
hereabouts, your frank and friendly pleasure for my taking of
sport in the games here under your commandment; of which
offer as I have been bold to make trial, so have I found more
than required therein afforded. Thanks is the least therefore
that I can render, and yet thanks is all that for the present I
can yield you in requital of your gentleness, which I give
you in infinite wise, and do further bind the uttermost of
my power upon any occasion to be ever acknowledging
your honourable kindness. In the mean while hold me still,
I pray you, in your good love and opinion, as you shall unfeignedly rest with me not the least beloved and esteemed.
And so, wishing you and my other great friends there at
Court, with your great honours, part of that quiet yet which
I here in my poor lodge enjoy, which makes me in private
not to envy your fortune's babe there, howsoever for other
cause I little brook him, I betake yourself to all welfare and
happiness. From Northampton, this 8th of August 1584.
Your most fast friend and loving kinsman,   A. Grey.[a]

A reference to the former Order of Council respecting horses affords an explanation of the following document:—

FROM THE LORDS OF THE COUNCIL.

After our hearty commendations, Where, in the beginning
of this summer, we and some others, authorised by her Majesty's commission under her Great Seal, did, by virtue of the said
commission, name, ordain, and depute you to cause all manner of persons within that County (who, by their abilities in
lands or goods, were, according to the Statutes, chargeable to
have and keep horses and geldings for service, and mares for
breed,) to put in readiness such horses, with meet horsemen,
furnished accordingly with armour and weapon, and to show

[a] Additional MSS. 15891, f. 6b.

them before you this summer at times convenient, to be ready
at her Majesty's commandment for the service of the Realm.
And to this end we did send to you, with our letters and commissions, certain instructions in writing, hoping that you have
had due regard thereof. But yet, doubting that by reason of
some impediments in this summer and harvest-time this service
hath not been put in such due execution as was meet; and yet
not doubting but if you have not already mustered them, and
given order for reforming the defects, yet you have made out
your precepts to all persons to charge them against some day
prefixed, before the end of this month or shortly after, to
come before you with their horses; and therein we pray you
to continue such a course as the service may take good place,
as well to increase the number as to make the same serviceable as near as may be both for the horsemen and the horses.
And notwithstanding that you shall have thus determined of
some especial day for your musters before the receipt of these
our letters, yet, to the intent that all abuses may be avoided,
and all suspicion that no horse or gelding shall be showed in
muster at several places and times to supply two rooms by
way of borrowing or lending; it is determined that one
especial day shall serve in all parts of the Realm for the full
and perfect muster, which shall be upon the last day of September next. And so we will and require you, that (notwithstanding any other shows and musters to be made before you
at any time before the day which we allow and think needful
to be done to make the service more perfect,) that in anywise
you direct and command the universal muster for that Shire to
be made the last day of September. And we require you, as
earnestly as we may, that none of you being put in trust for
this service, be absent from the said musters without great
and necessary cause; and that if you cannot finish the same
upon that one day, in reforming the defects, we can allow you
to continue the same until the next day, and then also to continue the said muster, so as you receive the bills, according to
our former instructions, of all the horses the first day; and
that, if time may serve, you do also view them at the least,

whereby no abuse be of answering two rooms with one horse; and, after that you have made this last muster, we require you to make your books and certificates thereof ready, and to send them to us as soon as you conveniently may, that her Majesty may be certified thereof, according to that she expecteth. And we could be content to have your opinions who are meet and skilful persons within that shire to take charge, to lead any bands of these horsemen, as well for leading of twenty-five, fifty, or five hundred, so as hereafter, when her Majesty shall understand thereof, she may determine her pleasure for the same. And thus we bid you farewell. From the Court at Oatland's, this 18th of August 1584. Your loving friends,　　　　　W. BURGHLEY.　　RO. LEICESTER.

　　　　　　　　　　　CH. HOWARD.　　H. SIDNEY.

　　　　　　　　　　　　　CHR. HATTON.[*]

About September in this year, Hatton appears, from the following well written letter, to have been so much displeased with Mr. Cox, his Secretary, as to have suspended him from his employment. Cox's offence was his having taken fees to obtain his Master's influence with the Queen in granting suits; and it is curious to observe, that such was the universal corruption that Cox says the Clerk of every Judge in England took gratuities for what he calls the "expedition" of justice; adding, that such bribes formed their only means of support. Hatton's integrity is certainly placed in a favourable light by this letter; but he does not appear to have treated his dependants with much liberality. Several other letters occur on this subject, which show that Cox had quarrelled with his fellow-servants;—

[*] Additional MSS. 15891, f. 20.

MAY IT PLEASE YOUR HONOUR, I most humbly beseech you to vouchsafe so much favour to my poor painful unworthy service as to afford me your honourable patience in reading these disordered lines at your fittest leisure, and to pardon my boldness therein, or rather my just cause of grief that presumeth thus far to trouble you. I find, greatly to the touch of my poor credit, that my adversaries' accusations are of such force and moment with your Honour, that it should seem they do every day more and more kindle your displeasure against me, and increase my disgrace; and that there want not some charitable, well-disposed ministers in store, (according to the course of the world,) who, taking opportunity of time, as delighting to fish in other men's troubled streams, are glad to put oil to this fire, in hope, by bringing it sooner to a flame, they may the better work me a quick dispatch out of your Honour's service. Of these men I will say nothing, but that I assure myself your justice and wisdom will easily distinguish them from other men by their manners, and conceive of them in the end as they deserve. For my own particular, I thank God I need not fear their malice; for I know I am innocent, and I have as little cause to doubt of justice, for that I am sure of the goodness of an honourable and a just judge, who will not credulously believe whatsoever ill-will shall say, that never said well; but will, in the equal balance of indifference, according to the fame of his virtue and worthiness, judge that only to be true, against his poor servant especially, which by honest, credible, unsuspected persons is substantially proved and testified. I know not what the witnesses are which, in these false objected crimes, are appointed to be censors of my shame and ill-fortune. I only crave that they may be more than one for one matter, and not such as are said *albo reti aliena captare bona;* men seeking to please and win favour by slander, or such as have borne spleen and former malice against the man accused; which if they have, I hope your Honour will not think them fit men to condemn me, but such as make up their own buildings with other men's ruins, and delight to say anything that may entrap the guiltless. Whatsoever they are, I dare boldly say thus much, with your honourable favour and patience, that if some of them shame not to say that again which they have many times spoken heretofore, they shall confess in your own presence that I have served you as carefully, and with all honour possible, both in word and deed, by my duty and diligence, as any man in Court that had so little countenance of his Master as myself in the poor place which I supplied. I understand I am charged to have sold such justice and favour as your Honour was wont to afford to your friends and poor suitors. It is a great fault, I confess, to sell the favour of so noble a personage, and a greater to sell justice; I know it well. Yet I hope your Honour will be pleased to think, and I may speak it truly without offence, that there liveth not so grave nor so severe a Judge in England, but he alloweth his poor Clerk under him, even in the expedition of matters of greatest justice, to take any reasonable consideration that should be offered him by any man for his pains and travail. It is the poor man's whole maintenance, and without it he could not live. I know your Honour will think it reason he should have it. If this be to sell justice and favour, sometimes to take a gratuity of 10s. for one letter among one hundred, sometimes more, sometimes less, according as the party was benefited, or as myself had deserved, I then confess with all humbleness, that as a poor scribe under your Honour (though unworthy), not knowing else how to live, I ignorantly erred, (as all the rest of your servants have done,) where I thought in that kind I should never have offended; and so might I in truth justly deserve this shame, which in Court and Country your Honour hath heavily laid upon me. Yet am I induced to think in reason, that if all the letters and other matters which I have written for you, early and late, were laid together before your Honour in your chamber, that you might but take a view of them to see how large and infinite they were in number which have passed my pen, howsoever this accusation (as it were to make

up the tale) is inserted among the rest, you would, in the virtue
of your own nature and noble condition, rather pity the
writer, and vouchsafe him a far more large reward than think
him unworthy of such little benefit as, through his painful
attendance, he hath reaped in your service towards the relief
and comfort of his poor estate; which though it be very small,
and in respect of other men's gains under you not worthy
speaking of to trouble your Honour withal, yet, as it is, it
may be happily one day a sufficient cause to an honest, grateful servant, when sickness shall by course of nature fall upon
him, to make him pour out his prayers to God for the comfort
and goodness of so honourable a Master. And I beseech your
Honour, that I may say thus much without your dislike of
him that accuseth me in this point, who hath most deeply, and
greatly to your dishonour, as I will show you when place and
time shall serve, offended in that which he now objecteth, to
the reproach of his fellow. If he had spent seven summers
and as many winters with that continual attendance and pains
that I have done, (though I humbly acknowledge I did no
more than my duty,) and had reaped no more fruit of his travail, in recompense of his service, than I have gotten since my
first repair to Court, I am sure he would either have thought
him a very malicious man that should have repined thus at his
poor relief, or would, ere this, have shamelessly importuned
you for some more honourable increase of your bounty and
goodness. The silliest soul that is would be glad to eat, and
to better his estate if fortune served. If, now and then, I got
some small relief towards my charges, (which God knoweth
was very small, and sometimes not 10s. in a twelvemonth,)
which, being little or much, is left as the only and ordinary
mean to your poor men wherewith to help themselves in your
service, shall this be imputed to me as a corruption, or a buying and selling of justice, when neither I nor any of your
servants (I except not those whom you have enriched by your
offices and liberal ways) either can do or will live without it;
and when other Masters in Court (considering the hardness of
this age) allow it commonly to their servants, without the

least dislike, as a necessary succour? I most humbly crave of
you, that in your honourable patience you will vouchsafe me
leave to be plain with you, without offence, in the submission,
reverence, and duty of my honest poor love towards you. I
neither let nor set your lands nor leases. I am no Deputy
Officer to enrich myself with continual fees; I never charged
you with any kind of wages, nor other gift or bounty of your
own whatsoever; I was never worthy to be any of those whom
you have advanced to reputation and wealth by your service.
In seven years my ill-fortune would not that ever I should
obtain anything by your goodness of her Majesty, but only a
lease in reversion, which hath yielded me, I confess, two hundred and odd pounds. I have had nothing to help myself but
the labour of my pen and the diligence of mine own study,
which your Honour knoweth, much better than I can imagine,
is able at this day to get me in . . . . living. I only thirsted
to please my Master, as a matter which I made my greatest
wealth in this world. How should I possibly maintain myself,
or in truth serve your Honour, with the comeliness which is
fit, having no more relief than the ordinary contentment of
your service, and being barred of such small benefit for soliciting of suits as I am now blamed for? It is no honest man's
part, but a base disposition, to accuse any man, much more his
fellow; yet, if I should say generally in this point what I
think, I am persuaded your Honour would have few left to
serve you in your chamber, or to wait on you at Ely House,
if it should please you to be as severe to all those as you have
been to me, which might be any way touched with taking of
rewards for soliciting of suits. Your wisdom foreseeth more
than I can conceive; and no doubt you do it all to a good
end. I must, therefore, and will think the best of the course
you take, and bear my burden with patience and duty. Some
of my friends have let me understand that your Honour
meaneth nothing less than my discountenance in this inter-
mission of service, nor will leave me to the infamy of my accusations, whatsoever should happen. I do herein acknowledge in most dutiful part, as becometh me, your singular

goodness. God make me thankful for it, and requite it in you with increase of His manifold graces and richest blessings. It is some comfort to a man in misery to enjoy his favour that hath cast him down: but, *fides semel amissa nunquam rediit ;* and a man once wounded in his fame shall never rid of the scar. What other men's stomachs will digest in matter of shame and infamy I know not; but for mine own part I protest (such is my folly) that if I did conjecture any man's malice could so much vanquish the noble disposition, which hath been always commended in your Honour, as to make you think any one part of those calumniations to be true, which you know his spleen and ill-will only hath objected against me, who hath ever hated me, God is my witness, I would rather banish myself to the uttermost parts of Egypt, to eat my tears instead of bread among the barbarians, than live tainted with villany and infamy in England in the best favour and countenance that it might please you to afford me: no, I hope I shall never live to be reputed so shameless as to look my Master on the face every day in Court, that shall every hour judge me in his heart a villain and a varlet. I beseech God rather shorten my days than suffer me to live in such reproach. I most humbly crave pardon of your Honour for my bold presumptuous writing. It is my fault, I confess to my shame, and yet in yourself I have ever thought . . . . virtue. I will be so no more, if it mislike you. I will do everything with all humility and duty that may best content you. I will, in the devotion of my heart, hold up my hands, and make my prayers to God to bless you, and to abridge their days that love you not, and love those that wish you all prosperity and happiness; not desiring to live longer myself than your Honour may conceive I have, and will ever serve you faithfully and truly. From Northall, the 4th of October 1584. Your Honour's most humble, poor, dejected servant,   S. Cox.*

* Additional MSS. 15891, f. 129b.

Considering the mess on which the Queen had break-
fasted, it is not surprising that it disagreed with her.
The delivery of the staff was apparently the appointment of Lord Hunsdon to the office of Lord Chamberlain,
which had become vacant by the death of the Earl of
Sussex in the preceding year; but, singular as it must
appear, no list of the great Officers of State has ever
been compiled, the accuracy of which can in any degree
be relied upon;—

TO LORD BURGHLEY.

My singular good Lord, Her Majesty, since your
going hence, hath been troubled with much disease in her
stomach. The cause thereof, as both herself thinketh and we
all do judge, was the taking in the morning yesterday a con-
fection of barley sodden with sugar and water, and made exceeding thick with bread. This breakfast lost her both her
supper and dinner, and surely the better half of her sleep.
But, God be thanked, I hope now the worst is past, and that
her Highness will shortly recover her old state of health, to
the comfort of us all.

I have considered the speeches your good Lordship used to
me touching the great Office at your last being here; and finding the time of this great feast of All Saints most apt for the
accomplishment of so great a grace from her Majesty, and
that my Lord might receive much the more honour by this
occasion taken of so timely a calling, I thought it not amiss to
put your Lordship in remembrance thereof, to the end that, if
it pleased you to be here somewhat the timelier on Saturday
next, you might possibly work the delivery of the staff either
that even, or in the morning before her Majesty's going to the
closet. My Lord Chancellor is looked for here, and many
more Lords, in respect of the solemnity of the day; and we
agree here the time will be most fit. I assure your good
Lordship that your earnest kindness herein will be most gratefully taken; and if the cause should fail, yet this course in

your good-will cannot be but most acceptable.   And so, your pardon prayed for this hasty rude letter, I humbly take my leave.   In the Privy Chamber on the Queen's side, where now her Majesty is determined to lie, this 29th of October 1584.   Your good Lordship's most bound,

CHR. HATTON.[a]

SIR CHRISTOPHER HATTON TO MR. SAMUEL COX.

As I am right sorry for your separation from my poor service, so should I have been very glad to have found you more desirous of the same.   In the sight of your letters I have found some show of your love towards me, but in the disposition of your actions there appeareth not so much as a proffer to make good your reconciliation with me.   It is true, that through the height of your heart and disdain of your fellows in domestical conversation, you have given them cause to fear your credit and hate your person; besides that, they have discovered some petty practices of yours, tending rather to their undoing than disgrace.   But of these their griefs it seems you be not only reckless, little weighing me, whom the quiet of this concord might most comfort, but them also, whom it doth most concern; but God would it were otherwise; and for your duties' sake in Christianity I was persuaded this office should not have been neglected.   Pride and wrath have brought forth these malicious dissensions to the great . . . . ature and discretion, and to the great grief and offence of me your poor friend.   But, for conclusion, I say, alter the course, or you may not be mine.   That you have been hardly handled, I will not deny; and that you have deserved it, I must likewise needs confess.   Appease your nature, with the even and considerate weighing of all matters on both sides, and then do that you ought, and you shall find of me what you would wish.   For causes touching myself I will first tell you, I find them not so forcibly proved, as they were plainly informed; neither am I of so light belief that thereby I will be carried to leave the men I have loved for

---

[a] Autograph in the State Paper Office.

such reports as have been uttered. I will not touch your fame without the warrant of justice, nor be your enemy before I feel your injury. I know you to be wise, and therefore these few may suffice you. I have showed you the way; I trust therefore, you will travel therein so as you may bring peace home with you, and so should I be right glad of such a servant. As sedition is a thing most dangerous, so is domestical faction most pernicious, and to me most hateful. Know me thus hereafter and please me for ever. Return your purpose of proceeding herein to Mr. Bruskett and then shall you receive my further resolution and determination towards you. From the Court this 26th of October 1584. Your loving master,   CH. HATTON.*

MR. SAMUEL COX, TO SIR CHRISTOPHER HATTON.

MAY IT PLEASE YOUR HONOUR, I find that the long suspense of your favor, hath bred an opinion amongst most men, that my offence towards you is so great and notorious, as you have utterly cast me off, for an unworthy servant, which the world taking notice of daily to my shame, increaseth my grief more than I will mention, and my discredit more than I am sure you wish for. Your Honour easily seeth it yourself in your wisdom. I most humbly beseech you, (if that faithful poor merit past, of your disconsolate servant may anything move you,) to redress it timely in your wonted goodness. All I crave, is an end for mine own discharge, to restore me again to your good opinion, without the which my languishing mind, looking back continually to storms that are past, shall have small comfort to serve you cheerfully : though I hope, as carefully, as any man towards you. God I take to witness (whose only wisdom sifteth the cogitations of all men's hearts) I have been always so far from detracting anything from your worthiness, that I never wittingly offended you so much as to conceive an unreverent thought of you. What I have often spoken to others, of the rare and singular blessings which God hath given you, I will now forbear to say to your-

* Additional MSS. 15891, f. 126b.

self, for modesty.   They are tokens of his divine love and
fatherly goodness in you, such as all men see, have made you
a most worthy minister under her Majesty, to dilate His glory
and her Highness's service.   God increase them manifoldly in
your Honor through the access of his highest favor, and make
me, and many other poor wretches, as thankful for them as
we ought to be in respect of the inestimable fruit and comfort
which in the . . . . of our Country, we have liberally
reaped by them.   And so wishing all prosperity to your honour
agreeable to your virtue and worthiness, most humbly craving
pardon for my presumption, I commend you in my prayers to
God, who ever bless you.   From my lodging in Cornhill,
the 26 of Oct. 1584, Your Honour's poor servant, most humbly devoted in all faithful duty,

S. Cox.*

DR. MATTHEW TO MR. SAMUEL COX.

Mr. Cox, Now I wish I had staid my last letter for answer
to both yours, I wrote upon Monday last, by reason Mr.
Walby remained longer at Newcastle, than that I looked
for him again here, knowing nothing of his going thither, but
doubting he had been departed southward.   But at his return
hither within two hours of my said letter sent, we conferred
at the full of both those things, that you made choice of.
The particulars whereof, I dare refer to the report of his indifference ; albeit to say the truth, he hath been more importune on your behalf, than I think was needful.   If that accord
which he and I have agreed on, do like you I am glad, and
shall be to perform it; if otherwise I shall be sorry, and yet
ready to yield you, if not a better yet a sooner satisfaction.
But if you had been mine own natural brother, as I have . .
. . . . my very good friend I could have used no
more either inquisition into the state of the lease, or expedition to compass it to your hands than I have carefully and
faithfully done, the late death of the lessee, and present
childhood of his widow considered.   I hope only to find in
you that courtesy, as to regard partly my credit, though spe-

* Additional MSS. 15891, f. 125ᵇ.

cially your profit; which truly I shall be as willing to further, as yourself to desire. It will be near Easter before I
can call for the lease to be shewed in court, which I am certainly informed is either none or nought. If between this
and that, it please you any further to impart unto me, I pray
you do it by this gentleman, with whom (for his experience
and faithfulness to you) I do best like to deal. In Easter
term, I hope to bring you your lease, under seal, as I have
said to him ; taking his word for the performance of your
part thereof. I offered him his charges that (as you wrote) he
might not return empty handed ; but I could fasten nought
upon him. And thus I most heartily betake you to God.
From Durham, 27th October 1584. Your assured ever,

TOBIE MATHEW.[*]

Mr. Dutton was the father of the Peter Dutton whom
Hatton, in a former letter, calls " his cousin and servant;—"

TO THE BISHOP OF CHESTER.

MY GOOD LORD, I am let to understand to my exceeding
great grief, there is some matter of suit depending before
your Lordship, between my very good friends Mr. John
Dutton of Dutton, and Mrs. Eleanor his wife, upon certain
complaints which she hath lately exhibited against him. And
(for the earnest good will which I have always borne them,
both in respect of alliance and of other good friendship passing between us) I am moved to write these few words unto
you, and heartily to entreat you to be pleased to take some
careful regard of this cause and of the weightiness of the
sequel thereof, in case it be not timely prevented. Your
Lordship knoweth how ungodly a course of proceeding this
is between man and wife, like to breed utter discredit to them
both if it should go forward as it hath begun. If therefore it
might be stayed and the cause ended with quietness through
your Lordship's good and godly means, I should have cause
greatly to rejoice thereat. But if this may not conveniently

* Additional MSS. 15891, f. 132.

be brought to pass, then am I earnestly to pray your Lordship, to set such good order for a direct course of proceeding to be observed therein, as the cause may be dealt in with all the indifferency that may be ; so as there ensue no obloquy or . . . . . . to touch the name of Mr. Dutton, which otherwise would leave too great a scar in his credit and reputation, being a principal gentleman of the Shire, who may hardly endure any such disgrace, and the same perchance because of further inconvenience hereafter.   Herein your Lordship shall do a most Christian act, worthy of your calling and function, and make me exceedingly beholden unto you for it. The performance whereof I refer to your most grave and wise consideration, with this addition only, that concerning the exhibition to be allowed unto Mrs. Eleanor it may please you to set down such an indifferent rate therein as may be to the good contentment of them both, if this possibly can be performed.   And even so, recommending your Lordship to the gracious protection of Almighty God, I take my leave.   From Hampton Court the 27th of October 1584. Your good Lordship's very loving assured friend,

CHR. HATTON."

MR. SAMUEL COX TO SIR CHRISTOPHER HATTON.

MAY IT PLEASE YOUR HONOUR, I am grievously sorry to perceive by your most honourable letters that you still remain in opinion that the factious quarrels risen of late in your service have been chiefly moved by me, whom you suppose to be a principal author and stirrer of the same; and that, unless I will reconcile myself to my enemies who have sought my destruction and ruin, you have determined utterly to abandon me as unworthy to be accounted yours.   God, who pardoneth the heaviest sins of us all, forgive them I humbly beseech him, and I do even as freely as yourself would wish me, that have cast these nets to ensnare me, poor wretch, of purpose to bring me, through your disgrace, to confusion.

Peck's Desiderata Curiosa, vol. I. p. 157.

The revenge is not mine, but his only; and it is enough I
know there is a blessing laid up for those that suffer.   To
obey your Honour's commandment, the rather concurring in
this point with my duty to God, to whose Holy table I may
not approach with malice in my heart, I will direct my
prayers to his fatherly goodness to give me patience and grace
to quench the passions which flesh and blood have kindled
within me against the injuries of my unkind fellows, which I
am now willingly content to tread under foot, as desirous
from henceforth to forget and forgive them, after the example
of Christ himself, who most graciously forgave us all.   And
for mine own particular cause of grief, in respect of your
Honour's displeasure, which I would God had not so wrath-
fully stirred up against me, I conceive it was but my unworthiness to serve you that hath justly laid the burden thereof
upon me.   You have but deservingly disgraced a poor silly
wretch, in whom, I confess, there is nothing to merit any better regard at your hands, much less the love and favour
wherewith you are wont to embrace and advance those whom,
for their necessary service, you are pleased especially to affect.   God give me comfort and more quiet after these storms
to serve your Honour cheerfully: more faithfully, and with
greater zeal of love, I shall never do than I have done: and
so I most humbly commend your Honour to the heavenly
blessings of his grace and favour.   From Cornhill, the 29th
of October 1584.   Your Honour's obedient poor servant.[*]

MR. SAMUEL COX TO . . . .

GOOD MR., I perceive by your last that it should seem you
understand by my Master that I misinterpreted the sense of
his honourable letters which he wrote last unto me, in thinking that he intreated me to a reconcilement with my fellows
where it were rather my part, of myself, to seek it.   I would
be loth to be reputed so simply graceless, or so grossly undutiful, as to think it fit for a Master, especially of his quality,

---

[*] Additional MSS. 15891, f. 126.

to intreat his servant, whom he may justly command, much
less so poor a wretch as myself, who am infinitely bound to
his goodness, to lay down my life at his feet to serve him.   I
rejoiced greatly at his letters, for that they were indeed to me,
a disconsolate poor man, most sweet and comfortable; tending
partly (as I took them) to rebuke me, that I had so long
omitted such charitable Christian office of reconciliation with
those with whom he thought it my duty to God and himself
to make atonement, which I was gladly willing to yield unto,
and in every respect to show myself careful to satisfy his
Honour, as well in this as in any thing else that might hereafter increase the quiet of his service, or breed friendly good-
will and acceptation between me and my fellows; being so
far from imagining he should intreat my return again, by his
letters, as in mine to his Honour (if you remember) I did dutifully acknowledge mine own unworthiness to serve him; and
that he had deservingly laid his disgrace upon an abject, unfortunate poor wretch, whose merit had not deserved any
better regard at his hands.   I have often most humbly sought,
and will ever seek to please and submit myself to his Honour
in all singleness of heart and faithful duty, as becometh me;
and when any of my fellows which have taken offence against
me shall be content, as I am, to cast off former malice, and to
end all private jars and unkindnesses, his Honour shall find
that, (how hardly soever they have dealt with me,) I will yet
freely forgive them all their discourtesies whatsoever, as more
worthy (respecting that even . . . . have wrought)
to be written in dust than in marble: nay, more than that, if
I had caused the disgrace of any of them as (with the peril of
my utter ruin,) they have procured mine, or if I had brought
any of them into the open scorn and rebuke of the world,
through the disfavour and ill-opinion of my Master, as they
have done me, to my greater grief and touch of credit than
ever they will be able to repair, I assure you I would have
sought them all England over, long ere this, but I would have
craved pardon of them; and should have thought it my duty
to have done so, howsoever they disdain once to make any

proffer of good-will or satisfaction to me, that am made by
their means a spectacle of shame and infamy; and this I know
standeth with the course of justice, and his Honour cannot
but conceive of it so in his wisdom, nor, I am sure, will not.
I refuse not to be as ready to reconcile myself as any of them.
I would be glad matters were so justly weighed as they might
receive a peaceful and a charitable end; but, to be plain with
you, (as with one whom I love,) I should think it hard measure to do sacrifice for another man's sins, or acknowledge a
fault in desiring favour, where the Judge himself hath justly
acquitted me. I will only seek and serve my Master, whom I
have offended, and endeavour to deserve the love of my fellows, either by way of reconciliation, or by any other honest
mean as they shall think me worthy of it. Some of them
sent me word of late that they will bring me to their bent, or
I shall never come more into service. Truly these words are
no good workers of concord, for the dutiful love and regard I
owe to my Master I should grieve in my heart to leese him;
but whatsoever should happen, better or worse, I promise you
I think I should sooner forsake life, liberty, and what favour
soever, than be a footstool to the frowardness of those that
hate me, especially of such as seem, by their own sayings, to
rule the reins as they list, and have credit to check and disgrace me when they please. If there be not some order taken
to bridle these men's tongues, or liberty given to other men
to speak what they will as well as they, for mine own part I
shall have small comfort to serve, especially, finding that all I
am able to say or do, and that the honest, painful duty of my
many years' service . . . . . . so much regarded as the blast
of one word only from the mouth of my accuser. This I say
boldly to you, my good friend, who I hope will interpret it
well. Think not much if my tongue do more liberally deliver
than is requisite, what my heart conceiveth without any ill
meaning. I have already borne so much, that my back is almost broken with the burden of it; and yet I must go pray
forgiveness of the workers of my woe, to make them insult
the more over me. There is a better and more indifferent

mean, as you know, than this to effect our reconciliation, which I pray you further with your best care of your poor friend, to keep our Master from offence, and myself from scorn; for the which I will ever love you and thank you accordingly. And so I commit you to God. From Cornhill, the 4th of November 1584. Your most beholding poor friend,

SAMUEL COX.[a]

MR. SAMUEL COX TO SIR CHRISTOPHER HATTON.

MAY IT PLEASE YOUR HONOUR, according to my obedience and bounden duty in seeking to do that which might best content you, I have used means to speak with Mr. . . . . twice or thrice since the receipt of your most honourable letters, of purpose, to grow to some such reconciliation and agreement with him as might be charitable and fit for us both in course of Christianity to accept of. At the length he sent me word he was presently to go into Northamptonshire, at his return from whence he would appoint time and place where we should meet and talk together; in which, mean while, I have thought it my duty the rather to avoid all suspicion of slackness, in these few lines to signify thus much to your Honour, whose commandment shall bind me as a law while I live to do that which may best please and satisfy your most grave and honourable desires. . . . . endeavoured to do the like towards my fellows Mr. . . . and . . . who finding your disgrace to lie so heavily upon me as it doth, are animated I doubt, to insult the more over me, and will by no means be intreated to have conference with me. When my friends come to move them to any such end, they cast them off slightly as if I were unworthy of their society, and themselves of better account than to regard the good-will of so poor a man as myself. To show your Honour their indecent speeches were too much trouble to you, and if you heard them, I am bound to believe by the experience I have of your goodness, that you would not think well of them in your justice. I see it is your honourable pleasure I

<hr>

[a] Additional MSS. 15891, f. 127ᵇ.

D D 2

should suffer all, and so I will do with patience, but yet ill words are no good workers of concord. And I most humbly beseech you to regard me among the rest as your poor servant, who in the place which I supply under you, hath been, is, and ever will be as careful to serve you, as the best of them, though as insufficient I confess as the meanest, but yet not unworthy of better usage than they have given me, which referring to the wisdom of your Honour's grave judgment, and myself and service to your further pleasure and direction, I beseech God to bless you with health and with the comfort of his highest favours. From my poor lodging in Cornhill this 9th of November 1584. Your Honour's most bound, unfortunate poor servant,   SAMUEL COX.[a]

MR. SAMUEL COX TO SIR CHRISTOPHER HATTON.

MAY IT PLEASE YOUR HONOUR, Yesternight Mr. Flowers[b] and I met together at your house in Holborn, where, according to our bounden duties, and your honourable pleasure directed to me in particular, we made such reconciliation and good end of all unkindnesses as was fit for us both to yield unto in regard of our faithful obedience to your Honour's service, and hath amply satisfied and contented each of us with all due respect of charity, to which effect Mr. . . . . courteously wrote his letters to Mr. Marb— and John, friendly wishing and advising them therein to take the like course with me, and to come to Mr. Bancroft's chamber at your Honour's house as we did, to satisfy and agree ourselves in anything that had bred cause of discontentation and ill liking heretofore betwixt us : whereunto they returned him answer, that they had business to attend of their own and could not come; for so Mr. Bancroft hath told me. Thus have I willingly sought them there three or four times in the zealous care of my duty to testify the most humble and earnest desire to do all that I can to please your Honour; but I fear it is labour lost and not unlikely to turn to smoke, unless you shall think it meet in your wisdom to interpose your com-

---

[a] Additional MSS. 15891, fol. 128[b].   [b] The name is, however, deleted.

mandment and authority, without the which I fear my devotion to serve you shall hardly receive that comfort which I have ever greedily thirsted to [enjoy through] the wonted favour and goodness of your Honour, which of all mortal blessings I repute the greatest that can happen to so poor a wretch, and without the which I shall think all life to be woful and miserable: and so, I end with all humility and most humble intreaty of pardon for my presumption herein: commending your Honour and your most virtuous actions to the favourable regard and protection of the Almighty. From my poor lodging in Cornhill the 28th of November 1584. Your Honour's faithful, most bounden poor servant,

SAM. COX.[a]

Another letter from the prolix Mr. Cox will be inserted here, though it belongs to the next year:—

MR. SAMUEL COX TO . . . .

SIR, I am sorry to hear that, of late, you are grown more subject to melancholy, and more desirous of solitariness than heretofore you have been. You shall find it (if I be not deceived) an humour sooner come than gone, and such as breedeth more contention for awhile, than bringeth good or commendation in the end. I pray you remember, that the wise patient must as well consider what will hurt him as what will help him, and always eschew the one and insue the other. If you think to receive any solace by means of a solitary life, you greatly deceive yourself, and fill your body full of raw humidities and ill affected humours, which having once taken root in you, will ever lie ready in wait, to search out secret and solitary places conformable to their nature, and forcibly keep you from all mirth and good company. Such false imaginations, instead of consuming and starving your evil, will give it nourishment, and as the fly, which flieth about the candle with pleasure, is burnt at the last, so will they at the length, purchase you pain, yea and death too, if you seek not remedy the sooner. Take heed to it therefore in time; as hidden flames kept down by force are most ardent, so these

* Additional MSS. 15891, f. 131[b].

corrupt humours, covertly lurking, do with more force consume and destroy the fair palace of man's mind. If you love
yourself, have regard to redress this evil, and to change the
order of your proceeding in the course of your health, which,
if you will do to your comfort, you must then account solitariness for a poison, and company for an antidote and the foundation of life, frame yourself to cast off the one, as a concu-
bine, and take the other into your favour as a lawful spouse.
Go unwillingly to melancholy, as the tortoise doth to the
enchantment, she will make you lean, forlorn, and fill you full
of putrefied blood, and in the end, draw both your life and
manners into corruption. The hasty departure of this messenger will here force me to close up my letter, you see how
bold I am, where I think my poor advice may be welcome.
It is a duty of courtesy, which I was loth should be wanting,
when I thought it might do good and be acceptable to so dear
a friend as yourself, whom God ever bless with his manifold
gracious favours. From the Court at Greenwich the 20th of
July 1585. Your assured poor friend,   SAMUEL COX.*

The following letter is without any date, but it seems
to have been written towards the end of 1584 :—

DR. MATHEW TO SIR CHRISTOPHER HATTON.

MY humble duty remembered unto your Honour. Albeit, since my placing in Duresme, it hath not pleased you to
command myself or my service in anything ; yet, for that I
cannot but acknowledge my preferment thither was greatly
furthered and specially followed by your honourable means,
I thought it the part of a thankful man to renew my acknow-
ledgments thereof unto your Honour, and withal to make humble offer of what I may do there, to be ready at your devotion,
as the person whom I do much honour, more for your many
virtues than for your place ; and to whom I am much bound-
en, not for this alone, but for divers other favours. That I
have not oftener attended upon your Honour, and visited
you according to my duty and ceremony of Court, hath not

* Additional MSS. 15891.

proceeded from any forgetfulness of that I owe you, but
rather of some scruple that I make to be cumbersome to
such persons as make more precious account of their time
than to idle it out in entertainments.   And so, trusting this
will be taken, if not for a sufficient amends, yet for a reasonable excuse both of my silence and of my absence, here
would I put an end to my letter, but that I cannot so refrain
my pen from scribbling somewhat of the abundance of my
heart, not as one curious in your causes, but yet bound to be
careful of your estate.   I am very sorry, Sir, to hear you
give yourself to be more private than you have been wont,
for solitariness is a certain humour sooner come than gone;
and it rather bringeth contentation for a while, than breedeth
commendation or good in the end.   You be not the first, Sir,
that have lost a good servant, or kept a bad; or that have
found both friends unfast and neighbours unthankful, undutiful followers, and professed enemies.   These thwarts are
incident, yea, and convenient too sometimes, not only to
check our joys and to prove our patience, but to let us see
and make us feel the odds between God and men, between
this and that other world.   And happy is he that with a
good stomach can brook the perils of these unkindnesses,
which are not piecemeal to be eaten and fed on, but rather to
be swallowed and devoured whole.   Happy is he at last that
is occasioned at first to try all before he need trust any, and
so to make both proof of his friends and profit of his foes.
A nobleman of Germany gave for his words *concussus surgo*,
and bare for his device a great stone in a palm-tree, to show
that as the palm riseth against and resisteth the burthen, so
it becometh men of council and courage, such as he was, (and
such as you be,) the more heavy they be laden the more
strongly to overbear it.   Like advice gave Sybilla to Æneas
before his travel, amidst his trouble, *Tu ne cede malis, sed con-
tra audentior ito.*   But to your Honour I will say no more
but ' Show yourself to be yourself, and give to your adversary
no one foot unless it be to gain two.'   I am not of the sword,
but of the robe; neither is mine ability much, though mine

affection be great: but what I am is at your commandment,
as I have good cause and am desirous to make some proof as
it shall like your Honour to minister the occasion. And thus,
not doubting but as after close weather the sun shines brighter
and warmer too, so your condition of honour and virtue shall
daily increase from good to better before God and man, I
will humbly crave pardon for my boldness, and so betake you
to the gracious protection and direction of the Almighty.
From the Savoy, this Thursday morning. Your Honour's
humble and most bounden,   To. MATHEW.[*]

Sir Christopher Hatton gave a remarkable proof of
his religious zeal in this year. A bill against Jesuits
and Seminary Priests having passed the Commons, it
was proposed, on the 21st of December, that the members should repair to their own homes; but, before sepa-
rating, "Hatton stood up again, and putting the House
in mind of her Majesty's most princely and loving kindnesses signified in her former messages and declarations,"
of which he had always been the bearer, "of her Highness's thankful acceptations of the dutiful cares and
travails of this House in the service of her Majesty and
the Realm," moved the House, "that, besides the rendering of our most humble and loyal thanks unto her Highness, we do, being assembled together, join our hearts
and minds together in most humble and earnest prayer
unto Almighty God for the long continuance of the most
prosperous preservation of her Majesty, with most due and
thankful acknowledgment of his infinite benefits and blessings, poured upon this whole Realm through the mediation of her Highness's ministry under Him." He added,
that he had "a paper in writing in his hand, devised
and set down by an honest, godly, and learned man;

* Additional MSS. 15891, f. 122.

and which, albeit it was not very well written, yet he would willingly read it as well as he could, if it pleased them to follow and say after him, as he should begin and say before them; which, being assented unto most willingly of all the whole House, and every one kneeling upon his knees, the said Mr. Vice-Chamberlain began the said prayer."[a]

Sir John Perrot, Lord Deputy of Ireland, proposed to the Government to found a University in Dublin, and to appropriate the revenues of St. Patrick's Church to its support.[b] This was naturally resisted by the Archbishop of Dublin and the Prebends, and some letters from the Archbishop will be found on the subject.

FROM THE LORDS OF THE COUNCIL TO THE LORD DEPUTY.

AFTER our very hearty commendations to your good Lordship. Whereas among other matters appertaining to the good government of that Realm, your Lordship hath, as we well perceive by sundry your late letters, a very special care to have a University erected there, according to an article of instructions given you in this behalf, before your departure from hence, for the converting of the revenues of the Cathedral Church of St. Patrick in that Realm towards the erecting of a University, and the maintenance of certain Readers and Scholars: for as much as we are given to understand that the said revenues do consist altogether of tithes, and that the Prebendaries there are persons impersonees, and have peculiar charges of sundry parish churches, the tithes whereof do make the revenues of the said College, without any temporalities or lay fees, we cannot resolve to dissolve or suppress the state of such a Church, considering it is of such pastoral cures, and to turn the living due to the Minister for the said

[a] Parliamentary History, vol. i. p. 827.   p. 385 ; and Monk Mason's History of the Cathedral of St. Patrick.
[b] Vide Harris' History of Dublin,

cures to other uses, without further information how the
same may be more lawfully done, and without inconvenience.
Therefore we have thought good to require your Lordship to
call unto you the Archbishop of Dublin, and together with
him to consider somewhat better thereof, as well of the
means how the said revenues growing of tithes might be
converted in some part to such use as your Lordship hath set
down; as also, if any alterations may be suffered, how much
thereof may be converted, without taking from the ministry
and the cures that which appertaineth unto them by all right
and conscience; as also of those letts which shall appear
unto you to hinder that alteration, and the inconveniences
that thereby might arise: whereof we pray your Lordship
we may receive from you, and from the Archbishop of Dublin, particular information, with your advice therein, to the
end that we may be thoroughly instructed in the cause, and
better able to yield you some resolution therein; and we
will not fail, as we shall see cause, to let your Lordship understand of our opinion, and what we shall think convenient to
be done in that behalf. But, upon the debating thereof with
Sir Lucas Dillon, we do think that by Parliament there might
be some device made of a contribution out of parsonages
impropriate, and some other ecclesiastical promotions, not
subject to the charge and cure of souls, to serve for maintenance of certain Public readers both in sciences and divinity,
and for relief of some convenient number of Scholars, whereby some beginning might be seen of a kind of public
schools, and by access of men's devotions it might be hoped
to have such a University planted in that Realm, rather than to
make a spoil of parishes with cures, as we see the intention
of dissolving of that College would work. And yet we can
wish that the disorders and misusages of those cures by the
Prebendaries (if any be) were reformed, to the which we will
yield our helps. So, until we receive further information from
your Lordship, we do bid you right heartily farewell. From
Greenwich, the 3rd of January 1584 [1585]. Your Lordship's
loving friends.[a]

[a] Additional MSS. 15891, f. 144.

The meeting of Parliament, about which the Queen was anxious, took place on the 4th of February; but it was prorogued on the 20th of March, and dissolved on the 14th of September:—

SIR CHRISTOPHER HATTON TO LORD BURGHLEY.

MY SINGULAR GOOD LORD, I have moved her Majesty, according to your Lordship's desire, touching the office of the Duchy. I find she hath passed her gracious grant of the same unto the Lord Willoughby two days since, for the which she blameth your Lordship, and is right heartily sorry. Her Majesty marvelleth that, having any liking to those small things, you caused nobody about her to speak of them. I perceive she hath some desire to reclaim her promise, wherein what will be done I am not able to certify your Lordship. I can assure your Lordship her Majesty dealeth most graciously, kindly, and lovingly towards you in her speeches and meaning, whereof I beseech you take comfort according to your wisdom.

The Queen requireth your good Lordship, with the Lord Chancellor and the Lord Steward, who is presently at London, to be here the morrow at night, about the matter of Parliament, wherewith I find her Majesty somewhat troubled. Her pleasure is, Sir, that you should advertise these Lords, that they fail not to be here; at which time I shall attend you according to my love and duty. And so I humbly take my leave in haste, this 26th of January 1584 [1585]. Your good Lordship's most bound poor friend,

CHR. HATTON.[a]

Mr. Davison was sent, early in 1585, to the Elector of Cologne, to deliver to him 6000*l.*; and he remained in the Low Countries until April, when he was commanded to return to England:—

[a] Autograph in the State Paper Office.   [b] Harleian MSS. 285, f. 122, 129.

MR. DAVISON TO SIR CHRISTOPHER HATTON.

IT may please your Honour, Since the last dispatch of this
bearer my servant, I have had little to write unto your
Honour, the mean time affording us nothing from the States
Commissioners in France since their departure from Abbe-
ville, so as hitherto we remain in a doubtful expectation
what issue their ambassade will take; whereof all men here,
of any judgment, do in the mean time carry a very hard
and jealous opinion, as of a remedy far more dangerous than
either helpful or proper to the disease of this troubled and
languishing commonwealth. Of the late attempted surprise
of Bois-le-duc, succeeded with dishonour and loss of four or
five hundred men at the least, amongst which was a brother
of the Elector Truchses*, this bearer can particularly inform
your Honour. Since the enemy hath recovered the forts
before Zutphen, some by force, the rest by composition, and
hath now free passage into Deventer, where the States
are driven by this means to reinforce their garrisons, Brussels is reduced to some strait, and without hope to hold long,
being only sustained with the vain expectation of the unlikely or untimely succours of their new-chosen saint. In
Gueldres there is some doubt of alteration by the means of
some principal seduced or corrupted by the enemy. In
Flanders he turneth all upside down: he hath begun to
redress and enlarge the old citadel at Ghant, already de-
fensible, and hath projected another (as we hear) about St.
Peter's within the same town, to hold the people the better
in devotion. At Bruges the necessities are said to be great,
especially through the want of Sluse, where the garrison is
now in mutiny for their pay. There was of late some expectation of a meeting at Liege by the Archbishops of Mentz and
Treves, with other Princes and Commissioners of the Empire,
to revive some motion and treaty of peace; but, since the
bruit is that their Commissioners should be deputed into
France, whether to effect the same the better with that King's
concurrency, or else to divert him from embracing the cause

* Sic.

or, under either pretext, to resolve something else that hath
been long since in hatching against the surety of religion and
the state of others, I leave to the better and more certain
advertisement of our Ambassador in France.   Some here,
that pretend to know something, do give out that the Spaniard, willing to leave a peaceable estate behind him, is both
inclined to peace, and minded to bestow these Countries, with
his eldest daughter, upon the Cardinal of Austria, now in
Spain, the better to satisfy other Princes jealous of his
greatness, and to incline this people the rather therewithal
to a reconcilement; in which respect, as some think, or rather
to countermine the doings of these States Commissioners, the
Prince of Parma hath sent thither the Marquis of Haverech
and Berques with the Prince of Chimay. But that this over-
ture hath any better scope, or will yield any better fruit than
the last treaty or colloquy, is of all wise men suspected; the
disposition whereof I leave to His providence that overruleth
all, to whose safeguard and protection I humbly commend
your Honour. And so, in haste for this time, I take my leave.
At the Hague, the 12th of February 1584 [1585]. Your
Honour's most bounden to do you service,   W. Davison.

Postscript.—The fleet prepared in Zealand for the relief
of Antwerp is, as we hear, gone up, with the only loss of
four vessels, whereof the one is sunk, the other taken. I
have likewise even now received advertisement that Brussels
is entered into some treaty with the enemy; and look to
hear by the next of their agreement, so as their expected
succour out of France shall come to them a day, as we say,
after the fair.[a]

In December 1584, when the bill against Jesuits and
Seminary Priests was read in the Commons, a Dr.
William Parry, "a man," says Camden, "passing
proud, neat, and spruce," was the only member who
spoke against it, declaring the proposed laws to be

[a] Additional MSS. 15891, f. 140.

"cruel, bloody, full of desperation, and hurtful to the English nation." For this offence he was committed to custody, and afterwards charged with treasonable matters. Being examined by three members of the Privy Council, Lord Hunsdon, Sir Christopher Hatton, and Sir Francis Walsingham, he acknowledged his fault, and begged the Queen's forgiveness. On the 25th of February 1585, Parry was tried for high treason before a Special Commission, consisting of Lord Hunsdon, the two Chief Justices and Chief Baron, the Master of the Rolls, Sir Francis Knollys, Sir James Croft, Sir Christopher Hatton, and Sir Thomas Heneage, and pleaded guilty. Hatton took a very prominent part in the proceedings;[a] and, according to Camden, "When the prisoner's confession was recorded, and judgment demanded him, Hatton thought it necessary, for satisfaction of the multitude that stood round about, that his crime might be manifestly laid open out of his own confession."[b] Parry was executed in Great Palace Yard on the 2nd of March.[c]

Sir Thomas Heneage was again made the channel of conveying some "tokens" and a letter from Hatton to the Queen. He sent her a true love's knot, with which she was much pleased, and wrote him a gratifying acknowledgment; but the most curious part of this letter is that which relates to Sir Walter Raleigh, and Elizabeth's indignation that he should be supposed to equal Hatton in her estimation. Varney will be recognised by all readers of "Kenilworth." The "priest" was Higgins, who is often mentioned:—

[a] State Trials, i. 133.
Camden's Annals, b. iii. p. 45.

[c] Stow, p. 701.

SIR, Your bracelets be embraced according to their worth, and the good-will of the sender, which is held of such great price as your true friend tells you, I think in my heart you have great cause to take most comfort in, for seldom in my life have I seen more hearty and noble affection expressed by her Majesty towards you than she showed upon this occasion, which will ask more leisure than is now left me particularly to let you know. The sum is, she thinks you faithfullest and of most worth, and thereafter will regard you : so she saith, so I hope, and so there is just cause. She told me, she thought your absence as long as yourself did, and marvelled that you came not. I let her Majesty know, understanding it by Varney, that you had no place here to rest yourself, which after standing and waiting you much needed; whereupon she grew very much displeased and would not believe that any should be placed in your lodging, but sending Mr. Darcy to understand the matter, found that Sir Wa. R. lay there, wherewith she grew more angry with my L. Chamberlain than I wished she had been, and used bitterness of speech against R. telling me before that she had rather see him hanged than equal him with you, or that the world should think she did so. Messengers bear no blame; and though you give me no thanks, I must tell you, that her Highness saith you are a knave for sending her such a thing and of that price, which you know she will not send back again ; that is, the knot* she most loves, and she thinks cannot be undone; but I keep the best to the last. This enclosed, which it pleased her to read to me, and I must be a record of, which if I might see surely performed, I should have one of my greatest desires upon earth; I speak it faithfully. The Queen is glad with me that the priest is taken; I pray God you may make him open all truth that may advance her surety, and to your Honour, which I wish in all kind as long and as happy as any man's living, and so commend me all unto you till I see you,

* " The true love knot."—Marginal note.

which I hope and think best to be as her Highness cometh home to-morrow at night. From Croydon the 2nd of April 1585. Your own ever sure so,   THO. HENEAGE.[*]

The Countess of Sussex's applications to be restored to the Queen's favour having failed, she renewed her efforts in a letter to Hatton in April of this year:—

THE COUNTESS OF SUSSEX TO SIR CHRISTOPHER HATTON.

SIR, I must and will confess while I live, that I have found that virtue, courtesy, and friendship in you that I have wanted in many others of whom I have deserved better than I have or ever shall be able to deserve of you: and therefore have thought good to make bold of you and to beseech your pains once again in soliciting her Majesty's most gracious favour towards me, the which if I found to be taken from me, by any my wilful offence towards her excellent and incomparable goodness, I would hate my life and think myself the most accursed creature that ever had breath; but for as much as my greatest fault (I hope) is nothing else but some error or oversight (in the midst of my miseries being overwhelmed with sorrow) which might have made the wisest and perfectest to slide, and yet perhaps my sliding, enforced and aggravated by evil will, (and made much more than it was) I trust in God, her most gracious nature and princely heart will not keep so straight an eye upon any oversight of mine, that spareth to see and to know and to revenge many offences and offenders in higher degree.   Howsoever it be, I have with all humility and duty sought her Majesty; and though I be eftsoons repulsed, yet will I ever seek her with as great lowliness as ever poor wretch that lay prostrate at her feat.   And if any particularity have been sinisterly brought to her sacred ears, that I have not heard of, if it might stand with her gracious favour to be satisfied from mine own mouth, I shall for ever think myself most bound to her excellency: and if I clear not myself of the most of that I have been charged withal, I

* Additional MSS. 15891, f. 147.

will condemn myself as unworthy of her princely presence, and live for ever in exile and disgrace.   And if I be able to perform this and to disprove the sinister informations of my contraries, alas! why should I wear out my life with this note of her Highness' indignation by which the world cannot but fancy some great enormity in me?   Sir, I beseech you, let me entreat you once again to plead mine innocency to her Majesty with a most humble mind to submit myself and to satisfy her Highness.   And if my hap be so hard as to be the only unfortunate woman of the world, your deserts and goodness are not the less, and my bond to you greatly increased, as knoweth the Almighty.   Bermondsey, the 12th April 1585.   Your assured friend,   FRAN. SUSSEX.[a]

TO MR. EGERTON, HER MAJESTY'S SOLICITOR.

SIR, Her Majesty being moved lately touching Mr. Doctor Dale's bill for his right of presentation in the Hospital of Sherborne, is graciously contented to sign the same, so the proviso contained therein be a sample as it ought to be, which if you shall find to be so, her Majesty's pleasure is, you shall subscribe his bill with present expedition, that it may be returned immediately, for such is her Highness' direction. And so, I commit you to God.   From the Court at Greenwich the 15th of April 1585.   Your very loving assured friend,   CHR. HATTON.

Sir, If you find not this bill formally drawn according to the law, you must presently make up another and deliver it to Mr. Dale, subscribed with your own hand.[b]

Philip Sidney had married Sir Francis Walsingham's daughter, and not only was the Queen reconciled to the match, but she Knighted Sidney at Windsor Castle in January 1584:—

---

[a] Additional MSS. 15891, f. 135.   [b] Egerton Papers, p. 113.

SIR FRANCIS WALSINGHAM TO SIR CHRISTOPHER HATTON.

Sir, Before my departure from the Court I did recommend unto her Majesty a suit of Sir Philip Sidney's, whereunto it pleased her to give a very favourable ear and to promise speedy resolution therein, now for that by reason of my absence it may depend longer than the necessity of the gentleman may well bear: I am therefore to pray you as my good and assured friend, to put her Majesty in mind thereof, and so shall you bind us both to be at your devotion. This bearer shall acquaint you with the suit, and in what sort the same hath been proceeded in. And so, not doubting of your most friendly furtherance therein, I commit you to God. At Barn Elms the 26th of April 1585.. Your assured friend,

FRA. WALSINGHAM.[a]

This and the following letter appear to relate to the arrest of the Earl of Arundell. The severity of the laws against the Catholics induced the Earl to take measures for quitting England, but he was apprehended through the treachery of his own followers, and committed to the Tower on the 25th of April. He wrote a long and eloquent letter[b] to the Queen, which was not to have been delivered until after his departure; but, being found, the reproaches it contained exasperated his enemies. He was tried and condemned, but the sentence was not executed, and he died a prisoner in the Tower in November 1595. The person indicated as "D" of this and the following letter has been identified:—

SIR FRANCIS WALSINGHAM TO SIR CHRISTOPHER HATTON.

Sir, I have perused the examination it hath pleased you to take of D——, and finding by your report of the man that

[a] Additional MSS. 15891, f. 146.   [b] This letter is printed at length by Stow, p 702—706.

he is but simple, and that the last year he was somewhat distracted of his wit, I see no cause but upon bond of good behaviour he may be set at liberty.   And so, I commit you to
God. At Barn Elms the 28th of April 1585.   Your most
assured friend,   FRA. WALSINGHAM.[a]

The Earl mentioned in this letter was clearly the Earl
of Arundell:—

SIR FRANCIS WALSINGHAM TO SIR CHRISTOPHER HATTON.

SIR, I return unto you D——'s examination; it were hard
(though it might be sufficiently proved,) that the Earl's reconciliation should be urged against him, being a matter rather
of conscience than of State.   And seeing her Majesty hath
heretofore (in point of conscience) dealt gratiously towards
Jesuits and Seminaries, men of worse desert, it would be ill
thought of that one of the Earl's quality should receive harder
measure than those that are reputed the poisoners of this
estate.   Touching the . . . . wherein it is said there were
certain hallowed grains, I received it from my Lord Treasurer, who can give particular information about whom it was
found.   And so praying God to send you continuance of
health, which I lack, I commit you to his protection.   At
Barn Elms, the 29th of April 1585.   Your most assured
friend,   FRA. WALSINGHAM.[b]

Arundell seems, in his misfortunes, to have shewn a
magnanimity becoming his race, though Walsingham
says he was by nature fearful.   The Lieutenant of the
Tower was Sir Owen Hopton, who was not, however, as
Walsingham recommends, removed from his office.   Mr.
Henry Macwilliam, to whose custody the Earl of Arundell was entrusted, was one of the Gentleman Pensioners, and his eldest daughter and co-heiress married
Sir John Stanhope, from whom several letters occur:—

[a] Additional MSS. 15891, f. 147ᵇ.   [b] Additional MSS. 15891, f. 146.

SIR FRANCIS WALSINGHAM TO SIR CHRISTOPHER HATTON.

SIR, The view of your letter hath made me change my opinion, touching the proceeding with the Earl, whose courage is to be abated, and no advantage to be lost until he be drawn to use some other language, seasoned with more humility. You shall do well to advise Mr. Macwilliam to look well to his charge: it cannot be but that he receiveth some comfort, and that not from mean persons, that putteth him in this courage. No man is of his own nature more fearful. It will behove her Majesty to make choice of some other, to supply the place of the Lieutenant of the Tower: it sufficeth not for him that shall hold that place to be only faithful, but he ought to be wise. I know it now to be the corruptest prison in England; which in these dangerous times standeth not with policy.

The force of the Guisans increaseth, and so much the more for that he daily getteth into his hands the King's treasure. The Queen Mother adviseth her son to grow to a peace: at the said Duke's price, few or none are willing to serve the King, but those whom he dare not use. Cardinal Montalto,[a] sometime a grey friar, by the favour of the Spanish faction is elected Pope: a man most furiously bent against those of the religion. There lacketh now, to bring our danger to the height of his pride, only the King of Spain's full possession of the Low Countries, which in the course we hold, will in a few days come to pass. And so with my most hearty thanks for your promised favour to Sir Philip Sidney, I commit you to God. At Barn Elms, the 1st of May 1585. Your most assured friend,   FRANCIS WALSINGHAM.[b]

The Archbishop of Dublin's second letter respecting the proposed University was probably written in April or May of this year:—

---

[a] Felix Peretti, Cardinal of Montalto, was elected Pope on the 24th of April, 1585, and took the title of Sixtus the Fifth.

[b] Additional MSS. 15891, f. 147.

ARCHBISHOP LOFTUS TO SIR CHRISTOPHER HATTON.

IT MAY PLEASE YOUR HONOUR, It pleased the Lords of her
Highness' Privy Council in February last, by letters sent
over by Sir Lucas Dillon to my Lord Deputy, to signify their
opinions touching the Cathedral Church of St. Patrick's, that
it should remain in the state wherein it was; notwithstanding
which letter, my Lord Deputy hath ever since continued his
former purpose to dissolve the same and to convert it to a
University.   And because in the livings of that Church
I have a special interest, (being ordinary Patron of the most
of them,) his Lordship acquainted me with his intention,
namely, that the Church should be turned to a place for the
Temporal Court, and the Prebends to the maintenance of
Colleges to be erected; which motion when I misliked for
many reasons heretofore signified by me unto your Honour
and the rest of her Highness' Council, his Lordship conceived
great offence and displeasure against me, threatening me
with these terms, that, if herein I would not yield unto him,
he would be my utter enemy, sift me, disgrace me, and make
me lose as much as I might lose in Ireland.   And whereas in
the letter sent from the Lords his Lordship was required to
call me unto him, and to confer privately with me touching
that matter, the letter was detained by his Lordship and
kept from me until the 11th of this instant.   These things
proceeding from a man of his authority and ability, and the
due care I had of that poor Church, whereof I have the pastoral charge, enforced me to solicit my dearest friends in England for the procurement of her Majesty's letter to his Lordship to stay him from that attempt; which being lately delivered unto his hands was so grievously taken, that I find
thereby his Lordship's displeasure to be increased against me,
and have just cause to fear, that whatsoever things can be
devised for my disgrace with her Majesty, or to discredit me
with their Lordships, shall not be omitted.

After the delivery of her Majesty's letter concerning her
express resolution for the continuance of the Church in the

state wherein it is, the 11th of this instant his Lordship sent
for me, and then, first showing the letter of the Lords sent in
February, required me to enter into conference with him how
most conveniently either the whole Church, or some good
part thereof, might be converted into an University; withal
laying before me a platform of a University drawn by himself,
consisting of many impossibilities, and for sundry just causes
to be misliked. Mine humble answer to his Lordship was
this: that, forasmuch as her Majesty had signified her gracious resolution touching my Church (for the which I most
humbly thank God and her Highness), I would not now presume to enter into any new device in this matter. His Lordship, being grievously offended with this my answer, forthwith
burst forth into these speeches, 'So I think; nor in any
other good things.'

I am secretly informed his Lordship intendeth to seek
some advantage out of this mine answer against me, and that
he doth inform the same into England by Mr. Secretary Fen-
ton, of whose forwardness in aggravating any cause against
me I nothing doubt, for that he hath professed himself an
utter enemy to me and my poor Church, by the ruin and
overthrow whereof he hath conceived an undoubted hope to
enrich himself.

I have further learned, by secret intelligence from some
which are familiarly acquainted with his Lordship's dealings,
that, upon this his Lordship's offence conceived against me, he
taketh occasion to seek my utter discredit with your Honour
by certain most untrue and malicious informations suggested
by mine enemies, the effect whereof ensueth: That in this
cause of the Church I oppose myself against his Lordship
only in respect of the private gain and commodity which
yearly I reap out of the same, thereby to pamper myself and
my children; that I have purchased one hundred pounds per
annum; that I have matched in marriage four of my daughters to four principal gentlemen, and am in readiness to bestow
the fifth; that I have builded a house, which already hath

cost me fifteen or sixteen hundred pounds; that all this wealth and substance I have gained by corruption in mine office of Chancery, and in the High Commission for the Ecclesiastical Causes; and, finally, that I am altogether degenerate, and become mere Irish.

The information, I confess, is of itself most odious, especially against a person of my place and calling; but because it containeth manifest untruths, and is reported to my honourable friend, whose knowledge of my life and conversation sufficeth to disprove so malicious suggestions, I have conceived firm and stedfast hope that before mine answer I shall not be condemned, but shall be admitted to use my purgation in sort as followeth: First, protesting before Almighty God that private respect have not induced me to stand in the defence of my poor Church, or therein to oppose myself against his Lordship, whom I honour; but the pastoral charge thereof committed unto me, which in conscience pricketh me thereunto, with many other reasons which have been alléged. I confess I do enjoy out of the livings of the Church an hundred pounds per annum, granted unto me by special *commendam* from her Highness under her Great Seal of England; the confirmation whereof my Lord Deputy at sundry times hath offered unto me during my life, in case I would yield my consent to the suppression of the Church; which honourable offer, made to me at sundry times and by sundry messengers of special trust and credit, I always refused, having had a greater care of the charge committed to me than mine own commodity.

The value of my purchase wanteth a good deal of two hundred marks per annum, which, by keeping of her Majesty's Great Seal in the time of Sir William Fitzwilliam's government, by her Majesty's entertainment, I gained; and now do humbly thank the Lord that it is so well bestowed for the relief of my poor wife and fifteen children living, which, otherwise, after my death would live in extreme beggary. Her Highness' entertainment was the only means thereof which, during my life, I will acknowledge. My four daughters are in truth married, and the fifth I hope shall be, to the sons and heirs of five honest and virtuous English gentlemen. But God is witness that all this hath been wrought by God's special providence with a small sum of money, in regard rather of their favour to my religion, they being all Protestants, (for which I thank God and the good education of my daughters,) than of any portion of money, which, in respect of the slenderness of my living, I was able to disburse.

The building of my house, which is newly reared, hath not in truth been half so chargeable as is suggested; but, whatsoever it hath cost me, I do confess that I gained the same wholly by her Majesty's bountiful entertainment bestowed upon me in the time of the late joint Government, committed to my partner, Sir Henry Wallop, and me; wherewith I have builded a poor castle, of threescore feet long, for the maintenance of my poor wife and children. The only founder under God of this poor work was her Majesty's liberality, which I and my children will never forget.

The Lord doth know right well that this hath been the only mean of my gain or lucre I have attained since my coming into this land, which, I trust, hath been bestowed upon good and godly uses; for as for the suggestion of indirect or corrupt means by me used to enrich myself, either in the Chancery or in the High Commission, (my duty and reverence reserved to the informer and his plan,) I do defy the whole world, and stand wholly upon my innocency, refusing no censure, but most humbly beseeching that my dealings might be tried at the Council-board, either to my utter discredit and undoing, or to the shame and confusion of mine enemy and accuser, whatsoever he be. Lastly, concerning that most odious suggestion that I am now degenerate, and become mere Irish, I refer the trial of this report to the long experience which both you and the rest of the Lords of her Majesty's Council have had of my faithful and loyal service in most dangerous times, wherein I dare be bold to challenge your Honour to be my witness how far I have hazarded my whole estate;

and, to disprove this malicious and most untrue suggestion, I am contented to submit myself to the meanest gentlemen of our nation.

These causes of my grief and great discomfort offered by his Lordship, I have made bold truly (even as before God bemoaning mine estate) to set down before your Honour, protesting before God that I am innocent of any evil or unkind practice towards my Lord Deputy, being no oppugner, but the defender in this cause both of myself and of my poor children. I have from time to time most diligently sought, both by my obedience and service, his Honour's favour; but by no means can obtain the same. My professed enemy is the Master of the Rolls, (who, even for religion itself, doth chiefly hate me,) and beareth so great a sway with his good Lordship, both in this particular cause and in many other against me that he daily incenseth his displeasure, and generally almost in all actions concerning her Majesty's service, that as many others are very much discontented, so in particular I find myself very much discouraged. I have no refuge to fly unto in these or any other injuries but only her Highness and that honourable Board, to whom I must and will appeal, referring the consideration of my twenty-eight years' service to her and their grave wisdoms. I wish from my heart the comfort of my Lord Deputy's favour and friendship, which in most humble manner I have required, and daily do sue for, praying your Honour to be a means to his good Lordship for the procurement thereof. And for my Cathedral Church, since her Highness hath signified her gracious resolution that it shall continue in the state wherein it is, without any innovation, I humbly beseech your Honour to persuade his good Lordship to desist from the purpose he hath conceived for the suppression and dissolution of the same. Your Honour's most humble to command.[*]

This and the next letter arose out of the persecutions to which Catholics were exposed after the passing of the Act against Jesuits and Seminary Priests :—

[*] Additional MSS. 15891, f. 150ᵇ.

SIR FRANCIS WALSINGHAM TO SIR CHRISTOPHER HATTON.

SIR, I will give present order, throughout the ports for the stay of the party, according to the description contained in your letter. It may please you to give some charge to your servant Pyne, to look well to the port of London, for that most of the profession do pass that way. And so I commit you to the protection of the Almighty. At Barn Elms, the 1st of May 1585. Your most assured friend,

FRA. WALSINGHAM.[a]

SIR THOMAS HENEAGE TO SIR CHRISTOPHER HATTON.

SIR, I have showed her Majesty your letter, this bearer brought me for answer, whereof her Highness's pleasure is, I should let you know, that she would have Isaac Higgins, now in your custody yet detained three or four days, and in the mean season, that he should be again better examined; and that Mr. Secretary should be sent to, and likewise Mr. Topcliffe with those in that commission, to know if the name of this man be in any of their rules, which they keep of such bad fellows as carry and re-carry books and letters into this Realm, and out of it, which being certainly known, that he be kept or let go, as shall be thought best by you for her Majesty's service. This is all I was willed to say, but this withal, that her Highness thinketh your house will shortly be like Gravesend barge, never without a knave, a priest, or a thief, &c. So loving you and leaving you, I commend me humbly to you. From the Court at Croydon, this 2nd of May 1585. Your own at commandment,   THO. HENEAGE.[b]

Only thirteen years had elapsed since the Duke of Norfolk, when under sentence of death, advised his eldest son to rely upon Hatton's friendship,[c] before that son was himself a supplicant to Hatton to save him from a similar fate:—

---

[a] Additional MSS. 15891, f. 147[b].   [b] Ibid, f. 148[b].
[c] Vide p. 9, *ante.*

I PRAY pardon me good Mr. Vice-Chamberlain, that I sent not this letter yesternight. The cause of my stay was, because I have greatly offended her Majesty, and therefore am desirous for as full a satisfaction as lieth in me to make, truly of myself to confess the sum of my offence, wherefore I staid this morning to see if I could any way call to mind anything that yesternight I had forgotten. That I have been both confessed and absolved, I cannot deny; but I protest, led unto it merely by conscience, without intending either to offend her Majesty or her State. My sending to Doctor Allen,* I have already acknowledged. Two things only I am now to add. The first, that I offered to be at his direction. The second that I wrote a letter unto him, and that was the only letter which ever I wrote, wherein I did signify, as much by writing of my being at his direction, and in this I must needs confess I offended her Majesty. And I protest afore God was so sorry for it after myself, as when the messenger which should have carried it, had not opportunity at the first to go over, I desired that it might be burnt; and what is done with it, I know not, but Brydges told me it was burnt. Now having in these points laid open fully and thoroughly wherein I have offended her Majesty, I protest afore God, as far as I can call to remembrance, I do utterly deny and disavow, that ever I was privy to any plot or practice laid or made against her Majesty, or her state; and if it can be proved, that I was made privy either to any former plot, or any new practice, I desire no favour, otherwise, I hope so much in the goodness and mercy of her Majesty, as she will take some pity and compassion upon me. I must confess I was slipping, but not fallen. I call God to witness she hath raised many that have slipped more, and therefore I cannot despair but that she can raise me, and as her goodness in that shall be exceeding great towards me, so I doubt not but my deserts towards her shall be such, as her

* Cardinal Allen, vide p. 16, *ante.*

Majesty shall well find, that I desire to be thankful, and that
I strive by all means to make satisfaction for this my offence.
And thus laying myself at the feet of her Majesty's mercy,
and commending my cause to your favour, I cease further to
trouble you.   From the Tower, the 7th of May 1585.   Yours
most faithful and assuredly for ever,   ARUNDELL.[a]

During his long career, though exposed to all the
jealousies that attend a Royal favourite, Hatton had
hitherto preserved an unsullied reputation.   An event,
however, occurred which afforded his enemies an opportunity of fixing a suspicion upon him; and, though
the charge may be safely pronounced scandalous and
untrue, it is nevertheless material for Hatton's justification that all the facts of the case should be stated.

On the 21st of June 1585, Henry Percy, Earl of
Northumberland, who had been for a year a close prisoner in the Tower for high treason, was found dead
in his apartment.   An Inquest was held in the Tower
on the day of his death before the Coroner and a Jury,
who found that the Earl, intending to kill himself, had,
five days before, caused a kind of pistol called a "dag,"
with bullets and gunpowder, to be brought into his chamber by one James à Price a yeoman, and had hidden
the dag in the mattress under the bolster of his bed;
that, between the hours of twelve and one in the night
of the 21st, he "did bolt the door of the aforesaid chamber, and the inner part of his chamber towards himself,"
lest any one should prevent his effecting his design; that
the Earl then lay down in his bed, and, taking the dag,
which was ready loaded with three bullets, in his
hands, "put it to the left part of his breast, near unto

---

[a] Additional MSS. 15891, f. 148[b].

the pap," and then discharged the contents "into his body and heart, and through his chine bone even into his right shoulder;" thereby "giving unto himself one mortal wound of the depth of twelve inches, and of the width of two inches, of which he instantly died."[a] Camden says that the Jury "found the dag, or pistol, with gunpowder in the chamber, and examined his man, who had bought the dag, and him which had sold it."

Two days afterwards, many Peers and Privy Councillors[b] met in the Star Chamber; when Sir Thomas Bromley, the Lord Chancellor, stated the cause of the Earl of Northumberland's imprisonment, and the manner of his death; "but, to satisfy the multitude, which are always prone to believe the worse," he desired the Queen's Attorney and Solicitor-General to state plainly all the facts. After specifying the particulars of the offence for which the Earl was imprisoned, "the manner of his death was related out of the testimony of the Inquest, the Lieutenant of the Tower, certain of the warders, and Pantins; and therefore it was concluded that he had murdered himself with his own hands, out of fear lest his house should be quite overthrown and attainted." After saying that the Earl was, by many good men, much lamented, Camden cautiously adds, "What the suspicious fugitives muttered of one Bailiff that was one of Hatton's men, and was a little before appointed to be the Earl's keeper, I omit as being a matter alto-

[a] Stow's Annals, pp. 706, 707, where a full copy of the Inquisition is given.
[b] Namely, the Lord Chancellor, Lord Burghley, the Earls of Shrewsbury, Derby, and Leicester, the Lords Howard of Effingham and Hunsdon; Sir Francis Knollys, Treasurer; Sir James Croft, Comptroller; Sir Christopher Hatton, Vice-Chamberlain; the Lord Chief Justice of the Queen's Bench, and Chief Baron of the Exchequer, and the Master of the Rolls and others : the audience very great of Knights, Esquires, and men of other quality.—Somers' Tracts, I. 213.

gether unknown unto me, and I think it not meet to
insert anything upon vain hearsays."[a]

The proceedings to which Camden refers are, however, more fully stated in a pamphlet[b] printed in that
year, and apparently by authority, the object of which
publication may be inferred from the opening para-
graph:—" Malice, among other essential properties appertaining to her ugly nature, hath this one not inferior to
the rest, and the worst incredulity wherewith she commonly possesseth the minds and affections of all those that
are infected with her; so blinding the eyes and judgment
of the best and clearest sighted, that they cannot see or
perceive the bright beams of the truth, although the
same be delivered with never so great purity, proof, circumstance, and probability." The author says, he was
present in the Star Chamber when the statements respecting the Earl of Northumberland's death were made, and
took notes of the several matters declared by the Lord
Chancellor, the Attorney-General and Solicitor-General,
the Lord Chief Baron, and the Vice-Chamberlain. Great
part of the pamphlet is occupied with proofs of Northumberland's treasonable conduct; and it was then said by
the Solicitor-General, that, while the Earl was a prisoner
in the Tower, he had, by corrupting his keeper, kept up

[a] Annals, Book III. pp. 50, 51.
[b] "A true and summary Report of
the Declaration of some part of the
Earl of Northumberland's Treasons,
delivered publickly in the Court at
the Star Chamber by the Lord Chancellor and others of her Majesty's
most Honourable Privy Council and
Council learned by her Majesty's
Special Commandment; together
with the Examinations and Depositions of sundry persons touching the
manner of this most wicked and violent Murder, committed upon himself with his own hand in the Tower
of London, the 28th day of June
1585. In ædibus C. Barker, Printer
to the Queen of England her most
excellent Majesty." Reprinted in
Lord Somers' Tracts, ed. Scott, vol.
I. p. 212; and in Howell's "State
Trials," vol. i. p. 1111 et seq.

a communication with Shelley, through his servant James
Price, and had thus learnt, on Friday or Saturday before
Trinity Sunday, (*i. e.* the 4th or 5th of June,) that Shelley had in his confessions so deeply implicated him, that,
" fearing the justice and severity of the laws, and also the
ruin and overthrow of his house, he fell into desperation,
and so to the destruction of himself:" that one Jacques
Pantins, a groom of the Earl's chamber, had stated, that,
on hearing of Shelley's confession, the Earl had declared
he was undone, often with tears lamenting his condition, and wished for death.   The Lord Chief Baron then
described the particulars of the Earl's death, "and in
what sort he had murdered himself."   After mentioning
the Coroner's inquest, he said, that, "upon the discovery
of the intelligence conveyed between the Earl and Shelley, it was thought necessary, for the benefit of her Majesty's service, by such of her Majesty's most honourable
Privy Council as were appointed Commissioners to examine the course of these treasons, that Jacques Pantins,
attending upon the Earl, and the Earl's corrupt keepers,
should be removed; whereupon Thomas Bailiff, gentleman,
sent to attend on the Earl of Northumberland upon the
removal of Palmer and Jacques Pantins from about the
said Earl, who, from the beginning of his last restraint,
attended on him, for the reasons lastly before mentioned,
was, by the Lieutenant of the Tower, on the Sunday,
about two of the clock in the afternoon, being the 20th
of June, shut up with the Earl as appointed, to remain
with him, and serve him in the prison for a time, until
Palmer, Pantins, and Price, then committed close prisoners, might be examined how the Earl came by such
intelligences as were discovered to have passed between

the Earl and Shelley, and between the Earl and others. Bailiff served the Earl at his supper, brought him to his bed about nine of the clock; and after some services done by the Earl's commandment, departed from the Earl to an outer chamber, where he lay part of that night; and being come into his chamber, the Earl rose out of his bed, and came to the chamber door and bolted the same unto him on the inner side, saying to Bailiff, he could not sleep unless his door were fast.   And at about twelve of the clock at midnight, Bailiff being in a slumber, heard a great noise, seeming unto him to be the falling of some door, or rather a piece of the house. The noise was so sudden and so great, that he started out of his bed, and crying out to the Earl with a loud voice, said, 'My Lord, know you what this is?'   The Earl not answering, Bailiff cried and knocked still at the Earl's door, saying, 'My Lord, how do you?' but finding that the Earl made no answer, continued his crying and calling, until an old man that lay without spake to him, saying, 'Gentlemen, shall I call the watch, seeing he will not speak?' 'Yea,' quoth Bailiff, 'for God's sake.'   Then did the old man rise and called one of the watch, whom Bailiff entreated with all possible speed to call Master Lieutenant unto him.   In the mean time, Bailiff heard the Earl give a long and most grievous groan, and after that gave a second groan; and then, the Lieutenant being come, called to the Earl, who, not answering, Bailiff cried to the Lieutenant to break open the Earl's chamber door, bolted unto him on the inner side, which was done, and then they found the Earl dead in his bed, and by his bed-side a dagge, wherewith he had killed himself." Sir Owen Hopton, the Lieutenant of the Tower, deposed upon oath, that on Sunday night, about

a quarter before one o'clock, he was called up by the
watch to come to the Earl of Northumberland, who had
been called to by Mr. Bailiff, his keeper, and would
not speak (as the watch told him); whereupon he went
to the Earl's lodgings, opened the outer doors till he
came to the chamber where Mr. Bailiff lay, which was
next to the Earl's bedchamber; and when he entered
the room, Bailiff said to him that he was wakened with
a noise as if a door or some large thing had fallen, and
that he had called to the Earl, but could obtain no
answer.   Hopton then went to the Earl's chamber;
and, "finding the same bolted fast on the other side
within the Earl's lodging, so as he could not go into
the Earl," he called to him, telling him the Lieutenant
was there, and prayed his Lordship to open the door.
" But, receiving no answer, and finding the door fast
bolted on the inner side of the Earl's chamber with a
strong iron bolt, so as they could not enter into the
same out of the lodging where the said Bailiff lay without breaking up the chamber door, caused the warders,
who were with this examinate, to thrust in their hal-
berds, and to wrest the door thereby as much as they
could, and withal to run at the door with their feet,
and with violence to thrust it open, which they did
accordingly.   And when this examinate came into the
chamber, in turning up the sheets, he perceived them
to be blooded; and then, searching further, found the
wound, which was very near the pap, not thinking at
the first sight but that it had been done with a knife.
This examinate went thereupon presently to write to
the Court, and took the warders into the outer chamber, and left them there until he returned, bolting the
door of the Earl's bedchamber on the outside.   And,

F F

as soon as this examinate returned from writing of his
letter to the Court, he searched about the chamber, and
found a dagge on the floor, about three feet from the
bed, near unto a table that had a green cloth on it,
which did somewhat shadow the dagge; and, after turning down the bed-clothes, found a box, in the which the
powder and pellets were, on the bed under the coverlet.
And saith, that the chamber where the Earl lay hath no
other door but that one door which was broken open
as aforesaid, save one door that went into a privy,
which hath no manner of passage out of it; and that
the Earl's lodging chamber and the entering into the
privy are both walled round about with a stone wall
and a brick wall; and that there is no door or passage
out or from the said Earl's bedchamber or privy but
that only door, which was broken open by the appointment of this examinate."*

Sir Owen Hopton then mentioned the names of the
four warders, who, with his own servant, were present
with him "at the breaking up of the Earl's chamber
door," all of whom were likewise examined, and who confirmed Sir Owen's statements in every point. With respect to there being but "one door in the Earl's chamber,
saving the door of the privy, which, together with the
chamber, was strongly walled about with stone and
brick, the Lord Chief Baron confirmed the same, having
viewed the chamber himself where the Earl lodged, and
was found dead."

At the Coroner's Inquest, James Pantins, the Earl's
groom, confessed that James Price had given the
dag or pistol to the Earl in his, (Pantins') presence,
on which he suspected that his Lordship " meant

* Page. 221.

mischief to himself, and did all he could to persuade
the Earl to send away the dag, but could not prevail;" but that he was commanded to hide it, whereupon he hanged it on a nail within the chimney
in the Earl's bedchamber; where the Earl thinking the
same not to be sufficiently safe in that place, it was by
the Earl's appointment taken from thence and put into
a slit in the side of a mattress, that lay under the Earl's
bed, near to the bed's head; and that the same Sunday
morning that the Earl murdered himself at night, he saw
the dag lying under the Earl's bed head.   The dag
was bought not many days before of one Adrian Mulan,
a dag-maker, dwelling in East Smithfield, as by the
said Mulan was testified, *vivâ voce*, upon his oath, in the
open Court, at the time of the public declaration made
of these matters in the Star Chamber."

It was declared by the Lord Hunsdon and the Lord
Chief Baron, "that the dag wherewith the Earl murdered himself was charged with three bullets, and
so of necessity with more than an ordinary charge of
powder, to force that weight of bullets to work their
effect. The Earl, lying upon his back on the left side
of his bed, took the dag charged in his left hand, (by
all likelihood,) laid the mouth of the dag upon his
left pap, (having first put aside his waistcoat,) and his
shirt being only between the dag and his body, which
was burned away the breadth of a large hand, discharged the same, wherewith was made a large wound in his
said pap, his heart pierced and torn in divers lobes or
pieces, three of his ribs broken, the chine bone of his
back cut almost in sunder, and under the point of the
shoulder-blade, on the right side within the skin, the
three bullets were found by the Lord Hunsdon, which he

caused the Surgeon in his presence to cut out, laying all three close together within the breadth and compass of an inch or thereabout. The bullets were shewed by his Lordship at the time of the publication made in the Court of the Star Chamber." The Lord Chief Baron then noticed the reports that were spread abroad, that the Earl had grown sickly and become weary of his life, from the small and unhealthy apartments in which he was confined, which he refuted by stating their size, having himself measured them; adding, that during the day the Earl had the range of five large chambers, and two long entries.

When the Chief Baron had concluded his address, Sir Christopher Hatton, who, " as it seemed, had been specially employed by her Majesty, among others of her Privy Council, in the looking into and examining of the treasons aforesaid, as well in the person of the Earl as of others, and was at the time of the Earl's commitment from his house in St. Martin's to the Tower of London, sent unto him from her Majesty, to put the Earl in mind of her Majesty's manifold graces and favours in former times conferred upon him, proceeding from the spring of her Majesty's princely and bountiful nature, and not of his deservings, to advise him to deliver the truth of the matters so clearly appearing against him, either by his letters privately to her Majesty, or by speech to Master Vice-Chamberlain, who signified also unto him that if he would determine to take that course, he should not only not be committed to the Tower, but should find grace and favour at her Majesty's hands, in the mitigation of such punishment as the law might lay upon him. And here Master Vice-Chamberlain repeated at length the effect of her Majesty's message, at that time sent to the Earl, beginning first with the remembrance of his practice, undertaken for the conveying away of the Scottish Queen, about the time of the last Rebellion, (as hath been declared in the beginning of this tract,) and that he confessing the offence, being capital, her Majesty nevertheless was pleased to alter the course of his trial by the justice of her laws, and suffered the same to receive a slight and easy punishment by way of mulct or fine of five thousand marks, whereof before this his imprisonment (as it is credibly reported) there was not one penny paid, or his land touched with any extent for the payment thereof; which offence was by her Majesty not only graciously forgiven, but also most christianly forgotten; receiving him not long after to the place of honour that his ancestors had enjoyed for many years before him, and gave him such entrance into her princely favour and good opinion, that no man of his quality received greater countenance and comfort at her Majesty's hands than he; insomuch that in all exercises of recreation used by her Majesty, the Earl was always called to be one; and whensoever her Majesty showed herself abroad in public, she gave to him the honour of the best and highest services about her person, more often than to all the noblemen of her Court."[*]

The evidence that the Earl of Northumberland committed suicide is so satisfactory, that it seems difficult for even religious bigotry or sectarian malice to have raised a doubt on the subject. Independently of the design to destroy himself, and the delivery of the dag, as stated by his servant Pantins, the testimony of Sir Owen Hopton, whose integrity has never been questioned, corroborated by that of five other persons, that the door of the Earl's chamber was so strongly fastened on the inside as to require considerable force to

[*] Somers' Tracts. I. 223.

break it open, that there were no other means of access
to it, and that he himself first·discovered the Earl's
body pierced with bullets, is not to be controverted
by such remarks as that "the change of his keeper,
the great difficulty of conveying fire-arms to a prisoner
in the Tower, and even the solicitude of the Court to
convict him of suicide, served to confirm in the minds
of many, a suspicion that his enemies, unable to bring
home the charge of treason, had removed him by assassination."[*]   But Dr. Lingard's account of Northumberland's death is not written with the impartiality which
distinguishes the earlier part of his valuable work.   He
does not state the cause of the removal of the Earl's servants or keeper, nor that it was done by a committee
of the Privy Council; no notice is taken of the evidence
of Sir Owen Hopton and the warders; the delivery of
the pistol by Price is doubted; and he refers to a letter
from Sir Walter Raleigh to Sir Robert Cecil, in 1601, to
show that "it was assumed as a fact known to them both,
that the Earl was murdered by the contrivance of
Hatton."   In that letter, which was written by Raleigh, to advise Cecil not to relent toward the "tyrant"
Essex, from any fear of consequences to himself, he
says:—"For after-revenges, fear them not; for your
own father, that was esteemed to be the contriver of
Norfolk's ruin, yet his son followeth your father's son,
and loveth him.   Humours of men succeed not, but
grow by occasions and accidents of time and power.
Somerset made no revenge on the Duke of Northumberland's heirs.   Northumberland that now is thinks not
of Hatton's issue.   Kelloway lives that murdered the
brother of Horsey, and Horsey let him go by all his life-

* Lingard, History of England, vol. viii. p. 237.   Murdin's State Papers,
p. 811.

time." Here Raleigh (who was, it may be remarked, Hatton's rival, if not •enemy) first enumerates the persons whose ruin, not murder, had been caused by political enmities; and there is no more reason to believe that Raleigh meant it to be inferred that Hatton had assassinated Northumberland, than that he meant to say that Burghley had murdered Norfolk, or that Dudley had killed the Protector Somerset; and when Raleigh did really mean to allude to "murder," he expressly said so in a separate sentence.

Bishop Kennett relates two traditions in the Percy family, respecting the Earl of Northumberland, which, however valueless, show at least that they did not believe in the assassination of their ancestor. It should be remarked, that the Earl of Essex, who had married this Earl's granddaughter, being a prisoner in the Tower on account of the Rye House Plot, he committed suicide in the same chamber in which Northumberland killed himself. "I have heard a tradition," says Bishop Kennett " from some of the family, that the dag or pistol was sent him inclosed in a cold pie, carried to his table without suspicion. I have heard Dr. Mapletoft, who travelled with the last Earl of Northumberland, say, that it helped much to confirm him in a belief of the Earl of Essex murdering himself in the Tower, because he had seen him pointing at the picture of this Henry Earl of Northumberland, and telling the then heir of the family, ' You owe more to that brave man than to any one of your ancestors; he had the courage to save your estate for you,"ᵇ Meaning that, by having taken away his own life, he had saved his lands from forfeiture.

It has been pertinently observed,ᵃ that Price, who, ac-

ᵇ Lansdowne MSS. 982, f. 75ᵇ.

cording to Pantins, brought the dag to the Earl, was
"not produced, though in custody." It certainly is not
expressly stated that Price was examined; but the printed
accounts of the transaction do not give the names of *all*
the witnesses at the Coroner's Inquest, and it is impossible to believe that Bailiff was not one of the principal,
though his name, like that of Price, is not mentioned.
The insinuation as to the presumed non-examination of
Price is, that the dag, instead of having been brought to
the Earl, belonged in fact to his assassin, which involves
the whole question of the manner of the Earl's death.

The suspicious circumstance of the removal of the
Earl's keeper and servants is explained by their having
conveyed communications to his confederates; and it was
the act of the Privy Councillors, who had been appointed
Commissioners to investigate the subject. Hatton was
no doubt a member of that commission, and may probably
have recommended one of his own retainers to supply their
place, from being well acquainted with his trustworthiness.
That very night, however, the prisoner is found dead in
his bed of a gun-shot wound; and if it were inflicted by
any other hand than his own, suspicion would of course
fix itself very strongly upon Bailiff, as the person nearest
to him, and in whose custody he was; and if he were
thought guilty, it is not surprising that Hatton should
have been suspected, by his enemies, of having prompted
the deed.

To these remarks it will only be added, that there
is not the slightest evidence of any enmity or unkindness
having ever been between the Earl of Northumberland
and Hatton; that, as is well remarked in the pamphlet,
"if men consider the inconvenience happened thereby, as

d Lingard.

well in matter of State as commodity to the Queen's Majesty lost by the prevention of his trial, who can in reason conjecture the Earl to have been murdered of policy or set purpose, as the evil affected seem to conceive ? If the Earl had lived to have received the censure of the law for his offences, all lewd and frivolous objections had then been answered, and all his goods, chattels, and lands by his attainder had come unto her Majesty, and the honour and State and prosperity been utterly overthrown ;" that, if it were desired to assassinate a prisoner, poison or the dagger were far preferable instruments to fire-arms; and that, though Hatton and other courtiers might, and probably would, have gained by the forfeiture of the Earl's lands had he been executed, they derived no advantage whatever from an act which secured his estates to his family.[a]

The Letter Book contains few letters written in 1586, and scarcely any of them are of much interest. No fact relating to Hatton has been found before August, except that in February, when the Earl of Leicester had excited the Queen's anger by his proceedings in the Low Countries, Hatton, knowing her weak point, advised him " to bestow some two or three hundred crowns in some rare thing for a token to her Majesty."[b]

MR. SAMUEL COX TO   . . . . .

SIR, Your letter being so full freighted with matters of great moment, makes me fear what to write, in respect of my inabi-

[a] It is much to be regretted that Lord Campbell did not, as might reasonably be expected of the biographer of a Lord Chancellor charged with so foul a crime as assassination, investigate all the evidence on this subject; for, had it been sifted by his great legal acumen and practical experience, the conclusion to which he might have arrived would have had great weight. As, however, his Lordship has merely mentioned facts, in a single sentence, without referring to any authority whatever, it may be doubted if he even saw the Inquisition in Stow, or the pamphlet in Somers and Howell.

[b] The Hardwicke State Papers, I. 299.

lity to answer it to your good contentment. Your news of the
blustering winds abroad, threatening (as you fearfully suspect)
some approaching inward storms at home, will, I hope, deceive you, and show you to be no great divine. The Pagan
philosophers that would take upon them to prognosticate over
boldly, would yet plainly affirm for truth, that *nulla est astro-
rum necessitas.* I am no philosopher, but your poor friend,
and I may say to you, I hope, without offence, man's conjec-
tures of future things, are but dreams and mere imaginations,
no divinations when reason hath well wakened his spirits.
Our long blessings of peace are the wonderful graces of God,
collated upon us, his unworthy people, for the which I
beseech him to make us thankful. Yet am I afraid, that they
do many times fare with us, as our sweet things do with man's
body; which corrupt nature with their great dulcetness, and
filleth the blood with undigested waterishness, making it apt
to boil and putrefy: such peril carrieth security with it, and so
sweet hath our peace been, that I fear it will bring somewhat
with it, that will be sour and loathsome in the end. Dulce
things are nourishing, but yet (as the physician saith) accompanied with loathing, honey is sweet and comfortable, but yet
it inflameth swiftly, engendereth choler: our long happy peace,
through her Majesty's provident care and goodness hath been
a restorative, or rather a preservative as you term it, of the
Kingdom and poor people; but I doubt greatly that (as dulce
things carry with them their dregs, which we take great delight to taste of notwithstanding, whereof oppilations do rise in
the stomach, through the operation of the gross substance,
wherein the savouriness of sweetness is grounded,) so will the
over sweet food of our long tranquillity so comfort and restore
the liver and spleen of our estate and country, (members
naturally thirsting after sweetness,) that the pure fine blood
of it (which is religion and justice) will be corrupted, and the
lungs, lights, and the very heart itself, shortly putrefied, if
(like good physicians) we look not to the nocuments in time,
and first remove their causes, whereby to avoid the perilous
effects, which otherwise must needs ensue; which I pray God

her Majesty may do happily and timely, but ever safely for the preservation of her royal person, whose health is our earthly life, and whose death will be the destruction and desolation of us all, as in the which we shall most miserably stifle and perish. God direct it from us in his clemency and goodness, to whose gracious favour I commit you. From the Court at Greenwich, the 7th of July 1586. Your poor friend fastly faithful,   SAMUEL COX.[a]

The following letter shows that Hatton, being seriously ill, had retired to Holdenby towards the end of August. The "horrible practices" to which he alludes, was the well-known conspiracy of Babington to assassinate the Queen;

SIR CHRISTOPHER HATTON TO LORD BURGHLEY.

ASSUREDLY, my good Lord, I find myself much bound to you for your oft and most honourable letters. I find thereby the time is deferred, and I fear the cause in this course will receive some prejudice. Is it not possible that, with the eye of her Majesty's wisdom, these most horrible and dangerous practices may be thoroughly looked into? Surely, Sir, if she did, there would be no days given to the prevention of them. God hath mightily defended us. He is all and *EveR* one. I beseech Him that these our negligences may not tempt Him.

I am come sick to my poor house, full of a fever, with stitches, spitting of blood, and other bad accidents. I must commit myself to God and the physician for awhile; and though your access hither be further off than before, yet, Sir, by reason of my sickness I cannot return; whereof (because such it seemed was her pleasure,) I most humbly beseech you to excuse me, for in truth I am very evil. God bless your good Lordship for *EveR*. Haste, from my poor house at Holdenby, the 2nd of September 1586. Your good Lordship's most bound poor friend,   CHR. HATTON.[b]

[a] Additional MSS. 15896, f. 137.   [b] Autograph in the State Paper Office.

Sir Christopher Hatton was, it appears, also one of the Privy Councillors by whom Mary's secretaries, Nau and Curle, were examined; for on the 4th of September, Burghley wrote to him, "that they would yield somewhat to confirm their mistress, if they were persuaded that themselves might escape, and the blow fall upon their mistress, betwixt her head and shoulders."[a]

Ill as Hatton describes himself to have been on the 2nd of September, he was able to return to London, and to sit as one of the Commissioners on the trial of the conspirators, Babington, Chidoke, Titchbourne, Savage, Abington, Ballard, Gage, Donn, and others, for high-treason, at Westminster, on the 13th, 14th, and 15th of that month. It is deserving of attention, as accounting in some degree for his subsequent elevation to the Woolsack, that Hatton took as prominent a part in those proceedings as any of the Judges.[b] When Savage had pleaded "guilty" to two and "not guilty" to one of the charges against him, and was told by Chief Justice Anderson and Chief Baron Manwood, that he must answer directly "guilty" or "not guilty," Hatton added, "To say that thou art guilty to that, and not to this, is no plea; for thou must either confess it generally, or deny it generally; wherefore delay not the time, but say either guilty or not; and if thou say guilty, then shalt thou hear further, if not guilty, her Majesty's learned counsel is ready to give evidence against thee." On the Attorney-General's saying "Now I hope is Savage's indictment sufficiently and fully proved," Hatton observed, "Savage, I must ask thee one ques-

[a] Lingard's History of England ed., 1838, vol. VIII., p. 219, who refers to this letter in Leigh's collection.

[b] Lord Campbell considers, that, "although the two Chief Justices and Chief Baron were present, Hatton took the lead in the conduct of the trial," p. 142.

tion: Was not all this willingly and voluntarily confessed by thyself, without menacing, without torture, or without offer of any torture?" to which he simply replied "Yes."* When it was proposed to adjourn the Court, Hatton signified its consent, and stated what would be the course of proceeding on the next day.

On the 14th, Ballard was called upon to plead, and saying "I answer as my case is," he, like Savage on the preceding day, was told by the Chief Justice either to deny the indictment generally, or to confess it generally; and Hatton added, "Ballard, under thine own hand are all things confessed; therefore now it is much vanity to stand vaingloriously in denying it."—"Then, Sir," said Ballard "I confess I am guilty." The Vice-Chamberlain's indignation against the prisoners was sometimes displayed in a manner which would not now be considered decorous in a Judge, though such conduct was then by no means uncommon. Donn confessing, that, when he was made privy to those treasons, "he always prayed unto God that that might be done which was to his honour and glory;" Hatton observed, "Then it was thus, that they said 'The Queen should be killed,' and thou saidst 'God's will be done!';" and Donn answering, "Yes, Sir," Hatton exclaimed, "O wretch! wretch! thy conscience and own confession show that thou art guilty."—"Well, Sir, then I confess I am guilty."

There was much of natural pity in Hatton's remark on Babington's statement, that he was partly seduced by Ballard's persuasions. "O Ballard, Ballard, what hast thou done? A sort of brave youths, otherwise endued with good gifts, by thy inducement

* Lord Campbell says, "the poor wretch, in the vain hope of mercy, eagerly replied 'Yes;'" but the motive and the eagerness of the reply are known only to his Lordship.

hast thou brought to their utter destruction and confusion." Ballard finished his reply to Babington's charge with the words "Howbeit, say what you will; I will say no more:" on which Hatton said "Nay, Ballard, you must say more, and shall say more, for you must not commit high treasons, and then huddle them up. But is this thy *Religio Catholica?* nay rather it is *Diabolica!*"

Barnwell declared that what he had done was only for conscience sake, and that he never intended any violence to her Majesty's person; on hearing which Hatton broke out with, "O Barnwell, Barnwell, didst thou not come to Richmond, and, when her Majesty walked abroad, didst not thou there view her and all her company, what weapons they had, how she walked alone? and didst traverse the ground, and thereupon coming back to London, didst make relation to Babington how it was a most easy matter to kill her Majesty, and what thou hadst seen and done at the Court: Yes, I know thou didst so. How canst thou then say that thou never didst intend to lay violent hands on her Majesty? Nay, I can assure thee moreover, and it is most true which I say, that her Majesty did know that thou didst come to that end, and she did see and mark thee how thou didst view her and her company; but had it been known to some there as well as unto her, thou had never brought news to Babington. Such is the magnanimity of our Sovereign, which God grant be not over much in not fearing such traitors as thou."[*] Barnwell replied.—"What I did was only for my conscience sake, and not for any malice or hatred to

---

* Upon this speech Lord Campbell, with some justice, remarks, that Hatton, "taking all this for confessed, he then, without being sworn, gives some evidence himself." It is, however, probable that most of the facts had been stated by Barnwell in his previous examination before the Privy Council.

her Majesty's person," upon which Hatton said, " Then wouldst thou have killed the Queen for conscience. Fie on such a devilish conscience!"[a]

At the conclusion of the proceedings "then began Sir Christopher Hatton, and made an excellent good speech in opening and setting forth their treasons, and how they all proceeded from the wicked priests, the ministers of the Pope. And first he showed how these wicked and devilish youths had conspired to murder the Queen's most excellent Majesty; secondly, to bring in Foreign invasion; thirdly, to deliver the Queen of Scots and make her Queen; fourthly,[b] to sack the City of London; fifthly, to rob and destroy all the wealthy subjects of this Realm; sixthly, to kill divers of the Privy Council, as the Earl of Leicester, the Lord Treasurer, Mr. Secretary, Sir Ralph Sadler, Sir Amias Paulet; seventhly, to set fire on all the Queen's ships; eighthly, to cloy all the great ordnance; ninthly, and lastly, to subvert religion and the whole state of government. The inventors and beginners whereof were these devilish priests and seminaries, against whom he doubted the Parliament had not yet sufficiently provided, who now a days do not go about to seduce the ancient and discreet men, for they (as the priests say) be too cold; but they assail with their persuasions the younger sort, and of those the most ripe wits, whose high hearts and ambitious minds do carry them headlong to all wickedness. In the end he concluded with remorse for the youth of some of these unhappy men, and with detestation of the facts of Ballard; and also shewed forth a notable proof of the falsehood of these lying Papists, which was a book printed at Rome, and made by the Papists, wherein

[a] Page 134.
[b] These charges were, Lord Campbell observes, " unsupported by any evidence."

they affirm, that the English Catholics, which suffer for religion, be lapped in bear-skins, and baited to death with dogs,—a most monstrous lie and manifest falsehood.

"Then spake my Lord Anderson to the like effect, almost in every point, in abhorring the abomination of the Jesuits and Seminaries; and in the end concluded with an exhortation for the health of their souls; and last of all pronounced the terrible sentence of their condemnation."[a]

On the trial of Abington, Tilney, Jones, and others, on the 15th of September, Sir Christopher Hatton again took a prominent and less creditable part.   When Abington asked to be allowed a pair of writing-tables, to set down what was alleged against him, and was informed by the Clerk of the Crown that "it was never the course here," Hatton said, "When you hear anything you are desirous to answer, you shall speak an answer at full, which is better than a pair of tables."   In the course of the proceedings, the Attorney-General, addressing Hatton, said, "Mr. Vice-Chamberlain, you desired Abington to set down the truth of these things; thereupon he set down a great deal in writing, and yesterday he tore it in a hundred pieces, and here Mr. Lieutenant of the Tower hath given me the pieces, and here they be." On which Sir Christopher Hatton observed, "Abington, you be very obstinate, and seem indurate in these treasons." The prisoner then answered the charges at some length; and concluded by saying that Babington's accusation was of no weight, for, having committed and confessed treason in the highest degree, "there was no hope for him but to accuse."—"For Babington's hope thereof," said Hatton, "I am persuaded he hath no hope at all; and my Lords here can assure there is no hope at all of his life: but

* Hargrave's State Trials, folio I., pp. 127-134.

he confessed what he knew for discharge of his conscience, and what he did, he did it willingly and voluntarily; for had not Babington voluntarily named Abington, who could have named Abington? and had he not also willingly accused Tilney, who could have accused Tilney?" Hatton showed some kindness to one of the conspirators called Charnock, for when he entreated him to induce the Queen to pardon him, he said, " Charnock, thy offence is too high for me to be an obtainer of thy pardon, but I am sorry for thee, if thou hadst applied thyself the best way, thou mightest have done thy Country good service." The prisoner said, " I beseech you then that six angels, which such a one hath of mine, may be delivered unto my brother to pay my debts." " How much" asked Hatton " is thy debts?" and being told that the six angels would discharge it, Hatton replied, " then I promise thee it shall be paid."[*]

The following letter from Babington was probably addressed to one of the conspirators, two of whom were called Robert, namely, Barnwell and Gage:—

ANTHONY BABINGTON TO . . . .

Robyn, *Non solicitæ possunt curæ mutare rati stamina fusi.* I am ready to endure what shall be inflicted: *Et facere et pati magna, Romanum.* What my courses have been towards Mr. Secretary you can witness; what my love towards you, yourself will confess. Their proceedings at my lodging have been strange. Look to your own part, lest of these my infortunes you bear the blame. I am the same I pretended. I pray God you have been and ever remain so towards me. *Est exilium inter malos vivere.* Farewell, my sweet Robyn, if (as I take thee,) true to me; if not, adieu, *omnium bipedum iniquissimus.* Return thine answer for my satisfaction, and my

* Howell's State Trials, vol. i. pp. 1127—1162.

diamond, and what else you wilt. The furnace is made, wherein thy faith must now be tried. Farewell till we meet, which God knows when. Yours, you know how far,

ANTHONY BABINGTON.[a]

The disclosures of the conspirators caused a Commission to be issued on the 6th of October for the trial of the Queen of Scots. Hatton was appointed one of the Commissioners, and they left London for Fotheringay before the 8th, and assembled there on the 11th of that month. It appears, that when not engaged in the proceedings, Hatton remained at Apthorpe, the seat of Sir Walter Mildmay, another of the Commissioners, which was about five miles from Fotheringay; and that on the 13th, Mr. Conway arrived from the Queen, with some special communication which had a "little daunted" him, and who brought back the following reply:—

SIR CHRISTOPHER HATTON TO THE QUEEN.

MAY IT PLEASE YOUR SACRED MAJESTY, Your princely goodness towards me is so infinite, as in my poor wit I am not able to comprehend the least part thereof. I must therefore fail in duty of thankfulness as your Mutton, and lay all upon God, with my humble prayers to requite you in Heaven and Earth in the most sincere and devout manner, that, through God's grace, I may possibly devise. Your Majesty's good servant, Mr. Conway, hath taken a wonderful sore journey. He hath from your Majesty a little daunted me. I most humbly crave your Majesty's pardon. God and your Majesty

[a] Additional MSS. 15891, f. 135b.

be praised I have recovered my perfect health; and if now for my ease or pleasure I should be found negligent in your service, I were much unworthy of that life which many a time your Royal Majesty hath given me. I might likewise sustain some obloquy, whereof I have heard somewhat; but my will and wit, and whatever is in me, shall be found assuredly yours, whether I be sick or whole, or what *EveR* become of me deem they what pleaseth them. God in Heaven bless your Majesty, and grant me no longer life than that my faith and love may *EveR* be found inviolable and spotless to so royal and peerless a Princess. At Apthorpe, this 13th of October 1586. Your Royal Majesty's most bounden poor slave,

Chr. Hatton.*

Mary, having refused to acknowledge the competency of the tribunal, or to appear before it, Hatton represented to her on the 13th, that she "was accused (but not condemned,) to have conspired the destruction of our Lady and Queen anointed. You say you are a Queen. Be it so. But in such a crime the Royal dignity is not exempted from answering, neither by the Civil nor Canon law, nor by the law of nations nor of nature. For if such kind of offences might be committed without punishment, all justice would stagger, yea, fall to the ground. If you be innocent, you wrong your reputation in avoiding trial. You protest yourself to be innocent, but Queen Elizabeth thinketh otherwise, and that neither without grief and sorrow for the same. To examine, therefore, your innocency, she hath appointed for Commissioners most honourable, prudent, and upright men, who are ready to hear you according to equity with favour, and will rejoice with all their hearts if you shall clear yourself of this crime. Believe me, the Queen herself will be much

---

* Autograph in the State Paper Office.

affected with joy, who affirmed unto me, at my coming from her, that never anything befel her more grievous than that you were charged with such a crime.   Wherefore lay aside the bootless privilege of Royal dignity, which now can be of no use unto you, appear in judgment, and show your innocency, lest, by avoiding trial, you draw upon yourself suspicion, and lay upon your reputation an eternal blot and aspersion." [a]

The next day, Mary sent for some of the Commissioners, and said she consented to appear, as " she was very desirous to purge herself of the crime objected against her, being persuaded by Hatton's reasons, which she had weighed with advisement." [b]   The trial accordingly took place on the 15th; and at its conclusion Mary, being asked if she wished to say any more, replied that " she required that she might be heard in a full Parliament, or that she might in person speak with the Queen and with the Council; " and then, " rising up with great confidence of countenance, she had some conference with the Lord Treasurer, Hatton, Walsingham, and the Earl of Warwick, by themselves apart." [c]   The Commissioners re-assembled at Westminster on the 25th of October, and pronounced their iniquitous sentence.

To the new Parliament, which met on the 15th of October, but was adjourned to the 29th, Hatton was again returned for Northamptonshire; and he resumed his position as Leader of the House of Commons.   On the 5th of November he declared, that the principal cause of summoning Parliament arose out of the late conspiracy against her Majesty, at the instigation of the Queen of Scots, tending to the ruin of the true religion established,

---

[a] Camden's Annals, b. iii. p. 37.   [b] Ibid. p. 88.   [c] Ibid. p. 96.

the invasion of the Realm, rebellion and civil wars :
" Yea, and withal, which his heart quaked and trembled
to utter and think on, the death and destruction of the
Queen's most sacred person, to the utter desolation and
conquest of this most noble realm of England!" After
dilating, at some length, on the execrable treacheries
and conspiracies of the Scottish Queen, he said, that
" speedy consultation must be had by this House for the
cutting of her off by course of justice;" for that otherwise the Queen's person would not be safe; and concluded his speech with these words, "Ne pereat Israel,
pereat Absolon."[a] Both Houses agreed to present a petition to the Queen, entreating her to order the execution
of the Queen of Scots; and the following letter, which
was marked to be sent "with all possible speed," relates
to the presentation of that petition, which took place on
the 12th of November. Davison had been made Secretary of State, and sworn of the Privy Council on the
30th of September :—

LORD BURGHLEY AND SIR CHRISTOPHER HATTON TO MR. SECRETARY DAVISON.

MR. SECRETARY, Whereas I the Treasurer perceive by the
report of me the Vice-Chamberlain, that her Majesty could
be content that the coming of the Lords of Parliament and
the Commons should be rather to-morrow than on Saturday.
In very truth so would we both have it ; but the dispersing of
both Houses is such, as the Lords have prorogued their Sessions until Monday or Tuesday, and therefore not possible to
give the Lords appointed warning to come afore Saturday,
and in like sort it will be to-morrow nine o'clock before the
Commons assemble ; wherefore we both pray this night you
to make our excuse herein to her Majesty, and in the morning

---

[a] Parliamentary History, vol. i. p. 836.

also there will be two or three Lords with her Majesty, to require audience of her Majesty; and thus being late in the evening, this Thursday, the 10th of November 1586, we bid you farewell.   Your assured loving friend,

W. BURGHLEY.   C. HATTON.[*]

On the 14th of November, after the Speaker had reported the Queen's answer to the petition, Hatton rose, and having first affirmed that the Speaker's report was true, he added, that the Queen had commanded him that morning to signify to the House, "that her Highness, moved with some commiseration for the Scottish Queen, in respect of her former dignity and great fortunes in her younger years, her nearness of kindred to her Majesty, and also of her sex, could be well pleased to forbear taking of her blood, if by any other means, to be devised by the Great Council of this Realm, the safety of her Majesty's person and government might be preserved without danger of ruin and destruction.   But herein she left them, nevertheless, to their own free liberty and dispositions of proceeding otherwise at their choice; for as her Majesty would willingly hearken to the reasons of any particular Member of this House, so, he added, they might exhibit their thoughts in that case, either to any of the Privy Council, being of that House, or to the Speaker, to be by him delivered to her Majesty."   He then reminded the House, that at the commencement of the Session the Queen had intimated her pleasure that no laws should be made in this Session; and moved the adjournment of the House to the 18th of November, during which interval the Queen might, he said, send some other answer to their petition, which she had not yet read.

* Original in the State Paper Office.

On that day the House again met, and, after many speeches, came to the resolution, "That no other way, device, or means whatsoever could or can possibly be found or imagined, that such safety can in any wise be had, so long as the said Queen of Scots doth or shall live." [a]

The French Ambassador was suspected of having tampered with William Stafford, the son of one of the Ladies of the Queen's bedchamber, to take away her life, through Du Trapp, his secretary; " but Stafford as detesting the fact refused to do it, yet commanded one Moody, a notable hackster, a man forward of his hands, as one who, for money, would, without doubt, despatch the matter resolutely :" [b]—

TO LORD BURGHLEY.

MAY IT PLEASE YOUR GOOD LORDSHIP, This evening we have had Moody before us, with whom notwithstanding we have dealt very roundly, yet can we draw nothing of substance from him. We have, therefore, thought it convenient to send to Mr. Randolph for his prisoner to be brought hither to-morrow, very early in the morning, to the end, that if we find this man to persist in his denial, he may be confronted with him as one that hath opened matter enough to touch them both by his own confession. We have likewise thought it fit to send very early in the morning for the keeper of Newgate, and one Romane his servant, with two other prisoners named by Stafford to have been by at his access to Moody, to examine them, touching the point of Du Trapp's resort unto him, wherein, as in the rest of our proceeding, we will use that care of secrecy which both the matter requireth, and her Majesty expecteth,—and in the meantime beseech your Lordship to advertise us, whether you think this course of confronting the parties fit or no for this first meeting, that we

[a] Parliamentary History, i. 843.   [b] Camden's Annals, b. iii. p. 105.

may proceed accordingly.   And if in the morning we find any
further matter worthy the advertisement, we will not fail
immediately to make your Lordship partaker thereof, otherwise, at our return to the Court in the evening, to bring the
report ourselves how we find the same.   And so we humbly
and heartily take our leaves this Friday night, at ten of the
clock the 6th of January 1586 [1587.]   Your Lordship's at
commandment,   CHR. HATTON
                                                    W. DAVISON.*

SIR CHRISTOPHER HATTON AND MR. SECRETARY DAVISON TO LORD BURGHLEY.

MAY IT PLEASE YOUR GOOD LORDSHIP, According to that
I the Secretary did signify to your Lordship this morning,
Du Trapp was brought very closely to this place; where,
after some little stay, we thought it good for the better clearing of the truth to sound what he could say to the matters objected against him by Stafford; who, after some vehement protestations, that he would deal plainly, as before God, respecting
more his Honour than either Ambassador, or any other whatsoever, he offered to set down as much as he could say with his
own hand, which we thought not amiss to yield unto, till we had
prepared some other matter to offer unto him by way of examination; whereof at the return of me, the Secretary, to the
Court this evening, your Lordship shall receive the particularities.   Since, we have again called Moody before us, and
spent some time and labour with him, who standing resolute
in his denial at his first coming, doth now begin to relent; and
having confessed the access of Du Trapp unto him, we nothing doubt his coming on with the rest.   We find already
that Stafford's discoveries are no fables; albeit Moody seems
resolved to lay the original and ground of this practice upon
Stafford, protesting his own fault to be chiefly in concealment
thereof; which, as he saith, he did for the respect of his brother being his master, and the rest of that honourable House

* Original in the State Paper Office.

of which Stafford is descended: he hath now likewise offered to discourse the whole cause in writing, wherein he is presently occupied. What it will fall out to be, your Lordship shall understand this evening. In the meantime it may please your Lordship to acquaint her Majesty with our proceeding thus far, to the end we may have her Highness' most gracious directions for our dealing in this unhappy action. And so we humbly take our leaves. At Ely-place, this 7th of January 1586 [1587]. Your Lordship's at commandment,

CHR. HATTON. W. DAVISON.*

Parliament met on the 15th of February; and on the 22nd Sir Christopher Hatton, by the Queen's command, acquainted the House of Commons with the threatened invasion by Spain. In a long speech he said, that the dangers the Nation then stood in arose from ancient malice against the Queen, and traced them to their root, the Council of Trent, "which agreed to extirpate the Christian religion, termed by them heresy, to which divers Princes had assented, and solemnly bound themselves." He divided his speech into five heads; the Catholics abroad, the Pope, the King of Spain, the Princes of the League, the Papists at home and their Ministers. After adverting to the various proceedings against this Country by the Pope, and the intended invasion by the King of Spain, he observed, that, "if we serve God in sincerity of heart, we need not fear." He then stated the force of the Spanish Armada in ships and troops, and pointed out the expediency of assisting the Low Countries, "the head of whose miseries was the Spanish Inquisition, by placard, using strange tortures not to be suffered." He repeated that "the great grief was religion," said, that all godly persons were bound to defend it; and

* Murdin's State Papers, p. 578.

concluded his address by commending the Queen's courage, "which was not less than that of the stoutest Kings in Europe."[a] On the 1st of March, several questions were submitted by Mr. Wentworth, respecting freedom of debate,[b] which the Speaker refused to put; but having showed them to Sir Thomas Heneage, Wentworth, and four other Members who had spoken on the subject, were committed to the Tower. On the 4th of March, it was moved that the Queen be petitioned to restore those Members to the House, when Hatton said, "that if the gentlemen were committed for matter within the compass of the privilege of the House, then there might be room for a petition; but if not, we shall occasion her Majesty's further displeasure." He rather advised them to stay till they heard more, which could not be long; and further, as to the book and petition, her Majesty had, for divers good causes best known to herself, thought fit to suppress the same, without any further examination of them; and yet he conceived it very unfit for her Majesty to give any account of her actions.[c] Parliament was dissolved on the 23rd of the same month.

Between the years 1582 and 1587, Hatton received large grants of lands. In August 1582, he obtained the manor of Parva Weldon, in Northamptonshire, and various lands in other counties; in 1585, the keepership of the Forest of Rockingham and the Isle of Purbeck were granted to him; in 1586, the site of the monastery of Buer, in Oxfordshire, and several manors in other parts of England; in January 1587, the domain of Naseby, in

[a] Parliamentary History, i. 847—850.
[b] Dr. Parry, in his very accurate, useful, and learned, though little known, "Parliaments and Councils of England," says, "No historian takes notice of the commitment of Mr. Wentworth and his companions." 8vo. 1839, p. 230.
[c] Ibid, pp. 852, 853.

Northamptonshire; and in July, being then Chancellor, the manor and rectory of West Drayton, and a tenement called Perry Place, in Middlesex, part of the lands forfeited by Lord Paget, were bestowed upon him.[a] It appears, moreover, that he had partaken largely of the estates forfeited by the rebels in Ireland, as, in September 1587, he held the castles and lands of Knockmoan, Cloyne, Kill, and Ballynecourty, alias Courts Town, with various baronies and other lands in the county of Waterford, which had belonged to Richard Fitz Morice, the Fitz Thomases, or to the Earl of Desmond.[b] On the 21st of May he was authorised to grant letters of denizenship to aliens, at his discretion, during the Queen's pleasure, though it is laid down in the strongest terms by Lord Coke and Blackstone, that the Crown cannot delegate that power to any Subject, "it being by the law itself so inseparably and individually annexed to the Royal person;"[c] and on the same day he received a warrant for the payment of the "fees, reward, and diet" appertaining to his office of Chancellor.[d] On the 12th of September he was appointed Lieutenant, or as that officer is now called, Lord Lieutenant of Northamptonshire.[e]

In the proceedings respecting the dispatch of the warrant for the execution of the Queen of Scots, Hatton took a prominent part. On the 2nd of February 1587, when Davison began to feel uneasy about the Queen's intentions, he went to the Vice-Chamberlain and communicated all the circumstances, adding that he was determined not to proceed any further in the affair by himself,

---

[a] Rot. Patent, 27, 28, 29, Eliz. passim.

[b] Book entitled "The Undertaker's Lands in Munster," sent on the 4th of September, 1587, in the State Paper Office.

[c] Seventh Report 25[b]. Calvin's Case.

[d] Rot. Patent, 29 Eliz.

[e] Ibid.

but would leave it to Hatton and others to determine what should be done. The Vice-Chamberlain then said, that, "as he was heartily glad the matter was brought thus far, so did he for his own part wish him hanged that would not join with Davison in the furtherance thereof, being a cause so much importing the common safety and tranquillity of her Majesty and the whole Realm;" and resolved to go with Davison to Lord Burghley, and confer with him on the subject. They accordingly did so, when it was determined to assemble the Council the next day; and in the mean time Burghley undertook to draw up the letters necessary to accompany the warrant, which Davison delivered into his hands. The next morning Burghley sent for Hatton and Davison, and showed them the draught of the letters; but Hatton finding them "very particular, and such as, in truth, the warrant could not bear," showed his disapprobation of them, and appeared to dislike their contents even more than he expressed. Burghley offered to write others in more general terms by the afternoon; and they agreed to assemble the Privy Council immediately, which met within an hour in Burghley's chamber. His Lordship then addressed them on the Scottish Queen's offences, and the necessity of executing the sentence; said that in signing the warrant, the Queen had done all that either reason or the law required of her; stated what had taken place between Her Majesty and Davison, but that Davison had refused to act alone; that as they were all equally interested, he thought they should make it a general and common cause; and that the warrant should be despatched without any further reference to the Queen. Each of the members of the Council having offered to take his share of the responsibility, it was resolved to for-

ward the warrant by Mr. Beale, the Clerk of the Council;
and the letters proposed by Burghley to accompany it,
being approved, they were ordered to be drawn up by
the evening.   The Council then separated, and went to
dinner, but met again at two o'clock, when the letters
were signed, and given to Beale, with express and urgent
directions to use the utmost expedition in proceeding to
Fotheringay.[a]   The Privy Councillors who were present
at those proceedings, and who signed the letters, were
Lord Burghley, the Earls of Derby and Leicester, Lords
Howard, Hunsdon and Cobham, Sir Francis Knollys,
Sir Christopher Hatton, Sir Francis Walsingham, and
Mr. Davison.[b]   No sooner had information arrived that
the sentence was executed than Elizabeth sent for
Hatton, and assured him that she was ignorant of the
act, and that it was entirely against her intentions.
Though her assumed indignation lighted upon all her
Ministers, it fell principally upon Davison, who was
committed to the Tower on the 14th of February; and
while in confinement he underwent three examinations.
Sir Christopher Hatton and Mr. Wolley, were first sent
to him on the 12th of March, when the following " articles were ministered to him :"—

WHETHER upon signing of the warrant, her Majesty gave it
not in express charge and commandment unto you to keep the
same secret, and not to utter it to anybody ? He answereth that
he hopeth her Majesty doth not forget how she commanded
my Lord Admiral to send for him to bring the warrant to her,
having, as his Lordship told me, resolutely determined to go
through with the execution.   Upon my coming to her, it
pleased her to call for the warrant, and voluntarily to sign it,

---

[a] Life of Davison, 8vo. 1823, Appendix A and B.

[b] Ibid p. 97, and Ellis's Original
Letters, Second Series, vol. III. p. 111.

without giving me any such commandment as is objected,
which he confirmeth in the presence of God. Other interrogatories made and bold answers given, 16th March 1586-7.[a]

Davison's own account of the examinations contains
the "other interrogatories," and his "bold answers."[b]
It does not appear by whom the examinations on the
14th and 16th of March, were made; but, as is well
known, Davison was sacrificed to the Queen's cruel and
selfish policy. It is remarkable, however, that neither
Hatton nor any other of the Queen's Ministers, who
signed the letters that accompanied the warrant for
Mary's execution, was present in the Star Chamber on
the 28th of March, when Davison was sentenced to be
heavily fined and imprisoned, except Sir James Croft, the
Comptroller, who, however, had the modesty and good
sense to say little on the occasion.

Great as had been the favours lavished upon Hatton
-by his Sovereign, the Country was not prepared for the
extraordinary promotion which raised him to the highest
office in the Realm, and imposed upon him judicial duties
of the most important nature. On the 12th of April,
Lord Chancellor Bromley died, and the Great Seal was
sent in the evening to the Queen, at Greenwich; and
except on two pressing occasions, it remained in her
hands. The Queen appointed the Earl of Rutland, " a
profound lawyer, and accomplished with all excellent
learning," to succeed Bromley,[c] but he died six days

[a] Lansdowne MSS. 982, f. 97.
[b] Life of Davison, Appendix E.
[c] Camden, b. III. p. 127. In his
original work (ed. 1615, p. 475)
Camden, after mentioning the death
of Chancellor Bromley, says, "Et
sexto post die, qui illi successor à
Regina destinatus, Edwardus Rut-

landiæ Comes ex Maneiorum," &c.
In his own translation, Camden's
words are, "And the sixth day after
[died] Edward Earl of Rutland,
whom the Queen had appointed to
be his successor," &c. This posi-
tive statement of a learned contemporary writer is thus misrepresented

afterwards, before he had received the Great Seal; and on Saturday, the 29th of that month, she delivered it to Sir Christopher Hatton, and appointed him Lord Chancellor of England. The ceremony is thus described: the Court was then at the Archbishop of Canterbury's palace at Croydon; and about four o'clock in the afternoon, in a private ambulatory or gallery, near her private chamber, and in the presence of the Archbishop and some other personages of high rank, her Majesty took the Seal, which was lying in a red velvet bag in a window, into her own hands, and carried it to the centre of the gallery. She then delivered it to Hatton, but immediately received it back again, and commanded it to be taken out of the bag. The Seal was then affixed to an instrument, and replaced in the bag, when the Queen re-delivered it to Hatton; and she "then and there made and constituted the said Sir Christopher Hatton, Lord Chancellor of England."[a]

It was to be expected that the appointment of any one, except an eminent lawyer, to the office of Lord Chancellor, would excite the astonishment, if not the enmity of the Bar. "The great lawyers of England," says

---

by Lord Campbell:—"Camden says, there was a speculation likewise at Court, that Edward Earl of Rutland would be appointed Chancellor, had he not suddenly died," p. 137.

[a] Rot. Claus. 29 Eliz. p. 42, [d] printed in Lord Campbell's Life of Hatton, p. 147. No authority has been found, and his Lordship does not cite any, to justify the following observations. After the execution of Mary, says the noble biographer, "balls and masques were resumed, and being still the handsomest man and the best drest, and the most gallant, and the best dancer at Court, he gained new consequence, pretend-ing to become an orator and a statesman." "Love and gratitude filled the mind of Elizabeth, and after some misgivings, whether he who would have made a most excellent Lord Chamberlain, was exactly fitted for the duties of Lord Chancellor, resolved to appoint him. The intention was, however, kept a profound secret from all except Burghley, till the time when the deed was done." "Some of the Courtiers at first thought that this ceremony [the delivery of the Great Seal] was a piece of wicked pleasantry on the part of the Queen," &c. pp. 146, 147.

Camden, "took it very offensively, for they, ever after the ecclesiastical men were put from this degree, had with singular commendations for equity and wisdom, borne this highest place of gowned dignity, bestowed in old time for the most part upon churchmen and noblemen. But Hatton was advanced thereunto through the cunning Court practices of some, that by his absence from Court, and troublesome Office of so great a magistracy, for which they knew him to be insufficient, his favour with the Queen might be abated. Yet bare he the place with the greatest state of all that ever we saw, and what was lacking in him in knowledge of the law, he laboured to supply by equity and justice."[a]

Speaking of Hatton's appointment, Fuller says, " The gownsmen grudging hereat, conceived his advancement their injury, that one not thoroughly bred to the laws, should be preferred to the place. How could he cure diseases, unacquainted with their causes, who might easily mistake the justice of the Common law for rigour, not knowing the true reason thereof? Hereupon it was that some sullen Serjeants at the first, refused to plead before him, until partly by his power, but more by his prudence, he had convinced them of their errors and his abilities."[b] No letter or other document exists to shew that Hatton himself sought this great Office; and it may be inferred from Camden's remark, that it was given to him through the intrigues of his enemies: nor

[a] Annals, b. III. p. 127.
[b] Fuller's Worthies ed. 1811. vol. II. p. 165. Lord Campbell, who quotes part of the above passage, erroneously assigns it to Naunton, and says that " Meetings of the bar were held, and it was resolved by many Serjeants and apprentices that they would not plead before the new Chancellor ; but a few who looked eagerly for advancement, dissented," p. 148. All that has been found on the subject is stated in the text ; and there is nothing whatever to show that there were " any meetings of the bar," or any general resolution of the profession not to plead before the new Chancellor.

has any allusion to his appointment been found in the
correspondence of the period.

The Chancellor, on the 3rd of May, the first day of
Trinity Term, rode from Ely Place, in Holborn, in great
state to Westminster, to take the oaths.   He was preceded by about forty of his gentlemen, uniformly dressed
in a blue livery, wearing gold chains, and by several
Pensioners and other gentlemen of the Court, on foot,
and was attended by the officers and clerks of the Chancery.   On his right hand rode Lord Treasurer Burghley,
and on his left the Earl of Leicester ; and he was followed by some of the Nobility, the Judges, many
Knights, and a great troop of their retinue.*   The following account of Hatton's reception in the Court of
Chancery, stands only on the authorities referred to ;—

"It is said," by Lord Campbell, "that Hatton was
received in the Court of Chancery with cold and silent
disdain.   Nevertheless, there was, from the first, some
little business brought on before him.   The Attorney and
Solicitor-General, lest they should themselves be dismissed, were obliged, however discontented they might
be, to appear to countenance him.   He made no public
complaint of his reception, and gradually gained ground
by his great courtesy and sweetness, to say nothing of the
good dinners and excellent sack, for which he was soon
famous.   It would appear that there was much public curiosity to see 'the dancing Chancellor' seated upon his
tribunal; and the crowds of strangers in the Court of
Chancery were so great, that there came out an order ' by
the Right Honourable Sir Christopher Hatton, Knight of
the Most Noble Order of the Garter, and Lord Chancellor
of England,' in these words :—' For the avoiding of such

* Stow's Annals, p. 741.

H H

great numbers of suitors and others as do daily pester
the Court in the time of sitting, by reason whereof heretofore it hath many times happened that the due reverence and silence which ought to be kept and observed in
that honourable Court hath been undutifully neglected,
and contrariwise much unmannerly and unseemly behaviour and noise hath been there used, to the hindrance of
the due hearing of such matters and causes as were there
to be handled, and to the great derogation of the honour
of this Court, and due reverence belonging to the same'
—Then follow regulations, by which none were to come
into Court but counsel, attorneys, officers, and their
clerks and parties, who were ' to continue so long as the
cause shall be in hearing, and no longer; and all other
suitors whatsoever (except Noblemen, and such as be of
her Majesty's Privy Council) were to stand without the
Court, and not suffered to come in without special licence.'ᵃ He was quite at home when presiding in the Star
Chamber, where he had before been accustomed to sit as
a Privy Councillor, and he had the Chiefs of the Common
Law to assist him. To this Court, according to usage, he
dedicated Wednesdays and Fridays. On other days he
sat for Equity business in the Court of Chancery; in
Westminster Hall in the mornings, and in his own house
in the afternoons. He made an order that four Masters
in Chancery should always attend, and sit on the bench
with him in Court, and two in his own house.ᵇ

   "He was exceedingly cautious, ' not venturing to wade
beyond the shallow margin of Equity, where he could
distinctly see the bottom.' He always took time to con-

ᵃ "Reg. Lib. B 31 and 32 Eliz.
1589, p. 498."—Lives of the Chancellors.

ᵇ "Ordo Curiæ, decimo viii.º die
Aprilis Anno Regni Elizabethæ Re-
ginæ xxx.º "—Ibid.

sider in cases of any difficulty; and in these he was guided by the advice of one Sir Richard Swale, described as his 'servant-friend,'[a] who was a Doctor of the Civil Law, and a Clerk in the Chancery, and well skilled in all the practice and doctrines of the Court. By these means Lord Chancellor Hatton contrived to get on marvellously well; and though suitors might grumble, as well as their counsel, the public took part with him, and talked with contempt of 'the sullen Serjeants,' who at first refused to plead before him. All were dazzled with the splendour of his establishment; and it was said, that he made up for his want of law by his constant desire to do what was just.[b] But the more judicious grieved; and, in spite of all his caution and good intentions, he committed absurd blunders, and sometimes did injustice."[c]

Upon this statement it may be observed that as "none of Hatton's decisions have come down to us,"[d] and as there is no report of his proceedings in his Court, the evidence of those "absurd blunders," and of his occasional "injustice," is wholly wanting; while even his learned biographer admits, that, in the cause of which a report[e] is preserved, he "presided with great gravity, and, with many apologies for the leniency of the sentence, he fined the defendant 2000l., and directed the Judges to testify this punishment on their circuits, to the end the whole Realm might have knowledge of it, and the people no longer be seduced with these lewd libellers." As Hatton "shewed great industry," and "made himself tolerably well acquainted with the practice of

[a] Fuller's Worthies.
[b] "Camden."
[c] Lord Campbell's Life of Hatton, pp. 149—151.
[d] Ibid. p. 158.
[e] Regina v. Knightly, in the Star Chamber. Howell's State Trials, I. 1270.

the Court of Chancery;" and as he "issued several
new orders to improve it, which were much applauded,"
it may be inferred, with more probability, and certainly
with more candour, that he performed the duties
of his high office with satisfaction to the public and
credit to himself. The fact, that none of Hatton's de-
crees were reversed, is met by the remark, that, "if he
and his adviser, Dr. Swale, had erred ever so much,
there were hardly any means of correcting them; for
there was no appeal to the House of Lords in Equity
suits till the reign of Charles II., and there was no chance
of bringing, with any effect, before the Council the
decree of a Chancellor still in power."[a]

"To give the public a notion," says his biographer,
"that he had attended to the study of the law, he actually published a 'Treatise concerning Acts of Parliament, and the Exposition thereof;'[b] but it was well
known to be written by another, and was withal a very
poor production;" but the fact is, that the work thus
positively said to have been "actually published" by
Hatton, with so unworthy an object, was not printed
until he had quietly reposed in his grave for eighty-
six years![c] Even the boldest and most important act
which a Chancellor can be called upon to perform,—
the refusal of his Sovereign's command to affix the

---

[a] Lord Campbell, p. 157.

[b] Ibid, p. 158.

[c] "A Treatise concerning Statutes,
or Acts of Parliament, and the exposition thereof; written by Sir Christopher Hatton, late Lord Chancellor
of England. London; printed for
Richard Tonson, at his shop under
Gray's-Inn Gate, next Gray's-Inn
Lane. Anno 1677." 12mo. Barrington, who appears really to have

seen the book, has formed a higher
opinion of its merits than Lord
Campbell. Speaking of Hatton he
says, " There is also a short Treatise on the Construction of Statutes,
which was printed in 1677, after his
death; if this was really written by
him, it must be allowed not to be
entirely destitute of merit."—Observations on the more Ancient Statutes, p. 405.

Great Seal to letters-patent, conferring an unconstitutional office upon the most powerful man in the Realm, —elicits no other praise than that it showed the mistake of supposing that "he would be utterly disgraced by the incompetent manner in which he must discharge his judicial duties;" and it is insinuated, that but for the opportune death of the party, he might have been induced to comply.[a] Though represented as having been so incompetent a Chancellor, Hatton is nevertheless said to have been so incessantly occupied with his judicial duties, as to have lost the Queen's regard by his absence from Court, where he was supplanted by Essex and Raleigh; and "on his occasional visits to Whitehall, or St. James's, to Richmond, or Greenwich," he had, it is added, "the deep mortification of finding himself entirely neglected and slighted for younger men.[b]" It was "on one of these occasions" that "he saw" Raleigh attract the Queen's notice by throwing his "brave silken cloak" before her when he was "instantly taken into favour by her, and appointed to the post which he himself had once held;" and so intimately acquainted is the noble biographer with the Chancellor's private feelings, that he says, Hatton "would now have been delighted to exchange "that post" for the Great Seal.[c]"

It unfortunately happens, however, that there is not the slightest foundation for this pathetic story, inasmuch as Raleigh was taken into favour by the Queen, and was an object of Hatton's jealousy, at least five years before the Vice-Chamberlain was raised to the

[a] Lives of the Chancellors, p. 153.   [c] Ibid. p. 155.
[b] Ibid. pp. 154, 155.

woolsack;[*] and Raleigh had obtained the post of Captain of the Guard nearly twelve months before that event.

On the 12th of May the Lord Chancellor received the following letter from Lord Burghley :—

TO THE LORD CHANCELLOR.

MY LORD, I am sorry that my pains are such as I cannot attend on you to-day in the Star Chamber, having yesterday, by more zeal of service in the Exchequer Chamber, than of regard to my harms, so weakened and pained my leg, as I cannot stir it out of my bed ; but this my declaration of my state is to no purpose to occupy your Lordship withal. This great matter of the lack of vent, not only of clothes, which presently is the greatest, but of all other English commodities which are restrained from Spain, Portugal, Barbary, France, Flanders, Hamburgh, and the States, cannot but in process of time work a great change and dangerous issue to the people of the Realm, who, heretofore, in time of outward peace, lived thereby, and without it must either perish for want, or fall into violence to feed and fill their lewd appetites with open spoils of others, which is the fruit of rebellion; but it is in vain to remember this to your Lordship, that is so notorious as there need no repetition thereof. The evil being seen and like daily to increase beyond all good remedies, it is our duties that are Councillors to think of some remedies in time, before the same become remediless ; and briefly the best means of remedy must follow the consideration of the causes of this evil, and so " *contrariis contraria curare.*" The original cause is apparently the contentions and enmities betwixt the King of Spain and his countries, and her Majesty and her countries. The reduction hereof to amity betwixt the Princes, and to open traffic according to the ancient treaties of intercourse, would be the sovereign remedy; but this may be wished sooner than speedily effectuated. But yet, seeing there is a signification notified of the good inclination of both the Princes,

* Vide, p. 275—278, *ante.*

and a great necessity to press them both thereto for the sou-
agement of their people, it were pity any course should be
taken either to hinder this or not to hasten it, which surely in
the Low Countries would be done, with whatsoever a reasonable cost may be, to keep the enemy from victuals, and to
withstand his enterprises against our friends until this next
harvest; and by this proceeding against him, there is no doubt
but he will yield to all reasonable conditions meet both for
her Majesty and her protected friends ; otherwise, if the good
fortune of our friends do decay, and the enemy recover that
which he now lacketh, that is store of victuals, he will either
underhand make peace with our friends, whom he shall find
both weak and timorous, and leave her Majesty in danger for
recovery of all that she hath spent, and in greater charges to
maintain her two cautionary towns against the whole Low
Countries than two Boulognes were, or else he will, being
puffed with pride, make a very Spanish conquest of Holland
and Zealand,—a matter terrible to be thought of, but most
terrible to be felt. But to insist upon this remedy is as yet in
vain, and therefore such other poor helps are to be thought of
as may somewhat mitigate the accidents present, and stay the
increase thereof, whereof when I do bethink myself, I find no
one simple remedy, but rather compounded of divers simples,
and to say truly they are but simple remedies, until peace may
ensue, which is the sovereign sole medicine of all. To have
vent increase, there must be more buyers and shippers than
there are, and seeing our merchants say that they cannot have
sales sufficient,

1. It were good that the Steelyard men were licensed to
trade as they were wont to do, with condition upon good
bouds that our merchants adventurers shall have their former
liberties in Hamburgh.

2. These Steelyard merchants must also have a dispensation
to carry a competent number of unwrought cloths that are
coarse, which are the cloths whereof the great stay is in the
Realm.

3. Beside this, the merchant strangers might have a like

dispensation for the buying and shipping of a competent number of like white coarse cloths.

4. And if her Majesty, for some reasonable time, would
abate only 2s. upon a cloth, I think there would grow no loss
to her Majesty, having respect to the multitude of the cloths
that should be carried, whereas now the strangers carry few,
but upon licences, for which her Majesty hath no strangers'
customs but English.

5. The strangers also must have liberty to buy in Blackwell
Hall, or else there may be a staple set up in Westminster, out
of the liberties of the City of London, which, rather than
London would suffer, I think they will grant liberty to strangers in respect of the hallage money which they shall leese.
Notwithstanding all these shows of remedies, I could wish
that our merchants adventurers were made acquainted herewith, and to be warned, that if they shall not amend the prices
to clothiers for their coarse cloths, whereby the clothiers may
be reasonably apparent gainers, and that to be put in practice
this next week, that then her Majesty will give authority to
put the former helps in practice. Thus, my good Lord,
because I understand you are to go to the Court this afternoon, I have thought good to scribble, as I do (lying in pain),
these few cogitations, submitting them to a more mature disquisition. Your Lordship's most assured, W. BURGHLEY.*

FROM THE LORD CHANCELLOR TO SIR FRANCIS WALSINGHAM.

SIR, This afternoon Sir Rowland Hayward and Sir Edward
Osborne have been with me to deliver an answer in the matter of buying and selling of cloths in Blackwell Hall. They
have assembled their Common Council upon this cause,
wherein by a general consent their resolution is this—That
with all reverent duty they submit themselves to anything it
shall please her Majesty to command them. But in this matter, that Strangers and other Subjects not being of their Company should have to do in Blackwell Hall (the same being an

* Original in the State Paper Office, indorsed, " 12th May, 1587."

express breach of their liberty,) they most humbly crave to be excused. It is directly (as they affirm) against their oath, to admit any others into this freedom, and the only recompence reserved for their servants, in hope of this future benefit and commodity, which being taken away by communicating the same indifferently unto others, would exceedingly discourage them, and perchance enure to farther inconvenience hereafter. They do therefore earnestly entreat me to be a mean their humble excuse may be received in this behalf, and that her Majesty will graciously vouchsafe to accept thereof. It may please you, Sir, in your wisdom, to deliver the effect hereof to her Highness, in such terms as may best be fitting with the cause, which referring to your good consideration, I bid you most heartily farewell. From London, the 27th of May 1587. Your assured loving friend,   CHR. HATTON, CANC.*

THE LORD CHANCELLOR TO WILLIAM CLOPTON, ESQ. AND JOHN GURDON, ESQ., JUSTICES OF THE PEACE IN SUFFOLK.

AFTER my very hearty commendations, by this . . . . I am informed of some unseemly and unnatural contention growing between this gentleman and his mother, for the suppressing whereof (being a matter of much rebuke unto them both) I find an honest disposition in him to have the cause taken up by any indifferent gentlemen for the avoiding of such a trouble or obloquy unto them in this behalf. I have therefore thought fit (being very desirous to further so good and godly a purpose) to refer the consideration of this suppliant grief unto you, as gentlemen of whose integrity and upright dealing in causes of like trust I am right well assured. Earnestly praying you upon the receipt hereof to call both parties before you, and upon due examination of the matter and original cause of their strife and unkindness, to seek (if you can) to reconcile the same, and to take such indifferent course for a final end between them as you shall find to be most agreeable with equity and justice. And in case that either of them

* Original in the State Paper Office.

shall refuse to stand to your order therein, then my desire is
you should advertise me thereof, and by whose default the
same shall happen, to the end [that I] may take such other
course as in that behalf shall . . . . . fit and convenient.
And so not doubting of your w . . . . . pains and travail
for so good a purpose, and the rather . . . . st for
which I shall have cause to thank you, and . . . .
you to . . . . . some good course of love and friendship between them if you possibly may, I bid you very heartily farewell. From London, the last of May 1587. Your very
loving friend, CHR. HATTON, CANC[a].

As the " Peerages" do not mention the death of any
child of Sir John Stanhope, afterwards Lord Stanhope,
there is nothing to fix the date of the next letter, except
that in his letter of the 8th of October 1587, he speaks
of " untimely death having bereft him of the fruit of
his youth and stay of his age." His son and successor
was born in 1592;—

MR. JOHN STANHOPE TO SIR CHRISTOPHER HATTON.

SIR, It is God's pleasure I should be left a sorrowful and
desolate father, by the death of my only child, and since it is
his doing, I must bear the cross thereof as quietly as he will
give me grace, though nature being strong, in a weak mind,
work according to natural passions; which, being unfit to be
spent in this place, makes me desirous to wait on you afore my
going, at your good leisure; hoping to find such continuance
of your favour, as I have ever, since my first coming hither,
been partner of. In requital whereof, I can but rest yours,
and pray for the continuance of your health, with increase of
all honourable comforts. Your Honour's humbly,
JOHN STANHOPE.[b]

---

[a] Autograph in the Harleian MSS. 286, f. 112.
[b] Additional MSS. 15891, f. 119.

MR. JOHN STANHOPE TO SIR CHRISTOPHER HATTON.

SIR, Since it hath pleased you something to relieve my afflicted spirits with the honourable offer of your friendly dealing, I thought it my part for your better remembrance, to add such notes thereunto, as, bearing a true date, may induce a readier dispatch in all good consideration. My time of attendance hath been here about sixteen years, with extraordinary charges, and all dutiful and ordinary care, without either fee, pension, or wages, during all which time I can never remember that I was so much as six weeks absent at once, and that not past twice in all. And though I know all is but duty, and nothing worth, yet have I been ever ready to supply one place or other, to be commanded as there was cause of service, never without that faith that was fit, nor such diligence as might deserve good opinion. Her Majesty's goodness being infinite, I humbly acknowledge to have been singularly bound unto her, and do rest with the burthen of an infinite debt; but for any portion befallen either to my preferment or profit I have never reaped any but that which yourself best knoweth of, who were the chiefest means to further in my behalf the fruit of her Majesty's gracious favour. Since which time (which is seven years past and more,) believe me, Sir, it is too true, I have both spent the last penny of that benefit, and sold   *l.* land of inheritance, which was my mother's gift. Yet still in debt, but not out of heart, if untimely death had not bereft me of the fruit of my youth and stay of my age, by whose convenient match I might have reared something to my advantage. But it hath now pleased the Almighty to leave me wholly to her Majesty's goodness, whereof, as I never had cause to doubt, so this, my present suit, being without charge to her Majesty, and without trouble to any, may both in part repair my ruin, and settle my mind to some better stay, which shall then be most quiet, when I shall know myself fittest to serve her Majesty as I desire, contented ever with the mean estate of a well-measured mind. In the meanwhile my humble prayer shall never cease for her prosperous and blessed estate,

nor my good-will to do you any service I shall be able. From
the Court at Whitehall, the eighteenth of October 1587.
Your Honour's humbly,   JOHN STANHOPE.[a]

So far from Hatton having lost any part of the Queen's
regard, he received a distinguished mark of her favour in
April 1588. On Saint George's Day, in a Chapter of the
Order of the Garter, held at Greenwich, four Knights were
elected by the Companions; but the Sovereign's pleasure
was not made known until the following day, the 24th,
when Robert Devereux, Earl of Essex, Thomas Butler,
Earl of Ormond, President of Munster, and Sir Christopher
Hatton, the Lord Chancellor, were declared Knights of the
Order. Being introduced into the Chapter, the Knights
Elect fell upon their knees, and were severally invested
with the insignia by the Queen's own hands; and they
were installed on the 23rd of May. It appears, however, that on Saint George's day, in the preceding year,
Hatton received eight, being the greatest number of votes;
but, as the Queen refused to attend when the scrutiny was
taken, on the pretence that she was not attired in the
mantle of the Order, no election took place.[b]

Lord Campbell's researches have discovered an admirable speech which was made by Lord Chancellor Hatton
on the elevation of Mr. Robert Clarke, to the dignity
of Sergeant-at-law, who attained that degree on the 12th
of June, 1588:—

" 'No man can live without Law, therefore I do exhort
you, that you have good care of your duty in the calling,
and that you be a father to the poor ; that you be careful
to relieve all men afflicted. You ought to be an arm to
help them ; a hand to succour them. Use uprightness

---

[a] Additional MSS. 15891.   [b] History of the Order of the Garter, 4to. p. 199.

and follow truth. Be free from cautel. Mix with the
exercise of the law no manner of deceit. Let these
things be far from your heart. Be of an undoubted resolution. Be of good courage, and fear not to be carried
away with the authority, power, or threatenings of any
other. Maintain your clients' cause in all right. Be not
put to silence. As it is alleged out of the Book of Wisdom,
' Noli quærere fieri Judex, ne forte extimescas faciem
potentis, et ponas scandalum in agilitate tua.'   Know no
man's face. Go on with fortitude. Do it in uprightness. ' Redde cuique quod suum.'   Be not partial to
yourself. Abuse not the highest gifts of God, which no
doubt is great in equity. These things be the actions of
nobility. He that doth these things duly, deserves high
honour, and is worthy in the world to rule. Let truth be
familiar with you. Regard neither friend nor enemy.
Proceed in the good work laid upon you. And the last
point that I am to say to you, use diligence and careful-
ness. And although I have not been acquainted with the
course of the Law, albeit, in my youth, I spent some time
in the study thereof ; yet I find by daily experience that
diligence brings to pass great things in the course and
proceeding of the Law ; and contrarily negligence overthrows many good causes. Let not the dignity of the
Law be given to men unmeet. And I do exhort you all
that are here present, not to call men to the Bar, or the
Bench, that are so unmeet. I find that there are now
more at the Bar in one House, than there was in all the
Inns of Court, when I was a young man. He concludes by
an exhortation to avoid Chancery, and to settle disputes
in the Courts of Law. We sit here to help the rigour and
extremities of the Law. The holy conscience of the
Queen for matters of Equity in some sort, is by her Majes-

ty's goodness committed to me, when *summum jus* doth minister *summam injuriam*. But the Law is the inheritance of all men. And I pray God bless you, and send you as much worship as ever had any in your calling.'"[a]

In June 1589 Sir Christopher Hatton's nephew, Sir William Newport *alias* Hatton, who had taken his uncle's name, was married to Elizabeth, the daughter and heiress of Judge Gawdy. The ceremony took place at Holdenby, and was honoured with the Chancellor's presence; but during the festivities news arrived of the murder of the French monarch. "Upon this news," says Mr. Gilbert Talbot, in a letter to his father, on the 1st of July 1589, " My Lord Chancellor, who was then at Holdenby, at the marriage of his nephew, was sent for up again with all speed, and this night he will be in London. He purposed to have tarried there ten or twelve days longer."[b] It was on this occasion that the following trifling circumstance occurred ; and, considering the universal practice of dancing at weddings, that Hatton was not then quite fifty years old, and that it was at the marriage of his nearest relative and adopted heir, his having cast aside his judicial gravity, and joined the dancers, scarcely justifies the inference, that, " while holding the Great Seal, his highest distinction continued to be his skill in dancing, and as often as he had an opportunity he abandoned himself to this amusement."[c] In a letter from a Captain Allen, dated on the 17th of August 1589, to Mr. Bacon, he says, "My Lord Chancellor's heir, Sir William Hatton, hath married Judge Gawdy's daughter and heir; and my Lord Chancellor

---

[a] " Reg. Lib. B. 1586 [1588?], f. 661." Lives of the Chancellors, pp. 158, 159.

[b] Hunter's History of Hallamshire, p. 91.

[c] Lives of the Chancellors, p. 159.

danced the measures at the solemnity.   He left the gown
in the chair, saying, ' Lie thou there, Chancellor.'"[a]

While alluding to the Chancellor's dancing, it is proper
to notice Gray's well-known lines, in his " Long Story" on
Stoke Pogeis, in Buckinghamshire.   Referring to Sir
Christopher Hatton, he says,

> " Full oft within the spacious walls,
> When he had fifty winters o'er him,
> My grave Lord Keeper led the brawls,
> The Seals and maces danced before him."

Lord Campbell states, that Hatton had, "at Stoke Pogeis
in Buckinghamshire, a country house, constructed in the
true Elizabethan taste.   Here, when he was Lord Chancellor, he several times had the honour to entertain her
Majesty, and shewed that the agility and grace which had
won her heart when he was a student in the Inner Temple
remained little abated."[b]   It appears, however, that both
Lord Campbell and Gray were quite mistaken in supposing
that Sir Christopher Hatton ever owned Stoke Pogeis, or
ever resided there.   The manor-house was re-built, in the
reign of Queen Elizabeth, by Henry Earl of Huntingdon ;
and Sir Edward Coke, who had married Elizabeth,
daughter of Thomas Earl of Exeter, and second wife
and widow of Sir William Hatton, the Chancellor's
nephew, held it as lessee under the Crown in 1601,[c] in
which year he entertained the Queen there ;[d] and about
1621 it was granted to him by King James the First.
Moreover, there is no trace of Hatton's having ever pos-

[a] Additional MSS. 4109, fo. 352,
printed in Birch's Memoirs of the
Reign of Queen Elizabeth, vol. i.
p. 56.

[b] Page 164.
[c] History of Buckinghamshire in
Lyson's Magna Britannia.
[d] Nichols's Progresses, III. 568.

sessed Stoke Pogeis : it is not mentioned among the lands
of which he died seised, nor among those which belonged
to his nephew and heir-at-law.   After Lady Coke's death,
on whom the property was settled, it went to Lord Purbeck,
the husband of Frances,[a] her only surviving child by Lord
Coke; whereas, if it had been inherited from Sir William
Hatton, it would have devolved upon his daughter, the
Countess of Warwick, or have gone with Lord Chancellor
Hatton's estates, on the death of Sir William without
issue male, to his next heir male, Sir Christopher Hatton.
Lord Coke's marriage with the widow of Sir William
Hatton may have given rise to the tradition that it once
belonged to Lord Chancellor Hatton, and misled Gray, who
has misled the author of the " Lives of the Chancellors."

The preparations to repel the Spanish Armada being
completed, the Queen visited the camp at Tilbury on the
8th of August; and, though it is positively said that "the
Chancellor attended her," and that "if the Spaniards had
landed was ready to have fought valiantly by her side,[b]"
the authority cited[c] for his having been present is scarcely
weighty enough to be set against the omission of his
name in all the accounts of her Majesty's visit ; and the
fact that on that very day Walsingham wrote a report to
Hatton of what was going on in the camp,[d] is almost
conclusive evidence that he was at some distance from
Tilbury.

Towards the end of August, or early in September, a
circumstance occurred, which has been before adverted to,

---

[a] Her sister, Elizabeth, to whom
the Queen was godmother in August, 1599, died unmarried.—Nichols's Progresses, iii. 465.
[b] Lord Campbell, p. 156.

[c] "The Critic," Ibid p. 152.

[d] Original in the Harleian MS.
6994, and printed in Wright's Queen
Elizabeth and her Times, p. 385.

when Hatton showed his knowledge of the constitution, a proper sense of the duties of his high office, and the firmness to oppose the Queen's will if her commands were illegal. "In the very end of this life," says the learned historian of the period, Leicester "began to enter into new hope of honour and power," by endeavouring to obtain from Elizabeth the appointment of Lieutenant of England and Ireland, for which office the letters-patent were actually drawn. Lord Burghley, and the Lord Chancellor, however, interposed, and prevented their being executed ; "and the Queen in time foresaw the danger of too great a power in one man."[a] Further proceedings on this subject, of which little is known, were prevented by the sudden death of this remarkable person, as he died suddenly on the 4th of September. By a codicil to his will, dated on the 30th of September 1587, the Earl of Leicester appointed Sir Christopher Hatton, his brother the Earl of Warwick, and Lord Howard of Effingham, overseers of his will, entreating them "to help, assist, and comfort his dear and poor disconsolate wife;" and he thus affectionately mentions Hatton:—"To my Lord Chancellor, mine old dear friend, I do give one of my greatest basins and ewers gilt, with my best George and Garter, not doubting but he shall shortly enjoy the wearing of it, and one of his armours which he gave me."[b] By the decease of Leicester, the Chancellorship of the University of Oxford became vacant, and Hatton was elected his successor.[c]

[a] Camden, b. iii. 145.
[b] Sidney State Papers, i. 74, 75.
[c] The speeches and proceedings on the occasion are in the Additional MS. 5845, in the British Museum.

Parliament met on the 12th of November, when Mr. Serjeant Snagge was elected Speaker of the House of Commons :—

SIR CHRISTOPHER HATTON TO MR. SERGEANT PUCKERING.

SIR, I am to pray you to take the pains to repair unto this town about the latter end of this week, that I may have some conference with you concerning matters of Parliament to this purpose; because the use of the higher House is not to meddle with any bill until there be some presented from the Commons; and so, by reason thereof, the first part of the sitting should be spent idly, or to small purpose, I thought it fit to inform myself what bills there were remaining since the last Parliament, of the which the Lords had good liking, but could not be passed by reason of want of time, and those I meant to offer to their Lordships till such time as there came some from the Lower House. And sending to Mr. Mason, the Clerk of the Higher House, to confer with him touching the same, I understand by him that most of them remain in your hands; wherefore I desire to have some speech with you herein. Further, I have thought good to let you understand how the world goes here, touching the Speaker of the Lower House, which charge her Majesty hath now resolved to lay on Mr. Sergeant Snagge. Other matters you shall understand at our meeting. In the mean time I commend you to the good keeping of Almighty God. From London, the 2nd of September 1588. Your assured loving friend,

CHR. HATTON.*

Though Parliament met on the 12th of November, it was prorogued to the 4th of February 1589, on which day the Lord Chancellor explained the cause of its being called together, in an able speech. After stating that peace had ever been the object nearest the Queen's heart, and that neither the infant state of Scotland, the treachery of

---

* Autograph in the Harleian MS. 6994, f. 148.

France, the divisions of her enemies, nor the frequent
solicitations of the Dutch, had provoked her to make war ;
and that, while she was endeavouring to prevent hostilities
with Spain, the Armada had approached our coasts, but that
the Almighty had graciously rendered their designs fruitless, and enabled her ships, though far inferior in number,
to defeat and put them to flight ; he then described the
subsequent fate of the Spanish fleet, and thus concluded:—

"But to what end do I by this recital endeavour to
make you secure and void of fear ?   Do not you imagine,
I say, that they are ardently studious of revenge, and that
they will not employ the power, the strength, the riches
of Spain, and the forces of both Kingdoms, to accomplish
it ?   Know you not the pride, fury, and bitterness of the
Spaniard against you ? Yes, this is the great cause of
summoning this Parliament; that in this most full assembly of the wisest and most prudent persons, called together from all parts of this Kingdom, as far as human
counsel can advise, a diligent preparation may be made,
that arms and forces and money may be in readiness ;
and that our navy, which is the greatest bulwark of this
Kingdom, may be repaired, manned, and fitted out for all
events with the utmost expedition."[a]

In the spring of 1589, an expedition, under the joint
command of "the two Generals," Sir John Norris and Sir
Francis Drake, was sent against Spain ; and it is said that
"the Earl of Essex, though much suspected, yet unknown
to the Queen, made arrangements to meet the Generals on
the coast of Portugal ;[b] but this letter shows that Essex's

---

[a] Lords' Journals, vol. i. ; and
Parliamentary History, vol. i. p.
854. Lord Campbell considers " this
speech of the dancing Chancellor is
in better taste than any performance
of his predecessors, either ecclesiastical or legal," p. 153.

[b] Stow, p. 751.

design was known to the Queen. Captains Crosse and Plott
appear to have belonged to the army :—

MY VERY GOOD LORD, For my opinion touching Captain
Crosse, I do think that upon her Majesty's late speeches with
him, he hath received some particular directions from herself,
concerning the two Generals, as also touching the Earl of
Essex, in which respect it seemeth fit he should be sent unto
them. This commodity there will come of it, that so her
Majesty's pleasure shall be delivered to the Generals, and their
desire therein also satisfied, who wish that he might be sent,
because he hath been made thoroughly acquainted with the
particular state of the army, as your Lordship may partly
perceive by the letter you require, which I send you here enclosed. Now for that divers ships are appointed for the carriage of the provisions, as appeareth by Captain Plott's own
note, the charge in my opinion may well be divided between
him and Captain Crosse, wherein, nevertheless I refer me to
your Lordship's better advice, and so commend you to the
Lord Almighty. From Ely-place, the 15th of May 1589.
Your Lordship's most assured poor friend,

CHR. HATTON, CANC.

Postscript.—My good Lord, as I conceive the victuals for
their supply cannot conveniently be sent all at one time ; and
therefore the one of these gentlemen may be sent before with
a part, and the rest come after with the other.*

MY VERY GOOD LORD, Being desirous to gratify my good
friend Sir Richard Knightley, I make bold to entreat of your
Lordship the gift of one stag and a brace of bucks, to be taken
in any place in Derbyshire wheresoever you shall think good
to appoint; which, being more than were convenient I should

* Original in the State Paper Office.

require but thus in my friend's behalf, yet will I be most willing to requite this your honourable courtesy whensoever it shall please you to command the like in any ground of mine or within my charge. And so, my good Lord, praying pardon herein, and always ready at your good commandment, I take my leave. From Holdenby, 30th July 1589. Your Lordship's poor friend, very assured,   CHR. HATTON, CANC.

I beseech your good Lordship to pardon this exceeding boldness, and give me leave humbly to pray you to command in anything whatever I have power to do you any acceptable service, &c.[a]

On the 2nd of September the Lord Chancellor drew up the following "Memorial" of business to be transacted :—

FROM HER MAJESTY.

Remembrances to my Lord Treasurer, the second of Sept. 1589.

1. That resolution be taken with the States; and that presently, because they desire to depart.

2. That her Majesty's affairs there in the Low Countries, concerning her forces and assistance, may be thoroughly considered of; wherein she greatly commendeth the opinion of Mr. Bodley.

3. That it be considered what personage of estate is fittest to be sent into Scotland, to the end that warning may be given unto him to make himself ready.

4. To speak with the Aldermen touching money.

5. Then the causes to be thoroughly dealt with concerning this last voyage, and to call Sir John Norreys and Sir Francis Drake to answer to the articles resolutely and directly.[b]

6. That care be taken to disperse these seditious soldiers out of hand.[c]

---

[a] Original in the Shrewsbury Papers, Vol. "I." in the College of Arms.

[b] "Their accounts are specially to be hastened," &c.

[c] "L. Buckhurst," added in Lord Burghley's hand.

7. Order should be taken in these countries that these soldiers, as they pass, should not outrage upon the people.

8. Item the examination of Martin Marprelate to be thoroughly proceeded in.[a]

Nothing of any importance relating to Hatton occurred in 1590. Parliament did not meet, and the Country was in a state of tranquillity in her foreign and domestic relations.

TO THE EARL OF SHREWSBURY.

MY VERY GOOD LORD, I have received that fair and honourable present which it hath pleased you to send me at the beginning of this new year; for the which, and many other your honourable kindnesses towards me, as I must acknowledge myself much bounden and indebted unto your Lordship, so I assure you, that wherein I may, and it shall please you to use me, I will not fail, by all good endeavours, to discharge the part of a true friend towards you; and so, wishing your Lordship a happy beginning and ending of many years to come, I take my leave. From the Court at Richmond, 2nd January 1589 [1590]. Your good Lordship's very assured,

CHR. HATTON, CANC.[b]

The following is the only letter of that year in the "Letter Book," and with its subject the Lord Chancellor had little concern :—

FROM THE ARCHBISHOP OF CANTERBURY TO THE CANONS OF LINCOLN.

I WAS desirous that the controversy lately between Mr. Griffin, Dean of Lincoln, and you, by occasion of his two erro-

[a] Autograph in the State Paper Office. Indorsed by Lord Burghley, "3rd Aug. 1589. A Memoriall by my Lord Chancellor."

[b] Original in the Shrewsbury Papers, Vol. "I." in the College of Arms.

neous sermons made severally at divers times, might have been ended by your Ordinary, the rather to avoid the offence that might be generally taken by the publishing and public prosecuting of that question, especially seeing the Dean doth utterly renounce the error in doctrine wherewith he is charged, although I cannot but in my heart mislike the words and his manner of teaching in that point. There are controversies enough in the Church of England, and they are not well advised, that will either take or give more, and especially above all other, any suspicion that any should think so basely and wickedly of the immaculate Lamb of Jesus Christ; but seeing my desire that way could take no place, I have myself, together with my Lord the Bishop of London, the Deans of Winchester and Paul's, Doctor Aubrey and Doctor Bancroft, taken knowledge of the matter, and thoroughly examined the Dean in all the articles wherewith he is charged; and though, notwithstanding we all with one consent did and do wholly mislike, and in our consciences condemn, the manner of speeches used in that sermon, and do think it intolerable for any man to use the like; yet because we find the Dean in substance of doctrine to differ from us in no point touching that article, and to promise that he will forbear hereafter such like kind or manner of speaking of the person of Christ, although he found the same in Luther and Calvin, and some others, whom we also in our judgments do therefore mislike; and for that also we are assured, that when occasion shall be offered unto him, he will notify unto the world that he is no way spotted with such kind of heretical and erroneous doctrine, we have thought good to rest in that persuasion, and so to end the matter, knowing the same to be most fit and convenient for the good and quiet of the Church, which could not but suffer great ignominy if any man of his calling should be touched with such errors; and therefore I, upon whom these burdens do especially lie, do heartily pray you to use him brotherly and friendly, and to conceive of him, as myself do, who have had full conference with him, and do know his mind and judgment in this case, requiring you likewise that if he, or any man else, shall hereafter use the like words, and so give the like offence, you advertise me with all speed thereof, that I may deal therein according to my duty. And because you shall not doubt of my opinion in this matter, I would have you to understand that I think Luther was in saying, ... was *omnium maximus latro, homicida, adulter,* . . . . and whosoever followeth . . . . speaking or writing so intemperately and unadvisedly, do write and speak contrary to the phrase of Scripture and to the truth, and indeed blasphemously; for although that the Scripture teacheth us that Christ was reputed such a one, yet to say simply that he was so, or that he had sin, or committed sin, or came properly or simply to be called a sinner, no Christian man will dare to affirm or justify. This is my resolution, which I would have you and all men to know; and those that shall impugn this, or teach to the contrary, I will prosecute with extremity and to the extremity. And so once again praying you to seek peace and ensue it, and friendly to confer one with another before you enter into judgment or condemnation, I commit you to the tuition of Almighty God. From Lambeth, the 29th of June 1590. Your assured, loving friend,   JOHN CANTUAR.

The indorsement of the following letter states that it was written by the "Lord Chancellor from Eltham, with the Lord Cobham:"—

TO LORD BURGHLEY.

MY VERY GOOD LORD, We have received your honourable letters, and can well witness your endless travails, which in her Majesty's princely consideration she should relieve you of, but it is true the affairs are in a good hand, as we all know, and thereby her Majesty is the more sure, and we her poor servants the better satisfied. God send you help and happiness to your best contentment. Surely, Sir, we have taken pains in reading Lilly's letters; and my Lord Cobham and I rely upon this hope of Parry's, wherein we pray God he be not deceived. I hope the morrow to be at London, where, if your Lordship will command me any service, I shall be ready for you. This 15th of July 1590. Your good Lordship's most bound,   CHR. HATTON, CANC.[a]

FROM LORD CHANCELLOR HATTON TO LORD BURGHLEY.

MY VERY GOOD LORD, The times being now full of troubles, and our shipping and warriors diversely employed about reprisals, so as the trade for wines is like thereby to be very much hindered; and that the law inhibiting the bringing in of wines in strangers' bottoms doth not only withdraw all strangers, and hath done of late years from that trade, but also is a fear to our Nation to lade home their wines in such strange vessels, as many times, for their better safety, they might and would do, if they were not subject to the danger of those statutes: I am therefore earnestly to pray your good Lordship that you would be pleased to write your letters to the Officers of Custom in the port of London, and to all others whom it may concern, that, during these troubles, no molestation be used, or trouble offered to any such as shall bring in wines in strangers' ships, contrary to the said statute, which I hope your Lordship will not think inconvenient, the time considered, and as it hath pleased you to do in the like case heretofore; and even so I bid your good Lordship right heartily farewell. From Ely place, the 20th of November 1590. Your Lordship's most bound poor friend,   CHR. HATTON, CANC.[b]

Only one year of Hatton's life remains; and it was not marked by any important event except, to himself, the most important of all. Though his health had gradually declined, he continued to sit in the Court of Chancery and in the Star Chamber. On the 17th of May he wrote a letter to Lord Burghley respecting the execu-

---

[a] Autograph in the State Paper Office.   [b] Lansdowne MSS. 65, art. 42.

tion of Udal, the Puritan minister, for felony, of which
letter Strype* gives the following abstract:—" He requested that the letter might be altered and drawn up
speedily for Udal and the rest ; because the time of their
execution, as it stood then appointed, drew near ; and
since there was not such haste to confer with those
others, which might be done, he said, with more leisure and advisement taken ;" and therefore, "that he
thought it best for some expedition to be used in conference with them ; and prayed his Lordship to give directions for the speedy drawing of this letter for Udal
and the rest to that purpose, that those two reverend
men might confer with them, and that, if they could by
good persuasions draw them to the acknowledgment of
their faults, to be set down in such a submission as the
Lord Anderson (Lord Chief Justice,) should draw up,
then the Queen's mercy to be extended towards them ;
otherwise, that they might repair by the execution of
justice on them, the harm they had done in sowing
sedition."

Among his letters of 1591 were those to his friend, Sir
Henry Unton, Ambassador Leiger at Paris, in September and October 1591, but they are now in a very imperfect condition:—

SIR CHRISTOPHER HATTON TO SIR HENRY UNTON,
AMBASSADOR IN FRANCE.

. . . . . disease since reporting it to be . . . . . the yellow jaun-
dice. Let me, ... for mine own quietness sake, understand in what . . . . . you are; that in case you should need any
help . . . . hence order may be taken for it. Nothing shall . . . .
I can assure your Lordship, that possibly may be had . . . . .

* Life of Archbishop Whitgift, ii. 97.

My late being at the Court, I heard nothing of your . . . . .
sickness; but that since from Sir Robert Cecil, ... good
friend, I received understanding of it, and with . . . . . how much
her most excellent Majesty was perple[xed] to hear thereof,
what care her Highness took for [your recov]ery, and the gracious great good opinions, conceiveth . . . . . of. This I signify to your Lordship, that you [may take] comfort to consider
her princely care over you both [for your]self (in that she
esteemeth so of you) as also in [regard] of her own service,
which she hopeth cannot but be . . . . . exceeding well through
your negotiation, wherein she hath settled an especial affiance
in the whole course of the . . . . . action. Sir, this want of
health which so unseasonably . . . . . unto you had almost brought
the good Lady, your wife, to death's door. But I hope you
shall receive . . . . . of each other, and I most earnestly wish
it. I have been visited myself of late with some distempera-
ture of body, and therefore conform the longer to write unto
you[r Lordship.] But this must not breed any conceit in your
Lordship, for you know the ground of my affection towards
you. News I have none to impart unto you; for . . . . . receive them altogether thence as the occurrences of the world
frame at this present. I will be always careful for your Lordship as a friend in anything which may concern your benefit,
honour, or reputation; and so, dear good . . . . . I commend
you to the . . . . . Almighty, who send you perfect health.
From London, the 5th of September 1591. Your Lordship's
most assured, true friend,   CHR. HATTON.*

SIR CHRISTOPHER HATTON TO SIR HENRY UNTON.

. . . . . and of all other particularities . . . . . enquired of so
dear a friend. In . . . . . hath satisfied me very well, and to
my great . . . . . I assure you. I must requite your Lordship,
but . . . . . answer at this time, being busy with a . . . . . dispatch to the Court. My absence from . . . . . this great while
by occasion of her Majesty's . . . . . City hath been the only

* Autograph in the Cotton MS. Caligula, E. VIII. f. 153.

cause of my seldom . . . . . unto you, but no want of good will
my . . . . . to . . . . . any office to do you good, either in . . . . .
in the execution of your great charge, which . . . . . [advance]
by all the means I can, as your true [friend] as occasion shall
serve. My next . . . . . will give me better opportunity to advertise . . . . . both how things are accepted from you, and what
. . . . . are fit for your further proceeding, which you understand from me in all plainness. But . . . . . comfort I doubt
not, as of whom we can . . . . . nothing but exceeding well, by
the taste of . . . . we see already. I must likewise forbear . . . . . advertisement to your Lordship until my being
this place, yielding no argument of matter fit . . . . . . knowledge, but only the discovery of certain . . . . . brained . . . . .
persons, who fall into strange . . . . . and, upon examination,
are found to be men distempered [in] their wits and under-
standings, and are dealt with accordingly; as, namely, one
Galliarde, who is carried . . . . . a strong imagination that he
shall be King after a short time; and another, called Elliott,
who . . . . . punishable in the highest degree, ... of sound
discourse, I must feed your Lordship for the présent with these
trifles. It may please you to accept all in good part, and expect amends upon better opportunity. I will not fail to do all
due compliment with Sir Robert Cecil on your Lordship's
behalf. And so thanking your Lordship for your favourable
advertisement, with an earnest desire of your continuance in
health even as if mine own, I recommend you to the holy
protection of the Almighty. From London, the 18th of September 1591. Your Lordship's most assured, true friend,

CHR. HATTON.*

SIR CHRISTOPHER HATTON TO SIR HENRY UNTON.

. . . . . you for the advertisement which . . . . . welcome unto
me both in itself and . . . . . in that it came from your Lordship.
Since . . . . . coming to the Court (where I made stay . . . . .
few days) I find that her Majesty hath hard conceit as well

---

* Cottonian MSS. Caligula, E.viii. f. 157.

towards your Lordship . . . . . as . . . . . for your going to the
Marshal Biron, of . . . . . as), seconding his Lordship's error,
whereof the . . . . . is grown.   Her Highness, taking it for an
. . . . that her General or Ambassador should all . . . . . follow
any person whatsoever other than . . . . . of the King himself,
to whom you are sent . . . . . that her forces should be employed in any other . . . . .   According to the form of the con-
tract, ... it had been far more fit for the Marshal to . . . . .
did upon either of you, than you upon him . . . . . upon her
express pleasure is, I should advise . . . . . from henceforth to
consider well upon . . . . . of your commission, and in no wise
to exceed the . . . . . thereof.   Howbeit, the news of the . . . . .
Gournay hath somewhat qualified this displeasure . . . . . as
her Highness hath granted to the Lord . . . .
months further stay; whereof your Lordship shall receive
more particular advertisement by . . . . from my . . . . .   Her
Majesty doth resemble this going of the Lord General. . . . . .
Your Lordship and of Sir Thomas Leighton to the sw . . .
dance; three on a row, forwards and backwards, as . . . . .
journey taken ·to very small purpose.   It . . . . . therefore,
. . . . . and may best content her Highness . . . . .   Some un-
pleasing conceit may grow which afterwards may hardly be removed.   My endeavours shall not fail, either herein or in anything else, to do all good office, both to uphold and to increase her Majesty's gracious opinion of your Lordship, I assure you; and I nothing doubt of your Lordship's wise consideration upon these points; and that such amends shall be
made by your discreet managing of this matter as shall be a
full satisfaction, and breed effect in her Highness of exceeding
good liking towards you.   Wherewith, my very good Lord, I
bid you most heartily farewell.   From London, the 4th of
October 1591.   Your Lordship's very assured, true friend,

                                        CHR. HATTON.*

Sir Christopher Hatton's last letter is that of the 5th of

---

* Cotton MSS. Caligula, E. viii. f. 239.

October to the Earl of Essex, then in command of a small
auxiliary force in France, advising him not to expose his
person to needless danger. The brother, who is alluded to
in this letter, was Walter Devereux, who was killed under
the walls of Rouen by a musket-shot :*—

SIR CHRISTOPHER HATTON TO THE EARL OF ESSEX.

October 5, 1591.

MY VERY GOOD LORD, Next after my thanks for your
honourable letters I will assure your Lordship that for my
part I have not failed to use the best endeavours I could for
the effecting of your desire, in remaining there for some longer
time : but withal, I must advertise you that her Majesty hath
been drawn thereunto with exceeding hardness; and the chief
reason that maketh her stick in it is, that for she doubteth
your Lordship doth not sufficiently consider the dishonour
that ariseth unto her by the King's either dalliance or want of
regard, having not used the forces sent so friendly to his aid
from so great a Prince, and under the conduct of so great a
personage, in some employment of more importance all this
while. Wherefore, both by her Majesty's commandment, and
also for the unfeigned good-will I bear your Lordship, I am
very earnestly to advise you that you have great care for the
accomplishment of her Highness' instructions effectually, and
according to her intention, in those things wherein you are to
deal with the King. Further, my good Lord, let me be bold
to warn you of a matter that many of your friends here greatly
fear, namely, that the late accident of your noble brother, who
hath so valiantly and honourably spent his life in his Prince's
and Country's service, draw you not through grief or passion
to hazard yourself over venturously. Your Lordship best
knoweth that true valour consisteth rather in constant performing of that which hath been advisedly forethought, than
in an aptness or readiness of thrusting your person indifferently into every danger. You have many ways and many

* Camden's Annals, b. IV. p. 2G.

times made sufficient proof of your valiantness; no man doubteth but that you have enough, if you have not overmuch; and, therefore, both in regard of the services her Majesty expecteth to receive from you, and in respect of the grief that would grow to the whole Realm by the loss of one of that honourable birth, and that worth which is sufficiently known, as greater hath not been for any that hath been born therein these many and many years, I must, even before Almighty God, pray and require your Lordship to have that circumspectness of yourself which is fit for a General of your sort. Lastly, my Lord, I hope you doubt not of the good dispositions I bear towards your Lordship, nor that out of the same there ariseth and remaineth in me a desire to do your Lordship all the service that shall lie in my poor ability to perform; and, therefore, I shall not need to spend many words in this behalf, but with mine earnest prayers for your good success in all your honourable actions, and after, for your safe return to the comfort of your friends and well-willers here, I leave your Lordship to God's most holy and merciful protection. From London, the 5th of October 1591.   Your good Lordship's most assured and true friend,   CHR. HATTON.[a]

Soon after these letters were written, Hatton was seized with his last illness. His mind had been greatly harassed by the Queen's insisting upon the payment of a large sum of money which he owed to the Crown from the receipt of Tenths and First-fruits,[b] amounting, it is said, to 42,139*l*. 5*s*., for which, after his decease, an extent was laid on his house in Hatton Garden.[c] Though the nature of the debt[d] is expressly stated by Camden, the

[a] Murdin's State Papers, p. 646.
[b] Camden's Annals, b. iv. p. 34.
[c] Nichols's Progresses, iii. 123, and p. 503, post.
[d] Among the charges brought against Lord Chief Justice Coke, in July 1616, he was accused of having while "he was in a place of trust concealed a statute of 12,000*l*., taken of Sir Christopher Hatton to the use of Sir Edward Coke, when he was your Majesty's Attorney-General, not to pay a debt of good value due unto your Majesty, nor to accept of a discharge for the same. And for the better strengthening of the statute,

latest biographer[a] of Hatton says that it was partly created by the loans which she had advanced to him on his "bonds and statute merchant," when he first attracted her notice.[b] "It brake his heart," says Fuller, "that the Queen (which seldom gave boons and never forgave due debts) rigorously demanded the payment of some arrears, which Sir Christopher did not hope to have remitted, but did only desire to be forborn. Failing herein in his expectation, it went to his heart, and cast him into a mortal disease."[c] The following letter was, it has been supposed, sent by him to the Queen on this occasion; but, as it is without date, and as he often incurred her temporary displeasure, it may have been, and probably was, written long before. "Your Turk" was, no doubt, one of her courtiers:—

SIR CHRISTOPHER HATTON TO THE QUEEN.

If the wounds of the thought were not most dangerous of all without speedy dressing, I should not now trouble your Majesty with the lines of my complaint. And if whatsoever came from you were not either very gracious or grievous to me, what you said would not sink so deeply in my bosom. My profession hath been, is, and ever shall be to your Majesty, all duty within order, all reverent love without measure, and all truth without blame; insomuch as, when I shall not be found such to your Highness as Cæsar sought to have his wife to himself, not only without sin, but also not

there was likewise a bond taken of 6000l., with sureties to the same effect. So that Sir Christopher Hatton lay charged, under the penalty of 18,000l., not to pay the debt, nor agree to any surrender, discharge, or release, nor any ways to assent thereunto." That this offence was aggravated by the denial and protestation made of late by the Lord Chief Justice, that he was not privy to the condition of the defeasance, whereas the statute was taken to himself by indenture, whereof Sir Christopher Hatton's part was found, but the other was not found. That he was privy to the penning of it, inserted words with his own hand, and that Mr. Walter and Mr. Bridgman, his own counsel, were witnesses thereunto."—Life of Sir Edward Coke in the "Biographia Britannica," Vol. II. p. 690.

[a] Lord Campbell, pp. 155, 156.
[b] Vide, p. 5, ante.
[c] Worthies, II. 165.

to be suspected, I wish my spirit divided from my body as his spouse was from his bed.   And therefore, upon yesternight's words, I am driven to say to your Majesty, either to satisfy wrong conceit, or to answer false report, that if the speech you used of your Turk did ever pass my pen or lips to any creature out of your Highness' hearing but to my Lord of Burghley, (with whom I have talked both of the man and the matter,) I desire no less condemnation than as a traitor, and no more pardon than his punishment.   And further, if ever I either spake or sent to the ambassadors of France, Spain, or Scotland, or have accompanied, to my knowledge, any that confers with them, I do renounce all good from your Majesty in earth, and all grace from God in heaven. Which assurance if your Highness think not sufficient, upon the knees of my heart I humbly crave at your Majesty's hands, not so much for my satisfaction as your own surety, make the perfectest trial hereof.   For if upon such occasions it shall please your Majesty to sift the chaff from the wheat, the corn of your commonwealth would be more pure, and mixt grains would less infect the sinews of your surety; which God most strengthen to your Majesty's best and longest preservation.[a]

When the Queen was informed of Hatton's danger, her old affection for him, as on a former occasion, revived.[b] Though she "visited and comforted him,"[c] on the 11th of November,[d] yet "having once cast him down with a word, she could not raise him up again."   According to Fuller, she brought, " as some say, cordial broths unto him with her own hands, but all would not do.   Thus no pulleys can draw up a heart once cast down, though a Queen herself set her hand thereunto."[e]   Sir Christopher

[a] Copy in the Harleian MSS. 993, f. 75.
[b] Vide, p. 22, ante.
[c] Camden's Annals, B. IV. p. 34.
[d] Nichols's Progresses, III. 122.

[e] Worthies, II. 165. Lord Campbell puts Fuller's remark *into Hatton's mouth*, and thus amplifies Fuller's account of his decease, without citing any authority whatever;—" In

K K

Hatton died at his house in Ely Place, on Friday, the
20th of November 1591, in the fifty-first year of his
age.[a] Though his death has been ascribed to the Queen's
conduct, the statement is very doubtful. His health
had long been impaired, and he died of diabetes,[b] a disease almost always mortal, and to which his constitution
seems to have long had a tendency.[c]

Sir Christopher Hatton was buried with great state in
Saint Paul's Cathedral. The corpse was preceded by one
hundred poor people who had gowns and caps given
them ; and more than three hundred gentlemen and
yeomen, in gowns, cloaks, and coats, as well as the Lords
of the Council attended, besides four score of the Queen's
guard.[d] A splendid monument[e] was erected to his memory by his nephew and heir, Sir William Hatton.

Lord Chancellor Hatton appears to have been sincerely
lamented. Camden describes him so well, as "a man
of pious nature, great pity towards the poor, singular
bounty to students of learning, (for which those of Oxford
chose him Chancellor of that University) and who in the
execution of that most weighty office of Lord Chancellor
of England could comfort himself with the conscience of a

Trinity Term, it was publicly observed that he had lost his gaiety and
good looks. He did not rally during
the long vacation, and when Michaelmas Term came round he was confined to his bed. His sad condition
being related to Elizabeth, all her
former fondness for him revived, and
she herself hurried to his house in
Ely place, with cordial broths, in
the hope of restoring him. These
she warmed, and offered him with
her own hand, while he lay in bed,
adding many soothing expressions,
and bidding him live for her sake.
'But,' he said, 'all will not do. No
pulleys will draw up a heart once cast
down, though a Queen herself should
set her hand thereunto.' "—p. 154.

[a] Monumental Inscription.—Lord
Campbell says erroneously that Hatton was in the 54th year of his age.

[b] Camden, p. 34.

[c] Vide p. 23, ante.

[d] Stow, p. 763.

[e] An Engraving of Sir Christopher
Hatton's Monument, and a copy of
the inscription upon it, is given in
Dugdale's History of St. Paul's. The
inscription will be found in the AP-
PENDIX.

right will to do equity.[a]" In a fragment of a letter from
Mr. Fortescue to Sir Henry Unton, written on the first
of December, ten days after his death, he speaks of the
death of their good friend the Lord Chancellor, "which
must be most grievous to him," and alludes to Hatton's
" broken estate and great debts." [b]

Upon the character of Hatton it is not necessary to
make many remarks, since it has been now so fully deve-
loped. That his talents were little inferior to those of
the greatest of his contemporaries will scarcely be denied ; and, however inadequate he may have been to perform all the duties of Lord Chancellor, few will agree that
in that station " his highest distinction continued to be his
skill in dancing."[c] He was of opinion that " in the cause
of religion neither searing nor cutting was to be used,"[d]
and he accordingly often interceded to preserve his enemies, the Puritans, and his supposed friends, the Catholics, from persecution. It is difficult to understand
for what reasons he was suspected of being favourable
to the ancient faith, and still less of having secretly
professed the Catholic religion. His correspondence
shows that he was the refuge alike of Puritan and
Catholic ; and that the distressed, whether arising from
offences against the State, from having incurred the
Queen's displeasure, or from sickness or poverty, always
appealed with confidence to his humanity and goodness.
His love of literature was well known; and, as Churchyard's letters, and the numerous dedications of books to
him show, he did not merely " affect to be a protector of
learned men,[e]"—a crime, however, with which no modern

[a] Camden, B. IV. 34.
[b] Cotton MSS. Caligula, E. VIII.
f. 180.
[c] Lord Campbell, II. 159.
[d] Camden, b. IV. p. 34.
[e] Lord Campbell.

K K 2

Chancellor is likely to be reproached. Of Hatton's own
erudition and acquirements there is certainly little other
evidence than the high opinion entertained of him by the
wisest and best of his contemporaries, and by his own letters and speeches. The imaginary " scapegrace student of
the Temple," and the imaginary " plucked" member of the
University, to whom, with the same flight of imagination
it is said, the University would not grant a degree,[a] was
accurate in his knowledge, could, at least, write his own
language without flippancy, and maintained a correspondence with some of the most learned men of his age.
Ockland,[b] in his description of the characters of Elizabeth's
Ministers, says of Hatton,—

> " Splendidus Hatton,
> Ille Satelitii regalis ductor, ovanti
> Pectore, Mæcenas studiosis, maximus altor
> Et fautor veræ virtutis, munificusque."

A far more grateful literary compliment was however
paid to Hatton than the dedications of obscure writers,
in the following sonnet of Spenser :—

TO THE R. H. SIR C. HATTON, LORD HIGH CHANCELLOR OF ENGLAND.

> Those prudent heads, that with their counsels wise,
>   Whilom the pillars of th' earth did sustain ;
> And taught ambitious Rome to tyrannise,
>   And in the neck of all the world to reign.
> Oft from those grave affairs were wont abstain,
>   With the sweet lady-muses for to play.
> So Ennius, the elder Africain ;
>   So Maro oft did Cæsar's cares allay.

---

[a] Lord Campbell.
[b] Christopher Ockland's Ειρηναρ-
χία, or Elizabetha, written in elegant
Latin Heroic verse, and containing
characters of all that Queen's great
Ministers. Strype's Annals, ed. Oxon.
1824, vol. III. pt. L. p. 234.

> So you, great Lord! that with your counsel sway
>   The burden of this kingdom mightily ;
> With like delights sometimes may eke delay
>   The rugged brow of careful policy ;
> And to these idle rhymes lend little space,
>   Which, for their title's sake, may find more grace.

Very few personal anecdotes of Hatton have been preserved. He is reported to have once said of Elizabeth
that the Queen did fish for men's souls, and had so sweet
a bait that no one could escape her net work.[a] Harington relates that on one occasion the Queen appeared displeased, and that on Hatton's leaving her presence with
an ill countenance, he pulled him aside by the girdle,
and said, privately, " If you have any suit to-day, I pray
you put it aside, the sun doth not shine; 'tis this
accursed Spanish business, so I will not adventure her
Highness's *choler*, lest she should *collar* me also."[b]

From this pun it has been gravely inferred that the
Queen once actually " collared Hatton before the whole
Court," and the letter before given[c] is said to have been
written to try and " appease her," on that occasion,[d]
though, as has been before observed, there is not the
slightest evidence to show when it was written.

A happier witticism is, however, recorded of Hatton.
" In Chancery, one time when the counsel of the parties
set forth the boundaries of the land in question, by
the plot; and the counsel of one part said, ' We lie
on this side, my Lord;' and the counsel of the other
part said, ' And we lie on this side :' the Lord Chancellor Hatton stood up and said, ' If you lie on both
sides, whom will you have me to believe?'"[e]

---

[a] Nugæ Antiquæ.
[b] Ibid, p. 176.
    Vide page 589, *ante*.
[d] Lord Campbell, II. 162.
[e] Bacon's Apothegms, ed. Mon-
tagu, 367.

Sir Christopher Hatton did not leave a Will. He had settled his estates upon his nephew Sir William Newport, *alias* Hatton, and the heirs male of his body; failing which, on his Godson, and collateral heir-male Sir Christopher Hatton.[*] Sir William succeeded accordingly to Holdenby and Kirby, and all the Chancellor's other property. He married first in June 1589, Elizabeth, daughter and heiress of Sir Francis Gawdy, Justice of the King's Bench, by whom he had a daughter, Frances, who was born in 1589, and in February 1605, became the wife of Robert Rich, second Earl of Warwick. Sir William Hatton's second wife was Elizabeth, daughter of Thomas Cecil, first Earl of Exeter, by whom he had an only child, who died an infant. He died on the 12th of March 1597, and his widow became the second wife of Sir Edward Coke, the celebrated Lord Chief Justice of England, by whom she had two daughters, Elizabeth who died unmarried, and Frances who married John Villiers, Viscount Purbeck. The quarrels of Lord Coke and his wife have rendered the name of Lady Hatton famous in the history of her time. On the death of Sir William Hatton without male issue, in 1597, Benefield and the Newport estates descended to his two daughters and co-heiresses; but Holdenby and the other Hatton estates passed under the Lord Chancellor's settlement to Sir Christopher Hatton, abovementioned. He obtained an Act of Parliament in 1605, to enable him to sell part of those lands; and in February, 1608, he conveyed Holdenby to Trustees, for the use of the King for life, with remainder to Charles Duke of York, in tail male. One of

[*] Baker's History of Northamptonshire, p. 195. Sir Christopher Hatton was the grandson and heir of John Hatton of Gravesend in Kent, younger brother of William Hatton of Holdenby, father of the Lord Chancellor.

the conditions of the sale was, that the King should grant to Sir William Hatton, all his Majesty's interest and reversion in any of the lands of the late Lord Chancellor, by virtue of any extent issued for the debts due by him to the late Queen, provided that the residue of the said debt should be paid off by 1500*l.* yearly, on the days appointed in an instrument made by the late Queen for securing payment of the debt.   The King further agreed to grant the custody of Holdenby house and park, with a fee of forty marks to Lady Elizabeth, widow of Sir William Hatton, and then the wife of Lord Chief Justice Coke, for her life, with the building called the Dairy House, belonging to the Mansion House for her lodging.*   The present representatives of Lord Chancellor Hatton are the heirs of the three daughters and co-heirs of Robert Rich, third Earl of Warwick, son and heir of Frances Countess of Warwick, the only child of his nephew Sir William Newport, *alias* Hatton ; namely :—

1. Lady Anne Rich, who married Thomas Barrington, Esq., son and heir-apparent of Sir John Barrington, Bart., and who is now represented by William Lowndes, Esquire, of Chesham, and William Selby Lowndes, Esquire, of Whaddon, in the County of Bucks.

---

* Baker's History of Northamptonshire, p. 195.   Lord Campbell says, (p. 165) that, by his marriage with Lady Hatton, "Lord Coke got possession of Hatton's estate ; " and that, " Christopher Hatton, who, by a collateral branch, was the heir at law of the Lord Chancellor, was ennobled in the reign of James I., by the titles of Viscount Gretton and Baron of Kirby, in the county of Northampton."   Every one of these statements is erroneous.   Lord Coke never got possession of Lord Chancellor Hatton's estate ; because, after Sir William Hatton's death, it devolved upon his heir male, Sir Christopher Hatton.   Christopher Hatton was not the heir *at law* of the Chancellor, but his heir of entail ; he was ennobled by Charles the First in 1643, and not by James the First : he was created Baron Hatton of Kirby, and not Viscount Gretton or Baron Kirby ; and it was his son who was created a Viscount in 1682, by the title of Viscount Hatton of Gretton, and not as Viscount Gretton.

2. Lady Mary Rich, who married Sir Henry St. John, and had an only child, Henry, the famous Viscount Bolingbroke, who died without issue in 1751.

3. Lady Essex Rich, who was the first wife of Daniel, second Earl of Nottingham and sixth Earl of Winchelsea, and whose present representatives are the Duke of Devonshire and the Earl of Thanet.

The Earl of Nottingham and Winchelsea married secondly, Anne, only daughter of Christopher second Lord and first Viscount Hatton of Kirby, son of Christopher first Lord Hatton, and grandson of the Sir Christopher Hatton, who inherited the Chancellor's estates in 1597. The Honourable Edward Hatton, a younger son of this marriage assumed the name of Hatton, and succeeded to Kirby, and was grandfather of George William Finch Hatton, the present Earl of Winchelsea and Nottingham.

APPENDIX.

SIR, Your sharp letters, proceeding as it should seem from
an intemperate humour of ill speaking, do make me much
marvel to see you changed so greatly as you are from the man
whom I have heretofore known you. The right colours of a
gentleman's coat arms are the virtues of the mind wherewith
he is clothed; but such are your actions to the show of the
world, and so fully fraught with malice, as howsoever your
body be derived from the loins of your ancestors, which I
confess were gentlemen of good fame and memory, (yet is
your mind) which ought to be the habitation of virtue, and
the image of God, through the force of reason so far from the
true merit and reputation of a gentleman, as to be plain with
you, I can hardly think you worthy of so good a title. I hold
him not to be deemed a man of any account, who, besides the
reverend commemoration of his parents' deserts, hath nothing
of his own worthy of the title and commendation of the personage which he sustaineth. Such a gentleman was Catiline,
in pre-eminence of blood and nobility of stock, but yet most
innoble for his vice, and for degenerating from the worthiness
and heroical virtues of his ancestors. Anthonius was said to
challenge great nobility from his house, but his friends told
him it was external, and appertaining to those which were
dead. Tully gloried in that he was noble by his own desert,
and builded not his honour upon the merits of dead men, as
Sallust did. Iphicrates being upbraided by Hermodius for

that he was the son of Cordo, a base parent, answered, my
house taketh beginning from me, but thine taketh her end in
thyself. When the Lacedæmonians bragged that they had derived their nobleness from Hercules, Lycurgus would oftentimes tell them that their brags would nothing avail them, except they did those things whereby Hercules became so noble.
Even so must I boldly say to you, my good friend, that unless
you add some egregious desert of your own to increase the
glory of your house, by the example of the worthy actions of
your ancestors, you shall but live still in obscurity, without all
good fame, as the son of the earth, come from an unknown
generation though men know you, through the ancient blood
and industry of your parents' virtues, to be a gentleman.   It
is not the producing forth of the ancient statues, nor smoky
images, neither yet the authentic coat armour, or torn and
rotten guidons of your worthy ancestors, now dead and con-
sumed to ashes, which can suppress either the foreign hostility
of the invading enemy, or pacify the civil sedition (if any
were stirred up at this present) against your Prince and
country, *nam genus et proavos et quæ non fecimus ipsi, vix ea
nostra voco.*   It is not the vain jactation or boast of authentic
stock (if virtues fail) which can relieve the need of common
peril, or make you truly worthy of the reputation of a gentleman.   To spend the day in surfeit and delicacy; to sit in
purple upon theatres, to go clothed in silk, your feet attired
with golden spurs, your fingers full of gems, a hawk on your
fist, to be perfumed with sweet ointment, and to lead a long
train of idle attendants after you, are not the notes of nobility,
but the marks of effeminacy, than which nothing can be more
contrary, or ought to be further removed from true generosity.
Thus much I have been bold to write unto you, because (when
I friendly admonished you of some things which methought
touched you to take care of) you sent me word, with some show
of offence, that you were a gentleman ; such snarling at every
man's manners (to be plain with you,) when you find they
square not to your own appetite, is neither commendable nor
comely, I gave you my poor advice for the best, and I meant

you no harm, but did rather expect thanks indeed at your hands for my good will, than any such unthankful and unkind acceptation of my well meaning towards you. I know well enough the antiquity of your stock, and the descent of your virtuous parents, yet must I say to you, as I have done often, that your large revenues and ample possessions be but as nurses of vice, and provocations of much evils, (notwithstanding the worthiness of your ancestors) unless yourself, the possessor of the same, have also your portion in valour and virtue, as without the which your gentility in truth is but a veil of licentiousness, a cloak of sloth, and a vizard of cowardice, from the which, I beseech God evermore defend you, to whose gracious favour I commit you. From my lodging in Cornhill, the 20th of November 1586. Your plain true friend,   SAMUEL COX.*

MR. SAMUEL COX TO . . . .

SIR, Among many other your good friends, who do wish you all comfort and relaxation of your present grief, there is none I assure you that bewaileth more heartily the late unfortunate loss, and untimely death of your dear son, than myself, as one whom I have ever loved much, for the many virtues and valuable parts which were in him. But seeing God for some secret causes best known to himself, hath now taken him from you, as more fit for him than for us, and more worthy of his Heavenly kingdom, than of this earthly mansion, (a place in truth not of dwelling but of burial,) I hope you will in your wisdom patiently accept of his divine pleasure, and attribute all to his goodness. So vain and variable (we see) is the joy of this world, and so transitory the state and condition of man's life, that when we think ourselves farthest from death we are nearest our end, and while we be speaking, this flower withereth: as passengers by sea we are all carried away in the ship and feel not how, being many times at our journey's end before we be aware; as well the

* Additional MSS. 15891.

3 A 2

dainty gallant young man, as the rough and wrinkled old man
fadeth away suddenly and consumeth to nothing: most happy
therefore is he, whose course in his lifetime is safe and
straight through virtue, as your son's was, which ought now
after his death to be your greatest comfort: he had long
opened his earthly slumbering eyes before his end, to behold
and think upon God's eternal . . . . . Heaven . . . .
he condemned all transitory and worldly vanities as vapours
of no continuance, which must now be the only joy to relieve
your sorrowful over loving heart. Whereunto wishing always
as to myself, I commit you to the merciful favour of the
Almighty, who ever comfort you with his goodness. From
my lodging in Cornhill, the 17th of December 1586.   Your
assured poor friend,   SAMUEL COX.*

MR. SAMUEL COX . . . .

Sir, I am sorry to hear that your pain is so grievous and
violent as I understand it is. The iliac passion is ever accompanied with such kind of gripings, but being once come to the
uttermost degree of extremity, the malice of it commonly
assuageth and is of small continuance. One contrary spring-
eth from the end of another; and as extreme joy commonly
is the beginning of sorrow, so intolerable and violent grief is
many times the beginning of consolation and pleasure. That
which comforteth me most is your physician's opinion that you
are free from all danger, though your own conceit, through
your sudden sounding and often fainting much abateth the
hope of your health and will not let you believe it. Take
comfort, I pray you, in the goodness of God and in the manifold virtues of your life, and let not any vain dread of sudden
death possess you; easily are the credulous brought into
hope and the timorous into fear; and fear itself is the one-
half of all our worldly miseries: conceive not timorously the
worst because your sickness taketh you usually with a trance;
think with yourself that your pain is the less and passeth over

* Additional MSS. 15891.

as it were with our breathing; it is sooner come than felt, and presently depriveth you of all force of understanding, which, to a man that hath the fear of God before his eyes, should be no discomfort, though it be sudden. I have ever known you studious in all godly zeal and true religion; you have ever lived in such sort, that howsoever it shall please God to dispose of your body, yet shall nothing happen so suddenly or unlooked for to your mind but that it shall always be prepared by the duty of Christian faith to receive God's mercy. We read that Cæsar in his later time was often subject to sudden faintings as now you are; and being present at a disputation where it was debated what kind of death was most easy and least painful, he answered at the length, (to conclude the controversy) that to the virtuous minded man, sudden death was most commodious, as void of all bitter pangs and passions which commonly accompanieth the patient that liveth long and grievously tormented with sickness. Though you be not of Cæsar's mind, yet let not your courage and comfort in sickness be less than his, seeing you are a Christian as he was not; and your disease is as his was, whereof beseeching God to deliver you I end with as many hearty prayers for your restitution of health as your piety of life and manifold virtues deserve, which I commend to the gracious and fatherly blessings of the Almighty. From the Court at Richmond the 17th of December 1586. Your assuredly bounden poor friend, Samuel Cox.[*]

MR. SAMUEL COX TO . . . .

Sir, I have lately received your very long letter, more bitterly written to offend your poor friend, than is fit to proceed from any man of religion and modesty, whereof you seem to make profession. Among other matters therein you charge me somewhat sharply with my disliking of Puritans, in that I should say they were *pietatis simulatores potius quam cultores,* men nourishing popularity under a shew of piety, and working

[*] Additional MSS. 15891.

confusion under the colour of perfection. I cannot deny what
I have said, though I protest I spake it not with any intent to
offend you: and to recant my opinion I may not, for (seeing
you are a sectary brought up in that school) I take it to be as
far from error as yours is from truth. But yet, if I have
spoken anything which is not justifiable in learning and reason I will always willingly submit myself to the correction of a
better judgment, *errare possum, hereticus esse nolo*: and I will
rather sit on the ground with little ease than rise and fall with
great danger. The author of strife, saith Solomon, is as one
that openeth the waters. I pray you, what are your preci-
sians? If any man be contentious, saith St. Paul, (speaking
of external things) we have no such custom, nor the Churches
of God: how then can you excuse your Puritans? that wheresoever they come do raise contention and kindle the fire of
discord, that without any consultation first had with the
Church, are bold to broach new fancies among the people of
their own devising, that take from Princes their due authority in ecclesiastical matters, that bring into contempt such as
be in authority, and make the ignorant subject lofty and arrogant: is not this a sowing of darnell where the light of the
word is revealed? and a laying of grievous stumbling-blocks
to stop the passage of the Gospel? Is it tolerable think you in
these perilous times to dream of alteration and to disturb the
peace of the Church with new contentions of external things
nothing pertinent to faith and salvation, when the Pope is so
vigilantly watchful in every corner to leap in at every little
breach to seek our confusion. If my disallowing hereof have
moved you to think amiss of me, I am sorry any such matter
should procure me your ill-will; but seeing it is for the
truth's sake, I will hope you will not stop your ears against it,
nor think sinisterly of him that hath ever in truth and plainness unfeignedly loved you. And so, I commit you to God.
From Whitehall the 20th July 1587. Your very plain poor
friend, SAM. COX.

MR. SAMUEL COX TO . . . .

SIR, Your servant coming lately forth of the country informed me of an inclosure which you have made not many
days since, to your great increase of benefit, which I was right
glad to hear of. Nevertheless, remembering how well I have
ever loved you, and how it standeth not with the duty of a
friend to cover with any mask of flattery, or other deceitful
colour of plausibility, the imperfections of him whom I affect
so dearly as yourself, I could not choose but open the plain
wonted meaning of my well-wishing and good-will towards you
in these few lines which I have written unto you, not so much
to please you, (though haply in policy another man would
think it fit I should do so for mine own good,) but plainly and
faithfully to advise you, in the sincerity of my love, what is
meetest for you to regard in this matter, for the particular respect of your own reputation and credit. If in turning your
land to pasture, which hath been accustomably occupied in
tillage, you have first considered your public duty to your
natural Country, before you descended into the private care of
your own commodity, it is tolerable and lawful to do that
which you have done: if not, be not offended with me, I pray
you, (for bitter medicines may profit, though they please not,)
if I be bold to tell you that it were better you had no land
than you should so abuse it; no private possessions, than so
to pervert them to the public desolation of your country. I
need not show you what enormities rise in the Commonwealth
by such manner of enclosures. You know as well as I how
they engender idleness, the ground . . . .
all were . . . . . : how they enfeeble and impair the defence
and strength of our Country, by reducing multitudes of people
living honestly by their lawful labours, to the number of two
or three idle herdsmen. You are not ignorant how Churches
are destroyed, and the service of God in many places thrown
down to the ground, the Patrons and Curates wickedly
wronged, and all by the decay of husbandry, one of the
greatest commodities of our Country. If, therefore, it pleased

you to lay these things wisely before your eyes, as considerations worthy to be called to council before you entered to make your enclosure, no doubt it will prosper and succeed well, as a building laid upon a sure foundation: if not, persuade yourself the ground-work was naught, and, therefore, must needs shortly perish, and bring with it more increase of late repentance than of honest benefit; whereof, the best will be this, the justice of the law will pronounce judgment against you: her Majesty, or next immediate Lord of the fee, shall possess half the value of the issues of your land so inclosed: the whole Country which once dearly loved you for your well living, will now justly hate you for your lucre; and the end will be nothing else but loss of reputation with your friends, and increase of defamation among your enemies, from which God ever keep you by his gracious goodness, to whose blessed favour I heartily commend you. From my lodging in Cornhill, the 19th of October 1587. Your faithful assured friend,

SAMUEL COX.

MR. SAMUEL COX TO . . . .

SIR, Your news of the hostile preparations in Spain are somewhat strange unto me, but yet not such as can make me fearfully think that they tend to the invasion of England, as many men conceive. I was in good hope that our troubles had been now at an end, and that the peace so generally spoken of would have concluded ere this time our lingering and languishing wars; but I perceive the King keepeth his old wont, and, like a greedy horse-leech, will not let go the skin till he be full of blood, delighting rather with the wilful mariner, to sail still in the tempestuous broad sea, than with the wise pilot to withdraw himself after storms into the calm and quiet haven. So Scotland stand firm and sure unto us, I am of opinion we shall not need to fear the Spanish brags. It is not here that they mean to land, where they shall have neither faction to back them, nor haven to harbour them; but in Scotland, rather, where they shall have both these wants plentifully supplied, and where their weak, sea-beaten, sick

soldiers may have quiet landing and good cherishing till they
may be able and fit to assail their enemies. The Frenchmen
did so (if you remember,) in King Edward the Sixth's time,
who, attempting to land their forces at Hythe, were all scattered and discomfited, by good fortune, at their first arrival.
They found no faction armed in England to receive their foreign forces at their landing, and therefore they repaired with
their power into Scotland, hoping by that means to invade
England, both with success and facility; and so will they do
now, in my opinion, wanting confederates here to succour them
in the execution of their malice against us . . . . . If they
should attempt to invade us alone of themselves, they must
look for no other fortune than they met with in King Henry
the Eighth's time, twice in Sussex and once in the Isle of
Wight, where, offering to make certain incursions with their
galleys and galliasis, they were all overthrown and discomfited,
though we had wars, even at the same instant also, with the
Scots, which gave them great opportunity and advantage
against us. I do not remember that there hath been any sea
conflict of moment at any time between the Englishmen and
Spaniards, unless it were once in King Richard the Second's
time, who, understanding of a great fleet that should go out of
Spain into Flanders, sent and set forth a navy with all speed
to meet with them, with whom, entering into battle, it fortuned
that the Englishmen and their ships were all scattered and
overthrown; and other than this precedent of sea-fight between
us and them I cannot call to memory, but examples are rife
and frequent of sea-battles between the Frenchmen and us,
though, in truth, ever fearfully foreseeing how perilous a train,
and what hazard of ill-success an invasion might draw with it,
they have seldom attempted at any time to invade us. It is
true that, in King Richard the Second's time, the French galleys destroyed and burnt divers towns upon the English coasts, as
Rye, Hastings, Portsmouth, and Gravesend; but they did it not
by a settled invasion, but by a sudden incursion, and departed
with all possible speed as soon as they had done that they came for.
At another time they burnt Plymouth and many towns in the

Isle of Wight in the same manner; but they did it by stealth, and fled immediately. In the civil war which King Henry the Fourth had waged with Owen Glendower, the Frenchmen invaded England with a hundred and forty ships, and landed twelve thousand men in Milford Haven, to aid Owen Glendower: but the end of their enterprise was miserable; for the Lord Barkley burnt divers of their ships as they lay at road in the haven, and the rest escaped by fleeing and retiring themselves into Brittany. King Edward the Fourth, making war at the entreaty of the Duke of Burgundy against the French King, invaded France with five hundred ships; but the Frenchmen never attempted, for all that, to invade England. So, likewise, in the great wars which King Henry the Fifth made against the French King, the Englishmen invaded France, and at the battle of Harfleur sunk five hundred French vessels, almost the whole navy of France; but the Frenchmen had patience with this overthrow, and never sought any revenge by invading England. The Scots, in truth, took their opportunity in the meanwhile to exercise their malice upon us, but the Duke of Exeter, the King's uncle, and the Archbishop of York, having raised a power to march against them, made them retire themselves into Scotland with shame, and to repent their rashness. So that, for mine own poor opinion, the state of England being naturally strong by the opportunity of the scite and sea as it is, we need not greatly fear the peril of any foreign invasion, so we be true and faithful within ourselves; for unless we be divided by faction or evil sedition, it will be a most difficult and dangerous enterprise for any stranger to invade us, much more, in his invasion, to have the upper hand over us. In King Henry the Third's time, Lewis, the Dauphin of France, invaded England with seven hundred ships. He possessed all the east part of it; he had the sea open to pass to and fro at his commandment; he had divers fortresses and strongholds in his possession, whereby to entertain a defensive war. The City of London and the Tower had submitted themselves to his mercy; the Barons had crowned him King; the Warden of the Cinque Ports, who kept the Keys of England under his girdle, confederated with him as one at his devotion. He had maintained wars the space of three years in England, and Henry the Third, his enemy, being but a child, and unfit, for the imbecility of his youth, to wrestle with so potent a Prince in wars, all which helps and benefits of fortune and force notwithstanding, when the nobility of the realm began once to forsake him, he was glad to make peace with King Henry, and to renounce all his interest and title in the Crown, together with all such possessions, castles, and holds as in three years' space he had recovered into his hands. So did Robert Duke of Normandy, another invader in the time of King Henry the First. The . . . . had called him in to make him a King; he landed at Portsmouth quietly, with a great power of men; he had many great helps to advance himself to the title and fortune of a King; but in the end, though he had reduced a good part of the realm under his subjection, yet was he forced to offer conditions of peace, and was contented to avoid the country: and as neither of both these last Princes had invaded England but by the aid and confederacy of the Barons, so were they both forced to flee and abandon their enterprise as soon as they saw themselves forsaken of the nobility, which, in respect of our present fear of trouble, is not unworthy of observation. I could tell you, that the King of Norway invaded England while William Rufus was absent, and occupied in the wars of Normandy; but to what purpose? The Welshmen called him in, and thought the King himself were absent; yet did the Earls of Chester and Shrewsbury give him battle, and overthrew him with great honour and victory: whereby we may easily perceive how hard an enterprise it is to invade England, and to what infinite perils the invader is subject that maketh any such attempt. He must be first sure of a faction, readily prepared and armed to receive him, of the inhabitants of the country, whom, if he be not able to bridle and command with forces of his own, and to overrule them as he shall see occasion, let him trust to it he shall never be assured of his new-conquered estate: on the other side, if his own . . . . . power be so great as may move fear or offence to the

people which called him in, it is to be thought they will jea-
lously suspect that Prince's greatness, and abate it by all the
timely means they may, to avert from themselves and children
the fearful yoke of servitude which must needs fall upon them
by suffering such dreadful multitudes of foreign forces to occupy and possess their country.   But it is more than time to
make an end of my tedious scribbling; wherein as I must earnestly pray your patience not to confirm, but without offence
to tolerate only my poor opinion, so would I be glad you would
be pleased to examine it thoroughly in your grave judgment,
and to vouchsafe me some few lines from yourself, in answer
thereof, as your leisure shall serve you.   With reference to
your own discretion and best opportunity, I commit you to the
gracious direction of the Almighty.   From Fulbrook and
Westhall Hill, the 2nd of Nov. 1587.   Your very assured
friend,   S. Cox.

MR. SAMUEL COX TO . . . .

Sir, If your evil speeches did not proceed more of spleen
than of judgment, I should hardly digest your petulancy, and
I could answer you if I listed, that seeing you speak what you
should not, you must be content to hear what you would not:
but I will rather bear injury and be patiently silent, than co-
piously eloquent, as you are, in this kind of immoderate railing
rhetoric.   I will only say thus much unto you; if the laws
were duly executed as they should be, if virtue were not trodden down and vice advanced; if perfidy had not place and
preferment before piety; if public authority were not contemptible and little regarded; if magistrates in their offices
were not commonly vendible and corrupted, so wicked a man
as yourself, in your words so venomously slanderous, in your
deeds so hatefully impious, and in the whole action of your
life so foully infamous, could never be suffered to live and insult as you do in all lawless liberty.   If you had not made
shipwreck of all shame, you would have forborne, in common
humanity, to have spoken so unreverently of my Lord as you
did.   It had been your duty to have known him to be a man

that is your superior, and to have used him with reverence fit and due to his place, but when you have said all that you can, and that malice hath left nothing unsearched that may nourish the vein of her humour, yet shall you not find him to be any of those that have raised sumptuous buildings *ex sanguine et miseriis civium*, or that do maintain the domestic pomp and magnificence of their own houses, with the lamentable spoils and rapines of the poor subject, which some men do, not unknown to yourself, with no small touch and imputation to their credits. My Lord, your brother is a noble personage, much beloved for his gentleness, and openly praised of all men for his wisdom, he is one whom I have ever honoured greatly, but I could never be so fortunate as to be worthy of his favour. I am none of those in truth that cause him as other men do, these mighty personages fall down and worship them, and offer up incense unto them as to hallowed altars. If I could, I might peradventure have tasted as liberally of his goodness, as I now feel deeply his undeserved displeasure; but I hope in the end he will look upon my poor merit and service with the eye of justice, and give to yourself, and such other bold and thick skinned faces the reward due to pickthanks and backbiters: and so I end for this time, wishing you more grace to make you acceptable to God, and more gratitude to use your friends more kindly than you do in your slanderous unkind speeches. Your over wronged poor friend, S. Cox.

MR. SAMUEL COX TO LADY ——.

MAY IT PLEASE YOUR LADYSHIP, My desire hath been ever great to do your Ladyship some acceptable service, in part of requital and satisfaction of the many singular favours which you have often vouchsafed to show me. But such hath my hard hap been, and still is to this day, that where I owe most in all humbleness of duty, there am I least able and most unworthy to perform, or show myself such as I ought to be; which I humbly beseech your Ladyship to excuse, not as a wilful fault, (for I would willingly redress it if I knew well

bow,) but as an imperfection of necessity, which (will I or no,)
I must needs obey.   Meeting by chance with this gentleman,
and inquiring of your Ladyship's health, he told me that which
I was most sorry to hear, and would be glad (by any service I
could do you,) to remedy, if it lay in my little power. I understood by him, that your Ladyship hath been lately so shrewdly
shaken with a fever, that it is strange to see so goodly and
beautiful a lady altered and estranged so much, in so short a
space, from the wonted excellence of beauty which heretofore
made you so perfect, rare, and peerless, in comparison of all
other ladies.   This is but to make you call to memory (my
most honourable good Lady,) how brittle a foundation the
gentlewomen build on, that ground all their glory upon beauty;
a thing naturally flitting, and no more permanent than the
time itself that cometh with it; a transitory accident of the
body, not able to continue, seeing the body and all, by course
of nature, must pass away at the length like a shadow.   It was
truly said of the philosopher to the noble Lady Cornelia, that
among all the qualities which pass away with this mortal body,
none is more swift than beauty; which, so soon as it hath
showed itself as a pleasant flower, it vanisheth even in the sight
of them that wonder at it, and most commend it. It is quickly
nipt with the least frost, and beaten down with every small
wind, and either suddenly pinched off with the nail of some
enemy's hand, or overthrown with the heel of some sickness
passing by: neither doth it bring so much delight when it
cometh, as it procureth grief when it departeth.   Domitian,
the Emperor, wrote unto a friend of his, whom he esteemed a
paragon of beauty, that there was nothing more acceptable
than beauty, nor more brittle; no gift of nature more glittering
for the time, and less durable in respect of the end; resting
only upon the uppermost part of the party which possesseth
it, covering many filthy and horrible things, flattering and de-
luding the senses with a simple and slight overcasting of the
naked skin. Whatsoever they be, therefore, Madam, that are delighted with its vanity, they carry a veil before their eyes, a
snare before their feet, and bird-lime upon their wings, which

will not easily suffer them to discern the truth, or follow virtue, much less erect their minds to the contemplation of heavenly happiness. If the comeliness and colour of your Ladyship's face be changed with a few fits of a fever, in so short a time, you may easily conjecture what it would be with continual sickness and access of old age. Give me leave to be bold with you, my honourable good Lady, in telling you the truth. Those yellow locks of yours shall fall away, and such as remain shall wax hoary; the scaly wrinkles shall plough the loathsome furrows upon your tender cheeks and glistering forehead; a sorrowful cloud shall cover the cheerful beams and shining stars of your beautiful eyes; rotten raggedness shall consume and fret away the smooth and white ivory of your fair teeth, not changing them only in colour, but disordering them also in place; your straight neck and well-proportioned shoulders shall wax crooked, your smooth throat curled, and you shall think those dry hands and crooked feet were never your own. Such an enemy hath she always at home that carrieth beauty in her face: a misspender of time; an occasion of pain and trouble; a plentiful matter to minister peril; a maintainer of lust and unclean affection, if she have not the singular fear and grace of God before her eyes. If your Ladyship do live, these things will come upon you almost sooner than it can be spoken; and if it please you now to believe me, you shall then less wonder to see how you are transformed. As the beauty and joy, therefore, of the body is but vain and transitory, so must I greatly commend your Ladyship (reputing it of so small price,) in that you do so worthily apply yourself to exercise the beauty of the mind; a thing far more precious, pleasant, and sure than the other, consisting, likewise, of semblable laws and comeliness of order, with apt and due disposition of the parts; a treasure which neither length of time shall consume, nor sickness extinguish, nor death itself overthrow. To let pass to speak of other. Spurina was renowned, not for her natural beauty's sake, but for her procured deformity. Her virtue made her truly fortunate; her beauty therein was most excellent and acceptable, even as your Ladyship's is. As your grace of beauty is joined with virtue, it is an ornament not unpleasant to sight, though short and frail; otherwise, it is but as a burthen to the owner's mind, and an unlucky sign of sorrowful deceit; from the which God evermore preserve your Ladyship, and give you the fulness of His heavenly grace and beauty, to make you eternally happy and fair in His eyes and blessed favour. Your Ladyship's most bounden at commandment,

SAMUEL COX.

MR. SAMUEL COX TO . . . .

SIR, I thank you much for your late letter, advertising me of the apprehension of the fisherman. I do not doubt but that he will be made discover some things that may greatly import the quiet state and safety of the realm, if he be well and thoroughly sifted. Truly, Sir, these foreign fishermen, under colour of fishing, do much harm, and are notable spies for strange Princes to work us privily great mischief. They secretly sound and search our channels, our deeps, our shoals, banks, and bars along the sea coasts: they run up into our havens, our creeks, our bays, and into our very roads. They take the best marks for the avoid of danger, they try the safest landings, and become perfecter in the knowledge of our sea coasts than our own masters and pilots, which even in peace bringeth great peril, but in time of war double danger. It is injury enough, and more than tolerable, that her Majesty suffereth at their hands to be deprived yearly of so many hundred thousand pounds as she is, by abusing her rich fishing upon her sea coasts, and, if ancient records be true, the Low Countries do not make so little yearly as 490,000*l.* sterling only by the herring which they take in the seas appropriate to her Majesty's dominions, a great mass of treasure, and a commodity which few Princes would lose, that might have so good right to it as her Majesty hath: at the least, she might in honour and justice require the tenth, though of her gracious goodness she would grant the stranger the rest. Seeing they receive greater benefit, and with less charge by the sea than the poor labouring husbandman doth within the land, by the tilth of the earth, what reason is there (especially taking their fish within her Majesty's peculiar seas and sea coasts) that they should be wholly exempt of all tithing? The tenth is a duty, Sir, as you know, which every man oweth to God in token of his thankfulness for those benefits which it pleaseth him to give us; and seeing God and nature hath established the royalty of our British seas and coasts in her Majesty, there is just cause in my opinion that they should yield her the tenth, as well in respect of God's part, to whom all tithe is due, as also for a grateful acknowledging of the great commodities which they receive within the royal sea limits of her Highness' dominions. It is a hard thing when ourselves, being beaten from our own fishings and fishing places, must be glad to buy our own commodities of strangers, a matter against all reason, conscience, law, and good civil policy. But Sir, pardon me, I beseech you, that I am so bold to run into so large a field and discourse of this matter, it is a thing, I know, that many men have spoken of in highest places, and could have no redress *locutores permulti, pauci sunt agentes.* Yet, Sir, let it not offend you that I, poor fisherman, do lay my hook also among others to catch the fish which hath been so long hoped for. I am glad to understand that her Majesty hath entertained that worthy preacher to attend on her Highness in Court whom you so highly commend. I know the man well, and have been long acquainted with him; he is, in truth, an honest, zealous minister, full of God's spirit, a man brought up in righteousness, ready to all good works; I would in God we had more such labourers in his holy vineyard. We have many that preach unto us in the lamb's weeds, but are inwardly ravening wolves: many, that with their premeditated painted orations thrust out the Pope at the fore gate, but receive him in again by the example of their lewd lives at the privy postern. God frame their hearts to embrace his word, and to follow it! for the godliness and virtue of Prince and Prelate is a great help to universal holiness; and if these be remiss and unclean, the rest (finding open the gate of licentious liberty) run headlong by throngs into the immeasurable field of errors, sects, and blasphemies. From the which God ever preserve us, to whose gracious favour I commend you. From London, the 18th of April 1588. Your assured friend,

SAMUEL COX.

MR. SAMUEL COX TO HIS COUSIN AND NAMESAKE.

MY GOOD COUSIN, You are now called, as I hear, from your private pleasant studies, wherein you might safely take delight without danger, to the public office and function of an Ambassador, which you shall hardly execute without peril. Many men, for vain glory sake, have unadvisedly desired such places, which afterward, instead of reputation, have justly yielded them ruin and repentance; but I assure myself, good Cousin, that you are none of those; and I beseech God rather keep you from the office than call you to it for any such reward. I do not doubt but that the very name of an ambassador is enough to make you fear the place, and to show you what the office importeth, and requireth in sufficiency at his hands that must discharge the same. In ancient times past Princes were so exquisite in the choice of their Ambassadors, that they employed no man in that function but such as had integrity, learning, and wisdom; how you find yourself, good Cousin, furnished with these perfections I refer to your own judgment. They were always men publicly noted for their virtues, and were called *legati a legendo*, because they made a public lecture; and so likewise they bear the name of orators, for that they were, or should be, eloquent, that is, learnedly able, by the help of long experience, to deliver all matters committed to their charge in apt and good words. Such an ambassador was that noble Cyneas, for King Pyrrhus, of whom it is written that *omnium animos facunda et diserta oratione sic quoquo vellet pelliciebat, ut Pyrrhus ejus opera, plures sese urbes recepisse, quam catafractorum viribus et impetu, sæpenumero gloriaretur*. Demosthenes was such another; highly commended for his learning and eloquence, and openly praised of all men for his wisdom. But, Cousin, the excellence of those times and persons is not to be stained with the comparison of this ignorant, barren age of ours. Their ambassadors were all grave, wise orators, and such as had been fathers of long and great experience: ours in respect of theirs (I am sorry to say it) are little better at this day than grammarians and sophisters, *qui verborum flosculis, nulla rerum scientia pollent,* and therefore forbidden by the law in truth to be ambassadors, though the weakness of the time do for necessity sake allow them. I speak not this as one thinking you unworthy of the place, for I know the contrary, but only to show you what an ambassador ought to be, that will worthily discharge such an office; and yet, to be plain with you, I had rather you went without it than had it if you might conveniently avoid it, as I am persuaded you might if you would humbly seek to be freed of it. Titus Manlius Torquatus (if I forget not the story), having an infirmity in his eyes when he was chosen Consul, refused for that cause to take it upon him, alleging that there was no reason that the fortune and state of others should be committed to his care that had no eyes to see or foresee what was fittest for himself. The Senate well accepted of his reason, and spared him the election; and so I think her Majesty would do, you having as just cause of excuse as he had, if you would seek it, on your knees, at your Prince's gracious hands, as he did. You see yourself feeble and sickly, and an ambassador's office requireth a strong body; he must be up early and down late, watch long and with little ease, make many sudden and painful journeys, and those accompanied also with divers and sundry perils, for the King's service, which asketh a body of sound health, not crazed and subject to many infirmities as yours is. More than that, where the law prescribeth that he should be five-and-twenty years old at the least that should be called to be a Prince's Ambassador, you know your years are not yet so many, and therefore as yet unmeet to be so employed. Your poverty, besides, (which is a dangerous temptation, if God should not the better guide you with his grace,) might be some reason in this case to move her Majesty to think you unfit for the place. It is not unknown to her high wisdom that foreign Princes used many

times to lay their hooks baited with rich presents to catch ambassadors withal that are poor and needy; and though it be
known well enough that no man can corrupt you with gifts,
nor possibly allure you with any unhonest lucre, yet is it
perilous that an ambassador should *ob facultatum inopiam, tur-
piter quæritare victum;* which your indigent estate might be
apt enough to force you unto, if her Highness (before she called
you to this place) should not bountifully supply your great
want; which, if she should do on the other side according to
the measure of your necessity, your service might happily be
over dear to her, especially in these frugal times when rewards
are so scant, even where they are best deserved. But, Cousin,
I will say no more to you, as you know the commonwealth's
sore, so am I sure that you understand your own grief best,
and are best able to use best means to cure it. To be short,
I will only wish you such a course in fortune as may be safest,
both here and elsewhere for yourself, and not thought fraudulent in your absence to your many poor creditors, who, now
with open gorge, are ready everywhere to exclaim on you, for
that they say you have sought this preferment as a place of
immunity and privilege, of purpose to defraud them of their
debts; and some of them stick not to allege for themselves,
that so deep a debtor by the justice of the law ought not to be
employed in any such public office; and that, *ei qui ære alieno
obstructus est, legatione interdicitur.* I would be glad, my good
Cousin, that I were able either to say or do anything to free
your shoulders from the burden of so weighty a charge; but
being an unfit instrument to deal in so great a cause, I remit
the use of these and such other reasons wholly to the consideration of your own judgment, resting ever as faithfully
yours as you have justly bound me. From my lodging in
Cornhill, the 20th of April 1588. Your very fast true friend
and kinsman,   SAM. COX.

MR. SAMUEL COX THE YOUNGER TO MR. SAMUEL COX.

SIR, Among so many notable benefits, whereby you have
made me very liberally and deeply beholden to you, there

hath been nothing more beneficial to me I confess in my life-
time, than your grave and friendly advice, always readily given
me, in all times of my need, both for my commodity and comfort. I cannot deny but that the office of an Ambassador
(according to your opinion,) is in some sort accompanied with
many perils, for that was the reason indeed why the law at
the first, (considering to what dangers ambassadors are daily
subject unto) did grant them such large and honourable privileges: and I remember, that Cneius Octavius, being sent
ambassador by the Romans to King Antiochus, was slain
at Laodicea by a lewd abject fellow of no account, for which
cause the Romans made war against the King: so were
Tullius Clinius, Lucius Roscius, Spurius Manlius, and Caius
Flaminius, all Roman ambassadors, cruelly put to death by
Tolominus, King of the Fidenates and of the Veientes. The
Sibaritæ also executed thirty ambassadors sent to them by the
Crotoniatæ, and caused them to be thrown out of the gates of
the city, and laid as a rueful spectacle before the walls un-
buried, which are examples, I must needs say, very manifestly proving that ambassadors live not without peril. Yet,
Sir, let me desire you also to remember withal, the care that
the law hath taken to provide for their safeties: which saith,
that *legatus totaque ejus familia et comitatus, est inter hostium
tela sacrosancta et inviolabilis.* If any man do offer an ambassador, or any of his train, any manner of violence to the touch
or violation of the honourable prerogative which the law of
nations hath given him, as a guard to defend him from all
hurt and injury, *qui eam violaverit aut pulsaverit, traditione ac
deditione plectendus est.* If he or any of his train, were but
stricken only, not hurt, and much less slain, yet, for this presumption and inhumanity, the law maketh the ambassador
judge and revenger of his own cause and injury. We read,
therefore, that Lucius Minutius and Lucius Manlius, for
striking the ambassadors of Carthage, in a general and public
council and assembly of the people, were forthwith delivered
to the ambassadors themselves, to be punished for their
offence, as they should think good. Quintus Fabius and

Cervius Apronius, were served in like sort, for the like violence offered to the ambassadors of the Apollonians: so that,
considering how strong a defence an ambassador's privilege is
unto him in peril, and that he carrieth evermore the justice of
the law, yea, rather the sword of punishment about with him,
wheresoever he goeth, to correct and revenge all such wrongs
as any man shall dare to proffer him, I see not (if I were
worthy of the place, as I am not,) why I should fear more to
be an ambassador abroad for the public service of my country,
(having those regal liberties to defend me,) than a private
man at home without them, to follow and attend mine own
particular causes. One privilege among the rest encourageth
me as much as anything else to take the office upon me, and
it is this, that for three years' space after my time of legation
expired, the law doth freely exempt and spare me from all
public services. *Nam qui legatione functus est,* as you know
better than I can tell you, *intra triennium ad aliud publicum
negotium compelli non potest.* Beside this, it will be some
restraint to bridle mine enemies' malice, who (having now, in
the flame of their rage, commenced many wrongful suits
against me, in hope, by their indirect practices, to consume
me by the misery of the same) shall be commanded by her
Majesty to surcease their suits, and the judges to forbear to
give judgment until my return; in which mean while I shall
win the benefit of time to relieve me of their grievous and unjust vexations: which, otherwise, without this privilege of her
Majesty's service, might peradventure be my utter undoing.
Omnibus, saith the law, *qui reipublicæ causa absunt, jure civili
conceditur, ut quamdiu suo munere funguntur judiciorum aleam
subire non cogantur:* which favour among the rest (though I be
most unworthy) I hope her Majesty, in her gracious goodness
will not deny me. I could extenuate by many reasons the
perils which you object to see so great in the exercise of this
office, if I thought it fit in so small a matter to trouble you
any longer. But, Sir, to what purpose? I could put you in
mind of many women (who in the imbecility of their sex,
being naturally fearful to incur dangers,) have, notwithstand-

ing, taken upon them to be ambassadors in great and weighty causes : but to what end should I labour *tanquam Phormio*, to teach Hannibal the stratagems of war? You know that the thirty Sabine virgins were sent as ambassadors to the Romans to entreat for peace, and the Princes of . . . . when they would celebrate the Olympic games, used commonly to send women of honourable quality as their public ambassadors, to solemnize the same. You may remember also, that Volumnia and Vatuiria, most modest and virtuous matrons, were sent as ambassadors unto Coriolanus. And the senate of Rome sent the Vestal virgins, by the advice and persuasion of Aulius Vitellius, unto Vespasianus the Emperor, to beseech him to incline to peace : whereby you may perceive, that, if women, by nature weak, by want of wisdom imperfect, and by the frailty of their sex timorous, have discharged these high offices without fear of peril, and without those singular perfections which you think needful in ambassadors, there is no such great cause as you pretend in respect of danger, to dissuade any man from the exercise of the same. Pardon me, therefore, I beseech you, Sir, if for my country's cause I submit myself willingly to the fortune of this place, what misfortune soever do befal me. We are all bound by God's word, not for fear like men pleasers, but for conscience sake like christians, to serve him truly, to obey our Prince faithfully, and to travail in our vocation, like subjects, honestly: and seeing the Prince, who is God's ordinance, hath commanded me to this service, I should think not to do it, were to leave my true duty, to fall from my faith, and rashly to judge her Majesty unjust and cruel in her commandments, whom all men have ever found most just and gracious. And so I commit you to God. From my lodging in Cornhill, the 27th of April 1588. Your very assured friend.   S. Cox.

Sir, Your fear of foreign invasion by strangers' power is much greater in my opinion, than you have just cause to conceive, if you would with light of understanding look well into the present strength and state of England, as it standeth at

this day. If Pericles said to the Athenians, who had not by
many degrees so large and absolute dominion of the sea as
her Majesty, *magnum est potiri mari, si insulani essemus, inex-
pugnabiles essemus*, what may her Majesty say of England, and
how much are we bound to thank God, that it is not only an
island, but the best fortified island, with shipping, men, munition, this day in all Christendom. I am glad to hear that the
Lords of her Majesty's privy council have providentially
taken such order as you advertise me they have, to prevent
the misery which is like generally to fall upon us, through the
scarcity and want of corn. Yet can I not a little marvel, how
this great lack should arise, considering the late seasonable
and fruitful years which we have had. All dearth groweth
either of ordinary causes natural, taking effect according to
the pre-destined plat of the whole world's economy ; or of extraordinary means of God's sending : as for natural impediments, either by excessive moisture or abundant heat, or howsoever else, they have not been such as can give any man just
cause to think that they have been the motives of this universal
sterility : neither hath God taken the blessings and fruit of the
earth from us, by any extraordinary mean of his heavenly
divine power, so that this want which we feel must needs be
altogether fraudulent, and falsely pretended in my opinion, by
some caterpillars and ravening wolves, who have either purely
stolen and conveyed away our corn and victual to the enemy,
whereby they have procured this dearth, or else have made
the Commons believe, in times of great abundance, that there
was great scarcity and want of things, which they have done
only to advance their own private gains, an abuse too common
in these days, and unfit to be suffered. I have many times
wished that we were well acquainted here in England with
the secret of Nuremberg, in reserving and keeping their corn
sweet and unputrefied many years together, as in those parts
they do. In these perilous times of scarcity, it were a most
necessary thing for our relief, and worthy to be put in practice.
It is thought that the fertility of England is such, if men do
but use their common industry, that it is plentifully and

wholesomely able, one year with another, to victual and feed twice as many more as it doth: so that if the surplusage were by good order reserved within the realm, and some part of it every year laid up in store, no doubt we might enjoy continued plenty, or at least sufficiency of all manner of needful victuals, at competent and reasonable prices. But, Sir, leaving these sores and griefs of commonwealth to the skilful judgment of such as understand them better than myself, I end in some haste as you see with my earnest intreaty, that you will pardon my boldness. From the Court at Greenwich, the 2nd of May 1588. Your assured friend,   S. C.

MR. SAMUEL COX TO . . . .

SIR, My brother Mardin taketh it unkindly, that you reproach him so often as you do with his father's late offence, and myself (to be plain with you) if his case were mine, would be loath to hear of a fault so often, that had so much discomfitted or grieved the offender. Christ was born for us all, and yet himself, touching his humanity, came of some evil disposed ancestors, though his person were sacred and unspotted, and solely and singularly holy. But being God and man he wiped away (which we cannot do) that stain of iniquity with the most divine and omnipotent power of his Deity, and was only pure and perfect. Thamar committed a fault with her husband's father; and Judas the patriarch lay incestuously with his son's wife: and yet this adulterous seed (through the incomparable bounty of God) enjoyed the Royal sceptre. We may not therefore disdain, or reproach any man for the frailty of his ancestors, for what is he, whose house and blood (if it were well sifted) carrieth not with it, in some sort or other, the spots of humanity and of Adam's fall. *Christus est heri et hodie et usque in secula futurus*, he was the son of Adam, as well as of David; the publicans and sinners sat with him at his table, as well as his disciples, he died for those that were dead before him, as well as for those which lived after him, and though some of us be more sinners than others, yet may we all go hand in hand together in that Baby-

lonical captivity of sin, and no man can say but he is an exile
from God, and a banished man from Heaven and his own Country, through the bondage and punishments of sin, unless it
please God to manumit him by his mercy, and restore him
again as a lost sheep to everlasting liberty.   But Sir, here I
will make an end, and pray you to pardon me that am so suddenly of a prater become a preacher of divinity, to one that is
more able to teach me, than I am able to learn.   From Westhallhill, the 11th of May 1589. Your well affected poor friend.

S. Cox.

MR. SAMUEL COX TO . . . .

Sir, I am requested to desire your favour in the behalf of
an old soldier, now lately pressed (as I hear) to go to these
new wars.   I beseech you, Sir, be as good to him as you may,
and remember his long absence already for his Country's
cause from his wife and children. It is a privilege due, as
you know, to old soldiers, not to be constrained, but to serve voluntarily; *nec quem militem veterem invitum ducendi jus est, sed
voluntarium.* If any home forces or urban bands be levied to remain within the Realm (as commonly there are in such perilous times to meet with intestine tumults if any shall happen)
this man is as fit as any I know to be employed in such a
service.   I am glad it pleaseth her Majesty to send a power
into Spain to prevent their coming hither.   It was the council of Sulpitius the consul to the people of Rome, in the wars
intended by the Romans against the Macedonians.   *Macedonia potius quam Italia bellum habeat, hostium urbes agrique
ferro atque igni vastentur;* and we may as truly say as they,
*Expecti jam sumus foris nobis quam domi fœliciora potentiora-
que arma esse.*   You remember the story better than I.   If
the Romans had sent forth their armies to succour Sagunt,
when the Carthaginians besieged it, they had diverted the war
in Spain, which afterward Hannibal brought into Italy, and . .
. . . . . the second war with the Carthaginians, when experience and their former careless cunctation had made him wise
too late, they sent their armies into the enemy's country to

keep their own home from foreign spoil. And I could wish, Sir, before the going forth of the army, that there might be some solemn public thanks given to God, used generally throughout the realm, both by prayer and preaching; no doubt he looked for such a sacrifice at our hands; and it were needful, and more than needful for the expiation of our foul and heavy sins: even the pagans in like troubles *solebant majoribus hostiis rem divinam facere.* The Romans did it after their superstitious blind manner in all their wars, especially in those which they made against Philip, King of Macedonia. If they did it to their false painted images, shall not we do it to our ever living true God against the King of Spain?

As for the late Scottish road into England it makes me remember Amilcar's case toward the Romans. This Carthaginian captain, contrary to the league, seduced certain French subjects to stir rebellion against the Romans, even as Bonner hath done lately, being a Scot, against England. The Carthaginians could not get Amilcar, for if they could, they had delivered him unto them; but they banished him for his offence and confiscated his goods, which is as much in this case as her Majesty can require at the King's hands in satisfaction of justice. And so, Sir, I leave any longer to trouble you, wishing I were able in any sort to requite your manifold and undeserved courtesies. From Westhallhill the 12th of May 1589. Your beholding poor friend, S. Cox.

A LETTER TO HIS FRIEND THAT HAD GIVEN MONEY FOR AN OFFICE.

Sir, It is an ordinary custom among friends to congratulate with one another upon any advancement or increase of good fortune, and so should I do and would do most willingly with you for your late preferment, were it not that I hear that you have rather purchased it with money than deserved it by virtue. To desire any office as a man is tolerable, but to solicit or sue for it as an ambitious seeker thereof is uncomely and hately. Whatsoever is procured by unlawful means is unlawful, and having obtained your office, (being a place of justice) by unjust and corrupt solicitation doth more justly give me cause to condole than congratulate with you for your preferment. Seldom or never prospereth the magistrate that buyeth his office, nor the commonwealth that tolerateth any such enormity. The wise man is admitted to give council for his judgment; the learned man for his much reading; and the old man for his experience: if for any of these respects you had been admitted to your office, men would then have reverenced you for your virtue, where now they do yield it you but only for your place. He that sits to judge many, must expect in reason that many will judge him: therefore assure yourself, however men may fear your authority, they will afford you little love unless you deserve it. He that hath liberty, with little knowledge how to use it, is as a ship without a pilot; and he that hath . . . . integrity without desert is . . . . . sepulchre; I may not say as a dye in purple. The surest estate is that which is most remote from envy. Before you were a magistrate you lived in safety, what you will or shall do now I know not; only this I know, that in mine own opinion, it is better to contemplate with the poor philosopher than to practise government with the rich rulers. And so praying your patience to judge the best of my boldness, I wish you all joy and good desert in the late increase of your new good fortune. From Westhallhill the 7th of July 1589. Your very assured plain poor friend,

SAM. COX.

MR. SAMUEL COX TO . . . .

SIR, I am sorry to perceive your offence conceived against me for little or no cause, if I be not deceived; but my hope is, that in the end you will have patience to hear the truth, as no doubt you have wisdom to resist all such as are apt without cause to reprove other men of error. Many men love to warm themselves with the wool of other men's sheep, and to accuse others unjustly, to the end themselves may in show seem, though not in deed, worthily blameless. But, Sir, I beseech

you do not, as many times ill judges do, pardon the crow and
punish the dove, neither be over hasty to give ear to informers, for they that so do must needs have guilt. The
proverb is . . . . I find to . . . true in
mine own case. I have been as careful as might be possible
not to offend you. I have many times made a curtesy to necessity because I would not displease you; I have ever desired
to love you, more for your virtue than to fear you for your
authority, and yet can other men that reverence you with
their lips, when their hearts are far from you, find more favour
at your hands than myself, that am more willing than any
man to enjoy your good opinion, and inferior to none in the
honest course of true friendship to deserve it. But, Sir, innocency in peril is a strong defence, which is all the comfort
I have in the accusation which you lay to my charge; and so
hoping that you will hear patiently and judge justly, and that
you will not over credulously give ear to informers, who as
wasps among bees, rather live to sting than to gather honey, I
end most dutifully obedient to all your commandments, as one
more ready to stoop and to kneel with the camel when he is
to take his burden, than frowardly with the stubborn Pharisee
to justify myself in any of my actions that do any way offend
you. And so I most humbly take my leave. From Westhallhill, the 7th of July 1589. Your Honour's at commandment,

SAM. COX.

MR. SAMUEL COX TO . . . .

SIR, Your yesterday's letter reprehending me in some sort
for my sharpness against the use of plays I received this day by
your brother Mr. Lewin, for the which I heartily thank you,
especially for your friendly care and regard which I find in
them, to satisfy me in some points which I stood in doubt of;
I must confess unto you I am somewhat scrupulous for the
tolerating of these stage-plays which are now adays without
respect of person, time, or place, so much used and allowed
among us. They were pastimes, very odious to the ancient
Fathers, and first instituted in the beginning for the honour

of idols: and (being commonly full of vile and unhonest words, intermingled with much lightness, lack of gravity, and comeliness,) I see no cause in my poor opinion why they should not rather be suppressed than suffered; forbidden as hurtful than borne withal as meet exercises in any Christian regiment. This made Chrysostom say, that the Devil builded stages in cities, and first invented plays to delude the people; that they contained the wicked acts and whoredom of the Pagan false Gods, grievously wounding the consciences of good men, and many ways kindling the flame of hateful lust in such as were addicted to frequent them. And David himself crieth out, saying turn away mine eyes, O Lord! that they behold not vanity: Can there be any greater vanity than these dangerous schools of licentious liberty, whereunto more people resort than to sermons or prayers? Can any corruption be more perilous or intolerable (especially in these latter times, in which by teaching we ought to amend) than to nourish the people in idleness (which is your . . . . advice) and not compel the loiterer to labour, who bringeth infamy and slander to the Commonwealth? What greater deformity can there be in any well reformed state than to see the folly of a few fools bring divers wise men out of their wits? To see the gates of Magistrates open for the one and shut up against the other? To see rich men give more to a player for a song which he shall sing in one hour, than to their faithful servants for serving them a whole year? To see infinite numbers of poor people go a begging about the streets for penury, when players and parasites wax rich by juggling and jesting? It is said that the great and noble temple of Diana was built by the Amazons with the only money and riches taken from a player, and that the very pagans themselves did lament it, even in the time of blindness and ignorance, how much more may we Christians (enjoying the benefit of the Gospel) bewail the miseries of these times wherein we see more houses built for these lewd assemblies than for preaching or praying: *alios mores hæc ætas, aliam vitam postulat:* It was wondered at that two parasites gave more money to King Cadmus toward the building of the famous city of Thebes (which had a hundred gates unto it) than all his subjects did besides: and is it not as strange and much more lamentable in these days that (professing Christ as we do) we should suffer men to make professions and occupations of plays all the year long, whereby to enrich idle loiterers with plenty, while many of our poor brethren lie pitifully gasping in the streets ready to starve and die of penury? In my poor opinion the building of Thebes with the parasites' ill-gotten . . . . . cannot be more detestable, nor the . . . . more miserably wicked in this . . . . if we must needs tolerate these spectacles of folly for the vain recreation of the people.   I could wish that players would use themselves now adays, as in ancient former times they have done, which was only to exercise their interludes in the time of Christmas, beginning to play in the holidays and continuing until twelfth tide, or at the furthest until Ashwednesday, of which players I find three sorts of people: the first, such as were in wages with the King and played before him some time at Hallowmass, and then in the later holidays until twelfthtide, and after that, only in Shrovetide; and these men had other trades to live of, and seldom or never played abroad at any other times of the whole year.   The second sort were such as pertained to noblemen, and were ordinary servants in their house, and only for Christmas times used such plays, without making profession to be players to go abroad for gain, for in such cases they were subject to the statute against retainers.   The third sort were certain artisans in good towns and great parishes, as shoemakers, tailors, and such like, that used to play either in their townhalls, or some time in churches, to make the people merry; where it was lawful for all persons to come without exacting any money for their access, having only somewhat gathered of the richer sort by the churchwardens for their apparel and other necessaries, in which manner if our players now adays used their sports and pastimes (not making their playing an occupation of idleness all the whole year, but an occupation only at certain festival times of rest when the people are free from labour,) in my opinion they should less offend God in playing, and the magistrate for granting them a moderate kind of liberty.   And so, praying pardon of you for my troubling of you so longwith a matter of so idle and playing a subject, I commend you to God's merciful and richest blessings. From Westhallhill the 15th of January 1590. Your very true friend,

SAMUEL COX.

MR. SAMUEL COX TO MRS. E———.

IT is much against my will, good Mrs. E., and I beseech you think so, that I have been forced all this while to forbear in any sort to visit you; but seeing the cause comes from above, and not from any careless thoughts of mine own, my hope is, you will be favourably pleased not to interpret my long silence unkindly; how often I have wished you well, and how dearly I love you, were but in vain to tell you. Such tales need not but where the truth is not known; but if mere cogitations were spirits, and could flee through the air invisibly, as undoubtedly spirits do, I dare say to you boldly, you had had more messengers from me ere this time than you could have well devised matters to have sent them. Let it suffice then, I beseech you, good Mrs. E., that these few lines do faithfully assure you (though they come but slowly) that he which wrote them affected you soundly, and meaneth as sincerely towards you as any friend you have living. Excuse me, I humbly pray you, if I seem too rude a scholar to you in this unaccustomed style of writing. You may see it is not my profession to make love, and my years (as you know) require other cares ; neither am I skilful in truth in these kind of fanciful studies; and yet seeing men in my case, know what we wish, but not what is wisdom; and love (as the proverb is) knoweth no laws, give me leave for once to be of his opinion, that thought it not fit for a lover to make any conscience of idle ceremonies. There was a law among the Lacedæmonians that he which loved youthfully at forty should lose the liberty of a citizen till fifty: do but remember it, and then think, I beseech you, how far I hazard myself for your sake, that am

content for the love of your favour not only to incur the peril
of law, but also to abandon the sweetness of mine own liberty,
the most precious possession that God can give me; but in
truth what would I not, nay what should I not do, for so rare
a virgin, such a virgin especially whose eyes (all men see) are
but as lights of modesty, whose ears listen after nothing but
piety, whose thoughts savour nothing but chastity, whose virtues are such as need no other means to publish her praise
than the merit of her own integrity?   I could say more if I
would, but that I know you covet not to hear your own commendation, which is none of the least of your virtues.   Well,
good Mrs. E., you see you have that you deserve, I mean my
love, though happily not that you desire, more virtue in me to
be worthy of your favour.   Imagine I am not the worst, though
I be not the best, and then, I dare assure you, the golden Indies
shall not better content you for their riches, than the plain well
wishing of so poor a friend for his fidelity; for so I will be,
and so I must be, unless I should do you injury.   God bless
you, good Mrs. E, and give you the effect of your best desires,
and me his favour, and yours to make me happy here and
elsewhere for ever.   From W . . . . . , the . . of May 1590.
Your very true friend,   SAM. COX.

DR. SEAMES TO MR. SAMUEL COX.

SIR,   I have talked with our Miller whom I find, as before,
resolute (if he can choose) not to marry, and if he be constrained, not to love: and in such a case what I should say I
know not.   When marriages that should be comforts are
turned to dislikes, then the law, *propter nimiam sevitiam*, or
the like, granteth separation *a thoro et mensa.*   As I do not
well see how it may be broken off, so I do not conceive how
it may be comfortable to either party, in which respect I
think it not amiss (if it may possibly be done) that he should
dotare et dimittere, which, in some reasonable sort, though his
ability be but small, he may peradventure be brought unto ;
and yet hitherto I cannot find that he will yield to anything,
being already persuaded that the witnesses will not swear

APP*.   3 C   .

that which they have said.   I have occasion myself to be absent in the term, and in the mean space to be much at Oxford.   If the parties should, by common consent, refer it to some indifferent friends, we might be eased, and the thing I hope well ended; but if it be to be dealt in while I remain here, I will either be glad to see you here at a Scholars' Commons, or meet you where you shall appoint.   And so, with my very hearty commendations, I commit you to God.   From Kinghame the 22nd of April 1594.   Your assured loving friend,   W. SEAMES.

WRITTEN BY MR. SAMUEL COX FOR A FRIEND.

SIR, I beseech you pardon me, if being possessed with some passion by reason of my grief, I do not so fully answer your letters and the effect of your desire as should become me.   I know you can conceive, and will easily consider in your wisdom, how heavy a cross it is to the father, to see his child, by wilfulness and want of grace, cast away and ruined ; of whom he expected greatest comfort and obedience.   Children are bound by a natural band of piety, to honour and obey their parents, to whom, if they owe humanity and thankfulness in anything, it is chiefly requisite in so necessary a thing as marriage ; wherein they ought not to deal without their parents' knowledge and consents, to whom both by the law of God, and by the light of nature, it appertaineth most properly, to have care to determine of their children's marriages. But my daughter, who was the chiefest cause of my care and my greatest hope of comfort, having taken upon her this weighty vow of marriage, directly contrary to my mind, as wilfully bent in the frowardness of her heart to disobey me, and violently as it were, to carry me into my grave with tears, hath contemptuously trodden under foot all humanity and duty, both to God and to me her poor father, to whom she was more bound to be thankful, for the manifold heavy cares which I have taken for her well doing than I can easily mention.   I concur not in opinion with those who think the parent's consents in these cases to be more convenient than necessary.   It

is a perilous gap of liberty opened to this and such other ungodly matches, which in many ancient common weals, have
been deemed so odious, as such contracts have not been only
frustrated and disannulled, but the disobedient children and
persons so offending have been severely punished.   Adam
himself did not chuse Eve to be his wife, it was God his
father, that brought her unto him: no more did Isaac, but
his father Abraham sent his servants to his kindred, to provide
one for him.   So did Isaac send Jacob unto Mesopotamia, to
the end he might there make choice of a convenient match
for him.   After this followed the law given of God, by Moses,
that children should honour and obey their parents.   But, Sir,
to what end should I trouble him with these examples, whose
wisdom knoweth them much better than I am able to imagine,
I beseech you pardon my presumption, and let the zealous love
of a father to his child excuse this boldness of mine to so
honourable a personage as yourself: unto whom, though fewer
words might suffice in respect of your grave judgment, yet,
being uttered in sorrow and grief, they may humbly (I hope)
impetrate favour and pardon of you.   Your assured true
friend.

UNKNOWN, TO SIR CHRISTOPHER HATTON.

Sir, So great a hope have I in my long trial of your merciful disposition, as it emboldeneth me to tie your leisure to
an unpleasant but needful repetition of Mr. Gifford's great
extremities, which have banished all hope if they be not,
through your goodness, mitigated before the Parliament, that
time yielding little leisure or leave for such unregarded suits.
It is your Honour's wisdom that can best determine my humble petition; therefore, reposing my only hope alonely in
your accustomed favour, and laying at your feet our great
mishaps, I forbear any longer to trouble you. Your Honour's
most bounden.

THOMAS CHURCHYARD TO SIR CHRISTOPHER HATTON.

Sɪʀ, The duty I owe you, the friendship found, and my
desire to continue in your favour, makes me watch occasion
to write and seek such matter as may be delightful for the
worthy person to whom I send it. I have presumed to show
you a piece of the honourable entertainment that Monsieur
and his princely company hath here received. I remit the
circumstances to this bearer, but cannot omit myself to tell
you how glad I am to see the people's affection to follow
my Lord of Leicester, as it doeth, by means of his wonted
courtesy. I dare boldly assure you he hath lighted such a
candle, both for hospitality and noble train, to all this country,
that few or none can show the like, or come any thing near him.
The marvellous dearth of victual, the greedy nature of this
people, and the hardness of all good things to be gotten,
maketh his honourable dealing shine the more, and seem in a
manner wonderful; the covetous cruelty of the common sort, by
their eager biting at gold, being such as it were enough to eclipse
the brightness of a Prince's bounty. The prices of all things
are so extremely unreasonable, as I am persuaded a King's
purse would scarcely reach with ease to the performance of
that which we find his Lordship hath with great good fame
and commendation most nobly discharged. You may think
it strange that I dwell so long upon so small a matter; but if
you were here to behold it in substance, you would pardon
my pen, and think it worthy of a larger discourse. For my own
part, I am but a looker-on, and a well-wisher to those whom
of right I reverence, and desire to serve in all faithful duty;
but yet is there no man that for the honour of his Country is
more glad than I to see this spectacle of true honour and
virtue in our Nation so far shadowing all others that would
contend to come near it. Now I have betaken myself to this
course of service, my desire is here to leave my bones, the
rather because I see my country hath no grave for a *Churchyard*. In furtherance of my intention herein, I must intreat
boldly, as I am wont, the mediation of your goodness by

writing a word or two to my Lord of Leicester, to prefer me
to the battle, to the breach, or to some noble Seignior whose
service may help me to find that which I have long sought
for, and could never with contentation obtain.   The last reward of a soldier is death ; this do I desire, as a man that have
made choice, though unworthy, of that profession.   I seek no
farm, I sue for no pension, nor I love not to live as an alms-
man : I covet to die like a Soldier and a true Subject, as loath
to live any longer in misery, when I see the world waxeth
weary of my well-doing.   If I may entreat a few lines from
you, I shall conceive good hope to obtain my request; if not,
I shall doubt I am forgotten there, where virtue hath most
bound me to bestow my love and service.   God increase your
good fame, and make you happy in His grace and all other
prosperity!   Your Honour's so bound in duty,

THOMAS CHURCHYARD.

MR. SAMUEL COX TO SIR HENRY LEE.

SIR, I had not thought that my mild and meek manner of
writing unto you could have possibly deserved so unkind an
answer as you sent me by your servant Beaumond ; much less
that so small a matter could draw you so quickly to forsake
your friend, who hath ever so faithfully loved you; neither can
I easily believe (whatsoever it please you to write,) that, having loved a man once with discretion, you will hastily leave or
lose him without cause ; for I pray you, Sir, admit the worst.
I presume you made me a promise, and you say you did not.
Shall this be sufficient to make you reject your friend, or to
wish you had left him five years sooner?   Truly, Sir, I am
sorry to hear it; and I must conceive so well of Sir H. Lee,
both for his particular kind merits to myself, for his wisdom
generally in the choice of his friends, and for the constancy of
his love and good usage to all men, that, though there were a
much greater cause than this, it could hardly make him contemn or condemn his poor friend so lightly.   I have heard of
a bird, called Ephemeres, in Scythia, that is bred to-day and
dead to-morrow.   I beseech you, Sir, let our friendship live

longer; let it not flee and fleet away so suddenly to give men
cause to think us mutable. You are a gentleman whom I have
long loved too dearly to lose so lightly, if I may be so happy
as to hold you. I have made choice to live near you, for the
special regard which I bear to your virtue, and (though I speak
it to yourself,) I have not been a little proud of the comfort of
so singular a friend, and so good a neighbour. It was the
least part of my thought to offend you; and, seeing I have paid
the money, let not him that is beaten make the amends. I
assure you, Sir, if you knew all, and what shift I was forced to
make upon the sudden to serve your turn, I am persuaded you
would sooner thank me than think me worthy of blame for my
labour: but I will tell you more when I speak with you, in
which meanwhile I will ever love you, and pray you to do so
by me till I deserve the contrary, which I will never do by
dealing with you unjustly, though, by misconstruction, you
may take me unkindly. And so I commit you to God. From
my lodging in Cornhill, the 2nd of Nov. 1587. Your assured
poor friend to command,   SAMUEL COX.

SIR, Being by occasion come hither to Frankfort, to confer
with Monsieur de Legure, he shewed me a letter of Monsieur
Buzenvall, wherein he writeth that some of my good Lords
and friends in England, were of opinion that I should be there
shortly, because they had written unto me to that effect. But
I received no such letters, neither from my Lord of Leicester,
nor you, to whom I acknowledge myself to be much beholding,
and to be altogether at your disposition. And though they
had come to my hands, yet could I hardly have done that you
desired, by reason of a piece of business, which is fallen upon
me, and concerneth the well-doing of a great many wherewith
I am entertained, and cannot but embrace it, as well for my
credit as my duty sake; and this it is, Sir. The Duke of
Bouillon, who is lately dead at Geneva, (finding himself near
the point of his departure,) requested me as earnestly as a man

might do, and so did likewise other of my friends, that I
would take into my care the towns he holdeth in sovereignty,
over which he gave me full power and authority, together
with the tutelage of his sister, whom he appointed his heir.
And whereas since his decease, the Duke of Lorrain hath laid
siege to Jametts, and threateneth also Sedan; the inhabitants
of the town understanding of the Duke's will, have requested
me to assist them in this time of need, which I have resolved
to do, seeing that, thereby I shall not break any point of my
promises, and the King if he weigh well the matter, cannot
justly mislike of my doing, being to no other end but to confirm the places under . . . . and to preserve the towns
against the practices and attempts of the Spaniard.   So taking myself to have a lawful calling in this action, I am upon
my return to Geneva, meaning from thence to advertise the
King, how much it importeth him to impeach the attempts of
those who without any right or title seek to possess them, and
afterwards to restore them to the same state, by way of truce,
or peace, wherein they were, before the Duke's decease; and
I think his Majesty will hearken thereunto, and that the matter may, by way of negociation, being well handled, be
brought to good pass, to the profit and surety of the said
towns; and if I can so end my business, (which I make no
great doubt of,) then shall I be more at liberty to acquit myself
towards my other friends whom I hold in no less recommenda-
tion, and thereof I will not fail to send you word.   This siege
whereof I have spoken, is but of the effects of the victory,
which those of the league have gotten, whereof they do not
forget to prosecute the fruits that are easiest to be gathered.
And to speak the truth, they have used singular diligence,
upon the general amazement which the unexpected fall of
this great giant hath wrought, to show their power, as well for
the increase of their reputation, as to make the world believe
that the same force, which had beaten it down, was likewise
ready to scourge those which had set it up.   So they came
within five leagues of Geneva, and put it in some fear; from
thence they were extending along by the frontiers of the Canton

of . . . . who thereupon took arms . . . . a good
countenance. They in Barill, were put in great alarm, afterward they staid in the county of Mountebilliard, where they
burned and spoiled all they met with, to the loss of above
2,000,000 crowns redouning . . . . who thereupon
retiring himself in a great fright to the Duke of Wirtemberg,
they both levied men, out of hand, for redress of that insolency. The town of Strasburgh, seeing such neighbours
drawn towards them, began to doubt the worst, and put themselves in readiness.   The Duke Casimer, seeing them so
near him, was in doubt to be visited in the Palatinates, and if
they had cast themselves into it, all that part which is beyond
the river of Rhone, had been their prey; and last of all, as I
have said, they have settled themselves before Cedan and
Jametts, having left all the borders of the Rhone amazed and
affrighted with their audaciousness and celerity; and as I have
heard this manner of prosecuting their victory, hath wrought
an apprehension in the inward parts of Germany; at the same
time was I at Hidelberg, and, considering with myself the
smallness of their forces, being not above four thousand men,
ill paid, ill led, and brought rather to make a brag, than any
great effect, I could not but marvel, or rather laugh, to see
what a terror they had wrought in those, who, being disunited,
improvident, and unprepared against the accidents of this
troublesome time, have escaped danger rather by the secret
providence of God, than by the greatness of their own means
wherein they abound . . . . using therein, but when it
is. . . . .   The Duke Casimer, upon this
occasion, assembled certain Lansquenets and Rayters, but it
was after the storm was past, and I think that now he shall
have no use of them. If they of .this country would make
their profit of these insolencies, (which are sensible and visible
arguments of the common danger that threateneth them,)
they would join with an other, in courage and fidelity, as well
for their own defence as to repress the bravery of this league,
which hath made so much ado in all Christendom. I know no
better way how to join together all these ragged and unpo-

lished stones, and to be the mortar of the whole building, than
the Queen's Majesty of England, if she might be well dealt
withal, to be the instrument thereof: for the great honour
which she hath gotten by daring alone to lay hands on him
that was tearing in pieces both France and the Low Countries,
hath brought her such credit and reputation, that her advice
would prevail much in these parts, to induce them to make a
like union for the defence of our cause, as our enemies have
done to assail us; and, in my opinion, the time is now very
seasonable, to deal with them, while the terror is yet alive in
their minds, of these late dangers; which, when it shall be
overpast, they will hear without understanding, and see without perceiving, and falling back again to their own accustomed
security, will leave time to the conquerors either to weaken by
force or abuse by subtlety, those who do oppose themselves to
their ambitious attempts. And if your treaty succeed not well,
you and your confederates will be constrained to seek such an
union to the end, that, after so great expences and travail lost,
you may be backed and sustained by assistance from hence,
and it is not to be doubted, but that our adversaries, what
show soever they make, have their necessities and are not so
lusty, but that another fresh assault, well-grounded, and well-
led, may make them shake and conform themselves to agreement. Some have caused bruits to be cast abroad here, but
I know not from whence it cometh, that the King of Navarre
made so slender account of the Dutch army, that partly it was
the cause of the overthrow thereof; but he is greatly wronged
by that slander, which I perceive doth by little and little wax
cold; for he hazarded his own life to make himself a way to
come to them; and it may be justly said, that courageous
Prince is to those of his party, instead of a mighty bulwark to
stop the swing and fury of this persecution, he is of an invin-
cible stomach, and spareth not his own wealth, which he be-
stoweth bountifully, after the manner of Alexander, to make
him way to greater things, retaining for himself only hopes, as
the other did, but that they are grounded upon a better foundation, and have respect to an object of far greater worth. He

might easily preserve that which he hath, but his mind cannot be restrained within such bounds, but seeketh by force to do vengeance on the authors of all those evils, and to compel . . . . . . to be . . . . of this Kingdom, to the accomplishment of which purpose he hath need of assistance from abroad, which, joined with the small means he hath within the realm, may altogether be able to frame a new body, and to do some notable effect this year, which would greatly amaze the enemy, where otherwise he will be bold and audacious, if, either by negligence or disability there should not be something attempted against him. If there be good ministers employed in this matter, it may be brought to good pass, as Monsieur Legure shall be better able to conjecture, and will advertise you, otherwise it will be but a grief to spend our money, to bring honour and credit to those which are the authors of our troubles, as it hath happened this last year. And now I pray you give me leave to speak a word of your negotiation of peace, which, when I think upon it, breedeth some doubts in my head, to see that those whom you have preserved from destruction, should give you occasion (by their suspicions, fearful and offensive pertinents) to hearken to this treaty, you and they not being soundly united together. The Spaniard will fear your holding together, and despise you being divided; and there is no doubt, but they are very cunning in treaties; for on the one side, with the ostentation of his great preparations he will engender a fear, and on the other side preach pretence of oblivion of things past, with observing his promise in small matters, and . . . . pleasant title and hope of a peace he shall easily make an impression of that which every man longeth for; for my own part I love no wars, and I think they only ought to be referred to this end, to deliver men from greater mischiefs, and that (by obtaining that which a man striveth for,) he may be assured to enjoy the conditions he hath purchased. The Queen's Majesty of England hath begun this action with great honour, having showed herself to be provident, in preventing the danger that was ready to fall upon her head, and magnanimous in sustaining an honest cause ready to be overthrown; and as many have in admiration, her perseverance, so it resteth to get out of it with like reputation, providing in such sort for her safety and theirs, whom she hath hitherto defended; and likewise for their well-doing, that, if they shew themselves worthy of that favour, she may leave engraven both in their hearts the remembrance of her great deserts; and in the enemy's minds an opinion that the unity and allegiance between her and them can never be dissolved, which is to be accounted so much the stronger, as it shall be less in their power to break it. I pray God give you wisdom to conduct well this matter, being so full of difficulties, to be brought to a good end; for if he do not accompany us, with his grace, as well in matters of peace as of war, both will re . . . . struction as it hath happened in our Dutch army, in the dissipation whereof, and in many other accidents, we might and ought to observe that the purposes of God are far other than the purposes of men; for where the glorious entry thereof struck terror into the hearts of our adversaries, and gave courage to our friends to sing an untimely triumph, we have suddenly seen it thrown down even lower than the earth; and on the other side the King of Navarre, accompanied with a handful of men, and in a manner fleeing from his adversary, obtained a famous victory. That mighty King, and that great Captain, who tumbled at their feet so many goodly cities, and saw himself round beset with monuments of conquest, hath been checked in the midst of his course, and by whom, but by a magnanimous Princess? The King of Poland, who wanted nothing of the Kingdom but to sit in the throne, hath been disgraced and taken prisoner by a Chancellor of small experience in matters of war. What should we think of your Sir Francis Drake, who hath been the scourge of that proud nation, and done shame to them at home in their own bosoms! and here in our country of France a mean gentleman of Dauphiny commandeth in the field and groweth greater . . . . . . where as our Princes, oftentimes with loss, have been fain to shut themselves within towns. And besides it may be noted that the diligence and good success of poor Skynk doth sometimes cross the enterprize of the greatest soldiers. By all which effects we ought to perceive, that God, by small and slender means, will abate the pride of great and haughty persons, which set themselves against His will, and he will have to himself the honour of our deliverance, for that we are so apt to steal it from him to ourselves, whensoever any good hap lighteth upon us; and for my part it maketh me hope well of the affairs of the Church to see God hold this kind of proceeding, for it is his manner of doing, and now that he beginneth to beat down the proud ones, it is to be looked for that he will advance those that are held in contempt.[*]

MR. SAMUEL COX TO . . . .

Sir, I understand that you are lately married, which is now the special cause that makes me bold to trouble you, being moved only to write these few lines unto you, that you might see how your poor well wishing friend congratulateth with you for your happy marriage. You are both of you very young, and have in all likelihood many years to enjoy the company and comfort of each other. God keep you both from discomfort, that have so long to live linked in the society of marriage together. I understand you conceived unkindly of your father, that he would not suffer you to marry sooner. If you knew what it were for a wife of fifteen years, and a husband of seventeen to entertain the charge and government of a family, you would say your father were cruel in marrying you so soon, and yourself unadvised in entering so hastily into so weighty a charge. The Athenians were commanded by Solon not to match themselves in marriage before they were twenty years old. Lycurgus made a law among the Lacedemonians, that no man should marry before he had accomplished the age of five and twenty years. Prometheus forbade the Egyptians to marry before thirty, and yet you think much to stay till seventeen years expired. There are certain laws and conditions in marriage, whereunto the husband is bound, as soon as he hath betaken himself to a

[*] Additional MSS. 15891, f. 169.

wife, as to be modest in manners, gentle in conversation, faithful in things committed to your trust, wise in counsel, provident for your family, sober in speech, careful of your children's education, and such a one as must always have truth and honesty as the object of commendation to guide and direct all your actions. If being but seventeen years old, you be furnished with these virtues, you are fit for marriage, if not, assure yourself more experience had been meet for you, before you had undertaken so heavy a burden. Plato would not have the children of his Commonwealth to marry before they had understanding and discretion to govern so great a charge, but having wisdom to guide them, he thought marriage to be a second Paradise, and a very hell when good government wanted in the parties married. I must commend one thing in your marriage as an argument of good judgment in you: that is, the equality between you and your wife in blood, in birth, and in state. No disparity, which many times bringeth with it perpetual captivity; but semblable and like conditions, which engender perfect love and good liking with freedom: which I beseech God ever make most happy and comfortable unto you, as no doubt he will the rather, for that you lovingly followed therein your good father's advice and direction, whose assent in such cases is necessary for him to give, and as dutiful for you to crave. Among the Lacedæmonians, he was disinherited that matched without his parents' licence, and among the Grecians he received sharp correction. God make you his, and guide you with his heavenly wisdom, that you may perfectly know him in the goodness of his mercy, and be ever here and elsewhere eternally happy. Your assured friend and kinsman,   SAMUEL COX.

MR. SAMUEL COX TO MRS. E——.

GOOD MRS. E. . . . , I have sent this bearer to inquire of your health, as desirous by others to hear how you do, seeing I cannot be admitted to see you myself. I have been many times at your house to visit you. I have earnestly entreated the favour to speak with you. I have sought you in the zeal of my honest love, with the best affection that so poor a friend can yield you. But what shall I say? Mistress E., my dearest love, is not at home; or she is sick, and may not be seen; or so busy as she will not spare any idle time to spend in visitation with so unwelcome a guest. What discomfort these unkind answerless answers have given me, I may not be bold to tell you; nor what grief I conceive of these undeserved disgraces. I take them but as worldly accidents, necessary sometimes to check our sudden joys, and I will swallow them, as I may, like bitter pills, in hope they may in the end prove more wholesome than loathsome. But yet, my sweet Mrs. E., let me beseech you to forbear in this sort any more to grieve me; know that I profess, as your poor friend, to love you. Bestow these crosses upon those (if any be,) that hate you, and not upon him that seeketh, by true affection, to enjoy you. Think with yourself, if you loved me as I do you, what thorns you would find then to tread on; what provocations of dislike, if good-will were not already well grounded; leave them as . . . . . . those that deserve them, and vouchsafe me more comfort that am carefully desirous, by all due means of good-will, to please you. So shall you ever bind me most faithfully to love you, and God, I hope, shall bless us both the better, and bid the banns in a happy hour, which I beseech him to send quickly and speedily to his gracious good pleasure, and both our comforts; to whose favourable tuition I commit you. Your most bound faithful poor friend,   S. C.

MR. SAMUEL COX TO MRS. E———.

Good Mrs. E., I received lately a letter by the hands of my servant, but from whom I know not, for I find no subscription under it, and lacking the appearance of some star, or, at least, the skill of some Persian astrologer, to tell me in what region the child was born, I can neither worship it as I would, nor present the myrrh and frankincense due to the birth of so sweet a creature as I should. Born it is; but whether at Bethlehem or Judæa, or at Capernaum in Galilee, I cannot show you. I like the aspect and countenance of it exceed-

ingly. If you know the mother, I . . . . . signify her name
unto me in a line or two . . . . her no harm, I assure
you, but happily love the child the better for the mother's
sake; neither need you fear Herod's cruel proclamation for the
destruction of children. It is Samuel, no Herod, that desires
to see it. At the foot of the letter there was written (as I take
it,) a certain Hebrew character, or else some hidden enchantment, fitter to be sent to a necromancer to conjure, than to a
friend to read; and surely, if it were put in a circle, I believe
it would prove some notable spirit that wrote it; for so I must
conceive, both by the witty and pithy inditing of it. I imagine
it came from some gentlewoman, for it was full of courtesy;
but uncourteously concluded, by the lack of a name. Yet
must I think myself beholding to her, because she meant
kindly towards me; for the which, let me entreat you, good
Mrs. E., to thank her if you chance to see her, and desire her
not to think it strange if I put that spirit in a circle that she
sent me to conjure. I will command it not to hurt her. And
so, with her own manner of subscription, I commend me to
you. Wishing you as well as he that best loveth you, your
true friend,   Nobody.

MR. SAMUEL COX TO MRS. E——.

Good Mrs. . . . . . . , a gentleman, loth to have his name
known, hath willed me to send my servant to see how you do.
What he is you must conjecture yourself; for I am warned I
may in no wise tell you. When I found him so scrupulous, I
asked the reason. He answered me, that a gentlewoman lately
taught him, that wisdom in matter of love never to subscribe
his name, which (saith he,) since I have ever observed. I told
him, for mine own part, honest love needed no such secrecy;
truth seeketh no corners, and virtue should not be ashamed to
show her face; and though that gentlewoman would not write
her name the first time for modesty, yet the second time, no
doubt, she would think it needless to use any such curiosity.
Thus I was glad to excuse her, whatsoever she was; and I
would do as much for you, if you should happen at any time

to commit so modest an error. Only this moveth me not a little, that such a gentlewoman's letter written without a name must now make me to be nameless in this paper, by his commandment, whom she so offended; and so must I ever be till she make him amends by another letter, wherein he may see her hand and name subscribed. Your fast friend,

Sam. C.

MR. SAMUEL COX TO . . . .

Mr. T., I have received your letter, and though I have no cause to thank you for your news (as you say yourself,) yet the remembrance of old friendship, that hath been of long time between us, makes me take anything kindly that comes from one who I think meaneth honestly. Touching the matter you write of, I must deal plainly with you, and I hope I may do so without your offence; as I have some cause to mislike it for my own private, having but one poor thing to live on, which I have bought and over-bought once or twice already, even to my utter ruin and undoing, and yet cannot enjoy it quietly for statute and other incumbrances; so am I sorry, in regard of the public, that any such thing should be set abroach, as this is, that might in any respect, in these dangerous days especially, give any the least occasion that may be to move so loving and obedient a people as her Majesty hath, and justly deserveth to have, to any manner of discontentment, as I fear this will, that toucheth so many, (for all cannot be wise,) if it be not very temperately and mildly handled; which, for my own part, I do nothing doubt of, considering the most honourable and grave Commissioners that are to deal in it. I have heard it said, and not without great reason, that the law rather suffereth a mischief than an inconvenience: that is, it rather tolerateth a wrong done to some one singular person only, than a hurt popularly grievous and offensive to many; and though I wish with all faithful humility and lowliness of duty, as much good to my most sacred dread Sovereign Princess, both for opulency of riches, and all other worldly felicity, as the commendation, or rather admiration of her divine virtues and most

merciful government doth justly merit; yet I would to God in
this matter (I speak like a fool,) it would please those good
sides of hers, I mean those worthy Counsellors which her
Highness hath about her, to observe in this point, as they do
in everything else most justly, the wisdom of the law, and
rather heed what is good for many, than what is hurtful to one
only, that it might be said, the Prince, as well as the law,
rather suffereth a mischief, and is content to endure that is
a hurt unto herself alone, than bring upon her people, by
avoiding such particular mischief, a general inconvenience
grievous to many; and then do doubt this untimely tossing
and tumbling up of men's estates : this ransacking of old titles,
and raking up, as it were, dead men's bones out of their graves,
which by her Majesty's peaceful blessed reign have long lain
asleep in their quiet possessed lands, would not now be so
favourably suffered. The Emperor Vespasian was called the
jewel of the world, and the darling of mankind, for his singular deserts of probity, piety, and pity, towards his poor people;
but was there ever any Vespasian, or other Cæsar whatsoever,
of more singular merit to their subjects, than our gracious
Sovereign Lady is to hers? No truly, she passeth them all,
both in mercy for pardoning, and in modesty and mildness for
governing; she spareth, commonly, when she may spill, she
stayeth when she may strike, and we see daily that she saveth
with mercy, when she might, if she would, destroy with justice;
which makes me poor wretch think assuredly, that if her
Majesty knew how many men are like to be hurt and utterly
ruined in this case, some by ancient warranties which have
been made in the sale of these lands to others; some by statute, some by recognizances, and some by infinite suits of law
that must needs depend upon the sequel of this matter, I am
persuaded her Majesty would rather lose, and forego her benefit, and say as that God of mercy said (whose image she is,)
ignosce illis, quia nesciunt quid fecerunt, they purchased lands
which they knew not to be mortgaged, and therefore they shall
have no harm by it, than any way take the advantage and
increase of gain, that the law, I confess, and the pre-eminence

of her Royal prerogative in this case giveth her. Men say,
the ignorance of the fact may excuse, though the ignorance of
the law cannot; and yet I have heard the learned are of opinion
that in some cases the ignorance of the law may excuse, and if
ever it did, or may excuse, either for fact or for law, or if it
may be termed true innocency, which hath no intent or cogita-
tion to offend, then surely, they that were not born when the
land was mortgaged, and have bought it since without any
knowledge of fact or law, that might in any sort prejudice them
in their purchases, ought in all reason and conscience to be
favoured and justly excused, both for their innocency and ignorance, that never heard, nor knew anything till now, after the
happy reign of so many Princes, why they should not peaceably and quietly possess their inheritances; and yet, I confess
it becometh us all, whatsoever we have, to lay it down at the
feet of her Majesty's mercy, if she have either cause to use it,
or will be pleased to command it, and much better we were to
do so, than trust to the courtesy of the law, that saith *caveat
emptor*, or impeach your Prince's prerogative, which is nothing
in effect, if we take it absolutely, but *licet si libet*, if I be not
much deceived. To make an end, I have but a piece of a poor
manor to live upon, and God knows indeed but a very small portion. I have sold a great part of it to supply my wants, the rest
hath been extended for debt ever since I bought it, till within
this year or two, and I owe yet, I protest unto you, above a
thousand pounds upon interest, which the rent of Fulbrook will
not discharge. I have served her Majesty first under her Ambassador Mr. Dale, in France, and then under her Vice-Chamberlain Sir Christopher Hatton, as a poor scribe in Court twenty
years together, without any manner of recompense, which I think
no man can say, that hath served so long. Now, if my desert,
which I confess is very small, be worthy of anything; or if my
unfortunate estate may move any commiseration in the eyes of
those that are the Commissioners, I hope, and will humbly sue
that they will spare me from the composition which you speak
of. If not, I am but a beggar, as I was before, and so I must
by this means even desperately continue still, and will thank

God for it, even as well as he that hath the philosopher's stone
to play withall, which I assure you I would not desire, (for the
best gold is but worldly dross,) but only to enable me to serve
my Prince and Country; and so, meaning very shortly to speak
with you at London, I forbear at this time any longer to trouble you. From Fulbrook, the same day that I received yours,
being the 29th of April 1599.   Your old fellow and friend
most assuredly,   S. Cockx.

A LETTER WRITTEN TO THE LOWER HOUSE OF THE PARLIA-
   MENT BY KING JAMES, TOUCHING THE MATTER OF UNION,
   WHICH THEY IMPUGNED.

You see with what clearness and sincerity I have behaved
myself in this errand, even through all the progress thereof,
though I will not say too little regarded by you, but I may
justly say not so willingly embraced by you as the worthiness
of the matter doth well deserve. I protest to God the fruits
thereof will chiefly tend to your own weal and prosperity, and
increase of strength and greatness. Nothing can stay you
from hearkening unto it but jealousy or distrust, either of me
the propounder, or of the matter by me propounded. If of
me, then do you both me and yourselves an infinite wrong, my
conscience bearing me record that I ever deserved the contrary
at your hands; but if you distrust me of the matter itself, then
you distrust nothing but your own wisdoms and honesty, for as
I have given over wrangling upon words with you, so crave I
no conclusion to be taken at this time herein, but only a commission, that it may be disputed and considered upon, and reported unto you, and then will you be your own cooks to dress
it as you list: so that, as I have already said, since the conclusion hereof can never be without your own assents, if ye be true
to yourselves, no man can deceive you in it. Let not yourselves,
therefore, be transported with your curiosity of a few giddy
heads, for it is in you now to make the choice, either by yielding to the providence of God, and embracing of that which he
hath cast in your mouths, to procure the prosperity and increase of greatness to me and mine, you and yours, and by

3 D 2

the way-taking of that partition wall, which already by God's Providence in my blood is rent asunder, to establish my throne and your body politic in a perpetual flourishing peace, or else contemning God's benefits, so freely offered unto us, to spit and blaspheme in his face, by preferring war before peace, trouble before quietness, hatred before love, weakness before greatness, and division before union, to sow the seed of discord to all our posterities, to dishonour your King, to make me and you a proverb of reproach in the mouths of all strangers and enemies to this nation and envyers of my greatness, and our next labour to be to take up new garrisons for the borders and to make new fortifications there, *sed meliora spero.* I hope that God, in his choice and free will of you, will not suffer you with old Adam to choose the worst, and so to procure the defacing of this earthly paradise; but, by the contrary, that he shall inspire you so as, with the second Adam, ye shall produce peace, and so beautify this our earthly kingdom herewith, as it may represent and be an earnest penny unto us of that eternal peace in that spiritual kingdom which is prepared for the perpetual residence of all his chosen children.

THE EARL OF ESSEX TO LORD KEEPER EGERTON.

MY VERY GOOD LORD, There is not the man this day living, whom I would sooner make a judge of any question that did concern me, than yourself; yet, you must give me leave to tell you, that in some causes, I must appeal from all earthly judges, and if in any, then surely in this, when the highest judge on earth hath imposed upon me, the heaviest punishment, without trial or hearing. Since then I must either answer your Lordship's arguments, or forsake mine own defence; I will enforce my aching head to do me service for one hour. I must first deny my discontentment (which was forced,) to be any humorous discontentment, and in that it was unseasonable, or is too long continuing, your Lordship should rather condole with me than expostulate. Natural seasons are expected here below, but violent and unseasonable storms come from above. There is no tempest to the passionate indignation of a Prince nor yet at any time so unseasonable, as when it lighteth on those that do expect a harvest of their careful and painful endeavours; he that is once wounded must feel smart, till his wound be cured, or the part senseless be cut off. I expect not her Majesty's heart, being obdurate; and be without sense I cannot, being made of flesh and blood; but then you may say I may aim at the end; I do more than aim, for I see an end of all my fortunes, and have felt an end to all my desires. In this course do I anything for my enemies? When I was present I found them absolute, and therefore I had rather they should triumph alone, than have me attendant on their chariots. Or do I leave my friends? When I was a courtier, I could yield no fruit of my love to them; now I am an hermit they shall bear no envy for their love to me; or do I forsake myself because I enjoy myself? or do I overthrow my fortune because I build not a fortune of paper walls, which every puff of wind bloweth down? or do I ruin mine honour, because I leave following the pursuit, or wearing the false mark of the shadow of honour? do I give courage or comfort to the foreign enemies, because I reserve myself to encounter them, or because I kept my heart from baseness, though I cannot keep my fortune from declining? No, no, I give every one of these considerations his due weight, and the more I weigh them, the more I find myself justified from offending in any of them. As for the two last objections that I forsake my country when it hath most need of me, and fail in the indissoluble duty which I owe to my Sovereign, I answer, that if my country had at this time any need of my public service, her Majesty that governeth it would not have driven me to a private life; I am tied to my country by two bands, one public to discharge carefully and painfully and industriously the trust that is committed unto me; and the other privately to sacrifice my life and carcase, which hath been nourished in it. Of the first I am free, by being dismissed by her Majesty; of the other nothing can free me but death, and therefore no occasion of performance shall offer itself but I will meet it half way. The indissoluble duty which I owe unto her Majesty, is only the duty of allegiance which

never can nor shall fail in me; the duty of attendance is no
indissoluble duty; I owe unto her Majesty the service of an
Earl and of a Marshal of England. I have been content to
do the service of clerk, but can never serve her as a villain
nor a slave; but yet you say I must weigh the time, so I do,
for now I see the storm come, I have put myself in harbour.
Seneca saith, we must give way to fortune; I know that Fortune
is both blind and strange, and therefore I go as far out of her
way as I can. You say the remedy is not to strive; I neither
strive nor seek remedy;—but I must yield you say and submit;
I can never yield myself to be guilty, nor this imprisonment
lately laid upon me to be just; I owe so much to the author of
truth, as I can never yield truth to be falsehood, nor falsehood to be truth. Have I given cause you ask, and take a
scandal? No, I gave no cause to take up so much as Fimbria
his complaint, for I did *totum telum corpore recipere*, I patiently
bear and sensibly feel that, that I then received, when this
scandal was given me,—nay, when the vilest of all indignities
were done unto me, doth religion force me to sue? Doth
God require it? Is it impiety not to do it? Why cannot
Princes err? Cannot subjects receive wrong? Is any
earthly power or authority infinite? Pardon me, pardon
me, my good Lord, I can never subscribe to these prin-
ciples. Let Solomon's fool laugh when he is stricken;
let those that mean to make their profit of Prince's faults,
shew to have no sense of Prince's injuries; let them acknowledge an infinite absoluteness on earth, that do not
believe in an absolute Infinite in heaven: as for me I have
received wrong; I feel it: my cause is good, I know it;
and whatsoever come, all the power on earth can never shew
more strength and constancy in oppressing than I can shew in
suffering whatsoever shall or can be imposed upon me. Your
Lordship, in the beginning of your letter, maketh yourself a
looker-on and me a player of mine own game, for you may
see more than I, but you must give me leave to tell you in the
end of mine, that since you but see, and I do suffer, I must of
necessity feel more than you; I must crave your Lordship's

patience to give him that hath crabbed fortune leave to use a crabbed style; but whatsoever my style is, there is no heart more humble or more affected to your Lordship than is that of mine. Your Lordship's poor friend, Essex.

LORD KEEPER EGERTON TO THE EARL OF ESSEX.

MY VERY GOOD LORD, IT is often seen, that a stander-by seeth more than he that playeth the game; and for the most part, every man in his own cause standeth in his own light, and seeth not so clearly as he should: your Lordship hath dealt in other men's causes and in great and weighty affairs with great judgment and wisdom, now your own is in hand you are not to contemn or refuse the advice of any that love you, how simple soever. In this order I range myself; of those that love you none more simple, and yet none that loveth you with more true and honest affection, which shall plead my excuse if you shall either mistake or misconstrue my words or meaning; but in your Lordship's whole wisdom I neither doubt nor suspect the one nor the other: I will not presume to advise you, but will shoot my bolt, and tell you what I think. The beginning and long continuance of this unseasonable discontentment you have seen and proved, by which you may aim at the end if you hold still this course, which hitherto you find to be worse and worse; and the longer you go the further out of your way, there is little hope the end will be better; you are not yet so far gone but you may well return; the return is safe, the progress dangerous and desperate. In this course you hold; if you have any enemies, you do that for them which they could never do for themselves; your friends, you leave open to scorn and contempt: you forsake yourself, overthrow your fortunes, and ruin your honour and reputation; you give that comfort and courage to the foreign enemies—as greater they cannot have, for what can be more welcome or more pleasing news unto them than to hear that her majesty and the realm are maimed of so worthy a member, who hath so often and so valiantly quailed and daunted them? you forsake your country when it hath most need of your

counsel and help; and lastly, you fail in your indissoluble
duty which you owe unto your most gracious Sovereign,—a
duty imposed upon you, not by nature and policy only, but by
religious and sacred bond, wherein the divine majesty of Almighty God hath, by the rule of Christianity, obliged you.
For the four first, your constant resolution may perhaps move
you to esteem them as light, but being well weighed, they are
not light or little to be regarded: and for the two last it may
be, that the cleanness of your inward conscience may seem to
content yourself, but that is not enough.   These duties stand·
not in contemplation or inward meditation, and cannot be performed but by external actions, and where that faileth the
substance faileth.   This being your present estate and condition what is to be done? what is the remedy?   My good
Lord, I lack judgment and wisdom to advise you, but I will
never lack any honest true heart to wish you well, nor, being
warranted by a good conscience, will fear to speak what I
think.   I have begun plainly, be not offended if I proceed so,
bene cedit qui cedit tempori : and Seneca saith, *lex si nocentem
punit cedendum est justitiæ : si innocentem, cedendum est fortunæ.*
The medicine and remedy is not to contend and strive, but
humbly to yield and submit.   Have you given cause and yet
take a scandal unto you? then all is too little that you can do
to make satisfaction; is cause of scandal given you? yet let
occasion, policy, duty, and religion enforce you to yield, sue
and submit to your Sovereign, between whom and you there
can be no proportion of duty, when God requireth it as a principal duty and service to himself, and when it is evident that
great good may ensue thereof to your friends, to yourself and
country, and to your Sovereign, and extreme harm to the contrary; there can be no dishonour or hurt to yield, but in not
doing thereof, dishonour and impiety.   The difficulty, my
Lord, is to conquer yourself, which is the height of true valour and fortitude, whereunto your honourable actions have
ever tended, do it in this and God will be pleased; her Majesty, I doubt not, well satisfied; your country will take good,
and your friends comfort by it, and yourself; I mention you

the last, for I know that of all these you esteem yourself least
that shall receive honour ; and your enemies (if you have any)
shall be disappointed of their hope: I have delivered what I
think simply and plainly; I leave you to determine according
to your wisdom; if I have erred, it is *error amoris*, not *amor
erroris :* confer and accept it I beseech you as I meant it, not
as an advice but as an opinion, to be allowed or cancelled at
your pleasure. If I might have conveniently have conferred
with yourself in person, I would not have troubled you with so
many idle blots : whatsoever you judge of this mine opinion,
yet my desire is to further all good means that may tend to
your good.   And so, wishing you all honorable happiness, I
rest your Lordship's most ready and faithful, though unable
poor friend.

ADDRESS OF THE CATHOLICS OF ENGLAND TO JAMES I.

MOST PUISSANT AND ORIENT MONARCH, Such are the rare
perfections and admirable gifts of wisdom, prudence, valour,
and justice, wherewith the bountiful hand of God's divine Majesty hath endued your Majesty, as in the depth of your provident judgment we doubt not but you foresee what concerneth
both the spiritual and temporal government of all your kingdoms and dominions. Notwithstanding your Grace's most
afflicted subjects and devoted servants, the Catholics of England, partly to prevent sinister informations which haply may
possess your forced ears before our answer be heard, partly as
men overwhelmed with persecution for our consciences, we
are enforced to have speedy recourse, in hope of present redress from your Highness, and to present these humble lines
unto your royal person to plead for us some commiseration and
favour.   Alas! what allegiance or duty how many noble men
and worthy gentlemen, most zealous in the Catholic religion,
have endured! Some loss of lands and livings ; some exile,
others imprisonment; some the effusion of blood and life for
the advancement of your blessed mother's right unto the
sceptre of Albion.   Nay; what finger did ever ache but Catholics' for your present title and dominion ? How many fled to

your Court, offering themselves as hostages for their friends to
live and die in your Grace's quarrel, if ever adversary had opposed himself against the equity of your cause: if this they
attempted with their Prince's disgrace to obtain your Majesty's
grace; what will they do now? What will they not do to live
without disgrace in your Grace's favour? The main of this
realm, setting petty sects aside, consisteth of four parts,—
Protestants, who have domineered all the former Queen's
days; Puritans, who have crept in apace among them; Athe-
ists, or Politicians, who were bred upon their brawls and contentions in matters of faith; and Catholics, who, as they are
opposite to all, so are they detested of all, because error was
ever an enemy to truth. Hardly all or any two of the first three
can be suppressed; and, therefore, we beseech your Majesty
to yield us as much favour as others of contrary religion to that
which shall be publicly professed in England shall obtain at
our hands; for if our fault be like, or less, or none at all, in
equity our punishment ought to be like, or less, or none at all.
The gates, arches, and pyramids of France proclaimed the
King *Pater patriæ et pacis restitutor*, because that kingdom,
well nigh torn in pieces with cruel wars, and made a prey to
foreign foes, was, by his provident wisdom and valour, ac-
quieted in itself, and hostile strangers expelled; the which he
principally effected by conditioning to tolerate them of an adverse religion to that which was openly professed. Question-
less, (dread Sovereign,) the Kingdom of England, by cruel
persecution of Catholics, hath been almost odious to all Christian nations; trade, and traffic, is exceedingly decayed; wars
and blood hath seldom ceased; subsidies and taxes, never so
many; discontented minds innumerable: all which your Majesty's princely countenance to your humble suppliants, the
afflicted Catholics, will easily redress, especially at this your
Highness' first ingress. "*Si loquatur ad eos verba levia erunt
tibi servi cunctis diebus,*" said the sage Councillors of Solomon
to Roboam; for enlargement after affliction resembleth a pleasant gale after a storm; very vehement, and a benefit in distress, doubleth the value thereof. How grateful will it be to

all Catholic Princes abroad, and honourable to your Majesty,
to understand how Queen Elizabeth's severity is changed to
your royal clemency; and that the lenity of a man re-edified
that which the misinformed anger of a woman destroyed; that
the Lion rampant is *passant*, whereas the *passant* had been
rampant! How acceptable shall your Highness' subjects be to
all Catholic countries, who now almost are abhorred of all,
when they shall perceive that your Highness prepareth not
pits and prisons for the professors of their faith, but admitteth
them temples and altars for the use of their religion. Then
shall we see with eyes, and touch with our fingers, that happy
benediction in Esaye, in this land, that swords are changed into
ploughshares, and lances into scythes; and all nations will say
hi sunt semen cui benedixit Dominus. We request no more favour
at your Grace's hands than that we may securely follow and
profess that Catholic religion which all your happy predecessors professed, from Donaldus' first converted soul, to your Majesty's peerless mother, last martyred; a religion so venerable
for antiquity, majestical for amplitude, constant for continuance, irreprehensible for doctrine, inducing to all kind of virtue
and piety, dissuading from all sins and wickedness; a religion
believed by all primitive pastors, established by all academical
councils, upheld by all ancient doctors, maintained by the first
and last Christian Emperors, recorded almost alone in all Ecclesiastical histories, sealed with the blood of millions of mar-
tyrs, adorned with the virtues of so many Confessors, beautified
with the purities of thousands of virgins, so conformable to natural sense and reason; and, finally, so agreeable to the sacred
text of God's word and gospel. The free use of this religion
we request, if not in public churches, at least in private houses;
if not with approbation, yet with toleration, without molestation. Assure, your Grace, that howsoever some Protestants
or Puritans, incited by moral honesty of life, or incited by instinct of nature, or for fear of some temporal punishment, pretend obedience to your Highness' laws, yet certainly and honestly Catholics, for conscience, observe them; for they,
defending that Prince's precepts and statutes, oblige no sub-

jects, under the penalty of . . . . will little care in conscience to transgress them which principally is tormented with
the guilt of sin. But Catholics, confessing merit in obtaining
and severity in transgressing, cannot but in soul be religiously
. . . . . for the least prevarication thereof. Wherefore, most
merciful Sovereign, we, your long afflicted subjects, in all dutiful submission, protest before the Majesty of God and all his
holy angels, as loyal obedience, and as immaculate allegiance
unto your Grace as ever did faithful subjects in Scotland or
England unto your Highness' progenitors; and, indeed, as sincerely with our goods and lives to serve you as ever did the
loyalist Israelites King David, or the trustiest legions the Roman Emperors. And thus, expecting your Majesty's cus-
tomary favour and gracious bounty, we rest your devote suppliants. Committing your Majesty to Him whose hands do
manage the hearts of Kings, and with reciprocal mercy will requite the merciful, your sacred Majesty's most devote suppliants,   THE CATHOLICS OF ENGLAND.

ARCHBISHOP HUTTON TO LORD CRANBORNE.

SALUTEM IN CHRISTO, I have received a letter from your
Lordship and others of his Majesty's Most Honourable Privy
Council, containing two points. First, that the Puritans be
proceeded against according to law, except they conform themselves. Secondly, that good care be had unto greedy patrons;
that none be admitted in their places but such as are conformable and otherways worthy for their virtue and learning. I
have written to the Bishops of this province, and, in their absence, to their Chancellors, to have a special care of this service; and therewith have sent copies of your Honour's letters,
and will take present order within mine own diocese. I wish,
with all my heart, that the like order were given, not only to
all Bishops, but to all Magistrates and Justices of the Peace,
to proceed against Papists and Recusants, who of late, partly
by this round dealing against the Puritans, and by some extraordinary favour, are grown mighty in number, courage, and
insolency. The Puritans, whose fantastical zeal I mislike,

though they differ in ceremonies and accidents, yet they agree with us in substance of religion; and I think all, or most of them, do love his Majesty and the present State, and I hope will yield to conformity: but the Papists are opposite and contrary in very many substantial points of religion, and cannot but wish the Pope's authority and religion to be established. I assure your Honour it is high time to look unto them. Very many of them are gone from all places to London, and some are come down to this country in great jollity, almost triumphantly. But as his Majesty hath been brought up in the Gospel, and understandeth religion exceeding well, so will he no doubt protect, maintain, and advance it, even to the end. If the Gospel should fail, and Popery prevail, it would be laid and imputed principally to you great Councillors, who either procure or yield to grant toleration to some of them. Good my Lord Cranbourn, let me put you in mind that you were born and brought up in true religion. Your wise father was a worthy instrument to banish superstition, and to advance the Gospel. Imitate him in this service especially. As for other things, though I confess I am not to deal in State matters, yet, as one that honoureth and loveth his most excellent Majesty with all my heart, I wish less wasting of the treasure of the realm, and more moderation to be used of the lawful exercise of hunting, both that the poor men's corn may be less spoiled, and other his Majesty's subjects more spared. The Papists give it forth, that they hope the Ecclesiastical commission shall be no more renewed; indeed, it stayeth very long, considering the great want thereof. I pray your Honour further it. Sir John Bennett will attend your Lordship's pleasure. Thus beseeching God to bless you with his manifold graces, that you may as long serve his most excellent Majesty as your most wise father did serve most worthy Queen Elizabeth, I bid your Lordship most heartily farewell. From Bishopthorpe, the 8th of December 1604.

THE KING OF MOROCCO TO THE KING OF ENGLAND, DELI-
VERED 5TH NOV. 1687.

WHEN these our letters shall be happy to come to your Majesty's sight, I wish the spirit of the righteous God may so direct the powers of your mind, that you may joyfully embrace
the messenger I send, presenting to you the means of exalting
the Majesty of God and your own renown amongst men. The
regal power allotted to our charge makes us first common servants to our Creator; then of these whom we govern the people: so that, in observing the duty we owe to our God, we
deliver blessings to the world; and in providing for the public
good of our States, we magnify the honour of God like the ce-
lestial bodies, that though they have much . . . . . serve only
to yield benefits to the world. It is the excellency of our
office to be the instruments whereby great happinesses are delivered to the nations.   Pardon me; this is not to instruct, for
I know I speak to one of a clearer and quicker sight than myself: but I speak this because God hath pleased to grant me
happy victory on some part of those rebelling pirates that have
so long molested the peaceful trade of Europe, and have present further occasion to root out the generation of these that
have been so pernicious to the good of our nations. I mean,
that since it hath pleased God to be so auspicious to our beginning in the conquest of Sallee, we might join and proceed
with hope of like success of war against Tunis, Argier, and
other places, ... and the receptacles for the inhuman
villanies of those that abhor rule and government herein; whilst
we extirpate the corruptions and malignant spirits of the
world, we shall glorify the great God, and perform a duty that
will shine as glorious as the sun and moon, which all the earth
will also adore and reverence; a work which shall ascend
sweet as the perfume of the most precious odour in the nostrils
of the Lord; a work grateful and happy to men; a work,
whose memory shall be reverenced as long as there shall be
any that delight to read the accounts of heroic and magnanimous spirits,—that shall last as long as there are remaining

amongst men that love and honour the piety and virtue of noble minds. This account I here willingly present to you, whose pious virtues are equal to the dignity of your power, that we, who are both servants to the great and mighty God, may, hand in hand, triumph in the glory which this action presents us. Now, because the islands which you govern have been ever famous for the unconquered strength of their shipping, I have sent these my trusty servants and Ambassadors to know whether, in your princely wisdom, you shall think fit to assist me with such forces by sea as shall be answerable to those I provide by land, which, if you please to grant, I doubt not but the Lord of Hosts will protect and assist those that fight in so glorious a cause. Nor ought you to think this strange, that I, who so much reverence an accord of nations, should first exhort to a war. Your great Prophet, Christ Jesus, was the Lion of the tribe of Judah, as well as the Lord and Giver of peace, which may signify to you, that he who is a lover and maintainer of peace must appear with the terror of the sword, and, wading through seas of blood, must arrive to tranquillity. This made your father James, of glorious memory, so happily renowned amongst all nations. It was the noble fame of your princely virtue which resoundeth even to the uttermost corners of the earth, that persuaded me to interest you to partake of that blessing wherein I boast myself most happy. I wish God may heap the richest of his blessings on you, increase your happiness with your days, and hereafter perpetuate the greatness of your name in all ages.

INSCRIPTION

ON THE TOMB OF SIR CHRISTOPHER HATTON, KNIGHT OF THE GARTER, AND LORD HIGH CHANCELLOR OF ENGLAND.

Sacrum memoriæ
D. Chr. Hattoni, Guil. fil. Joh. nepotis,
antiquiss. Hattonorum gente oriundi ;

Regiæ Majestatis D. Elizabethæ ex nobilibus stipatoribus L. vici ; Sacratioris Cameræ Generosorum unius ; Prætorianorum Militum Ducis ; Regii procamerarii ; Sanctioris Consilii Senatoris ; summi Angliæ ac Oxon. Acad. Cancellarii : Ordinis nobiliss. San. Georgiani de Periscelide Equitis. Maximo Principis omniumq; bonorum mœrore (cùm LI annos cœlebs vixisset) 20 Novembris anno 1591, in ædibus suis Holburnæ piè fato functi.

Guil. Hattonus, Eques auratus, ejus ex sorore nepos, adoptione filius, ac hæres mœstissimus, pietatis ergo, Posuit.

ON ANOTHER PART OF THE SAME TOMB.

Quæ verô, quæ digna tuis virtutibus (Heros)
Constituent monumenta tui ? si qualia debet
Posteritas, si quanta tibi prudentia, justi
Quantus amor, si quanta fuit facundia linguæ,
Et decus et pulchro veniens in corpore virtus,
Illaq; munificæ semper tibi copia dextræ :
Deniq; quanta fuit magna tibi gratia quondam
Principis, éque tuis quæ creverat inclita factis
Gloria, tanta tibi statuant Monumenta Nepotes,
Ipsa tuos caperet vix tota Britannia Manes.

ON A TABLET AFFIXED TO A COLUMN NEAR THE SAME MONUMENT.

Stay and behold the mirror of a dead man's house,
Whose lively Person would have made thee stay and wonder :
Look, and withal learn to know how to live and die renowned,
For never can clean life and famous Herses sunder.

Hatton lies here, unto whose name Hugh Lupus gave
(Lupus the sister's sonne of William Conquerour)
For Nigel his dear servant's sake worship and land :
Lo there the Spring ; look here the honour of his ancestry.
When Nature molded him her thoughts were most on Mars,
And all the Heavens to make him goodly were agreeing ;
Thence was he valiant, active, strong, and passing comely,
And God did grace his mind and spirit with gifts excelling.
Nature commends her workmanship to Fortune's charge.
Fortune presents him to the Court and Queen,
Queen Eliz. (O God's dear handmaid) his most miracle ;
Now hearken, Reader,—raretie not heard or seen,—
This blessed Queen, mirror of all that Albion rul'd,
Gave favour to his faith and precepts to his hopefull time ;
First trained him in the stately band of Pensioners.
Behold how humble hearts make easie steps to clime.
High carriage, honest life, heart ever loyall,
Diligence, delight in duty, God doth reward :
So did this worthy Queen, in her just thoughts of him,
And for her safety, make him Captain of her Guard.
Now doth she prune this vine, and from her sacred breast,
Lessons his Life, makes wise his heart for her great Councells,
And so Vice-Chamberlein, where forreign Prince's ey's
Might well admire her choyce wherein she most excells.
So sweetly temp'red was his soul with vertuous balme,
Religious, just to God, and Cæsar in each thing ;
That he aspired to the highest Subject's seat,
Lord Chancellour (measure and conscience of a holy King),
Robe, Collar, Garter, dead figures of great Honour,
Alms-deeds with Faith, honest in word, franke in dispence ;
The Poor's friend, not popular ; the Churches pillar,
This Tomb shews th' one ; th' Heavens shrine the other.

Franciscus Florus ad memoriam heri sui defuncti, luctusq' sui solatium,
Posuit. Anno Domini 1593.*

* Dugdale's History of St. Paul's, by Ellis, p. 56.

THE END.

LONDON:
Printed by S. & J. BENTLEY, WILSON, and FLEY
Bangor House, Shoe Lane.

Printed in the United States
86567LV00005B/8/A